Youth Justice

Youth Justice

Critical
Readings

edited by
John Muncie
Gordon Hughes
Eugene McLaughlin

SAGE Publications
London • Thousand Oaks • New Delhi

in association with

TheOpen
University

SAGE Publications Ltd
6 Bonhill Street
London EC2A 4PU

SAGE Publications Inc
2455 Teller Road
Thousand Oaks, California 91320

SAGE Publications India Pvt Ltd
32, M-Block Market
Greater Kailash - I
New Delhi 110 048

British Library Cataloguing in Publication data

A Catalogue record for this book is available
from the British Library

ISBN 0 7619 4913 5
ISBN 0 7619 4914 3 (pbk)

**Library of Congress Control Number
2001 135909**

Typeset by SIVA Math Setters, Chennai, India
Printed in Great Britain by The Cromwell Press,
Trowbridge, Wiltshire

Contents

Acknowledgements   ix

Preface   xi

1   Modes of youth governance:
political rationalities, criminalization and resistance   1
John Muncie and Gordon Hughes

**Part I   Folk devils: constructions and
reconstructions of youth and crime**   19

2   Constructions and reconstructions of British
childhood: an interpretative survey,
1800 to the present   22
Harry Hendrick

3   Youth crime and moral decline: permissiveness
and tradition   45
Geoffrey Pearson

4   Lesser breeds without the law   50
Paul Gilroy

5   Rethinking moral panic for multi-mediated
social worlds   68
Angela McRobbie and Sarah Thornton

6   The vilification and pleasures of
youthful transgression   80
Keith Hayward

Part II   The origins of youth justice   95

7   Innocence and experience: the evolution of the
concept of juvenile delinquency in the
mid-nineteenth century   98
Margaret May

8   The invention of juvenile delinquency in early
      nineteenth-century England   115
      Susan Magarey

9   The three Rs – repression, rescue and rehabilitation
      ideologies of control for working-class youth   123
      John Clarke

10   The government of a generation:
      the subject of juvenile delinquency   138
      Peter Rush

11   Reforming the juvenile: gender, justice and
      the child criminal in nineteenth-century England   159
      Heather Shore

      Part III   Positivism and welfarism   173

12   The triumph of benevolence: the origins of the
      juvenile justice system in the United States   177
      Anthony Platt

13   Penal strategies in a welfare state   197
      David Garland

14   On the decriminalisation of English juvenile courts 216
      Anthony Bottoms

15   Children's hearings and children in trouble   228
      Janice McGhee, Lorraine Waterhouse
      and Bill Whyte

16   Restorative youth justice: the last
      vestiges of welfare?   238
      Loraine Gelsthorpe and Allison Morris

      Part IV   Justice, diversion and rights   255

17   Wider, stronger and different nets:
      the dialectics of criminal justice reform   258
      James Austin and Barry Krisberg

18 Justice, retribution and children 275
Stewart Asquith

19 Whose justice? The politics of juvenile control 284
John Clarke

20 'Troublesome girls': towards alternative
definitions and policies 296
Annie Hudson

21 Challenging the criminalization of children and
young people: securing a rights-based agenda 311
Phil Scraton and Deena Haydon

Part V Detention and retribution 329

22 Failure never matters: detention centres and the
politics of deterrence 332
John Muncie

23 The boot camp and the limits of modern penality 345
Jonathan Simon

24 The reductionist agenda 359
Andrew Rutherford

25 The future of imprisonment 373
Thomas Mathiesen

26 New punitiveness: the politics of
child incarceration 386
Barry Goldson

Part VI Risk management and prevention 401

27 Corporatism: the third model of juvenile justice 404
John Pratt

28 The end of an era 413
John Pitts

29   Understanding and preventing youth crime   425
         David Farrington

30   Expanding realms of the new penology:
         the advent of actuarial justice for juveniles   431
         Kimberly Kempf-Leonard and Elicka Peterson

31   The contemporary politics of youth crime prevention   452
         Tim Newburn

                                                     Index   464

Acknowledgements

The authors and publishers wish to thank the following for permission to reprint copyright material:

Part I   Folk devils: constructions and reconstructions of youth and crime
Falmer Press for *Constructions and reconstructions of British childhood: an interpretative survey, 1800 to the present* by Harry Hendrick, edited by A. James and A. Prout, 1997

The Magistrates Association for *Youth crime and moral decline: permissiveness and tradition* by Geoffrey Pearson in The Magistrate 1993/1994

Routledge for 'Lesser breeds without the law' by Paul Gilroy from *There Ain't No Black in the Union Jack*, 1987

Taylor and Francis for 'Rethinking moral panic for multi-mediated social worlds' by Angela McRobbie and Sarah Thornton in *British Journal of Sociology* 46:4

Part II   The origins of youth justice

Indiana University Press for 'Innocence and experience: the evolution of the concept of juvenile delinquency in the mid-nineteenth century' by Margaret May in *Victorian Studies*, March 2002

Edinburgh University Press for 'The invention of juvenile delinquency in early nineteenth century England' by Susan Magarey in *Labour History Review* No 34, 1978

University of Birmingham for 'The three Rs: repression, resuce and rehabilitation' by John Clarke in *Centre for Contemporary Cultural Studies, Stencilled Paper* 1975

Kluwer Academic Publishers for 'The government of a generation: the subject of juvenile delinquency' by Peter Rush in *The Liverpool Law Review*, 14:1 (1992) pp. 3–41, with kind permission from Kluwer Academic Publishers

Part III   Positivism and welfarism

Little, Brown and Co for 'The triumph of benevolence: the origins of the juvenile justice system in the United States' by Anthony Platt in *Criminal Justice in America* edited by R. Quinney, 1974

Ashgate Publishing Ltd for 'Penal strategies in a welfare state' by David Garland, in '*Punishment and Welfare*'

'On the decriminalisation of English juvenile courts' by Anthony Bottoms, reprinted with the permission of The Free Press, a Division of Simon and Schuster, Inc., from *Crime, Criminology and Public Policy: Essays in Honour of Sir Leon Radzinowicz*, edited by Roger Hood. Copyright © 1974 by Heinemann Educational Books

Part IV   Justice, diversion and rights

Sage Publications Ltd for 'Wider, stronger and different nets: the dialectics of criminal justice reform' in *Journal of Research in Crime and Delinquency*, 18:1, 1981

A. Morris and H. Giller for 'Justice, retribution and children' by Stewart Asquith in *Providing Criminal Justice for Children*, 1983

Reprinted from *International Journal of the Sociology of Law*, vol. 13, no. 4, John Clarke 'Whose justice? The politics of juvenile control', pp. 407–421, 1985, by permission of the Academic Press

Sage Publications Ltd for 'Troublesome girls: towards alternative definitions and policies' by Annie Hudson from *Growing up Good* by M. Cain, 1989

Part V   Risk management and prevention

Sage Publications Ltd for 'Failure never matters: detention centres and the politics of deterrence' by John Munice in *Critical Social Policy*, no. 28, 1990

Social Justice for 'The boot camp and the limits of modern penality' by Jonathan Simon in *Social Justice* vol. 22, no. 2, 1995

'The reductionist agenda', extract from *Prisons and the Process of Justice* by Andrew Rutherford, published by Heinemann. Used by permission of The Random House Group Ltd

Continuum for 'The future of imprisonment' by Thomas Mathiesen from *Prison on Trial*, 1990

John Pratt, 'Corporatism: the third model of juvenile justice', *British Journal of Criminology*, 1989, vol. 29, no. 3, pp. 236–254, by permission of Oxford University Press

Blackwell Publishers Ltd for 'The end of an era' by John Pitts from *Howard Journal of Criminal Justice*, v31 (1992) pp. 133–149

Joseph Rowntree Foundation for 'Understanding and preventing youth crime' by David Farrington from *Social Research Findings*, no. 93, 1996

Sage Publications Ltd for 'Expanding realms of the new penology' by Kimberly Kempf-Leonard and Elicka Peterson in *Punishment and Society*, vol. 2, no. 1, pp. 66–97, 2000

Preface

This collection of readings is designed for use as a key text for the Open University postgraduate course D864 *Youth Justice, Penality and Social Control*, one of the courses in the university's Master's programme in Social Policy and Criminology. The course is concerned with exploring the historical origins, discursive practices and governmental initiatives that make up the complex of contemporary systems of youth justice.

The volume brings together for the first time some of the most influential and compelling analyses of youth crime and youth justice that have appeared in journals and books over the past thirty years. Each has been selected because of the critical insights it delivers to understanding the multiple, competing rationales of Western systems of youth justice. These reprinted pieces are supported by seven specially commissioned articles, which review the past literature and explore its relevance to understanding contemporary youth justice theory and practice. These chapters work specifically to show how each new 'turn' in youth justice has worked with, incorporated or transformed earlier approaches. In this regard we are grateful to Loraine Gelsthorpe, Barry Goldson, Deena Haydon, Keith Hayward, Allison Morris, Tim Newburn, Phil Scraton and Heather Shore for opening up new directions and providing new challenges for youth justice analysis.

As an organizing device the book is presented in six separate, but in reality overlapping, parts. Part I provides a vital contextualization by detailing how the key signifiers of childhood, youth, delinquency and moral panic can be considered as social constructions. Part II brings together the most influential analyses of the origins of youth justice in the early nineteenth century: a field which even today remains relatively under-researched. Part III focuses on the nature of penal welfarism and explores the degree to which the goals of care and rehabilitation continue to have purchase in contemporary systems. Part IV examines the vexed question of providing young people with justice and rights and how these have tended to be subverted, not simply by the counter-discourse of welfare, but by adult power in all its caring and disciplining guises. Part V explores the continuing centrality of punitive custodial institutions for youth justice, despite a long history of their 'failure' and numerous campaigns for their abolition. Finally, Part VI considers the impact that new modes of actuarialism, corporatism, community responsibilization and managerialism have made within the new premise of youth justice 'to prevent offending by children and young people'.

Collectively these parts offer a systematic examination of youth justice history and policy by drawing upon a number of different theoretical frameworks derived from such diverse sources as cultural criminology, social constructionism, Marxism, critical criminology, discourse analysis and the governmentality theses. Most of these theoretical frameworks are implicit within chapters and are not the subject of discussion in their own right. However, it is not necessary to be a student of the differing frameworks to appreciate the analysis offered by each chapter, though in themselves they do provide a rich basis for further analysis. As such, the book is not simply aimed at students and academics. It is also designed to appeal to the rapidly expanding range of practitioners, managers and policy makers in this increasingly important field of professional practice.

Although we are named as editors of the book, its development has relied on the considerable support given by numerous others, in particular Hilary Canneaux, Ross Fergusson, Fiona Harris and Rebecca White. Particular thanks are due to Mike Presdee, who acted as external assessor for the postgraduate course to which this volume is linked.

As ever we are indebted to Sage – and Miranda Nunhofer in particular – for their continual enthusiasm for our collective project of developing criminological studies at the Open University.

John Muncie
Gordon Hughes
Eugene McLaughlin

1

Modes of youth governance

Political rationalities, criminalization and resistance

John Muncie and Gordon Hughes

The history of youth justice is a history of conflict, contradictions, ambiguity and compromise. Conflict is inevitable in a system that has traditionally pursued the twin goals of welfare and justice. Welfarism promises a focus on meeting needs and rehabilitation but has always been compromised by an enduring neo-conservative framework of moral culpability and punishment. Justice implies a commitment to individual rights and due process but has readily been translated into neo-liberal responsibilization and neo-conservative retributive strategies. A narrow justice *v.* welfare debate is thus particularly moribund, for neither model has ever been fully realized in practice. Rather, youth justice tends to act on an amalgam of rationales, oscillating around and beyond the caring ethos of social services and the neo-liberal legalistic ethos of responsibility and punishment. As a result it continually seeks the compromise between youth as a special deserving case and youth as fully responsible for their own actions. Such a compromise tends to be reached by expanding the remit of the system, whether this is justified in the name of bifurcation, diversion or crime prevention. Welfarist goals are pursued for some, whilst in other arenas justice as retribution dominates. This expansionary tendency – both in sentencing powers and in system reach – is also reflective of a general ambivalence towards young people. Youth justice is not simply concerned with the offender but with those 'at risk' or thought likely to offend. The story is further complicated by the fact that, whilst problems of control and order have always been central to youth justice discourses, they have also been underpinned by concern for vulnerability and protection.

This chapter examines the extent to which these continually shifting contours and discourses of youth justice have established a structuring context in which 'what

SOURCE: Commissioned for this volume. John Muncie is Senior Lecturer in Criminology and Social Policy and Gordon Hughes is Senior Lecturer in Social Policy, both at the Open University, UK.

it means to be young' has become increasingly tightly defined and regulated. It does so by casting a critical eye on the burgeoning literature on regulation, governance and governmentality (for example, Burchell *et al.*, 1991; Rose, 1996b; Smandych, 1999; Stenson and Sullivan, 2001) and assesses its value for understanding the complexity of contemporary youth justice policy and practice. The chapter explores how youth governance, particularly in England and Wales, is embroiled in the collective impact of competing and contradictory discursive practices. It concludes by noting how these contradictions also produce significant moments of resistance, absence and closure.

POLITICAL RATIONALITIES: WELFARE AND NEO-LIBERAL GOVERNANCE

Nikolas Rose (1989, p. 121) has argued that 'childhood is the most intensively governed sector of personal existence'. Reviewing the past 150 years of youth justice history, it seems hard to disagree. Since child offenders were first tentatively separated from adults in youth prisons and subsequently in reformatories, discourses of youth and childhood have emphasized not only indiscipline but also vulnerability. Both constructions have legitimated innumerable programmes designed to mould and shape child development, whether by coercion or seduction, education and persuasion. The casting of children as in need of guidance and support has enabled virtually every aspect of childhood development to be subject to regulation, surveillance and inspection. In this analysis, then, social control is achieved through processes of 'normalization'. Notions of 'normality' and 'deviance' are continually fed to us through professional discourses and have become progressively more internalized. It is never a matter of overt coercion. The subjects of government may have been characteristically viewed as 'members of a flock to be shepherded, as children to be nurtured and tutored', but governmentalists also view them as 'citizens with rights, as rational, calculating individuals whose preferences are to be acted upon' (Rose, 2000, p. 323).

Moreover such processes are never static but subject to historical contingency. Rose (1996b) identifies three modes of governance that have dominated since the eighteenth century: the 'liberal', the 'welfare liberal' and the 'advanced liberal'. Following Foucault (1977, 1991), classical liberalism is depicted as allowing individuals the freedom to govern their own lives. The disciplinary logic of the reformatory, for example, is to produce the subjective conditions of self-regulation necessary for the governance of a society of free and civilized individuals. Governance is achieved through 'authorities of expertise'. Rose contends that, by the twentieth century, this liberal project had failed, as evidenced by greater social fragmentation and individualization. Increases in crime and unemployment attested to the dangers of *laissez-faire*. Penal welfare emerged as one formula for reorganizing social, political and economic affairs (see Chapter 13 of this volume). The state took on a greater responsibility for guaranteeing not only individual freedom but also collective security. Social insurance and social work were its hallmarks — both ostensibly inclusionary by guarding against the economic vagaries of systems of wage labour whilst establishing the parameters of 'correct' behaviour in return. Security and protection were provided in return for social obligation and social responsibility.

Many authors (for example, Garland, 2001) have recognized how since the 1960s this penal-welfare framework has been systematically undermined by the development of forms of neo-liberal (or in Rose's more generic term 'advanced liberal') governance. This can be broadly characterized as placing less emphasis on social contexts, state protection and rehabilitation and more on prescriptions of individual responsibility, an active citizenry and governing at a distance. Welfare liberalism was increasingly critiqued for encouraging state dependence, overloading the responsibilities of the state and undermining the ability of individuals to take responsibility for their own actions. 'Old' notions of *social* engineering, *social* solidarity, *social* benefits, *social* work, *social* welfare, for example, were transformed to create responsible (that is, not welfare-dependent) citizens.

Rose (1996a) characterized this shift as amounting to a 'death of the social' throughout entire frameworks of government (not simply youth and criminal justice). It involved:

- Changing governance to reflect market-like conditions and processes.
- Privatizing the state sector.
- Remodelling the remaining state agencies to become enterprises.
- Devolving responsibility for self-government to individuals, families and communities: the active citizen.
- Exposing professional practice to fiscal accounting, audit and evaluation research.
- Promoting individual choice and individuals' desire to govern their own conduct with *freedom*.
- Replacing professionals with individuals as 'experts of themselves'.

In youth justice these new modes of governance are most clearly visible in the twin strategies of responsibilization and managerialization.

Neo-liberal responsibilization

A discourse of responsibility lies at the heart of neo-liberal modes of governance. It characteristically takes two forms:

- Individuals should be held responsible for their actions.
- Families and communities should take primary responsibility for crime prevention away from the state.

It is largely in the latter sense that Garland (1996) refers to a responsibilization strategy involving 'central government seeking to act upon crime not in a direct fashion through state agencies (police, courts, prisons, social work, etc.) but instead by acting indirectly, seeking to activate action on the part of non-state agencies and organizations'. For example, in the United Kingdom from the mid-1980s onwards numerous campaigns (such as Neighbourhood Watch), organizations (such as Crime Concern) and projects (such as Safer Cities) were established to encourage inter-agency co-operation and local initiative. The message was that everyone – from property owners to manufacturers to school authorities, families and individuals – has a responsibility to reduce criminal opportunities and increase formal controls. Rose and Miller (1992) reasoned that this was not a simple case of state abrogation, nor of privatization of public issues, but of a new mode of 'governing at a distance'. The state may issue directives, but responsibility for their enactment is passed down to local bodies and ultimately individuals themselves. In the field of youth justice this has developed into a simultaneous devolution and centralization of youth justice policy.

By the late 1990s all local authorities were given the statutory duty to 'prevent offending by young people'. A plurality of expertise – police, probation, social services, health authorities, education authorities – are now required to have regard to that aim. All aspects of local authority work have become infused with crime prevention responsibilities. For example, every local authority with social service and education responsibilities is required to formulate and implement an annual youth justice plan setting out how youth justice reform is to be funded and put into operation. It is also required to establish a youth offending team (YOT), consisting, on a statutory basis, of representatives from each of social services, probation, police, health and education authorities: what were formerly youth *justice* teams are replaced by youth *offending* teams. These agencies are to 'pull together' to co-ordinate provision, ensure that each agency acts in tandem and to deliver a range of interventions and programmes that will ensure that young people 'face up to the consequences of their actions'. In effect the youth offending team displaces the statutory child care operations of social services departments (Goldson, 2000b). But each YOT plan also has to be submitted for approval to a national body – the Youth Justice Board – which, by 2000, had formulated a set of practice criteria to act as national standards (Youth Justice Board, 2000). Moreover, their work will be constantly scrutinized through budgetary planning and auditing for cost and effectiveness. The youth justice plan enables local agencies to be held to account for their 'success' or 'failure'. Local ownership is circumscribed by national standards, performance targets and statutory limits (Vaughan, 2000; Muncie, 2002).

At an individual level the responsibilization ethos finds its practical expression in principles of restorative justice. Whilst radical advocates of restorative justice speak of replacing formal justice with processes of reconciling conflicting interests and of healing rifts (see, for example, De Haan, 1990), the incarnation of restoration in New Labour's reform programme appears most interested in ensuring that offenders face up to the consequences of their actions. In legislative terms, restorative principles are typically cited as being present in referral, reparation and action plan orders (see Chapters 16 and 31 of this volume). Here the burden of responsibility falls on individuals to atone or change their behaviour, rather than on the state to recognize that it also has a responsibility (within UN conventions and rules) to its citizens. The axiom that youth justice is to 'confront young offenders with the consequences of their behaviour and help them to develop a sense of responsibility' (Youth Justice Board, 2000) also extends to ten-year-olds. In many crucial respects the distinction between adult and youth justice was eroded in the 1990s. Fionda (1998) cites several legislative changes and reformulations of policy in England and Wales which have 'an almost stubborn blindness' to welfare principles. The 'adulteration' of youth justice is most marked for ten to fourteen-year-olds, who now face almost the same sentencing powers as were previously restricted to those aged fourteen or over. Since the 1970s numerous commentators have remarked on the slow erosion of the juvenile court as a social welfare agency geared to rehabilitative ideals and, since the 1980s, its failure to recognize the mitigating circumstances of age. In the United Kingdom such shifts were epitomized by the abolition of the presumption of *doli incapax* for ten to fourteen-year-olds in 1998, but arguably reached their apogee in the United States, where, for at least a decade, most state legislatures have moved to change their laws so that young people charged with serious crime are tried and punished as if they were adults. The purpose of juvenile codes has also been reformulated to prioritize punishment and to facilitate the use of punitive training and boot camps. In some states there is now no age limit at all to adult criminal prosecution and trial (Grisso and Schwartz, 2000). In these ways any residual language of 'justice and rights' has been appropriated by one of 'self responsibility and obligation'. Garland (2001, p. 165) refers to this adulteration as symptomatic of a 'reactionary thematization of late modernity' through which politics and culture have become saturated with images of moral breakdown, incivility and the decline of the family.

Managerialization

The key problem of youth justice, which for many years was reducible to a simple welfare/justice dispute, is now expanded to marrying demands for retribution and responsibility with new discourses of crime prevention, crime reduction and community safety. By the early 1990s it was being increasingly argued that no one agency could achieve crime control alone. What was required was a 'joined-up' system of youth justice stretching from families, through schools to policing, courts and correction. In short, a new mode of governance was required to draw all these agencies together and effect a suitable *management* of youth crime, in particular, and of youthful behaviour in general. Managerialism stresses the need to develop a connected, coherent, efficient and above all *cost-effective* series of policies and practices. It is ostensibly governed by pragmatism rather than any fundamental penal philosophy. Managerialism provides the means by which philosophical dispute can be sidestepped. Its concern is not necessarily reform, training or punishment, but implementing policies that 'work', whether pragmatically or politically. Its key concern is with maintaining internal system coherence.

In the United Kingdom managerialism was first absorbed into criminal justice by the Conservatives in the early 1990s. In the field of youth justice the 1996 Audit Commission 'value for money' report on waste and inefficiency was pivotal. New Labour enthusiastically embraced its agenda and identified new public managerialism (NPM) as the route through which an economical and accountable system could be created. In line with previous public-sector reforms, NPM involves a simultaneous centralization and devolution of state responsibility. It is characterized by increased emphasis on achieving results rather than administrative processes; the setting of explicit targets and performance indicators to enable the auditing of efficiency and effectiveness; the publication of league tables illustrating comparative performance; the identification of core competences; the costing and market testing of all activities to ensure value for money, the externalization of non-essential responsibilities, the establishment of a purchaser–provider split, the encouragement of multi-agency co-operation, and the redesignation of clients as 'customers' (McLaughlin *et al.*, 2001).

Such principles have impacted on youth justice by:

- Recasting the past as 'failure' in order to clear the ground (despite the 'successes' of the late 1980s in reducing youth crime and custody rates).
- Identifying risk conditions, rather than the causes of youth crime.

- Setting statutory time limits from arrest to sentence.
- Establishing performance targets for youth offending teams.
- Discovering 'what works' via evidence-based research.
- Establishing the Youth Justice Board as a central body.
- Establishing youth offending teams to 'join up' local agencies.
- Establishing a statutory obligation on local authorities to 'prevent offending by young people'.
- Establishing means of standardizing risk conditions (e.g. by formulating ASSET assessment tools).
- Disseminating efficient practice via communication.

It is an environment in which the multi-agency co-operation of 1980s corporatism (Pratt, 1989: see Chapter 27 of this volume) and the risk assessment strategies of actuarialism (Feeley and Simon, 1992; and see Chapter 30 of this volume) are fused into an overarching 'task environment' based on audit, market testing, performance targets, productivity remits, cost-effectiveness and the quantifiable ethos of 'what works'. Within its own terms it is capable of subjugating the entire purpose of youth justice to the meeting of what in crime reduction parlance is termed SMART targets (those that are specific, measurable, achievable, realistic and timetabled) (Audit Commission, 1999). For example, the combining of social programmes with managerial practices raises the spectre not only of acting in the short term but of adding to the depth and intensity of social control. Complex social issues are depoliticized and subjected to the logic of financial audit whilst the pursuit of 'what works' legitimates further surveillance and monitoring.

BRINGING THE 'SOCIAL' AND THE STATE BACK IN

The prescriptions of neo-liberalism may be evident in the managerial and responsibilizing aspects of modern youth justice but the 'death of the social' thesis on its own fails to capture the nuances and complexities of recent youth justice reforms. The continuing problem for neo-liberalism is how to rejuvenate a sense of autonomy without abandoning the simultaneous project of monitoring and regulating social, particularly family, life. The neo-liberal is also in constant danger of unravelling in the face of neo-conservative tendencies to remoralization and authoritarianism (see below). Moreover, as law and order have been consistently placed towards the top of the media, public and political agendas, governments are expected to act quickly and decisively: 'the political culture of crime control now takes it for granted that the state will have a huge presence' (Garland, 2001, p. 173). A mixed economy of state sovereignty *and* devolved power to non-state agencies is the result.

Alongside numerous responsibilization strategies also lies a rhetoric of remoralization: developing a social basis of inclusion through appeals to the work ethic, the provision of universal nursery education and measures to assist single parents back to work. State initiatives such as the New Deal, Sure Start and the restorative elements of the 1998 Crime and Disorder Act have been viewed as a 'reformulation of holistic social strategies' (Stenson, 2000, p. 239). However, it is also a holism that potentially draws numerous aspects of social policy into a criminal justice agenda, creating the conditions for a 'criminalization of social policy' (Crawford, 1997, p. 228;

Muncie, 1999, pp. 247–8; Stenson, 2000, p. 239) when the boundaries between welfare and punitive interventions become increasingly blurred.

In such ways the 'social' is not so much denied as reconfigured within a reinvention of welfarism and reworkings of neo-conservatism which stand alongside the neo-liberal. All this makes a straightforward reading of contemporary youth justice problematic. The system appears to have little in the way of a fundamental philosophy but rather is marked by a series of overlapping – sometimes complementary, sometimes conflicting – discourses. Arguably one of its greatest hallmarks is now the promotion of myriad agendas of governance.

Reinventing the past 1: welfare paternalism

Governing in the name of 'the social' is widely viewed as the underlying principle of welfare states, particularly from 1945 to the 1970s. These have been characterized as advocates of the necessity of state intervention to protect citizens from unemployment, sickness and old age and to regulate the uncertainties of market exchange. As part of this process youth crime was viewed as stemming from neglect and deprivation, which could be ameliorated by various community-based treatment programmes to assist in youth's rehabilitation. In fact, in youth justice the salience of social programmes specifically targeted at the *needs* of youth arguably dates back at least to the establishment of the juvenile court at the end of the nineteenth century (first established in Chicago in 1899 and subsequently in England in 1908). Since then the key formal principle underlying all work with young offenders has been to ensure their general welfare. For example, in England and Wales the 1933 Children and Young Persons Act established that 'every court in dealing with a child or young person who is brought before it, either as an offender or otherwise, shall have regard to their welfare' (Section 44). It is a principle that has remained untouched to the present, although what actually constitutes 'welfare' and how it may be achieved are continually subject to dispute (see Chapter 16 of this volume).

In the United Kingdom the heyday of youth justice welfarism is usually taken to be the series of debates in the 1960s from which the 1969 Children and Young Persons Act in England and Wales and the 1968 Social Work Act in Scotland emerged. Both advocated a rise in the age of criminal responsibility and sought alternatives to criminalization and custody by way of treatment, non-criminal care proceedings and care orders. It was one element in the Labour Party's vision of a society based on full employment, prosperity, expanded educational opportunities and an enlarged welfare state which would overcome social inequalities and thus remove a major cause of young offending (Pitts, 1988, p. 3). Moreover, the prevailing political view of the late 1960s was that young offending was largely trivial and transient in nature and above all was so commonplace that the full weight of the law was unjustified and counterproductive (see Chapter 14 of this volume). In England the 1968 White Paper *Children in Trouble* argued that 'It is probably a minority of children who grow up without ever behaving in ways which may be contrary to the law. Frequently such behaviour is no more than an incident in the pattern of a child's normal development' (Home Office, 1968, pp. 3–4).

In Scotland the Kilbrandon report described delinquency as a 'symptom of personal or environmental difficulties' (cited by Morris and McIsaac, 1978, p. 26).

Young offending was seen as an indication of maladjustment, immaturity or damaged personality: conditions which could be treated in much the same way as an illness or disease. Kilbrandon advocated the abolition of the juvenile court and its replacement by a welfare tribunal. Local authority social workers were to play a more pivotal role in deciding who were 'delinquent' and how the 'delinquent' should be treated. Authority and discretion were notably shifted out of the hands of the police, magistrates and prison department and into the hands of the local authorities and the Department of Health and Social Security (see Chapter 15 of this volume). Reviewing these developments, some declared that 'the hour of the "child-savers" had finally arrived' (Thorpe *et al.*, 1980, p. 6).

All this was justified in the name of the state acting in a child's best interests. Whilst in England much of this welfare endeavour was undermined by non-implementation and police and magisterial non-compliance, in Scotland a children's hearing system was established to replace the juvenile court with a welfare tribunal serviced by lay people from the community. Although not without its own political contestation, the hearing system is still held to be one of the few bastions of a welfare-based youth justice system throughout the world. But elsewhere by the late 1970s the forces of neo-liberalism were gathering strength (Rose, 1996b). Beginning with von Hayek's immediate post-war critique of welfare interventionism as inefficient, self-defeating and totalitarian, the principle of freedom based on individual responsibility became firmly entrenched. The economic argument that the welfare sector was unproductive and parasitic on market capitalism fed into a range of critiques of social governments as arrogant, overloaded and failing to ameliorate social inequalities. Welfare practice and professionals were attacked from all parts of the political spectrum as unaccountable, overbearing and destructive of other forms of support such as community and the family.

In the youth justice context civil libertarians and radical lawyers also sought to establish due process in judicial decision making to overcome arbitrary and discretionary court outcomes. The left condemned welfare expertise as nothing but covert social control by the state and the neo-liberal right contented itself with the argument that the youth justice system had throughout gone 'too soft'. Eventually what emerged was a technique of government based on creating a 'distance between the decisions of formal political institutions and other social actors', a conception of 'actors as subjects of responsibility, autonomy and choice' and a project to 'act upon them through shaping and utilizing their freedom' (Rose, 1996b, pp. 53–4). Bringing responsibility back into youth justice was initially aligned with the 'just deserts' movement of the 1980s whose central liberal tenet was to establish sentencing proportionate to the offence, to remove professional discretion and to focus on the offence rather than individual circumstances (see Chapters 18 and 19 of this volume). As a result it appeared to expunge all elements of welfarism from the system. In England such principles were given a statutory footing in the Criminal Justice Act 1991. However, from 1993 to 1997 a 'prison works' Conservative mentality seemed to appropriate any liberal just deserts/individual rights elements into further advocacy of a punitive retribution.

Yet it would be misleading to view contemporary youth justice as completely bereft of the welfare principle. Elements remain in systems such as that in Scotland, and if the New Labour 'third way' project can be read as a reconfiguration of the social, then possible vestiges remain in the linkage between economic, welfare, health and youth justice policy and the partial recognition that enhancing opportunities is crucial to social exclusion and tackling crime reduction. The United Kingdom is also a signatory to UN conventions which state that in all legal actions concerning those under the age of eighteen the 'best interests of the child shall be a primary consideration' (United Nations, 1989, article 3). In turn, however, it should also be pointed out that New Labour's particular reading of welfare often involves sleight of hand whereby help is couched in the language of protection and used to justify interventions that penetrate deep into child-rearing and parental practices. Thus curfews and powers to criminalize parents are justified as an entitlement and any measure deemed to be preventive is simultaneously cast as acting with the welfare of children in mind. In such cases it is clear that whilst a discourse of welfare and the principles of 'the social' may have been reconfigured, even subverted, they cannot be considered to have been completely lost.

Reinventing the past 2: neo-conservative remoralization

Whilst responsibilization strategies have been read as a partial withdrawing of state intervention, the techniques of remoralization typically involve a strengthening and deepening of state interventionist programmes. As the 'problem' is perceived to be greater than offending *per se*, involving rather a break-up of the moral fabric and cohesion, targeting the non-criminal is also legitimized. Whilst responsibilization tends ultimately to find individual targets, remoralization – as a mode of governing – is based on the regulation, surveillance and monitoring of entire families and communities. In crucial respects strategies to remoralize the labouring classes through family targeting have been a pivotal and defining element of youth justice since the onset of reformatories and industrial schools in the mid-nineteenth century. In its contemporary guise it is invoked in a prevention discourse which targets not only the criminal but that which is perceived to be 'disorderly' and 'antisocial'. It rests crucially on the identification of a feckless, 'at risk' underclass who through a combination of refusal to work, teenage parenthood and single parenting threaten to undermine the entire moral fabric of society (Murray, 1990).

By proclaiming that the principal aim of the youth justice system is to *prevent* offending, action against legal *and* moral/social transgressions is legitimized. For example, one of the most radical initiatives of the 1998 Crime and Disorder Act is the availability of new orders and powers that can be made other than as a sentence following conviction. Child safety orders, local child curfews, antisocial behaviour orders and sex offender orders do not necessarily require the prosecution or indeed the commission of a criminal offence. The contention that crime runs in certain families and that antisocial behaviour in childhood is a predictor of later criminality opens the door to a range of legislative initiatives which draw children below the age of criminal responsibility into formal networks of social control. Children can be targeted as 'offenders' before they are old enough to be criminally responsible. Clouded in a rhetoric of 'child protection' or 'family support', behind this new remoralization strategy lies the objective of compelling parents to take 'proper' care and control of their children, whilst by the age of ten children will be held fully responsible themselves. This overt deepening of early intervention is justified as 'protecting the welfare of the young offender' (Home Office, 1997) because 'if a child has begun to offend they are entitled to the earliest possible intervention to address that offending behaviour and eliminate its causes' (UK government, 1999, para. 10.30.2, emphasis added).

The representation as progressive of criminalizing measures that penetrate deep into the everyday lives of young people and their families is clearly designed to ward off criticism and potential contradiction with the 1998 Human Rights Act implemented in 2000. This Act incorporates the European Convention on Human Rights into British law. Article 6 provides for the right to a fair trial with legal representation and the right to appeal. Youth offender panels deliberating on referral orders would appear to be in denial of such rights. Article 8 confers the right to respect for private and family life and protects families from arbitrary interference. Parenting orders, child curfews and antisocial behaviour orders, in particular, would again appear to be in contempt (Dinham, 1999; Muncie, 2002).

At the heart of Labour's new youth justice, then, lies a familiar analysis of family breakdown, poor parental control, failing child-rearing practices and a dependency culture (Muncie, 2001). Inevitably, the policy prescriptions flowing from this analysis are governed by assumptions about the 'normal orderly family' and the necessity to inculcate a work ethic at all costs. Social programmes such as the national parenting help line, welfare to work and Sure Start are presented as opportunities; parenting orders, compulsory curfews and antisocial behaviour orders await those who fail to voluntarily seek their 'benefit'. Workfare programmes 'seek to micromanage the behaviour of welfare recipients in order to remoralize them … This is "tough love", "compassion with a hard edge". It is through moral reformation, through ethical reconstruction, that the excluded citizen is to be reattached to a virtuous community' (Rose, 2000, pp. 334–5).

Much of this flies in the face of repeated research findings that young people in trouble with the law have complex and systematic patterns of disadvantage which lie beyond any incitement to find work, behave properly or take up the 'new opportunities' on offer. The percentage of children in poverty is higher in Britain than in any other country in the European Union: rising from some 10 per cent in 1979 to 35 per cent in 1999. Family difficulties and prior contact with the care system are also notable characteristics of 'known offenders' (Crowley, 1998; Haines and Drakeford, 1998; Goldson, 2000a). Moreover, these technologies of remoralization may have shown some promising results in some places at some times (Farrington, 1996; Sherman *et al.*, 1997; Graham, 1998), but the evidence also shows that they work best with those who concern us least: the petty offender from relatively stable home backgrounds (Wikstrom and Loeber in Pitts, 1999/2000). For the remainder any inclusionary programme which does not simultaneously advocate a redistribution of power, wealth and opportunity is likely to be seriously flawed.

Reinventing the past 3: neo-conservative authoritarianism

Perhaps the greatest anomaly in all modes of youth governance is that, however pervasive and seductive their welfarist, responsibilizing, reintegrative or restorative aims, youth justice has also been underpinned by a persistent coercive and authoritarian rationale. Discourses of neglect, immaturity and poor parenting have always sat uneasily against those of incorrigibility, persistent offending and dangerousness.

As a result, some of the most punitive regimes of incarceration have repeatedly been reserved for the young. The anomaly is somewhat 'solved' by clouding youth incarceration in a welfarist treatment discourse. Thus in the United Kingdom reformatories were legitimized in the name of reform via disciplined labour and religious education. Borstals were places of training. Approved schools were for re-education. Detention centres and youth custody centres were alternatives to prison. And currently secure training centres (for twelve to fourteen-year-olds) are ostensibly concerned with education as well as correction.

The Detention and Training Order introduced by the 1998 Act explicitly incorporates an element of training, to be carried out in the community under the supervision of a social worker, prison officer or YOT member. Yet the recurring critique of youth custody, in whatever form, is that it is self-defeating and counterproductive (see Chapter 26 of this volume). Preventive rhetoric has done nothing to undermine the pivotal position of youth custody. Inclusion is sanctioned only if exclusion is retained for particular groups of young offenders. This authoritarian mood has persisted despite compelling evidence of custody's harmful effects. In England and Wales the number sent to young offender institutions (YOIs) has continued to grow since 1994. The UK countries not only have some of the lowest ages of criminal responsibility but also lock up more young people than most other countries in Western Europe. For reasons which appear political rather than pragmatic, the example followed is usually that of the United States, whose punitive values are legendary – so much so that Simon (2001) refers to an emergent 'penality of cruelty' characterized in the United States by the death penalty for juveniles, boot camps and numerous shame sanctions (see Chapter 23 of this volume). Yet, as various campaign groups have maintained, vengeance and retribution through custody are demonstrable failures in preventing reoffending. Reconviction rates in England and Wales are well established and if anything are worsening. Young offender institutions are beset with brutality, suicide, self-harm and barbaric conditions. Moreover, custody diverts considerable resources from community provision to high-security institutions. It has long been maintained that the great majority of young people sentenced to custody pose no serious risk to the community, and indeed by leading to broken links with family, friends, education, work and leisure they may become a significantly greater danger on their return (Goldson and Peters, 2000; Muncie, 2002).

It is difficult to marry the ongoing incarceration of the young with a discourse of crime prevention or a philosophy of acting on the basis of what is known to 'work'. Rather, the rationale for the use of custody must be found elsewhere. The down side of the neo-liberal desire to break state dependence is the growing visibility of the homeless and unemployed young on the streets. This in turn plays on public anxieties and insecurities that creep into everyday life when structures of welfare support have been removed. In the process new conceptions of dangerousness have emerged (Pratt, 1999, p. 156) and the prison has been relegitimated. But in the youth justice field it is a reinvention of a responsibilization strategy that offenders are free to choose; if their choices lead to offending they must take the full consequences. As Tony Blair put it, 'Don't be surprised if the penalties are tougher when you have been given the opportunities but don't take them' (Blair, 13 June 1997, cited by Vaughan, 2000).

In tandem, a discourse of training and providing support to change behaviour continues inside youth custodial institutions. So progress through the penal system also becomes something of a matter of personal decision – whether or not to attend anger management or drug rehabilitation, or agree to sentence planning programmes. These attempts to rationalize incarceration aside, it is also clear that authoritarianism in general is driven by an ongoing political dynamic. Being 'tough on crime' inevitably leads to punitive 'solutions' in which a fearful public may be persuaded that 'something is being done'. To resort to custody or not is fundamentally a political decision. For example, the increase in the prison population in the United Kingdom since 1993 can in many ways be tied to the fallout from the murder of two-year-old James Bulger by two ten-year-olds. Although exceptional, the horror had to be atoned. And in the process a politics of fear, even of 'child hatred', emerged (Scraton, 1997 and see Chapter 21 in this volume). Notably, this demonization and child blaming has led to a paradigm shift in the treatment of girls, with misbehaviour (for example, fighting) being defined as criminal and immorality (for example, teenage pregnancy) being constructed as pre- or near criminal. Further, the celebration of punitiveness appears self-perpetuating. For example, youth justice initiatives, subsequent to the 1998 Act, which promised a new ethos of prevention, have been driven by a punitive and coercive mentality. This has involved:

- Withdrawal of benefit for those who fail to comply with community sentences.
- Electronic monitoring of ten to fifteen-year olds.
- Expanding local child curfew schemes to include fifteen-year-olds.
- Mandatory drug testing of all those arrested.
- Increasing fines on the parents of truanting children.
- Renaming community service as community punishment.
- Urging greater use of antisocial behaviour orders.
- Advocating on-the-spot fines for drunken, noisy and antisocial behaviour.
- Imposing 'lifestyle' sentences, such as driving licence confiscation, for disorderly behaviour.

The attractiveness of such authoritarianism lies in the appearance that 'something is being done' swiftly and decisively. For all the tendency of the state to govern at a distance, it reasserts a sovereign mode of state action: to evoke the continuing primacy of absolute power. Far from responsibilizing or managing, this neo-conservative mode of governance is concerned simply to demonize, promote hostility and pursue the politics of vengeance. Here questions of 'what works' and effectiveness appear to have no place.

HYBRID AGENDAS OF YOUTH GOVERNANCE: CRIMINALIZATION, RIGHTS AND RESISTANCE

In the field of youth justice it is difficult to prioritize any one mode of youth governance as ascendant or as above contestation, or indeed as acting in isolation from other modes. Managerialism may come closest to drawing the threads together, but only within the terms of its own strictly confined agenda. Similarly, neo-liberal readings may appear to chime with many of the responsibilizing trajectories of current reforms, but they do not adequately recognize the significance of those continuing strategies which allow the state to maintain sovereign power.

What is less open to dispute is the diverse and expanding array of strategies that is available to achieve the governance of young people. It is an array that is capable of drawing in the criminal and the non-criminal, the deprived and the depraved, the neglected and the dangerous. This broad ambit is secured because the discourse of crime prevention/reduction/safety is sufficiently imprecise to be all-encompassing. It is generated from the continuing ambiguities surrounding the place of young people in society. The precise boundaries and meaning of youth and adolescence remain uncertain. Moreover a period of 'youth' (and increasingly of the 'child') is rarely evoked with the same impersonality as that of 'adulthood'. Rather, the term is used as shorthand for a series of emotive and troubling conditions.

Youth is largely defined in terms of what it is lacking rather than by what it is (Muncie, 1999, p. 3). This is one reason why young people are afforded a central place in law-and-order discourse. They remain the touchstone through which crime and punishment can be imagined and re-imagined. Simon (1997) has argued that the salience of law and order in the United States is such that its citizens are continually governing themselves through their reaction to crime. Arguably, more accurately, it is the constellation of images thrown up by youth, disorder *and* crime that provide the basis of contemporary contexts of governance. The continual reworking and expansion of youth justice systems; a never-ending stream of legislation apparently dominating all other government concerns; the political use of crime as a means to secure electoral gain; the excessive media fascination – both as news and entertainment – with all things 'criminal'; and the obsession with regulation whether through families, schools or training programmes, all contrive to raise anxiety and encourage a punitive response to disputes and conflicts of whatever sort. Youth, crime and disorder are prioritized as the 'occasions and the institutional contexts in which we undertake to guide the conduct of others (and even of ourselves)' (Simon, 1997, p. 174). In crucial respects numerous aspects of social policy – whether regarding parenting, health, education, employment – appeared to have been captured within a youth justice discourse. Attempts to formulate 'joined-up' partnership approaches have drawn all manner of 'early interventions', from pre-school education to parenting classes, into a crime control discourse. Crime prevention has in effect activated a simultaneous criminalization of social policy. A focus on disorder and misbehaviour has blurred the boundaries between deviant and non-deviant, between the public and the private (Cohen, 1985).

Such readings of contemporary policy formation seem to give further weight to a 'death of the social' thesis and the growing primacy of ascribing the multivariate modes of youth governance to neo-liberal prescriptions and technologies. It seems to have an even greater resonance when governance is achieved not simply through crime, but also through disorder. An ensuing focus on *potential* for harm (rather than harm itself) clears the way for multiple possible strategies in the quest for risk management: a quest that can easily be turned toward exclusionary ends. Strategies of 'making people feel secure', through zero tolerance of the 'antisocial' for example, necessarily broaden the remit through which voluntary and statutory, public and private, collective and individual agencies can find legitimacy in acting against the 'undesirable'.

To the critical criminologist such developments chime easily with notions of an ever more repressive and intolerant state in which the coercive takes precedent over the persuasive (Muncie, 1999). But the complex and contradictory nature of modes of youth governance also suggests the possibility of continual conflict, struggle and resistance. As Foucault put it: 'if one governed too much, one did not govern at all – one provoked results contrary to those one desired' (cited by Barry *et al.*, 1996, p. 9). For example, the sheer cost of wholesale adoption of neo-liberal and neo-conservative rationalities conflicts sharply with simultaneous insistence on achieving managerialized cost-effectiveness. In essence, as Simon (1997, p. 185) acknowledges, governing through crime threatens to marginalize and criminalize entire sections of the population, which inevitably makes the process of governance more difficult: 'governing through crime reproduces the mentalities and strategies that have helped bring us to this impasse'. It is a strategy that is corrosive of any democratic ideals.

As a result, the 'catastrophic' images raised by some neo-liberal readings of governance must be subjected to their own revision. They may help us to identify significant social changes, but are less attuned to resistance to change, to the inherent instability of neo-liberal strategies and to the simultaneous emergence of other competing transformational tendencies. For example, O'Malley (2000) argues that broad governmental mentalities will always be subject to revision when they are activated on the ground. And at this level youth justice practice is likely to continue to be dominated by a complex of both rehabilitative 'needs' and responsibilized 'deeds' programmes. The language of social work reports on clients may, for example, have changed from 'social enquiry' to 'risk assessment' but the information is still likely to be dominated by traditional considerations of offender history, reports from psychologists and evaluations based on the clinical expertise of the human sciences (O'Malley, 2000, p. 161). Whatever the rhetoric of government intention, the history of youth justice is also a history of active and passive resistance from the magistracy, from the police and from youth justice workers through which such reform is to be effected. For example, in England and Wales, despite powers of three years' standing, no local authority has moved to implement a local child curfew. Moreover, we should also remind ourselves that many of the 'new' targets of intervention – inadequate parenting, low self-esteem, poor social skills, poor cognitive skills – are remarkably similar to those targets identified by a welfare paternalist mode of governance. The incongruity between such latent welfarism and the clearly retributive nature of a 'no more excuses' agenda may well create some space in which the complex welfare needs of children in trouble can be re-expressed (Goldson, 2000b). Equally, an ill-defined rhetoric of crime prevention has enabled social programmes to be once more elevated as those most likely to secure 'community safety'. Thus even in the United States – reputedly the bastion of neo-liberalism – we can still find numerous programmes funded by justice departments and run by welfare/police partnerships which appear more concerned with social support (for example, providing housing, health care, employment opportunities) than with overt crime control. Moreover, such reinventions of the social can also be based on long-term and large-scale programmes which address such issues as poverty, powerlessness, discrimination, and so on, which fly in the face of neo-liberal, short-term, 'what works' evaluative, or neo-conservative punitive, agendas. As O'Malley (2000, p. 162) argues, 'driven by discourses and agendas generated by the human sciences that were foundational of the welfare state long-range projects of "the social" survive or are reborn'.

We also need to be mindful of the significant legal purchase afforded to those who continue to advocate a rights-based agenda for young people. Such an agenda arguably comes closest to cutting through the internal disputes of modes of governance in that it draws attention to the limited nature of a debate primarily focused on *how* we govern rather than *why* we govern. In other words, the governmentality theses often lack a fundamental element of critique. And such partiality is reflected in the current emphasis on forging a youth justice system that draws together a multiplicity of agencies to pursue some coherence without addressing philosophical disputes about purpose. Thus governmental debates circulate around how to responsibilize, how to manage, how to control, rather than challenging established discourses about youth and childhood. These, as Haydon and Scraton (2000) record, tend to circulate around notions of care *and* control, liberation *and* confinement, freedom *and* discipline. Throughout non-intervention is deemed unthinkable. And in the process the protection of individual rights, such as those established by UN conventions, is given only secondary consideration. In most youth justice systems rarely are young people allowed the right to speak for themselves. A rights-based agenda notes the general 'disdain for children as active participants in their own destinies'. Adult power is frequently imposed without negotiation or consultation. Thus a politics of adultism, driven by professional discourses of protection (but realized as surveillance), discipline (but realized as subservience) and correction (but realized as punishment) confirms children and young people as outsiders; the 'other' to adult essentialism (Haydon and Scraton, 2000, pp. 447–8). Children's rights or child-centred advocacy-based initiatives are excessively marginalized: 'It is not simply that adults conspire to exclude or marginalize children and young people from the processes of consultation, decision making or institutional administration but that there is no conceptualization or recognition that such processes might be appropriate' (Scraton, 1997, p. 164).

Youth justice is underpinned by the paradoxical prescription that young people are not rational and responsible enough to be fully empowered but are deemed fully rational and responsible if they offend. A neo-liberal mode of government may pay lip service to recognizing the limited rights of the mature child but maintains that children need to be governed differently from adults and where the law does intervene it characteristically assumes legal power over both child and parent (Bell, 1993, p. 403). In contrast a positive rights agenda seeks children's full and active participation, as providers of knowledge and information rather than as passive recipients and as oppressed victims of adult power (see Chapter 21 of this volume). As Cuneen and White (1995, p. 267) put it: 'If young people's rights are not respected, if young people do not receive respect, then why should they respect law and state institutions?' Such an approach to understanding youth justice ultimately concerns itself less with the processes and procedures of governance than with establishing new terrains for progressive youth justice reform. Crucially, this depends on full recognition that the problem to be confronted is not necessarily one of youth but of the exercise of adult power in all its caring, responsibilizing, protective, disciplining and corrective guises.

Youth justice is a confusing and messy business. It is likely to remain that way. This chapter suggests that, whilst young people may be subject to expansionary modes of governance, complete, coercive control of them is unlikely ever to be achieved (see Chapter 7 of this volume). This elusiveness of control appears to rest on the continual recasting of youth as simultaneously in need of control but also in need of protection. The adult gaze is fixed on youth as something both desirable and threatening. Desirable because youthful energy remains a part of adult longing; threatening because freedom is deemed dangerous when unsupervised and unregulated

(Muncie, 1999, p. 11). In this sense the youth question is 'the site of a singular nexus of contradictions' (Cohen, 1986, p. 54). And as a result it is perhaps unsurprising to find that youth justice is also a prime site of confusion and ambivalence. Whatever unity is aspired to within the rubric of prevention it is likely to be achieved only by the growing insistence that all policy, practice and intervention should be made to run through and with certain standardized, financially accountable and managerialized procedures. Managerialism, because it has no higher purpose, may be the only available thread that can tie the contradictory, the volatile and the inconsistent together. No reading of the future can ever be clear. The logics of welfare paternalism, justice and rights, responsibilization, remoralization, authoritarianism and managerialism will continue their 'dance' and new spaces for resistance, relational politics and governmental innovation will be opened up.

REFERENCES

Audit Commission (1999) *Safety in Numbers: Promoting Community Safety*, London, Audit Commission.

Barry, A., Osborne, T. and Rose, N. (eds) (1996) *Foucault and Political Reason*, London, UCL Press.

Bell, V. (1993) 'Governing childhood: neo-liberalism and the law', *Economy and Society*, vol. 22, no. 3, pp. 390–403.

Burchell, G., Gordon, C. and Miller, P. (eds) (1991) *The Foucault Effect: Studies in Governmentality*, Hemel Hempstead, Harvester.

Cohen, P. (1986) *Rethinking the Youth Question*, Post-16 Education Centre, Working Paper no. 3, London, Institute of Education.

Cohen, S. (1985) *Visions of Social Control*, Cambridge, Polity Press.

Crawford, A. (1997) *The Local Governance of Crime: Appeals to Community and Partnership*, Oxford, Clarendon Press.

Crowley, A. (1998) *A Criminal Waste: A Study of Child Offenders Eligible for Secure Training Centres*, London, Children's Society.

Cuneen, C. and White, R. (1995) *Juvenile Justice: An Australian Perspective*, Melbourne, Oxford University Press.

Dinham, P. (1999) 'A conflict in the law?', *Youth Justice Matters*, December, pp. 12–14.

De Haan, W. (1990) *The Politics of Redress*, London, Unwin Hyman.

Farrington, D. (1996) *Understanding and Preventing Youth Crime*, Social Policy Research Findings no. 93, York, Joseph Rowntree Foundation.

Feeley, M. and Simon, J. (1992) 'The new penology: notes on the emerging strategy of corrections and its implications', *Criminology*, vol. 30, pp. 449–74.

Fionda, J. (1998) 'The age of innocence? The concept of childhood in the punishment of young offenders', *Child and Family Law Quarterly*, vol. 10, no. 1, pp. 77–87.

Foucault, M. (1977) *Discipline and Punish*, London, Allen Lane.

Foucault, M. (1991) 'Governmentality' in Burchell *et al.* (eds) *The Foucault Effect*.

Garland, D. (1996) 'The limits of the sovereign state', *British Journal of Criminology*, vol. 36, no. 4, pp. 445–71.

Garland, D. (2001) *The Culture of Control*, Oxford, Oxford University Press.

Goldson, B. (ed.) (2000a) *The New Youth Justice*, Lyme Regis, Russell House.

Goldson, B. (2000b) 'Children in need or young offenders?', *Child and Family Social Work*, vol. 5, pp. 255–65.

Goldson, B. and Peters, E. (2000) *Tough Justice*, London, Children's Society.

Graham, J. (1998) 'What works in preventing criminality', in P. Goldblatt and C. Lewis (eds) *Reducing Offending*, Home Office Research Study no. 187, London, Home Office.

Grisso, T. and Schwartz, R.G. (eds) (2000) *Youth on Trial*, Chicago IL, University of Chicago Press.

Haines, K. and Drakeford, M. (1998) *Young People and Youth Justice*, Basingstoke, Macmillan.

Haydon, D. and Scraton, P. (2000) '"Condemn a little more, understand a little less": the political context and rights implications of the domestic and European rulings in the Venables–Thompson case', *Journal of Law and Society*, vol. 27, no. 3, pp. 416–48.

Home Office (1968) *Children in Trouble*, Cmnd 3601, London, HMSO.

Home Office (1997) *No More Excuses: A New Approach to Tackling Youth Crime in England and Wales*, Cm 3809, London, HMSO.

McLaughlin, E., Muncie, J. and Hughes, G. (2001) 'The permanent revolution: New Labour, new public management and the modernization of criminal justice', *Criminal Justice*, vol. 1, no. 3, pp. 301–18.

Morris, A. and McIsaac, M. (1978) *Juvenile Justice?*, London, Heinemann.

Muncie, J. (1999) *Youth and Crime: A Critical Introduction*, London, Sage.

Muncie, J. (2002) 'A new deal for youth?' in G. Hughes, E. McLaughlin and J. Muncie (eds) *Crime Prevention and Community Safety: New Directions*, London, Sage.

Murray, C. (1990) *The Emerging British Underclass*, London, Institute of Economic Affairs.

O'Malley, P. (2000) 'Criminologies of catastrophe? Understanding criminal justice on the edge of the new millennium', *Australian and New Zealand Journal of Criminology*, vol. 33, no. 2, pp. 153–67.

Pitts, J. (1988) *The Politics of Juvenile Crime*, London, Sage.

Pitts, J. (1999/2000) 'New youth justice, new youth crime', *Criminal Justice Matters*, no. 38, pp. 24–5.

Pratt, J. (1989) 'Corporatism: the third model of juvenile justice', *British Journal of Criminology*, vol. 29, no. 3, pp. 236–54.

Pratt, J. (1999) 'Governmentality, neo-liberalism and dangerousness' in Smandych (ed.) *Governable Places*.

Rose, N. (1989) *Governing the Soul*, London, Routledge.

Rose, N. (1996a) 'The death of the social? Refiguring the territory of government', *Economy and Society*, vol. 25, no. 3, pp. 327–46.

Rose, N. (1996b) 'Governing "advanced" liberal democracies' in Barry *et al.* (eds) *Foucault and Political Reason*.

Rose, N. (2000) 'Government and control', *British Journal of Criminology*, vol. 40, no. 2, pp. 321–39.

Rose, N. and Miller, P. (1992) 'Political power beyond the state: problematics of government', *British Journal of Sociology*, vol. 43, no. 2, pp. 173–205.

Scraton, P. (1997) 'Whose "childhood"? What "crisis"?' in P. Scraton (ed.), *'Childhood' in 'Crisis'?*, London, UCL Press.

Sherman, L., Gottfriedson, D., M'Kenzie, D., Eck, J., Reuter, P. and Bushway, S. (1997) *Preventing Crime: What works, What doesn't, What's promising*, Washington DC, US Department of Justice.

Simon, J. (1997) 'Governing through crime' in L. Friedman and G. Fisher (eds) *The Crime Conundrum*, Boulder CO, Westview Press.

Simon, J. (2001) 'Entitlement to cruelty: neo-liberalism and the punitive mentality in the United States' in Stenson and Sullivan (eds) *Crime, Risk and Justice*.

Smandych, R. (ed.) (1999) *Governable Places: Readings on Governmentality and Crime Control*, Aldershot, Ashgate.

Stenson, K. (2000) 'Crime control, social policy and liberalism' in G. Lewis S. Gerwitz and J. Clarke (eds) *Rethinking Social Policy*, London, Sage.

Stenson, K. and Sullivan, R. (eds) (2001) *Crime, Risk and Justice*, Cullompton, Willan.

Thorpe, D.H., Smith, D., Green, C.J. and Paley, J.H. (1980) *Out of Care: The Community Support of Juvenile Offenders*, London, Allen & Unwin.

UK government (1999) *Convention on the Rights of the Child: Second Report to the UN Committee on the Rights of the Child by the United Kingdom*, London, HMSO.

United Nations (1989) *The United Nations Convention on the Rights of the Child*, New York, United Nations.

Vaughan, B. (2000) 'The government of youth: disorder and dependence', *Social and Legal Studies*, vol. 9, no. 3, pp. 347–66.

Youth Justice Board (2000) *National Standards for Youth Justice*, London, Youth Justice Board.

Part I

Folk devils

Constructions and reconstructions of youth and crime

The question of whether and to what degree 'childhood' is being undermined or eroded will continue to generate one of the most emotive debates of the first decades of the twenty-first century. The changing status of 'the child', the restructuring of 'childhood' and appropriate child-rearing practices will reverberate across public discussion about the condition of the family, parenthood, education, community and the nation. And there is every indication that this discussion will be fed by an ongoing sense of anxiety and panic. Two important, overlapping areas of the discussion will be notable among increasingly heterogeneous and often contradictory contemporary images and representations of 'the child' and 'childhood'. First, deliberation will persist about how to protect the innocence conventionally associated with childhood from the threats posed by the transformation of the traditional family and parenthood, the assumed damaging influence of all aspects of popular culture, the destructive intentions of the 'dangerous stranger', and child abuse. Local and national debate will lock into progressively more global debates about child soldiers, child prostitution and child workers.

Coexisting alongside the discourse of children as innocent victims will be one that highlights the problems that 'delinquent' children are seen to pose for social order. Local authority surveys indicate that, on many housing estates, the antisocial activities of bored and disaffected children and young people generate anger, despair and fear among older residents. How to respond to the threat posed by a 'post-innocent' generation of children – who, it is claimed, do not know the difference between right and wrong – is expressed most obviously and dramatically in the debate about children who murder other children.

In November 1993 two eleven-year-olds, Jon Venables and Robert Thompson, were found guilty of the murder of two-year-old James Bulger. Venables and Thompson were sentenced to a minimum of eight years' detention. The Lord Chief Justice subsequently raised their sentence to ten years and the then Home Secretary, Michael Howard, in turn raised it to fifteen years. The European Court of Human Rights, however, declared this extension of the boys' minimum sentence to be unlawful. Throughout their time in detention a highly polarized debate took place about how society could have produced such 'killer children'. The parents of James Bulger led a campaign against the release of the two boys. Venables and Thompson were consistently characterized in sensational and extensive tabloid newspaper headlines as 'evil', unreformable and unpunished. The announcement of their release in June 2001 was accompanied by threats of vigilante action. Not surprisingly, given the core concerns of public discussion, 'the child' and 'childhood' will continue to be the subject of intensive surveillance and supervision and of the intervention of a multitude of governmental agencies. As a result, it is vital that social scientists should examine the representations of the child and childhood that are embedded in the practices and ideologies of the criminal justice and social welfare professions.

Part I explores how childhood, adolescence and youth are constructed and reconstructed. Since the publication of Philip Aries's seminal text *Centuries of Childhood* (1962) social scientists have explored a central tenet that childhood is socially constructed – thus challenging the pervasive notion of childhood as a natural biological fact. Research across a variety of time periods has illustrated how childhood is a constant process of contestation and negotiation. The opening chapter in this part, by Harry Hendrick, discusses the variable constructions of childhood that were characteristic of nineteenth and twentieth-century England. Hendrick details the shift from a fragmented notion of childhood to a much more uniform and coherent one; the rise and development of idealized notions of the domesticated family; the evolution of statutory relations between 'state', 'family' and 'welfare'; and the political and cultural struggle to extend the changing concept of childhood among the population throughout that time. Amidst various nineteenth-century reconstructions and rerepresentations of 'the child' we witness the appearance of the fully fledged 'delinquent child'. This particular child deviated from the emergent Victorian ideal and the struggle between the conflicting perspectives of the criminal justice system and welfare reformers for his or her soul. Hendrick also alerts us to the importance of researching how these constructions were contested and resisted, not least by the children themselves.

Chapter 3 by Geoffrey Pearson was written in the context of the 'moral panic' about the youth crime wave that engulfed the United Kingdom in the early 1990s. He challenges the implicit claims in much public discussion about 'youth crime' of a 'golden age' of stability and order when young people behaved themselves and children were seen and not heard. Pearson's historical sweep is intended to illustrate the almost continuous concern about the nation's children and youth and how knee-jerk moral condemnation undermines attempts to formulate an adequate understanding.

There is increasing awareness among historians of the need to contextualize the history of childhood and youth within understandings of the United Kingdom as an imperial and post-imperial nation. This broader conceptualization is particularly important in understanding the recurring depiction of a 'golden age' against which the present is viewed as a moment of steep national decline. In Chapter 4 Paul Gilroy makes this connection explicit through his analysis of the racialization of crime since the Second World War.

He analyses how, during the 1970s and 1980s, existing discourses of 'youth' and 'crime' were joined with a post-colonial discourse which constructed 'black youth' as an instantly recognizable criminal group and generated a 'moral panic' about 'mugging'. Gilroy's work also pinpoints the remarkable durability of the criminal images of 'black youth' first forged in the 1970s and 1980s, and how the racialization of crime is constantly being reworked to include other categories of youth.

As these readings point out, the United Kingdom suffers periodic 'moral panics' about youth crime, engendered by the news media. First coined by Stanley Cohen in *Folk Devils* and *Moral Panics* (1973) and subsequently reworked by various social scientists, the term 'moral panic' is now one of the most insistently used in journalistic commentary and is routinely brought into play in public debates about a multitude of issues. In Chapter 5 Angela McRobbie and Sarah Thornton question the analytical relevance of the 'moral panic' concept to media-saturated societies such as the United Kingdom. After tracing the genealogy of the concept, they detail how media-conscious youth cultures of the 1990s subverted conventional social scientific usage of it. First, young people associated with the acid house and rave scene made conscious efforts to generate a sensational 'moral panic' in order to produce a sense of 'authenticity' and 'transgression'. Second, because of the defining features of the evolving dance scene and the face of the 'chemical generation', the news media could not maintain the hard-and-fast distinctions between 'deviant' and 'normal', 'disreputable' and 'respectable' and 'acceptable' and 'unacceptable' that had been the hallmark of the sensationalized reporting of previous youth cultures and fads. Finally, those involved fashioned new modes of resistance that effectively neutralized the state's attempt to criminalize the scene.

In Chapter 6 Keith Hayward concludes this part of the volume with a discussion of the excitement, pleasures and opportunities afforded by participation in certain forms of youthful deviance and criminality. Developing some of the key ideas of cultural criminology, he insists that we need to recognize the emotional and subjective qualities of criminal activity and the transgressive practices of youth in late modern societies which are marked by ontological insecurity, risk taking, hyper-individualization and the hedonistic pursuit of maximum self-fulfilment. Attempts to control 'youth crime' through criminalization and penalization are counterproductive because they will inevitably generate new modes of resistance, and are undermined by the corresponding popular cultural process of commodification and celebration of the excitement and emotional rush associated with transgression and its criminalization.

2

Constructions and reconstructions of British childhood: an interpretative survey, 1800 to the present

Harry Hendrick

The purpose of this chapter is to survey some of the most important social constructions of British childhood since the end of the eighteenth century in order to illustrate the historical variability of the concept. Such a brief account is unable to do little more than point towards the principal identities, and the attributable 'prime movers of social change' (Anderson, 1980: 61). My hope is that a familiarity with these perceptions, as held by dominant interests within our society, will help to explain both the tenacity and the self-confidence of western interpretations of 'childhood'. The focus here is on four related themes. First, the gradual shift from an idea of childhood fragmented by geography – urban/rural – and by class life-experiences, to one that was intended to be much more uniform and coherent; second, the rise and development of what historians refer to as the 'domestic ideal' among the nineteenth-century middle classes, which helped to present 'the family' as the dominant institutional influence on age relations; third, the evolution of an increasingly compulsory relationship between the State, the family and child welfare; and, fourth, the political and cultural struggle to extend the developing constructions (and reconstructions) of childhood through all social classes, to *universalize* it.

INTRODUCTION

Let us begin by making clear what is meant by 'social construction'. The term has nothing to do with 'the cultures which children construct for and between themselves'. During our period, 'childhood' – both the institution and the construction of – was composed by adults; usually those of the professional middle class. This is not meant to sound conspiratorial. No attempt is being made to suggest that children's condition is entirely devoid of a biological dimension, nor to deny the effects of physical being, though the nature of the consanguinity between the social, the

SOURCE: This chapter is taken from A. James and A. Prout (eds) *Constructing and Reconstructing Childhood*. London, Falmer, 2nd edn, 1997, pp. 34–62.

psychological and the biological is extraordinarily problematic. All the same, historians agree that 'ideas like parenthood and childhood are socially constructed and thus can be put together in diverse set of ways' (Anderson, 1980: 60). We know also that whatever its historical mutability, there is always a relationship between conceptual thought, social action and the process of category construction and, therefore, definitions of childhood must to some extent be dependent upon the society from which they emerge.

Thus the supporting premise of what follows is that the numerous perceptions of childhood, which have been produced over the last two hundred years or so, can only be fully comprehended within the context of how different generations and social classes have responded to the social, economic, religious and political challenges of their respective eras. Throughout the nineteenth century, for example, the influences of Romanticism and Evangelicalism, the social and economic impact of the industrial revolution, and the combined effects of urban growth, class politics, the 'rediscovery' of poverty, imperialism and the 'revolution' in the social sciences, all made necessary new understandings and new practices. As these changes were involved with the building of an industrial state and, later on, a liberal industrial democracy, no part of the societal fabric was left unattended, or unreconstructed, not least those areas most relevant to this essay: family relationships, concepts of health, welfare and education, and the value of children as investments for the future. Similarly, twentieth-century influences, such as popular democracy, world wars, psycho-analysis and the 'Welfare State', have profoundly altered the ways in which 'childhood' has been 'put together'.

In 1800 the meaning of childhood was ambiguous and not universally in demand. By 1914 the uncertainty had been virtually resolved and the identity largely determined, to the satisfaction of the middle class and the respectable working class. A recognizably 'modern' notion of childhood was in place: it was legally, legislatively, socially, medically, psychologically, educationally and politically institutionalized. During these years the making of childhood into a very specific kind of age-graded condition went through several different stages or 'constructions' (and 'reconstructions'). Each new construction, which was manifested in a kind of public identity, may be observed in approximate chronological order as pertaining to Rousseauian Naturalism, Romanticism, Evangelicalism, the shift from wage-earning labour to 'childhood', the reclamation of the juvenile delinquent, schooling, 'Child Study', 'Children of the Nation', psycho-medicine, and 'Children of the Welfare State'.

PRELUDE: EIGHTEENTH-CENTURY INFLUENCES – THE NATURAL CHILD

There is a general agreement among historians of the modern period that from the late seventeenth century a new attitude towards children (and notions of childhood) began to manifest itself, so much so that the eighteenth century has been claimed as a 'new world' for them (Plumb, 1975). In the 1680s, the Cambridge neo-Platonist philosophers asserted the innate goodness of the child and in 1693 Locke published *Some Thoughts Concerning Education*, which included an attack on the idea of infant depravity, and portrayed children as *tabula rasa* (although with respect to ideas rather than to temperament and ability). Not that Locke was revolutionary in relation to child rearing methods, though he tended to oppose corporal punishment. Much more significant was his recognition that children were not all the same – they differed and, therefore, they were individuals (Sommerville, 1982: 120–7; Cunningham, 1995: 63–4; Hardyment, 1995: 1–15).

In effect, the eighteenth century heard a debate on the child's nature. At one extreme stood the infamous statement of John Wesley, the Methodist leader, which urged parents to 'break the will of your child', to 'bring his will into subjection to yours that it may be afterward subject to the will of God'. At the other extreme stood Rousseau, author of the seminal *Emile* (1762), and all those who, under his influence, invested their children with a new understanding and affection (Sommerville, 1982: 127–35; Hardyment, 1995: 24–9). In *Emile* Rousseau captured the imagination of Europe with his validation of Nature, which espoused the natural goodness of children and the corrupting effects of certain kinds of education. He was not alone in his attachment to Nature for the age was one of profound social changes, many of which expressed themselves in more sensitive responses to the natural world in general and, in particular, to animals, women and slaves (Plumb, 1975: 70; Thomas, 1983: 172–91, 301; Porter, 1982: 284–8).

Part of the originality of the educational theory propounded in *Emile* lay in the claim that from both the physiological and the psychological perspectives, the educator was to treat the child as 'a little human animal destined for the spiritual and moral life' who developed 'according to certain laws whose progression must be respected above all' (Boutet De Monvel, 1963: vii). No less significant in inspiring a new outlook was the book's philosophical emphasis on the child as *child*: 'We know nothing of childhood' – 'Nature wants children to be children before they are men'. Thus could children be valued as children, and not merely as adults in the making (although this view of childhood still saw it as a stage on the route to adulthood (Sommerville, 1982: 127–31; Cunningham, 1995: 65–9; Pattison, 1978: 58). This was the essential feature of Rousseau's radicalism and of his contribution to the new construction of childhood. Moreover it was reiterated by numerous reformers throughout the nineteenth century, even though the majority of them lost the subtlety of Rousseau's innovative understanding of the child–nature relationship, reducing it to a crude view of children as distinguished merely by 'natural' incapacity and vulnerability' (Coveney, 1967: 40–4; Sommerville, 1982: 127–31).

THE ROMANTIC CHILD

The 'natural' child soon met up with the influences of Romantic and Evangelical revivals at the end of the eighteenth century, as well as the effect of the political economy of a growing child-labour force in factories and mines. Where the Romantics were concerned, in the works of Blake, Coleridge and Wordsworth, the child – enveloped in a concept of 'original innocence' derived from Rousseau – stood centrally in the search to investigate 'the self' and to express the Romantic protest against the 'Experience of Society'. In time, these objectives became sentimentalized and static in the hands of Victorian literature, but they began full of nuance and did much to provide children with an identity, not just of 'naturalness', but of significance for the evolution of humanity itself.

There were, however, initially two different views authenticated by Romanticism. One, associated with Blake, saw childhood not as a preparation for what was to come, but as the *source* of 'innocence', a quality that had to be kept alive in adulthood in order to provide nourishment for the whole life. Blake's vision, however, was confused by that of Wordsworth who changed the emphasis by bestowing upon children an infancy endowed with blessings from God, so much so that childhood came to be seen as the age where virtue was domiciled, and everything thereafter was downhill rather than upward towards maturity. The influential Wordsworthian perception of childhood was of a special (genderless) time of life, filled with childlike qualities, which was lost at the moment of its completion – it becomes 'a lost realm' since 'Growing up becomes synonymous with the loss of Paradise' (Cunningham, 1995: 73–5; Pattison, 1978: 58; Carpenter, 1985: 9; Sommerville, 1982: 168–9).

Notwithstanding that one particular Romantic view came to dominate the continuing construction of childhood, we need to see that we are witnessing the putting together of a particular childhood, narrowly confined to an elite, as a literary, social and educational theme. Furthermore, we are witnessing a contest for a particular set of beliefs, to represent a particular form of society, which was to stand between eighteenth-century rationalism and nineteenth-century industrialism. In this struggle, the child was to be central to the 'reinstatement of Feeling' (Coveney, 1967: 29–33, 37, 40).

THE EVANGELICAL CHILD

In some respects the 'Romantic Child' was short-lived. Poets are no match for political economy. Both the reaction to the French Revolution – the suppression of liberties – and the impact of the industrial revolution – the demand for free labour and the destruction of the old 'moral economy' – pushed adult–child relations in the opposite direction to that promised by Romantic aspirations. Besides the reactionary political climate of the early nineteenth century, and the aggressiveness of the new capitalism, optimistic notions of childhood also found themselves pitted against the weight of the Evangelical Revival, with its belief in Original Sin and the need for redemption. In evangelical hands, human nature, having been tarnished in the fall from grace, was no longer 'pleasing to the author of our Being'. Thus in 1799 the *Evangelical Magazine* advised parents to teach their children that they 'are sinful polluted creatures'.

Hannah More, the evangelical founder of the Sunday School movement and 'scribe of the counter-revolution', not only denounced 'the rights of man' and of women, but warned that in future society would be subject to 'grave descants on the rights of youth, the rights of children, the rights of babies' (Walvin, 1982: 45). 'Is it not', she wrote 'a fundamental error to consider children as innocent beings, whose little weaknesses may, perhaps, want some correction, rather than as beings who bring into the world a corrupt nature and evil dispositions, which it should be the great end of education to rectify?' (quoted in Robertson, 1976: 421; but see also Rosman, 1984: 97–118). By the 1820s More had overtaken Maria Edgworth, a disciple of Rousseau, and author of the influential *Practical Education* (1801), in popularity, which suggests a retreat from the 'rational tenderness' approach to child-rearing and with it the view of the child as being not only of Nature, but also of Reason (Hardyment, 1995: 19–30).

In opposing both Rousseau and the Romantics, Hannah More never underestimated the importance of educating and rearing children. In part her conviction was rooted in a tradition born during the Reformation, which sought to register childhood as an age that warranted the investment of time, thought, concern and money. However, the nineteenth-century discussion on the meaning of childhood in an industrializing and urbanizing nation was very much the work of evangelicals who produced their own agenda for child welfare reform, largely through the promulgation of a Domestic Ideal with its emphasis on home, family, duty, love and respect (Heasman, 1962; Davidoff and Hall, 1987: 321–56). During the many debates, the optimism of the Rousseauian and Romantic views gave way to the pessimism and alarmism of evangelical thought. The loss occurred despite the continued, though fragmented, influence of the Romantic ideal where childhood was portrayed as being fundamentally different from adulthood; different, that is, in the sense of having its own nature, and not simply being an immature condition. The evangelicals grasped this difference, but they used it for their own purposes.

FROM WAGE-EARNING TO 'CHILDHOOD'

Prior to the closing decades of the eighteenth century, there were few voices, if any, raised against child labour. For most children labouring was held to be a condition which would teach them numerous economic, social and moral principles. By the end of the century, however, this view was being challenged as first climbing-boys and parish apprentices in cotton mills and then factory children in general came to be regarded as victims, as 'slaves', as innocents forced into 'unnatural' employment and denied their 'childhood'. During the course of the debates, between, say, 1780 and 1840s, a new construction of childhood was put together by participants, so that at the end of the period the wage-earning child was no longer considered to be the norm. Instead childhood was now seen as constituting a separate distinct set of characteristics requiring protection and fostering through school education.

There are several explanations for this fundamental change of attitude towards the capabilities and responsibilities of children. Broadly speaking, many contemporaries were appalled, not only by the scale and intensity of the exploitation of young wage earners, but also by what was seen as their brutalization. These critics were equally appalled by the scale and intensity of the industrialization process itself, and they regarded the plight of the factory child – since factories were the most vivid representation of this process – as symbolic of profound and often little-understood changes in British society, changes that appeared to threaten what was held to be a *natural* order. In campaigning to restrain child labour, reformers – of varying persuasions – were in effect arguing about much else besides, including the direction of industrialization and, within this context, the meaning of progress. The 'childhood' they wished to promote was one that would be suitable for a civilized and Christian nation.

These objections, along with many others, to child labour had their roots in those eighteenth-century psychological, educational and philosophical developments already mentioned. For example, in opposition to, and paralleling the development of, *laissez-faire* capitalism, many critics projected the notion of a 'natural' and 'innocent' childhood, one opposed to the unremitting debasement of children through long hours, unhealthy conditions corporal punishment and sexual harassment (of girls) (Cunningham, 1995: 138–45; Thompson, 1963: 331–59). Similarly, the evangelical attitude to children, though in conflict with the Romantic, also opposed their unregulated economic activity. This attitude emanated from the combined, and often contradictory, influences of evangelical opinion concerning human nature, the gathering pace of the bourgeois 'domestic ideal' and fears about the social and political behaviour of the mass of labouring men and women – a class in the 'making' – in the first few decades of the century. It saw the brutalization of children as contributing to the dehumanization of this class and, therefore, was to be avoided (many Romantics also shared this view to a certain extent). A not unconnected theme here was the anxiety of the middle and upper classes who looked on Chartism (the first mass working-class political movement) as indicative of unstable conditions which, in common with the recurring economic distress of the period, turned issues relating to public order into matters of national security (Rosman, 1984: 47–53; Davidoff and Hall, 1987: 93–4, 343; Hall, 1979; Pearson, 1983: 156–62).

The Health and Morals of Apprentices Act, 1802, which was intended to control conditions primarily for parish apprentices, proved ineffective with the expansion of industry and the introduction of steam power. But thereafter the reform campaign grew in vociferousness, assisted as it was by government investigative committees, agitational publications and rallies. If the Rousseauian, Romantic and Evangelical understandings of childhood underpinned much of the reformers' campaign, there were more specific arguments against child labour that also pointed to the child's special character. Reformers were quick to identify the physical and moral dangers. The former referred to damage to children's bodies through long hours, debilitating temperatures, polluted atmospheres, and beatings. The moral dangers were perceived chiefly as a lack of education and religious instruction and general precociousness. These 'utilitarian' arguments amounted to a warning that child labour threatened the reproduction of society (Cunningham. 1991: 65).

In addition, there were three critical factors in the reconstruction process (and the emphasis is on the prefix here since the arguments achieved so much of their power through being diffused with Rousseauian, Romantic and Evangelical sentiments). The first was the emergence of the view that child labour was not 'free' labour. A basic principle of *laissez-faire* political economy was that labour was free and, therefore, could make its own contract with employers. However, during the debate on the above mentioned Factory Act of 1802, it became clear that children were not equal participants in the making of a contract and, once this was accepted, therefore, it followed that child labour was different in kind from adult labour (Cunningham, 1991: 69–71; Driver, 1946: 47, 243).

Second, the image of the child as being 'unfree' soon came to be associated with another and in some respects more vigorous image, that of slavery. Many reformers from the late eighteenth century onward looked for inspiration to the anti-slavery movement of the period, and were quick to draw analogies between the lives of West Indian slaves and those of factory children. The analogy had first been used in respect of climbing boys, but it became much more potent in connection with factory children since both textiles and slavery were central to the British economy (Cunningham, 1991: 72; Drescher, 1981; 11–13; Driver, 1946: 53, 104–5). The effect of the comparison of child wage-earners to slaves furthered the view that their condition rendered them unfree.

The third factor was the debate concerning 'The Order of Nature'. The fear was that a natural order of parents, and more likely of fathers, supporting their children, was being inverted through the demand for child (and female) labour in factories at the expense of adult males. This was important since it affected not only the role of children, but also that of women as wives in relation to men as husbands and, more generally, the 'natural order' of patriarchal domesticity. Moreover, it had ramifications for the growing tension throughout industrialization between this 'natural' order (of course, itself a social construction) and the order of capitalist political economy. This led on, in the minds of those, like the Evangelical Tory, Lord Ashley, to a consideration of the 'order' of the nation at a time of great social and economic upheaval, where the neglect of children could easily lead not only to the damnation of souls, but also result in social revolution (Cunningham, 1991: 83–96: Thompson, 1963: 331–49; Pearson, 1983: 156–62).

In the debates of the 1830s, the 'fundamental categories' of analysis had become 'childhood–adulthood' (Driver 1946: 244). Thus the substance of the child 'nature' in question was that it differed in kind from that of the adult. The age at which adulthood began had been undecided, but in 1833 a Royal Commission, drawing upon physiological evidence concerning puberty and having identified the associated change in social status, declared that at the age of 13 'the period of childhood ... ceases' (quoted in Driver; Cunningham, 1995: 140). The Commission led on to the Factory Act, 1833, the first piece of effective legislation, which prohibited selective employment of children under 9, and limited the working day to eight hours for those aged between 9 and 13. This was the principal success of the reformers' campaign: to establish the distinctive quality of child labour and, thereby, of children. It soon followed that such a quality implied a nature that should be common to all children, after allowing for the 'natural' differences of social position. By 1837, a reformer compaigning on behalf of climbing boys, who were still unprotected by legislation, could claim: '*They* are, of all human beings, the most lovely, the most engaging, the most of all others claiming protection, comfort, and love. They are CHILDREN' (quoted in Cunningham, 1991: 64). In this sense, the campaign to reclaim the wage-earning child for civilization was one of the first steps along the road of what can be described as the social construction of a *universal* childhood. Although at the time this made little difference in practice, the ideal situation had been formulated and posed, and for the rest of the century, reformers, educationalists and social scientists strove to make real the ideal through two further reconstructions: the reformed juvenile delinquent and compulsorily schooled child.

THE DELINQUENT CHILD – THE CHILD AS *CHILD*

Perhaps there was no more obvious attempt at the conscious universalization of 'childhood' than that which occurred with the mid-nineteenth-century reconstruction of juvenile delinquency (Pearson, 1983, Ch. 7). The arguments surrounding the evolution of the concept of juvenile delinquency focused upon the perceived conflict between 'Innocence and Experience' (we shall see here the perversion of these Romantic virtues). The clue to the new attitude being proclaimed by reformers can be found in this quotation from M.D. Hill, the Recorder of Birmingham:

> The latter [the delinquent] is a little stunted man already – he knows much and a great deal too much of what is called life – he can take care of his own immediate interests. He is self-reliant, he has so long directed or misdirected his own actions and has no little trust in those about him, that he submits to no control and asks for no protection. He has consequently much to unlearn – he has to be turned again into a child (quoted in May, 1973: 7).

No wonder, then, that Micaiah Hill, in a prize-winning essay, asked 'Can these be children?' Hill voiced a common theme throughout the literature when he wrote that understandings of middle or upper-class childhood were 'utterly inapplicable to that of a child brought up to vagrant habits' (quoted in Pearson, 1982: 167). Of course, this implied that he and other reformers were using a concept of childhood that was at odds with what they saw as the childhood of the poor and the neglected. Clearly, by this time (1850s) the intention was to make these children conform to a middle-class notion of a properly constituted childhood, characterized by a state of dependency.

The campaign for reform produced the Youthful Offenders Act, 1854, which, together with further Acts in 1857, 1861 and 1866, was significant for a number of reasons. Most importantly, for our purposes it provided the initial recognition in legislative terms of juvenile delinquency as a separate category (prior to the Act only children under 7 were presumed to be incapable of criminal intent), thereby extending 'childhood' beyond the traditional first seven years to under 16 (for non-indictable offences). Accordingly, the legislation defined the extended childhood' as 'different'; reinforced the view that they were not 'free' agents; drew attention to the child–parent relationship with the latter being expected to exercise control and discipline; and emphasized the danger of those in need of 'care and protection' becoming delinquents (Walvin, 1982: 152–3; May, 1973: 7–29; and see Chapter 7 of this volume).

Here was a critical turning-point in the legislative history of age relations, second only in significance to the Education Acts of the 1870s and 1880s. For under construction was a carefully defined 'nature', albeit the subject of much debate, which also contained a return to a mythical condition of childhood. Hence the phrase 'he has to be turned *again* into a child' (my emphasis). At the heart of this particular reconstruction process lay the 'care and protection' clauses of the legislation. These clauses took the Romantic approach to childhood and fused it with Evangelical convictions to produce an image of the 'innocent' child, who needed to be given the protection, guidance, love and discipline of what Mary Carpenter called *'the family'*, by which she meant an idealized notion being generated through the Domestic Ideal. However, where poor parents failed to rear such a child, it was determined that 'parental' discipline for delinquents should be provided by reformatory schools (Carpenter, 1853: 298–99; May, 1973: 7–29; Pearson, 1983: 165; Pinchbeck and Hewitt, 1973: 471–7).

At the core of the reconstruction as a whole, and the reason why it is so important in the history of childhood, was the successfully advanced belief of Carpenter that 'a child is to be *treated as a child*' (quoted in Manton, 1976: 109). 'What physiologists tell us', she wrote, justifies representing 'the child in a perfectly different condition from the man' (Carpenter, 1853: 293). The problem was believed to be that young delinquents and, by implication, all those neglected working-class children exhibited features which were the reverse of 'what we desire to see in childhood'. Such children were 'independent, self-reliant, advanced in knowledge of evil, but not of good, devoid of reverence for God or man, utterly destitute of any sound guiding principle of action ...' In a revealing passage, Carpenter continued: 'That faith or trust so characteristic of childhood, which springs from a sense of utter *helplessness* [my emphasis], from a confidence in the superior power and wisdom of those around' scarcely existed in the child in need of proper parental care. Thus children had to be restored to 'the true position of childhood'. The child must be brought to a sense of dependence by re-awakening in him new and healthy desires that he cannot himself gratify, and by finding that *there is a power far greater than his own to which he is endebted for the gratification of these desires* [my emphasis]' (*Ibid*: 297–9).

In order to understand the significance of developments in the concept of juvenile delinquency for this particular construction of childhood, it has to be remembered that the movement to create a separate order of juvenile justice emerged from three sources: the debate on child labour, the economic and political upheavals of the 1830s and 1840s, and the increasing popularity of the school as a means of class control. Consequently, the writings of reformers were the products of deeply held and widely debated convictions about the nature of the social order at a time when the middle class was anxious about what it deemed to be the rebellious and aggressive attitudes and behaviour of those young people (and their parents) who frequented the streets of urban areas (May 1973). On the broader level, the question facing politicians, philanthropists and reformers was how to build a healthy, co-operative society, one with a cohesive social and moral fabric, to replace the chaos and immorality that appeared to be widespread, even in an increasingly respectable mid-Victorian Britain (Selleck, 1985: 101–15; Pearson, 1983: 162–7, 171–9). The new conception of juvenile delinquency, with its implications for the universalization of an ideal childhood, was part of the answer (May, 1973: 29).

THE SCHOOLED CHILD

In their approach to the reformation of the juvenile delinquent, many commentators made the implicit assumption that, in the long run, only education would prevent the 'dangerous classes' from continually reproducing their malevolent characteristics. The work of reform of 'habits of order, punctuality, industry and self-respect', advised one enquirer, must 'begin with the young … They are the depositories of our hopes and expectations' (quoted in Pearson, 1983: 182); while a Justice of the Peace warned: 'I have no other conception of any other means of forcing civilisation downwards in society, except by education' (quoted in Johnson, 1970: 96–8, 104). Similarly, a government report noted that there was a need to produce educated men who 'can be reasoned with' (quoted in Colls, 1976: 97). Mary Carpenter had these sentiments in mind when she portrayed reformation as the necessary step towards 'willing obedience' which, in the coming age of industrial democracy, was an essential condition of 'rule by consent' (quoted in Pearson, 1983: 179–82).

The evolution of the concept of delinquency and the introduction of compulsory schooling, while not exactly chronologically hand-in-hand, were, as has just been shown, ideologically related. Thus there was nothing coincidental in mid-nineteenth-century penologists and social investigators seeking to return children to their 'true position', as it also involved making them more amenable to the classroom. The fact that it was a minority of children who were delinquent in some way or another was irrelevant to the basic restructuring of what a proper childhood should be. The notion of this childhood was as much concerned with images and establishing norms as with real rates of delinquency. For the reformers, precocity (and the perceived independence of spirit that accompanied it) and effective schooling were irreconcilable. The reconstruction of the 'factory child' through the prism of dependency and ignorance, was a necessary precursor to mass education in that it helped to prepare public opinion for shifts in the child's identity: from wage-earner to school-pupil; for a reduction in income of working-class families. as a result of loss of children's earnings; and for the introduction of the State into the parent–child relationship.

But in what ways did the school seek to alter children's 'nature', thereby creating a virtually new construction of childhood? It threw aside the child's 'knowledge' derived from parents, community, peer group, and personal experience. Instead it demanded a state of ignorance. Secondly, it required upon pain of punishment, usually physical, a form of behaviour, accompanied by a set of related attitudes, which reinforced the child's dependence and vulnerability and, in terms of deference towards established authorities, its social class (Humphries, 1981, Chs 2–3; Hendrick, forthcoming). Thirdly, the ability of children to work for wages was no longer viewed from the perspective of their exploitation by adults, but rather from that of their own moral weakness: wage-earning children were not 'proper' children and, therefore, had to be made 'innocent' of such adult behaviour, and the school was the institutional means of achieving this end. Fourthly, in claiming the legal and moral right to inflict physical punishment upon children, the school reinforced the idea of the child as being in 'need' of a *particular* form of discipline, for, although children had always been assaulted in their capacity as employees, wage labour had obscured what was coming to be regarded as an essential feature of their new condition (Hendrick, 1992: 42). Fifthly, it further institutionalized the separation of children from society, confirming upon them a separate identity: their proper place was in the classroom. Finally, the school emphasized the value of children as investments in future parenthood, economic competitiveness, and a stable democratic order.

There is no doubt, then, that in the last quarter of the nineteenth century the school played a pivotal role in the making of a new kind of childhood. It was not alone in this process, for as the century came to a close other agencies and philosophies were also reconceptualizing the child's condition (Hendrick, 1994, part II and Hendrick, forthcoming). But the classroom and the ideological apparatus of education were crucial because they demanded – indeed, could not do without – a truly *national* childhood, one that ignored (at least theoretically) rural/urban divisions, as well as those of social class (Hurt, 1979, *passim*). Schooling, as has just been shown above, did more than merely declare a particular definition of childhood. By virtue of its legal authority, and on a daily basis through teachers and school attendance officers, it was able to impose its vision upon pupils (many, perhaps the majority, of whom were unwilling to accept this 'reconstruction' of what they should be) and upon their parents (many of whom showed a similar reluctance) (Hurt, 1979, Chs 7 and 8). This construction was intended to directly involve *all* children and was meant to be as inescapable as it was visible, for in denoting them as 'pupils', the school was a constant and omnipotent reminder of who they were.

THE 'CHILD-STUDY' CHILD

One reason why the schooling process was so significant was that it helped to give rise to what became known as the Child Study movement (1880s–1914). The 1880s was an important decade in the history of children's welfare since, partly under the impact of schooling and partly as a result of a growing concern about poverty and its possible political consequences, it saw the beginning of 'a prolonged and unprecedented public discussion of the physical and mental condition of school children' (Sutherland, 1984: 6–13). One development, above all others, turned children into attractive research-subjects, namely, the opportunities afforded to investigators by mass schooling. Earlier in the century the focus of attention had been on distinct groups of children, such as factory workers and delinquents, but now it was the entire school population. In fact, the school was crucial in making children available to professionals: sociologists, psychologists, doctors and educationalists, all of whom sought to produce 'scientific' surveys of the pupils (Sutherland, 1984: 5). In this way, just as children were being dramatically constructed as 'school pupils' under the weight of 'education' (itself searching for scientific status as a subject), they also found themselves being examined under the influence of 'science', whose main institutional forum was the Child Study movement.

For some time there was a growing interest in how children developed, the immediate origins of which were separate articles published in *Mind* by Darwin and Hippolyte Taine in 1877, followed in 1881 by 'Babies and Science', written for the *Cornhill Magazine* by James Sully, Professor of Philosophy and Psychology at London University. These articles heralded a number of important studies in the closing decades of the century, the most notable being, from Germany, Wilhelm Preyer's *The Mind of the Child* (1888) and, from the USA, Stanley Hall's seminal essay on 'The Content of Children's Minds' (1883) (Wooldridge, 1995).

Besides the influence of Hall's writings, the impetus behind the movement came from three main sources. Mass schooling had revealed the extent of mental and physical handicap among the pupils and this attracted the attention of politicians and philanthropists, as well as of social and natural scientists: biologists and natural historians saw a close affinity between racial development and that of the child and looked to Child Study to further their knowledge; and, at a time when poverty was being 'rediscovered', there was a growing anxiety about racial degeneration. In general, teachers, doctors, psychologists, scientists, sociologists, educationalists and middle-class parents were anxious about the quality of the child population and this was combined with an interest in the details of human development (Wooldridge, 1995: 19).

Child Study spawned two organizations in the 1890s: the first, the Child Study Association (1894), was formed largely under the inspiration of Hall, and argued for 'a scientific study of individual children by psychological, sociological and anthropometric methods' and for the examination of the 'normal as well as the abnormal' (Keir, 1952: 10). The Association's journal, the *Paidologist* claimed that it would help parents 'with observations of the periods and aspects of child life'; it would attract teachers by offering them 'guiding principles'; and that it would prove to be of interest to those involved in 'education, psychology, biology and medicine'. The emphasis of the Association was on the individual child, rather than the condition of the child population as a whole. It wished to gain 'insight into child nature' in order to offer 'a more precise unfolding of the human mind, and of the way in which this was modified by the environment'. The second group to be founded was the more medically oriented Childhood Society (1896), which owed its origins to two committees: one established by the BMA in 1888, and the other by the 7th International Congress of Hygiene and Demography in 1891. The membership tended to come from medicine, education and statistics. The main interest of the Society lay in the mental and physical condition of children, especially racial considerations. In 1907 the two groups merged to become the Child Study Society, but by 1914 the movement as a whole was in decline as educational psychology rapidly fulfilled its role (Wooldridge, 1995, Ch. 2).

None the less, during its brief life the Society conducted a number of investigations and actively promoted its findings, thereby diffusing knowledge about the nature and conditions of childhood. In effect, Child Study helped to spread the techniques of natural history to the study of children, showing them to be 'natural creatures'; through its lectures, literature, and the practice of its influential members, it popularized the view that the child's conception differed from that of adults, that there were marked stages in normal mental development; and that there were similarities between the mental worlds of children and primitives (Wooldridge, 1995: 47).

The significance of the movement in the reconstruction of childhood (along 'scientific' lines) was that (in conjunction with developments in educational psychology), it was part of a more comprehensive movement towards enveloping childhood in a world of scientific experts of one sort or another. Childhood was no longer something that occurred 'naturally'. As we have seen, from the eighteenth century onwards there had been a growing interest in the nature, meaning and specificity of childhood, and of how it related to the big questions of human development. Under the impact of post-Darwinian science, the fear of racial deterioration, the ongoing revolution in the social sciences and the beginnings of preventive medicine, Child Study was seen to be increasingly relevant to understandings of, and solutions to, a number of dominant problems of the period and, therefore, it was considered to be socially and politically important. Thus the movement served to position the social, educational, psychological and racial importance of childhood, and of children, in terms of education, social welfare and mental and physical health.

'CHILDREN OF THE NATION'

Child Study, as has been observed, owed its inspiration to 'a heady combination of utilitarian calculation and romantic sentiment' (Wooldridge, 1995: 19). However, the movement was itself part of a much broader development concerning children and childhood in the late nineteenth century. We have already noted the importance of schooling in terms of providing opportunities for 'scientific' research, and for providing the stimulus for the 'unprecedented' public discussion of the physical and mental condition of children. Given this to be so, it has been suggested that between the 1880s and *c.* 1914, children, and child welfare, achieved a new social and political identity as they came to be seen, in the words of Sir John Gorst, the Tory reformer, as being 'of the Nation' (quoted in Hendrick, 1994: 41; also Hendrick: forthcoming). This can best be understood as a shift of emphasis from the mid-nineteenth-century concern with rescue, reform and reclamation, mainly through philanthropic and Poor Law interventions, to the involvement of children in a consciously designed pursuit of the national interest, which included the post-Boer war movement for 'national efficiency', education, racial hygiene, responsible parenthood, social purity and preventive medicine. The latter was of particular significance as the emphasis in children's health changed from 'sickly survival to the realisation of potential' (Baistow, 1995, title).

In each of these areas the State was becoming more interventionist through legislation (and through forming new relationships with local government authorities and charitable agencies). It is well known that among the most significant legislative Acts were those covering the age of consent (1885), infant life protection (1872 and 1897), the prevention of cruelty to, and neglect of, children (1889), the school feeding of 'necessitous' children (1906), school medical inspection (and treatment) (1907), a juvenile justice system (1908), and infant welfare (1918). The implementation of these measures meant that through their everyday involvement in children's lives, welfare bureaucracies of national and local government, and of philanthropy, imposed what, to all intents and purposes were, certain class dominated, and 'expert' formulated, concepts of childhood on the general population. Both state and charitable welfare provision made a number of assumptions (many of which were derived from psycho-medicine) about what constituted a proper childhood and its 'natural' conditions.

However, it could be argued that an important feature of this reconstruction of childhood, and of child welfare legislation in particular, was a concern with children's rights, and that 'it was the state alone which could enforce these rights' (Cunningham, 1995: 161). This view necessitated a sharp separation of childhood from adulthood, and the recognition of children's peculiar needs and characteristics. 'Childhood and adulthood ... became almost opposites of one another' (*Ibid*.: 160). Of course, protecting children, and their rights, was in harmony with the larger purposes of the state in securing the reproduction of a society capable of competing in the harsh conditions of the twentieth century' (*Ibid*.: 161). This was clearly expressed by Dr T.N. Kelynack, a leading medical journalist and public health activist, who wrote:

> the world of childhood has been an undiscovered or at least unexplored land. The child is a new discovery. Realizing at last the wealth, power, requirements of this long-neglected treasury, minds and hearts everywhere are awakening to a realization of opportunities and responsibilities, and in all sections of society eagerness is being manifested to understand and serve the child (quoted in Hendrick, 1994: 42).

And why was this?

> The child of today holds the key to the kingdom of the morrow; the child that now is will be the citizen of coming years and must take up and bear the duties of statesmanship, defence from foes, the conduct of labour, the direction of progress, and the maintenance of a high level of thought and conduct ... (Kelynack quoted in Wooldridge, 1995: 23).

Such assumptions and aspirations, whether focusing on children's 'rights' or their role as 'the citizen of tomorrow', demanded a subject conformity, that not only continued to *universalize* childhood, making it even more coherent and ordered, but also consolidated the idea of it as a period marked by vulnerability and, therefore, requiring protection. The incapacitated child, vulnerable, innocent, ignorant and dependent, was entirely suited to be a member of the twentieth-century family, the 'haven' within a liberal-capitalist system, sustained by a popular vote (Hendrick, 1992: 49). In an age of fierce imperial, political, military and economic national rivalries, in addition to domestic anxieties regarding poverty, class politics, social hygiene and racial efficiency, children were being reconstructed as material investments in national progress.

THE PSYCHOLOGICAL CHILD (IN THE PSYCHOLOGICAL FAMILY)

By 1918, childhood was well on its way to being conceptually 'modern': it had been broadly shaped by nineteenth-century notions derived from Romanticism, Evangelicalism and middle-class 'domesticity', it was increasingly defined in relation to educational, medical, welfarist and psychological jurisdictions, and was clearly separate from adulthood. However, given the importance of 'time' in understandings of child-hood, it is important to recognize that the inter-war period saw further significant refinements of the conceptualization of childhood, through, on the one hand, psycho-logy, in particular the work of Cyril Burt on individual differences and that of Susan Isaacs on child development and, on the other hand, through the psychiatrically dominated Child Guidance movement (Wooldridge, 1995: 73–135; Thom, 1992; Rose, 1985: 176–96). The different strands of psychology, psychoanalysis and psychiatry are extremely complex and difficult to disentangle and, therefore, the emphasis here is not on describing them, but on claiming their importance for yet another reconstruction of childhood. If the earlier reconstruction through welfare (1880–1918) had emphasized the child's body (though with a mental health dimen-sion), the psychological child would be one of the Mind in terms of emotions, fantasies, dreams, instincts and habits (Hendrick, 1994: 1–7).

The specific targets for Burt's applied psychology were three groups of abnormal children: the delinquent, the backward and the gifted (this focus alone, from an influential psychologist, put child nature in general under the spotlight). Within this framework Burt developed a moral psychology in which mental conditions were given pre-eminence over the economic. Thus he attached great importance to the family, and to the role of the mother in the rearing of emotionally balanced children. Strained family relations produced the nervous child, for it was in family relation-ships that 'the real difficulty resides'. A properly functioning family was essential for mental health since 'Nearly every tragedy of crime is in its origins a drama of domestic life' (quotations in Wooldridge, 1995). This was particularly true of juvenile delinquents, whose condition, said Burt, arose from a misdirection of a high level of 'energy' which produced unconscious 'complexes' (Rose, 1985: 195). These complexes related to the child's mental life involving fantasies and conflicts, the resolution of which was to be solved through psychoanalysis striving to 'disengage all the implicated motives of the child, unconscious as well as conscious' (*ibid.*). Such a view of the child's emotional world pointed towards a depth and breadth of meaning that had hitherto been barely appreciated.

Susan Isaacs was probably the most significant child psychologist of her genera-tion and, therefore, was extremely influential in promoting a psychological construc-tion of childhood since her ideas reached a wide and varied audience via a number of avenues: published studies of the intellectual and social development of children; her experimental school – Malting House – in Cambridge; the establishment by her of the Department of Child Development at the London Institute of Education; her work as a propagandist for nursery education; her problem page in *Nursery World* and in *Home and School;* her evidence to the Consultative Committee of the Board of Education; and her role in introducing educational psychologists to the work of such seminal figures as Freud, Piaget and Klein (Wooldridge, 1995: 111; Rose, 1985: 189–90; Urwin and Sharland, 1992: 185–7).

In her examination of children's intellectual growth, Isaacs showed that they have the same mechanisms of thought as adults do. 'They know less than adults and have less developed minds than adults; but they do not understand the world in fundamen-tally different ways from adults' (Wooldridge, 1995: 121). Where the social develop-ment of young children was concerned, she portrayed them as 'naive egoists' and claimed that their aggressiveness was due to their egotistical desire for 'possessions, power and attention'. The reasons for this lay in the unconscious, a world for the infant that was dominated by basic wishes, fantasies and fears. Isaacs informed mothers as to the importance of these and advised that leaving the child free to choose its own form of expression was usually the best course (Rose, 1985: 189). Much of the early life of children was taken up with the control of their impulses and the understanding of their anxieties. Only in this way could the child's ego be free 'for the possibility of real development – in skill and understanding, and stable social relations' (quoted in Wooldridge, 1995: 126). In essence, an 'understanding, liberal, tolerant attitude was to be encouraged to the vicissitudes of the mental and emotional growth of the child' (Rose, 1985: 189).

If two strands of psychological reconstruction of children are evident in the work of Burt and Isaacs, the third and most overtly institutional influence was in the development of Child Guidance Clinics of the 1920s and 1930s, through both their practice and their research (Rose, 1985; Thom, 1992). The significance of the clinics was that they took 'nervous', 'maladjusted' and delinquent children and 'treated' them, producing as they did a new perspective on the nature of childhood. Under the clinics' influence child psychiatry was consolidated as a distinct realm of medicine as childhood was given 'its own repertoire of disorders: ... of personality (timidity, obstinacy ...); behaviour disorders (truancy, temper tantrums ...); habit disorders (nail biting, thumb sucking ...); "glycopnec" disorders (migraine, insomnia ...)' (Rose, 1985: 179). However, perhaps the special significance of the clinics was their role in distributing a new understanding of childhood among a number of different professionals: teachers, probation officers, social workers, school attendance officers, and doctors and psychiatrists. This made it possible to 'regard the clinic as the fulcrum of a comprehensive programme of mental welfare'. Furthermore, the clinics were propagandist, through radio talks, popular publications, lectures and its association with parent–teachers organizations, in promoting certain views of happy families and happy children which were dependent upon a new tolerance of, and sympathy for, the child (*ibid*: 203–4).

From Burt and Isaacs, from psychological and psychiatric textbooks, from the clinics and from educational psychology came the message, actively promoted throughout the professions of psycho-medicine, teaching, social work, and penology, that 'childhood' mattered. This significance bestowed upon childhood was made visible in three main contexts: the mind of the child; the child in the family; and child management. Childhood, it was explained, had an inner world, one that reached into the unconscious and was of great significance for adult maturity, the efficient functioning of family and, ultimately, for political stability: 'The neglected toddler in everyone's way is the material which becomes the disgruntled agitator, while the happy contented child is the pillar of the State' (Riley, 1983: 59–108; Rose, 1985: 188–91; quotation in Urwin and Sharland, 1999: 191; see also 174–99).

THE CHILD OF THE WELFARE STATE

This child had two main identities: as a *family member,* and as a *public responsibility.* These identities, insofar as they were 'new' (and both were heavily dependent upon the psychologizing of the child throughout the inter-war period), were rooted in three main sources: wartime experiences, in particular the evacuation process; the theories of maternal deprivation and family cohesion associated with the leading figures in Child Guidance; and the Curtis report on child care in children's homes, which was followed by the Children Act, 1948.

The evacuation process in 1939 (described by one psychoanalyst as 'a cruel psychological experiment on a large scale') had involved the removal of nearly one million unaccompanied children together with half a million mothers with pre-school children from their urban homes in large industrial cities to reception areas in regions less likely to be bombed. The main social and psychological impact of this mass movement of children and mothers was to reveal the extent of urban poverty and slum housing, the tenacity of the ordinary working-class family in sticking together, the relatively poor physical and mental condition of thousands of children, and the existence of what was coming to be known as the 'problem family' (that is, the family who found it difficult or impossible to cope emotionally, economically, mentally, physically, and so on, without assistance from social workers and other state agencies). Evacuation, it was claimed, had shone a torchlight into the darkest corners of urban Britain, and what was revealed was both shocking and frightening in its implications for racial efficiency, emotional stability and post-war democracy (Macnicol, 1986; Calder, 1971; Inglis, 1989; Holman, 1995).

But the evacuation experience also had important consequences for theories of child care and for the psychological significance of family relationships. The Cambridge Evacuation Survey, conducted by a team of psycho-medics, revealed, as had Child Guidance Clinics, 'the crucial importance of family ties and of the feelings of parents and child towards one another'. But whereas the clinics had a small number of patients, evacuation provided the experts with many hundreds of thousands of subjects (Rose, 1990: 161). For those psychiatrists, such as John Bowlby, who had researched the effects of early separation of young children from their mothers, the evacuation experience confirmed their views. Separation produced an 'affectionless character' and it was character disorder that was the root cause of anti-social behaviour (quoted in Rose, 1990: 162; see also Urwin and Sharland, 1992: 194, and Riley, 1983). This line of thinking about children's mental health became significant in the post-war climate as concern was expressed about the mental hygiene of the population. In such a climate of opinion, 'The troubles of childhood were of particular concern ... [for] ... a scheme of preventive mental health, not only for themselves, but because they were sure warning of greater problems to come, and they were treatable by early intervention' (Rose, 1990: 163). Here, then, was a portrait of childhood, couched almost entirely in psycho-analytical terms, which looked upon children as being significant members of an organic population.

Furthermore, where the reconstruction of childhood is concerned, all these influences played a part in what might be called the 'discovery' of children 'in care'. Nor should the influence of the pronatalist drive to rejuvenate the family be overlooked (pronatalism grew out of an anxiety about the low birth rate) (Riley, 1982: 150–96). However, first we need to remind ourselves that the politics of the 1940s brought forth what was conspicuously thought of as a 'Welfare State' in which citizens had evidence of their *citizenship* through their right to free social and health services. This deliberate democratization of citizenship began to be formulated during the wartime debates on post-war reconstruction with one eye on sustaining a healthy and growing population and the other on the growth of communism throughout Europe and Nationalism throughout the Empire. In addition to the government's commitment to full employment, and the Education Act, 1944, there were four major welfare Acts regarded as underpinning the creation of the Welfare State: the Family Allowances Act (1945), the National Health Service Act (1946), the National Insurance Act (1946) and the National Assistance Act (1948).

The Children Act, 1948, has to be set within the context of this legislative record. Prior to the passing of the Act, the Curtis Committee on children in care (1946) found:

> a lack of personal interest in and affection for the children which we found shocking. The child in these Homes was not regarded as an individual with his rights and possessions, his own life to live and his own contribution to offer. He was merely one of a large crowd, eating, playing and sleeping with the rest … Still more important, he was without feeling that there was anyone to whom he could turn who was vitally interested in his welfare or who cared for him as a person (quoted in Rose, 1990: 167; see also Hendrick, 1994: 214–17).

This sentiment was enshrined in the Act, whose main principles included the establishment of local-authority Children's Departments, a new emphasis on boarding-out in preference to residential homes, restoration of children in care to their natural parents, and greater emphasis on adoption where appropriate.

In many respects, the principal theme of the Act, distinguishing it from previous child welfare legislation, was that local authorities responsible for a child in care were 'to exercise their powers with respect to him so as to further his best interests and to afford him opportunity for the proper development of his character and abilities' (quoted in Hendrick, 1994: 218). The child 'was a citizen of a democracy, a citizen with rights, and these included the right to a family life' (quoted in Rose, 1990: 167). Thus the publicly cared-for child was to be treated as an individual, to have rights and possessions, to be treated as a person; and wherever possible to be put into either an adoptive 'family' or returned to his or her natural parents. Childhood had been reconstructed on two levels, both of which had their origins throughout the inter-war period: as an *individual* citizen in a welfare democracy, and as a member of a family (Hendrick, 1994: 22–8). Moreover, insofar as the child in care was a 'public' child, it was viewed from the perspective of a kind of 'domestic ideal' (itself driven by pronatalism), whose late eighteenth/early nineteenth-century paternity was now emblazoned with psychoanalytic understanding.

'CONTEMPORARY' CHILDHOOD

Thereafter, identifying constructions or reconstructions of childhood in the 1960s, 1970s or 1980s becomes more difficult, at least for the historian. In many respects the 1960s stands as an enigmatic decade, so commonly referred to by a generation of the 'chattering classes' (of both the Left and the Right) while so far from being known in any accurate historical sense. Images of youth cultures and 'teenage' revolts are one thing, but notions of childhood, as far as this decade is concerned, are something altogether different.

The golden age of welfare was already beginning to tremor with self-doubt by the end of the 1960s, and its end was confirmed by the Labour Minister Anthony Crosland in 1975, long before the New Right gained the political and intellectual ascendancy, when he publicly warned that 'The party is over' (quoted in Glennerster, 1995: 167). And yet, at the same time as right-wing think tanks saw some of their more extreme ideas being put into practice in relation to economic and to a lesser extent social policy, and the Children's Rights Movement of the 1960s seemed to have lost ground, a new attitude towards children developed through the 'rediscovery' of child physical abuse to which was added, in the 1980s, child sexual abuse. It hardly needs to be said that media and political campaigns around child abuse were never straightforward in their concern for children, whose sufferings have often been hijacked by special interest groups in order to spread their own and primarily adult influences, whether they be of the feminist, Marxist, medical or religious variety. However, to his credit, Nigel Parton, one of the most influential left-wing figures in the debate, admitted that in his earlier work he ignored 'the child in child abuse' as well as 'the impact of power relations on children's lives' (Parton, 1990: 10–18. See also the influence of Ennew, 1986). And Parton is only one of many social scientists who have begun to recognize the existence of children as people [that is] the growing appreciation of the need for adult society to look beyond the traditional interest of psychologists in child development, to a deeper and more subtle understanding of the child's social world and of the adult–child relationship (Chisholm, *et al.* 1990; James, 1993; Qvortrup, *et al.* 1994; Mayall, 1994; Jenks, 1996).

Equally significant in the continuing, but often contradictory, processes of reconstruction are organizations that have emerged since the Year of the Child (1979), whose objectives are not those of the traditionally passive and often repressive protection of children. Instead, they represent a new Children's Rights Movement as they seek to listen to children's grievances and to campaign on their behalf: e.g., the Children's Legal Centre, Childline, and EPOCH (End Physical Punishment of Children), and the Children's Rights Development Unit. Similar progressive develop-ments include the famous Gillick judgement of 1985, where the House of Lords upheld the legality of doctors giving contraceptive advice to children without parental knowledge or consent, and the abolition in 1986 of corporal punishment in state schools. On the other hand, the much vaunted The Children Act, 1989, though providing provision for 'listening' to children's viewpoint has, it seems, done little to enhance their rights. In sexual abuse cases children's evidence is no longer so uncon-ditionally accepted as true and, since the murder of James Bulger in 1993 by two 10-year-old boys, most commentators agree that public and legal attitudes towards children have hardened. It is difficult to assess the extent to which all this constitutes a meaningful reconstruction of childhood.

But another aspect of this question is the popularity in certain quarters of the belief that childhood has been eroded, lost or has suffered a 'strange death' (Jenks, 1996). While the wide gulf between the poor child and the majority of more affluent children troubles many contemporary observers, others are equally concerned that there has been an 'increase of violence and disturbance among the young' who, hav-ing been given 'the best of everything', nevertheless feel 'cheated, purposeless and confused' (Seabrook, 1982). There is a similar concern for the so-called end of innocence (or the 'fall' of childhood), important features of which are said to be the 'sexualization of childhood from the innocence – and ignorance – of the past to the more worldly wise child of today … in a commercial, fashion-conscious age, boys and girls are so preoccupied with how they look and dress that they can no longer enjoy mucking about and having fun – that they are missing out on the pleasures of child-hood' (Humphries, *et al.,* 1988: 147). A recent twist to this theme has been the suggestion that with the Bulger murder, 'the innocence of childhood has finally come of age' (Jenks, 1996: 118).

However, the most controversial thesis (advanced by Neil Postman, an American media sociologist) claims that childhood is 'disappearing', mainly through the influence of television, but also by the use of child models in the advertising of children's clothes and adult products, the tendency of children's clothes to resemble adult fashions, the increasing violence of juvenile crime, and the gradual replacement of traditional street games by organized junior sports leagues (in America). The child, in having gained access to the world of adult information (mainly through television) has been 'expelled from the garden of childhood' (Postman, 1983: 192).

In such a climate of opinion, 'children become alien creatures, a threat to civilisation rather than its hope and potential salvation' (Cunningham, 1995: 179). Television is regarded as dangerous because 'it places before children images of the good life hardly consonant with the delayed gratification endorsed by Postman and before him by a long tradition within Christianity'. This vision of the good childhood, is not one of freedom and happiness; 'rather it is good behaviour, a deference to adults, and a commitment to learning skills essential for the adult world' (ibid.: 180). Notwithstanding this critical appraisal, it has been suggested that modern society has seen a 'collapse of adult authority', which 'took effect at varying rates'. The 'collapse' is said to be witnessed by the growth in parental spending on children, and the search by parents for 'emotional gratification' from children (ibid.: 182–5; also Zelizer, 1985).

This view, together with that of 'disappearing' childhood, is countered by those who argue that children 'remain subject to authority relations' (Hood-Williams, 1990). The power and control of adults over children is described with reference to Weber's notion of 'patriarchal authority' (meaning 'the probability that a command with a specific content will be obeyed by a given group of persons'), as 'age-patriarchy', which refers to an imbalance of power, control, and resources manifesting themselves through adult control – expressed as a demand for obedience – over children's space, bodies and time. This is not to say that there is an absence of affection between parents and children, for, just as between husband and wife within the patriarchal marriage, so 'one of the tasks of some modern childhoods is to be companionable, to be fun, to be loved and loving as well as to meet the more traditional requirements to respect, honour and, above all, to obey' (ibid.: 158).

We have here an answer to the claim that the parental search for 'emotional gratification' has entailed a shift in power towards children. On the contrary, it has positioned children in a similar fashion to the ideal 'bourgeois' wife and mother in her historical role as 'the angel in the home': pampered and loved, an essential ornament serving as testimony to domestic bliss, but subservient to male power (Davidoff and Hall, 1987). With reference to the heaping upon children of consumer goods, we know that adults have far greater control over 'the meaning and availability of consumer goods', which subordinates children's choices 'towards consumption patterns that do not seriously conflict with those of adults' (Oldman, 1994: 47–7). Moreover, since toys usually reach children as 'gifts', and we know from anthropological studies that gifts 'are a very special form of exchange which require their own reciprocities', clearly 'gifts are not given "freely". Some return is expected' (Hood-Williams, 1990: 162).

CONCLUSION

This survey has shown that since at least the eighteenth century there have been several authoritative social constructions (and reconstructions) of childhood. From the perspective of adults, these different understandings have shared the intention to identify the existence of 'childhood'; to define the desirable state of 'childhood'; to incorporate the concept into a larger philosophy concerning the meaning of life; and to control 'childhood', whatever its nature. From the beginning of our period, each construction sought to mould 'childhood' as a singular noun; the plural posed too many conceptual and political problems. In the eighteenth and for most of the nineteenth century, the plurality of 'childhoods' made it difficult to capture the desired condition and to secure agreement on what it should be. Consequently, disciples of Rousseau, Romantics, Evangelicals, child-labour reformers, anti-slavers, penologists, educationalists, moralists, psycho-medics and advocates of all aspects of child welfare struggled to regularize competing identities, through what was a developing conception of *proper* 'childhood', designed to secure universal approval. For most of this century what became a widely accepted construction of childhood by, say, 1914, has been elaborately and carefully refined in accordance with the principles of medicine, psychology and education on the one hand and, on the other, in relation to the political goals of universal welfare and a popular commitment to the family.

The extent to which each 'construction' was a 'reconstruction' is difficult to determine and, ultimately, it is not that important an issue. Contemporaries probably assumed conceptual originality, but there was always some degree of overlap among the expanding and changing perceptions, certainly in their ideological imperatives (and we should never forget the *political* nature of the social construction of childhood). The different constructions stretched out towards three related and paralleling objectives. The first was a uniformity and coherence necessary to unite the urban and the rural, capable of embracing different social-class experiences, and focusing on the supposedly 'natural' state of childhood. Secondly, the font of this uniformity and coherence was to be the family, sanctified by religion and personified from the early nineteenth century by a largely middle-class 'domestic ideal', with its emphasis on order, respect, love, duty and clearly defined age and gender distinctions. Here the child could live out a *proper* childhood in a *natural* environment. Thirdly, from the end of the nineteenth century a compulsory relationship involving the State, the family and public health and welfare services was legislated into practice. This built upon ideals of domesticity and, through psycho-medicine, reinforced the 'natural' childhood in terms of education, socialization and the culture of dependency. Of course, none of this just happened. It was a consciously executed political and cultural enterprise and, therefore, was often fiercely contested territory as the different beliefs concerning the 'nature' of childhood struggled for supremacy. And not least important among the contestants were children themselves.

REFERENCES

Anderson, M. (1980) *Approaches to the History of the Western Family: 1500–1914*, London, Macmillan.

Baistow, K. (1995) 'From sickly survival to the realisation of potential: Child health as a social project', *Children Society*, 9, pp. 20–35.

Boutet De Monvel, A. (1963) 'Introduction', Rousseau, J.J., *Emile*, London, Dent.

Calder. A. (1971) *The People's War*, London, Panther.

Carpenter, H. (1985) *Secret Gardens: The Golden Age of Children's Literature*, London. Allen and Unwin.

Carpenter, M. (1853) *Juvenile Delinquents: Their Condition and Treatment,* London, Cash.

Chisholm, L. *et al.* (1990) *Childhood. Youth and Social Change: A Comparative Perspective,* London, Falmer Press.

Colls, R. (1976) '"Oh happy English children": Coal, class and education in the North-East', *Past and Present,* 73, pp. 74–99.

Coveney, P. (1967) *The Image of childhood,* 2nd ed., Harmondsworth, Peregrine Books.

Cunningham, H. (1991) *The Children of the poor: Representations of Childhood Since the Seventeenth Century,* Oxford, Basil Blackwell.

Cunningham, H. (1995) *Children and Childhood in Western Society since 1500,* London, Longman.

Davidoff, L. and Hall, C. (1987) *Family Fortunes: Men and women of the English middle class 1788–1850,* London, Hutchinson.

Drescher, S. (1981) 'Cart Whip and Billy Roller: Or anti-slavery and reform symbolism in industrializing Britain', *Journal of Social History,* 15, 1, pp. 3–24.

Driver, C. (1946) *Tory Radical: The Life of Richard Oastler,* New York, Oxford University Press.

Ennew, J. (1986) *The Sexual Exploitation of Children,* Cambridge, Polity Press.

Glennerster, H. (1995) *British Social Policy since 1945,* Oxford, Blackwell.

Hall, C. (1979) 'The early formation of Victorian domestic ideology', in Burmanm, S. *Fit Work for Women,* London, Croom Helm, pp. 15–32.

Hardyment, C. (1995) (ed.) *Perfect Parents: Baby-care Advice Past and Present,* Oxford University Press.

Heasman, K. (1962) *The Evangelicals in Action,* London, Geoffrey Bles.

Hendrick, H. (1992) 'Changing attitudes to children, 1800–1914', *Genealogists' Magazine,* 24, 2, pp. 41–9.

Hendrick, H. (1994) *Child Welfare England: 1870–1989,* London, Routledge.

Hendrick, H. (forthcoming) *Children, Childhood and English Society, 1880–1990,* Cambridge University Press.

Holman, B. (1995) *The Evacuation,* The Lion Press.

Hood-Williams, J. (1990) 'Patriarchy for children: On the stability of power relations in children's lives', in Chisholm, L. *et al., Childhood, Youth and Social Change: A Comparative Perspective,* Basingstoke, Falmer Press, pp. 155–71.

Horn, P. (1974) *Children's Work and Welfare 1780s–1880s,* London, Macmillan.

Humphries, S. (1981) *Hooligans of Rebels? An Oral History of Working Class Childhood and Youth, 1889–1939,* Oxford, Blackwell.

Humphries, S., MACK, J. and PERKS, R. (1988) *A Century of Childhood,* London, Sidgwick and Jackson.

Hurt, J.S. (1979) *Elementary Schooling and the Working CLasses: 1860–1918,* London, RKP.

Inglis, R. (1990) *The Children's War: Evacuation 1939–45,* London, Fontana.

James, A. (1993) *Childhood Identities: Self and Social Relationships in the Experience of the Child,* Edinburgh University Press.

Jenks, C. (1996) *Childhood,* London, Routledge.

Johnson, R. (1970) 'Educational policy and social control in early Victorian England', *Past and Present,* 49, pp. 96–119.

Keir, G. (1952) 'A history of child guidance', *British journal of Educational Psychology,* 22. pp. 5–29.

Macnicol, J. (1986) 'The effect of the evacuation of schoolchildren on official attitudes to state intervention', in Smith, H.L. *War and Social Change: British Society in the Second World War,* Manchester University Press.

Manton, J. (1976) *Mary Carpenter and the Children of the Street,* London, Heinemann.

May, M. (1973) 'Innocence and experience: The evolution of the concept of juvenile delinquency in the mid-nineteenth century', *Victorian Studies,* 17, 1, pp. 7–29.

Mayall, B. (1994) (ed.) *Children's Childhoods: Observed and Experienced,* London, Falmer Press.

Oldman, D. (1994) 'Adult–child relations as class relations', in Qvortrup, J. *et al., Childhood Matters: Social Theory, Practice and politics,* Aldershot, Avebury, pp. 43–58.

Parton, N. (1990) 'Taking child abuse seriously', in Violence Against Children Study Group, *Taking Child Abuse Seriously,* London, Unwin Hyman, pp. 7–24.

Pattison, R. (1978) *The Child Figure in English Literature,* Athens, University of Georgia Press.

Parson, G. (1983) *Hooligan: A History of Respectable Fears,* London. Macmillan.

Pinchbeck, I. and Hewitt, M. (1973) *Children in English Society,* London, RKP.

Plumb, J.H. (1975) 'The new world of children in eighteenth-century England', *Past and Present,* 67, pp. 74–95.

Porter, R. (1982) *English Society in the Eighteenth Century,* Harmondsworth, Penguin.

Postman, N. (1983) *The Disappearance of Childhood,* London, W.H. Allen.

Qvortrup, J. *et al.* (1994) *Childhood Matters: Social Theory, Practice and Politics,* Aldershot, Avebury.

Riley, D. (1983) *War in the Nursery: Theories of the Child and Mother,* London Virago.

Robertson, P. (1976) 'Home as a nest: Middle class childhood, in nineteenth-century Europe', in De Mause, L. *The History of Childhood,* London, Souvenir Press.

Rose, N. (1985) *The Psychological Complex: Psychology, Politics and Society in England, 1869–1939,* London, RKP.

Rose, N. (1990) *Governing the Soul: The Shaping of the Private Self,* London, Routledge.

Rosman, D. (1984) *Evangelicals and Culture,* London, Croom Helm.

Seabrook, J. (1982) *Working-Class Childhood: An Oral History,* London, Gollancz.

Selleck, R.J.W. (1985) 'Mary Carpenter: A confident and contradictory reformer', *History of Education,* March, pp. 101–15.

Sommerville, J. (1982) *The Rise and Fall of Childhood,* London, Sage.

Sutherland, G. (1984) *Ability, Merit and Measurement: Mental Testing and English Education,* Oxford, Clarendon Press.

Thom, D. (1992) 'Wishes, anxieties, play, and gestures: Child Guidance in inter-war England', in Cooter, R. *In the Name of the Child. Health and Welfare, 1880–1940,* London, Routledge, pp. 200–19.

Thomas, K. (1983) *Man and the Natural World: Changing Attitudes in England, 1500–1800*, Harmondsworth, Penguin.

Thompson, E. (1963) *The Making of the English Working Class*, London, Gollancz.

Urwin, C. and Sharland, E. (1992) 'From bodies to minds in childcare literature: Advice to parents in inter-war Britain', in Cooter, R. *In the Name of the Child. Health and Welfare, 1880–1940*, London, Routledge, pp. 174–99.

Walvin, J. (1982) *A Child's World: A Social History of English Childhood, 1800–1914*, Harmondsworth, Penguin.

Wooldridge, A. (1995) *Measuring the mind*, Cambridge University Press.

Zelizer, V. (1985) *Pricing the Priceless Child: The Changing Social Value of Children*, New York, Basic Books.

3

Youth crime and moral decline: permissiveness and tradition

Geoffrey Pearson

'In the last 30 years, the balance in the criminal justice system has been tilted too far in favour of the criminal and against the protection of the public', said the Home Secretary in his speech to the recent Conservative Party conference, adding that 'The time has come to put that right'. This kind of complaint against rising crime and moral decay – characteristically invoking a generational timescale of '20 or 30 years ago' – is one which we have heard many times since the Second World War. It looks back to a 'golden age' before 'permissiveness' had worked its damage, to a fondly remembered past of civility and order when the traditions of family and community were still intact. As Lady Thatcher expressed the sentiment in her memoirs, reflecting on the Brixton and Toxteth riots of 1981, 'Authority of all kinds – in the home, the school, the churches and the state – had been in decline for most of the post-war years'.

What I wish to do in this article is to suggest that these ways of thinking about youth crime can be deeply misleading. We think of these problems as new, but both the problem and its encircling discourse are by no means new. Young people can, and do, commit serious crimes. Some of them are difficult and persistent offenders. However, what is not at all clear is whether these matters have any connection with jeremiads of national decline.

THE POSTWAR DILEMMA: WHICH WAR WAS THAT?

What is not in question is the sense of conviction and purpose in these debates according to which standards have come tumbling down in the postwar years, the police and magistrates have had their hands tied by the sentimentality of penal reform and 'do-gooders', while the defiant young laugh in the face of the law. Part of the seductive appeal of these ways of thinking is that they are part of a wider structure

SOURCE: This chapter is taken from *The Magistrate* December 1993/ January 1994, pp. 190–2.

of feeling that the process of change and modernity has gone too far and that we must get back to basics. For example:

> 'That's the way we're going nowadays. Everything slick and streamlined, everything made out of something else. Celluloid, rubber, chromium steel everywhere ... radios all playing the same tune, no vegetation left, everything cemented over. ... There's something that's gone out of us in these 20 years since the war'.

Or again:

> 'The passing of parental authority, defiance of pre-war conventions, the absence of restraint, the wildness of extremes, the confusion of unrelated liberties, the wholesale drift away from churches, are but a few characteristics of after-war conditions'.

This sorry postwar blues is such a familiar lament as to be almost unremarkable. And yet, the immediate complicating difficulty is that these are both complaints from *before* the war. The first is George Orwell's pre-war novel *Coming Up for Air*. The second is a Christian youth worker, James Butterworth, writing in 1932 about his experiences in the boys' club movement in the Elephant and Castle district of working class London amidst the sweeping changes of the 'postwar' years.

Nor was it only youth workers or fictional characters in novels who succumbed to this 'postwar' malaise in the 1920s and 1930s. One active focus of discontent was F.R. Leavis's 'Scrutiny' group at Cambridge, repeatedly thundering against 'this vast and terrifying disintegration' of social life. 'Change has been so catastrophic', wrote Leavis in 1930, that it had 'radically affected religion, broken up the family ... the generations find it hard to adjust themselves to each other, and parents are helpless to deal with their children'. T.S. Eliot's writings were drenched in the same anxieties. 'We have arrived', he thought, 'at a stage of civilisation at which the family is irresponsible ... the moral restraints so weak ... the institution of the family is no longer respected'. F.W. Hirst in his summary of *The Consequences of the War to Great Britain* (1934) agreed that, 'Post-war people, as compared with Pre-war people, have lost confidence in things human and divine. ... The post-war generation suffers from a sort of inward instability. ... There seems nowadays to be no desire to provide for the future or look beyond tomorrow'.

Then as now, these sentiments were linked directly to problems of crime and criminal justice. In addition to common allegations that the family, community and authority were in disrepair, a key cause of crime among the young was seen to be the influence of American gangster movies which offered incitements towards imitative crime and immorality. 'This rejection of conventional standards' and 'the greater freedom from restraint which is characteristic of our age' meant for Roy and Theodora Calvert writing on *The LawBreaker* in 1933, that 'we are passing through a crisis in morals'.

For some, one further aspect of this crisis was the new juvenile justice system installed by the 1933 *Children and Young Persons Act*. As Winifred Elkin described in her account of *English Juvenile Courts* (1938) the new arrangements were often criticised, unfairly in her view, as 'our drawing room courts' and 'our "namby-pamby" methods'. In context such as this, A.E. Morgan in his King George's Jubilee Trust report of 1939 on *The Needs of Youth* summed up a catalogue of complaint which has an uncannily familiar ring:

'Relaxation of parental control, decay of religious influence, and the transplantation of masses of young persons to new housing estates where there is little scope for recreation and plenty for mischief ... a growing contempt by the young person for the procedure of juvenile courts. ... The problem is a serious challenge, the difficulty of which is intensified by the extension of freedom which, for better or worse, has been given to youth in the last generation'.

VICTORIAN VALUES AND QUEEN VICTORIA'S HOOLIGANS

In so many ways these inter-war complaints seem like a carbon-copy of our own postwar ennui, and those who voiced them were often to be found looking back to happier times 'before the war'. Indeed, even today the late Victorian and Edwardian years – from the 'Gay Nineties' until the outbreak of the Great War – are often remembered as a time of unrivalled domestic harmony. The cosy fug of the Music Hall. The unhurried pace of a horse-drawn civilisation. The rattle of clogs on cobbled streets. Here, perhaps is the true home of 'Old England' and unfettered tradition. This was not, however, a picture of itself which late Victorian England would always have found recognisable.

'The tendencies of modern life', as Mr C.G. Heathcote the Stipendiary Magistrate for Brighton explained in 1898, 'incline more and more to ignore or disparage social distinctions, which formerly did much to encourage respect for others and habits of obedience and discipline'. Submitting evidence to the Howard Association on the subject of juvenile offenders, Mr Heathcote was in no doubt that 'the manners of children are deteriorating' and that 'the child of today is coarser, more vulgar, less refined than his parents were'. Nor was he alone in taking such a gloomy view. In the following year 'the break-up or weakening of family life' was on the editorial agenda of *The Times,* no less than 'the break-up or impairment of the old ideas of discipline or order' in the cities.

With the old traditions already in eclipse amidst the dying embers of Queen Victoria's golden reign in the late 1890s, and with crime and immorality seen to be on the rampage, the decline of the family and the increase of irresponsible parenthood were often a central concern in the years which followed. 'A somewhat unlovely characteristic of the present day', wrote Mrs Helen Bosanquet in her book on *The Family* (1906), was that 'there is among the children a prevailing and increasing want of respect towards their elders, more especially, perhaps, towards their parents'. A few years later Mrs Mary Barnett in *Young Delinquents* (1913) would agree. 'One of the most marked characteristics of the age is a growing spirit of independence in the children, and a corresponding slackening of control in the parents'.

Already, the rising generation was seen to be beyond control at the turn of the century – vulnerable to the vulgarity of the Music Hall, and to the copy-cat lure of crime and sensation at the silent cinema. That young people 'have tasted too much freedom', 'had no idea of discipline or subordination' or had 'emancipated themselves from all home influence and restraint' was a tireless accusation. Reginald Bray, who was by no means an unsympathetic observer, expressed the fear in 1911 that 'The city-bred youth is growing up in a state of unrestrained liberty' as 'the habits of school and home are rapidly sloughed off in the new life of irresponsible freedom'. Whereas, a government report of 1910 went so far as [to] allege that, 'The gamins of our large towns live a bandit life away from their homes, free of all control'.

This was the era in which the word 'Hooligan' first entered into common English usage, to describe what was widely seen as a new streak of violence among the rising generation: assaults on police, robberies, vandalism, and pitched battles between rival neighbourhood gangs. London's Victorian Hooligans of the late 1890s were what we might nowadays call a 'youth culture', having adopted a uniform dress-style of peaked caps, neck scarves, bell-bottom trousers cut tight at the knee, heavy leather belts with designs worked in metal studs, and a hairstyle which was cropped close to the scalp with a 'donkey fringe' hanging over the forehead. In other cities, similar gangs with the same dress-style were known and feared by different names: the 'Scuttlers' and 'Ikes' of Manchester and Salford; the 'Peaky Blinders' of Birmingham. In London it was a common allegation that the Hooligan gangs regularly engaged in armed combat with pistols and revolvers.

For many of their contemporaries, these gangs were a sure sign of a novel deterioration among the nation's youth and one of the missions of Baden-Powell's Boy Scout movement which was launched in 1908 was to rescue a generation which was said to be 'drifting towards "hooliganism"'. For others, such as the distinguished Police Court Missioner Thomas Holmes, the matter was no more than 'press-manufactured Hooliganism' which had been magnified by newspaper sensationalism. Holmes would have agreed, nevertheless, that the original Hooligans were symptomatic of an often turbulent street life. As the Metropolitan Police Commissioner's annual reports indicated, each year around the turn of the century one-in-four of London's policemen were assaulted in the course of their duty and one-in-ten of these would be on the sick-list for a fortnight or more. The policeman's lot was not a happy one.

Nor were these mere scuffles. As an illustration of different standards of civility and justice, we can note a case from 1898 when a man was killed amidst a bottle-fight among holiday-makers returning to London one Sunday evening from a railway excursion to the seaside. The only action taken was that three men were hauled before the magistrate the following day on a charge of 'assault' where they were each fined twenty shillings and required to pay the doctor's bill on the dead man. Life was evidently cheap in the streets of 'Old England'.

CONCLUSION: TURNING THE CLOCK BACK, BUT HOW FAR?

What is the meaning and significance of this history? It is certainly not a question of denying or diminishing the importance of crime in the community. Rather, it involves an acknowledgement of a long connected history of involvement with juvenile crime. One in which the same rhetoric has, unhappily, often been applied to the problem. It is a rhetoric, moreover, which is utterly misleading in its emphasis on the novelty and unprecedented dimensions of juvenile crime, thus failing to recognise the ways in which youthful crime and misconduct are firmly embedded aspects of the social landscape. The fact that we seem to be able to persuade ourselves in the 1990s that we are passing through an unprecedented crisis of public morals, while expressing our fears in a language which is indistinguishable from that of generations which are long dead, is an extraordinary historical paradox which reflects an equally extraordinary historical amnesia about even the more recent past.

It is not that the world does not change. Indeed, there are aspects of the crime question in contemporary Britain which *are* novel, and which will require new remedies:

the increasing use of firearms; certain kinds of drug-related crime; new styles of robbery such as 'ram-raiding'. However, the tired vocabulary of 'permissive decline' is one which somehow fails to keep pace with a moving world. If it is to be our guide for thought and action, this will guarantee failure in the future just as it has often been associated with failure in the past.

If 'permissiveness' is a concept which fails to measure up to the historical evidence, then what of 'tradition'? Here again there are problems. If tradition – in terms of the integrity of family and community in the past – means anything, then why were earlier generations unable to recognise that they lived in a stable and ordered social universe? 'I think morals are getting much worse', 60-year-old Mrs Charlotte Kirkman informs us. 'There were no such girls in my time as there are now', she adds 'When I was four or five and 20 my mother would have knocked me down if I had spoken improperly to her'. Once more, a familiar lament involving however what by now is a familiar difficulty: Mrs Kirkman's voice echoes down to us across a century-and-a-half as part of the evidence marshalled by Lord Ashley before the House of Commons in 1843 to argue the case for an effective system of education for the children of the poor. *Plus ca change?*

4

Lesser breeds without the law

Paul Gilroy

[...]

The ability of law and the ideology of legality to express and represent the nation state and national unity precedes the identification of racially distinct crimes and criminals. The subject of law is also the subject of the nation. Law is primarily a national institution, and adherence to its rule symbolizes the imagined community of the nation and expresses the fundamental unity and equality of its citizens. Beyond this general level, the importance of law and constitution in Britain is understood to be a unique and important cultural achievement. As Britain, stressed by crisis, has moved in the direction of a 'law and order' society, popular politics have infused legality with the capacity to articulate the very core of national identity. This idea [was] central to the rise of Margaret Thatcher. Discussion of the vicious conflicts between blacks and the law's agents has been prominent. These conflicts have sometimes been seen as a self-fulfilling prophecy of black externality and alienness which are in turn confirmed increasingly by vivid images of the particular crimes and criminals that are understood to be the anti-social effects of black settlement. In recognition of this and of its role in more authoritarian and populist forms of government regulation and intervention, following Hall *et al.* (1978) it has become commonplace to see the history of 'mugging' as the history of just such a racial category of crime. The moral panics which have attended the deployment of this concept in popular politics are interpreted as evidence that representations of the black presence in terms of its illegality are bound up with the experience of national crisis and decline. They provide at a visceral level contradictory, common-sense explanation, symbols and signs which render the shock of Britain's loss of status intelligible and enable it to be lived out in 'racial' terms. The fundamental process of fragmentation and chaos engendered by the crisis are contained in the images of a disorderly and criminal black population. However, the association of blacks and criminality in political discourse turns out to be more complex than this. The representation of black crime has taken several quite different forms, some of which do not draw on the image of

SOURCE: This chapter is taken from Gilroy, P. *There ain't no Black in the Union Jack*. London, Hutchinson, 1987, pp. 74–9; 85–102; 109–10.

'mugging' at all. Indeed blacks have not always been thought of as a high crime group in British society. The changing patterns of their portrayal as law-breakers and criminals, as a dangerous class or underclass, offer an opportunity to trace the development of the new racism for which the link between crime and blackness has become absolutely integral.

If the black presence in post-war Britain has been constantly identified as a source of problems, the precise shape and dimensions of these problems have constantly changed, reflecting a shifting balance of political forces in the struggles between black settlers and both institutional and popular racisms. It has been mistakenly argued, particularly in the aftermath of the 1981 street protests, that the identification of blacks with crime is simply a consequence of their membership of a disadvantaged and politically marginal group. This peripheral position is thought to make them more likely to engage in criminal acts. The distinct forms of criminality they practise are both sanctioned by the 'residual ethnic factors' in their inner-city culture and invited by its decaying environment. Their criminality triggers a militaristic police response, creates a white backlash and thereby inaugurates a 'spiral of conflict' in the inner city (Lea and Young, 1982).

This schema, which is not without support on the Labour left, contains a number of propositions which will be challenged below. The extent to which it is empirically demonstrable is not of primary concern here. The argument against it should not be read as a denial of the fact that blacks engage in criminal acts, though there are a number of unresolved questions around the extent of black participation – in particular around the role of official statistics in verifying their involvement. It is no betrayal of black interests to say that blacks commit crime, or that black law-breaking may be related to black poverty as law-breaking is always related to poverty. The possibility of a direct relationship between ethnicity, black culture and crime is an altogether different and more complex issue. It will be examined only as part of my consideration of the growth in new types of racial meaning and racist ideology during the 1970s.

In using the archaeological method this chapter is addressed not to epistemological questions which would seek to evaluate discourses relative to some norm of truth, but to the exploration of the conditions under which the discourse of black crime has become central to contemporary 'race' politics while other discourses have faded out. I am concerned here with the history of representations of black criminality and in particular with the elaboration of the idea that black law-breaking is an integral element in black *culture*.

[...]

Explanations of criminal behaviour which make use of national and racial characteristics are probably as old as the modern juridical system itself. The process in which the nation state was formed in Britain in the eighteenth and nineteenth centuries also provided the context in which modern legal institutions grew and developed. The moral regulation of citizens and their property became a primary object of state intervention. The identification of law with national interests, and of criminality with un-English qualities, dates from this process of state formation and has a long history which remains relevant to the analysis of 'race' and crime today.

The garotting panic which gripped London in 1862 is a well known early example of moral and political alarm about law-breaking which involved focusing the crime on a particular group of people whose deviancy was then conceived in terms of national and cultural differences. Reference was made to the alien, un-English quality which the garotters' activities lent to the areas of the metropolis in which it was practised: 'Highway robbery is becoming an institution in London and roads like the Bayswater Road are as unsafe as Naples.'[1] Once prisoners paroled on 'tickets of leave' were identified as the source of these outrages, the solution to the problem which caught the popular imagination was a revival of transportation abroad beyond the boundaries of the national community. As Jennifer Davis (1980) puts it, once it was concluded that ticket-of-leave men were members of a dangerous and irredeemable class, the liberties of free Englishmen were not to be extended to them.[2]

Sixteen years later, the 'Jack the Ripper' murders in Whitechapel were to provide a second illustration of how particular crimes could be categorized as un-English in inspiration or execution. This time it was a settler community, the Jews of the Spitalfields neighbourhood in East London, who were to be harassed and abused as part of popular outrage against murders which the *Daily News* identified as being 'foreign to the English style in crime'.[3]

Anxiety about the criminal predisposition and activities of the immigrant population inspired demands for the introduction of immigration controls in the first years of this century. When the issue of alien criminality was debated in Parliament, the settlement of Russians, Rumanians and Poles in the East End of London was described by the Tory member Major William Evans-Gordon in military metaphors no less potent than those chosen by Enoch Powell. Though he did not define the entire immigrant population in criminal terms he was firm that a 'considerable proportion of bad characters' were among them and that 'their competition with the home industries extends to burglary and other cognate crimes'. He concluded:

> I should have thought we had enough criminals of our own ... surely the executive government should have the power to deport such persons as were recently referred to by the chairman of Clerkenwell sessions who stated that 'foreign criminals had recently been landing by hundreds in London, formed themselves into gangs and carried on a systematic series of burglaries'.[4]

Historians of Jewish settlement have also identified concern with what were perceived to be the characteristic manifestations of Jewish crime during the Edwardian period. Here concern centred on the involvement of the community in a 'white slave traffic' which involved in the procurement of reputable white women for immoral purposes in cities as diverse as Buenos Aires, Bombay and Constantinople (Holmes, 1979; Gartner, 1973).

In 1912, the Criminal Law Amendment Act introduced flogging for the men of 'almost entirely foreign origin' who were engaged in this vile trade.[5] There was, however, no more general popular panic about the criminal behaviour of the East End Jews. Indeed when the Metropolitan Commissioner and his deputy were summoned to the Royal Commission on Alien Immigration in 1903, the relationship between their force and the Jewish settlers was not discussed as a problem.

The idea that immigrants engaged in higher rates of criminal behaviour and committed crimes which were essentially un-English bears the imprint of a second set of social theories. This tendency has been identified by David Garland (1985a, 1985b) as being central to the development of criminology in Britain and saw the racial deterioration and the criminal propensities of the urban population as related features of moral and physical degeneration which were the consequences of city life.

This association of criminality with urban living is closely connected with discussion of 'race'. It has at various points both supported and provided an alternative explanation to the more obviously biologically based theories. The fact that urban criminals had been identified as a 'race' apart, long before the wave of post-war black settlement, contributes to the potency of today's racial imagery of crime. It may also have strengthened the metaphor for urban crisis and decay which has been provided by black criminality. The appearance of metropolitan criminals with visibly apparent 'racial' characteristics is, in this context, the final proof that earlier anxieties about the effects of urban life had been justified. This is particularly true where, as we shall see below, the racial and cultural characteristics of the black population have been identified as contaminants of their white neighbours.

Anxiety about these harmful aspects of city life was integral to concern about the state of 'national efficiency' which Gareth Stedman Jones and others have argued was widespread in late Victorian and Edwardian England.[6] It endured beyond the 1914–18 war and can be discerned in the language of jungle and tribe with which Cyril Burt described the culture of the Young Delinquent (Humphries, 1981). It reappears not only in the idea of hooliganism as a disease that emerged in discussion of the 'boy labour problem' but in the notion of 'the unfit' that connects discussions of alien criminality in the post-war period[7] with a pathological view of the urban working class which defined the origins of their criminal inclinations in feeblemindedness and pauperism.[8]

[…]

FROM QUANTITY TO QUALITY – POWELLISM, PICCANINNIES AND PATHOLOGY

It is only by looking in detail at the language and imagery of this discourse on 'race' that the extent of changes which followed Enoch Powell's 'river of blood' speech of April 1968 (Powell, 1969) can be appreciated. […] If it can be read as a break in the epistemology of contemporary racism, this speech also provides an extended commentary on the way in which legality, the ultimate symbol of national culture, is transformed by the entry of the alien wedge.

Powell first defined the central problem of black settlement as a 'preventable evil' and gave it substance in the fearful notion that 'in fifteen or twenty years' time the black man will hold the whip hand over the white man', an image which derives its potency from a striking inversion of the roles of master and slave, covertly acknowledging guilt while summoning fear. He moves into the main body of the text with a section entitled. 'A matter of numbers'. He conceded that 'numbers are of the essence' and specified the proper object of government policy as their diminution by the encouragement of what is called 're-immigration'. However, this is not the main thrust of his argument. The problem introduced by the blacks is not reducible to a matter of numbers […] The issue is not the volume of black settlement but rather its character and effects, specifically the threat to the legal institutions of the country made concrete by the introduction of new race relations laws. As he puts it: 'If all immigration ended tomorrow … the prospective size of this element in the population would be unaffected.'

It is not then a matter of how many blacks there are, but the type of danger they represent to the nation. The rest of the speech is dominated by a polemic against the new race legislation which would afford black settlers the protection of the law where discrimination was proven. It was the contemplation of this bill which led Powell to compare himself to the ancient Roman with the grizzly vision of the Tiber foaming with much blood. His horror was at the prospect of blacks being afforded limited legal protection and it was this debasement of the legal sanction which appalled him rather than the issue of mass immigration itself.

The letter from an anonymous Briton which comprises the centrepiece of the speech has a double importance. It provides the proof required to legitimate Powell's view of the dire effects of black settlement and does so through a discussion of the perversion of the traditional legality which has been the result of the new legislation. Inseparable from this is the identification of young blacks as both a visible political problem in the public sphere and as a metonym for the incompatibility of blacks as a whole with English (city) life. The moment at which crime and legality begin to dominate discussion of the 'race' problem is thus also the moment when 'black youth' become a new problem category, conceived in the combination of youth and 'race'.

The anarchy represented by black settlement is counterposed to an image of England in which Britannia is portrayed as an old white woman, trapped and alone in the inner city. She is surrounded by blacks whose very blackness expresses not only the immediate threat they pose but the bleak inhumanity of urban decay. The letter describing her plight generates racial meanings from an accumulated tension between a series of neat binary oppositions – white/negro, clean/dirty, noisy/quiet. Its racial imagery is also striking for the way in which the conflicting colours are also gendered. The principal character, the aged white woman, is introduced first as 'a white' as if her other attributes are secondary. The word 'negro' is used similarly to signify the maleness of those it identifies. Where black people or children are referred to, other words are introduced – immigrants and piccaninnies.

The old woman's house, in the 'once quiet street which has become a place of noise and confusion', is beset early one morning by 'two negroes who wanted to use the phone to contact their employer'. These were the days in which 'negroes' had jobs. Their approach suggests the encroachment not just of alien blacks into the national heartland, but of the public sphere in which blacks are defined as being 'at home' into her private, domestic environment. The intrusion of the immigrants is initially by the threat of violence. She is verbally abused by them for her refusal to let them use the phone even though 'she would have refused any stranger at that hour'. She fears that they may attack her.

Her financial plight eventually forces her to seek replacements for the white tenants who have fled the black takeover of their once respectable street – an allusion to the mother country's post-war need for colonial labour. However, the only lodgers she can find are blacks and she will not accept them. Thus cut off, she begins to feel too afraid to go out and the negroes who have offered to buy her home for a paltry sum gradually institute a campaign of harassment and violence against her. They use their children as weapons in this war.

> Windows are broken. She finds excreta pushed through the letter-box. When she goes to the shops, she is followed by children, charming wide-grinning piccaninnies. They cannot speak English, but one word they know. 'Racialist' they chant.

What will become of this woman when the new race relations bill becomes law, wonders Powell's anonymous correspondent? The letter concludes speculatively: 'This woman is convinced she will go to prison. And is she wrong? I begin to wonder.'

The national tragedy described by the letter hinges on the transformation of English legality. The innocent are to be consigned to prison after being found guilty of racialism while the really guilty ones – the blacks who push excreta through letter-boxes and know just one word of English – are left to roam free. The inversion echoes the transposed master/slave image which opens the speech. The national constitution is distorted and destroyed by the presence of the alien blacks. They are the criminals, not the old woman, and their criminality is the central expression of their alien status. It expresses their distance from the authentic Englishness signified in the life which the law-abiding old woman was able to enjoy before their noisy arrival.

Legality is the pre-eminent symbol of national culture and it is the capacity of black settlement to transform it which alarms Powell rather than the criminal acts which the blacks commit. The discursive frameworks and textual strategies which define the new racism are all present in Powell's speech. The basic images and signs recur time and again in subsequent debate and commentary on 'race'. The portrait of white female vulnerability, the noise, the shit through the letter-box, endures into the 1980s as imagery for the effects of black settlement. It continues to connote immigration long after immigration ceased, and rests on the stain of illegality which has expanded to encompass a more detailed account, even a theory, of black propensities towards crime and disorder. Powell's wide-grinning piccaninnies were soon to grow up, and with the onset of their adolescence, the image of young black muggers stalking mean inner-city streets in pursuit of the old and infirm entered the syntax of British racism.

[...] The political language of Powellism that followed, secured the crucial link between 'race' and nation by focusing attention on the issue of legality and then on the violation of the constitution by blacks. The debate over the effects of the race relations legislation led directly into anxiety over black crime, and Powell played an integral role in the transition from one to the other.

By the time in 1976 when he declared 'mugging' to be a racial crime'[9] a complex combination of common-sense definitions and explanations of the 'race' problem had become fully operative. [...] It is important, however, to emphasize that the 'mugging' label did not arrive here initially as an expression of the deterioration in relations between blacks, particularly young blacks, and the police. There is plenty of evidence to substantiate the view that this conflict emphatically preceded both the use of the 'mugging' term and the official view of blacks as a high crime group in the population (Humphry and John, 1972; Hunte, 1965).

The 1971–2 session of the Home Affairs Select Committee on Race Relations and Immigration chose to inquire into the issue of 'Police/Immigrant Relations'. Their report (HMSO, 1972) refers to the relations between police and young blacks as 'difficult and explosive' and quotes a spokesperson from the West Indian Standing Conference who had said:

> To state that a sizeable proportion of the West Indian Community no longer trust the police is to confer a euphemism upon a situation which, for many, has reached a level equal to fear.

He continued:

> The Conference is convinced that if urgent action is not taken to give effect to the grave issue at hand, violence on a large scale cannot be ruled out. The solution rests largely in the hands of the police.

Another witness identified among police 'a tendency ... to consider that because a man was black he was a potential criminal'.

These perspectives seem familiar today but the arguments with which the police answered them show that any resemblance to more recent views of conflict between blacks and the police is only superficial. Evidence from the Police Federation, the rank and file police officers' 'union', concluded with the view that 'there was no serious problem in police/immigrant relations', but warned that the position of 'vociferous militants' in the black communities would be strengthened unless more was done to improve education and employment prospects for immigrants.

The Metropolitan Police evidence noted that: 'We often find that although we are prepared to talk to some of them [immigrant communities] they do not seem willing to talk to us.' Both submissions stated their opposition to the idea that blacks were naturally, socially or constitutionally disposed to higher levels of criminal behaviour than whites. The Federation said that 'if [a man] does a gas meter it is because he wants money, not because he has a black skin', while the Met. went so far as to endorse a view of the relationship between the environment and crime which had gained currency as a result of the publication of John Lambert's *Crime, Police and Race Relations* in 1970: 'There was not so much a problem of immigrant crime as of crime in over-crowded areas, where immigrants tended to live.'

The overall view which emerged from the committee's report swings between the idea that blacks were less criminal than whites and the idea that they were more or less similar in their criminal habits. The former position was propounded by the Chief Constables of Sheffield and Leeds who respectively stated that 'the crime ratio is far less with the immigrant people than it is with white people' and 'the immigrant areas are less of a problem to us from the police point of view than the skinheads or the crombies'.

The Chief Officer from Leeds identified a 'special difficulty', though not a criminal offence, in the 'number of West Indian girls leaving home and sleeping rough for one or two days at a time'. In spite of this, he added, prostitution problems with coloured girls were 'far less' than with white ones. One Metropolitan Police division, covering Notting Hill and Notting Dale, submitted a special comparative study of black and white crime statistics to the committee. Although the black population of the district was estimated at around 12 per cent, some 30 per cent of the callers at Notting Hill police station were revealed to be black.

This survey, together with similar, less detailed figures from Wandsworth, drew attention to the apparently disproportionate involvement of young blacks in robbery. Yet this observation is remarkable for its distance from the stereotype of the 'mugging' which was to follow it.

> Immigrant crime rates were, if anything, a little lower than those for the indigenous population. The only exception to this was robbery. Of 38 robberies in Notting Hill in 1971, 30 involved coloured people, mainly teenagers. These robberies were not organised or premeditated, but were usually things such as snatching handbags ... the coloured population does not feature largely in the drug scene (HMSO, 1972, p. 23).

Where the crimes, which were to become known as 'muggings', were identified, they were seen as a minor issue which was insufficient to dent the fundamental belief that immigrant criminality was low. Similarly, this report was written long before the phrase 'black youth' had acquired its fearsome contemporary power to signify disorder and national decline. Where West Indian youths are recognized as constituting 'special difficulties' for the police this is a result of their homelessness rather than their lawlessness.

Though the first stirrings of an explanation of black family life in pathological terms are undoubtedly present, the main reason given in the report is the parental insistence that by 15 the (male) youth should be able to support themselves by the fruits of their own work. The overcrowding of family homes was also mentioned as a contributory factor.

The gulf between this report and subsequent theories of 'race' as the effect of separable, antagonistic national cultures cannot be overemphasized. West Indians, it explained, were 'British in way of life, language and laws: only their culture and colour [are] different.' This is an interesting formulation because it excludes 'way of life' from the definition of culture which is being used. The content of this cultural difference is not revealed, but the suggestion that ethnic cultures amount to a complete discontinuity if not conflict between 'racial' groups is nowhere to be found. The same view emerges from the report's discussion of West Indian shebeens and noisy parties, a subject deemed important enough to be the first of the special difficulties listed. The committee began by denying that 'noisy parties are necessarily more attributable to black than white people'. They do, however, go on to criticize one particular type of party.

The shebeen was identified by police witnesses as a 'thorn in the flesh' of the force in various urban areas. These self-made leisure institutions were identified as a problem for the police but again there was no attempt to connect the patterns of consumption and recreation of which they are part to any idea of a characteristically West Indian culture or way of life. The fulcrum of official anxiety in this area is the suggestion that licensing laws are being broken as a matter of routine.

More significant for future common-sense theorizations of black criminality was the report's grasp of the political problems which lay beneath the surface of the black communities and its sense that conflict with the police was guided by a form of political antagonism rooted in the American ideology of 'Black Power'. The evidence submitted by the Police Federation had sought to turn the official mind towards consideration of the Black Power and Black Alliance movements which were thought to be recruiting among the young unemployed. There is no suggestion that these groups and movements were either representative of the community as a whole or of any innate West Indian predisposition to disorder. The Metropolitan Police evidence admitted that the force was 'worried' about the rise of isolated local pockets of militance but not 'unduly worried about it'. Young people were again identified as being 'ripe for plucking' by older, more experienced agitators. No direct connection between the rise of Black Power and unemployment was apparent to the committee.

A Police Federation representative from Coventry expressed concern about the publication of literature inciting young West Indians to violence and identified 'back street organizations ... composed of coloured ex-students who are maoists and revolutionaries' as the culprits. Where the two themes of youth and militancy come together in this way it was the role of the militants which caused the greater alarm.

These representations of criminality were centred primarily but not exclusively on the West Indian communities. The problem of Asian criminality was presented around different themes, particularly illegal immigration, which was also identified by the committee as a special difficulty. The traffic in illegal immigration was viewed as a minor but none the less significant problem for police forces, particularly as it offered a gateway into other important areas of criminal activity, such as blackmail and forgery. Significantly, the need to circumvent immigration control was not viewed as anything to do with Asian culture, family size, or a distinct way of life. The report concluded: 'in general legal immigrants are as opposed to it [illegal immigration] as anyone else'. The distinction drawn here [...] separates criminals from the law abiding, the disreputable from the respectable, in a manner which makes no concessions to the idea that blacks are a priori criminals, or even the suggestion that their patterns of criminal behaviour are culturally determined.

The governmental response to the committee's report was published in late 1973. It persists with the view of black criminals and disorderly types as minority within an overwhelming majority of solid citizens. The immigrants, it begins, 'are not in themselves a problem for the police' (HMSO, 1973). The white paper went further than the committee document by suggesting that the truculence and disorderly behaviour of black youth might originate in their frustration at not being 'accepted on the same terms as others regardless of colour'. [...] [T]he paper contextualizes discussion of the policing problems presented by black youth with an extended reference to the problems which police have had with other groups of (white) young people. The open acknowledgement of youth subculture and style as expressions of disorderly orientation is offered as the key to interpreting the behaviour of the 'small minority of young coloured people ... apparently anxious to imitate the behaviour amongst the black community in the United States' (HMSO, 1973).

These views of the relationship between 'race' and crime recede rapidly in the period between the arrival of the 'mugging' concept and the 'long hot summer' of 1976 which hosted the most bitter confrontations to date between blacks and the police.

Those years saw the definition of blacks as a low crime group turned round 180 degrees. They also witnessed the formation of a politicized roots culture among the black populations of the inner city. [...] What is important here is the extent to which that culture's political expressions, symbols, themes and modes of organization are themselves bound up with the new definition of blacks as a law and order problem. When the Metropolitan Police returned to the House of Commons Home Affairs Select Committee to give evidence in the 1975–6 session, their submission not only sought to withdraw the mistaken impression they had given five years earlier in suggesting that blacks were a low crime group but also identified the malevolent activities of

> 'certain individuals, organisations and journals' which 'consistently demonstrate their antipathy to the police and ... signal their intent to sabotage police/community relations ... continued editorial vilification of the police and other social agencies, distorted accounts of court proceedings, and repetition and exaggeration of unsubstantiated and one-sided complaints of police "brutality" which forms the sterile basis of a number of ethnic newspapers and periodicals, have a cumulative effect on the state of police/black relationships, and provide a false justification for extremes of group behaviour' (HMSO, 1976, p. 182).

These activities were denounced by the police as attempts to politicize the merely criminal actions of a disorderly and youthful minority. The phrase 'West Indian Community' was used in quotation marks, presumably intended to be ironic in tone. These sentences in the police submission conceal a commentary on the growth of articulate antagonism towards the police and detailed criticism of their practice. The ironic reference to the West Indian community can be read as an acknowledgement of the degree to which the community was being defined and organized politically around the policing question during this period. A series of well-publicized cases in London and elsewhere had provided disturbing evidence of the degree of conflict which had developed as well as the degree of organization in the black communities around the policing theme.

If the 1970 conflict around Notting Hill's Mangrove restaurant and the subsequent trial on charges of riot and affray fed anxiety about the role of 'Black Power Militants' in the growth of crime and disorder, the tone of panic in the mid 1970s was set by a sequence of bitter confrontations in and around other black cultural institutions – the dance-halls and clubs where the bass-heavy beat of the sound systems pumped righteous blood to the political heart of the community.

Predictably concern was greatest where 'black youth' were involved and the first of these confrontations also took place in Notting Hill at the Metro youth club in August 1971. The confrontations which followed are noteworthy not only for the consistency with which they originate in institutions which were cultural and recreational rather than formally political but for the new types of political organization and struggle which were constructed as part of the various campaigns to defend those who had been arrested. While the law was recognized as a repressive force there was no reluctance to use what constitutional and democratic residues it contained. The strategy which was devised sought to reveal and then exploit the political dimensions of the legal process by using the dock as a platform for the critical perspectives of the defendant while combining this legal struggle with popular, local agitation and organizing of community support. Those campaigns were aimed at maximizing mobilization rather than membership of the various organizations involved.[10]

[…]

The best known examples of this type of protest are provided by the large-scale cultural events of the community which drew national and regional rather than merely local support: the Bonfire Night riots in Chapeltown, Leeds, in 1973, 1974 and 1975; the running battle between police and youth at Brockwell Park in Brixton and, most famous of all, the Carnival riots of 1976, 1977 and 1978. Of these, the Notting Hill Carnival riot of 1976 will be examined in detail later, as a watershed in the history of conflict between blacks and the police and in the growth of the authoritarian forms of state planning and intervention during the 1970s.

It is important to remember that these major visible confrontations were exceptional only in their scale. By this time both police and black community sources agree that smaller conflicts were becoming routine events on the pavements of inner-urban areas. The Metropolitan Police's 1976 evidence to the Home Affairs Select Committee confided that 'the potential for conflict' was inherent in every law enforcement situation between police and West Indians (HMSO, 1976), and admitted that forty incidents between police and black youth with the potential for large-scale disorder had occurred in the twelve months before March 1976. Given the concentration of these events in the summer months, this total amounts to almost one major incident each week. The minor confrontations are not listed, but five incidents are cited and summarized in the report as typifying the broader problem. Of these, two originated in West Indian parties and the rest in a reggae festival, a youth club and local fair. All involved attempts by a crowd to release blacks who had been arrested and three of the five feature struggles over a black presence in public space which was thought to be illegitimate because of its size or character. Incident 2, for example, originated from a group of black teenagers who were thought by officers to be obstructing the entrance to a railway station. Incident 3 was provoked by forty black youths milling about in the road outside a club, and incident 4 by a group of blacks who were standing on the pavement outside a party.

The police memorandum observed that 'members of London's West Indian community do appear to share a group consciousness'. In each of the examples of black disorder listed, a cultural context is instrumental in establishing the extent and character of this collective, oppositional identity. Violence is seemingly formed by or in relation to, specific cultural institutions and events and identity is reproduced or transmitted by attacks on the police. Culture secures the link between the criminal minority and the mob who spring to their defence. Thus attacks on the police are also gradually seen to be expressive of black culture.

The Met. presented elaborate statistical proof of its revised thesis that blacks were after all disproportionately more criminal than whites. Their evidence dates their change of opinion from 1974 when 'concern began to grow ... about the degree of involvement by black youth in robbery and theft [from the] person offences in some areas' (HMSO, 1976). It concluded: 'Our experience has taught us the fallibility of the assertion that crime rates amongst those of West Indian origin are no higher than those of the population at large.'

The adequacy of the statistical material presented by the Met. can be questioned on a number of grounds. The compound 'circumstantial' category of robbery and other violent theft was used to lump together fundamentally different types of offences: the violent (robbery) and the non-violent (theft) across the lines which the law had set between them. This had the effect of inflating the total. The new category rapidly became a synonym for 'mugging' (GLC, 1986). No information as to the 'race' of victims was included, thus inviting the conclusion that blacks were robbing whites rather than other blacks. The various 'non-white' groups were added together to produce a single 'racial' category. Most significantly, the figures were based on arrests and victims' perceptions of the assailant rather than any figures for convictions. These objections are not central to the argument here but they have been the focus of a long political and criminological controversy which was rekindled after the Met. again issued 'racialized' statistics of this type as part of their response to the Scarman Report on the Brixton riots and the criticism of the police which had greeted it. Joe Sim (1982) has argued that the decision to issue the statistics and the manner of their release can be interpreted as a political intervention by the Met. designed to undermine what were felt to be the unacceptable contents of Scarman's report. If this instrumental and calculated purpose is a plausible analysis of the 1982 figures, such an explanation could also apply to the release of identical figures in 1976. The political chemistry of the earlier moment had little in common with the post-riot atmosphere of 1982 when policing was enjoying an unprecedented level of public scrutiny and debate. However, there are several reasons to suggest that the release of the figures was a part of the Met.'s political strategy at that time.

First, the emphasis on brute and basic images of black criminality and on crime rather than politics as the motivation and the primary characteristic of black law-breakers must be set in the context of the London Spaghetti House siege of September 1975. The restaurant was held up and members of staff taken hostage by armed black activists who identified themselves as politically inspired. Robert Mark, the Met.

Commissioner, described the episode in his autobiography as 'the most difficult and potentially explosive of all the various problems which I had to deal with in my 20 years as a chief officer of police' (Mark, 1978). He continued: 'From the outset it was rightly assumed that this was a simple armed robbery that had gone wrong ... any attempts ... to represent it as a political act were received with the derision which they rightly deserved.'

It is conceivable then that this political initiative around the theme of black crime, coming, after all, from the Yard's most senior officers, was part of a plan to offset the possibility that other similar political criminality might develop. The emergence of the Police Federation on to the stage of national politics is a second important background factor. The Federation's 'Law and Order' campaign had been launched in the autumn of 1975. Black crime was again a major issue and may have provided common ground between the force's developing rank and file voice and the views of its senior officers. This agreement, which cemented unity inside the force across the divisions of rank and bureaucracy, was matched by a populist politics. Mark had tried, in his own words, to engage the police service in 'the moulding of public opinion and legislation' (Critchley, 1978), and imagined a situation in which the force could draw a direct mandate from the population partly through more sophisticated use of the media. He had earlier referred to the relationship between his force and the press as an 'enduring if not ecstatically happy marriage' and he proved to be an effective communicator, politicizing his office in an unprecedented manner, particularly through television.

The political potential of the 'race' issue was readily apparent by this time and the Met. acknowledged as much when they admitted that their 1976 memorandum to the Select Committee 'will be taken by some people and used as racist propaganda against the black community' (HMSO, 1976). I am not suggesting that they intended to stir up racial sentiment for its own sake, but rather that the emphasis on black crime became a useful means to bolster the standing of the police, enhancing support for the organization at a difficult moment and winning popular consent which could no longer have been simply taken for granted.

Yet if the release of the racial statistics and new emphasis on the problem of black crime was a tactical ploy, the emphatic defeat of the Met. by 'howling mobs' of black youth during the 1976 carnival in Noting Hill suggested that it was an unpredictable and unreliable one. The aftermath of the riots saw the popular press extremely critical of the policing of the festival. An editorial in the *Evening Standard* was typical of some of the criticism expressed.

> It would be less than fair to aver that the police were in the right. All the reports suggest that Scotland Yard was far too heavy-handed on Monday. It should not have sent 1500 uniformed men to police the Carnival in the Notting Hill area. A force seven times as large as the one that attended last year's festivities must surely have contributed to the tension in a part of London in which, as the Yard knows very well, the police are regarded by many inhabitants as the natural enemy. The whole exercise was an error of judgement.[11]

The picture of black criminals being seen to get the upper hand was not, in the short term at least, a productive image for the police. The quality of their leadership was called into question and there was an increasing level of demand that something should be done.

Press reports of the carnival are interesting for what they reveal about the new conceptions of black crime and disorder. As in the Met. evidence of 1976, the carnival explosion was presented as the result of the crowd becoming involved in rescuing or preventing the arrest of black criminals out of some sense of racial solidarity. One police spokesman told the *Daily Mirror*: 'It's the same old story, a lot of West Indians who intervened and attacked our men did so without bothering to inquire why we were trying to arrest other coloureds.'[12] The rioters were described in several papers as the 'calypso mob' or 'calypso rioters'. This underlines the importance of the cultural dimension in creating the forms of racial solidarity which induced the mob to side with their criminal 'race' peers against the forces of law and order. The *Mirror* described the almost magical transformation which had occurred: 'suddenly the joyful smiles on the faces of the calypso revellers disappeared. They were replaced by an angry army of black youths'.[13] The *Financial Times* reported that the mob had been said to be heading towards Notting Hill police station which had been placed on siege alert. The *Daily Telegraph* invoked the memory of 1958 by pointing out that it was eighteen years to the day since the earlier conflicts. Alone among the press, that paper branded the disturbances 'race riots', suggesting that as far as the national race problem was concerned, nothing had changed in the intervening period. On closer inspection the meaning of the term 'race riots' in the *Telegraph* report is quite different from the conventional meaning of the words which are usually understood to refer to violent clashes between different racial groups. The 1976 riots were racial events for the *Telegraph* not because they involved racial conflict but because they expressed the 'race' of the blacks who had created them:

> Fierce race riots broke out in London's Notting Hill last night at the end of the three-day Caribbean carnival. At least 95 policemen were injured as coloured men in screaming groups attacked them with bottles and bricks. Several policemen were stabbed.[14]

Mark's autobiography compared the carnival riot to the 'sordid celebrations attending the hangings at Tyburn tree' and explained the unfavourable press coverage which his force had received by referring to the mendacity of newspaper reporters whom he identified as part of a stratum of politically motivated people urging 'a kind of black saturnalia in the interests of good race relations' (Mark, 1978). His final report as Commissioner of the Met. denied that the riots had been 'racist in nature' (HMSO, 1977), but indicated the direction of future police strategies in relation to race and crime in its declaration that there would be no 'no-go areas in London'. This comment betrayed an enhanced sense of the spatial and geographical dimensions to policing which became a feature of police practice in London as part of the response to the Notting Hill defeat. The pockets of black settlement in which the disorderly minority were thought to reside were subjected after the carnival riot to what can be described as a policy of containment. Runnymede Trust research into the use of the 'sus' law carried out during this period revealed that the law was not used uniformly, even within inner London, and that appearances on the charge were concentrated in courts serviced by police officers working in the West End of the city. If there were to be no no-go areas for the Metropolitan Police their practice suggests that they were keen to impose restrictions of this type on the freedom of movement enjoyed by 'black youths' (Demuth, 1978).

The containment policy identified certain neighbourhoods as high crime areas and proved this by reference to comparative statistics for 'muggings'. Special squads of anti-mugger police were set up in some areas.[15] The attempt to informally exclude blacks from certain central districts was matched by intense and aggressive policing in their home territory. The Special Patrol Group (SPG) was used in several of these operations, and particularly in South London and Hackney became the focus of community antipathy to the police.[16]

The story of street level conflicts between the various black communities and the police would fill a chapter on its own and has been recorded by other writers. It is not the principal issue here. The extension of containment policy under Sir David McNee's commissionership is important not for the local conflicts which resisted it but for the manner in which it marked a departure from a policing strategy based on the need to combat particular types of crime – burglary or 'mugging'. Instead, the direction shifted towards area-based strategies which assumed that any inhabitant of a high-crime district could be treated as a criminal. We shall see below how ideas like these have been refined and brought into the mainstream of police thinking under the leadership of Sir Kenneth Newman, the present Met. Commissioner.

In the 1976–8 period they were still in a preliminary stage and the concept of 'mugging' was still centrally featured as a part of the justification for differential police practice between areas.[17] However, 'mugging' was not the only mode of criminal behaviour which was used to prove the disorderly character of London's criminal areas. The growth of neo-fascist political activity during this period provided the context for an important encounter between the anti-police proclivities of black youth and those of white anti-fascist 'extremists' who attempted to smash the National Front and its associates off the streets wherever they organized public demonstrations. The right wing organizations rapidly developed the tactic of marching in a provocative manner through black districts. In recognition of its populist power and its congruency with their belief in black inferiority, concern about the level of black criminality was prominently featured in their propaganda. The counter-demonstrations instituted by the emergent anti-racist movement were joined in London and elsewhere by large numbers of black youth. In Lewisham and Ladywood in 1977 and in Southall as part of the run-up to the General Election in 1979, black protesters attacked both 'fascists' and the police who provided them with protection. Their resistance gave credence to the view of the decaying inner-city areas as rough and violent places, where anti-police attitudes were commonplace.

The black mob, either on its own or allegedly manipulated by white 'outside agitators', thus opened a new chapter in the lexicon of racialized crime imagery. Pictures of blacks collectively engaging in disorder began to confirm the suggestion that this type of behaviour had something to do with what made aliens distinct. Violence made the link between the blackness and disorder more complex and more profound.

The shift towards a plural collective image rather than the lone and isolated figure of the 'mugger' reflected the partial de-racialization of the mugging concept which had followed once white 'muggers' had begun to be caught. It also reflected the need to explain the public order problems which had become routine in the inner city areas. Groups of blacks engaging in disorder and moving to defend the criminal minority against arrest were seen as expressing the culture of the whole community: their cultural distinctiveness. Where the ethnic politics of community self-organization were also discernible, in a variety of guises: Black Power, Rastafari, or Asian militancy – they too acquired the taint of criminality. [...] It is important to remember that between 1975 and 1981 the symbols and rhetoric of that movement achieved a mass character in Britain's black communities, triggering official alarm in proportion to the degree to which they were adopted as a reference point by many people who did not choose to signify their allegiance or interest by wearing locks or colours.

The riots in Bristol during 1980 signalled that the containment strategy would not, on its own, be sufficient to deal with the problems of a disorderly black population. Containing a community successfully depended on an overall grasp of which communities and areas were volatile. The burning of St Paul's conveyed the message that bitter confrontations could erupt anywhere where blacks were settled, regardless of whether there had been any previous history of conflict with the police.

Fred Emery put it thus in *The Times:* 'No one at Westminster would have ... shortlisted Bristol as the potential powder keg'.[18] The much-publicized involvement of white residents in the protest, notably the participation of white pensioners in the looting of the supermarket, further complicated the picture. One local paper described the riot as '50–50 whites and blacks',[19] but the events were rapidly racialized with the theme of black culture as the catalyst of disorder becoming more and more dominant. Emery continued: 'It is no good pretending that "this was not in any sense a race riot" when there is, as Mr Merlyn Rees put it, "particular needle" between West Indian youth and the police.' The *Star* picked up this theme under its headline 'Race Mob Runs Riot'. The *Mirror* and the *Sun* made no overt reference to the 'race' of the rioters in their respective headlines 'Mob Fury' and 'Riot Fury'. The *Daily Telegraph* quoted a white bystander who identified the origins of the riot in 'a question of authority and the reaction to authority', but this observation was perversely used to confirm the special role of blacks in the events. By now, anti-authoritarianism was also being identified as a black cultural trait.

As the explanatory narrative of the events unfolded, the lawless character of the St Paul's area was traced back to its black settlers and their ways of life which had apparently rubbed off on their white neighbours. Black sociologist Ken Pryce was summoned to provide proof of this claim. He explained to the *Sunday Times* that 'ganja' (marijuana) which was alleged to have been sold at the Black and White cafe, the community institution with the usefully symbolic name where the riot had begun, was, in fact, a 'most important lifestyle trait' in the area.[20] Criminal use of drugs was revealed then not only as a means of recruitment of whites into this way life, but as a tangible link between the riots and the culture of the black Bristolians whose inability to live without their weed expressed their difference from true Britons. Ganja also linked their superficially different types of criminality. It made explicit the connection between the private and usually petty lawbreaking of the pot smoker and the expressive public disorder which had been symbolized most powerfully in St Paul's by the burning of the local Lloyds bank.

Pryce also drew attention to the role of ganja in the Rastafarian religion. Drug use has been a background theme in the representation of blacks as a criminal group for a long period. It was reflected in another drugs case in June 1982. This saw pupils at Eton, one of the country's most famous public schools and a symbol of the ruling class in its own right, detained by police. The *Daily Mail* reported the story prominently and sought to make the most of the contradiction between the popular image of Eton as a bastion of traditionalism and the tale of black-inspired drug use there. The transformation of the pupils and their descent into criminality was achieved by a Rastafarian who had sold them not only ganja but apparently his lifestyle too:

> Inquiries by housemasters have uncovered stories of boys as young as 14 smoking cannabis and reggae parties where cigarettes were handed round. ... [A] boy said that there were three sources for the drug ... a house owned by a Rastafarian in Slough and London street

dealers in the Railton Road area of Brixton and All Saints Road, Notting Hill. He claimed that … up to 10 boys would gather in a room to listen to Bob Marley records and roll hashish cigarettes.[21]

This example is less trivial than it might initially seem. It confirms first, the ubiquity of the threat to British life which is represented by the activities of black criminals; second, the power of that group who are able to secure entry into a secure and protected educational environment; and third, the pleasures involved in forsaking the duties and obligations of British discipline and replacing them with an idle and hedonistic lifestyle. The headmaster of Eton, Dr Eric Anderson, concludes the piece by warning that 'cannabis is a national problem among young people'. [...]

Hedonism and dangerousness are very closely entwined in imagery of the black criminal. We have already seen how black parties and shebeens were gradually identified as sources of anti-police violence rather than simply places in which the licensing laws were being broken. The most significant recent example of the fusion of these two themes in discussion of 'race' came in the reporting of a ten-day party which ended in injuries to six police officers when the mob who had been taking their leisure inside 'surged out' and attacked the police.[22]

The papers reported that the party had been a source of fear not only for the police but for local white residents who had had to sleep 'in their kitchens at the back of the house with the doors barricaded'. Officers who had been dispatched to quell the party after a reported ten days of continuous noise reported that as soon as the mob erupted into violence shouts of 'white bastards' and 'white pigs' were heard. The *Sun* which gave the duration of the party as only eight days, reported that the riot had ensued when 'West Indian party-goers thought the police were going to call time on their fun'.[23] The *Daily Mail,* which listed the party's length as nine days, referred to the mob as 'guests' at the party and claimed that the trouble had flared as police had gone to investigate a reported assault. Music from the party, claimed the *Mail,* was 'shaking houses nearby' and it warned that if disruption like this was allowed to continue then 'worried people will take the law into their own hands'. Later, the *Mail* continued, a 'knife was found in a nearby garden'.

The party was alleged to have run throughout the period between Christmas and New Year without a break. This context is significant because it is the tension between how 'normal' English people spend the holiday period and the way that the blacks have fun which forms the point at which their respective cultures can be seen to diverge and become antagonistic. The shouts of abuse from the party suggest that the police attempt to 'call time' had been interpreted by the blacks as a racial act, and the activity of the police seen to be expressive of whiteness, further cementing the view of the party as expressive of black culture and blackness.

The law, embodied in the police, erects a barrier, not just of respectability but of racial culture or ethnicity. The reports establish a supportive relationship between the police and the local white residents harassed by the noise. This image of the law intervening to contain and suppress black culture and disorder is very different from the portrait of law in the 'rivers of blood' speech examined earlier. The threat of blacks, specifically of black youth, appears essentially the same, but the thirteen years have seen the representation of law and legality in the popular politics of race turned right around so that the police were now acting not in favour of the blacks but against them.

[...]

CONCLUSION

[...]

The idea that blacks are a high crime group and the related notion that their criminality is an expression of their distinctive culture have become integral to British
racism in the period since the 'rivers of blood' speech.

I am suggesting that the view of the blacks as innately criminal, or at least more
criminal than the white neighbours whose deprivation they share, which became
'common sense' during the early 1970s, is crucial to the development of new definitions of the black problem and new types of racial language and reasoning. As culture
displaced anxiety about the volume of black settlement, crime came to occupy the
place which sexuality, miscegenation and disease had held as the central themes and
images in the earlier discourses of 'race'. Crime, in the form of both street disorder
and robbery was gradually identified as an *expression of black culture* which was
in turn defined as a cycle in which the negative effects of 'black matriarchy' and
family pathology wrought destructive changes on the inner city by literally breeding
deviancy out of deprivation and discrimination. To plead that this is recognized is
not to deny that blacks have sometimes been identified as the perpetrators of crimes
which resemble the stereotyped image of the 'mugging'.

What must be explained is the durability of these images and their remarkable ability to act both as a focus for popular anxiety about crime in general and as a sign for
national decline, crisis and chaos. The element of blackness is crucial to how they work.

NOTES

1 *Spectator,* 19.7.1862, quoted by Jennifer Davis (1980, p. 199).
2 Davis (1980), p. 203.
3 *Daily News,* 11.9.1888
4 House of Commons *Hansard,* 29.1.1902, col. 1278.
5 House of Commons *Hansard,* 1.11.1912, cols 768–99.
6 Stedman Jones, *Outcast London,* Chapter 6.
7 Cyril Osbourne MP, House of Commons *Hansard,* 5.12.1958, col. 1552.
8 *The Times,* 2.10.1911
9 *Daily Telegraph,* 12.4.76.
10 *Race Today,* October 1976.
11 *Evening Standard,* 26.4.78.
12 *Daily Mirror,* 31.8.76.
13 *Daily Mirror,* 31.8.76
14 *Daily Telegraph,* 31.8.76.
15 *Evening Standard,* 26.4.78.
16 The best sources here are The Institute of Race Relations' 1979 pamphlet *The Police
    Against Black People*; The Hackney CRE report *Policing in Hackney. A record of
    HCRE's Experience 1978–82 (1983)*, and *The Final Report of The Working Party
    into Community/Police Relations in Lambeth* (London Borough of Lambeth, 1981).
17 *Evening News,* 25.9.78.

18 *The Times*, 5.4.80.
19 *Bristol Evening Post*, 3.4.80.
20 *Sunday Times*, 6.4.80.
21 *Daily Mail*, 4.6.82.
22 *Daily Mirror*, 3.1.81.
23 *Sun*, 3.1.81.

REFERENCES

CCCS (1982) *The Empire Strikes Back*, Hutchinson, London.
Critchley, T.A. (1978) *A History of Police in England and Wales* (2nd edn), Constable, London.
Davis, J. (1980) 'The London Garotting Panic of 1862: A Moral Panic and the Creation of a Criminal Class in mid-Victorian England', in Gatrell, Lenman and Parker (eds) *Crime and the Law: The Social History of Crime in Western Europe since 1500*, Europa Publications, London.
Demuth, C. (1978) *'Sus': A report on the Vagrancy Act 1824*, Runneymede Trust, London.
Garland, D. (1985a) *Punishment and Welfare: A History of Penal Strategies*, Gower Press, Aldershot.
Garland, D. (1985b) 'Politics and Policy in Criminological Discourse', *International Journal of Law and Society*, February.
Gartner, L.P. (1973) *The Jewish Immigrant in England 1870–1914*, Simon, London.
GLC (1986) *Policing London: Collected Reports of the GLC Police Committee Support Unit*.
Hall, S., Clarke, J., Critchley, C., Jefferson, T. and Roberts, B. (1978) *Policing the Crisis: Mugging, the State and Law and Order*, London: Macmillan.
HMSO (1977) *Report of the Commissioner of Police of the Metropolis for the year 1976*, Cmnd. 6821.
HMSO (1976) Select Committee on Race Relations and Immigration Session 1975-6, *The West Indian Community*, Metropolitan Police Evidence Thursday 25 March (47–vii).
HMSO (1972) Select Committee on Race Relations and Immigration Session 1971-2, *Police/Immigrant Relations*, 1, 471–1.
Holmes, C. (1979) *Anti-semitism in British Society 1876–1939*, Edward Arnold, London.
Humphries, S. (1981) *Hooligans or Rebels? An Oral History of Working Class Childhood and Youth 1889–1939*, Basil Blackwell, Oxford.
Humphry, D. and John, G. (1972) *Police Power and Black People*, Panther, London.
Hunte, J. (1965) *Nigger Hunting in England?*, West Indian Standing Conference, London.
Lea, J. and Young, J. (1982) 'The Riots in Britain 1981: Urban Violence and Political Marginalisation', in Cowell, D. *et al.* (eds) *Policing The Riots*, Junction Books, London.
Mark, R. (1978) *In The Office of Constable*, Fontana, London.
Powell, E. (1969) *Freedom and Reality*, Paperfront, Kingswood.
Sim, J. (1982) 'Scarman The Police Counter Attack', in Eve and Musson (eds) *The Socialist Register 1982*, Merlin, London.

5

Rethinking 'moral panic' for multi-mediated social worlds

Angela McRobbie and Sarah Thornton

'Moral panic' is now a term regularly used by journalists to describe a process which politicians, commercial promoters and media habitually attempt to incite. It has become a standard interview question to put to Conservative MPs: are they not whipping up a moral panic as a foil to deflect attention away from more pressing economic issues? It has become a routine means of making youth-orientated cultural products more alluring; acid house music was marketed as 'one of the most controversial sounds of 1988' set to outrage 'those who decry the glamorization of drug culture'. Moreover, as moral panics seem to guarantee the kind of emotional involvement that keeps up the interest of, not just tabloid, but broadsheet newspaper readers, as well as the ratings of news and true crime television, even the media themselves are willing to take some of the blame. Sue Cameron, discussing 'new juvenile crime' on BBC2's *Newsnight*, asks, 'Is it not the media itself which has helped to create this phenomenon?'

Moral panics, once the unintended outcome of journalistic practice, seem to have become a goal. Rather than periods to which societies are subject 'every now and then' (Cohen, 1972/80: 9), moral panics have become the way in which daily events are brought to the attention of the public. They are a standard response, a familiar, sometimes weary, even ridiculous rhetoric rather than an exceptional emergency intervention. Used by politicians to orchestrate consent, by business to promote sales in certain niche markets, and by media to make home and social affairs newsworthy, moral panics are constructed on a daily basis.

Given their high rate of turnover and the increasing tendency to label all kinds of media event as 'moral panic', we think it is time to take stock of the revisions, then consider the strengths and weaknesses of this key concept. Although both the original model of moral panics and the reformulations which introduced notions of ideology and hegemony were exemplary interventions in their time, we argue that it is impossible to rely on the old models with their stages and cycles, univocal media, monolithic societal or hegemonic reactions. The proliferation and fragmentation of mass, niche and micro-media and the multiplicity of voices, which compete and contest the meaning of the issues subject to 'moral panic', suggest that both the original

SOURCE: This chapter is taken from *British Journal of Sociology*, 1995 Vol. 46, No. 4, pp. 559–74.

and revised models are outdated in so far as they could not possibly take account of the labyrinthine web of determining relations which now exist between social groups and the media, 'reality' and representation.

THE ORIGINAL THEORY OF MORAL PANICS

Although the argument that media coverage can have an active role in creating deviant behaviour owes its existence to symbolic interactionist theories of 'labelling' (cf. Becker, 1963; Wilkins, 1964), it was the pioneering studies of Jock Young (1971) on the social meaning of drug-taking and Stanley Cohen (1972/1980) on the media-inspired confrontations between mods and rockers, and their edited collections (Cohen, 1971; Cohen and Young, 1973) which developed and effectively launched the concept of 'moral panic'. Not only did their studies explore how agents of social control like the police played a role in 'amplifying' deviance, but they developed a vocabulary for understanding the powerful part played by the media. This meant going beyond the sociological accounts which looked at patterns of ownership and control as signs of complicity between media and government. Attention was now being paid to the ideological role of the media and the active construction of certain kinds of meaning.

  In addition, this work explored how deviant behaviour was interactive rather than absolutist. It was more often the outcome of complex chains of social interaction than the product of young people with a predisposition, individually or environmentally, towards crime or rule-breaking behaviour. Finally this approach challenged moral guardians by suggesting that their overreaction was counterproductive. The media coverage of deviance acted as a kind of handbook of possibilities to be picked over by new recruits. Worse still, segregating young people away from the community created a greater risk of long-term social disorder since 'a society can control effectively only those who perceive themselves to be members of it' (Young, 1971: 39). Overreaction, therefore, contributed to further polarization, though this might have been the desired effect, as Stuart Hall *et al.* (1979) later argued.

  Cohen's *Folk Devils and Moral Panics* is rightfully a classic of media sociology, embracing a greater degree of complexity than the many summaries of the work indicate. He acknowledges that social control is uneven and much less mechanistic than the model of deviancy amplification suggests. Indeed one group of respondents (drawn from the non-mod, non-rocker public) criticizes the media for over-reporting the clashes, while others describe how they came down to the beach to have a look at the 'fun'. Cohen has a sophisticated grasp of how these events fed into popular folklore ('Where are the mods and rockers today?' was a question he was repeatedly asked while carrying out his fieldwork) and when the panic had finally run its course and de-amplification had set in, the characters in this drama settled into history as recognizable social types belonging to a particular period, sometimes referred to, even by the agents of social control, with a hint of nostalgia.

HOOLIGANS, HISTORY, AND HEGEMONY

Engaging directly with the law and other rhetoric of Thatcherism in the late 1970s and into the 1980s, Geoff Pearson's *Hooligans: A History of Respectable Fears* (1983) focuses on the way moral panics often entail looking back to a 'golden age' where social stability and strong moral discipline acted as a deterrent to delinquency and disorder. However, twenty years previously, the same process could be seen in operation: the 'kids' were seen as unruly and undisciplined, unlike their counterparts of the previous decade. The same anxieties appear with startling regularity; these involve the immorality of young people, the absence of parental control, the problem of too much free time leading to crime, and the threat which deviant behaviour poses to national identity and labour discipline. Pearson shows how, during the 1940s, there were scares about 'cosh boys' and Blitz kids and how, in the 1930s, there were a string of moral panics about the misuse of leisure time and the decline of the British way of life through the popularity of Hollywood cinema. Pursuing this chain of investigation back through the nineteenth century, Pearson argues that the nature of the complaints and the social response to them provides a normative and consensual language for understanding the turbulence of social change and discontinuity [see Chapter 3 of this volume]. The value of this historical study is to cast a critical shadow over any claims about the dramatic rise in violent crimes carried out by young people. Instead, it shows how moral panics in society act as a form of ideological cohesion which draws on a complex language of nostalgia.

The studies of Cohen, Young and Pearson show moral panics as acting on behalf of the dominant social order. They are a means of orchestrating consent by actively intervening in the space of public opinion and social consciousness through the use of highly emotive and rhetorical language which has the effect of requiring that 'something be done about it'. The argument about deviancy amplification is precisely that where such strategies are indeed followed by social and legislative action, they also reassure the public that there is strong government and strong leadership.

It is only with theories of ideology that the idea of the media's moral panics as defining and distorting social issues gives way to a more integrated and connective understanding of the construction of meaning across the whole range of media forms and institutions. *Policing the Crisis* (1979) by Stuart Hall and his colleagues at the Centre for Contemporary Cultural Studies (CCCS), University of Birmingham marks a turning point in this respect. They introduced a more Marxist and a more theoretical vocabulary to the terrain, which was more palatable to British sociologists than much of the structuralist and semiological analysis of the mass media which followed it, first, because it drew on the empirical model of the moral panic and, second, because of its concern for history and political culture. As a result, *Policing the Crisis* can be seen as bridging the gap between sociology and cultural studies.

Policing the Crisis introduced the Gramscian concept of hegemony to analyse the way in which moral panics around mugging and the alleged criminality of young Afro-Caribbean males created the social conditions of consent which were necessary for the construction of a society more focused towards law and order and less inclined to the liberalism and 'permissiveness' of the 1960s. This particular analysis of the moral panic shows it not to be an isolated phenomenon but a connective strategy, part of the practice of hegemony which enlarges the sphere of influence which Gramsci labelled 'civil society'. The moral panic then becomes an envoy for dominant ideology. In the language of common sense, it operates as an advance warning system, and as such it progresses from local issues to matters of national importance, from the site of tension and petty anxieties to full-blown social and political crisis. The authors are alert to the complexity of historical and social breakdown which, they claim, can then be managed only through the escalation of the control and coercion. This begs many questions in relation to the scale of social control, but what is particularly important is the recognition that ideology is a suffusive social process, and that it is not a simple question of the distortion of truth, but rather that ideology is a force which works continuously through the mobilization of 'common sense'.

Despite the pivotal position *Policing the Crisis* occupies in the history of the concept of moral panic, the panoramic sweep of its Gramsci-influenced argument across the entire landscape of post-war Britain makes it more a work of classic neo-Marxist scholarship than a sociology of deviance. Critical response has thus been divided between those sociologists who take issue with the study's empirical claims, suggesting as Waddington does that

> the evidence cited in support of the view that the situation with regard to crime in general and 'muggings' in particular was not getting dramatically worse, and in some respects shows an improvement, does not in fact support this contention (Waddington, 1986: 257)

and writers like Paul Gilroy who draw from the study a vocabulary for developing further an analysis of race and ethnicity, relocating *Policing the Crisis* within a more distinctly Cultural Studies perspective (Gilroy 1987 and see Chapter 4 of this volume). More recently Schlesinger and Tumber (1994) have returned to the sociology of crime reporting and both responded to Hall *et al.* (1981) and re-visited moral panic theory as a whole.

As its title suggests, Simon Watney's *Policing Desire* (1987) looks not at crime but at so-called deviant sexual practice, taking the debates of *Policing the Crisis* further by providing a foundation for a better understanding of how controversial social and sexual issues become inscribed with certain kinds of meaning across a wide variety of media forms. Watney rightly points out that the gradual and staged creation of a 'folk devil' as described by moral panic theorists applies to neither gay men and lesbians nor people who are HIV positive. Instead there is a whole world of 'monstrous' representations. Since sexuality is subjected to regulation and control through a multiplicity of institutions each with their own distinctive discursive practices and textual strategies, moral panics are not, as some have suggested, the key to understanding fears and anxieties about AIDS. As Watney puts it

> the theory of moral panics is unable to conceptualise the mass media as an industry intrinsically involved with excess, with the voracious appetite and capacity for substitutions, displacements, repetitions and signifying absences. Moral panic theory is always obliged in the final instance to refer and contrast 'representation' to the arbitration of 'the real', and is hence unable to develop a full theory concerning the operations of ideology within all representational systems. Moral panics seem to appear and disappear, as if representation were not the site of *permanent* struggle of the meaning of signs. (Watney, 1987: 41)

Classic moral panic theorists would ignore the daily endorsement (not to say enjoyment) of heterosexuality as an ideological norm and the consequences this has for those who are excluded. Policies and practices which are concerned with 'policing desire' do not, according to Watney, emanate from one or two centralized agencies of social control. They are endemic in media and society, and in this context the moral panic is best seen as a local intensification or 'the site of the current front line' rather than a sudden, unpleasant and unanticipated development (Watney, 1987: 42).

Watney suggests that our understanding of moral panics might be fruitfully informed by psychological models which seek to understand the ambivalence, excessive interest and even fascination displayed by moral guardians for the objects of their distaste.

Through considering the meanings which have developed around AIDS and homosexuality, Watney replaces the vocabulary of the moral panic with that of representation, discourse and the 'other'. In so doing, he is able to bring to his work concepts drawn from fields of psychoanalysis, film studies and cultural studies to produce a deeper account of processes of exclusion and regulation than that available in the traditional sociology of social control.

CONTESTING 'SOCIETY' AND 'HEGEMONY'

British society and media, youth culture and 'deviance' have changed considerably since the 1960s, and these historical transformations bring to light some of the theoretical and methodological limits of these various studies. In original moral panic theory, 'society' and 'societal reactions' were monolithic and, as others have already argued, ultimately functionalist. Similarly, Hall *et al.*, Pearson and Watney perhaps over-state hegemony and overlook the counter-discourses from which they draw and to which they contribute. In the 1990s, when social differentiation and audience segmentation are the order of the day, we need to take account of a plurality of reactions, each with their different constituencies, effectivities and modes of discourse.

Given the kinds of moral panic to which they attend, it is problematic that Cohen's 'society', Pearson's description of collective memory and Hall *et al.*'s 'hegemony' exclude youth. Ethnographies of contemporary youth culture (cf. Thornton, 1995) find that youth are inclined *not* to lament a safe and stable past *but* to have overwhelming nostalgia for the days when youth culture was genuinely transgressive. The 1990s youth culture is steeped in the legacy of previous 'moral panics'; fighting mods and rockers, drug-taking hippies, foulmouthed punks and gender-bending New Romantics are part of their celebrated folklore. Whether youth cultures espouse overt politics or not, they are often set on being culturally 'radical'. Moral panic can therefore be seen as a culmination and fulfilment of youth cultural agendas in so far as negative news coverage baptizes transgression. What better way to turn difference into defiance, lifestyle into social upheaval, leisure into revolt?

Disapproving mass media coverage legitimizes and authenticates youth cultures to the degree that it is hard to imagine a British youth 'movement' without it. For, in turning youth into news, mass media both frame subculture as major events and disseminate them; a tabloid front page *is* frequently a self-fulfilling prophecy. Sociologists might rightly see this in terms of 'deviancy amplification', but youth have their own discourses which see the process as one in which a 'scene' is transformed into a 'movement'. Here youth have a point, for what gets amplified is not only a 'deviant' activity, but the records, haircuts and dance styles which *were said* to accompany the activities.

Knowledge of this youth-culture ethos is such that its exploitation has become a routine marketing strategy of the publishing and recording industries. For example, the 'moral panic' about 'Acid House' in 1988, 1989 and 1990 began with a prediction on the back of the album that launched the music genre. The sleeve notes described the new sound as 'drug induced', 'sky high' and 'ecstatic' and concluded with a prediction of moral panic: 'The sound of acid tracking will undoubtedly become one of the most controversial sounds of 1988, provoking a split between those who adhere to its underground creed and those who decry the glamorization of drug culture.' In retrospect, this seems prescient, but the statement is best understood as hopeful. Moral panics are one of the few marketing strategies open to relatively anonymous instrumental dance music. To quote one music monthly, they amount to a 'priceless PR campaign' (*Q*, January 1989).

Following London Records' sleeve notes, the youth-orientated music and style press repeatedly predicted that a moral panic about Acid House was 'inevitable'. Innuendo, then full-blown exposés about Ecstacy use in British clubs, appeared in the music press for months before the story was picked up by the tabloids. By the end of August, many magazines were wondering why the tabloids were ignoring the issue, while others, confident of eventual moral panic, imagined possible headlines like 'London Gripped by Ecstasy!' or 'Drug Crazed New Hippies in Street Riot' (*Time Out* 17–24 August 1988). In September 1988, during the 'silly season', the tabloids finally took the bait and subjected the culture to the full front-page treatment. The government, Labour opposition *and* the police were keen to ignore the topic for as long as they possibly could, only belatedly making statements, arrests and recommending legislation. This moral panic was incited by a couple of culture industries (e.g. recording and magazine publishing) well versed in the 'hip' ideologies of youth subcultures.

In addition to the difficulty we have in excluding rather large social groups and industrial activities from accounts of 'society' or 'consensus', so we can't ignore the many voices which now contribute to the debate during moral panics. In the 1990s, interest groups, pressure groups, lobbies and campaigning experts are mobilized to intervene in moral panics. For example, the spokeswoman of the National Council for One Parent Families, Sue Slipman, played a leading role, on an almost weekly basis over a period of three or six months, in diminishing the demonization by the Tories of young single mothers for having children without being married.

One of the main aims of pressure groups is timely intervention in relevant moral panics – to be able to respond instantly to the media demonization of the group they represent, and to provide information and analysis designed to counter this representation. The effectiveness of these groups and in particular their skills at working with the media and providing highly professional 'soundbites' more or less on cue make them an invaluable resource to media machinery working to tight schedules and with increasingly small budgets. They allow the media to be seen to be doing their duty by providing 'balance' in their reporting. At the same time, they show how 'folk devils' can and do 'fight back'.

This phenomenon of becoming an expert, having been a deviant, has a long history in the field of serious crime, drug abuse and juvenile delinquency. However, the proliferation of groups recently set up to compaign on behalf or with folk devils and the skill with which they engage with media is an extremely important development in political culture. When Labour and Conservatives take the same line on law and order, arguing for 'effective punishment' and the need for the moral regeneration of society, many media are inclined to give voice to other, sometimes dissenting, groups. In the absence of an immediate and articulate response from Labour, such groups occasionally function as a virtual form of opposition to the government. A new political sociology, taking into account the prominence of the media, might fruitfully explore the precise sphere of influence and the effectiveness of these organizations.

This marks a series of developments which have occurred perhaps in response to the impact of moral panic theory itself, i.e. the sociologist as expert. At least some of the agents of social control must have been listening when figures like Jock Young and Geoff Pearson were invited to add their voices to these debates, because in recent incidents where there have been fears that disorder or outbreaks of rioting might spread to other areas or to other cities, the playing down of the scale of such incidents has been a recurrent feature and a point of recommendation by the police in relation to the media.

Although moral panics are anti-intellectual, often characterized by a certain religious fervour, and historically most effectively used by the right, only a predominantly right-wing national press arguably stops them from being amenable to the current left. Of course, government is always advantaged, due to higher number of authoritative news sources and to institutionalized agenda-setting. But, there is always the possibility of backfire. For example, when John Major attempted to build upon the moral panic around 'single mothers' (if not initiated, then certainly fuelled by government spokespeople because it helped legitimize welfare cutbacks) with his 'Back to Basics' campaign, the media, followed by Labour, deflected the empty rhetoric back on to the Tory party, turning the campaign into an ad-hoc investigation into the personal morality and sexual practices of Tory MPs.

The delicate balance of relations which the moral panic sociologists saw existing between media, agents of social control, folk devils and moral guardians, has given way to a much more complicated and fragmented set of connections. Each of the categories described by moral panics theorists has undergone a process of fissure in the intervening years. New liaisons have been developed and new initiatives pursued. In particular, two groups seem to be making ever more vocal and 'effective' intervention: pressure groups have, among other things, strongly contested the vocality of the traditional moral guardians; and commercial interests have planted the seeds, and courted discourses, of moral panic in seeking to gain the favourable attention of youthful consumers.

This leads us to query the usefulness of the term 'moral panic' – a metaphor which depicts a complex society as a single person who experiences sudden fear about its virtue. The term's anthropomorphism and totalization arguably mystify more than they reveal. Its conception of morals overlooks the youthful ethics of abandon and the moral imperatives of pressure groups and vocal experts. In the 1990s, we need to acknowledge the perspectives and articulations of different sectors of society. New sociologies of social regulation need to shift attention away from the conventional points in the circuit of amplification and control and look instead to these other spaces.

MORAL PANICS FOR EVERY MEDIUM

Not only need the attitudes and activities of different social groups and organizations be taken into account and not subsumed under a consensual 'society', but also the disparate perspectives of different mass, niche and micro-media need to be explored. Britain saw a remarkable 73 per cent increase in consumer magazine titles during the 1980s – the result of more detailed market research, tighter target marketing and new technologies like computer mailing and desk-top publishing (*Marketing* 13 August 1993). Crucially, the success of many of these magazines has been in the discovery and effective representation of niches of opinion and identity.

As seen above, moral panic is a favourite topic of the youth press. When the mass media of tabloids and TV became active in the 'inevitable' moral panic about 'Acid House', the subcultural press were ready. They tracked the tabloids' every move, re-printed whole front pages, analysed their copy and decried the *misrepresentation* of Acid House. Some 30 magazines now target and speak up for youth.

[…]

Despite their proliferation and diversification, however, the media are obviously not a positive reflection of the diversity of Britain's social interests. This is partly because there are large groups of people in which the media are not economically, and, therefore, editorially interested – crucially, the D and E 'social grades' which are categorized by the *National Readership Survey* as the unskilled working class and 'those at the lowest levels of subsistence', in other words, the long-term unemployed and poorly pensioned. But even here, there are glimmers of hope. The *Big Issue* is now perceived as the newspaper voice of the homeless. Other groups and agencies produce a never-ending flow of newsletters and press releases many of which are written in a house-style customized to the needs of the journalists on national and local media. So-called folk devils now produce their own media as a counter to what they perceive as the biased media of the mainstream.

Moreover, these niche and micro-media can even attempt to incite their own moral panics. Take, for example, two rival political groups, the Socialist Workers Party (SWP) and the British National Party (BNP) – both of which have their own tabloid papers, which speak to their members and attempt to reach out beyond. In the wake of the election of a BNP councillor in Tower Hamlets in autumn 1993, the fascist BNP paper wrote hysterically about the lost neighbourhoods of the white working class and vilified members of the Anti-Nazi League (ANL, a branch of the SWP) as 'ANAL' scum. The SWP paper, on the other hand, recounted how fascism was sweeping the country and full-out Nazism was just around the corner, due to the actions of their chief 'folk devil', not the BNP hooligan, but the police – those 'traitors' to the working class who gave the BNP the protection of the state. Both attempted to fuel violent political action with their respective moral panic discourses – arguably with a measure of success. This case suggests that moral panics, of this localized variety, are not necessarily hegemonic.

But one needn't turn to specialist magazines and newspapers to find the plurality and divergences of opinion that characterize today's (and probably yesterday's) 'moral panics'. Even the national dailies have dependably different stances. The paper whose tone and agenda is closest to 1960/1970s-style moral panic is probably the *Daily Mail*. During the Thatcher years, the *Daily Mail* practised and perfected the characteristics of hegemony, in a way which was in uncanny harmony with Thatcherism. It was a daily process of reaching out to win consent through endlessly defining and redefining social questions and representing itself as the moral voice of the newly self-identified middle class as well as the old lower middle class. The fact that the *Mail* is the only national daily with more female than male readers – if only 51 per cent female – undoubtedly informs its respectable girl's brand of moral indignity. Hence, hysteria about single and teenage mothers is perfect material for a *Daily Mail* moral panic.

Tabloids like the *Sun* prefer to espouse an altogether different brand of moral outrage. With a topless sixteen year old on page 3 and a hedonistic pro-sex editorial line, their moralism need be finely tuned. But that doesn't stop them from being the most preachy and prescriptive of Britain's daily papers, with page after page of the '*Sun* says ...' However, the *Sun*'s favourite moral panics are of the 'sex, drugs and rock 'n' roll' variety – stories about other people having far *too much* fun, if only because the paper is set on maintaining a young (and not greying) readership. Moreover, these kinds of story have the advantage of allowing their readers to have their cake and eat it too; they can vicariously enjoy and/or secretly admire the transgression one moment, then be shocked and offended the next. When considering the way moral panics work within different publications, one need keep in mind that *Sun* readers take their paper a good deal less seriously than *Mail* readers take theirs. As Mark Pursehouse discovered in interviewing *Sun* readers, one of the key pleasures in reading the *Sun* is the process of estimating what part of a story is true, what parts exaggerated or totally invented (cf. Pursehouse, 1991).

In the last few years, the broadsheets have not only made use of more visual and colour material, they also seem to have adopted tabloid-style headlines to accompany their tabloid supplements. For example, the covers of the *Guardian* G2 section frequently sport exaggerated, sensational headlines. 'BLOOD ON THE STREETS: They're Packing Pistols in Manchester' announces a story about the increasing use of firearms by young drug dealers on mountain bikes in Manchester's Moss Side (*Guardian* 9 August 1993). Given the more measured copy which follows, the *Guardian* would seem to be using this 'shock horror' language to lighten up the story – the capital letters signifying an ironic borrowing of tabloid style. But, as the *Sun*'s language is understood by many of its readers as tongue-in-cheek, the *Guardian*'s irony gives it an alibi, but not absolution. Moreover, these mixtures of outrage and amusement point to the 'entertainment value' of moral panics – something mentioned but not really integrated into previous models. (Cf. Curran and Sparks 1991 for a critique of the 'astigmatic perspective' of accounts of politics and the press which overlook entertainment.)

[...]

MEDIATED SOCIAL WORLDS

In addition to unpacking 'society', on the one hand, and the 'media', on the other, the third consideration in updating models of 'moral panic' need be that the media is no longer something separable from society. Social reality is experienced through language, communication and imagery. Social meaning and social differences are inextricably tied up with representation. Thus when sociologists call for an account which tells how life actually is, and which deals with the real issue rather than the spectacular and exaggerated ones, the point is that these accounts of reality are already representations and sets of meanings about what they perceive the 'real' issues to be. These versions of 'reality' would also be impregnated with the mark of media imagery rather than somehow pure and untouched by the all-pervasive traces of contemporary communications.

The media have long been seen to be embedded in the fabric of society. What may be constitutively new is the degree to which media have become something with which the social is continuously being defined. For example, characterizations like 'Mirror reader' or 'Times reader' often give us as good an indication of social class as the mention of a particular occupation. Social age and generation (rather than biological age) are played out in the relation between Radios One and Two or Capital FM and Capital Gold. Subtle differences of gender identity are negotiated when, say, a working-class woman says she dislikes all soap operas, preferring instead news, sport and nature programmes. Similarly, at the risk of being cliché, for a man to admit his devotion to the films of Joan Crawford and Judy Garland is, in some contexts, tantamount to 'coming out'.

At another level, the hard and fast divide between media professionals and media 'punters' seems to have broken down to some extent. The ownership of home video-cameras, the new space for broadcasting home video material on national television (in series like *Video Diaries*), the existence of 'right to reply' programmes, the possession of degrees in media studies all point in this direction. Audiences can be credited with possessing a greater degree of 'media literacy' than they did in the past. Also important here is the introduction of a distinctively amateurish (rather than professional) style of presentation, developed by Channel Four's *The Tube* in the early 1980s and best reflected in the 'fluffed' mannerism of its two presenters, Jools Holland and Paula Yates. Finally, the increasing reliance on the audience as a resource for successful television, either as visualized participants or audible internal audiences, seems to give a positive place to the audience in the process of programme production.

The strength of the old models of moral panic was that they marked the connection between 'the media' and 'social control'. But, nowadays, most political strategies *are* media strategies. The contest to determine news agendas is the first and last battle of the political campaign. Moreover, the kinds of social issues and political debates which were once included on the agendas of moral panic theorists as sites of social anxiety, and even crisis, could now be redefined as part of an endless debate about who 'we' are and what 'our' national culture is. These are profoundly 'home affairs'. The daily intensity and drama of their appearance and the many voices now heard [not] in the background but in the foreground, punctuating and producing reality, point more to the reality of dealing with social difference than to the unity of current affairs (cf. Hall, Connell and Curtis, 1981).

CONCLUSIONS

What has been argued here is that the model of moral panic is urgently in need of updating precisely because of its success. While the theory began its life in radical sociology, the strength of the argument quickly found its way into those very areas with which it was originally concerned, influencing social policy and attitudes to deviance generally. As a result, the police, as agents of social control now show some awareness of the dangers of overreaction, while sectors of the media regularly remind viewers of the dangers of moral panic and thus of alienating sections of the community by falsely attributing to them some of the characteristics of the so-called folk devils.

Crucially, the theory has, over the years, drawn attention to the importance of empowering folk devils so that they or their representatives can challenge the cycle of sanctions and social control. Pressure groups, lobbies, self-help and interest groups have sprung up across the country and effectively positioned themselves as authoritative sources of comment and criticism. They now contribute to the shape of public debate, playing a major role in contesting what they perceive as dangerous stereotypes and popular misconceptions.

The theory has also influenced business practice, albeit through an undoubtedly more circuitous route. Culture industry promotions and marketing people now understand how, for certain products like records, magazines, movies and computer games, nothing could be better for sales than a bit of controversy – the threat of censorship, the suggestion of sexual scandal or subversive activity. The promotional logic is twofold: first, the cultural good will receive a lot of free, if negative, publicity because its associations with moral panic have made it newsworthy; second, rather than alienating everyone, it will be attractive to a contingent of consumers who see themselves as alternative, avant-garde, radical, rebellious or simply young. In the old models of moral panic, the audience played a minor role and remained relatively untheorized. With few exceptions, they were the space of consensus, the space of media manipulation, the space of an easily convinced public. A new model need embrace the complex realm of reception – readers, viewers, listeners and the various social groups categorized under the heading of public opinion cannot be read off the representation of social issues.

The moral panics we have been discussing here are less monolithic than those the classic model implied. Recent moral panics do remain overwhelmingly concerned with moral values, societal regularities and drawing of lines between the permissible and the less acceptable. However, hard and fast boundaries between 'normal' and 'deviant' would seem to be less common – if only because moral panics are now continually contested. Few sociologists would dispute the expansion over the last decade of what used to be called, quite simply, the mass media. The diversification of forms of media and the sophisticated restructuring of various categories of audience require that, while a consensual social morality might still be a political objective, the chances of it being delivered directly through the channels of the media are much less certain.

REFERENCES

Becker, H. (1963) *The Outsiders*, New York: Free Press.

Cohen, S. (ed.) (1971) *Images of Deviance*, Harmondsworth: Penguin.

Cohen, S. (1972/1980) *Folk Devils and Moral Panics: The Creation of the Mods and the Rockers*, Oxford: Basil Blackwell.

Cohen, S. and Young, J. (eds) (1973) *The Manufacture of the News: Deviance, Social Problems and the Mass Media*, London: Constable.

Curran, J. (1978) 'The Press as an Agency of Social Control: An historical perspective' in G. Boyce *et al.* (eds) *Newspaper History*, London: Constable.

Curran, J. and Sparks, C. (1991) 'Press and Popular Culture', *Media, Culture and Society* 13: 215–37.

Gilroy, P. (1987) *There Ain't No Black in the Union Jack: The Cultural Politics of Race and Nation*, London: Hutchinson.

Hall, S. *et al.* (1979) *Policing the Crisis: Mugging, the State and Law and Order*, London: Macmillan.

Hall, S., Connell, I. and Curtis, L. (1981) 'The "unity" of current affairs televison' in Tony Bennett *et al.* (eds) *Popular Televison and Film,* London: BFI.

Pearson, G. (1983) *Hooligans: A History of Respectable Fears,* London: Macmillan.

Pursehouse, M. (1991) 'Looking at the Sun: Into the Nineties with a Tabloid and its Readers', *Cultural Studies From Birmingham* 1: 88–133.

Schlesinger, P. and Tumber, H. (1994) *Reporting Crime: The Media Politics of Criminal Justice,* Oxford: Oxford University Press.

Thornton, S.L. (1995) *Club Culture: Music, Media and Subcultural Capital,* Oxford: Polity.

Waddington, P.A.J. (1986) 'Mugging as a Moral Panic: A Question of Proportion', *British Journal of Sociology* 37 (2): 245–59.

Watney, S. (1987) *Policing Desire: Pornography, AIDS and the Media,* London: Methuen.

Wilkins, L.T. (1964) *Social Deviance: Social Policy, Action and Research,* London: Tavistock.

Young, J. (1971) *The Drugtakers: The Social Meaning of Drug Use,* London: Paladin.

6

The vilification and pleasures of youthful transgression

Keith Hayward

There can be few subjects as effective at setting in motion the meter of public opinion as youth crime. For many, it betokens a general erosion of public standards, providing visceral and compelling evidence of an ever more 'permissive society'. For others, such contemporary fears about the increased seriousness of youth criminality represent little new: simply the continuation of a centuries-old tendency to scapegoat and vilify the transgressions of the young (for example, Pearson, 1983), yet another moment in a long series of moral panics. This chapter, however, is not an attempt to retrace the contours of the debate (not least because the subject has been covered with considerable insight and authority in the preceding chapters of this volume). Nor should it be seen as an attempt to offer any practical political or social solutions for reducing or controlling the errant behaviour of young people. Instead, this chapter takes an altogether different tack. Following the theoretical approach of a group of scholars whose work is often collectively referred to as 'cultural criminology'[1] (see Katz, 1988; Lyng, 1990; Presdee, 1994, 2000; Ferrell and Sanders, 1995; Redhead, 1995), the chapter focuses on the excitement, pleasures and opportunities for psychic resolution involved in certain modes of youthful criminality.

The chapter will unfold in three sections, each drawing on a distinct facet of contemporary cultural criminology. It begins with a discussion of one of the pivotal texts in the postmodern reconstruction of aetiology, namely Jack Katz's *The Seductions of Crime: Moral and Sensual Attractions in Doing Evil* (1988). Katz's emphasis on the seductive quality of crime represents a refreshing alternative to much mainstream criminology and arguably has resonance for anyone wishing to understand the compelling and exciting nature of much youth crime. The chapter continues with an attempt to locate Katz's framework within a broader social context. More specifically, the section seeks to emphasize the dialectic between excitement, (self) control and crime under conditions of late modernity, arguing that, in an increasingly socially precarious world, many individuals are seeking to construct identity for themselves

SOURCE: Commissioned for this volume. Keith Hayward is a Lecturer in the School of Law, University of East London, UK.

by engaging in practices (including criminal practices) that involve what I wish to call a 'controlled loss of control'. The final section looks at the very different responses of the state and the market to such a set of circumstances, focusing in particular on what it is about contemporary culture, and the societal reactions to that emergent culture, that makes transgression and the consumption of transgression so seductive.

'THE SEDUCTIONS OF CRIME': JACK KATZ AND THE ATTRACTION OF TRANSGRESSION

As the title of his book suggests, the central contention of Jack Katz's (1988) theory of crime is that there are 'moral and sensual attractions in doing evil' and that a truly inclusive account of 'antisocial behaviour' has to start from this premise. However, as Katz stresses from the outset, while the subject of crime has been approached from numerous perspectives, very few explanatory accounts have focused on the varied emotional dynamics and experiential attractions that are an integral element of much crime (the notable exceptions being the works of David Matza and Howard Becker). Consequently the 'lived experience of criminality' rarely features in traditional criminological and sociological explanations of crime and deviance:

> Somehow in the psychological and sociological disciplines, the lived mysticism and magic in the foreground of criminal experience became unseeable, while the abstractions hypothesized by 'empirical theory' as the determining background causes, especially those conveniently quantified by state agencies, became the stuff of 'scientific' thought and 'rigorous' method.
>
> (Katz, 1998, pp. 311–12)

For Katz, causal explanations of criminality that stress the importance of structural, environmental, genetic or rational choice factors, over and above the emotional and interpretative qualities of crime, are often guilty of stripping away and repressing key individual emotions such as humiliation, arrogance, ridicule, cynicism (and importantly) pleasure and excitement – emotions that, in many cases, are central to the criminal event. In doing so they 'turn the direction of enquiry' around, so that the focus of criminological attention falls on the 'background' rather then the 'foreground' of the criminal act (ibid., p. 9). Thus, fundamentally, Katz poses a question that many criminologists either take for granted or completely ignore: namely 'why are people who were not determined to commit a crime one moment determined to do so the next?' (ibid., p. 4). The solution, he claims, can be found only by going beyond background factors and delving deeper into the criminal act itself. He argues that the various mechanisms which move actors between 'background factors and subsequent acts' have been a kind of 'black box', assumed to have some motivational force but left essentially unexamined (ibid., p. 5). Katz proposes to retrieve and prise open the contents of this 'black box'. In short, one might say that Katz's work can be seen as an attempt to reclaim the 'unexamined spaces in criminological theory' (Henry and Milovanovic, 1996, p. 60).

Using an eclectic array of sources, Katz builds up a picture of the sensual, magical and creative appeals of crime. Evoking the notion of the Nietzschean superman, Katz asserts that deviance offers the perpetrator a means of 'self transcendence', a way of overcoming the conventionality and mundanity typically associated with the banal routines and practicalities of everyday 'regular life'. At the subjective level, crime is stimulating, exciting and liberating. To think of crime as either another form of rational activity or as the result of some innate or social pathology is to totally miss the point.[2] At the same time, he urges more attention to the criminal act – for each specific crime, he maintains, presents the criminal with a distinct set of subjective experiences and existential dilemmas, and thus has its own singular attraction.

If emotions are major contingencies in the 'lived contours of crime', Katz's broad cross-section of crimes offers many resonances for anyone attempting to devise a theory of youth crime. The 'sneaky thrills' of juvenile shoplifting are discussed, from the 'sensual metaphysics', pleasure and 'ludic' quality of the act itself to the shame and embarrassment felt on apprehension. Robbery is also discussed at length. Katz builds up a picture of robbery as a spontaneous, chaotic and often hedonistic act. Also emphasized is the 'sense of superiority' involved in the act of 'stickup' and the pride that robbers take in their defiant reputation as 'badmen'. Katz even examines the lived sensuality behind events of cold-blooded, 'senseless' murder. In particular, he charts the role of 'defilement', 'sacrifice', 'righteous rage', 'vengeance' and 'hedonism' – emotions that are frequently at the root of most 'non-modal homicides'. Controversially, Katz explicitly extends this line of argument to include youth criminality – specifically, gang-related crime and other forms of street violence – and in doing so challenges the assumptions of broadly Marxist-inspired critical commentators who portray working-class youth delinquency as symbolic rebellion against the dominant values of society and the contradictions of capitalism (for example, Hall and Jefferson, 1976; Willis, 1977). At the same time, in some moments, his language is highly reminiscent of such work, notably in the emphasis on the 'transformative magic' of crime/deviance. The key difference is that Katz draws out the inherent 'emotionality' of the criminal act, as opposed to the emphasis on ideas in the analysis of ideology, the actor as a rational agent working with, as it were, 'corrupt information'.

Certainly, as I have argued elsewhere (Fenwick and Hayward, 2000, pp. 36–9), Katz's work on the thrill of transgression can easily be extended to include a range of other criminal activities – especially those perpetrated by young people – and to oppose any simplistic diagnosis in terms of immediate financial or practical benefits. Teenage criminal practices such as vandalism, theft and destruction of cars, firestarting, hoax emergency service call-outs, car 'cruising',[3] peer-group violence and other forms of street delinquency have much to do with youth expression and exerting control in neighbourhoods where, more often than not, traditional avenues of youthful stimulation and endeavour have long since evaporated.

> Similarly, graffiti 'artists' and members of 'tag crews' in both the United States and in Europe, often talk at length, not only about the thrill and emotional charge experienced when breaking into buildings and compounds and defacing private property, but also about how their work serves as a means of self-expression and a way in which they can make themselves heard (see Ferrell, 1995, Lasley, 1995) ... Arguably, if no material gain is likely to be forthcoming from this practice, then it must surely centre around either the excitement of perpetrating an illegal act or the exhilaration of wanton destruction. A similar argument might be put forward in relation to drug use which is probably the most prevalent of all youthful criminal transgressions. There can be little doubt that the drug sub-culture is inextricably linked with emotion: from the social circumstances in which the majority of teenage drug

use takes place (for example, bars, clubs, raves and so on); to the anticipation involved in the 'scoring' process; continuing with the heightened sensations experienced prior to and during ingestion of the drug; and finally, the roller-coaster of emotions one feels following the resolution of the process and the psychopharmacological high.

(Fenwick and Hayward, 2000, pp. 36–7)

Such examples serve to illustrate that, in many cases, individuals are seduced by the existential possibilities offered by criminal acts – by the pleasure of transgression. And, hence, a key advantage of this approach is that it helps us to understand why it is that youth criminality is not solely the preserve of those groups who are economically and socially disadvantaged. These groups may well be over-represented in the criminal justice system but – to make a familiar point – this may have more to do with the social construction of criminality than higher actual rates of criminal participation (see Chapter 4 of this volume). Youth crimes such as drug taking, 'twocking',[4] peer-group fighting and vandalism have an expressive element which (as I shall argue later) is inextricably related to excitement and the exertion of control; consequently, their motivation cannot be limited to any specific set of social circumstances or economic inequality. Such crimes are about the thrill of transgression and the pursuit of the limit.

Despite its originality,[5] Katz's work has been much criticized for failing to recognize the wider social and structural contexts within which all individual experience takes place. (For another version of this argument see O'Malley and Mugford, 1994; Van Hoorebeeck, 1997.) However, this line of argument itself seems to ignore Katz's criticism of the failure of 'background' structural theories of crime to address the fundamental question of why (under shared social conditions) one person rather than another commits a crime. (Katz is not even without precedent here: witness all the 'over-prediction of crime' critiques.) At this point we find ourselves traversing familiar ground – the 'structure versus agency' debate. However, rather than view Katz's work simply as resurrecting one side of this binary framework, I wish to proffer a very different claim. It is my contention that Katz's analysis is not so much about agency versus structure as about prioritizing emotionality in such a way that it neither reduces emotions purely to the level of individual psychology (Katz should be credited for taking emotions out of the realm of pathology) nor pre-locates the question of those emotions in the drama of state resistance and political rebellion.

It is this cultural line of enquiry that I wish to develop in the remainder of the chapter. Focusing on one particular emotion – excitement – I will explore what is particular about human experience and social conditions *today* that makes the pursuit of excitement so seductive. More specifically, it will be proposed that transgressive behaviour is becoming seductive not only because of the excitement it brings at the level of the individual experience (*à la* Katz) but also, importantly, because it offers a way of seizing control of one's destiny. This latter point is of increasing importance. For Katz, as stated above, the issue is escape from the mundane routines of everyday life. However, the contemporary milieu is now more complex. For not only do we inhabit an ever more complex and uncertain world in which control is frequently wrested from us, but, at the same time – in something of a social irony – late modern society responds to such circumstances by enacting a series of constraining so-called rational measures that, rather than creating order and stability, serve only to create a sense of what I will call here the 'hyper-banalization' of everyday life. Yet again, this movement interacts with that perverse cultural as well as economic agency – the market – too often overlooked by criminologists with their relentless focus on official agencies of social control.[6]

EXCITEMENT, 'EDGEWORK' AND RISK: AVENUES FOR A 'CONTROLLED LOSS OF CONTROL' IN LATE MODERN LIFE

As numerous commentators have suggested, late modern society (not least in the industrialized West) can be characterized by a pervasive sense of insecurity and disembeddedness: not just in the well documented areas of cultural production (Featherstone, 1991; Jameson, 1991) and industrial capitalism (Hall and Jacques, 1990; Harvey, 1990; Amin, 1994) but also importantly in the realm of everyday life (de Certeau, 1984) and at the level of individual consciousness and awareness. Everything, it seems, is subject to change and reconstitution, as seen in the apparent 'crises' in masculinity (Connell, 1995; Jefferson, 1997), the family (Wilson, 1975) and the demise of the nation state (Taylor, 1999, pp. 20–7). While such a chaotic and uneven world may, in the long term, offer society a whole new range of opportunities and possibilities, in the short term it often throws up feelings of melancholia and uncertainty as large numbers of people are forced to reconsider their past, present and future and face up to the fact that many of the teleological presuppositions they clung to for so long have collapsed and cannot be reconstructed. Grand narratives and individual narratives rise and fall together (Lyotard, 1984).

This has been the stuff of much observation. Giddens (1990), for example, colourfully equates everyday life in late modernity with trying to regain control of an out-of-control juggernaut. Mike Davis (1990, 1998) and Zygmunt Bauman (1987, 1998) meanwhile see the future only in terms of a new dialectic of social control predicated on each individual's ability to bridge the cultural/financial gap that dictates entry to the consumer society, creating a new category of the excluded urban repressed. However, from a purely criminological perspective, perhaps the best articulation of the impact of current social and economic conditions on individual subjectivity is the one set out by Jock Young:

> We live now in a much more difficult world: we face a greater range in life choices than ever before, our lives are less firmly embedded in work and relationships, our everyday existence is experienced as a series of encounters with risk either in actuality or in the shape of fears and apprehensions. We feel both materially insecure and ontologically precarious.
>
> (Young, 1999, p. vi)

What all these commentators have in common is the belief that success in tackling the contemporary crime problem depends upon acknowledging the 'ontological insecurity' of feeling physically and psychologically at risk in an unstable and changing world. In short, we must engage with the contingencies and dilemmas (the dilemmas of the contingent?) brought about by the late modern condition.

One form of social response to these fundamental transformations and uncertainties has been the emergence of various social agencies that attempt to deal with the changes through a non-judgemental, non-reductive form of 'risk management' (Giddens, 1990, 1991; Beck, 1992). However, as Beck suggests in his influential text *Risk Society*, often the very steps taken in a bid to stave off (or more accurately 'manage') risk serve only to produce new risks or exacerbate older ones. Thus this new awareness of the consequence of our actions – what Beck describes as a heightened 'reflexivity' – can only intensify and make more anxious the sense of the 'juggernaut out of control'.

It is, however, interesting to look at the subject of risk from a somewhat different perspective, specifically the way that many individuals are using risk (and associated practices) as a means of achieving a semblance of control – or, more accurately, (following Mike Featherstone, 1991) a 'controlled sense of loss of control' – in the face of the changes and upheavals associated with late modernity. One might say that, rather than eschewing risk, the modern subject is embracing it. Let us pause to consider this point in more detail. As alluded to above, one of the strange paradoxes of contemporary society is how, at the same moment, an individual can feel both onto-logically insecure *and* – as a result of the increasing drive within everyday life towards the 'hyper-banalization' of society – over-controlled. In other words, not only is it becoming more difficult to exert control and navigate a life pathway via the 'estab-lished' (and crumbling) norms and codes of modernity but, at the same time, the indi-vidual is confronted by a reactive and burgeoning 'culture of control' (Garland, 2001), whether in the form of state-imposed criminal legislation and other modes of rationalization or private, decentralized forms of surveillance and other techniques. Given such circumstances, might it not be the case that many individuals will wish to escape this conflicting situation by exerting a sense of control and self-actualization – to feel alive in an over-controlled *yet at the same time* highly unstable world? Moreover, might reflexive risk calculation (such a prominent feature of our times) be the very instrumental device that enables that escape?

Indeed, within the various cultural practices associated with contemporary youth culture there is much evidence to suggest that risk taking is becoming more pervasive. From the youthful (and not so youthful) excesses associated with 'E' and 'rave' culture, car 'cruising' and 'binge drinking' to the rise in dangerous extreme sports and the upsurge in socially risky practices such as unprotected sex and the use of hard drugs such as heroin and cocaine, it seems that, for many young people, the greater the risk the greater the attraction. Perhaps it should come as no real surprise, then, that many of the forms of crime identified above also become a way of navigating a path through such uncertain times. But I am getting ahead of myself. Let us return to the question of how the conditions of late modernity are affecting everyday life, and in turn contributing to much youth criminality.

Stephen Lyng (1990) has explored what one could call the existential nature of voluntary risk taking – or, as he prefers to call it, 'edgework' – in post-industrial society. According to Lyng edgework involves:

> [a] clearly observable threat to one's physical or mental well-being or one's sense of an ordered existence. The archetypal edgework experience is one in which the individual's failure to meet the challenge at hand will result in death, or at the very least, debilitating

injury. This type of edgework is best illustrated by such dangerous sports as skydiving, hang gliding, rock climbing, motor cycle racing/ car racing, and downhill ski racing or by such dangerous occupations as fire fighting, test piloting, combat soldiering, movie stunt work and police work. The threat of death or injury is ever-present in such activities, although participants often claim that only those 'who don't know what they are doing' are at risk.

(*Ibid.*, p. 857)

For Lyng, edgework activities are a means of seizing control, a way of reacting against the 'unidentifiable forces that rob one of individual choice' (*ibid.*, p. 870).

Despite raising many interesting ideas, Lyng's article has been criticized for overemphasizing prototypically masculine middle-class pursuits, while at the same time ignoring the risk-taking practices associated with other sections of society. Eleanor Miller (1991) has suggested that the idea of edgework or 'considered risk taking' as a means of exerting control should be extended to include women and other sections of society such as the poor and the socially excluded – the very individuals who appear in Bauman's and Davis's accounts of the urban 'repressed'. Such an assertion makes perfect sense. Given my earlier arguments, the search for risk, hedonism and excitement requires outlets – but the opportunities vary enormously, and in class/gender/neighbourhood-related ways – whether it be a certain activity, a form of experience or indeed a specific type of space. In Lyng's account such emotions are experienced on the cliff face, the racetrack, in the combat zone, during a sky-dive or in other demarcated spaces. However, if one is not able to escape one's social environment to engage in licit risk taking or edgework activities, one has to find alternative outlets to play out these emotions. In a great many instances the likelihood is that individuals will 'get their kicks' in spaces they know well (to use a term made famous by Brantingham and Brantingham, 1981, within the 'cognitively known area'). In other words, the run-down estate or ghetto becomes a paradoxical space: on one hand it symbolizes the systematic powerlessness so often felt by the individuals who live in such environments, and on the other the sink estate serves as a site of risk consumption that provides numerous illegal avenues. The ghetto becomes a 'performance zone' in which displays of risk, excitement, masculinity and even 'carnivalesque pleasure' in the form of rioting are frequently perpetuated (see Presdee, 2000).

This is the point at which we need to go beyond Katz's simple model of crime as escape from/transcendence of the routine to present instead a 'control–excitement' model (understood via risk, hedonism, expressivity and the concept of edgework). Put simply, many forms of crime frequently perpetrated in urban areas should be seen for exactly what they are, an attempt to achieve a semblance of control within ontologically insecure social worlds (O'Malley and Mugford, 1994; Morrison, 1995; Henry and Milovanovic, 1996).

This idea that deviance is connected with reality construction and identity in late modern consumer society has been explored in the fascinating book *Kamikaze Biker* by Ikuya Sato (1991). Sato's first-hand account of the motivation and phenomenology of *boso* driving culture in Japan sheds some light on the experiential feelings of individuals involved in risk-laden, illegal activities – not least, how certain feelings were common to the *bosozoku* when racing or eluding the police.[7] In particular, the sense that what they were doing was somehow 'bracketed off from everyday life'. Consequently *bosozoku* self-reported that they experienced a 'loss of self-consciousness', the feeling that 'means–ends relationships were simplified' and the sense that *boso* driving involved a different temporal framework from 'ordinary life'.

Obviously, this argument applies more to crimes with a strong so-called 'expressive' element than it does to other more utilitarian/rationalistic forms of criminality. (For example, joy-riding exemplifies these ideas in that it is both rich in excitement and may seem to offer a means of self-actualization, while at the same time providing the participant with a physical means of traversing (and escaping) the socially deprived neighbourhood.) But one should not forget that these are the very crimes that abound in troubled inner-city neighbourhoods. Consequently one may view such crimes as 'urban edgework', attempts to construct an enhanced sense of self by engaging in risk-laden practices on the metaphorical edge:

> On the one hand, there is the routinised alienation and boredom of everyday life – a world in which individuals find themselves over-controlled and yet without control. On the other hand, there are those activities which offer the possibility of excitement *and* control. Lyng's account focuses on extreme sports, whilst the new cultural criminology focuses on transgression. Although ostensibly dangerous, these activities offer a mode of being in which individuals take control through a calculated act of decontrol. The seductiveness of crime is not only linked to the inherent excitement of the acts involved, but also to the more general feelings of self-realization and self-expression to which they give rise. It might be an unpalatable thought, but it is through such activities that individuals come alive.
>
> (Fenwick and Hayward, 2000, p. 49)

THE 'CRIMINALIZATION OF EVERYDAY LIFE' VERSUS THE 'COMMODIFICATION OF TRANSGRESSION'

> Excitement, even ecstasy (the abandonment of reason and rationale), is the goal ... The quest for excitement is directly related to the breaking of boundaries, of confronting parameters and playing at the margins of social life in the challenging of controllers and their control mechanisms ... It is the realm of resentment and irrationality *par excellence* and also the realm of much crime. It is that part of social life that is unknowable to those in power and which therefore stands outside their consciousness and their understanding. They cannot understand it or indeed even 'read' it as real life, but only as immoral, uncivilised, obscene and unfathomable social behaviour.
>
> (Presdee, 2000, pp. 7–8)

In his book *Cultural Criminology and the Carnival of Crime*, Mike Presdee (2000) argues that, for many young people, the pleasure and excitement of transgression are double: not only as a direct corollary of a society currently undergoing pronounced change and reconstitution, but also as a reaction against a situation in which the only response of the state is to impose more intense forms of social control. Evoking Weber's (modernist) rubric of rationalization, Presdee asserts that, in an effort to curb the apparent increase in youth crime (cf. Zimring, 1998), Western governments have enacted a series of measures that add up to what he describes as 'the creeping criminalization of everyday life'. The result, he argues, is that, in certain social settings, ours is a world in which 'dominant and seemingly rational logics' act upon us and constrain us: 'As the individual becomes more and more trapped by applied science and the rational, so we become more and more enmeshed and oppressed within the so-called scientific measurement of our lives' (Presdee, 2000, p. 159; on this point see also Chapters 1 and 27–31 of this volume).

At this point it is worth reflecting on the exact nature of these 'rational logics'. On the one hand, there is the clearly punitive form (that is, prohibitive legislation, the move towards harsher punishment regimes for young offenders, and other reactionary measures), on the other hand, there are those measures based around an actuarial and calculative approach to the control and management of social problems – this latter approach being all about the creation of routines, conformity and acceptable social habits/behaviour. While traditionally these two forms of social control have been seen to have clear conceptual differences (for example, Foucault, 1977 on the juridico-dynamic versus the disciplinary form), in recent times the distinction between them has become noticeably blurred. In practice, a hybrid form of criminalization/social control has emerged. For example, curfew orders, while being punitive in essence, at the same time represent a move towards the conditioning and 'routinization' of individual action.

Homogenizing these two aspects, Presdee emphasizes the paradox that the more the state imposes rationalizing rubrics the more it provokes in its citizens/subjects not compliant rationality, but rather heightened emotionality: 'we respond with irrational emotions derived from desire, pleasure and the sensualness of a postmodern commodity culture' (ibid., p. 29). Hence a spiral in which this 'irrational response' provokes further punitive/rationalizing moves from the state. Culture therefore becomes at once the site of excitement and social contestation, of experimentation and dissonance: 'It is a world full of contradictions, inequalities and struggle, yet it is a world where ... the pursuit of pleasure is potentially antagonistic to the state' (ibid.)[8].

Presdee then reactivates the familiar language of moral panic (Young, 1971; Cohen, 1972). Indeed, on the face of it, little has changed: the transgressive nature of youth (sub)cultural practice still provokes a general sense of fear and moral indignation; mass media coverage still serves to 'amplify deviance'; complex social phenomena continue to be reduced to simple causal relations; and politicians continue to fall over themselves in their attempts to curry favour with the 'moral majority' by vilifying and condemning the 'immorality of contemporary youth'. This pervasive criminalization process, he argues, adds up to little more than a war against the young. From curfews to exclusion orders, from benefit reform to Public Disorder Acts, the government is turning the screw on the young, subjecting not only their 'oppositional forms of popular and personal pleasure' to increasing political arbitration and state agency sanction, but also their legitimate cultural practices and even, in many instances, their everyday round.

In a not unfamiliar twist of this same axis McRobbie and Thornton (see Chapter 5 of this volume) argue that moral panic in turn produces a response: for many young people a decent dose of moral outrage remains the only acid test of a truly oppositional, and therefore worthwhile, cultural practice. Indeed, even this response has been, literally, incorporated. Corporations are now actively using moral panics (in the form of 'a bit of controversy – the threat of censorship, the suggestion of sexual scandal or subversive activity') for their own ends. This point is illustrated in Presdee's memorable account of the way that successive governments attempted (largely in vain) to criminalize and regulate one of the most popular forms of youth expression, contemporary club ('rave') culture (see Presdee, 2000). In this account we see how such intense forms of social control are always destined to fail – one only need look at the abject failure of current anti-drug legislation to recognize this to be the case. Certainly the collective efforts of UK governments during the 1990s to regulate club culture and outlaw many of its associated *sub rosa* activities served only to train the spotlight of attention more firmly on the 'club scene' – both its underground and its more mainstream manifestations. Once again we are forced to consider just how entwined is the relationship between the various processes that serve to vilify and ultimately criminalize the cultural practices of the young, and the very reasons why many young people actually engage in those practices in the first place.

> Being 'young' is characterized by a culture created out of the tensions that emanate between regulation and rebellion; control and care; the civilised and the savage. The result is a carnivalesque culture that forever pushes at the boundaries of transgression ... Their culture, rather than being a search for the 'authentic' as in modern culture, is an endless search for the inauthentic; that is, a culture that is empty of the authority and the imperatives that come with authenticity. *It is this perceived 'emptiness as protest' that prompts panic from 'adult' society.*
>
> (*Ibid.*, p. 114, emphasis added)

As well as making the obvious (Foucauldian) points about repression/control proliferating rather than suppressing its object of alteration, what is interesting about Presdee's account is the notion of 'the search for the inauthentic' – indicating a social logic considerably altered since Cohen's classic work. Certainly this, in my opinion, can help us understand intensified social and state responses. For as Docker (1994, p. 117) has pointed out, while in cultural terms modernism protested against the contemporary world, the issues of young people could still be understood in terms of their search for an authentic self and the need to break free from the constraints of imposed rationality and authority. However, the 'search for the inauthentic', as Presdee seems to be suggesting, is something very different – a break with this modernist 'tradition' and a refusal to engage with established tropes of meaning making. No wonder such resistance produces a greater fury.

Yet it is not only as prohibition (or discipline or, indeed, administrative/actuarial criminology) that the 'wider society' engages with cultural forms that are tied in to the production of youth identity, including the way in which images of crime are inscribed in this process. (See Young, 1996, for a more developed version of this argument.) In what follows I intend to follow this line of enquiry by looking briefly at how that other great agent of social reaction – the market – is participating in the process of promoting and marketing transgression.

Postmodernism (as eloquently illustrated by Harvey and Jameson) celebrates heterogeneity, depthlessness, unpredictability, risk, *inauthenticity* and technological advances in communication, media and consumer culture (hence also a note of caution about the too easy use of such terms as 'self-actualization' and 'identity'). Nowhere are these cultural tendencies more in evidence than in contemporary youth culture (Fenwick and Hayward, 2000, pp. 43–6). What is important in this context, however, is the way that, in recent years, corporate capitalism has increasingly come to rely on images of crime as a means of selling products in the youth market. Certainly, crime has long sold. The compelling and salacious nature of certain criminal acts ensures a ready audience for crime and it has remained an enduring theme in popular culture throughout the twentieth century. What has changed, however, is both the force and the range of the message. Crime has been seized upon: it is being packaged and marketed to young people as a romantic, exciting, cool and fashionable cultural symbol. It is in this cultural context that transgression becomes a desirable consumer choice. Within consumer culture, crime is being aestheticised and stylised, presented in the mass media on a par with a fashion aesthetic. This is not to suggest any simple causal link between images of violence and crime in consumer culture and contemporary youth crime; rather what I am suggesting is that the distinction between representations of criminality and the pursuit of excitement, especially in the area of youth culture, is becoming extremely blurred.

> It is worth pausing to reflect on this 're-branding' of crime within contemporary culture. One obvious example of this process is the way in which 'gangster' rap combines images of criminality with street gang iconography and designer chic to create a product that is immediately seductive to youth audiences. For instance, in recent years it has become very difficult to tell whether gangster rap imagery and styling is shaping street gang culture in the US or vice versa. Since the 1980s, many cultural symbols of rap music, such as branded sports apparel and designer clothing, have been used by street gangs as a means of 'flagging' gang affiliations. Add to this the fact that several major rap artists like Tupac Shakur and the Notorious BIG have been murdered in a long-running feud between East and West coast rap artists, and it becomes immediately apparent that, at least in the field of gangster rap, art and real life are becoming ever more interwined. Stylized images of crime abound in many other areas of the mass media, sending mixed messages to a young audience who often take their lead from popular and consumer culture. In film, violent crime and drug dealing are glamorized by slick production values and carefully selected soundtracks. The central characters in films such as *Pulp Fiction, New Jack City, Reservoir Dogs, True Romance and Natural Born Killers* are then lionized as cool popular culture icons.
>
> (Fenwick and Hayward, 2000, pp. 45–6)

Likewise, on television, crime is being packaged as entertainment (Baudrillard, 1983). 'Reality' police shows are a staple of television schedules, despite being little more than a mixture of dramatic case re-enactments and real-life crime footage, cobbled together to provide audiences with a vicarious televisual cheap thrill. Crime also features prominently in the world of video gaming. Violent imagery has always played a major part in this pastime, most notably in role playing and 'shoot 'em up' games. However, in recent years, game developers have begun to produce games like *Kingpin* that use criminal activities as their central theme, two notorious examples being *Carmaggedon* and *Grand Theft Auto*, both of which had their release dates put back while the content of the games was reviewed by censors. *Carmeggedon* celebrates reckless and aggressive driving, while in *Grand Theft Auto* players traverse urban landscapes by hopping from one stolen car to another, gaining extra points by eluding the police. These games provide their predominantly young audience with vicarious excitement from activities that are at best questionable (Fenwick and Hayward, 2000, p. 45). Perhaps the most obvious example of this 'genre mixing' was the reaction to the murder of Jill Dando and the thought that it must in some way be linked with her role on the popular television show *Crimewatch*.

To conclude, while the state responds to the reconfigurations and transformations associated with the late modern condition by imposing what it believes to be more 'rational' forms of control and authority, the market takes a very different approach. Rather than attempting to curtail the excitement and emotionality that, for many individuals, is the preferred antidote to ontological precariousness, the market chooses instead to celebrate and, very importantly, commodify, these same sensations.

CONCLUSION

The themes and ideas presented in this chapter pose more questions than answers. For example, simply drawing attention to the various ways in which the vilification and pleasures of youthful transgression are inextricably linked provides little practical assistance to criminologists engaged in the fundamental task of reducing youth crime. Likewise, the recognition of the centrality of culture in the social production of crime also militates against any obvious solutions. However, it is hoped that this chapter has drawn attention to the role of excitement and emotionality in the commission of many forms of youth crime, and highlighted the ways in which many young people, faced with the contingencies and dilemmas brought about by the late modern condition, seek refuge in what I have called a 'controlled loss of control'. At a less explicit level the chapter has also attempted to highlight the ever changing nature of youth crime and therefore the need to subject it constantly to the lens of deconstruction, for only by undertaking this task will criminology be able to gain a more rounded picture of youthful transgression.

NOTES

I am indebted to Professor Beverley Brown for her helpful comments on drafts of this chapter.

1 Cultural criminology is a particular form of criminological theory that sets out to reinterpret criminal behaviour as a technique for resolving certain psychic conflicts – conflicts that in many instances are indelibly linked with various features of contemporary life. One might say that it represents a phenomenology of transgression fused with a sociological analysis of late modern culture. That said, cultural criminology should not be thought of as in any way oppositional to the more mainstream criminological enterprise. Rather it should be seen as a means of reinvigorating the study of crime. As Ferrell and Sanders have commented: 'bending or breaking the boundaries of criminology ... does not undermine contemporary criminology as much as it expands it and enlivens it' (Ferrell and Sanders, 1995, p. 17).
2 As Fenwick and Hayward have observed, 'It is worth noting that this argument challenges one of the central assumptions of much contemporary criminology, namely the belief that most crime is routinized and, in some way, banal. This is undoubtedly the case if one adopts the perspective of the police or other criminal justice and law enforcement agencies, however, it is not necessarily true for those participating in criminal activity, for whom the most innocuous transgression may well represent an exhilarating form of experience' (Fenwick and Hayward, 2000, p. 36).
3 'Cruising' is the cutting edge of *sub rosa* car culture and involves unauthorized high-speed city-centre car racing and mass car rallies at which dangerous driving practices are encouraged and their actors lionized.
4 'Twocking' refers to the practice of taking cars without their owners' prior consent.
5 It is worth emphasizing at this point that Katz is not alone in his attempt to reorientate criminology's gaze away from logos of materialism and rationalism towards a position on crime that more fully appreciates the existential nature of the criminal act. Authors such as Presdee (2000), Stanley (1996, chapter 7), Morrison (1995), Young (1996), Salecl (1993) and Henry and Milovanovic (1996), for instance, have all also contributed to this project.
6 On the subject of the interaction of the cultural and the economic see Michel Callon's (1998) *Laws of the Market*.

7 *Boso* driving refers to the practice of illegal street racing and high-risk, high-speed reckless driving displays undertaken by teenage Japanese car and motorcycle gangs or *bosozoku*.
8 On this point, I am reminded of a quote by Zizek (1999: 252): 'on this level power and resistance are effectively caught in a deadly embrace: there is no power without resistance (in order to function, power needs an X which eludes its grasp); there is no resistance without power (power is already formative of that very kernel on behalf of which the oppressed subject resists the hold of power).'

REFERENCES

Amin, A. (1994) *Post-Fordism: A Reader*, Oxford, Blackwell.
Baudrillard, J. (1983) *Simulations*, New York, Semiotext(e).
Bauman, Z. (1987) *Legislators and Interpreters*, Cambridge, Polity Press.
Bauman, Z. (1998) Work, *Consumerism and the New Poor*, Buckingham, Open University Press.
Beck, U. (1992) *Risk Society: Towards a New Modernity*, London, Sage.
Brantingham, P.J. and Brantingham, P.L. (1981) *Environmental Criminology*, Beverly Hills CA, Sage.
Callon, M. (ed.) (1998) *Laws of the Market*, Oxford, Blackwell.
Cohen, S. (1972) *Folk Devils and Moral Panics*, Oxford, Blackwell.
Connell, R. (1995) *Masculinities*, Cambridge, Polity Press.
Davis, M. (1990) *City of Quartz*, London, Verso.
Davis, M. (1998) *Ecology of Fear*, New York, Metropolitan Books.
de Certeau, M. (1984) *The Practice of Everyday Life*, Berkeley CA, University of California Press.
Docker, J. (1994) *Postmodernism and Popular Culture: A Cultural History*, Cambridge, Cambridge University Press.
Featherstone, M. (1991) *Consumer Culture and Postmodernism*, London, Sage.
Fenwick, M. and Hayward, K.J. (2000) 'Youth crime, excitement and consumer culture: the reconstruction of aetiology in contemporary theoretical criminology', in J. Pickford (ed.) *Youth Justice: Theory and Practice*, London, Cavendish.
Ferrell, J. (1995) 'Urban graffiti: crime, control and resistance', *Youth and Society*, vol. 27, pp. 73–92.
Ferrell, J. and Sanders, C.S. (1995) *Cultural Criminology*, Boston MA, Northeastern University Press.
Foucault, M. (1977) *Discipline and Punish*, London, Allen Lane.
Garland, D. (2001) *The Culture of Control*, Oxford, Oxford University Press.
Giddens, A. (1990) *The Consequences of Modernity*, Cambridge: Polity Press.
Giddens, A. (1991) *Modernity and Self-identity: Self and Society in the late Modern Age*, Cambridge, Polity Press.
Hall, S. and Jacques, M. (1990) *New Times: the Changing face of Politics in the 1990s*, London, Lawrence & Wishart.
Hall, S. and Jefferson, A. (1976) *Resistance through Ritual*, London, Hutchinson.
Harvey, D. (1990) *The Condition of Postmodernity*, London, Blackwell.
Henry, D., and Milovanovic, S. (1996) *Constitutive Criminology: Beyond Postmodernism*, London, Sage.
Jameson, F. (1991) *Postmodernism*, London, Verso.

Jefferson, T. (1997) 'Masculinities, crime and criminology' in M. Maguire, R. Morgan and R. Reiner (eds) *The Oxford Handbook of Criminology* (2nd edn), Oxford, Clarendon Press.

Katz, J. (1988) *Seductions of Crime: Moral and Sensual Attractions of Doing Evil*, New York, Basic Books.

Lasley, J.R. (1995) 'New writing on the wall: exploring the middle-class graffiti subculture', *Deviant Behaviour*, vol. 16, no. 2, p. 151.

Lyng, S. (1990) 'Edgework: a social psychological analysis of voluntary risk taking', *American Journal of Sociology*, vol. 95, pp. 887–921.

Lyotard, J. (1984) *The Postmodern Condition*, Manchester, Manchester University Press.

Miller, E.M. (1991) 'Assessing the risk of inattention to class race/ethnicity and gender: comment on Lyng', *American Journal of Sociology*, vol. 96, pp. 1530–4.

Morrison, W. (1995) *Theoretical Criminology: From Modernity to Postmodernism*, London, Cavendish.

O'Malley, P. and Mugford, S. (1994) 'Crime, excitement and modernity', in G. Barak (ed.) *Varieties of Criminology: Readings from a Dynamic Discipline*, Westport CT, Praeger.

Pearson, G. (1983) *Hooligan: A History of Respectable Fears*, Basingstoke, Macmillan.

Presdee, M. (1994) 'Young people, culture and the construction of crime: doing wrong versus doing crime' in G. Barak (ed.), *Varieties of Criminology: Readings from a Dynamic Discipline*, London and Westport CT, Praeger.

Presdee, M. (2000) *Cultural Criminology and the Carnival of Crime*, London, Routledge.

Redhead, S. (1995) *Unpopular Cultures: The Birth of Law and Popular Culture*, Manchester, Manchester University Press.

Salecl, R. (1993) 'Crime as a mode of subjectivism: Lacan and the law', *Law and Critique*, vol. 4, pp. 2–20.

Sato, I. (1991) *Kamikaze Biker: Parody and Anomy in Affluent Japan*, Chicago, University of Chicago Press.

Stanley, C. (1996) *Urban Excess and the Law: Capital, Culture and Desire*, London, Cavendish.

Taylor, I. (1999) *Crime in Context: A Critical Criminology of Market Societies*, Cambridge, Polity Press.

Van Hoorebeeck, B.V. (1997) 'Prospects of reconstructing aetiology', *Theoretical Criminology*, vol. 14, pp. 510–18.

Willis, P. (1977) *Learning to Labour*, Aldershot, Gower.

Wilson, J.Q. (1975) *Thinking about Crime*, New York, Basic Books.

Young, A. (1996) *Imagining Crime*, London, Sage.

Young, J. (1971) *The Drugtakers: The Social Meaning of Drug Use*, London, Paladin.

Young, J. (1999) *The Exclusive Society*, London, Sage.

Zimring, F.E. (1998) *American Youth Violence*, Oxford, Oxford University Press.

Zizek, S. (1999) *The Ticklish Subject: The Absent Centre of Political Ontology*, London, Verso.

Part II

The origins of youth justice

Radical reform of the youth justice system has been a central part of New Labour's agenda to reduce offending by children and young people, to build safer communities and to tackle social exclusion. Part II underlines the value of studying the nineteenth-century origins of youth justice in order to provide a context for our understanding of modern-day reforms. The history of youth justice reform goes largely unacknowledged in New Labour's proposals and initiatives. A fixation solely with the present and future is overly encouraged by New Labour's sweeping condemnation of everything to do with youth justice prior to the 1998 Crime and Disorder Act as a 'failure'. Who wants to be associated with failed histories? We would argue, however, that one of the most obvious tropes connecting nineteenth and early twentieth-century government programmes of youth justice reform with the present is the reformers' repeated utilization of an almost evangelical progressive discourse to justify their actions.

The introductory reading, Chapter 7 by Margaret May, analyses how the mid-nineteenth-century official recognition of 'juvenile delinquency' and the formation of 'children' as a distinct legal category were linked with the production and circulation of new social scientific knowledges and practices and emergent representations of 'childhood' (as discussed in Part I of this volume). The various shifts were consolidated into a reform movement that condemned the policy of imprisoning children by challenging the conventional discourses of criminal justice. Reformist legislation established that the nation's 'children' were in need of the state's care and protection, and mandated the creation of institutions such as industrial and reformatory schools that reinforced the distinction between 'child' and 'adult'.

Our discussion continues with Susan Magarey's detailed study, in Chapter 8, of the role played by the criminal law in 'legislating juvenile delinquency into existence' in the early nineteenth century. This chapter provides us with many examples of the ways in which the enlargement of the scope and the increasing severity of the criminal code, allied to the creation of the 'new police', impacted on leisure pastimes and petty criminal activities. Most notably, minor delinquency and nuisances by children came to be treated as grave offences, and new legislation effectively criminalized the 'antisocial behaviour' of street children. Magarey also makes the important point that examining the nineteenth-century transformations in terms of the shift from an 'unreformed' to a 'reformed' system of juvenile justice distracts us from thinking about the shifts as a strategy of power and morality of domination.

In Chapter 9 John Clarke argues that it is important to ask why 'youth' and 'youthful misbehaviour' are accorded such a privileged position in discussions about the nature of social order. 'Youth' for Clarke is such a potent social category because it has the power to convey a deeper message about the state of society and social change. His chapter provides an explicit critique of the humanitarian motives of the juvenile reform movement, pointing out how its presentation of the 'youth problem' was informed by bourgeois notions of the respectable family and childhood and the determination to turn out productive members of the industrial labour force. Clarke also shows how the reformers' determination to claim the body and soul of the delinquent from the penal system destabilized the classical view of crime, law and punishment and paved the way for the appearance of positivist criminology. Eventually the juvenile court became the institution that was given the impossible task of reconciling the tension between criminal justice and welfarist discourses (as discussed in Part III of this volume).

Peter Rush, in Chapter 10, assigns himself the task of complicating the critical history of juvenile delinquency. He recognizes the importance of questioning reformist intentions and unmasking the deeper, undisclosed and unrecognized social control implications of their proposals. However, he also believes that the 'grand sweep' of critical histories tends to overlook the contradictions and inconsistencies of motive and resistance. He explores how official understandings of 'the problem' in the nineteenth century centred, not simply on the existence of juvenile crime, but on explanations for the perceived increase in juvenile crime. It was this that triggered the quest to identify the causes of the problem, which in turn provided the discursive space within which the subject of juvenile delinquency could become possible, and a network of distinct disciplines and practices of control and subjugation could emerge. Rush also argues that it is important to examine how the juvenile delinquent appears across a series of disparate social problems, all of which demand a response from the state. The chapter concludes with a brief examination of the late nineteenth-century discovery of the 'incorrigible juvenile delinquent' who stands as proof of failure of the reformatory enterprise and of the need for reformation to be extended. In these ways, constructions of delinquency also play into and justify the existence of the adult prison and a much broader carceral discourse.

Finally, in Chapter 11, Heather Shore's revisionist reading challenges the idea that summary jurisdiction and separate custody for children were mid-nineteenth-century creations. This chapter also centres the importance of studying the shifting discourses about delinquency through the lens of gender and sexuality. She narrates how the formalization of summary justice for juveniles enabled the development of a custodial system that incorporated juvenile offenders, semi-offenders and 'at risk' children. The use of separate custody for juveniles in voluntary-sector institutions, from the late eighteenth century, was vital to the emergence of a state-sanctioned industrial and reformatory school system. Shore notes how concern over female delinquents was framed, for the most part, in terms of their sexual immorality. This was accompanied by further concern about the threat that these sexually mature or knowledgeable girls and young women were supposed to pose to 'innocent' boys. Whilst informal trial and punishment were the key mechanism for processing female juveniles, Shore also highlights the existence of specific institutions to deal with the juvenile prostitute.

7

Innocence and experience: the evolution of the concept of juvenile delinquency in the mid-nineteenth century

Margaret May

> The latter [the delinquent] is a little stunted man already – he knows much and a great deal too much of what is called life – he can take care of his own immediate interests. He is self-reliant, he has so long directed or mis-directed his own actions and has so little trust in those about him, that he submits to no control and asks for no protection. He has consequently much to unlearn – he has to be turned again into a child....[1]

Matthew Davenport Hill's portrayal of a juvenile delinquent epitomised the new attitude to the problem and treatment of delinquency in mid-nineteenth-century England. Hitherto the problem had received only limited attention and young offenders were punished in exactly the same way as adults. State recognition of Reformatory and Industrial Schools in 1854 and 1857 (17 & 18 Victoria, c. 86; 20 & 21 Victoria, c. 48) marked a radical change in penal policy. For the first time in a legislative enactment Parliament recognised juvenile delinquency as a distinct social phenomenon and accepted responsibility not only for young offenders, but also for children who, although not in conflict with the law, required 'care and protection'. Thus children coming before the courts were no longer regarded as 'little adults' but as beings in their own right entitled to special care because they lacked full responsibility for their actions. This change in status was accomplished by the introduction of reformatory rather than punitive treatment and also involved the assertion of new powers of state intervention in parent–child relationships. A reformatory system which clearly distinguished a child's offence from an adult's crime replaced a penal system which made little specialised provision for children. This departure culminated in Herbert Samuel's Children Act of 1908 (8 Edward VII, c. 17).

   Despite the significance of these innovations and the early Victorian obsession with rising crime rates, historians have largely neglected the subject.[2] The Reformatory School Movement has been interpreted simply as the product of religious concern and generous humanitarianism. Religious fervour and compassion for the 'waifs and

SOURCE: This chapter is taken from *Victorian Studies*, Vol. 17, No. 1, 1973, pp. 7–29.

strays' were certainly widespread, and the 'outcast child' was a familiar theme in Victorian literature well-calculated to boost an author's popularity and sales. However the segregation of child and adult offenders emanated from more complex motives. This paper traces the evolution from eighteenth-century attitudes to the redefined concept of juvenile delinquency in the mid-nineteenth century.

I

At the beginning of the nineteenth century few legal distinctions were drawn between the offence, mode of trial, or punishment of children and adults. But a limited concession was made for the capacities of infants. Centuries of judicial precedent had built up the principle of *doli capax* most clearly enunciated by Blackstone in 1796, 'the capacity of doing ill, or contracting guilt, is not so much measured by years and days, as by the strength of the delinquent's understanding and judgement.'[3] Up to the age of seven it was presumed that children were incapable of criminal intent and could not be held personally responsible for violations of the law; between the ages of seven and fourteen they were presumed innocent unless the prosecution proved their ability to 'discern between good and evil'; thereafter they were fully responsible.

These provisos were generally observed[4] but otherwise children were sentenced to the same retributive punishments as adults, graded by statute and judicial precedent according to the magnitude of the offence. Age by itself gave no right to special treatment and children were tried with the full publicity and formality of judge and jury or magistrate.[5] Young offenders were liable for all the main forms of punishment, capital conviction, transportation and imprisonment. They had no legal right to be treated differently, though individual magistrates might exercise a compassionate discretion. Thus although 103 children under fourteen received capital sentences at the Old Bailey between 1801 and 1836, all were commuted to transportation or imprisonment.[6] But such clemency was only a variant of a policy applied to all offenders in the early nineteenth century in the face of the stringent penal code (Radzinowicz, *Criminal Law*, I, 163). Children also shared the punishment of transportation; 780 males and 136 females under twenty-one were transported to Australia between 1812 and 1817 alone.

During the first half of the century, however, transportation and capital conviction gradually gave way to imprisonment as the chief form of punishment for all offenders. Again there was little differentiation between children and adults. Prisons at first were mere places of detention where offenders of all types and ages were huddled together indiscriminately. A Select Committee of 1818 found free association between prisoners common in most metropolitan and provincial gaols. Newgate, where 'children of the tenderest age were confined in the cells with prisoners of more mature age and more confirmed habits of crime,' was but the most notorious of many. Similarly in Bristol, Fowell Buxton, the prison reformer, found that boys were allowed 'to intermingle with men' and all 'without distinction of age were in heavy irons'. At the better disciplined Gloucester and Salford prisons 'boys were treated as adults' and subject to the rigours of the treadmill.[7]

Early efforts at prison reform continued to treat young and old alike. As early as 1777 John Howard had exposed the abuses and overcrowding which made gaols 'nurseries of crime.' He acknowledged the particular dangers to the young who were 'totally ruined' there.[8] But his concern, like that of his successors, focused on the question of mass corruption rather than on the needs of any particular group of inmates. Any consideration of the problem of protecting juveniles was incidental. The swelling prison population, however, stimulated efforts at reform and in the process the problem of the young offender was revealed.

Prison reform passed through several phases, each employing different devices for eliminating contact between individual inmates. The first limited step was the introduction of classification in 1823, following various local experiments. But this categorisation of offenders by character and seriousness of offence, whilst entailing the separation of the inexperienced and the hardened, did not necessitate segregation by age. The sheer size of the prison population did, however, force several prisons to allocate separate 'wards' for juveniles and to establish prison schools. The obvious inadequacies of classification led to a more vigorous campaign in the 1830s and 1840s based on American successes.[9] The rival Separate and Silent Systems were enthusiastically advocated. Both aimed at eliminating corruption; the former by physical separation, the latter by enforced silence. Their protagonists had high expectations of both general deterrence and individual reformation. Following the appointment of William Crawford and Whitworth Russell as Prison Inspectors in 1836, the Separate System was widely adopted as the best cure for all offenders. It was applied with equal rigour to young and old. At Reading the child offender was placed in solitary confinement 'like a dog in a kennel,' relieved only by the visits of officials, or, as at Wakefield, by extra schooling. Boys were even employed on the crank at Hampshire County Gaol. Meanwhile a parallel campaign to remove similar abuses from the transportation system brought some improvement but no change in status for the young offender. Efforts at classification included the introduction of a separate convict hulk in 1823 and a boys' penal colony at Point Puer in 1837; and as part of the general reorganisation of transportation, Parkhurst Prison was opened in 1838 to train boy transportees before embarkation. Despite all efforts at uniformity, however, the penal system was still characterised by great diversity.

But the strenuous attempts at improvement and the decline of association had an unexpected result. As mass contamination was reduced the special problem of the young offender was highlighted. New techniques of prison management and reform were allied with changing attitudes to the purpose of imprisonment itself. The reforms of the 1830s and 1840s with their emphasis on individual reformation shifted attention from the nature of the offence to the criminal himself. Significant changes in the character of penal administrators followed. Gradually the inefficient eighteenth-century gaoler was replaced by a new generation of prison governors and chaplains dedicated to proving the value of their reforms. They found the existence of ever-increasing numbers of children in the improved prisons an embarrassing impediment to reform. By 1850 Joshua Jebb, the Surveyor-General of Prisons, was admitting that he did 'not think that the present prisons are at all adapted to juveniles.'[10] It was this dissatisfaction, shared by prison officials, magistrates, and a small group of well-informed outsiders, which stimulated a search for new policies. Discontent was firmly based in their practical experience and drew its strength from clear evidence of failure. For the first time the crucial question of the suitability of imprisonment for children was raised.

The arguments familiar since Howard were given a new direction. Prisons were criticised not for mass corruption but corruption of the young. Recommittal statistics demonstrated that prison reform was producing the opposite effect to that intended. Juveniles were neither deterred nor converted, as the Reverend John Field, an assiduous supporter of the Separate System, was mortified to discover. John Clay was equally horrified to find a reconviction rate of 56 per cent in Preston in the 1840s. Juvenile recidivism was recognized by the Chaplain at Bath, the Reverend C.S. Osborne, who deduced 'once in gaol, always in gaol' was a truism for boys. 'They become trained to prison life' (S.C. on Prison Discipline, p. 343).

Failure was at first ascribed to individual aspects of prison administration, but later led to condemnation of the whole idea of imprisoning children. Imprisonment scarred the young with a life-long stigma which prevented respectable, honest employment and forced children back into criminal life. Children treated as adult criminals reacted accordingly. 'Branded as prison birds,' they played their role for the admiration of their peers; for a boy once labelled as a criminal 'regards himself as belonging to the criminal class' (S.C. on Prison Discipline, pp. 343–4). The policy of repeated short sentences reinforced this break with society. Detention was too short to effect any permanent improvement, but often provided an insight into the good food and shelter of the prison, removing any fear of recommittal and even encouraging it. State main-tenance in gaol was seen as an inducement to parental irresponsibility. Magistrates like Thomas Eastcourt warned that prison sentences were a 'boon' to negligent parents. Prisons were a premium on crime, and whilst parents evaded the duty of maintenance the public faced mounting expenditure. Moreover their money was poorly spent. Few prisons provided specialised schooling or retraining schemes for juveniles. Gaolers employed to discipline adults followed the same custodial approach with children, who were hardened into a criminal life.

Inevitably these widespread doubts culminated in an onslaught against the whole policy of imprisoning children. Such a radical contention was underpinned by both emotional and practical considerations. The contrast between a small vulnerable child and the fortress-like condition of the prison affronted the growing humani-tarian sentiment of the time. But it was the new awareness among prison officials of children's reactions to confinement which engendered reform. The all-embracing Separate System proved particularly unsuitable for children, endangering their health and providing no outlet for their 'restless minds.' The prison inspectors Frederick Hill and Captain John Williams discovered that offences within the Separate System were more frequent among children than adults. Even Crawford and Russell found that cellular isolation clearly revealed the mental and physical differences between children and adults, and concluded, 'so marked is the distinction in the feeling and habit of manhood and youth that it is quite impractical to engraft any beneficial plan for the lengthened confinement of boys upon a system adapted to adults.'[11]

These perceptions were firmly rooted in contemporary theory: associationist psychology maintained that children developed in response to external stimuli. This was precluded by prison confinement, which starved them of the very spirit of child-hood. The Governor of Cold Bath Fields, G.L. Chesterton, observed that 'the youth-ful mind is so elastic, the desire to play and the inclination for trifles are such that the bringing of boys like these under a strict system … which you assign to a grown-up person is a perfectly unnatural state for a boy' (S.C. on Prison Discipline, p. 634). Prisons not only failed to meet a child's physical and mental needs, but he or she was positively harmed by the experience. Young offenders were contaminated directly by promiscuous association with adults in the unreformed gaols and indirectly tainted by the 'moral atmosphere' of the prison. This was but one facet of the major change in attitudes to childhood that characterised mid-Victorian social reform. Just as the

Mixed General Workhouse, and indeed the early factory employment of children, were condemned for ruining childish innocence by the mere presence of adults, so prisons transmitted adult vices.

Disillusionment with imprisonment and fears that it only confirmed a criminal career extended beyond the prison walls. Uneven sentencing policy reflected the difficulties of many magistrates and judges in choosing the best procedure consistent with their knowledge of delinquency and the punishment permitted by law. The evidence of Graham Spiers, Sheriff of Edinburgh, to the 1847 Select Committee on Criminal Law exemplified long standing doubts: 'I have been puzzled, acting judicially, where a boy has been brought before me and found guilty of theft to know what to do.'[12] Some magistrates exercised their discretion through various devices for avoiding imprisonment. But the resultant inconsistencies in sentencing practice provoked further criticism on the one hand from those who felt juveniles were being treated too harshly and, on the other, from who those who felt uncertainty was encouraging impunity.[13]

The pomp and ceremony of trial by jury for juveniles accused of more serious offences also perturbed court officials. The majesty of the law was undermined by the 'mockery' of formal and expensive trials of children too young to appreciate the solemnity of the occasion. Moreover the lengthy pre-trial detention of juveniles, often on very trivial offences, exposed them to all the depravity concentrated in the prison. In the 1820s a Warwickshire magistrate, J.E. Eardley-Wilmot, in an effort to salvage legal dignity argued that minor offences by children should be classed as misdemeanours, not felonies, and children should be dealt with summarily. Magistrates in Petty Sessions should follow 'the domestic regulation of families,' and provide punishments appropriate to children in order to avoid the stigma of public trial and imprisonment.[14] But his proposals were attacked because such differentiation between the child and the adult would deprive the child of the right of all free-born Englishmen to trial by jury – an unwarrantable interference with the liberty of the individual. This traditional equation of children and adults was challenged by an influential group of lawyers who argued that a child's freedom was largely illusory. He was not a free agent.[15] After prolonged wrangling the 1847 Summary Jurisdiction Act was passed giving power to try children under fourteen summarily for petty larceny. In 1850 this was extended to include children up to sixteen.[16] A combination of judicial self-interest, the need to reduce costs, and a growing awareness of the special rights of children thus produced the first statutory distinction between children and adults.

II

The growing discontent among prison administrators and magistrates was based not only on disenchantment with defective sentencing and imprisonment, but also on a new awareness of the nature and extent of juvenile delinquency. Whilst prison experiments isolated the problem of the young offender from that of the adult, other developments highlighted the existence of a large group of children who, though not technically law breakers, shared their characteristics. Segregation of the neglected and ill-behaved child was one result of the growth of a system of public education which provided only for the more tractable and fee-paying working class, and a system of public assistance that made no direct provision for child neglect. Institutional differentiation was accompanied by the identification and delineation of delinquency as a special social problem, demanding distinctive action. Such categorisation was the direct result of the increasing availability of criminal statistics in the nineteenth century, and the corresponding growth in the scientific study of crime.

Early in the century knowledge of the problem was largely confined to the observations and conjecture of a few criminal law administrators. Criminal activities were frequently confused with the problem of mass pauperism and little attention was paid to the young. The most notable early attempt at analysis was that of the London police magistrate, Patrick Colquhoun, whose belief that crime was spiralling led him to describe the types of crime flourishing in the metropolis and attack the penal system which 'vomitted' criminals back on to society. Large numbers of human predators, many commencing their careers in infancy, were at war with society.[17] A more precise insight into the extent and changing pattern of crime followed the introduction of the Home Office Returns in 1805. Though they did not distinguish adults and juveniles, they did reveal an apparently rapid rise in crime. Witnesses at Select Committees in the 1810s and 1820s repeatedly attributed this to an increase in juvenile offenders. So widespread was this impression that special local inquiries were held, notably in London in 1816 and in Surrey and Warwickshire in 1828. All confirmed a 'perfectly appalling' rise in crime committed at a much earlier age than formerly. It was ascribed primarily to parental neglect.[18]

These findings were reiterated with new authority in the 1830s and 1840s when more refined methods of inquiry and diagnosis were developed. Under Samuel Redgrave's supervision from 1834 the national returns were improved, and for the first time information on the age and education of offenders was provided.[19] Parallel prison reforms replaced the erratic and limited prison registers with compulsory uniform records, including details of age. This sudden flow of information and the absence of long-term statistics fostered a widespread belief in the escalation of crime. Some contemporaries realised that factors independent of the activities of criminals might be partly responsible. The more general impression, however, was that, despite growing industrial prosperity, crime was apparently increasing out of all proportion to the rise in population, and this increase was greatest among the young. Redgrave revealed a massive 600 per cent rise in crime between 1805 and 1842.[20] Prison convictions of under-twenties increased from 6,803 in 1835 to 11,348 by 1844. By 1853 Sydney Turner, the future Inspector of Reformatory Schools and Chaplain of Red Hill School, estimated that 12,000 juveniles were being imprisoned annually. Anxious and frequently confused use of statistics generated the intense public alarm which was a major force behind the acceptance of new measures.

Such fears precipitated a flood of unofficial inquiries in the 1830s and 1840s, which both confirmed national trends and paved the way for social action. The emergence of juvenile delinquency as a distinct social problem can be traced through these investigations. The gradual accumulation of detailed information increasingly shifted from general studies of crime to specific consideration of delinquency. This was accompanied by various analytical processes which isolated juvenile delinquency from other social problems. The nature of the investigations was an important factor in this development. Most were empirical studies, the product of the daily experience and apprehensions of those whose occupations brought them into contact with young miscreants. Lawyers, magistrates, voluntary teachers and ministers of religion constructed a picture of delinquency which was widely accepted because of their professional status. Though the investigators claimed objectivity, their findings were inevitably coloured by their own prejudices and values. The concept of deviance implies behaviour which somehow differs from prevailing expectations.[21] The conditions discovered by these amateur social investigators violated their images of childhood. Throughout their writings comparison between the realities of slum childhood and their own sense of a protected childhood is implicit.

The most authoritative group of investigators was the self-styled 'moral statisticians' of the numerous statistical societies. Their work was of crucial importance in initiating the 'science' of criminology and in particular in drawing attention to the age of the offender. They developed the methods and tools of statistical inquiry, examining the 'moral topography' of different areas as well as the 'moral health' of the whole nation. In the words of R.W. Rawson, the first Secretary of the London Statistical Society, they believed that just as Newton had discovered universal laws governing the physical world, so 'moral phenomena may be found to be controlled and determined by peculiar laws.' A simple accumulation of facts and figures would reveal the laws which regulate criminality (*JSSL*, II [1839], 316–18).

In their search for verifiable facts and patterns of criminal behaviour they elaborated the first clear concept of juvenile delinquency. The key breakthrough was Rawson's demonstration in 1839 that the correlation between age and the type and number of offences was one fundamental 'law' of crime. Criminal activity began early in life and reached a peak between sixteen and twenty-five. Larceny and petty theft were the most characteristic offences. Joseph Fletcher, another prominent member, concluded that since over half of those sentenced were under twenty-five 'there is a population constantly being brought up to crime' (*JSSL*, VI [1843], 236).

His observation and the new consciousness of age were substantiated by a close scrutiny of criminal life and habits. Widespread concern with the early urban environment had produced a series of general studies of social conditions in the 1830s. J.P. Kay's influential survey of Manchester in 1832 revealed, among a mass of social problems, the prevalence of the 'moral leprosy,' crime.[22] By the 1840s crime and delinquency were being treated as separate social questions, and not merely as illustrations of a general social disease. W.A. Miles' experience in London led him to distinguish criminals from the respectable working class, particularly 'a youthful population ... devoted to crime, trained to it from infancy, adhering to it from education and circumstances ... a race "sui generis", differing from the rest of society not only in thoughts, habits and manners but even in appearance.'[23]

Another early study, William Beaver Neale's 'Juvenile Delinquency in Manchester,' stressed 'the existence of a class of juvenile delinquents,' concentrated in certain quarters of Manchester 'congenial to criminals.' Such areas were the source of both moral and physical 'contagion and pestilence'; children born and reared in them were 'predestined' to a life of crime. Neale traced the careers of such potential malefactors from 'the first step', juvenile vagrancy, through street selling which served as a guise for petty pilfering, to pickpocketing and organised crime. Parents often actively encouraged this process, forcing their offspring to beg and steal to satisfy their own whims. Lacking affection and supervision, the juvenile delinquent in consequence displayed his independence. He was 'in general a gambler and a drunkard' with an 'unnatural' interest in the opposite sex. But 'circumstances' and parental irresponsibility rather than 'innate depravity' produced such outrageous behaviour: of one hundred cases examined, sixty were the offspring of 'dishonest' and thirty of 'profligate' parents.[24]

Neale's account is dominated by the two recurrent themes of later more comprehensive inquiries, the precocity and promiscuity of his young subjects, and the close connections between adult and juvenile crime. Juvenile delinquents were identified through a process which emphasised those features which distinguish them both from other children and adults. To study the 'moral topography' of cities and to confine the delinquent to deteriorating and squalid areas involved a tendency to transfer the characteristics of the area to its inhabitants. In particular the coincidence of insanitary conditions and criminal areas led many investigators to adopt the rhetoric of the public health reformers as a method of identifying and classifying a separate sector of the population. Indeed many, such as Thomas Beggs and the Reverend John Clay, were themselves active in the public health movement. Sanitary and medical analogies were freely employed. Juvenile delinquents were frequently referred to as 'human vermin' and crime as a 'moral disease.' Imagery such as this reflected fears that crime, like cholera, was contagious and might infect not only the inhabitants of the immediate locality but the whole social fabric. Crime diffused 'a subtle, unseen, but sure poison in the moral atmosphere of the neighbourhood, dangerous as is deadly miasma to the physical health.'[25]

Conceptualisation of this kind was sharpened by a concentration on those attributes which most distinguished this youthful group from other respectable and well-tutored children. The behaviour and familiarity with the adult world and its pleasures found among slum children contradicted middle-class standards of childhood morality and propriety. Horrified investigators could only describe such behaviour in terms of a savage animal-like existence. 'English Kaffirs,' 'Street Arabs,' 'ownerless dogs' were the epithets commonly applied, and strong contrasts were drawn with an idealised obedient middle-class child, sheltered by stringent but affectionate parental supervision from both the snares of the world and his own inability to decide for himself. This use of racial nomenclature was another method of designating a special group and reflected the apprehensions which the inquiries inspired. Lower-class standards of child-rearing were denounced, and the conduct of street children received universal condemnation. Their restless, uncontrolled and nomadic existence embraced all the symptoms of social disorganisation, and challenged the very foundations of an ordered society. Mere exposure to crime-infested areas seemed to generate anti-social conduct, whilst careful studies of the new prison records and inquiries among offenders themselves confirmed that the massive problem of adult crime was rooted in the progressive career of the delinquent child. The solution lay in catching the young recruit before he became too accustomed to his irregular mode of life.

A nation-wide accumulation of evidence rapidly convinced the public of this threat. Edward Rushton, Stipendiary Magistrate for Liverpool, encountered 'Hottentots' in his courts, reared 'without the constant care and judicious guidance of a vigilant mother.' The London magistrate, J. Buchanan, plotted the geography of delinquency in the capital, as did the more famous accounts of criminal areas, Mayhew's *London Labour and the London Poor,* and Beames' *Rookeries of London.* The latter described the London rookeries as 'beds of pestilence' and 'rendezvous of vice,' nurseries of felons 'where children were trained as criminals under professional thieves and become addicted to drink and debauchery.' Even in Ipswich John Glyde's study of social conditions forced him to conclude that 'the mass of depravity among the rising generation is horrifying to witness.' Boys gambling openly on the streets on Sundays, and 'almost all, even from the boy of twelve, have acquired the habit of smoking; and obscene and disgusting language is continuously emanating from their lips.'[26]

'Can these be children?' was the inevitable question raised by the Reverend Micaiah Hill in his prize-winning essay of 1853, observing the amusements, the singing and dancing salons, and the extraordinary licentiousness shown by children at such gatherings. Young law-breakers and vagrants were 'never children in heart and mind,' and concepts of childhood taken from the upper or middle class were 'utterly inapplicable.' Their unchildlike behaviour was the result of the pernicious environment in which they lived, and particularly of 'parents destitute of all sense of parental responsibility,' who permitted 'licence of an extent ruinous to childhood.' Delinquency rose from 'too early an exposure to the hardships and temptations of life' caused by large scale desertion, broken marriages or orphanage. Many children were driven to crime and vagrancy by sheer necessity.[27]

Hill's consensus portrait of juvenile depravity drew freely on the mass of earlier local and national studies, and also on the work of prison officials whose case studies and personal observations added further insights into the problem. Many governors and chaplains extended their statutory duty to report on the state of the prison by narrative accounts of the inmates and analysis of their motives. Prominence was given to the size and composition of the prison population with its large proportion of juveniles, and they were especially struck by the prevalence of defective parental care. The Reverend John Clay was the pioneer of case histories and found large numbers of orphans, illegitimate and deserted children among his charges. He was disturbed by the fact that even children of parents with relatively high incomes were rarely visited by them. Their gross ignorance left a profound impression on him.[28] By 1853 it was estimated that 3,000 orphans annually were sent to prison. Crime was even shown to be hereditary, passing on from father to son like a disease. Children of criminals formed a substantial proportion of those imprisoned.

The full weight of prison officialdom was added to the definition of delinquency. Reforming chaplains such as Osborne, Field and Carter; governors such as Chesterton and Smith; and even police constables like Stephen Neal reported the neglect and especially the ignorance of delinquents. During the 1830s and 1840s there was a virulent controversy over the relationship of crime and education since earlier observations had pointed to a direct link between ignorance and crime. This assumption remained a strong force in all arguments for the advancement of education, though a few argued that education simply increased the criminal's proficiency. A more refined approach was adopted by influential chaplains like Clay and statisticians like Fletcher, who pointed out that crime was related not only to the quantity of education but its quality, particularly in morality and religion. It was not simply the illiteracy of prisoners which roused concern but their manifest lack of religious and moral instruction.

Thus whilst prison reforms exposed the problem of young offenders, a wide range of studies defined the delinquent in terms of his behaviour and conditions. A portrait of delinquency was built up by inference through detailed descriptions of criminal areas and evocative illustrations of the habits and manners of slum children. Concern with the young offender had extended to the 'embryo criminal.' But overwhelmed by the implications writers frequently magnified the problem. Depravity and youthful exuberance were often confused and the age groups included undefined. That most included children from the age of eight or nine up to eighteen or twenty as part of one single category is indicative of their basic approach in defining delinquency as a social problem. The description of the delinquent was a negative one, concentrating on the least child-like qualities exhibited. The fundamental issue was that of the 'hideous antithesis, an infant in age, a man in shrewdness and vice ... the face of a child with no trace of childish goodness.'[29] Both the offence and the associated patterns of behaviour roused concern. Implicit in the social reporting was a particular view of childhood as a period of dependency. Children should ideally be excluded form the adult world and restricted to their own closely regulated activities.

If the neglected and delinquent child was 'unlike other children,' he or she was still not an adult. The process of isolating young malefactors was accompanied by the belief that unseemly habits were the product of a defective environment and abnormal conditioning. Multifarious causes were assigned, ranging from the unchecked curiosity and adventurousness of childhood to bad housing and the temptations presented by the new urban society. Most interpreters did not question the social system but were moralistic and policy-oriented. It was generally agreed that the absence of proper parental care was most to blame. Indeed the topology of delinquency was commonly expressed in terms of the parents' condition, from the orphaned to the abandoned or neglected child through to the child deliberately instructed in theft. Diagnosis in terms of parental neglect facilitated concrete action. It mirrored current preoccupations with the supreme importance of the home and the family in child socialisation. Children were 'copyists' who developed the habits of honesty, diligence and obedience through imitating those around them. Constant and vigilant parental surveillance was necessary to prevent the mistakes of inexperience. The child could not be held fully responsible for misconduct; he or she was 'more sinned against than sinning.'

This evaluation of childhood derived from the contemporary proliferation of child guidance manuals. Overlaid with New Testament and Romantic sentiments of childish innocence, it was most clearly and sensitively expressed by Mary Carpenter. Her clarion-call of 1851, *Reformatory Schools for the Perishing and Dangerous Classes and for Juvenile Offenders,* defined the categories of children in a way which galvanized public opinion and led to the first positive state action. Her wide reading and personal experience of Ragged Schools led her to distinguish between the 'dangerous class' of young offenders, and the 'perishing class' of incipient criminals living a life of vagrancy or theft but not yet subject to the law and excluded from any schooling. The central characteristic of all wayward children was not physical destitution, nor lack of education, but moral destitution resulting from parental neglect. Her *Juvenile Delinquents – Their Condition and Treatment* in 1853 expanded this analysis. The young delinquent exhibited 'in almost every respect, qualities the very reverse of what we should desire to see in childhood; we have beheld them independent, self-reliant, advanced in the knowledge of evil....' Yet children were physically and mentally quite different beings from adults, less developed in both respects. By being placed in a position of 'dependence' within a properly organised family system they might be 'gradually restored to the true position of childhood' – the key to reformation.[30]

Her studies intersected the work of social investigators and the operation of the prison and education systems. As a teacher she had discovered the exclusivity of the British and National Schools which, for reasons of poverty, behaviour or appearance, did not admit the lowest social segments. Even the Sunday Schools, originally founded by Raikes for the very poorest, were by mid-century largely confined to the more industrious and respectable classes. Rudimentary literacy was, in her opinion, moreover, not the prime need of such children. Religious-based moral training was necessary to provide an understanding of the difference between right and wrong which parents had neglected. Even if moral instruction in schools were improved the lesson might be undermined in the home. Thus by restricting their curriculum and intake the existing schools had in fact helped to define the delinquent.

By aiding only those who sought assistance and dealing with children as appendages of their parents, Poor Law administration had a similar effect. The few suggestions for substituting the workhouse for prisons were sharply rebuked. Honesty and dishonesty were not to be confused; by breaking the law, the delinquent however destitute had cut himself off from the pauper. The future prison inspector, William Crawford, had as early as 1834 pointed to the folly of treating pauper and delinquent in the same way. In her evidence to the Select Committee of 1852, Mary Carpenter herself repeated the argument that 'the poorhouse is, in theory, a refuge for the physically destitute.' The victims of misfortune should not be tainted by association with the victims of vice, however similar their situation might appear.[31] The 'moral orphan' required separate treatment.

III

Demands for remedial state action inevitably followed the discovery of these social and institutional outcasts. Spearheaded by Mary Carpenter and Matthew Davenport Hill, a prolonged and well-organised campaign for reform was launched. A powerful cross-section of religious and political opinion adhered to it, harnessing the professional impetus to reform, from magistrates and prison administrators to the more emotional response of the humanitarians. The strength of their case lay with an influential group of lawyers led by Charles Pearson, the City of London Solicitor. New insights into the condition of delinquents prompted a re-evaluation of the ancient principle of *doli capax*. They argued that the child's 'incapacity' to distinguish between right and wrong should be more fully implemented, and 'that his age, the neglect or vice of his parents, and the depraving circumstances of his childhood should be taken into account.'[32] This was the basis of middle-class parental protection. The misbehaviour of their children brought parental chastisement, but lower-class children were sent to prison for similar faults. Moreover the civil law already made allowances for the young, and Mary Carpenter argued that the criminal law should be assimilated to it: 'The law of England does not recognise the right of a young person … to contract matrimony, or enter into solemn engagements without the consent of his parents…. The child is very rightly regarded in the eyes of the law as incapable of acting wisely for himself and therefore under the control of his parents' (M. Carpenter, *Reformatory Schools,* p. 286). Such comparisons were reinforced by the example of the French Code Napoleon which stipulated that children under sixteen acted *sans discernement* and acquitted them of the offence, placing them under the care of the state for retraining. The English reformers argued that all children lacked *discernement* and that the law should treat delinquents 'as a wise parent would in such circumstances.' Discipline commensurate with a child's nature, not adult punishment, was necessary when a child proved 'by his conduct that he is ignorant of his duty, deficient in principle and totally unfit to guide himself' (S.C. on Criminal and Destitute Juveniles, p. 118).

As well as demonstrating a child's irresponsibility the reformers exacerbated and manipulated public disquiet. Fears of the swarming numbers 'preying' on society and corroding the social order mounted with the imminent abolition of transportation in the early 1850s. The response of a threatened middle class was essentially defensive. Disruption was to be contained by reasserting their own values about home and family life. Pressure applied as a result of these fears induced the government to support C.B. Adderley's Youthful Offenders Bill of 1854. But impressionistic propaganda and philosophising on *discernement* was of limited use in producing an operational definition of juvenile delinquency. As the Reverend Sydney Turner pertinently remarked, 'what we want is a practical test which a policemen can apply and a magistrate decide upon.'[33] But controversy centred upon the definition of the child's culpability and age of discretion, and the state's right to interfere with the parent. Moreover many suggestions were opposed as a premium on crime and unjust to the honest poor.

The reformers themselves were uncertain where and by what criteria the line between child and adult should be drawn. In addition they disagreed about the degree of guilt exhibited by children and the purpose of punishment itself. The most obvious index of responsibility, age, was also the most disputed; and even the prevailing emphasis on the precocity of delinquents proved an obstacle. Many traditionalists argued that age in itself was an insufficient index. Children were often more vice-ridden than adults, and often committed more serious crimes. Age should not provide an escape from punishment, and clemency would only increase the incentive to crime. The child's dependence on parents for training and other extenuating circumstances were, on the other hand, pointed to by the reformers. Their confusion over the degree of guilt and the consequent propriety of some form of punishment persisted, however.

The 1852–1853 Select Committee heard conflicting evidence on the delinquent's capacity to distinguish between right and wrong and the age at which this capacity was reached. Opinion on the age of discretion ranged from ten to sixteen. Clay, while admitting that 'in many cases a child does not know he has committed a crime,' maintained that he knew it was wrongful as punishment would follow. Sydney Turner believed that children 'are in fact aware of what they do' and knew punishment would ensue, whilst Captain John Williams 'scarcely ever knew a case in which a boy did not know he was doing wrong.'[34]

The vehemence of this controversy was seen at a special meeting of the Royal Society of Arts in 1855. The main speaker, Jelinger Symons, attacked 'the belief that juvenile offenders are little errant angels who require little else than fondling,' arguing that they could discern between right and wrong and should be punished accordingly. Indeed reformation was impossible without such warning of the consequences of misbehaviour. David Power, Recorder of Ipswich, disagreed completely. Children should not be punished for their parents' neglect but rehabilitated. The traditionalists were represented by Mr Elliott who attacked 'effeminate and diseased sentimentality' and argued that 'juvenile offenders should be treated as all other offenders,' 'they must be hurt so that the idea of pain might be instantly associated with crime in the minds of all evildoers.' Aversion therapy had been a constant theme in utilitarian and traditional policy, and Elliott was supported by Lord Lyttleton who argued that *doli capax* had never meant 'that the crime of that child was not to be imputed to it because of a fault in the education of the child.'[35]

The sharp division of opinion led ultimately to legislative compromise. Mary Carpenter's proposals for Reformatory Schools for convicted offenders and Industrial

Schools for the incipient criminal and neglected child were accepted.[36] The former were recognised in 1854, the latter in 1857 and similar measures were passed for Scotland and Ireland. Under the 1854 Act a system similar to that governing education in general was established, based on a partnership of state and voluntary bodies. Judges and magistrates were empowered to sentence children under sixteen on indictable or non-indictable offences to Reformatory Schools for a period of two to five years. Reformatory treatment was preceded by a prison sentence of at least fourteen days, later reduced to ten. Schools were to be managed by voluntary associations subject to state inspection and certification. Maintenance costs were met by the state and also by a parental contribution of up to 5s. a week. In 1857 local authorities were also given powers to finance the schools.

The legislation epitomised the attitudes to delinquency held up to the 1880s and embodied fundamental changes in the state's attitude to children. A more liberal interpretation of *doli capax* was sanctioned, acknowledging the essential differences between children and adults. For Adderley, the crux of his Act was the recognition that 'children in the eyes of the law are not fully to blame,' since they committed offences 'for want of knowing better.' Children for the first time were accepted as wards of state and new rights of enforcing parental responsibility were asserted. The legal age of delinquency was set at sixteen, following the French precedent, and corrective detention in the Reformatory ensured a 'child's punishment for a child's crime.'[37]

The discrimination between children and adults was not complete, however. Old traditions and fears were still strong. The Act was only permissive and many magistrates continued to ignore it. Imprisonment of children, though at a dwindling rate, continued to the 1890s. Large sections of the public continued to regard delinquents as nuisances requiring a sharp lesson. Reformatory treatment itself was preceded by imprisonment, as a concession to those who maintained that without clear punishment the Reformatory would be an incentive to crime and parental neglect. Mary Carpenter and others continued to resent this, but the essential principle of a child's diminished responsibility was established.

This was particularly important in the context of a second dispute over state interference with parental rights. Reformatory Schools were intended to enforce parental responsibility, directly, by maintenance contributions and, indirectly, by warning that financial duties could not be avoided, as under the prisons, by child neglect. Parental maintenance was a new principle but its adoption was eased by the fact that convicted children were already in the state's custody. Industrial Schools raised the issue in a more acute form, embodying direct restrictions on parental control. Under the 1857 Act magistrates were empowered to sentence children aged between seven and fourteen to the Schools for any period up to their fifteenth birthday. The sentence was not preceded by imprisonment as the Act dealt only with children charged with vagrancy. Voluntary management was again combined with state aid.

The uncertain charge of vagrancy proved difficult to administer and was little used until an amendment in 1861 classified the children to be dealt with. This was broadened by a consolidating measure in 1866. A new category of children, those 'in need of care and protection' was thus introduced into English law. The 1866 Act defined those requiring state care as 'any child under the age of fourteen found begging or receiving alms ... wandering, and not having a home or settled place or abode, or any visible means of subsistence, or [who] frequents the company of reputed thieves; any child apparently under the age of twelve years who, having committed an offence punishable by imprisonment or some less punishment, ought nevertheless, in the opinion of the justices, regard being had to his age, and to the circumstances of the case, to be sent to an Industrial school.' For the first time children 'beyond their parents' control' were also included.[38]

The experimental time limit placed on the Industrial Schools by the first two Acts reveals their revolutionary implications. Again parents were to contribute to the maintenance of their children and be deprived of their right to bring them up as they wished. As early as 1834 William Crawford's monumental study of American institutions had declared, 'to separate children from their parents by committing them to a place of confinement ... for an act of vagrancy, or the mere accusation of such an act ... is a stretch of authority not reconcilable with the spirit of the English law.' Monckton Milnes, the presenter of a bill in 1849, found 'a strong objection to the enforcement of the responsibility of parents and guardians by legal means ... lay members of the House were unwilling to take upon themselves the establishment of so new a principle.'[39]

Yet the Reformatory and Industrial Schools permitted a substantial encroachment on parental freedom, by attempting to impose middle-class standards of child-rearing on lower-class parents. In declaring that 'we have proceeded on the principle that we must revere the parental duties as long as they are not abandoned,' Matthew Davenport Hill voiced the reformers' awareness of the novelty of the legislation (S.C. on Criminal and Destitute Juveniles, p. 41). Industrial Schools were founded on the belief that in some cases the welfare of the child and public safety necessitated the separation of parent and child. No parent should be allowed to bring up his child 'in such a way as to almost secure his becoming a criminal.'[40] Where a parent abrogated his duties the state had the right to act *in loco parentis*. Parents who failed to provide not only physical but mental and moral care had signed away their rights to their children. By upholding this fundamental principle, Industrial Schools provided the precedent for later legislation to protect the child, and paved the way for compulsory education.

Many of the promoters of Reformatory and Industrial Schools saw punishment of parents and enforcement of parental duties as the chief benefits of the Acts. The decline in delinquency from the 1850s was frequently attributed to greater willingness among parents to keep their children off the streets. Legal sanctions for improved standards of parental training were one aspect of the legislation. Equally radical was the approach to the treatment of children in institutions. The schools aimed 'to train up the child in the way he should go,' by providing all the elements for civilised development missing from the child's own home. Institutionalisation was based on the rehabilitative philosophy enunciated by Mary Carpenter, Hill, Turner, T.B.Ll. Baker and other contributors to the *Reformatory and Refuge Union Journal* and the *Transactions of the National Association for the Promotion of Social Science* from the 1850s.

There was general agreement on the main ingredients of reformation. Schools were to act as 'moral hospitals' and provide the corrective training to which children, as wards of state and victims of neglect rather than fully responsible law-beakers, were entitled. Treatment policies were based on a fixed concept of the needs of delinquents, who, reared to 'wild licence' and 'self-action,' needed in Turner's phrase to be 'remoulded and recast.' The Commander of the Reformatory Ship *Akbar* saw his task clearly, 'the first great change which has to be affected ... when they are received on board in their vagrant state is to make them "boys." They are too old, too knowing, too sharp when they come on board, too much up in the ways of the world.'[41] The re-creation of more acceptable patterns of behaviour was to be achieved by methods whose success had been demonstrated by a number of voluntary schools both in England and abroad before 1854.[42] Sentences should be sufficiently long to permit reformation and children should be removed from their 'haunts and associates' and placed in more amenable surroundings. The best situation was the countryside, the 'rural antidote to town poisoning.' Exemplary substitutes for defective parents and neighbourhood influences should be provided by a devoted staff who organised the school on the family system. The guidance of the upper classes missing in the slum areas was supplied by voluntary managers. A stringent retraining programme based on religion and work would prepare children for their restoration to society. Treatment of this nature, however, was not to elevate the child, but prepare him by the acquisition of industrious habits for a life of unremitting honesty and strenuous labour in his own social station. The 'object is not to make learned thieves but plain, honest men' (*Report of the Proceedings of a Conference ...*, p. 14).

Practical administration of these ideals proved another matter, and early optimism was often lost. Staffing and financial problems, the need to preserve less eligibility and safeguard the public, tended to outweigh child welfare. Hopes of providing a complete substitute for imprisonment were delayed to the 1890s. Defective enforcement of the Acts, and the later charges that the discipline was over-severe, should not be allowed to disguise the revolutionary implications for the position of the child in society. The establishment of separate institutions gave the juvenile delinquent a new legal status. The operation of the English penal and educational systems and the perceptions of social investigators had resulted in new distinctions between the child and the adult. The acceptance of Mary Carpenter's belief that 'children should not be dealt with as men but as children' was a seminal point in the evolution of the modern child (S.C. on Criminal and Destitute Juveniles, p. 119).

NOTES AND REFERENCES

1 M.D. Hill, 'Practical Suggestions to the Founders of Reformatory Schools' in J.C. Symons, *On the Reformation of Young Offenders* (Landon: Routledge, 1855), p. 2.
2 Some major historians such as David Owen, *English Philanthropy, 1660–1960* (London: Oxford University Press, 1964) and L. Radzinowiez, *History of the English Criminal Law* (London: Stevens, 1948–56) have accorded it serious study. Aspects of crime have also been studied by J.J. Tobias, *Crime and Industrial Society in the Nineteenth Century* (London: Pelican, 1972) and *Urban Crime in Victorian England* (New York: Schocken, 1972); A.F. Young and E.T. Ashton, *British Social Work in the Nineteenth Century* (London: Routledge and Kegan Paul, 1956); M. Gruenhut, *Penal Reform, A Comparative Study* (Oxford: Clarendon Press, 1948); and L.W. Fox, *The English Prison and Borstal Systems* (London: Routledge and Kegan Paul, 1952).
3 W. Blackstone, *Commentaries on the Laws of England* (London: John Murray, 1857 edition), IV, 19.
4 'Answers of Certain Judges, Select Committee of the House of Lords on the Execution of the Criminal Law, especially respecting Juvenile Offenders and Transportation,' *Parliamentary Papers*, 1847, VII, Appendix.
5 Like adults children were tried for lesser crimes before magistrates and for more serious crimes before the judges.

6 B.E.F. Knell, 'Capital Punishment: Its Administration in Relation to Juvenile Offenders in the Nineteenth Century and Its Possible Administration in the Eighteenth,' *British Journal of Criminology, Delinquency and Deviant Social Behaviour*, V (1965), 198–207.

7 'Select Committee within the City of London and Borough of Southwark and Newgate,' P.P., 1818, VIII, 5; T.F. Buxton, *An Inquiry Whether Crime and Misery are Produced or Prevented by Our Present System of Prison Discipline*, 3rd ed. (London: Arch, 1818), p. 133; 'Select Committee on Criminal Committals and Convictions,' P.P., 1828, VI, p. 77, 93.

8 J. Howard, *The State of the Prisons in England and Wales* (Warrington: n.p., 1777), p. 21.

9 For a history of prison discipline see L.W. Fox; M. Gruenhut; S. and B. Webb, *English Prisons under Local Government* (London: Longman Green, 1922); U.R.Q. Henriques, 'The Rise and Decline of the Separate System of Prison Discipline,' *Past & Present*, 54 (1972), 61–93.

10 'Select Committee on Prison Discipline', P.P., 1850, XVII, 29.

11 'Eighth and Eleventh Reports of the Inspectors of Prisons,' P.P., 1843, XXV; and P.P., 184, XXI; Third Report, P.P., 1837–8, XXX, 109.

12 'Select Committee on the Execution of the Criminal Law,' P.P., 1847, VII, 381.

13 M.D. Hill, for instance, introduced a system of probation in Birmingham.

14 J.E. Eardley-Wilmot, *A Second Letter to the Magistrates of Warwickshire on the Increase of Crime in General, but more particularly of Juvenile Delinquency* (London: Hodgson, 1820), p. 9.

15 See evidence in 'Report of the Commissioners for Inquiring into the County Rates and Other Matters,' P.P., 1836, XXVII and 'Third Report from the Commissioners on Criminal Law (Juvenile Offenders),' P.P., 1837, XXXI.

16 10 &11 Vic. c. 82; 13 & 14 Vic. c. 37; many of the legal protagonists were members of the Law Amendment Society and engaged in the reform and codification of the criminal law.

17 P. Colquhoun, *A Treatise on the Police of the Metropolis* (London: Fry, 1796).

18 *Report of the Committee for Investigating the Causes of the Alarming Increase of Juvenile Delinquency on the Metropolis* (London: Dove, 1816); J.E. Eardley-Wilmot, *A Letter to the Magistrates of England*, 2nd ed. (London: Hatchard, 1826); R. Jackson, *Considerations on the Increase of Crime* (London: Hatchard, 1828).

19 Age statistics in 1834, education in 1835. In 1841 age statistics were changed to accord with the census. Age, sex and education statistics were discontinued in 1849 since reliable information was provided through the Prison Returns, first published in 1820, and reorganised as appendices to the Prison Inspectors' Reports in 1836. In 1854 age statistics were again changed to allow for Reformatory Schools.

20 *Journal of the Statistical Society of London*, IX (1846), 177. Hereafter cited as *JSSL*.

21 S. Cohen, *Images of Deviance* (London: Penguin, 1971), pp. 9–24.

22 J.P. Kay, *The Moral and Physical Condition of the Working Classes Employed in the Cotton Manufacture of Manchester* (London: James Ridgway, 1832).

23 'Second Report of the Select Committee of the House of Lords on the Present State of the Several Gaols and Houses of Correction in England and Wales,' P.P., 1835, XI, 395.

24 W.B. Neale, *Juvenile Delinquency in Manchester, Its Causes and History, and Some Suggestions Concerning its Cure* (Manchester: Hamilton, 1840), pp. 8, 9, 13, 52 ff.

25 Mary Carpenter, 'Juvenile Delinquency in its Relation to the Education Movement,' in *Essays upon Educational Subjects*, edited by A. Hill (London: Longmans Green, 1857), p. 321. Gertrude Himmelfarb makes a similar point about Mayhew, in 'Mayhew's Poor: a Problem of Identity,' *Victorian Studies*, XIV (March 1971), pp. 307–20.

26 E. Rushton, *Juvenile Delinquency* (London: Simpkin Marshall, 1842), p. 13; W. Buchanan, *Remarks on the Causes and State of Juvenile Crime in the Metropolis* (London: Taylor, 1846); T. Beames, *The Rookeries of London: Past, Present and Prospective* (London: Bosworth, 1850), p. 119; J. Glyde, *The Moral, Social and Religious Condition of Ipswich* (Ipswich: Burton, 1857), pp. 50–1.

27 M. Hill and C.F. Cornwallis, *Two Prize Essays on Juvenile Delinquency* (London: Smith Elder, 1853), pp. 58, 59, 49.

28 *Report of the Proceedings of a Conference on the Subject of Preventive and Reformatory Schools, held at Birmingham* (London: Longmans Green, 1851), p. 53.

29 S. Robins, *A Letter to the Right Honourable Lord John Russell on the Necessity and Mode of State Assistance in the Education of the People* (London: Ridgway, 1851), p. 51.

30 M. Carpenter, *Reformatory Schools for the Children of the Perishing and Dangerous Classes, and for Juvenile Offenders* (London: Gilpin, 1851); M. Carpenter, *Juvenile Delinquents – Their Condition and Treatment* (London: Cash, 1853), pp. 292, 298.

31 'Report of William Crawford on the Penitentiaries of the United States,' P.P., 1834, XLV; 'Select Committee on Criminal and Destitute Juveniles,' P.P., 1852, VII, 466.

32 *Report of the Proceedings of a Conference ...*, p. 43.

33 [S. Turner], 'Juvenile Delinquency,' *Edinburgh Review*, XCIV (October 1851), 424.

34 'Select Committee on Criminal and Destitute Juveniles,' P.P., 1852, VII, 191, 7; P.P., 1852–3, XXIII, 255.

35 J.C. Symons, *On the Reformation of Young Offenders* (London: Routledge, 1855), pp. 82–118.

36 Her recommendations and the legislation also owed much to the experiments, both at home and abroad, in voluntary Reformatory Schools.

37 *Irish Quarterly Review*, IX (April 1859), 1.

38 29 & 30 Vic. c. 118; 25 & 26 Vic. c. 10. Under the 1857 Act Industrial Schools were placed under the Committee of Education and transferred to the Home Office in 1861.

39 'Report of William Crawford,' P.P., 1834, XLV, 44; *Report of the Proceedings of the Conference ...*, p. 38.

40 'Select Committee on Criminal and Destitute Juveniles,' P.P., VII, 119.

41 S. Turner, 'Reformatory Schools, A Letter to C.B. Adderley, MP.,' in J.C. Symons, *On the Reformation of Young Offenders*, p. 9; *Irish Quarterly Review*, VII (1857), xlix.

42 Red Hill and Stretton in England, Mettray in France, and the Rauhe Haus in Germany.

8

The invention of juvenile delinquency in early nineteenth-century England

Susan Magarey

By 1851 'juvenile delinquency' was established among journal-reading, servant-employing Britons as a major problem in the condition of England. It was, wrote J.S. More, a professor of civil law, 'next to slavery ... perhaps the greatest stain on our country'.[1] Matthew Davenport Hill, recorder of Birmingham, described it as 'the head-spring of that ever-flowing river of crime, which spreads its corrupt and corrupting waters through the land'.[2] Dickens pictured it as a 'bog', and prophesied that its 'seed of evil' would yield a 'a field of ruin ... that shall be gathered in, and garnered up, and sown again ... until regions are overspread with wickedness enough to raise the waters of another deluge'.[3]

[...]

Historians have paid little attention to these anxieties, or to the phenomena provoking them – children and adolescents in the streets and the prisons between about 1820 and about 1850. Those who have considered the subject, J.J. Tobias in *Crime and Industrial Society in the Nineteenth Century*, Margaret May in 'Innocence and Experience: the evolution of the concept of juvenile delinquency in the mid-nineteenth century'[4] [see Chapter 7 of this volume] Ivy Pinchbeck and Margaret Hewitt in *Children in English Society Volume Two*,[5] all have accepted the portraits of the 'problem of juvenile delinquency' drawn in the second quarter of the nineteenth century by property-owning, law-enforcing commentators. But such portraits are highly coloured, reflecting general fears of social disruption, pity for children who 'ought to have their Pinbefores instead of Iron Bars before them',[6] and an evangelical impulse to domestic missionary work, far more than close and dispassionate observation. This means that, as John R. Gillis has observed, casual delinquency and persistent criminality among children and adolescents in this period 'await further intensive study'.[7]

SOURCE: This chapter is taken from *Labour History* No. 34, 1978, pp. 11–25 (abridged).

This article is the beginning of a contribution to such a study. I want to explore the interplay between changes in some juvenile behaviour and changes in the criminal law and its enforcement, in Britain between the 1820s and the 1850s.

The article's title echoes that of Anthony Platt's book *The Child Savers: The Invention of Delinquency*,[8] a study of the child saving movement in the United States at the end of the nineteenth century. Platt is a sociologist, concerned with 'the ways in which certain types of youthful a behavior came to be registered as "delinquent"', and he contends that 'The child savers ... brought attention to – and, in doing so, invented – new categories of youthful behavior which had been hitherto unappreciated'.[9] [See Chapter 12 of this volume.]

[...]

[D]uring the second quarter of the nineteenth century three changes occurred which, in practice though not in law, altered the position of a child committing a criminal offence. The first was a broad change, affecting the whole society. The other two were narrower, following directly from what has generally been seen as the 'reform' of the criminal law and its enforcement.

Firstly, the presumption that a child under fourteen was *doli incapax* fell, as the recorder of Birmingham observed in 1852, 'into desuetude'.[10] This was, at least partly, the expression of a shift in opinion about children's capacity for understanding, which may have been linked to their increasing entry into the individually paid wage-labour force. It probably reflected, too, Beccaria's influence upon ideas about the criminal law.[11] The shift was evident from the bench to the police station. In 1830 Justice Littledale protested, 'I cannot hold that a child of ten years is incapable of committing a felony. Many have convicted [children] under that age.'[12] In 1852 a metropolitan police magistrate remarked that 'the characters of children brought up in town are so precociously developed that I should find it difficult to mention any age at which they should not be treated as criminals'.[13] The lapse in presumption to *incapacitas* also reflected, in part, the judiciary's helplessness before the destitution from which many offences clearly proceeded. The stipendiary magistrate of Liverpool complained of having had to try one of five children of a destitute Irish woman for 'begging about the streets'. The child said that she would not go home if she were released, so he committed her to prison.[14] Poor relief and punishment had been but faintly distinguished since 1834; it is hardly surprising that an inspector of prisons objected in 1847 that magistrates sent boys to prison 'for the Purpose not of punishing juvenile Offenders, but constituting these Establishments Receptacles of Poverty and Destitution'.[15] By 1855 such a policy was filling the Liverpool borough prison with children like Ann Philpin, a thirteen-year-old convicted of 'Frequenting', Michael Roan, aged twelve, and Ann Lewis, aged fourteen, convicted of not being able to give a good account of themselves, and ten-year-old Michael Brien, convicted of begging.[16] A fourteen-year-old in Millbank in 1835, one of ten children of an agricultural labourer receiving parish relief, had stolen 5s. because, he said, 'My Father had no Money'. He had not known that he was 'violating the Laws of God and Man', but he was still in prison.[17] It would appear, then, that trifling delinquencies committed by mere children probably had [...] come to be treated as grave offences.

The prison inspectors also claimed that recent statutes had criminalised a whole range of behaviour peculiar to the young. This was the second change which altered the position of a child in relation to the criminal law. The acts that they cited, the Vagrant Act and the Malicious Trepass Act, were both passed during Peel's administration of the home office in the 1820s, when he was working for sweeping reform of the whole criminal justice system – preventive police, systematisation and consolidation of the criminal law, reduction of the number of offences carrying the death penalty, and a more deterrent regime in prisons.[18] Both acts, as Radzinowicz has noted approvingly, 'adjusted the punishment to various modalities of the offence'.[19] They also reduced the severity of punishment for first offences. But at the same time, the Vagrancy Act of 1824 made it a criminal offence to be a 'suspected Person or reputed Thief'.[20] It also added to the description of people who could be classed as rogues and vagabonds, 'every Person playing or betting in any Street ... or other open and public Place ... at any Game or pretended Game of Chance', a provision which may have been directed at Mayhew's 'Bouncers and Besters' and Binney's 'Magsmen and Sharpers',[21] but one which could as well be applied to children playing marbles, pitch and toss, or gambling with halfpennies, farthings, or buttons, in the street.[22] Similarly, the Malicious Trespass Act of 1827, while revising the severity of an earlier statute which had made 'entering into any orchard, garden, etc., and carrying away any trees, plants, shrubs, fruit of vegetables ... a felony punishable by transportation',[23] nevertheless extended the range of behaviour proscribed as criminal by refining its definitions of kinds of offence. Under this act it became an offence to damage fruit or vegetables growing in a garden,[24] so that London urchins picking fruit hanging over the walls of orchards and market gardens on the outskirts of the metropolis were transformed from nuisances into criminal offenders.[25]

Such enlargement of the scope of the criminal code, made possible by the decrease in its bloodiness, was carried further when Peel finally achieved the Metropolitan Police Act of 1829. That listed among the 'offenders' a policeman might apprehend, without warrant,

> all loose, idle and disorderly Persons whom he shall find disturbing the Public Peace, or whom he shall have just Cause to suspect of any evil Designs, and all Persons whom he shall find between Sunset and the Hour of Eight in the Forenoon lying in any Highway, Yard, or other Place, or loitering therein, and not giving a satisfactory Account of themselves.[26]

These were categories which left much to the discretion of the policeman. And members of the 'new police' force which Peel established, on the foundations laid by the Fieldings, were probably not unwilling to exercise their discretion against children whom they considered a nuisance. The general instructions issued to the metropolitan police stressed that their 'principal objective' was *the prevention of crime*.[27] As policemen making arrests had to conduct their own cases in court, and were liable for costs and counter-prosecution if they did not secure a conviction,[28] they may have concentrated their efforts to prevent crime on juveniles, who were less likely than adults to present an able defence or to instigate counter charges. A shoemaker who lived with several boys who had been convicted often said that 'the boys know that the police had not always spoken the truth about them'.[29] Policemen were urged to be cautious: those in the metropolis were reminded more than once that 'the Police

Constable is not authorised to take anyone into custody without being able to prove some specific Act by which the law has been broken', and they were rebuked for officiousness in telling people to 'move along' or jostling them in the streets.[30] Yet the fact that such restraining directions had to be issued at all suggests that, as a police commissioner remarked in 1880, 'The Metropolitan Police in their early days were rather over-enthusiastic in enforcing the law and dealing with minor offences'.[31] And the necessity of making a specific charge on arrest was easily answered by the breadth and vagueness of the charges that they were entitled to bring. They acquired still greater powers under the Metropolitan Police Act of 1839. This extended the categories of people they might arrest to people in audiences – in unlicensed theatres, bear pits, at cock fights, dog fights, or badger-baiting; to people in gaming houses; and to people found in a thoroughfare or public place flying a kite, playing any game 'to the Annoyance of the Inhabitants or Passengers', or making a slide in the ice or snow.[32] Both of the Metropolitan Police Acts made a wholesale onslaught on the leisure occupations of the poor and labouring classes.[33] They also made London street-children particularly susceptible to arrest. Many were idle, like Mayhew's would-be nutseller, for want of employment or the means to acquire something to sell. Many were homeless; Mayhew said that most estimates of the numbers of 'outcast boys and girls who sleep in and about the purlieus of Covent Garden-market each night' were 'upwards of 200'. Many frequented penny gaffs which presumably were unlicensed since, by the time Mayhew was writing, a number of them had been suppressed.[34] And neither unemployed, homeless, or theatre-going children, nor 'new police' forces, were confined to the metropolis.[35] The numbers of juveniles convicted under the Police Acts rose from just over 2 per cent of all convictions in that category in 1840 to just over 12 per cent in 1843, and the number of juveniles convicted as 'known or reputed thieves' rose from just over 29 per cent of all convictions in that category in 1838 to almost 36 per cent on 1845.[36] It seems likely, then, that 'new' policemen were far from reluctant to prosecute juveniles. It seems likely, too, that [...] the increasing number of boys in prison could indeed be attributed to the criminalisation of behaviour characteristic of the poor and urban young.

The third change which, in practice, affected the position of a child who committed a criminal offence, was a further effect of Peel's efforts to make the administration of the criminal law more efficient. [...] Under the Malicious Trespass Act of 1827, for instance, first and second offenders were tried, not on indictment in open court by a jury, but summarily, by one or two justices of the peace. The Larceny Act passed in the same year also extended the judicial powers of the magistracy.[37] The Metropolitan Police Acts, likewise, provided for summary jurisdiction of any of the offences that they itemised, either by two justices sitting together or by a single police magistrate – an office created by the first act. Since the method of trial had formerly been one of the principal ways of distinguishing misdemeanours from felonies – misdemeanours were tried summarily, felonies on indictment – this change made that distinction, as Maitland was to observe in 1885, 'capricious and of no great substantive importance'.[38] The result was confusion about the cases in which young offenders were privileged, and those in which their privilege depended upon their *incapacitas doli*. In some cases judges simply dismissed young offenders, regardless of age or offence.[39] In others the children were savagely penalised. Lord Brougham told the House of Lords in 1847 of a magistrate so eager 'to show how active he was in the discharge of his duty' that he committed four boys aged about ten years for trial as felons for having 'in frolic taken a cap from the head of one of their comrades ... and thrown it into a field'.[40] In the same year the assistant judge of the central criminal court observed that 'Among those summarily convicted as 'reputed Thieves' there are no less than thirty-two Children of the Age of Seven Years', and a further eighty-seven aged eight. These convictions, he pointed out, had occurred during a period when only three eight-year-olds had been convicted of theft on indictment in open court.[41] Where, then, had all the others acquired their reputation as thieves? The magistrates, he implied, were either ignorant, or unjust, or both. It was a harsh judgement, but not entirely unwarranted. In July 1851 an Essex magistrate, the Reverend Henry Selby Hele, sitting in jurisdiction alone, convicted a boy called George Trigg of stealing about a pint of gooseberries worth one halfpenny, and sentenced him to seven days' imprisonment and two whippings. Trigg was spared the second whipping only because a prison inspector noticed the case. The home office reprimanded the clerical J.P. for a wholly illegal proceeding.[42] Yet again, it would seem, the increase in juvenile prisoners probably did represent an increase in the severity of punishment for offences which, as Crawford and Russell argued, 'were formerly disregarded, or not considered of so serious a character as to demand imprisonment'.[43]

Crawford and Russell based their remarks on a set of extremely deficient returns of juveniles under the age of sixteen in the metropolitan prisons. Their tables showed that of the total number of under sixteen-year-olds committed to the metropolitan prisons during the three years 1833–35, almost half in each year had been convicted summarily of misdemeanours, and offences defined by the Vagrancy Act, the Malicious Trespass Act and the first Metropolitan Police Act. As the other half included those committed to await trial, those subsequently acquitted or discharged, and those convicted and sentenced at the central criminal court of the Middlesex quarter sessions, the number convicted summarily of misdemeanours and newly defined offences probably formed a majority of the convictions of under sixteen-year-olds in each year.[44] Such evidence was suggestive, but hardly conclusive proof of their contention.

However, these prison inspectors were wiser than they could have known in 1836. The predominance of summary convictions for recently criminalised behaviour among all convictions of juveniles was not confined either to London and Middlesex, or to the mid-1830s. The prison returns for England and Wales show that from 1838 to 1856, summary convictions for vagrancy amounted to more than 20 per cent of all convictions of juveniles, and that summary convictions for malicious trespass, larceny and being a 'known or reputed thief', and other convictions under the Metropolitan Police Acts, all together accounted for roughly 30 per cent of all convictions of juveniles. The proportions in each category varied considerably. But combined, their proportion of the total number of convictions of juveniles remained fairly constant throughout the period. And that proportion amounted to roughly half, indeed at times more than half, of the total number convicted. So prison inspectors Crawford and Russell were right. At least half of the increasing number of juvenile prisoners, which so alarmed the property-owning classes, were in prison as a result of the creation of new criminal offences, an extension of the powers of justices of the peace, and a widespread readiness to treat children as young as nine or ten as fully responsible adults.

It is impossible to ascertain how many of these children were nevertheless [...] supporting themselves solely by thieving, and how many were, by contrast, casual pilferers like Binney's mudlark, children stealing from desperate necessity [...] or children convicted for behaviour which they did not know was an offence. But the very nature of the behaviour proscribed by Peel's 'reforming' statutes suggests that most were occasional, rather than regular, offenders. And as a far greater number of them were convicted under the Vagrancy Act than under the Larceny Act, it is likely that many had not stolen anything at all. There was little doubt in the prison inspectors' minds: they inveighed against the triviality of the offences for which children were sent to prison.[45] And one encounter with prison made these boys, with their gaol-cropped heads, into easy targets for further police enthusiasm. [...] The Liverpool magistrates noted in 1846 that of fourteen boys they had initially imprisoned, ten were eventually transported.[46] They might not have imprisoned even half that number if Peel had not extended the scope of criminal law twenty years earlier.[47]

Peel may not have intended to expand the scope and severity of application of the criminal law. His stated aim was merely 'to look at all the offences which are now punishable by death, [and] to select those ... which can be safely visited with a mitigated Punishment'.[48] He cannot be described as the deliberate inventor of juvenile delinquency. But his statutes did extend to certain previously only casually or domestically regulated behaviour of the young, all the means of state coercion provided by the criminal justice system. It might be an over-statement to maintain, as Platt does of the child-saving movement in the United States, that juvenile delinquency was 'invented', or, as might be a more appropriate way of characterising the changes that I have described, 'legislated into existence'. But such a representation of the origins of the problem of juvenile delinquency would not be entirely frivolous.

It would not be a new suggestion, either, except to those holding the view that the changes made by this son of a cotton mill owner to the Bloody Code of Old Corruption were unalloyed 'reforms'. This view is epitomised in the first sentence of the first volume of Radzinowicz's monumental *History of English Criminal Law and its Administration*, where he announced that

> Lord Macaulay's generalisation that the history of England is the history of progress is as true of the criminal law of this country as of the other social institutions of which it is a part.[49]

Such a view, which is still widely held, has militated against closer examination of the side effects of Peel's 'reforms'. But the moral teleology which it expresses is another Whig version of history. The questions which labour and social historians bring to their examination of the past are, by contrast, shaped by the conviction that such changes are more intelligible when they contrast not the 'unreformed' with the 'reformed', but rather one strategy of power, one morality of domination, with another.[50] The perception that 'law itself may not only punish crime, but improvise it'[51] is hardly recent.

NOTES AND REFERENCES

1 *Report of the Proceedings of a Conference on the subject of Prevention and Reformatory Schools, held in Birmingham on the 9th and 10th December, 1851*, London, 1851, p. 20.
2 *Op. cit.*, p. 12
3 Quoted in Mary Carpenter, *Reformatory Schools, for the children of the dangerous and perishing classes, and for juvenile offenders*, London, first pub. 1851, new imp. 1968, p. 59.

4 *Victorian Studies*, XVII, 1 (1973). This article is a useful survey of attitudes to juveniles in prison during the second third of the nineteenth century. But its argument confuses changes in legal status with change in form of punishment.
5 London and Toronto, 1973, ch. XVI.
6 *P.P.*, 1835 (441) XII, p. 248.
7 John R. Gillis, *Youth and History: Tradition and Change in European Age Relations 1770–present*, New York and London, 1974, p. 68. The number of girls committed to prison during this period was far smaller than the number of boys. Accordingly, most discussion of 'the problem of juvenile delinquency' was discussion of the condition and behaviour of boys. This article has followed the emphasis of its sources. But there is clearly need for detailed examination of the condition and behaviour of girls who were imprisoned, and of the reasons for their numbers being so much smaller than those of boys.
8 Chicago and London, 1969.
9 Platt, *The Child Savers*, pp. 9, 3–4.
10 *P.P.*, 1852 (515) VII, p. 71.
11 See, e.g., Frederick Engels, *The Condition of the Working-Class in England*, first pub. in England 1892, St Albans, 1974, pp. 172–3; J.A. Banks, 'Population Change and the Victorian City', *Victorian Studies*, XI, 3 (1968), p. 285; Radzinowicz, *Ideology and Crime*, pp. 12–13; Ian Taylor, *et al.*, *The new criminology*, London, 1973, p. 2.
12 *R. v. Owen*, 1830, E.R. 172, pp. 685–6.
13 *P.P.*, 1852 (515) VII, p. 91.
14 Mary Carpenter, *Juvenile Delinquents, their condition and treatment*, London, 1853, p. 147.
15 *P.P.*, 1847 (534) VII, p. 297.
16 Register of Juvenile Offenders committed to Reformatories by the Borough of Liverpool under the Act 17 & 18 Vict. c. 86, 1854–60.
17 *P.P.*, 1835 (438) XI, p. 337.
18 Norman Gash, *Peel*, London and New York, 1976, pp. 65–70.
19 Leon Radzinowicz, *A History of English Criminal Law and its Administration from 1750*, 4 vols, London, 1948–68, vol. 1, p. 585.
20 5 Geo. IV c. 83, cl. IV.
21 Mayhew, *London Labour and the London Poor*, vol. IV, pp. 24, 32; Binney, 'Thieves and Swindlers', pp. 385–8.
22 Mayhew, *London Labour and the London Poor*, vol. I, p. 469.
23 Radzinowicz, *A History of English Criminal Law*, vol. I, p. 585.
24 7 & 8 Geo. IV c. 30, cl. IV.
25 *P.P.*, 1852 (515) VII, p. 86.
26 10 Geo. IV c. 44, cl. VII.
27 Quoted in Radzinowicz, *A History of English Criminal Law*, vol. IV, p. 163.
28 *P.P.*, 1837 (79) XXXI, p. 23: K.K. Macnab, 'Aspects of this history of crime in England and Wales between 1805–1860', Ph.D. thesis, University of Sussex, 1965, p. 202.
29 *P.P.*, 1852 (515) VII, p. 210.
30 Quoted in Radzinowicz, *A History of English Criminal Law*, vol. IV, pp. 165–6; cf. Dickens: "'This boy,' says the constable, "although he's repeatedly told to, won't move on –"

"'I'm always a-moving on, sir,' cries the boy, wiping away his grimy tears with his arm. "I've always been a-moving and a-moving on, ever since I was born. Where can I possibly move to, sir, more nor I do move!"' Charles Dickens, *Bleak House*, first pub. 1852–3, London, 1907, last repr. 1962, p. 244.
31 Quoted in Tobias, *op. cit.*, p. 66.

32 2 & 3 Vict. c. 47. cl. XLVI, XLVII, XLIX, LIV.
33 Robert W. Malcolmson, *Popular Recreations in English Society 1700–1850*, Cambridge, 1973, chapters 6 and 7, esp. pp. 140–5.
34 Mayhew, *London Labour and the London Poor*, vol. I, pp. 469, 475, 476.
35 See, e.g., [H. Shimmin], *Liverpool Life: Its Pleasures, Practices and Pastimes*, second series, reprinted from the *Liverpool Mercury*, Liverpool, 1857. Liverpool and Bristol established police forces under the Municipal Corporations Act of 1835, 5 & 6 Will. IV, c. 76, see John Latimer, *The Annals of Bristol in the nineteenth century*, Bristol, 1887, p. 187; J.P. Martin and Gail Wilson, *The Police: A Study in Manpower*, London, 1969, p. 7. In 1839 the provisions of the first Metropolitan Police Act were applied to Manchester, Bolton and Birmingham, see 2 & 3 Vict. c. 87; 2 &3 Vict. c. 88; 2 & 3 Vict. c. 89.
36 Eade, *op. cit.*, p. 431.
37 7 & 8 Geo. IV, c. 29.
38 F.W. Maitland, *Justice and Police*, London, 1885, p. 16.
39 *P.P.*, 1847 (447) VII, p. 567.
40 *Hansard* III, 1847, vol. 90, c. 1136.
41 *P.P.*, 1847 (534) VII, p. 45.
42 W.J. Williams to H. Waddington, 16 July 1851; H. Selby Hele to Home Office, 17 July 1851, and notes on this, all in H.O. 12/3722.
43 *P.P.*, 1836 (117) XXXV, pp. 83–4.
44 *Op. cit.*, pp. 85–7.
45 *P.P.*, 1836 (117) XXXV, p. 84. They did not, however, propose decriminalisation of such behaviour, but rather a difference in the treatment of convicted juveniles.
46 [Liverpool magistrates], *Criminal Population: Petition of the Justices of the Borough of Liverpool, praying for inquiry*, Liverpool, 1846, in H.O. 45/1471; see also *Hansard* III, 1847, vol. 90, cc. 183–203.
47 The changes in England's criminal justice system described in this article raise questions about the 'hardened criminal' character of convicts transported to Australia.
48 Gash, *Peel*, p. 68.
49 Radzinowicz, *A History of English Criminal Law*, vol. I, p. ix.
50 E.g. Michael Ignatieff, 'A Just Measure of Pain: Penitentiaries in the Industrial Revolution in England, 1750–1810', Ph.D. thesis. Harvard University, 1976, pp. 39–43.
51 Karl Marx, 'Population, crime and pauperism', *New York Daily Tribune*, 16 September 1859. quoted in Taylor, *et al., op. cit.*, p. 217.

9

The three Rs – repression, rescue and rehabilitation: ideologies of control for working class youth

John Clarke

This paper is an initial and exploratory attempt at making some connections between themes discernible in the development of the English legal apparatus for the control of deviant working class youth. The concerns of the paper are shaped by an interest in the development of juvenile justice in the nineteenth century, and by an interest in the relation between dominant ideologies and the apparatus of social control developed by the dominant class.

[…]

[I]t asks the question of why youth and the question of youthful (mis)behaviour should be accorded a privileged position in discussions about the direction and nature of the Social Order. The substantive analysis is centred around major themes of what I have loosely termed the juvenile reform movement of the nineteenth century, and the subsequent trajectory of those themes in the later development of English juvenile justice.

[…]

THE JUVENILE OBSESSION: YOUTH AND THE SOCIAL ORDER

Youth has been identified as being of central social and political significance in the past three centuries, from the apprentices who provided an ever-present and excitable element of the London Mob, through Chadwick's concern in his report on the Sanitary Conditions of the Labouring Population to guard against the 'substitution for a population that accumulates and preserves instruction and is steadily progressive, a population that is young, inexperienced, ignorant, credulous, irritable,

SOURCE: This chapter is taken from Centre for Contemporary Cultural Studies, stencilled paper, University of Birmingham, 1975, pp. 1–22 (abridged).

passionate and dangerous' (quoted, Pearson, 1975: 170) right through to the post-war 'moral panics' about hooligans, bizarre youth cults, and gangs who make the streets unsafe for law abiding people.

In these various forms Youth as a social category seems to have the power to carry a deeper message about the state of society, the social and political changes taking place and so on, without recourse to the language of politics itself.

[...]

[T]he discussion of youth is made to carry more than its surface message, and operates, at a deeper level, as the vehicle for the discussion of society and social change. It will be part of the argument in this chapter that the concern with youth (and working class youth, in particular) is made to perform this double function, dealing directly with youth, but always with an eye on youth as an indicator or carrier of broader social messages.

This 'youthful obsession' is like all other ideological discourse, in that it is not without its 'rational core' – the real social base upon which it rests even in the same moment that it distorts it. The real key to the importance of youth lies in the question of the reproduction of the social conditions of production. Central among these conditions is that of ensuring the stable reproduction of the labour force over time – the guaranteed recruitment of the young to their role as the next generation of the proletariat (cf. Althusser, 1971). As the growth of a state educational system, to identify but one of a range of institutions, indicates, the task of ensuring this continuity is too complex and vital a task to be left to the traditional institutions of socialisation, especially that extremely unreliable institution, the working class family.

[...]

Innocence redeemed – the moral and political economy of juvenile rescue

The history of industrialism has always been a continuing struggle (which today takes an even more and vigorous form) against the elements of 'animality' in man. It has been an uninterrupted, often painful and bloody process of subjugating natural (i.e., animal and primitive) instincts to new more complex and rigid norms and habits of order, exactitude and precision which can make possible the increasingly complex forms of collective life which are the necessary consequences of industrial development.

Gramsci, 1973: 298

The sentiment of human benevolence, and its practical expression, derived directly from religious influence. It came from the quickened knowledge, born of the new religious revivalism, that all men were children of God, and loved by Him ... There is no doubt that the greatest single urge to help the less fortunate ... sprang from deep religious experience.

Young and Ashton, 1956: 41–2

The juvenile reformers appear in many of the works on the emergence of welfare and social work in Britain as among the principal agents of the new 'humanism' – springing from a deep religious experience or not – which sought to ameliorate the human tragedies of the Industrial Revolution. It is, however, my intention to treat them here as a prime example of Gramsci's process of subjugation of the 'natural' to the demands of industrial capitalism. First, though, a brief expansion – I do not wholly accept the connotations of the Gramscian 'natural' in this process. I would want to treat this as referring to both the continuities of pre-Industrial Revolution habits which were retained by the emergent industrial proletariat, *and* to the adaptations which they developed in the face of a tenuous and unstable existence in early nineteenth century cities.

I am taking as my starting point that instability of youth, and thus the uncertainty of their recruitment to the labour force [...] as focusing the efforts of the juvenile reformers. The first assault of the reformers (in the early nineteenth century) was on the need for separation of adult and juvenile offenders in prison. The mixture of the two groups was seen as the major cause of promoting a seemingly inevitable recruitment of the young offender to the criminal rather than the labouring classes. The logic of the position was eventually recognised by the State in the establishment firstly of the juvenile hulks, and subsequently the use of Parkhurst as a juvenile prison.

Subsequent debate attempted to build on this recognition by calling for a more broadly based recognition of youth as a special case in the eyes of the law, a case deserving of special treatment and exemption from the classical legal concerns of individual responsibility and punishment. It is the themes raised in the discussion of the causes and prevention of juvenile crime which I shall focus on here. The causes of delinquency (and what I offer here is an abstraction from the myriad explanations of what I feel are central coherent complexes) may roughly be represented in the interplay of *the nature of childhood, the functions of the family, and the effects of the neighbourhood*.

The family is given a central role to play in the stability of the social order in ensuring the correct upbringing of children. Margaret May has rightly argued (1973) that much of the heat of the reformers' drive to 'rescue' the children of the streets can be traced to the dissonance between their own experiences of bourgeois childhood and their subsequent contact with the more relaxed discipline of the working class family which 'abandoned' the children to the rigours of the outside world, often from a very early age [see Chapter 7 of this volume]. The recurrent theme of the reformers is of delinquents and pre or near delinquents being the result of abandonment or neglect by the family, where it is not the result of a more direct education for crime by the family itself. Thus, the driving force identified behind Mary Carpenter's first three classes of delinquents is the family:

> The first class consists of daring, hardened young offenders, who are already outlaws from society.... We need hardly ask what has been their previous history; it is certain that they have led an *undisciplined childhood*, over which no moral or religious influence has been shed, and which has been *untrained to any* useful, industrious habits....
>
> The second class is, if possible, more dangerous to society than the first, because more systematic in their life of fraud ... these are youths who are *regularly trained by their parents* or others in courses of professional dishonesty....
>
> A third class, and perhaps a still more numerous one, consists of children who are not as hardened or daring as the first, or as trained to crime as the second, but who, from the

culpable neglect of their parents, and *an entire want of all religious or moral influence at home,* have gradually acquired, while quite young, habits of petty thieving, which are connived at, rather than punished, by their parents....' (1853: 23) (My emphasis).

Implicit in this image of the family is an understanding of childhood as a special status, characterised above all else by its *dependency* on the parents. In the iron grip of the family, the child – the unknowing repository of innocence – was carefully prepared for its delayed entry into the real world. The exposure by working class parents of their children to the street and all that it contained thus precipitated the child from its privileged position of innocence and dependency into an *unnatural* knowledge and premature worldliness.

[...]

This 'hideous antithesis', where it does not derive directly from parental corruption, is attributed to their exposing the child to the 'moral sewer' of the streets, and the life style which they contained – the halfworld of the Victorian Underworld which enveloped (to the horror and terror of the Bourgeoisie) both the leisure pursuits of the labouring classes and the networks of the criminal classes. The reformers' commentary on the children of the streets thus has a double thrust – both at the moral condition of the children and at the leisure habits of the labouring classes which provide the sources of that corruption and unnatural knowledge. It is important not to underestimate the thrust of this 'double-edge', for it embodies a deliberate vagueness in its target. The problem is not that of the *delinquent* child, but those conditions of working class life which stand behind both the 'delinquent' and the 'neglected' child, the conditions of both family life and the recreational pursuits of the working class. Thus Samuel Wilderspin – like some intrepid participant observer – donned 'a dirty face ... long beard ... and a jacket' in order to 'see them as they are'. He was not, however, delighted with the richness of the ethnographic detail with which he returned:

... you find their conversation generally consists in immoral language and language of an obscene nature ... and young creatures of both sexes may be seen in the public houses hearing all this, pledging each other in their glasses and the boys with a pipe in their mouths smoking.

(quoted in Johnson, 1975: 8.)

In a similar vein, Mayhew's catalogue of the ills of the 'nomads' of the city streets bears more than a passing resemblance to those more scientifically phrased commentaries on the working class's inability to adopt a calculus of deferred gratification:

The nomad ... is distinguished from the civilised man by repugnance to regular and continuous labour – by his want of providence in laying up a store for the future – by his inability to perceive consequences ever so slightly removed from immediate apprehension – by his passion for stupefying roots and herbs ... and for intoxicating liquors ... by an immoderate love of gaming ... by his love of libidinous dances ... by his delight in warfare and all perilous sports – by his desire for vengeance – by the looseness of his notions as to property – by the absence of chastity among his women, and his disregard for female honour.

(quoted in Pearson, 1975: 153.)

It was into this morass of crime, debauchery and idleness that children were thrust by parental neglect, and the danger of allowing the young to 'idle away' their time on the streets was noted in the Report of the Society for Investigating the Causes of the Alarming Increase of Juvenile Delinquency in the Metropolis:

> He falls in with those gambling in the streets and becomes contaminated. In this manner has many a deluded youth been ruined, who was first incited to gamble in the streets from want of an industrious occupation; he graduates from petty pilfering to experienced thieving. Here he mixes with the most abandoned criminals and acquires a taste for the commission of crime.
>
> (quoted in Pinchbeck and Hewitt, 1973: 436.)

Here, then, the young were exposed to and contaminated and infected by the 'moral diseases' of the city streets and turned to the paths of gambling, licentiousness, drink and crime. Without the preventive inoculation of the moral guardianship of the family, the neglected young appeared to be doomed. In the absence of that other great resolver of all social ills – education – the law offered for the reformers the only available machinery through which these children could be 'rescued' and restored to their proper child-like nature (and, coincidentally, to a life of industriousness, sobriety, thrift and morality).

The mechanisms through which the voluntary agencies and individuals managed this rescue were many and varied, but, again, there are common threads running through them in the redemption of the innocents debauched. From the informal system of probation used by Hill, to the visiting of the delinquent in prison practised by the Society for Investigating the Causes ... where

> the youths in confinement (were to be) separately examined and privately admonished, the evil consequences of their conduct to be represented to them and every persuasion used for their recovery which kindness could suggest.
>
> (quoted in Pinchbeck and Hewitt, 1973: 433.)

and from the voluntary industrial and reform schools to the redemption through the countryside practised by Canon and Mrs Barnett's more forceful methods in which 'sometimes the circumstances made it necessary to kidnap a girl' (quoted, Pearson, 1975: 191) similar focal points recur: the family, the true nature of childhood, moral and industrial tutelage. Mary Carpenter once again provides the definitive statement of the first two aspects in her recommendation of systems of reform which approximate as closely as possible to the family:

> The child ... must be placed where the prevailing principle will be, as far as practicable, carried out – where he will be gradually restored to the *true position of childhood*.
>
> He must be brought to a *sense of dependence* by re-awakening in him new and healthy desires which he cannot himself gratify, and by finding there is *a power far greater than his own* to which he is indebted for the gratification of those desires. He must perceive, by manifestations which he cannot mistake, that this power, whilst controlling him, is guided by interest and love; he must have his own affections called forth by the obvious personal interest felt in his own individual well-being by those around him; he must, in short, be placed in a family.
> (1853: 298.)

Carpenter's argument is instructive as much for its revealing insights into the bourgeois family as for its detailing of the proper method of rehabilitation. It innocently reveals the 'deep structure' of the bourgeois conception of the family, casting aside its concealing appearances. It is, *apparently*, an institution which articulates around the giving and taking of love and affection, focusing on personal development and individual well-being. Carpenter reveals, inadvertently through the agency of the context into which it is being inserted, an institution of coercion, creating and enforcing dependency in the child through the calculated manipulation of those rewards which constitute its 'surface appearance' – love, affection and interest. The bourgeois family, stripped naked, becomes remarkably similar to other bourgeois institutions, concerned with the distribution and use of power, with the construction of hierarchies, deference and positionally ascribed responsibilities, duties and character. It is here that the appropriate character traits, habits and knowledges are inculcated and ingrained (both for bourgeois and proletarian children, though differentially structured) through the position of controlled dependency. In a more homely vein, Mrs Barnett tells the same story in writing of two correctional homes where 'sixteen girls are received and loved and scolded into training' (quoted in Pearson, 1975: 191).

The other central theme of 'rescue' is the creation of a self which is 'useful' – prepared to play the part of a proper citizen in labour and life. Lord Russell, introducing the 1854 Reformatory Schools (Scotland) Act to Parliament, expressed the hope that these institutions might 'be able to affect to some measure that the young offenders sent to these institutions would forget their vicious habits and be restored as respectable and useful members of society' (quoted in Boss, 1967: 26). The reformatory schools held out the prospect of industrial training and moral education. The work was not always directly suited to occupational rehabilitation on release – sometimes the emphasis tended towards work that made profits for the institution, as Carlebach describes:

> There was, first of all, a gradual trend from work carried out for training purposes to work which would increase profit. A number of institutions eventually confined themselves to employments which were not only useless in the training sense, but were very harmful to the children in order to achieve maximum profit from their labour. Amongst such employments were brick-making, wood-chopping and paper-salvage for boys, and laundry work for girls. (1970: 68–9.)

The development of such a tendency is perhaps not all that surprising within a system whose avowed aim was to prepare the child for a return to a life of labour from which maximum profit would be extracted. Mary Carpenter's preferred form of labour was also not noticeable for its direct connection with the likely future employment prospects of its graduates. Firmly convinced of the merits of the *colonie agricole* at Mettray, she thought agricultural labour to be most conducive to rehabilitation:

> The salutary fatigue of the body removes from the mind evil thoughts and renders it necessary to devote to repose the hours which in the towns are given to vicious pleasures ... (1853: 306)

However, in this industrial training, the content or type of work to be learnt was almost certainly of less relevance to the reformers than that the child should learn the *form* of work – its routines, habits and patterns. The provision ensured that the child would be normalised to work in general, rather than acquire specific skills.

FROM REPRESSION TO REFORM: THE ATTACK ON RESPONSIBILITY

Before pursuing some of these themes in the subsequent development of juvenile justice, I want to briefly consider a more abstracted theme raised by the reform movement activities. The state support for reformatory schools was not won without opposition – an opposition which often centred around those already in possession of the delinquents – the Prison Inspectorate (James, 1972). One focus of the reformers' attacks on the existing state system of juvenile hulks and prisons was that their traditional emphasis on a punitive character for imprisonment was particularly unsuited to the special needs of the young, that, as Carpenter put it, 'children should not be dealt with as men but as children'. In a more rhetorical vein, Brenton condemned the hulk, *Euryalus*, as a 'Floating Bastille; – children in iron cages who should have been in a nursery garden' (quoted in Pinchbeck and Hewitt, 1973: 455).

Such an attack constituted the first major assault (in practice rather than in the philosophy of law) on the classical view of crime, law and punishment which (in typically uncodified manner) forms the bedrock of the English criminal law, most notably in the subordination of questions of motivation to the questions of guilty knowledge and responsibility. This orientation has its roots in the image of bourgeois man generated in the formulations of classical political economy and political philosophy, the atomised, egotistic, rationally self seeking embodiment of individualism, bounded only by the 'social contract'. Taylor, Walton and Young, in their summary of classical law, make this observation on the central relation between the individual and the law:

> the individual is responsible for his actions and is equal, no matter what his rank, in the eyes of the law. Mitigating circumstances or excuses are therefore inadmissible. (1973: 2.)

The assumptions of rationality and knowledge, taken together with the formal equality before the law, constitute the ground on which the obsessive focus with guilt, responsibility and punishment of the criminal law is possible without the consideration of the conditions and motives of the act. It is against this, embodied in its practical form in the criminal law and the prison system, that the juvenile reformers mounted their attack based on the implicitly positivist premise that the young were not fully 'bourgeois men', but were subject, by virtue of their innocence and dependency, to contagion by the worst excesses of the real world, from which contagion the delinquent 'exhibited in almost every respect, qualities the very reverse of what we should desire to see in childhood' (Carpenter, quoted in May, 1973: 22). Thus, contrary to the prevailing legal principle, the reformers argued that 'his age, the neglect or vice of his parents, and the depraving circumstances of his childhood should be taken into account' (quoted in May, 1973: 23).

The exemption created by the acceptance in law of this determinist image of the child created the first major hole in the classical structure through which the subsequent armies of psychiatrists and social workers have run and thoroughly confused the law's focus on criminal responsibility (for a legalist discussion, see Jacobs, 1971). Crucially, this 'confusion' has broadened the conception of punishment to include a range of 'liberal' and 'humanitarian' interventions in the criminal's welfare – a scope far beyond the classical penologists' conception of the Law's function. Beccaria's ruling might well have been addressed to the reformers:

> Reformation is not to be thrust even on the criminal; and while, for the very fact of its being enforced, it loses its usefulness and efficiency, such enforcement is also contrary to the rights of the criminal, who can never be compelled to anything save suffering the legal punishment.
>
> (quoted in Radzinowicz, 1966: 12.)

Sentiments which expressed rather less regard for the 'rights of the criminal', but which share its logic in practice, were part of the punishment philosophy which the Prison Inspectorate were to deploy against the reformers. They held that the prisoner …

> has committed an offence; he must, therefore, be punished; he is depraved himself; he must, therefore, not be suffered to deprave others …

and he should be discouraged from further offences 'by a recollection of the privations, hardships and discomforts of a prison' (quoted in James, 1972: 18). From this classical position emerges one of the earliest articulations of what remains a familiar complaint against the modifications in the prison system which aim at rehabilitation:

> It is not merely sufficient to transfer the juvenile depradators to a charitable asylum … the imperfect and relaxed discipline of which is not calculated to produce any deep impression, or any permanent change in his habits and character.
>
> … if the juvenile depradators of the metropolis discovered that their offences would be merely visited by a short detention in a comfortable asylum, where they would be regarded as objects of compassion, and subjected to little privation and restraint, such a course would only tend to confirm the offender in his depradatory habits and invite others to follow his example. (Report of Prison Inspectors, 1838, quoted in James, 1972: 27–8.)

Similarly, as late as 1851, the Surveyor-General of Prisons could still thunder the warning that institutions modelled on Redhill and Mettray 'do not possess the PENAL features which are calculated to repress crime by the fear of its consequences' (James, 1972: 30). From the softness of the 'charitable asylums' to the contemporary mythology of colour TVs and bingo in the 'hotels for prisoners' is but a short step, and the classical equation of crime and punishment remains a key element in contemporary understandings of law and order.

It is in such debates as this and their outcomes within the system of justice and control that the 'practical logics' of the conflicts which Radzinowicz and other have treated at the level of legal and criminological theorising find their real consequences. In these logics in practice, the abstract philosophies do not remain visible in their 'pure forms' – they become adapted to the conventions of the already existing logics in use, shape themselves around those of the opposing tendencies, organise themselves to 'win' the support of public and political opinion and so on. Even in the case of the reformers themselves, one finds a strange mixture containing traces of both the classical view of the criminal and the emergent positivist conception of the delinquent. Their roots in investigative work – their concern with causation and classification – their deterministic conception of childhood all stress an affinity with a later positivist criminology, while their commitment to rescue and redemption contain a close approximation to the classical view of man – the installation of an ability to distinguish right and wrong, the acknowledgement of his responsibilities to society and so on.

JUVENILE WELFARE – *IN LOCO* (WORKING CLASS) *PARENTIS*

It remains to trace through two themes which emerged in the Reform Movement's re-creation of juvenile justice – the focus on the family, and the blurring of distinctions between the delinquent and neglected child – through their developments in the subsequent career of the juvenile court.

These two themes seem to determine both the shape and trajectory of the juvenile court up to the present and carry in the development of their logic the conditions and direction of a more extremely *interventionist* variant of social control than emerges anywhere else in the legal apparatus. They are also the bases for the more obvious controversy which focuses on the contradiction between criminal procedure and the welfare of the delinquent in juvenile court procedure.

In the establishment of the juvenile court as a distinct legal institution in the 1908 Act, the court was empowered to act upon two types of children – the delinquent, who appears before the court on a criminal charge, and the 'neglected' child, whom they were empowered to send to an industrial school. Neglected children were those who were found begging, having parents who failed to exercise proper guardianship, were destitute, or whose parents had criminal or drunken habits or were in prison; or who were associating with reputed thieves or common prostitutes. The significance of this lies not only in the breadth of the conditions which were taken to constitute neglect, but that from the first the court was empowered to intervene to rescue the child from the vagaries of working class socialisation.

The thorough conflation of the categories of delinquent and neglected had only to await the deliberations of the 1927 Home Office Departmental Committee on the Treatment of Young Offenders, who argued, in terms with which Mary Carpenter would have fully sympathised, that:

> ... there is little or no difference in character and needs between the neglected and the delin-
> quent child. It is often a mere accident whether he is brought before the court because he
> was wandering or beyond control or because he has committed some offence. *Neglect leads
> to delinquency.*
>
> (Cmnd. 2831: 6.) (my emphasis.)

Thus, albeit belatedly, the reformers' vision of the dependent and vulnerable child was enshrined at the very heart of the juvenile system, with the classical 'responsible individual' of bourgeois law being replaced by the 'responsible family' of juvenile law. The 'responsible family' was embodied in the juvenile court in the formulation, in the 1933 Children and Young Persons Act, of the child 'in need of care and protection' – if he was shown to be falling into 'bad associations' or being exposed to 'moral danger', through the absence or neglect of his parents. And in all cases before them, the court itself was enjoined to play the part of the responsible parent, by having regard to 'the welfare of the child' as the primary principle in the disposition of the child.

The 1908 and 1933 Acts command and shape the field of juvenile justice right through until the post-war upsurge of delinquency which threatened to mar the pleasant vistas of the 'Affluent Society'. The Conservative established Ingleby Committee was the first of a variety of contributions to the discussion of delinquency and the Juvenile Court which were to occur during the sixties. Their attention was focused squarely on the family in relation to delinquency, but we have to tread on more delicate ground with the use of the family in this and the subsequent debates, for it appears with differing political 'glosses'. The Ingleby Committee's view of the family bears the marks of its Conservative ancestry, its primary stress is on parental responsibility for the upbringing and proper discipline of the child, though with a by no means purely 'free enterprise' admission of the role which may be played by social services in helping the family carry out its responsibility:

> The child cannot be regarded as an isolated unit. The problem is always one of the child in his environment and *his immediate environment is the family to which he belongs*. It is the situation and the relationships with the family which seem to be responsible for many children being in trouble, whether the trouble is called delinquency or anything else. *It is often parents who need to alter their ways*, and it is therefore with family troubles that any preventive measures will be concerned. (quoted in Ford, 1975: 23) (my emphasis.)

The Ingleby Committee's concern with the family and the image of it which they articulate (parents who must 'mend their ways') are part of the Committee's overall focus on a conservative vision of the juvenile court, which centres on the allocation of 'responsibility'. Bottoms describes their reasoning as follows:

> By and large, children come to court because those responsible for their upbringing ... have 'been unable in different degrees and for various reasons to bring the child up in the way he should go. They have been unable ... to teach him to behave in an acceptable manner'. For the younger child, the responsibility lies 'squarely' with the upbringers; but later on 'the child must learn to stand on his own feet and accept greater responsibility for his actions'. (1974: 323–4.)

The ghost of bourgeois legal man still haunts these considerations, with their simple and specific concern with *moral education and responsibility*. The modest recommendations of the Committee were embodied, in diluted form, in the 1963 Children and Young Persons Act, which also expanded the category of 'in need of care and protection' to a somewhat 'tougher' version – that of being 'in need of care, protection or *control*' – presumably to include that new breed of delinquent who resisted even the efforts of morally upright and well intentioned parents to exercise parental authority.

THE FABIAN FAMILY AND SOCIAL RECONSTRUCTION

The family was to remain the key issue in the discussion of delinquency, dominated from now on by the Labour Party. The tone was set by a Fabian pamphlet criticising the Ingleby Report in 1962 which complained that 'those who hoped to find the outline of a *statutory service to help the family in need* looked in vain.' (Donnison *et al.*, 1962, my emphasis.) The social democratic image of the family is inextricably bound up with the whole Labour commitment to the construction of 'equality' and the meritocratic society.

Given the post-war social reconstruction and the seeming creation of an 'open society' via rehousing, educational change and so on (not to mention the all pervasive image of affluence), delinquency, from a social-democratic standpoint, was almost necessarily part of a category of residual social problems. These problems focused on the 'problem family' which, for whatever reason (and preferably, personal inadequacy, especially after the collapse of the economic base for Labour's 'social programme') had failed to adjust to take advantage of the new opportunities of a meritocratic Britain. This familial ideology was first propounded in relation to delinquency in the Longford study group's pamphlet 'Crime – a challenge to us all' of 1964, which stresses the problems of adjustment of working class children:

> Chronic or serious delinquency in a child is, in the main, we believe, evidence of the lack of care, the guidance and the opportunities to which every child is entitled. There are very few children who do not behave badly at times; but the children of parents with ample means rarely appear before juvenile courts. The machinery of law is reserved mainly for working class children who, more often than not, are also handicapped by being taught in too big classes in unsatisfactory school buildings with few amenities or opportunities for out-of-school activities.
>
> Anti-social behaviour in a child may arise from difficulties at home, from unhappiness at school, from physical and mental handicaps or maladjustment, or from a variety of causes for which the child has no responsibility. (quoted in Berlins and Wansell, 1974: 22.)

The sweep of causes is characteristically social-democratic both in its range and its limits – from environmental 'disadvantage' to personal and family 'maladjustment', though at this early stage, there is a stronger edge to the 'social disadvantage' theme than is subsequently visible. The question of 'responsibility' is firmly and abruptly swept off the agenda, in favour of more socially interventionist solutions to these 'disqualifying' factors, with the family-as-socialisation-for-healthy-participation at the centre:

> It is a truism that a happy and secure family life is the foundation of a healthy society and the best safeguard against delinquency and anti-social behaviour. (quoted in Berlins and Wansell, 1974: 23.)

Consequently, a central recommendation of the group was for:

> the establishment of a family service with the aim of helping every family to provide for its children the careful nurture and attention to individual and social needs that the fortunate majority already enjoy. (1964: 1.)

Thus, delinquency appears firmly on the agenda of the 'mopping up' work of the social services who are enjoined to intervene to promote the adjustment of 'problem families' to the healthy enjoyment of the good life that the 'fortunate majority' already participate in.

It was the Longford report, and its more formal development in the 1965 White Paper on *The Child, the Family and the Young Offender* which made possible the alliance between the emerging social work professions and the Labour position on delinquency. The vagueness of the identification of delinquency, and the role attributed to the family both allowed an entree for casework based conceptions of family socialisation processes. Bottoms offers the more cynical suggestion that the central role envisaged for the social worker in the Family Councils to be set up to replace the juvenile court had some appeal to an emerging profession attempting to set the seal of respectability on its status. [See Chapter 14 of this volume.]

The criticism of the White Paper meant that its proposals were dropped, but it reappeared in modified form in the 1968 White Paper *Children in Trouble*. Here the alliance with social work is accomplished, delinquency and the family are re-presented in a more psychoanalytically derived and social-work based frame of reference, though the intent – the possibility of intervention – remains the same:

> It is probably a minority of children who grow up without ever misbehaving. Frequently such misbehaviour is no more than an incident in the pattern of a child's normal development. But sometimes it is a response to unsatisfactory family or social circumstances, an indication of maladjustment or immaturity or a symptom of a deviant, damaged or abnormal personality. (quoted in Berlins and Wansell, 1974: 28.)

Delinquency now appears merely as the 'presenting symptom' of some deeper malaise and maladjustment – conceived in terms of deviations from the 'normal' pattern of child development. The terms may have changed to scientist ones, but the focus of attention remains the same as that of the nineteenth century reformers – how to ensure the *proper* socialisation of working class children, i.e., according to the pattern derived from the ideal (bourgeois) family structure. The 1969 Act establishes the conditions for intervention to ensure this standard is attained – what is now in the dock in the juvenile court is no longer the delinquent but the 'deviant, damaged or abnormal' *family*. The Act all but accomplishes the abolition of the troublesome distinction between the delinquent or neglected child, by demanding that an offence is not, of itself, sufficient basis for bringing a child (and his family) before the courts. In addition, the child must be shown to also fall within one or other of the categories which constitute 'neglect'. The Act also places the disposition of the child largely in the hands of the social work agencies.

I argued earlier that the juvenile reform movement embodied an implicit critique of the working class family arrangements and child rearing practices. Their solution was to find a 'substitute' family which would perform the necessary functions of training and discipline. That alternative has not been lost – community homes have replaced, in name, if nothing else, the old 'approved school' system as the alternative agencies of discipline and the development of the 'useful' citizen. But the 1969 Act culminates the deeper logic of the reformers by providing the mechanisms, not for the rehabilitation of the delinquent, but for the rehabilitation of the deviant family. Where the condemnation of the working class family was once indirect and polemical, the possibilities for the inspection, judgement and condemnation of working class families by the social work profession is now lodged at the centre of the juvenile justice system. The condemnation is now direct and practical.

CONCLUSION

The juvenile reform movement and its consequences for the development of the juvenile court articulates around very central core ideas of bourgeois ideology – especially those of the Family and Work. These terms are rarely given a detailed theoretical development, but are carried at a level of 'practical common-sense'. The very vagueness and appeal to 'verification' in everyday experience constitute the basis for their ability to create a deep and pervasive non-political consensus about English society. The vagueness and appeal to 'common-sense' allows the 'concepts' to address and cohere the disparate experiences of various class cultures. The themes take different forms in the different class experiences, but their thematization in the categories of the Family and questions of authority and discipline, and Work and notions of responsibility, respectability and self-hood can contain and hold these differences.

[...]

Such consideration must force an analysis of bourgeois 'social control' which goes beyond the relatively simple task of demystifying 'humanitarian' advances to reveal their contribution to 'controlling' the working class, to a more difficult level of attempting to untangle the ways in which bourgeois social control is both a means for repressing the working class *and* a 'civilising' force as well, which raises the development of the productive forces (in which I include the working class itself) to higher and more advanced (and at the same time, more contradictory) levels.

Within the more limited horizons of my argument here, I hope to have begun to open up the processes by which:

> each new class ... is compelled, merely in order to carry through its aim, to represent its interest as the common interest of all the members of society, that is, expressed in ideal form: it has to give its ideas the form of universality, and represent them as the only rational universally valid ones. (Marx and Engels, 1970: 65–6).

In juvenile justice, it is possible to follow the embodiment of the process of 'ideal' universalisation into the logics in practice of the apparatuses of the State with the power to 'realise' that universalisation. The juvenile court offers an illustration of the way in which the 'the conditions which make possible a certain way of life' are mediated through the 'ideal expressions' of bourgeois experience into direct and practical attempts to ensure their fulfilment.

The role of the juvenile court in such a process is, obviously, a relatively marginal one, especially given the development of other state institutions (centrally, a state education system) charged with the control of working class socialisation. But the court does have a privileged position by virtue of its legal power to intervene directly in the individual and the family, to be able to enforce, where necessary, the conditions of proper socialisation. That this logic should reach its consummation in the social democratic concern with the family's role in creating 'equality of opportunity' only indicates both the extent to which those 'universalised' ideas have taken hold, and the problems which are raised in understanding the bourgeois state and its relation to and adaptation of, 'pressure from below' for 'equality' and 'welfare'. [...]

REFERENCES

Althusser, L. (1971) 'Ideology and Ideological State Apparatuses' in *Lenin and Philosophy*. New Left Books.
Aubert, V. (ed.) (1969) *Sociology of Law*. Penguin.
Berlins, M. and Wansell, G. (1974) *Caught in the Act*. Penguin.
Boss, P. (1967) *Social Policy and the Young Delinquent*. RKP.
Bottoms, A.E. (1974) 'On the decriminalisation of the English Juvenile Courts' in Hood (ed.), 1974.
Carlebach, J. (1970) *Caring for Children in Trouble*.
Carpenter, M. (1853) *Juvenile Delinquents: their condition and treatment*. Cash.
Clarke, J. (1975) 'Style' in *Working Papers in Cultural Studies, 7/8*.
Clarke, J. *et al.* (1975) 'Classes, Cultures and Subcultures' in *WPCS, 7/8*.
Cohen, S. (1974) 'Criminology and the Sociology of Deviance in Britain' in Rock and McIntosh (eds) (1974).
Cooper, D. (ed.) (1968) *The Dialectics of Liberation*. Penguin.
Ford, D. (1975) *Children, Courts and Caring*. Constable.
Gouldner, A.W. (1971) *The Coming Crisis of Western Sociology*. Heinemann.
Gramsci, A. (1973) *The Prison Notebooks*. Lawrence and Wishart.
Hay, D. (1975) 'Property, Authority and the Criminal Law' in Hay, Linebaugh and Thompson (eds) (1975).
Hay, D., Linebaugh, P. and Thompson, E.P. (eds) (1975) *Albion's Fatal Tree*. Allen Lane.
Hood, R. (ed.) (1974) *Crime, Criminology and Public Policy*, Heinemann.
Jacobs, F.G. (1971) *Criminal Responsibility*. Weidenfeld and Nicolson.
James, D.W. (1972) 'The Origins of the Youthful Offenders Act of 1854.' M.Soc.Sci. diss., Dept. of Econ. and Soc. History, University of Birmingham.
Jefferson, T. *et al.* (1975) 'Mugging and Law 'n' Order'. CCCS Stencilled Paper.
Johnson, R. (1970) 'Educational Policy and Social Control in Early Victorian England'. *Past and Present*, 49.
Johnson, R. (1975) 'The Blue Books and Education: 1816–1896' CCCS Stencilled Paper.
Laing, R. (1968) 'The Obvious' in Cooper (ed.) (1968).
Marx, K. and Engels, F. (1970) *The German Ideology*. Lawrence and Wishart.
May, M. (1973) 'Innocence and Experience: the evolution of the concept of Juvenile Delinquency in the mid-nineteenth century'. *Victorian Studies*, XVII (1).
Pearson, G. (1975) *The Deviant Imagination*. Macmillan.
Pinchbeck, I. and Hewitt, M. (1973) *Children in English Society*, vol. II. RKP.
Radzinowicz, L. (1948) *History of the English Criminal Law*, vol. I. Stevens.
Radzinowicz, L. (1966) *Ideology and Crime*. Heinemann.
Renner, K. (1949) *The Institutions of Private Law and their Social Functions*. RKP. (Page refs. refer to the extract in Aubert (ed.) (1969).
Rock, P. and McIntosh, M. (eds) (1974) *Deviance and Social Control*. Tavistock.
Smith, A.C.H. *et al.* (1975) *Paper Voices*. Chatto and Windus.
Stedman-Jones, G. (1974) 'Working class culture and Working class politics in London, 1870–1900: Notes on the remaking of a working class'. *J. of Social History*.

Taylor, I., Walton, P. and Young, J. (1973) *The New Criminology*. RKP.

Taylor, I., Walton, P. and Young, J. (1975) 'Critical Criminology in Britain: review and Prospects' in *idem* (eds) (1975).

Taylor, I., Walton, P. and Young, J. (eds) (1975) *Critical Criminology*. RKP.

Thompson, E.P. (1967) 'Time, Work-discipline and Industrial Capitalism' *Past and Present*, 38.

Young, A.F. and Ashton, E.T. (1956) *British Social Work in the Nineteenth Century*. RKP.

Young, J. (1975) 'Working Class Criminology' in Taylor, Walton and Young (eds) (1975).

10

The government of a generation: the subject of juvenile delinquency

Peter Rush

[···]

The juvenile delinquent is the subject of an immense discourse. As such, I begin with two beautiful stories – narratives that define and delimit the field of questions possible for thinking the historicity of juvenile delinquency.

The discovery of the juvenile delinquent was one of the crowning achievements of the reforming sentiment in the early decades of the nineteenth century. Although the name had been coined in 1776, it was not until the nineteenth century that the actual size of the problem was revealed. It was the efforts of a disparate collection of well-intentioned philantropists that were decisive for the discovery of the problem. The philanthropists, and particularly Mary Carpenter, campaigned for the reform of the law, the reform of legal punitive practices, and the reform of the juvenile delinquent. For the first time, the reformers were able to formulate a knowledge of the juvenile and to use that knowledge to transform the ways in which society dealt with its juveniles. In short, the discovery of juvenile delinquency was integrated into the contemporary penal practices. Such an integration involved critique. The law had been punishing juveniles since time immemorial. In doing so, the law had overlooked the distinctiveness of these 'infant felons'. The juvenile delinquent was punished but she was punished as if she was an adult. Such an oversight had dramatic consequences. The infant felon was subjected to harsh, cruel and degrading punishments. Moreover, the severity of punishment meant that the legal institutions themselves were, in effect, criminogenic: they neither deterred nor prevented crime but rather encouraged and seduced their infant subjects into further illegalities. Faced with such problems, the reforming enterprise developed a series of explanations and campaigned for a number of solutions. The misrecognition of the infant felon would be matched by a story of her distinctiveness. The severity of the penal punishments would be met by a practice that would treat the newly-discovered juvenile with the care and kindness befitting her

SOURCE: This chapter is taken from *The Liverpool Law Review*, Vol. 14, No. 1, 1992, pp. 3–41 (abridged).

sovereign humanity. Such care was not only humanitarian, it was also more effective: it worked with and used the uniqueness of the juvenile so as to reform her. As such, a panoply of punishments were designed and built in order to differentiate the juvenile from other delinquents, and from the non-delinquent. Some fifty years after the discovery of the juvenile delinquent, the Reformatory School received its statutory recognition in the Reformatory Schools (Youthful Offenders) Act 1854 and the Reformatory Schools Act 1857. Reform had become law and legal punishment had become legal reformation. Of course, the victory was only partial. There was bound to be political and pragmatic setbacks: some politicians still needed to be convinced, the right staff for the institutions needed to be found and trained, old staff had to be persuaded of the efficacy of reform. Having discovered the juvenile delinquent, the knowledge of her ways and condition had to be improved. And then of course there was the problem of incorporating that knowledge into the methods used to deal with the delinquent juvenile. So the reforming enterprise continued apace into the twentieth century, trying to come up with a knowledgeable and practical solution to the problem of juvenile delinquency.

Such an apologia for reform is one story in the history of the methods of dealing with crime and criminals. It begins with the brute reality of that moral fixture, juvenile delinquency. From this empirical and problem based beginning, the story proposes explanations which in turn lead to solutions which in turn have varying degrees of success. Over the last decades, however, a considerable body of work has developed which criticises both the functions of the criminal justice system and its ideological representations. In elaborating this critique, a sociology of deviance has invariably had recourse to the problem of juvenile delinquency as it tells a tale of social control. This story assumes a different but no less real starting point – instead of the discovery of juvenile delinquency, the critical narrative begins with the administration of children.

Social control, the story runs, had existed before the nineteenth century. Nevertheless, with the emergence of the enterprise of reform, the process of control reorients itself so as to effectively deal with the new social problems being thrown up in the first half of the nineteenth century. The best representation of reform is not so much humanitarianism but social control, not care but moralisation. Ironically, care was at best a side-effect of control; at worst the essence of humanitarian reform was social control. This was evident not only in the horrific but subtle details of the reformatories but also in the texts of Mary Carpenter and other like-minded reformers. As such, juvenile delinquency is a social construction, an invention of the reformers. Urbanisation and industrialisation brought with them new needs and new problems for society, and particularly for the emergent middle classes. Among them was the problem of juvenile delinquency, and in particular the problem of working-class children. The juvenile was a problem for the middle classes because, if not actively working against them, the juvenile was at least resistant to or did not have the wherewithal to abide by bourgeois values. Juvenile delinquency was thus a label, a stereotype used to stigmatise and moralise that class of children who departed from the attitudinal and behavioural norms of the middle classes. In sum, juvenile delinquency is both a social construction and an invention of control: the latter because it is a representation, the former because it is an effect of social causes. The result is that many children are caught in the net of reform despite the fact that they have broken no law, committed no infraction of a legal rule. As such, intended or otherwise, the invention of juvenile delinquency ensues in the extension of the social control of children. The Reformatory School was the archetypal institution in the continuum of control that spread throughout society from the mid-nineteenth century onwards. Of course, that control is not total and all-successful; resistance existed. At worst, the ideology and the practice went hand in hand. At best, the reforming enterprise was only partially realised in practice.

Such is the critical story that elaborates an historical sociology of deviance and juvenile delinquency. It begins with the reality of social control. From this beginning, it goes on to discover beneath the representations of the reformers, a system that oppresses and confines deviant subjects. From such an empirical and problem-based beginning, it provides explanations of why particular targets, such as juvenile delinquency and working-class children, are selected: changes in social structure, departures from class-based norms, and so on. And only with such explanations in hand can we really understand the concept of juvenile delinquency.

[...]

A historical sociology of social control has become the doxa of (critical) accounts of juvenile delinquency. This story of control amounts to little more than a reinstatement of the narrative of reform – but in the mode of negation. Thus, radical criminologists have delighted in discovering control beneath the mask of benevolence. Moreover, this unmasking has been considered a critical task in and of itself. Criticism becomes little more than a denunciation – a denunciation of all that the debate condenses; a denunciation of the methods of dealing with juvenile delinquents and, more generally, crime and criminals; a denunciation of the nature of the social order itself; a denunciation of the criminological enterprise; and so on. In short, just as the history of juvenile delinquency is excessive, so too is the denunciation of social control.

Nevertheless, once liberal squeamishness is set aside, the task of a history of juvenile delinquency is necessarily more modest. If, in Jameson's words, 'history is what hurts',[1] then it becomes necessary to describe the *specific* ways in which it hurts. This does not require that the category of social control be jettisoned. Rather, it becomes necessary, at least in the first instance, to describe different styles of control in terms of their distinctive techniques, rationalities, and objectives. The concern of this essay then is to describe the particular ways in which the problem of juvenile delinquency is put together in the first half of the nineteenth century. How is juvenile delinquency constructed as a problem?

The essay consists of three movements. The first sets out the emergence of a discourse on the increase in crime, and in particular juvenile crime. The problem was not simply the existence of juvenile crime but, more importantly, the increase in juvenile crime. Having introduced 'the problem', the second movement is concerned to describe its contours. This entails a reconstruction of that discursive space within which the subject of juvenile delinquency becomes possible. That space is not confined to a specific discipline, although it perhaps has an elective affinity with what would by the end of the nineteenth century become the eclectic science of criminology. It may however be traced in the manuals, pamphlets, articles, journals and books of a panoply of social observers in the first half of the nineteenth century. The second movement of the essay thus describes the 'rules' of formation of a discourse of the increase in crime, and in particular juvenile crime. In doing so, the essay uses 'archaeology' to demarcate a space between the figure of the young offender (or 'infant felon') and the juvenile delinquent.[2] The third and final movement of the essay shifts the focus from the subject of juvenile delinquency to the distinctive practice of its subjection, in order to render intelligible the '*logic* of the specificity of power relations and the struggles around them'.[3] In the middle of the nineteenth century, the problem of juvenile delinquency becomes a problem of the individual and the class to which she belongs. The distinctive style of control that is imagined is one which, in the language of the childsavers, is described as 'moral discipline', 'moral management', and 'moral government'. On the field of juvenile justice, the particular apparatus is the Reformatory School, and the objective of the strategy within which the School had an effectivity is what Lord Ashley called 'the government of a generation'.

AN INCREASING PROBLEM

[···]

While Lord Ashley could claim that 'crime advances at a rapid pace', a Sussex magistrate could confidently assert in 1835 that 'the increase of juvenile offenders has been arithmetical within the last Twenty years.'[4] Statistical figures were often used when, from the second decade of the nineteenth century, all social observers begin to testify to an increase in crime, and particularly crime by children. As the Committee of the Society for the Improvement of Prison Discipline and for the Reformation of Juvenile Offenders reports: 'all the information, howsoever acquired, unites in demonstrating the lamentable fact, that juvenile delinquency has of late years increased to an unprecedented extent, and is still rapidly and progressively increasing.'[5] Although there are disputes over the accuracy of the statistics (disputes that have continued to the present day), what is being registered in the early nineteenth century by the use of statistics is a novel problem. The problem is an 'Alarming Increase' in juvenile crime.

Crime and Society are correlated with each other. In the context of youthful offending, an Inspector of Prisons could posit the more general rule that 'As society approaches perfection, there will be a diminution of crime.'[6] Within this teleology, the alarming quality of the problem is the converse rule: as crime increases, so society itself approaches collapse. Crime was understood as symptomatic of more generalised social practices. Moreover, the particular attention given to criminal juveniles in this symptomatic reading is linked to a historicisation of childhood: the child is our past, our present and our future. Mary Carpenter, doyen of the childsavers, writes of her juveniles as 'future actors in the world's theatre.'[7] Similarly the discourse of the childsavers argues that the increase in juvenile crime is a recent phenomenon – of seventy or eighty years' growth – which can be attributed to the galloping forces of urbanisation and industrialisation. And finally, the increase in juvenile crime was alarming because criminal juveniles were seen as implicated in the current economy and civil unrest. A Birmingham conference on reformatory schools notes the 'enormous expense' and 'serious loss' caused by the young property violators; while the mobs associated with the Gordon Riots and the Chartist turbulences are often characterised as populated to a large extent by juvenile 'depradators'. Horace Walpole finds it significant that 'of several persons, male and female, executed on account of the late [Gordon] riots, seventeen of them have been under 18 years of age, and three not quite 15.'[8]

The child as a mirror of social history and social order provides an intelligibility for the problem of the 'alarming' increase in juvenile crime. The problem is alarming because what is at stake is the very Condition of Society. The stakes are high: an increase in juvenile crime indicates impending social doom.

However, the problem of the increase in juvenile crime is not a discrete problem. Rather it is continuous with a more extensive concern with the child, with a fear of and for the child. From the late eighteenth century and throughout the nineteenth, a frenzy attaches to child-rearing practices; to itinerant pedlars selling blasphemous and obscene books to schoolchildren; to children discharged from gaol; to young people in gaols; to infamous Birmingham brothels in which juvenile, even infantile, prostitution is carried on. All of these problems take the child as their idea and target. In brief, the problem of the increase in juvenile crime emerges within a political economy of the child which constitutes its object as mirror of Society itself. It is as such that juvenile crime becomes a social imperative in the nineteenth century.

This much the conventional histories of juvenile delinquency exemplify, if sometimes unwittingly. But to identify where and when the problem of juvenile delinquency began is not a sufficient answer to the question 'what is the nature of this problem?'. While the question of the origins of juvenile delinquency has a place, it is also necessary to trace the specificity and complexity of the discursive fact of a social imperative to address the problem of juvenile crime. First, the problem addressed is not just the existence of juvenile crime; it is more importantly, an increase in juvenile crime. Second, this problem is formed and answered in the nineteenth century by a complex torsion between two related but different frameworks: one which produces the young offender, and another which produces the juvenile delinquent. It is to an excavation of these two related issues that we will first have to address ourselves.

THE MORAL DISCERNMENT OF THE YOUNG OFFENDER

The enterprise targeted two institutions: the discourse on the increase in juvenile crime fixed upon the administration of the prison and of the criminal trial. In the regularity with which these administrations are criticised, the young offender emerges as a discrete category.

The solemn majesty and justice of the trial, it was argued, had little if any effect. At the same time, the severity of the capital statutes contravened the 'humanity' of the magistrates, and as such was deleterious to any attempt to achieve an efficient system of punishment. What was important in both these situations was the *mentality* of the young offender. The critiques predicted the legal subject as possessing a capacity to discern between good and evil. The reformists argued that criminal legal practices were failing to regulate the exercise of the capacity to discern between good and evil.

The criminal legal narrative of capacity spells it out and is exemplary in this respect. According to the narrative, the child whose conduct broke a legal rule was not necessarily subject to legal punishment. The child was incapable of being a subject of law if it possessed a 'want or defect of *will*.'[9] As such, the exemption of the young offender was not a question of its chronological age: a defect in the will also exempted idiots, lunatics, and the intoxicated. Childhood – like these other exempted categories – enters the narrative of capacity as a matter of understanding. As Blackstone states, 'the capacity of doing ill, or contracting guilt, is not so much measured by years and days, as by the strength of the delinquent's understanding and judgement.'[10] The issue for Blackstone and for many others is whether or not the child could 'discern between good and evil.' Such discernment rendered the young offender no different to any other offender. In the phrase 'young offender', it was the dimensions of the term offender that were relevant and functional for the discourse. The young offender, like all other subjects of law, was 'a creature endowed with both reason and freewill' who was commanded by law 'to make use of those faculties in the general regulation of this behaviour.' Without the faculty of understanding, no will could guide the legal subject's conduct. As such, a knowledge of wrong-doing would inevitably and directly result in the commission of criminal acts; and conversely, if the child possesses a knowledge of what is right he will act accordingly and honestly.

If the criminal legal narrative of capacity is exemplary, it was no more so than the widespread reformist critiques which condemn popular amusements, unregulated fairs, the violation of the Sabbath, the lack of education, improper parental conduct, lack of employment. All were understood as confounding the discernment of the legal subject. All were singled out as causes of juvenile offending.

Again, the critique of the criminal legal administration in terms of solemnity, humanity and severity constructs the problem as a confounding of discernment and understanding. The severity of the criminal laws leads to their non-implementation because of the humanity (expressed in mercy) of the magistrates which, in turn, thwarts the efficiency of the criminal law. In effect the criminal law in no longer able to produce the necessary discernment in the (young) offender. Quite the opposite: 'the uncertainty of their operation encourages the offender to calculate, even if convicted, on a mitigated punishment.'[11] The specific problem here is that the severity and humanity of the criminal legal practice introduced an equivocation in the lesson of law. There is a confusion of legal representations, and the will of the offender exploits this ambiguity. The effect of the administration of the criminal law was to engender a forgetfulness on the part of its subjects. Such a loss of memory, such a confusion of representations, accounted for the existence of particular crimes.

But the problem that concerned the reformers was not just the existence of juvenile crime; it was the increase in juvenile crime. The increase is being prompted because not only is the administration of criminal law failing to prevent particular crimes, but its very practices are actively promoting the commission of criminal acts. The problem of the increase in juvenile crime was a problem of the criminogenic nature of the criminal legal practices, unreformed practices that confounded the discernment and knowledge of those children who broke the legal rules.

If this is the problem, the reformed practice would be its obverse. Against the equivocation and ambiguity of the criminal law, it would assert the certainty of punishment. Thus, the same sentence would be given for the same offence (a rule of uniformity of punishment); and sentences would be graduated according to the seriousness of the offence (a rule of hierarchised differentiation of punishment). The operation of these rules in the critique of capital punishment has been the subject of extensive exegesis. Its putative opposite – summary jurisdiction – has however been largely ignored. Nevertheless, the young offender has a role to play in the extension of this jurisdiction.

Summary jurisdiction emerged out of and was a reorganisation of the powers of the Justice of the Peace. It entailed trial by magistrate or magistrates without a jury. In the early nineteenth century, more and more offences – largely public order offences – became subject to trial without a jury. That extension of summary jurisdiction proceeded through the classification of offences and offenders. Thus, the Metropolitan Police Act 1829 provided that either a single police magistrate or two justices of the peace sitting together could deal summarily with particular types of offences. In a similar vein, under the Malicious Trespass Act 1827, it was enacted that first and second offenders could be dealt with summarily. In short, offences are increasingly being classified according to their 'seriousness' as the summary jurisdiction of magistrates is being extended. [See Chapter 8 of this volume.] One consideration in determining such seriousness was the number of prior offences. Magistrates would be allowed to deal summarily with the less serious offences, and a first offence would not be as grave as a second, third or fourth offence. The logic of prior records brings an increasing number of young offenders for summary trial.

In order to understand the particular use of age in such trials, however, it is necessary to note that the extension of summary jurisdiction is part of more general reorientation of judicial punishment. For much of the eighteenth century, the trial was the central apparatus of criminal justice. So much so that punishment was in effect part of the trial. In this situation, the execution of the offender was simply the end point of the majesty, mercy, and justice of the criminal trial.[12] By the beginning of the nineteenth century, trial and punishment are becoming disjoint. In the process, the trial is displaced from its focal position. Rather than the trial providing the site wherein moral knowledges could be regulated, the sentence and mode of punishment takes over. Now, in the early nineteenth century, the prison is to be the scene wherein the representation of law, the knowledge of morality, so essential to the discernment of the legal subject would be made certain. This is clearly the way that the Bill of 1821 for 'the Punishment, Correction and Reform of Young Persons Charged with Privately Stealing from Houses, or the Person in Certain Cases' is constructed. The Bill proposed that summary powers be given to two local justices of the peace so that, instead of the young offender being tainted by association during pre-trial imprisonment with hardened adult offenders, swift justice could be meted out and the young person committed to a the place of 'correction and reform'. In short then, the extension of summary jurisdiction brings with it a corresponding emphasis on the sentence and the mode of punishment. We can now see how the age of the offender takes on a significance. In the criminal legal narrative of capacity, the chronological age of the offender is irrelevant to guilt and responsibility. As long as punishment remained part and parcel of the trial, chronology could not become relevant. As the mode of punishment is gradually distinguished from the trial, the chronological age of the offender could become important at the stage of sentence and punishment. At first this appears as a residual element of the 'mercy' which had been condemned by the reforming enterprise. But it gradually comes to mitigate the seriousness of the offence.[13] The effect is that different sentences and different punishments for different ages are required. At this point, we are at the limit of the figure of the young offender.

Legal responsibility predicated that all offenders had the capacity for moral discernment; the offence of the offender was that in this particular situation their behaviour had not been guided by the dictates of their reason and their will. In this framework, law does not construct the young offender as ontologically distinct from the adult offender; the distinctiveness of the young offender could only be a matter of chronology, and could only enter where the attribution of responsibility was formally and administratively distinguishable from the application of punishment.

The struggles around capital punishment, the extension of summary jurisdiction, and pre-trial detention have been mentioned. In addition, the reformers took objection to the use of prison confinement under any circumstances – if that confinement involved association. In this struggle, as with the others, there is an interplay between the ontology of the offender and a chronology which separates the child from the adult.

Margaret May has convincingly argued that the separation of the juvenile as a distinct category of offender is a solution to the problem of a swelling prison population. It is certainly a solution but of itself the increasing prison population does not dictate a separate punitive regime for the young offender. [See Chapter 7 of this volume.]

The problem of the prison is a problem of the mind and its regulation. Edward Wakefield writes of the types of 'seducers' inhabiting Newgate Prison and who obtain 'a complete mastery over the mind' of the young inmate. Thirteen years earlier, H.G. Bennett had written of 'the vicious contagion that predominated' in the same prison. At the same time, John Harford finds an object lesson in the Bristol Gaol, the 'most affecting case' of a 'little boy only ten years old'. He concludes his lesson with an already answered question: 'Sad to say, there were four other young lads, mingled in the crowd – In what state of mind will these young offenders emerge from such society?'[14] Clearly, these statements are using miasmatic theories of the spread of disease. Association in the unreformed prisons provides the material pathways whereby contagion could be communicated. What is being communicated is a vicious knowledge: contagion is a matter of confusing the mental representations that guide the conduct of the legal subject.

Later, the discourse of contagion will become central to a new way of addressing the problem of the increase in juvenile crime. But here that discourse is still operating as if the problem of the offender is a confusion in her mental representations. And it is as such that the most horrific figure of the unreformed prison is the 'hardened adult offender'. Thomas Buxton has this to say about the Bristol Gaol yard: its inhabitants are a conglomerate of 'vice in all its stages; boys intermingle with men; accused with the convicted; the venial with the veteran and atrocious criminal'. The young offender is described as spending his nights 'taking lessons ... in blasphemy and dissoluteness, and ... imbibing the seeds of a disease which you shall carry home to your family.'[15] In short, the hardened adult offender usurps the place of law in directing the moral discernment of the young tentative and inexperienced offender. The atrocity of this figure is that he substitutes a pedagogy which corrupts the pedagogy of reason and law. As such, the young offender is not yet to be reformed; he is to remain innocent because he is prevented from learning the lessons of vice. Thus, the separation of young offender and adult offender will not be on the basis of an ontological difference in the capacity for moral discernment. That capacity she shares with the adult offender. What differentiates the young from the adult offender is the knowledge which guides the conduct of each. In 1823, classifications of crime and sentence are introduced. The chronological age of the offender is one factor in those classifications. 1823 is also the year in which separate convict hulks for young offenders are floated.

In sum, then, the young offender regularly appears in a series of disparate struggles. Within these struggles, there emerges a discourse on the increase in juvenile crime. This discourse is usually read as if it was youthfulness that defined and motivated the young offender. My argument has been however that the pertinence of youth is to mark out a difference *within* the ontological category of offender. As such, the young offender is first and foremost an offender and only secondarily a youth. In effect, the figure of the young offender is organic (and not genetic) to that other more familiar category, the juvenile delinquent. The problem of the young offender is a problem of regulating the exercise of the capacity for moral discernment. The problem of the unreformed practices is that they not only fail to regulate but actively promote the wayward exercise of that capacity. And finally, the problem of the *increase* in juvenile crime is that very promotion: whether it is by way of the equivocation introduced by a severity tempered by mercy in the criminal trial, or by way of the contagious association of hardened adult offenders, or by way of the unlicensed theatres… The purpose of the next section is to articulate the specificity of the juvenile delinquent – both in its distinctions from the young offender and in its specific positivity.

THE MORAL CLASS OF THE JUVENILE DELINQUENT

The phrase juvenile delinquency is first used in 1776. And by the middle of the nineteenth century it is in full bloom. The framework within which it flowers is one that constitutes 'the social' as its predominant concern.

The discursive problem remains the increase in juvenile crime. Within this problematisation, the child operates as an emblem of the condition of society. In framing the young offender, the predication of a moral discernment guiding the conduct of the offender had taken place within the arena of society, where society was understood as a homogeneous mass of individuals possessing a will. However, with the emergence of a concern with the social, this image of society is fractured. Now, it is a concern with society as a heterogeneous collection of typical groups. And where the young offender is capable of moral discernment, the juvenile delinquent is a person marked by the conditions of the group. Hence, those terms that have been seized upon by many historians of the nineteenth century: the dangerous, the perishing, and the honest classes who were said to exist within the more general class of the poor. It is in this concern with the classes that make up the domain of the social that the birth of the juvenile delinquent as subject is located.

The framework of the social can be read at the intersection of two ways of constructing the problem of an increase in juvenile crime: namely, a narrative of life and a narrative of place.

In 1852, Matthew Davenport Hill sees the town 'as containing within itself a great source of crime, both adult and juvenile.'[16] So too with the concern over the housing in which they lived. For Cornwallis, the filthy dwellings and squalid misery are an 'indication' of crime. In sum, there is a concern with the circumstances of the environment, with that which makes up a territory. Moreover, this concern with environmental circumstances is pursued within a model of cause and effect. The minutiae of the locality are elaborated as potential causes, the effect of which is criminal behaviour. And, of course, the more focused the investigation the more causes could be revealed. As such, an empiricist narrative of locality unearths a potentially infinite number of causes: the effect is an ever-expanding object of knowledge.

Similarly, with the narrative of life. Henry Worsley writes: 'If in the period of youth, and up to the very verge of maturity, they are degraded by vice and crime, it is but natural to suppose, that their confirmed manhood will be only the completion of their rudimental course'.[17] Here we have not the conditions of a life – a beginning, middle and end. The template is no longer, as it was for the young offender, discerning moral conduct but a pattern of upbringing, 'the habits of life'. Not simply or even, in Blackstone's phrase, the 'strength of understanding' but the delinquent's appearance, 'thoughts, habits and manners.'[18] And thus the 'moral state of the boy' is to be assessed and determined by recourse to 'a great number of collateral inquiries, the object of which is to know whether a boy is in a course of crime; whether he is one of those who has entered the lists of that large body who make crime their calling, profession, trade, or pursuit in life.'[19] The concern here is with a moral career, the style of life which defines the juvenile delinquent. As in the pursuit for geographical causes, the details of the juvenile's existence are scrutinised in order to uncover the temporal geneses of behaviours.

The elements that go to make up each of these narratives include: the uses of leisure, the type and condition of the dwellings and streets, the kind of employment, the amount of education, political and religious beliefs, reading habits (Bible or the story of Jack Sheppard) and styles of speech (the vernacular is invariably annotated). Each of these elements form a possible array of interminable variables in empirical investigations. It is this empiricist frame of reference which the philanthropic reformers share – whether they are secular of religious. It is also this frame that makes possible the widening of the childsavers' web.

But of all the variables with which the investigations come up, the family is the most prominent. No matter whether the issues be education, sanitation, prison or the criminal law, the enterprise of the childsavers formulates a number of diatribes that denounce the decadence of the 'residuum' and, in particular, the families of the residuum. The arrangement of houses is lambasted; while beer shops, gin shops, streetlife, are all constructed as refuges from the degrading conditions of the home. 'Home' becomes emblematic of both the local and life conditions that define the juvenile delinquent. The Reverend Sydney Turner asserts that 'the altered state of the family, the altered state of the home, does seem a very powerful incentive to criminality'. And Gilbert A'Beckett, a Metropolitan Police magistrate, links the procreative and environmental factors in the provocative home: 'I found the dwellings of the poor very much overcrowded, rendering it quite impossible that anything like morality or decency could be observed among the inmates, and leading, no doubt, to indiscriminate connection, bringing into existence a class of unfortunate children likely to prove very fertile sources of crime.'[20]

In all these statements that focus on the family, what emerges is the notion of a class. But the constituents of that class are not simply functions *of* the economic. Rather more diverse criteria are used, amongst which the economic is just one. Thus, it is the local and life conditions of a group which provide Mary Carpenter with what she calls the 'strong line of demarcation' between the classes.[21] It is these conditions which provide the childsavers with their narrative of morality. But whereas with the young offender the morality was a question of the exercise of the capacity to discern, with the juvenile delinquent it is an issue of moralities, of the mores and manners to which a class is disposed. In short, the category of class is both a personal and a social condition.

The notion of a class-bound delinquency entails a different ontology of childhood. For John Ellis, 'there is the Child, there is the youth' both of which form an internal structure to time 'before manhood'. The child is no longer the embodiment of an innocence to be preserved. Rather, the child is now the incorporation of an experience to be reformed. Now, as W.J. Williams argued, 'it must be considered also that these boys are singularly acute; they have a degree of precociousness about them which is quite surprising, therefore they are older when young than any other class.'[22] Whereas the young offender remains young even as she learns the lessons of the hardened adult offender, the juvenile delinquent goes beyond her chronological age. The ontology of childhood is neither chronological nor 'will'-based. The ontology of the juvenile delinquent is given by the experiences in his moral class. The class is defined as generating juvenile delinquency, as marking the individual by *promoting* a specific set of behaviours which are practised in a specific environment, in a specific context.

This is the force of William Neale's notion of a 'moral topography'. Writing about Manchester, he claims that children born and raised in districts which produced a moral physical 'contagion and pestilence' were 'predestined' to a life of crime.[23] The language of contagion was also used to describe the young offender, but there the miasmatic theory referred to the contagion of moral representations. Here, contagion is the spreading of mores and manners, of experiences. So, W.A. Miles describes a youthful population which is 'devoted to crime, trained to it from infancy, adhering to it from education and circumstances … a race sui generis, differing from the rest of society not only in thoughts, habits and manners but even in appearance.'[24] The experience of the child is thus the effect of her position within a class. Or, put the other way round, the conditions of the class generate and preserve the juvenile delinquent in her course of life. While giving a place to the free-will of the delinquent (Neale uses the language of devotion and adherence), the moral scene of the class is a positive force: it is one which promotes and trains. According to Mary Carpenter, the juvenile is an individual who uses her liberty but abuses it by grovelling in the structuring mire of her class.[25] The juvenile delinquent is thus formed in that space at the intersection of freedom and determination.

The young offender forgets and thus must be reminded of the dictates of his reason by certain example. Here, the juvenile delinquent remembers all-too-well, and thus a different memory must be created. While the young offender was an absence to be filled, the juvenile delinquent is a participant in circumstances to be replaced by a training in behaviours. It is this distinction which renders intelligible Davenport Hill's now classic description of the juvenile delinquent: 'a little stunted man already – he knows much, a great deal too much, of what is called life – he can take care of his own immediate interests. He is self-reliant – he has so long directed or misdirected his own actions and has so little trust in those about him, that he submits to no control, and asks for no protection. He has consequently much to unlearn – he has to be turned again into a child'.[26] The juvenile delinquent has to be turned – turned from the manners of the class that defines her and into the mores of another class.

A LOGIC OF CLASSIFICATION

The problem of liberal governance is how to control one and all, both the individual and society, without collapsing the one into the all and the all into the one. It is the notion of class which provides the solution: a hinge between the individual and society. In the present context, the juvenile delinquent is the subject of a social class. But the effect of a class analysis is not only to fix the individual, the little stunted man. It is also to arrange and divide the domain of the social.

The classification of the social domain falls into three generic categories in the discourse on juvenile delinquency – namely, the dangerous classes, the perishing clases and the honest classes (of the poor). Mary Carpenter's six classes of juvenile delinquent are produced according to whether or not they belong to either the dangerous or perishing classes which in turn are defined against the honest classes.[27] For example, the problem of dangerousness is a problem of crime which diffuses 'a subtle unseen, but sure poison in the moral atmosphere of the neighbourhood, dangerous as is deadly miasma to the physical health.'[28] Similarly, Edwin Chadwick formulates the 'important moral and political considerations' of the problem in the fact that '[T]hey substitute for a population that accumulates and preserves instruction and is steadily progressive, a population that is young, inexperienced, ignorant, credulous, irritable, passionate and dangerous ...'[29]

The young criminal class becomes synonymous with danger for the respectable classes, dragging them into youthful unrest, political sedition, crime. However, the dangerousness of this juvenile class consists not in the commission of illegal acts but in its character. A moral disposition constitutes the class as inherently dangerous. We have simply to read the flamboyant metaphors of Henry Worsley's prize-winning essay on juvenile delinquency: 'Even if he stops in his career before the commission of any such extreme act [as burglary or murder], he is scarcely less dangerous to the real prosperity of the community: corrupt himself and corrupting others; a centre to which those whose dispositions are similar, are naturally attracted, and round which they congregate; a bane to society, which like an ulcer on the body, is continually enlarging, and distributing far and wide its noxious influences.'[30]

What is implicit here is that the existence of crime substantiates the existence of a criminal class. As later criminologists have insistently argued, crime is taken-for-granted. However, the problem for the enterprise of the reformers is the *increase* in juvenile crime. It is this problem which is met by a 'social construction' type argument. For the reformism enterprise, it is the notion of a class which explains the increase. Firstly, as indicated above, the class is constituted as a positivity. The dangerous classes are described by Worsley as an active force, one that promotes its vices. Secondly, that positivity is a differential category. Thus, the problem of the increase in juvenile crime exists as a relation between the perishing and the dangerous. But these classes are not arranged as opposing forces. According to Worsley, the members of other classes are 'naturally attracted' to the dangerous class. In the language of Jelinger Symons, one type of perishing class is described as 'outcast children ... outside the gaol and the workhouse, though constantly hovering on the verge of both ... A large section [of these children] are on the threshold of destitution – some of whom it is fair to assume, are not yet actually criminal, and successfully resist the temptations of their position.'[31] In other words, the classification of the social domain is not a technique which divides the population into self-enclosed, discrete and coherent segments. The language is not that of barriers but of borders ('threshold' and 'verge') which are always liable to crossing. So paupers exist in a perishing relationship to criminal classes; criminals are dangerous to paupers and to honest labourers who themselves exist in a perishing relationship to the pauper. The categories of 'dangerousness' and 'perishing' are thus not attributes of a single class, but rather describe the positive relations of mutual influence between different classes. It was in this way that the classification of the social could account for the increase in crime and juvenile crime. The existence of crime self-evidently substantiated the existence of a criminal class, but it was the *positivity* of the relation between the classes which substantiated the possibility of the increase in juvenile crime. Thus, the apparatus of the reformatory school will have been designed to decrease the crime rate by governing the positive relations between the classes.

ETHICAL MACHINES

In 1851, some three years before the legislative enactment of a reformatory plan, Mary Carpenter is to write that '[W]e have also to view the child, not only in his individual position, but in his relation to the class among which he is placed, and above which we desire to raise him.'[32] As Mary Carpenter formulates it, the relationship is one internal to the class: a class that reproduces itself by promoting and training up its own offspring. But it also reproduces itself by recruiting from other classes. What is at stake then is the relationships *within and between* the social classes. In the context of the increase in juvenile crime, the Reformatory will exercise that 'species of silent but efficient control'[33] which treats with both these types of relationships.

The strategy of governing the relations within and between the classes may be defined by its objectives: one, to eliminate the dangerous classes; and two, to preserve and improve the perishing classes. Sydney Turner is concise: 'we cannot slay the monster while we are continually feeding and supporting him'. Lloyd Baker writes that 'Our object is not so much to benefit the individual as to benefit the children of the honest neighbour whom that criminal would corrupt.'[34] The two objectives of the strategy are thus complementary: to eliminate the dangerous is to prevent the decay of the perishing classes, and to improve the perishing would at least eliminate the increase in the dangerous classes.

The techniques elaborated within these objectives are numerous and varied. Some will have been: the extension of transport routes into and through those districts identified as squalid, the construction of parks and playgrounds, the building of model villages on the outskirts of town. All of these tactics are designed to alter the spatial context of a class's *habitus*. This tactic is complemented by a second type of technique. It is a type in which the juvenile delinquent is to be removed from the moral scene of its class and retrained, turned again into a child. The reformatory is of this type.

In characterising the moral scene of a class as a positive force, it was argued that the existence of a criminal class trained the juvenile delinquent to be 'independent'. Mary Carpenter and Henry Worsley write of the child as more an individual than a machine. There is then a strange symmetry between the unmachinelike nature of this delinquent and the analogues used for the function of the reforming practices: 'There might be a system of external machinery so perfect, that by its action upon the humble ranks, they would be controlled, kept in due discipline, and restrained in great measure from crime.'[35] In short, the plan would be what Mary Carpenter calls a 'machinery of goodwill'[36] which would work with and on the moral scenery of the juvenile class. The framework of this machine can be dismantled into two crucial components: one, the rule that defines the aim and character of personal reformation, and another, the architectural rule that places the administrative personnel as the lynchpin of the machine.

(i) Moral training: the pains of self-formation

Attending the construction of the young offender, the aim of the juridical practice was to regulate the confusion of mental representations. One tactic of this regulation was to separate the adult from the child. With the juvenile delinquent, another aim emerges. The reformatory machine is not simply to separate; its function is to retrain, to remodel, to refashion the juvenile. This is to be understood as an attempt to manage a lateral shift in the moral habits of the juvenile. As David Power suggested, '[T]he only punishment that I would have would be that which might be necessary in training a child out of the way in which he has been going into the way he should go.'[37] Whether it is a convict ship, a prison, or a reformatory, the effect promoted is the creation of a new and different set of dispositions.

The retraining is directed at a class of children. Davenport Hill is succinct: 'The main object – that which has excited so much benevolent activity – is to reclaim these wanderers, to reverse their outlawry, to bring them back into the brotherhood of society, to train them up so that they may be, in the expressive language of our old common law, true men, the friends and not the enemies of their honest and hard-working neighbours'. In addition, it is important that what is to be changed is not so much the moral discernment itself, but a moral knowledge buttressed by a set of ethical dispositions. Hill provides the rule in the context of a critique of prison discipline: 'When it [prison discipline] does affect him for the moment with a desire to change his course of life, he finds himself in no position, for want of training, to act upon his new-born resolutions ...'[38] Moral discernment is useless outwith a training that promotes a conformity to that discernment. More positively, a training in behaviours and aptitudes is necessary. In the Platonic language of Carpenter, the aim is to have 'a more true and powerful action on the soul of the child.'[39] A moral training of behaviours will create a memory for, leave marks on, the juvenile. The language of moral training is that of memories, habits, dispositions, behaviours.

According to a 'moralisation thesis' that has become orthodox in considerations of this period, the moral training advocated here by the reformist enterprise gives the lie to the benevolence of the philantropists. Such ironic criticism finds that under the guise of care, there is but control. Evidence for the irony is writ plain, it is argued, in the repeated references to both kindness and pain. True, the self-representations of the reformers are replete with such references. However, what is distinctive about moral training is that it was neither simply care nor simply control. For moral training to be effective, it was argued, the juvenile had to be willingly involved in her own reformation. Kindness would solicit that involvement in producing the proper dispositions and habits. Only then would the juvenile have a memory which would guarantee his conformity to the new dispositions when released from the reformatory. The ironic history of moralisation continually effaces this crucial feature of moral training.

Moral training is a promotion of self-government. In describing his managerial relation with the inhabitants of the Brook Street Ragged School, John Ellis's repetition is evocative: 'I used to tell them that they might, by governing their tongue, and governing their tempers, and governing their appetites, and governing themselves generally, be much more happy if they would put themselves in harmony with the laws of their own physical nature.' Some of the dispositions promoted in this government of the self are habits of order and regularity, of industriousness, of thrift and saving, of self-respect, and domesticity. As the last implies, and M.D. Hill states, these habits would be constructed by 'the action of the family principle.'[40]

As noted earlier, in the discourse on the increase in juvenile crime there was a great deal of criticism of families of the unrespectable classes – those classes which Booth would later call the residuum. This criticism was set against the norm of respectable working-class (as opposed to middle-class) lifestyles. Hence, the dispositions and habits – industriousness, regularity, and so on – were the values of and for the (better-off) respectable working-class. Middle-class reformers did not, I would argue, try to refashion delinquents into bourgeois gentlemen. Rather, the aim was to transform them into productive, self-supporting (hence the importance of thrift and saving) working-class citizens. It was the ideal 'labourer' rather than the ideal entrepreneur or capitalist that was the target of self-government and moral training. As Davenport Hill put it, after the reformatory those who had once been juvenile delinquents would become 'the friends and not the enemies of their honest and hard-working neighbours.'[41]

(ii) The turn of the screw

Moral training required that the individual juvenile had to be enlisted in her own reformation; she was required to work upon her self. So too the reformatory worker had to create a persona for himself. That persona would simulate the architectural principle of the reformatory machine itself.

Architecture had a central place in the project of reformation, of moral training. This concern with architecture meant that the reformatory programme was not simply a blueprint; through architecture, reformation became at once ideal and material. The preoccupation of the reforming enterprise was not just with timetables, teaching curricula, modes of instruction, forms of labour and so on, but also with *design*. Through a proper design, a *mood* of order, regularity and domesticity could be dispersed throughout the reformatory space.

The design of the reformatory was also the design of the reformatory worker's persona. According to G.H. Bengough, co-founder of the Hardwicke Reformatory School, '[O]n the manager, be he clergyman or layman, be he called master, or chaplain, or governor, or what not, the whole success indeed of the situation will, under God, depend. It is not the rules – they may hinder of help him – but it is only the man, by his personal action, that can reform.'[42]

The 'personal action' of the 'youthworker' is also that of the schoolteacher described by Richard Johnson, namely 'a subtle working upon the emotional economy of the child.'[43] Such work was created by extending the authority of the youthworker throughout the reformatory, into every nook and cranny. What is required was an all-pervasive tone which marks the machine with the reformer's indelible stamp. Perhaps the most extreme instance of this tonal ethic is John Ellis's story of an interminable holding in debt: 'Though I never use the rod, or anything else of that sort, there is a feeling in those lads that brings them to perfect submission; they dread my looks, or a frown, or a word from me, more than they would dread the lash ... these lads always feel that they were in my debt, and I never allow them to pay me.'[44] Family man, manager, chaplain, layman – these would be the names for that persona, the principle of which was shared by the architectural design of the reformatory: namely, to simulate a *mood* of order, submission, domesticity.

The youthworker is a technological principle of the reformatory apparatus. As such, he could be replaced by any other technological device which would simulate that mood of order, industriousness, and domesticity. But where the youthworker becomes indispensable is in his relations with the judicial administration. The knowledge that the youthworker gains from his 'personal action' in the reformatory will also function infra-legally. John Ellis was the manager of the Brook Street Ragged School. In his account above, he is an expert witness for the Select Committee on Criminal and Destitute Juveniles. Two years later a legislative plan for a system of Reformatory Schools is enacted. The judicial administration now relies on this nascent youthworker for its perception and authoritative enunciation of the problem of juvenile delinquency. In 1857, the Reformatory and Refuge Union offered to 'advise' the London magistrates on the availability of reformatories and on which would be more suitable for each class of juvenile with which the magistrate would deal. The offer was accepted and 49 years later the Union is still arranging confinements.[45]

What I have been describing so far is some of the ways in which the enterprise of reform was concerned to design a technology of the moral space *internal* to the reformatory school. That space is constructed, in the words of R. Hall, as a network of 'careful trainings and minute observances.'[46] Here the design is focused upon the moral training of the individual delinquent. That training was simultaneously to be a retraining. Thus, the design of the reformatory is simultaneously directed towards the delinquent class and its relationship with the other classes that constitute the social.

REFORMATION WITHIN THE SOCIAL

The social is the dominant category of liberal governance. Located between the civil and the political, it has also reorganised each of these terms: civility has become privacy, and politics has been reinvented as policy. My concern here is not with the genesis of the domain of the social. Nor is my overriding concern with the ways in which the problem of juvenile delinquency and its reform is connected up with other social problems and their reforms. Rather my concern here is somewhat more limited. It is with the way in which the formulation of juvenile delinquency as a social problem establishes the need for specific kinds of interventions; conversely, with the way in which the governance of juvenile delinquency is formulated as interventions into the domain of the social. The integration within the social of a reformatory designed for 'minute observances and careful trainings' is addressed through two problems: negatively, the problem of severance, and positively, the problem of replacement.

(i) The problem of severance

'In the great majority of instances, I do not hesitate to affirm that the only means by which reformation of such juvenile delinquents can be rationally expected, is by their thorough and permanent severance from those scenes and associations in which their evil habits are formed.'[47] The Inspectors of Prisons would have agreed with the Chief Bow Street Magistrate who, in his evidence to the Select Committee of the Metropolis, argued that 'to get away those boys before they are completely contaminated ... would be a great national object. I am talking of those children of eight to twelve; that if they could be taken from their parents when they are found in the streets, and put into some asylum, where they could be trained up to industry, it would be an immense thing, and then the gangs would want recruits, and would fall to decay.'[48] The individual is to be severed from the moral space that generates her deviance. Whereas the extension of transport routes and the construction of playgrounds function to remove the social space from the individual, the Reformatory School functions to remove the individual from the social space. The Reformatory School is designed as a solution to the need to remove the child from the delinquent class, from the moral space of juvenile delinquency. Such a process of severance is formulated in the context of a debate between punishment and reform.

By the mid-nineteenth century there is a battle waged over the administration of the juvenile delinquent. Modernist histories typically characterise this battle as one between two opposing camps: one, a philanthropic and 'welfarist' advocacy of juvenile reformatories and, the other, a juridical and 'punishment' advocacy of juvenile prisons. However, a reading of the contemporary accounts indicates that the two camps share a common objective. MacGregor had asserted that 'mere confinement' was in itself a punishment, and Mary Carpenter had characterised the forcible 'taking away' through reformatory confinement as a 'severe punishment.'[49] Not only is a language of punishment used by these philanthropists, but the institutions of prison and reformatory are positioned as variations on a strategy of severance. Thus, there was a two-way trade in inmates between Parkhurst Prison on the Isle of Wight and the Redhill Reformatory School. Furthermore, Parkhurst existed as a preliminary step to complete removal from England, namely transportation to Australia (the colony for juvenile boys at Point Puer in Van Diemen's Land). On the other hand, the Warwickshire County magistrates repeatedly used the reformatory at Stretton-on-Dunsmore as a means of removal. If the inmates ran away, legal 'fictions' were used by the magistrates to punish the escapees. Similarly, an entire separation had been attempted at the Hackney Wick School in the 1830s. The particular mode of this separation was a restriction and supervision of visitors and a careful governance of home leave. These several techniques of confinement functioned as complementary and harmonious variations which resolve the need for removal from the moral space of the juvenile class. And with the Reformatory School Act 1854, the reformatory school became the model apparatus for compulsory juridical confinement. By 1866, there were some 50 reformatory schools.

The reformatory school not only complemented the justice of the juvenile prison, it was also supplemented by other reformatory institutions: fostering, probation, 'after-care'. In relation to the former, the Recorder of Birmingham (M.D. Hill) instituted a programme whereby children coming before him were committed into the service of respectable tradesmen. When asked by the Select Committee on Criminal and Destitute Juveniles whether, if legal detention in reformatories was established, there was any necessity for continuing with his programme in Birmingham. Hill replied: 'There are some cases in which you have an opportunity of disposing of a child at a distance ... Under these circumstances it is still advisable to persevere in that plan [at Birmingham], for this reason, that it is quite clear that in an artificial establishment like a Reformatory, you can only imitate the action of the family principle. If you can send that child into the bosom of real families, who feel an affection for the child, who will show him good example and treat him with judicious kindness, you, I think, put him under circumstances of very superior efficacy for reformation'. Reform school or probation, simulated or real families, the reformist enterprise instituted 'action at a distance', action which was predicated on the violence of a prior removal. The question of what is to done after release from the reformatory is resolved in the same way. Sergeant Adams advocated expatriation to the colonies where they would be supervised by voluntary societies.[50] Such had been the practice of E.P. Benton's Society for the Suppression of Juvenile Vagrancy. Between 1830 and 1834, some 278 boys and 37 girls had been sent to the colonies by the Society. Many of them had come from the Hackney Wick Reformatory.

In sum, the problem of severance is met by a dual process. On the one hand, concentration and confinement through the prison and the reformatory (convict hulks also achieved a certain use). On the other hand, there is a process of dispersal: fostering, probation, after-care, expatriation. Moreover, these processes exist in a lateral relation to each other; they function alongside each other as techniques for the removal of juvenile delinquents *from* the moral scene that is proper to delinquency and *to* a moral space which will have promoted an other training, a retraining. The second problem through which the reformation of the juvenile is integrated in the reformation of the social is the dimensions of that retraining – the vertical relation between the scene of delinquency and the scene of reformation.

(ii) The problem of replacement

The need to replace one scene by another is constructed within a strategy concerned to produce an efficient and useful correspondence between the moral space internal to the reformatory and the external location of the juvenile class. Such a concern may be read in the narrative of the need for a distinct, rather than abstract, machinery.

Mary Carpenter begins her book *Reformatory School* by noting that the existence of the perishing and dangerous classes of children 'requires perfectly distinct machinery and modes of operation in dealing with them'. She then goes on to invent an awesome network of schools premised on a precise and finely-tuned adaptation of machine to subject. In relation to the delinquent, there is a three-tiered structure. For those who cannot attend other schools due to want of character or necessary clothing, there will be Free Day Schools. For those who through extreme poverty or vice become habitual vagrants and pilferers, there will be the compulsory Industrial Schools. And finally, for the juvenile criminal, there will be the Reformatory School.

The reformatory school is connected to the contemporaneous movement for popular education. This connection occurs, as Carpenter's plan above indicates, by way of a double series of distinctions. School is marked off from school, and class is marked off from class. Moreover, each series is given to and superimposed upon the other. The institutional division proceeds from the moral scenery, the habitus, of the group with which the school is to treat. The juvenile criminal requires special techniques because of its own history, its own locality. It is in this sense that the relationship between the reformatory and its subject is constituted as an efficient one: the reformatory is to suit the ethical nature of the juvenile. An efficient treatment is the very obverse of the moral scene to which the juvenile delinquent by definition is disposed. This rule of efficiency is evidenced in a letter sent by W.A. Miles to Lord John Russell: 'In order to reform these boys I should first consider the effects produced upon their minds by the utter hopelessness with which they are occasioned to view their present and ultimate situation, as well as the recklessness produced by punishments and the combinations of idleness and profligacy. Secondly, I should consider what method might be most beneficial to counteract that effect, and, by adapting it endeavour to introduce a new stimulus to their energies, and given another bias to their thoughts.'[51]

The efficient reformatory machine constructs a moral space that is a counter-weight to, the symmetrical opposite of, the moral scene of the juvenile class. The efficient reformatory machine is also the most useful for society. That which is most useful is a machine that will have replaced the memory of delinquent class with the memory of the honest and respectable classes. Lord Russell, when introducing the 1854 Reformatory Schools Act for Scotland to Parliament, asserted confidently that these machines would 'be able to effect to some measure that the young offenders sent to these institutions would forget their vicious habits and be restored as respectable and useful members of society.'[52] The replacement of memories will alter the course of the child's future life: rather than a repetition of his delinquencies, he will become the ideal 'labourer'. Hence, the utility of the reformatory machine [see Chapter 9 of this volume].

The distinct machines of reformation are thus a response to the need for useful efficiency. It is also within the terms of this response that the failure of the reforming enterprise is played out; namely, the obsessive fascination with reconviction studies, the language of cost-efficiency, even the New Humanitarianism of the 1960s which, in a refined form, is found in the minimal interventionism of 'juvenile justice' arguments in the 1980s. The failure is understood as an effect of the institution's integration in the strategic reformation of the social. In one aspect, the failure of the enterprise is a lack of correspondence between machine and juvenile. The machinery of moral training and the juvenile delinquent are not sufficiently calibrated. The continually receding horizon of this utopia is the elimination of the problem of juvenile delinquency.

It also ensues in an extension of the field of battle which the enterprise is waging. Here the classification of the social, of classes within classes, is not sufficiently acute. And thus the reformatory treats with those for which it is not designed. As a result, the enterprise cannot be held to account for the waywardness of some of its charges. The answer depends on the context. One solution to the problem of classification is a call for 'more research', the call so beloved of criminology's concluding paragraphs. As more evidence is collected, more classifications come to light and other machines will be designed to cater specifically for these new categories. The proliferation of precisely distinct machines finds its possibility in the failure of the enterprise to provide totally distinct machines. As the Reformatory and Refuge Union could comment in 1906. 'There are many in danger who are not old enough to find admission to certified schools. It would have been a short-sighted policy to have left these children until they became qualified for a Reformatory or for a Certified Industrial School, not a few were allowed to drift; but the rapid increase in the number of Voluntary Homes for the poor, neglected children especially in recent years, has prevented this.'[53] In 1856, there are 26 Voluntary Homes in England. In 1906, there are 449. With each new class of juvenile, there is a superaddition, another distinct machine to supplement existing ones.

It is thus apposite to end this essay with the incorrigible juvenile. He is a figure horrific precisely because he is a criminal who signs the failure of the reformatory enterprise. As such, he marks the limit of its utopia and yet evokes the incorporation of the institution within a strategy to reform the social, the class, and the juvenile delinquent.

Lieutenant-Colonel Jebb argued that we must retain Parkhurst Prison because we have to deal with the incorrigibles. He explains: 'the boys might be removed from one place to another; and that if they failed in the condition under which they were removed from the penal establishment, they would be liable to the entire sentence again.'[54] Under the sign of reformation, the prison sword is to be suspended, never abolished. If the child in the juvenile delinquent is so set in the lore of its class, then it is back to prison. Thus, just as there was to be a relation of correspondence between the reformatory and the juvenile delinquent, if it was to be efficient, so there is an homology between the failure of the reformatory and the failure of the juvenile delinquent. That figure of incorrigibility is formed in a push further along the failure of the reformative ideal: first, a removal from the moral scene of its class; and then a possibly endless removal from distinct machine to distinct machine. The possibility of the incorrigible juvenile is the condition of existence for the prison. Just as at the beginning of the nineteenth century, the hardened offender was the failure of the prison which established the need for the reformatory, so the incorrigible juvenile is the failure of the reformatory which simultaneously extends the reforming enterprise and maintains the prison. The generation of the juvenile delinquent is at the same time the generation of a carceral course.

REFERENCES AND NOTES

1 F. Jameson, *The Political Unconscious,* Cornell University Press, 1981, 102.
2 M. Foucault. *The Archeology of Knowledge,* Tavistock, 1974, 144–5.
3 M. Foucault, *Power/Knowledge* (ed. C. Gordon), Harvester, 1980, 145.
4 Quoted in S. Magarey, 'The Invention of Juvenile Delinquency in Early Nineteenth Century England', 34 *Labour History* (1978) at 12.
5 *First Report of the Committee of the Society for the Improvement of Discipline, and for the Reformation of Juvenile Offenders,* London, 1818.
6 *Report from the Select Committee on Criminal and Destitute Juveniles ... 1852,* Irish University Press, 1970, 14.
7 M. Carpenter, *Reformatory Schools,* Gilpin, 1851, 58.
8 *Report of the Proceedings of a Conference on the Subject of Prevention and Reformatory Schools ...,* Longmans Green, 1851. The quote from Horace Walpole is in L. Radzinowicz, *A History of the English Criminal Law and Its Administration from 1750,* Volume 1, Stevens and Sons, 1948, 14.
9 W. Blackstone, *Commentaries on the Laws of England.* University of Chicago Press, 1979 (orig. pub. 1765–69), vol. 4, 20 (emphasis in original).
10 *Supra* n. 9, at 23.
11 *Report of the Committee of the Society for Investigating the Causes of the Alarming Increase of Juvenile Delinquency in the Metropolis,* Dove, 1816, 10.
12 D. Hay, 'Property. Authority and the Criminal Law', in *Albion's Fatal Tree* (ed. D. Hay *et al.*), Penguin, 1977.
13 P. King, 'Decision-makers and Decision-making in the English Criminal Law, 1750–1800', 27 *The Historical Journal* (1984), 25–58.
14 E. Wakefield, *Facts Relating to the Punishment of Death in the Metropolis,* London, 1831; H.G. Bennett, *A Letter to the Common Council and Livery of the City of London, on the Abuses existing in Newgate ...,* London, 1818, 9; J. Harford, *Considerations Upon the Pernicious Influence of the Bristol Gaol ...,* Bristol, 1815, 23.
15 T. Buxton, *An Inquiry Concerning Whether Crime and Misery are Produced or Prevented by Our Present System of Person Discipline,* 2nd ed., J. and J. Arch, 1818, 155–9.
16 *Supra* n. 6 at 3–35.
17 H. Worsley, *Juvenile Depravity,* Gilpin, 1849, 1.

18 House of Lords Select Committee, *Second Report on The Present State of the Several Gaols and Houses of Correction in England and Wales,* Parliamentary Papers, XI, 1835.
19 *Supra* n. 6 at 55, 59.
20 *Supra* n. 6 at 31 (Turner) and 237 (A. Beckett).
21 *Supra* n. 6 at 90.
22 *Supra* n. 6 at 204 (Ellis) and 17 (Williams).
23 Quoted in May M. 'Innocence and Experience', 17/1 *Victorian Studies* (1973) at 17–18.
24 *Supra* n. 18.
25 *Supra* n. 7 at 321–2.
26 M.D. Hill, 'Practical Suggestions to the Founders of Reformatory Schools', in *On The Reformation of Young Offenders* (ed. J.C. Symons), Routledge, 1855, 2.
27 M. Carpenter, *Juvenile Delinquents: Their Condition and Treatment,* Patterson Smith, 1970 (orig. pub. 1853), 23–31.
28 Quoted in May, *supra* n. 23 at 18.
29 E. Chadwick, *Report on the Sanitary Condition of the Labouring Population of Great Britain,* Edinburgh University Press, 1965 (orig. pub. 1842).
30 *Supra* n. 17 at 2.
31 J.C. Symons, *On The Reformation of Young Offenders,* Routledge, 1855, 99.
32 *Supra* n. 7 at 77.
33 *Supra* n. 26 at 1–7.
34 In J. C. Symons, *supra* n. 31, 7–22 at 21 (Turner) and 22–37 at 37 (Lloyd Baker).
35 *Supra* n. 17 at 213.
36 *Supra* n. 7 at 151.
37 *Supra* n. 6 at 146.
38 *Supra* n. 6 at 59.
39 *Supra* n. 27 at 299.
40 *Supra* n. 6 at 198 (Ellis) and 70–1 (Hill).
41 *Supra* n. 26 at 4.
42 G.H. Bengough, 'Letter to Jelinger C. Symons', in J.C. Symons, *supra* n. 31, 123–31 at 128.
43 R. Johnson, 'Notes on the Schooling of the English Working Class', in *Schooling and Capitalism* (ed. R. Dale *et al.*), Open University Press, 1975, 48.
44 *Supra* n. 6 at 201.
45 Reformatory and Refuge Union, *Fifty Years' Record of Child-Saving and Reformatory Work (1856–1906), Being the Jubilee Report of the Reformatory and Refuge Union,* Charing Cross Office of the Union, 1906.
46 R. Hall, 'Extract from a Lecture on Mettray', in J.C. Symons, *supra* n. 31, 37–56 at 51.
47 *The Sixth Report of the Inspectors of Prisons, Northern and Eastern District* (1841), extract appended in the 1852 Report, *supra* n. 6 at 424.
48 Quoted in I. Pinchbeck and M. Hewitt, *Children in English Society,* Volume II, Routledge and Kegan Paul, 1973, 446.
49 *Supra* n. 6.
50 *Supra* n. 6 at 70–1 (Hill) and 215 (Adams).
51 W.A. Miles, *A Letter To Lord John Russell, Concerning Juvenile Delinquency...,* John Eddowes, 1837, 14.
52 Quoted in J. Clarke 'The 3 Rs – Repression, Rescue and Rehabilitation', University of Birmingham (1975) at 11.
53 *Supra* n. 45 at 56.
54 *Supra* n. 6 at 370.

11

Reforming the juvenile

Gender, justice and the child criminal in nineteenth-century England

Heather Shore

In the final volume of *A History of English Criminal Law*, Radzinowicz and Hood stated, 'The concept of the young offender, with all that implies for penal policy, is a Victorian creation' (1986, p. 133). By the mid-nineteenth century, according to this perspective, the rudiments of the juvenile justice system were in place. The Juvenile Offenders Act of 1847 confirmed the principle of summary trial for children up to the age of fourteen (10 and 11 Vict. c. 82, 1847), this was extended to sixteen in 1850 (13 and 14 Vict. c. 37, 1850). Whilst the juvenile court was not established until the early twentieth century (under the 1908 Children's Act), the Acts of the mid-nineteenth century made sure that, for most indictable crime, juveniles were separated from adult offenders (Radzinowicz and Hood, 1986, pp. 629–33). The Industrial and Reformatory Schools Acts of the 1850s established the principle of separate custodial provision for juveniles, to be finalized in 1876 under the Education Act, which established day industrial schools and truant schools.[1] Thus, it has been argued, this period experienced the 'invention' of the juvenile delinquent; for the first time the juvenile was seen as a distinct category of offender (see Chapters 7, 8 and 10 of this volume).

This chapter will consider the emergence of this category in the nineteenth century, and the corresponding development of the juvenile justice system, with particular reference to summary jurisdiction, punishment and gender. The main focus will be on the early and middle years of the nineteenth century, a period when many of the perennial features of juvenile justice were being debated. It will then consider the progress of juvenile justice after the mid-century, when a system recognizable to modern practitioners was gradually established. The significance of the early nineteenth century has become increasingly obvious from recent research, which has shown that the rise of indicted juvenile crime, and the merging of private and public-sector discourses about delinquency, were already apparent a couple of decades prior to

SOURCE: Commissioned for this volume. Heather Shore is Lecturer in Social and Cultural History at the University of Portsmouth, UK.

Radzinowicz and Hood's 'Victorian creation' (King, 1998; King and Noel, 1993; Shore, 1999a). Indeed, at the end of the French wars in 1815 there was a widespread belief in the increase of juvenile crime. A number of factors, such as population rise, urbanization, poverty and demobilization inter-reacted, leading to something of a 'moral panic' about such crime. Concern had been expressed about delinquent youth in previous centuries (Ben-Amos, 1994; Fielding, 1758; Griffiths, 1996; Hanway, 1759; Pearson, 1983; see also Chapter 3 of this volume); however, it was only from the 1810s that consistent representations and inquiries started to appear. Moreover, as was so often the case with law-and-order issues, London was a major focus. The metropolis was thought to be home to a criminal class of juvenile offenders, bred in the particular circumstances produced by urban life. There was concern about juvenile crime in places other than London. The industrial urban conurbations of Manchester, Birmingham and Liverpool provoked similar sentiments. However, London had long been the organizing focus of both debate and legislative enactment concerned with crime.

THE 'INVENTION' OF JUVENILE DELINQUENCY

The idea of the 'invention' of juvenile delinquency is supported by the development of what we may call a language of delinquency. Thus the terms 'juvenile delinquent' and 'juvenile offender' were rarely found prior to the early nineteenth century. Nevertheless, contemporaries were not always clear about what they actually meant by a juvenile delinquent, and there was much discussion about the specific age boundaries that defined juvenile crime. Hence it was imperative to decide the division between young and adult offenders and for that division to subsequently shape the response to juvenile criminals. Consequently there was a re-evaluation of criminal responsibility in the period. In Parliament the debate was based upon the doctrine of *doli incapax*. The presumption was that children between seven and fourteen could not be found guilty of a felony, unless it could be proved that the child had acted with malice.[2] With property crime, and other offences, this criterion of knowledge of self-guilt had to be established (Shore, 1999a, pp. 8–9).

For early nineteenth-century commentators the debate about criminal responsibility was fraught with confusion and dissatisfaction. One of the criticisms was the apparently arbitrary nature of the setting of age parameters. Critics of sharply defined age boundaries, the future Prime Minister Robert Peel among them, commented on the problem presented by very young recidivists. Should the child of twelve, for example, who had been in custody many times be treated differently from the youth of sixteen who had appeared in court on his first charge? Reclamation often depended less on the age of the juvenile than the degree to which he/she was 'hardened'. Clearly, it was felt that minority did not automatically correlate with innocence or inexperience. This fixing of boundaries and mapping out of the statutory juvenile offender was strongly intertwined with contemporary debates about the form and function of criminal trial. In particular, it was felt that young offenders should be processed by means of summary justice.

SUMMARY JURISDICTION

For those concerned about the welfare of juvenile offenders, one of the most controversial issues in the early decades of the nineteenth century was that of summary jurisdiction (Radzinowicz and Hood, 1986; Shoemaker, 1991). The advocates of summary justice felt that it should be available to try crimes below a certain value or level of seriousness, crimes below a certain value committed by juveniles, and crimes attracting a relatively 'mild' punishment: a fine, a flogging or a short term of imprisonment (Hansard, 1829, cols. 997–8). The main concern with the conventional procedure was for the moral well-being of the prisoner during the period of remand; even in those establishments that served as transitional prisons, such as Newgate, there were few attempts to separate boys from men, or known offenders from first-timers. Since children were viewed as fundamentally impressionable, the association of prisoners caused great disquiet. The effect of such intercourse was discussed in worrisome, invasive, corporeal terms – of 'contamination', 'contagion' and 'corruption'. Summary jurisdiction, its supporters argued, would decrease the potential for 'contamination' to a considerable extent by cutting out the remand period, and processing young offenders quickly and cleanly, avoiding the glare and ceremony of the superior courts. For inexperienced offenders, it was crucial that they did not get too established within the more formal mechanisms of the criminal justice system (Shore, 1999a, pp. 29–34).

Yet forms of summary jurisdiction were already being used to process an extensive range of actions and behaviour (Shoemaker, 1991, p. 6). Petty pilfering, trespass, prostitution, gambling, idleness, vagrancy, riot and assault were all offences that could be committed by young people. And indeed such activities were often seen as the provenance of delinquent youth, disorderly apprentices and girls of 'loose habits'. How did this change in the nineteenth century? Certainly the extension of summary jurisdiction to indictable offences was an innovation. As pointed out above, summary jurisdiction was extended to indictable crime committed by juveniles by the Juvenile Offenders Act of 1847. This Act empowered two magistrates to try children aged up to fourteen accused of simple larceny. Three years later the age was set at sixteen, and this eventually led to the Criminal Justice Act of 1855, which enabled all simple larcenies up to the value of 5s to be tried summarily (Radzinowicz and Hood, 1986, pp. 620–1; Shore, 1996, pp. 84–95). However, in the decades prior to this a wide range of Acts were being used by London's magistrates to process juvenile offenders. Susan Magarey has described the criminalization of what was effectively antisocial behaviour by the Malicious Trespass Act of 1820 and the Vagrancy Act of 1824, arguing that these Acts 'extended the range of behaviour proscribed as criminal by refining its definitions of kinds of offence' (Magarey, 1978, p. 20, and see Chapter 8 of this volume). Nevertheless the extent to which these Acts merely formalized the existing policies of many magistrates has to be considered (King, 1998, pp. 133–7). Hence, for many years prior to the Juvenile Offenders Act, juveniles in London were being processed summarily for a wide range of offences. And whilst the extensive summary processing of children for petty crime was broadly supported by contemporaries, there were conflicting views about how juveniles should actually be punished.

PUNISHMENT

In the post-Napoleonic War period corporal punishment was favoured by magistrates and police, who were in the front line of juvenile justice, and believed that it was enough to deal with most petty delinquency. Not surprisingly, there are indications that the police employed their own discretion on whether or not to use physical chastisement with juveniles. For example, eighteen-year-old Andrew Clarke, interviewed in prison in the mid-1830s, claimed to have been 'frequently let off with a thrashing or *box on the ear*' (PRO, HO73/2, pt. 2). However, this discretionary justice was not always acceptable. In 1828 Mr Richard Gregory, the treasurer of the watch in Spitalfields, described how it could backfire: 'sometimes our inspectors have caught the boys pilfering, and have given them a good thrashing with their ash sticks, and the parent has gone the next day to Mr Bennett, of Worship-Street, and got a warrant, and Mr Bennett has actually held them to bail for it' (SCPM, 1828, p. 98). Indeed, there was considerable concern about the effects of corporal punishment, and a number of commentators felt that it was too degrading and harsh a punishment for juveniles. The same commentators also recommended *short* correctional periods of custody for juveniles. Hence, even before the redefinition of the Vagrancy Act and the passage of the Malicious Trespass Act in the 1820s, substantial numbers of children were being committed to bridewells and houses of correction on charges of vagrancy and for other misdemeanours (Shore, 1999a, pp. 31–2). Giving evidence to a contemporary select committee, Francis Hobler, the clerk to the Lord Mayor, described the considerable discretionary powers which magistrates could employ to commit children to such institutions:

> The Lord Mayor frequently orders boys to solitary confinement; and though he has no power to confine them a certain time, yet he often exercises that parental authority at the request of parents, by putting the boys into the house of correction by way of remand; the hearing the irons and bolts and fastenings, and the chains (if he has any feelings left,) frequently produces the best effects, and he comes up quite penitent and full of promises for future behaviour.

> (SCPM, 1817, p. 495)

It is clear that summary justice, in the case of both trial and forms of punishment, was well established in London in the 1810s and early 1820s. Moreover, magistrates employed considerable discretion when dealing with juvenile offenders. Yet the crisis, or 'moral panic', of these years was heavily conditioned by the increasing number of children appearing in front of the higher courts, charged with felony. In parallel to this the debate about the punishment of juveniles was increasingly concentrated on those who were prosecuted for indictable crime, i.e. those who had travelled the extra length into the formal criminal justice system. And increasingly some form of custody was becoming the preferred option.

REFORMATION

By the 1820s and 1830s Peel's reform of the capital statutes was well under way: whilst juveniles were still sentenced to death for the remaining capital crimes, the actual numbers executed were tiny (Knell, 1965). Until the mid-nineteenth century, when the Industrial and Reformatory Schools Acts were passed, a variety of strategies to deal with convicted juveniles were tried out, with varying success. At the root of these strategies was the recognition that society had a larger constituent body of juveniles in the justice system to deal with – it is clear that the 'great confinement' of this period embraced youth (see Chapter 7 of this volume). Nevertheless, the increased juvenile prison population was not merely a reflection of the rise in indictable juvenile crime. Analysis of such crime in London suggests that a growing willingness to prosecute juveniles, combined with an increasing tendency to find them guilty, was the major momentum behind the rising number of juveniles in prison (Shore, 1999a, p. 103).

Ideas about the reformability of the convict had long been a theme of penal debate, but the specific reformation of the juvenile offender had taken on a new urgency by this time. This reformation was located strongly within institutional provision. As well as the bridewells, houses of correction and new penitentiaries of the state, this included a wide variety of comparative institutions which were aimed at the reform of the juvenile. The use of transportation and colonial emigration for juvenile offenders was also closely aligned with this debate. At the core was the need to remove children from their domestic surroundings, whether on the streets of London or their parents' hearth. In the post-Napoleonic War period the usual solution had been for children to spend a short time in a reformatory institution, usually a bridewell or house of correction, before returning to their parents. By the 1820s the emphasis increasingly shifted away from the community and towards some form of longer-term custodial punishment for juveniles. The problem was the exact form and function of that custodial punishment.

In the late 1820s and 1830s, for all convicts, the conflict between more punitive and more reformative systems of custody was in debate. The great theme of this period was the classification and separation of what were perceived as different groups of convicts (Henriques, 1972). Thus boys were to be removed from men, and bad boys were to be removed from those identified as less experienced offenders. The paradox of the situation was how to control the behaviour of both those children already labelled as criminal and those children on the periphery of the criminal justice system: the 'dangerous' and 'perishing' juveniles. Likewise, many of the children who spent time in the voluntary custodial institutions, such as the Refuge for the Destitute, and the School of the Philanthropic Society, were not specifically criminal. Often they were the children of convicts, or were children who had been committed for vagrancy. Consequently there was a drive to find a scheme that could incorporate both groups of children, using the systems of classification which were being recommended in legislation such as the 1823 and 1824 Gaol Acts, engineered by Peel himself (4 Geo. IV, c. 83 and 5 Geo. IV, c. 85).

The classification and grading of juveniles were already well established in the institutions of the voluntary sector. As early as the 1790s the Philanthropic Society had placed delinquent boys into the Reform, where they were provided with a moral and social education. Once 'sufficiently reformed' they were transferred to the Manufactory, where they were taught practical skills and undertook employment (Philanthropic Society, 1804; Carlebach, 1970). It is arguable that it was the representatives of this voluntary sector that provided much of the momentum for change. Whilst the parliamentary debate can be traced through the various 'crime' select committees of this period, a considerable number of independent philanthropists and researchers were actually going into the prisons of the metropolis and were clearly unhappy with what they found. The members of the Committee for Investigating the Causes of the Alarming Increase of Juvenile Delinquency in the Metropolis, established in 1815, emphasized the necessity for separate juvenile provision (Shore, 1996, p. 60). Moreover the later metamorphosis of this committee, the Prison Discipline Society, was the major penal pressure group of the period: a sort of proto-Howard League

(Highmore, 1822). During the 1820s and 1830s a myriad of evidence was submitted by these, and other, organizations which illustrated the beneficial effects of separate juvenile provision not only on the crime rates but also on the public purse. Moreover, as a result of time spent visiting children in prison, they stressed the counterproductive effect of traditional forms of custody from the early days of the debate.

As early as 1816 plans had been submitted for a juvenile penitentiary, by Samuel Hoare, the Quaker banker and philanthropist, and the architect James Bevan (SCPM, 1816, pp. 520–33). This plan intrinsically conflicted with the tenor of contemporary thought on penality. Whilst it was accepted that the new penality needed to be a reformatory experience, contemporaries were also aware of the need for the preservation of the principle of less eligibility (McConville, 1981, pp. 238–41, 354–6). As the Governor of Coldbath Fields House of Correction remarked of juvenile inmates in 1831:

> the punishment of prison is no punishment to them; I do not mean that they would not rather be out of prison than in it, but they are so well able to bear the punishment, and the prison allowance of food is so good, and their spirits so buoyant, that the consequences are most deplorable.
>
> (SCSP, 1831, p. 33)

In other words it would be unwise to make the prison too attractive. Consequently, despite calls for separate juvenile penitentiaries throughout the period, it took until 1838 for the first state-run juvenile institution, the ill-fated Parkhurst, to materialize, and it was not until the 1850s that the reform and manufactory of the Philanthropic Society were to be echoed in state-controlled institutions (Carlebach, 1970, pp. 25–46; McConville, 1981, pp. 204–10). Prior to this, attention was concentrated largely on the types of punishment and methods of control that could achieve the object of moral reformation.

GENDER

The reformability of the juvenile was the central theme of debates about penality in this period. Clearly, the reformation of all convicts was at issue, but the sub-group of juveniles were particularly focused upon for obvious reasons. As opposed to older convicts, juveniles were seen as reclaimable (although, as suggested earlier, contemporaries were keen to differentiate between different degrees of experience and maturity in crime). Juveniles were also an important focus since they represented a future generation of criminals. Thus not only would these juveniles progress into 'criminal careers' as adults, but they themselves could become the parents of a new generation of potential criminals: as the reformer Mary Carpenter put it, 'to rise up to be the parents of a degraded progeny of pauper children' (Carpenter, 1851, p. 352). Despite this rhetoric the discourse on juvenile crime at the time was heavily gendered. The preoccupation was with the male juvenile thief (Shore, 1999b, pp. 78–83). When girls were considered it was from the confines of narrow descriptive categories, which stereotyped them as either prostitutes or flash girls (an early nineteenth-century equivalent of a gangster's moll: Davies, 1999; Shore, 1999b, pp. 83–6). Representations of young offenders were generally based on the most extreme examples of juvenile crime: children who had reached the superior courts, who awaited transportation, and who lingered in the prisons and houses of correction, children who were invariably boys. The concern over girl delinquents was generally framed in terms of their sexual immorality, accompanied by a strong emphasis on the sexual threat which they apparently posed to boys (Miles, 1839, p. 45; Wakefield, 1968, pp. 200–1).

The division between juvenile boys and girls was expressed clearly in the report from the committee formed to investigate the causes of juvenile delinquency, referred to above. It published this pivotal, and at the time influential, document in 1816 (*Report of the Committee,* 1816). Committee members interviewed several hundred boys in Middlesex prisons and houses of correction in order to compile the report. Female juvenile offenders were not interviewed; typically girls were referred to only in the context of prostitution. Whilst this gender division was hardly new, the broader concentration on male juvenile property crime was (King, 1998, pp. 120, 122; Shore, 1999b, pp. 77–8). Thus in the commissions, reports and texts that appeared from the late 1810s there was little significant discussion of other forms of crime such as indirect property crimes like fraud and coining, assault or other physical violence. Moreover, while immorality was a concern, it was rarely stated explicitly as sexual immorality, except in cases of female juvenile prostitution (Shore, 1999b, pp. 83–6).

Consequently it seems that rather more substantial attention was lavished on male juveniles. However, other forces were at work in the concentration on male juvenile offenders. It is clear that not only did a far higher number of boys enter the criminal justice system, but that in the case of rising juvenile indictments the rise was much more markedly male than female (King, forthcoming). One of the implications is that juvenile girls may have been more likely to be dealt with informally by the magistrate or by some other agency than to go on to the superior courts. For example, the Refuge for the Destitute and the bridewell took in female juveniles, in some cases recommended by the magistrates, and in others brought by their guardians.

Other organizations were aimed specifically at juvenile prostitution. For example, the Society for the Suppression of Juvenile Prostitution was in operation in the 1830s, and the Birmingham Society for the Protection of Young Females and Suppression of Juvenile Prostitution in the 1840s. Within the voluntary sector there were also institutions solely designated for female juvenile inmates. For example, the Royal Victoria Asylum in Chiswick and the Chelsea School of Discipline in Middlesex. At the School of Discipline girls were not allowed skipping for exercise 'since it makes them bold in their manners' (SCG, 1835, p. 485). A set of admissions to the London bridewell in 1835 shows a healthy female presence: just under half the juvenile inmates were girls. The vast majority of the girls had entered the bridewell on the grounds of prostitution. Typical entrants were the fourteen-year-old brought in by her father: 'a Girl of violent, wild, and disobedient Character, quite beyond the Control of her parents', or another fourteen-year-old, brought by her friends. 'This young girl is addicted to pilfering, has followed loose habits, and associated with very bad characters' (SCG, 1835, pp. 419–25). Even where 'loose habits' were not expressly referred to, sexual transgression was implied. And once they were categorized as criminals, or more appropriately as prostitutes, far greater maturity was attributed to them than to boys. There was strong resistance to the idea that young, physically immature girls could be sexually knowledgeable. Consequently, such girls were often portrayed as hardened, corrupt women. In January 1831 two girls (aged eleven and twelve) were arrested and charged at Bow Street 'with walking the streets for the purpose of prostitution, and with uttering the most abominable language under the Piazzas of Covent-Garden ... although of such tender years, the defendants were hardened in vice, and the language which they were constantly in the habit of using was most obscene and disgusting' (*The Times*, 26 January 1831). Thus once a woman (or girl) had given herself up to 'immorality' she was seen as being capable of far greater depths of evil and vice than her male counterpart. Mrs Shaw of the Chelsea School of Discipline commented on the viciousness of her female charges in the 1830s. When asked about the girls' demeanour Shaw replied, 'their violence is really fearful, one or two have threatened to knock me down; they doubled their little hands,' though she acknowledged, 'we have never suffered anything serious; it's mere threat' (SCG, 1835, p. 487).

Whilst male juvenile behaviour was characterized by the conflict between innocence and experience, there was generally seen to be some force influencing their actions. Thus they were corrupted by parents, by other boys, by temptation, by older thieves, by women and girls. While juvenile girls had also been corrupted at some stage, they tended to be treated as part of the threat to boys, rather than assessed as offenders in their own right. There was much less discussion of saving and reforming these juvenile prostitutes, rather it seems that their role in these discourses was mainly that of cipher for the actions of male juvenile offenders. As one commentator remarked in 1835, 'these boys have their girls, who are more depraved even in their habits, who live extravagantly on the produce of the plunder, urging them on to guilt, and sinking these boys as low as they can be sunk in every species of debauchery and crime' (SCG, 1835, p. 513). Despite this rather heavyhanded rhetoric a substantial minority of girls were appearing in front of the criminal courts in their own right, charged with petty theft, pocket picking and other property crimes. Cases were typically like that of thirteen-year-old Lydia Moles, who was found guilty of stealing six printed books from an Old Street bookseller, John Hicks, in November 1800 (OBSP, first session, 1801, p. 17). She was confined to Newgate for a month. The number of girls indicted for the more serious larceny such as burglary and robbery, or for crimes against the person, was negligible. Where girls were indicted for robbery it was generally from the dwelling house, where the girls were often in service. For example, in 1814 fourteen-year-old Mary Cooley was found guilty of feloniously stealing £35 from the dwelling house of Margaret Dunnally in Clerkenwell, where she worked as a servant. Mary was sentenced to death (OBSP, first session, 1814, pp. 24–5). On the whole the crimes that girls and boys committed were much the same: petty, mundane delinquencies, theft from shops or from their place of work. Yet what the contemporary sources suggest is that boys and girls were treated differently, and that the differences extended to their likelihood of spending time within the formal mechanisms of the criminal justice system. Nevertheless, whilst boys were more likely to spend time in prison, girls were not left out of the institutional nexus. As we have seen, the correctional institutions and comparative institutions of the voluntary sector welcomed girl juveniles. This was underlined by the mid-century in the address for the opening of the female refuge of the Refuge for the Destitute:

the committal and re-committal of females to the metropolitan and suburban houses of correction, amounts to about 7,000 annually: and when this fact is taken into consideration, together with those of the privitations, and, too often excessive occupation, by which so large a proportion of our female population is predisposed and incited to crime and vice; the duty of affording an asylum to the penitent must be strongly felt, as well as the interest of society acknowledged, in withdrawing them from plunder.

(Refuge for the Destitute, 1849)

Moreover, with the establishment of the state-run industrial schools and reformatories after the mid-century the focus arguably shifted away from the gendered focus on the male juvenile thief to embrace a rather broader definition of juvenile delinquency.

THE REFORMATORY SYSTEM

Traditionally, historians have argued that after the mid-century juvenile crime declined. Certainly the number of children charged with felony, appearing in front of the higher courts and being committed to prison decreased. On the one hand criminal children were being diverted to summary jurisdiction, which was well established by the mid-century. On the other hand, the imprisonment of juveniles was increasingly giving way to the ascendancy of the industrial and reformatory school movement. Indeed, during the later nineteenth century, developments in juvenile justice were largely concerned with the reformatory school system. Parkhurst had not been a success, and had been the subject of substantial criticism from the influential philanthropist Mary Carpenter (Carpenter, 1851, pp. 317–23). Increasingly, contemporaries were turning to foreign models for inspiration (Leonards, forthcoming). Thus agricultural reform schools like the Rauhe Haus in Germany and Mettray in France were visited by the luminaries of the British juvenile justice system, who were impressed by the adoption of 'family' systems and the employment of religiously motivated staff (Driver, 1990). Agricultural and industrial training followed by colonial emigration was to be a core strategy in the design of the new reformatories. However, in reality emigration only accounted for a small proportion of juveniles discharged from the reformatory and industrial schools (Radzinowicz and Hood, 1986, pp. 214–20). In fact after-care was a neglected element of these institutions. Instead the energies of the reformers and managers of such institutions were concentrated on form and function. Radzinowicz outlined six core issues with which juvenile justice professionals were concerned in the later nineteenth century. First was the issue of preliminary imprisonment prior to entering a reformatory or industrial school; second was the management of the schools – should they be administered by the Home Office or as part of the growing educational system? Third, should the reformatory and industrial schools be kept separate or amalgamated? Fourth, what were the rights and obligations of the parents? Fifth, what should be done with the children upon discharge? Sixth, how far should the industrial and reformatory schools be extended – in other words how incorporative should such institutions be? (Radzinowicz and Hood, 1986, p. 202.)

In some ways the state juvenile justice system of the later nineteenth century adopted the methods and reformatory strategies of the philanthropic sector, which had identified industrial training for 'at risk' children and reformatory training for delinquent and criminal children. Thus both criminal children and the peripherally delinquent, or children of adult criminals, were absorbed into the state system from the mid-nineteenth century. This was further affirmed in an Amending Act of 1861 (24 and 25 Vict. c. 113) which redefined the 'vagrant child' as 'almost any child under fourteen found begging, receiving alms, of no settled abode or means of subsistence or one who frequented criminal company' (Springhall, 1986, p. 167; Stack, 1994, p. 65). A further Consolidating Act of 1866 widened the net even further by including orphans, children of criminal parents and children whose parents were undergoing penal servitude (29 and 30 Vict. c. 118). Moreover the industrial and reformatory schools increasingly became a substitute for the formal imprisonment of children. Thus the significant decline of child imprisonment from the mid-nineteenth century is partially explained by the impact of the reformatory movement. By the 1860s delinquent and semi-delinquent children were admitted to the industrial schools without previous imprisonment (Stack, 1994, pp. 64–5). Moreover, by the early twentieth century many of the differences between the industrial and reformatory schools had been eroded (Bailey, 1987, pp. 47–57; Cox, 1996, forthcoming; Humphries, 1981).

SEXUALITY

For girl inmates of reformatory and industrial schools, their treatment was once again subject to gendered understandings of male and female delinquency (Cale, 1993; Cox, 1996; Mahood and Littlewood, 1994; Mahood, 1995). Historians researching the administration and experiences of girl juveniles in the Victorian reformatory system have found very strong evidence that girls were more likely to be committed for sexual delinquency. To a large extent this reflected the contemporary preoccupation with the notion of the 'fallen' girl or woman. Whilst rescue homes for young prostitutes and vulnerable females had long been a feature of society, delinquency and youthful female sexuality were increasingly linked in the Victorian mind. Correspondingly, a number of institutions aimed at the rescue and reform of juvenile prostitutes emerged, such as the London Society for the Protection of Young Females, the Rescue Society and the Reform and Refuge Union (Jackson, 2000, p. 14). Moreover the connection between delinquency and female sexuality was emphasized in the reformatory school movement. Thus Louise Jackson has shown that not only delinquent girls, but also girl victims of sexual abuse, were placed in industrial schools. Therefore, such victims of abuse were tainted by sexual knowledge (Jackson, 2000, p. 65). Girls entering the industrial school had often been criminalized as a result of association with sexual immorality. In contrast, as Michelle Cale has pointed out, such circumstances were hardly significant in boys' cases, 'For example, of the 43 boys committed to the Stockport Boys' Industrial School in 1891, only two were recorded as having prostitutes for mothers, and almost a third were committed for failing to attend an elementary school' (Cale, 1993, p. 205). Boy inmates of the industrial schools were not immune from sexual surveillance. Perhaps unsurprisingly, masturbation and homosexuality among boy inmates were frequently cited as worrying features of institutional life (Mahood and Littlewood, 1994, pp. 564–5). Nevertheless the unavoidable conclusion is that it was the control of female sexuality that was a key aim of the reformatory movement (Cale, 1993; Cox, 1996).

CONCLUSION

To summarize the main points of this chapter: firstly, whilst the mid-nineteenth century was undoubtedly a turning point for juvenile justice, it is clear that we can no longer see the use of summary jurisdiction and separate custody for children as particularly innovative. For many years prior to the mid-century Acts, summary justice for juveniles was being negotiated and extensively utilized by magistrates in London and, as Peter King's work has suggested, in other urban centres. Moreover, for most of the period 'rescue and reform' was the key mechanism for processing female juveniles. Secondly, there was a shift from locally interpreted forms of summary justice for juveniles to more formal indictment and penality in this period (whether in the form of custody at home or transportation). By the late 1840s justice had shifted once again and summary jurisdiction became the main criminal process to which children were exposed, albeit in its new remodelled form: correspondingly, the number of indicted juveniles decreased. These jurisdictional shifts were paralleled by the development of a custodial system which incorporated both juvenile offenders and children 'at risk'. Whilst on the one hand the rhetoric of classification meant that children were graded by their apparent level of criminality, on the other, rather more children were now spending time in front of the magistrates, and inside the houses of correction, bridewells and prisons – and, after the mid-century, in the industrial and reformatory schools. Thirdly, the use of separate custody for juveniles, enshrined in the reformatory and industrial schools Acts of the mid-century, was already facilitated in the institutions of the voluntary sector from the late eighteenth century. Whilst the impact of the refuges and schools, in terms of the actual numbers of children they took in, is limited, their impact on the eventual shape and scope of the state-controlled institutions is marked. Moreover, the broader role of the philanthropic sector in providing the momentum for the development of juvenile justice in the early nineteenth century is notable. In fact, some of the philanthropists became the first penal professionals, taking up formal roles in the state system. For example, the Reverend Sydney Turner, of the Philanthropic Society, became the first inspector of the reformatory schools. Finally this period was characterized by a shifting discourse in terms of gender, which had very real implications for the treatment of female juveniles, though, as the work of historian Pam Cox has shown, by the turn of the century delinquent girls in state institutions were still being categorized by their apparent sexual knowledge. Thus the early nineteenth-century discourse can be seen as part of a continuum in attitudes to gender and justice that historians and criminologists alike have traced.

NOTES

1 Reformatory Schools Act, 17 and 18 Vict. c. 74; Reformation of Young Offenders Act (17 and 18 Vict. c. 86), Middlesex Industrial Schools Act [Local] (17 and 18 Vict. c. 169); 1855, Youthful Offenders Amendment Act (18 and 19 Vict. c. 87); Elementary Education Act, 39 and 40 Vict. c. 79 (1876).
2 The literal translation of *doli incapax* is 'incapable of being sorry'; that is, incapable of understanding.

REFERENCES

Bailey, V. (1987) *Delinquency and Citizenship: Reclaiming the Young Offender, 1914–48*, Oxford, Clarendon Press.
Ben-Amos, I.K. (1994) *Adolescence and Youth in Early Modern England*, London and New Haven CT, Yale University Press.

Cale, M. (1993) 'Girls and the perception of sexual danger in the Victorian reformatory system', *History*, vol. 78, pp. 201–17.

Carlebach, J. (1970) *Caring for Children in Trouble*, London, Routledge.

Carpenter, M. (1851) *Reformatory Schools for the Children of the Perishing and Dangerous Classes and for Juvenile Offenders*, London, Gilpin.

Cox, P. (1996) 'Rescue and Reform: Girls, Delinquency and Industrial Schools, 1908–33', unpublished Ph.D, University of Cambridge.

Cox, P. (forthcoming) *Gender, Justice and Welfare*, Basingstoke, Palgrave.

Davies, A. (1999) '"These viragoes are no less cruel than the lads": young women, gangs and violence in late Victorian Manchester and Salford', *British Journal of Criminology*, vol. 39, no. 1, pp. 72–89.

Driver, F. (1990) 'Discipline without frontiers? Representations of the Mettray reformatory colony in Britain, 1840–80', *Journal of Historical Sociology* (Great Britain), vol. 3, pp. 272–93.

Fielding, J. (1758) *A Plan for a Preservatory and Reformatory, for the Benefit of Deserted Girls, and Penitent Prostitutes*, London, Franklin.

Griffiths, P. (1996) *Youth and Authority: Formative Experience in England, 1560–1640*, Oxford, Clarendon Press.

Hanway, J. (1759) *An Account of the Marine Society*, London.

Henriques, U. (1972) 'The rise and decline of the separate system of prison discipline', *Past and Present*, vol. 54, pp. 61–93.

Highmore, A. (1822) *Philanthropia Metropolitania*, London.

Humphries, S. (1981) *Hooligans or Rebels? An Oral History of Working-class Childhood and Youth, 1889–1939*, Oxford, Blackwell.

Jackson, L.A. (2000) *Child Sexual Abuse in Victorian England*, London, Routledge.

King, P. (1998) 'The rise of juvenile delinquency in England, 1780–1840: changing patterns of perception and prosecution', *Past and Present*, vol. 160, pp. 116–66.

King, P. (forthcoming) *Crime and Law in the Age of Reform, 1750–1850*, Cambridge, Cambridge University Press.

King, P. and Noel, J. (1993) 'The origins of "the problem of juvenile delinquency": the growth of juvenile prosecutions in London in the late eighteenth and early nineteenth centuries', *Criminal Justice History: An International Annual*, no. 14, pp. 17–41.

Knell, B.E.F. (1965) 'Capital punishment: its administration in relation to juvenile offenders in the nineteenth century and its possible administration in the eighteenth', *British Journal of Criminology, Delinquency and Deviant Behaviour*, vol. 5, no. 2, pp. 198–207.

Leonards, C. (forthcoming) 'Border crossings in the field of juvenile care in the nineteenth century: European and Dutch discourses and practices on the criminal child', in P. Cox and H. Shore (eds) *Becoming Delinquent: European Youth, 1650–1950*, Aldershot, Ashgate.

Magarey, S. (1978) 'The invention of juvenile delinquency in early nineteenth-century England', *Labour History* (Canberra), vol. 34, pp. 11–27.

Mahood, L. (1995) *Policing Gender, Class and Family: Britain, 1850–1940*, London, UCL Press.

Mahood, L. and Littlewood, B. (1994) 'The "vicious girl" and the "street-corner boy": sexuality and the gendered delinquent in the Scottish child-saving movement, 1850–1940', *Journal of the History of Sexuality*, vol. 4, pp. 549–78.

McConville, S. (1981) *A History of English Prison Administration* I, *1750–1877*, London, Routledge.

Miles, W.A. (1839) *Poverty, Mendicity and Crime*, London, Shaw.

Philanthropic Society (1804) *An Account of the Present State of the Philanthropic Society*, London.

Pearson, G. (1983) *Hooligan: A History of Respectable Fears*, Basingstoke, Macmillan.

Radzinowicz, L. and Hood, R. (1986) *A History of English Criminal Law and its Administration from 1750* V, *The Emergence of Penal Policy*, Oxford, Stevens.

Shoemaker, R. (1991) *Prosecution and Punishment: Petty Crime and the Law in London and Rural Middlesex, c. 1660–1725*, Cambridge, Cambridge University Press.

Shore, H. (1996) 'The Social History of Juvenile Crime in Middlesex, 1790–1850', unpublished Ph.D., University of London.

Shore, H. (1999a) *Artful Dodgers: Youth and Crime in Early Nineteenth Century London*, Woodbridge, Boydell Press.

Shore, H. (1999b) 'The trouble with boys: gender and the "invention" of the juvenile offender in early nineteenth-century Britain', in M. Arnot and C. Usborne (eds) *Gender and Crime in Modern Europe*, London, UCL Press.

Springhall, J. (1986) *Coming of Age: Adolescence in Britain, 1860–1960*, Dublin, Gill & Macmillan.

Stack, J. (1994) 'Reformatory and industrial schools and the decline of child imprisonment in mid-Victorian England and Wales', *History of Education*, vol. 23, no. 1, pp. 59–73.

Wakefield, E.G. (1968) 'Facts relating to the punishment of death in the metropolis', in M.F. Lloyd Pritchard (ed.) *The Collected Works of Edward Gibbon Wakefield*, Glasgow, Collins.

Primary sources

'Juvenile offenders accused of larceny', Hansard, vol. 20 (1829), cols. 997–8.

Old Bailey Session Papers, 1801, first session, p. 17, no. 16.

Old Bailey Session Papers, 1804, sixth session, p. 341, no. 400.

Old Bailey Session Papers, 1814, first session, pp. 24–5, no. 34.

Public Record Office (PRO), HO73/2, pt. 2.

Refuge for the Destitute, opening address, 1849 Refuge for the Destitute Minutes, 1819–1847, Hackney, Rose Lipman Library.

Report from the Select Committee on the Police of the Metropolis, PP, 1816, V (SCPM, 1816).

Report from the Select Committee on the Police of the Metropolis, PP, 1817, VII (SCPM, 1817).

Report from the Select Committee on the Police of the Metropolis, PP, 1828, VI (SCPM, 1828).

Report from the Select Committee on Secondary Punishments, PP, 1831, VII (SCSP, 1831).

Report of the Committee for Investigating the Causes of the Alarming Increase of Juvenile Delinquency in the Metropolis (Dove, London, 1816).

Report from the Select Committee of the House of Lords appointed to Inquire into the Present State of Goals and Houses of Correction in England and Wales, PP, 1835, XI–XII (SCG, 1835).

The Times, 26 January 1831.

The Times, 30 July 1831.

Part III

Positivism and welfarism

For much of the twentieth century the virtues of welfarism were a taken-for-granted idiom of youth justice. Acting in a 'child's best interests' and making welfare considerations paramount in court proceedings have been its defining characteristics. The establishment of the juvenile court, probation, indeterminate sentencing, care orders, individualized treatment and separate custodial regimes have all been heralded as evidence of the centrality of welfare dispositions.

Welfare requires a reading of the state of childhood and youth not only as vulnerable, but also as particularly worrisome and disturbing. It is assumed that delinquency and criminality are symptomatic of some underlying problem, which can be diagnosed and treated in a therapeutic fashion either by removing the young from harmful environments or by providing intensive supervision. A myriad theories and regulatory practices have subsequently emerged to address such concerns. Numerous forms of positivist criminology – whether biological, psychological or sociological – have variously attributed adolescent delinquency to hormonal imbalances, peer-group pressure, personality deficits, dysfunctional families, and so on. Growing numbers of psychiatrists, social workers, philanthropists, psychologists and youth workers have been enlisted, not only to provide correctional services, but also to identify those who may be thought likely to offend.

The conventional wisdom is that this welfare ethos dominated youth justice until at least the 1970s and has ensured that young people are treated with a degree of humanity and social justice appropriate to their age. However, it has always had to sit alongside a prior and counter ethos that all offenders must be held responsible and punished for their actions no matter what their age. As a result, much of the literature on youth justice has been obsessed with unravelling the contradictions of delivering welfare *and* punishment. Since the 1970s this has been represented in even starker form through the recognition that welfarism has been progressively undercut by a punitive 'just deserts' mentality intent on responding to the nature of the offence rather than to the individual needs of the offender. The gradual importation of 'adult' proceedings and outcomes into the youth court system is widely viewed as dismissive of the welfare principle. Yet there are exceptions to the rule. In Scotland, for example, welfare tribunals established in the 1970s continue to operate in preference to juvenile courts. In New Zealand, Canada and in some Australian states, various forms of conferencing or sentencing circles empha-size the importance of supporting offenders by encouraging reintegration rather than seeking coercion and exclusion. We should remain mindful, too, that, enshrined in the UN Convention on the Rights of the Child (to which most of the world's governments are signatories) are substantial responsibi-lities on the part of governments and parents for the welfare of children. In these instances, although it may be considered that the pursuit of welfare has been redefined or reconfigured, it is by no means completely absent.

Part III brings together a number of critical readings of the role that welfare has played in the formation and subsequent development of separate systems of justice for young people. It opens in Chapter 12 with Anthony Platt's classic neo-Marxist critique of traditional liberal perspectives, which have hailed the late nineteenth-century reform movements in the United States as fundamentally humanitarian, benevolent and progressive. Platt argues that, instead, the rationale behind those reform movements lay more in the wider concern of powerful corporate interests to protect their own privileged positions. 'Child saving' was part of a larger movement to regulate capital and labour and to achieve cultural hegemony. Welfare pro-grammes were underpinned by the need to develop industrial discipline and new modes of social control for the 'delinquent', the 'pre-delinquent' and the 'neglected'. Juvenile court legislation enabled the state to extend its govern-mental gaze into all aspects of working-class family life. The child savers may have preached a benevolent rhetoric, but they were not averse to using severe disciplinary measures to ensure the compliance of youth. Acting in a child's 'best interests' did not preclude resort to austere and coercive punishment. In total, Platt argues, the welfare-based youth justice reforms of the late nineteenth and early twentieth centuries did more to consolidate state power than to afford greater democratic participation to those the reforms were supposed to benefit.

In some contrast, in Chapter 13 David Garland's revisionist history of this same period in the United Kingdom gives greater weight to the redistributive and integrative effects of liberal reform. Basic capitalist requirements may have remained in place, but order depended less on coercion and more on self-regulation. In the reading reproduced here Garland detects the emer-gence of a new penality in the early twentieth century, based on processes of normalization in which the new institutions of probation and supervision acted to support family life rather than simply to control it. A new language or 'ideological mode of address' shifted the function of penality to one of training, treatment, restoration, support and protection. Only for those who refused the benefits of conformity was segregation reserved. Above all, Garland advances the argument that, whilst welfare may always be contested, its effects are not completely coercive. Rhetoric and official representation are not merely smokescreens that render reality invisible, they too have real social consequences. Commitment to welfarism may have been variable, but the disagreements that followed in much of the twentieth century were more concerned with finding the right balance between welfare and punishment than with questioning the range of considerations that were legitimately involved. In this sense the emergence of penal welfarism gave rise to an influential new vocabulary and implicit set of rules for dealing with young people who find themselves in trouble with the law.

Nowhere was this more clearly in evidence than in the spate of welfare-inspired committee reports, official inquiries and policy proposals that emerged in Britain in the 1960s. Chapter 14 by Anthony Bottoms and Chapter 15 by Janice McGhee, Lorraine Waterhouse and Bill Whyte chart the different outcomes of welfare reform in England, Wales and Scotland. In England and Wales the 1969 Children and Young Persons Act, whilst retaining the juvenile court, advocated raising the age of criminal responsibility to fourteen. It also looked forward to developing alternatives to detention by way of treatment-focused community programmes and non-criminal care orders. As Bottoms records, the Act was consistently attacked as being too welfare-minded and permissive. The history of its development throughout the 1960s reveals the political disputes involved and the contradictory outcomes of attempts to combine philosophies of social work and welfare with those of criminal justice. Although heralded as the most decisive decriminalizing instance of penal policy, the 1969 Act was never fully implemented. The incoming Conservative administration, the magistracy, the police and some sections of the probation service consistently opposed it on the grounds that it undermined the due process of law by relying too heavily on social workers' discretion and evaluation of youthful behaviour. As a result, welfarism in English youth justice has been progressively ignored or undermined.

In Scotland, however, the Social Work (Scotland) Act of 1968 was successful in abolishing the juvenile court and replacing it by a welfare tribunal. The Kilbrandon Committee of 1964 had argued that there was little difference between offenders and those in need of care. It pursued the classic welfare/positivist argument that children who found themselves in trouble did so primarily because of a failure to be allowed to develop normally. Delinquency was described as a symptom of personal or environmental difficulties. This approach relied implicitly on a medical model in which delinquency and deprivation were seen as pathological problems that could be treated only by a welfare agency responding to individual needs. Children's hearings, in which social workers assumed a pivotal role, were first put into operation in 1971. Whilst McGhee *et al.* tend to be somewhat circumspect about actual outcomes and the long-term realization of welfarist goals, it remains the case that the Scottish system continues to offer more possibilities of welfare-based negotiation and intervention than that of England and Wales.

In England and Wales it has long been argued that, since the 1969 Act, there has been a marked and consistent retreat from welfare ideals and practices in favour of punitive justice-based initiatives. However, New Labour's emphasis on *preventing* youth crime does, in some respects, reopen the door to a reformulation of some quasi-welfare practices. Elements of the new referral order, for example, explicitly borrow from Scottish experience by requiring first-time offenders to attend a Youth Offender Panel which devises a contractual individualized programme designed to address the causes of the offending behaviour and to move to reparation, rehabilitation and restoration. In the final chapter in this part, Loraine Gelsthorpe and Allison Morris consider the extent to which this 'new' paradigm of restorative justice can indeed be read as a reconfiguring of welfare or whether it is a reassertion of the primacy of individual responsibility. In particular, they compare the meaning of restoration in New Zealand's family group conferences with its adoption in an English climate of 'no more excuses'. Despite recognizing the multiple good intentions and practitioner enthusiasm that restorative justice can claim, its effect will be tenuous, they argue, when pursued alongside systems that are otherwise dominated by punitive values.

12

The triumph of benevolence: the origins of the juvenile justice system in the United States

Anthony Platt

[…]

TRADITIONAL PERSPECTIVES ON JUVENILE JUSTICE

The modern system of crime control in the United States has many roots in penal and judicial reforms at the end of the nineteenth century. Contemporary programs which we commonly associate with the 'war on poverty' and the 'great society' can be traced in numerous instances to the programs and ideas of nineteenth century reformers who helped to create and develop probation and parole, the juvenile court, strategies of crime prevention, the need for education and rehabilitative programs in institutions, the indeterminate sentence, the concept of 'half-way' houses, and 'cottage' systems of penal organization.

The creation of the juvenile court and its accompanying services is generally regarded by scholars as one of the most innovative and idealistic products of the age of reform. It typified the 'spirit of social justice,' and, according to the National Crime Commission, represented a progressive effort by concerned reformers to alleviate the miseries of urban life and to solve social problems by rational, enlightened and scientific methods.[1] The juvenile justice system was widely heralded as 'one of the greatest advances in child welfare that has ever occurred' and 'an integral part of total welfare planning.'[2] Charles Chute, an enthusiastic supporter of the child-saving movement, claimed that 'no single event has contributed more to the welfare of children and their families. It revolutionized the treatment of delinquent and neglected children and led to the passage of similar laws throughout the world.'[3] Scholars from a variety of disciplines, such as the American sociologist George Herbert Mead and the German

SOURCE: Originally published in R. Quinney (ed.) *Criminal Justice in America*, Boston, Little Brown & Co. 1974, pp. 356–89 (abridged).

psychiatrist August Aichhorn, agreed that the juvenile court system represented a triumph of progressive liberalism over the forces of reaction and ignorance.[4] More recently, the juvenile court and related reforms have been characterized as a 'reflection of the humanitarianism that flowered in the last decades of the 19th century'[5] and an indication of 'America's great sense of philanthropy and private concern about the common weal.'[6]

Histories and accounts of the child-saving movement tend either to represent an 'official' perspective or to imply a gradualist view of social progress.[7] This latter view is typified in Robert Pickett's study of the House of Refuge movement in New York in the middle of the last century:

> In the earlier era, it had taken a band of largely religiously motivated humanitarians to see a need and move to meet that need. Although much of their vision eventually would be supplanted by more enlightened policies and techniques and far more elaborate support mechanisms, the main outlines of their program, which included mild discipline, academic and moral education, vocational training, the utilization of surrogate parents, and probationary surveillance, have stood the test of time. The survival of many of the notions of the founders of the House of Refuge testifies, at least in part, to their creative genius in meeting human needs. Their motivations may have been mixed and their oversights many, but their efforts contributed to a considerable advance in the care and treatment of wayward youth.[8]

This view of the nineteenth century reform movement as fundamentally benevolent, humanitarian and gradualist is shared by most historians and criminologists who have written about the Progressive era. They argue that this reform impulse has its roots in the earliest ideals of modern liberalism and that it is part of a continuing struggle to overcome injustice and fulfill the promise of American life.[9] At the same time, these writers recognize that reform movements often degenerate into crusades and suffer from excessive idealism and moral absolutism.[10] The faults and limitations of the child-saving movement, for example, are generally explained in terms of the psychological tendency of its leaders to adopt attitudes of rigidity and moral righteousness. But this form of criticism is misleading because it overlooks larger political issues and depends too much on a subjective critique.

Although the Progressive era was a period of considerable change and reform in all areas of social, legal, political and economic life, its history has been garnished with various myths. Conventional historical analysis, typified by the work of American historians in the 1940s and 1950s, promoted the view that American history consisted of regular confrontations between vested economic interests and various popular reform movements.[11] For Arthur Schlesinger, Jr., 'liberalism in America has been ordinarily the movement of the other sections of society to restrain the power of the business community.'[12] Similarly, Louis Hartz characterizes 'liberal reform' as a 'movement which emerged toward the end of the nineteenth century to adapt classical liberalism to the purposes of small propertied interests and the labor class and at the same time which rejected socialism.'[13]

Conventional histories of progressivism argue that the reformers, who were for the most part drawn from the urban middle classes, were opposed to big business and felt victimized by the rapid changes in the economy, especially the emergence of the corporation as the dominant form of financial enterprise.[14] Their reform efforts were aimed at curbing the power of big business, eliminating corruption from the urban political machines, and extending the powers of the state through federal regulation of the economy and the development of a vision of 'social responsibility' in local government. They were joined in this mission by sectors of the working class who shared their alienation and many of their grievances. For liberal historians like Richard Hofstadter, this alliance represented part of a continuing theme in American politics:

> It has been the function of the liberal tradition in American politics, from the time of Jeffersonian democracy down through Populism, Progressivism, and the New Deal, at first to broaden the numbers of those who could benefit from the great American bonanza and then to humanize its workings and help heal its casualties. Without this sustained tradition of opposition and protest, and reform, the American system would have been, as in times and places it was, nothing but a jungle, and would probably have failed to develop into the remarkable system for production and distribution that it is.[15]

The political and racial crises of the 1960s, however, provoked a reevaluation of this earlier view of the liberal tradition in American politics, a tradition which appeared bankrupt in the face of rising crime rates, ghetto rebellions, and widespread protests against the state and its agencies of criminal justice. In the field of criminology, this re-evaluation took place in national commissions such as the Kerner Commission and President Johnson's Commission on Law Enforcement and the Administration of Justice. Johnson's Crime Commission, as it is known, included a lengthy and detailed analysis of the juvenile justice system and its ineffectiveness in dealing with juvenile delinquency.

The Crime Commission's view of the juvenile justice system is cautious and pragmatic, designed to 'shore up' institutional deficiencies and modernize the system's efficiency and accountability. Noting the rising rate of juvenile delinquency, increasing disrespect for constituted authority and the failure of reformatories to rehabilitate offenders, the Commission attributes the failures of the juvenile justice system to the 'grossly overoptimistic' expectations of nineteenth century reformers and the 'community's continuing unwillingness to provide the resources – the people and facilities and concern – necessary to permit [the juvenile courts] to realize their potential....'[16] This view of the *unrealistic* quality of American liberalism was observed earlier by Richard Hofstadter:

> My criticism ... is ... not that the Progressives most typically undermined or smashed standards, but that they set impossible standards, that they were victimized, in brief, by a form of moral absolutism.... A great part of both the strength and the weaknesses of our national existence lies in the fact that Americans do not abide very quietly the evils of life. We are forever restlessly pitting ourselves against them, demanding changes, improvements, remedies, but not often with sufficient sense of the limits that the human condition will in the end insistently impose upon us.[17]

Or as the Crime Commission stated it, 'failure is most striking when hopes are highest.'[18]

In the following pages we will argue that the above views and interpretations of juvenile justice are factually inaccurate and suffer from a serious misconception about the functions of modern liberalism. The prevailing myths about the juvenile justice system can be summarized as follows: (1) The child-saving movement in the late nineteenth century was successful in humanizing the criminal justice system, rescuing children from jails and prisons, developing humanitarian judicial and penal institutions for juveniles, and defending the poor against economic and political exploitation. (2) The child-savers were 'disinterested' reformers, representing an enlightened and socially responsible urban middle class, and opposed to big business. (3) The failures of the juvenile justice system are attributable partly to the over-optimism and moral absolutism of earlier reformers and partly to bureaucratic inefficiency and a lack of fiscal resources and trained personnel.

These myths are grounded in a liberal conception of American history which characterizes the child-savers as part of a much larger reform movement directed at restraining the power of political and business elites. In contrast, we will offer evidence that the child-saving movement was a coercive and conservatizing influence, that liberalism in the Progressive era was the conscious product of policies initiated or supported by leaders of major corporations and financial institutions, and that many social reformers wanted to secure existing political and economic arrangements, albeit in an ameliorated and regulated form.

THE CHILD-SAVING MOVEMENT

Although the modern juvenile justice system can be traced in part to the development of various charitable and institutional programs in the early nineteenth century,[19] it was not until the close of the century that the modern system was systematically organized to include juvenile courts, probation, child guidance clinics, truant officers, and reformatories. The child-saving movement – an amalgam of philanthropists, middle-class reformers and professionals – was responsible for the consolidation of these reforms.[20]

The 1890s represented for many middle-class intellectuals and professionals a period of discovery of 'dim attics and damp cellars in poverty-stricken sections of populous towns' and 'innumerable haunts of misery throughout the land.'[21] The city was suddenly discovered to be a place of scarcity, disease, neglect, ignorance, and 'dangerous influences.' Its slums were the 'last resorts of the penniless and the criminal'; here humanity reached the lowest level of degradation and despair.[22] These conditions were not new to American urban life and the working class had been suffering such hardships for many years. Since the Haymarket Riot of 1886, the centers of industrial activity had been continually plagued by strikes, violent disruptions, and widespread business failures.

What distinguished the late 1890s from earlier periods was the recognition by some sectors of the privileged classes that far-reaching economic, political and social reforms were desperately needed to restore order and stability. In the economy, these reforms were achieved through the corporation which extended its influence into all aspects of domestic and foreign policies so that by the 1940s some 139 corporations owned 45 per cent of all the manufacturing assets in the country. It was the aim of corporate capitalists to limit traditional laissez-faire business competition and to transform the economy into a rational and interrelated system, characterized by extensive long-range planning and bureaucratic routine.[23] In politics, these reforms were achieved nationally by extending the regulatory powers of the federal government and locally by the development of commission and city manager forms of government as an antidote to corrupt machine politics. In social life, economic and political reforms were paralleled by the construction of new social service bureaucracies which regulated crime, education, health, labor and welfare.

The child-saving movement tried to do for the criminal justice system what industrialists and corporate leaders were trying to do for the economy – that is, achieve order, stability and control while preserving the existing class system and distribution of wealth. While the child-saving movement, like most Progressive reforms, drew its most active and visible supporters from the middle class and professions, it would not have been capable of achieving significant reforms without the financial and political support of the wealthy and powerful. Such support was not without precedent in various philanthropic movements preceding the child-savers. New York's Society for the Reformation of Juvenile Delinquents benefited in the 1820s from the contributions of Stephen Allen, whose many influential positions included Mayor of New York and president of the New York Life Insurance and Trust Company.[24] The first large gift to the New York Children's Aid Society, founded in 1853, was donated by Mrs William Astor.[25] According to Charles Loring Brace, who helped to found the Children's Aid Society, 'a very superior class of young men consented to serve on our Board of Trustees; men who, in their high principles of duty, and in the obligations which they feel are imposed by wealth and position, bid fair hereafter to make the name of New York merchants respected as it was never before throughout the country.[26] Elsewhere, welfare charities similarly benefited from the donations and wills of the upper class.[27] Girard College, one of the first large orphanages in the United States, was built and furnished with funds from the banking fortune of Stephen Girard,[28] and the Catholic bankers and financiers of New York helped to mobilize support and money for various Catholic charities.[29]

The child-saving movement similarly enjoyed the support of propertied and powerful individuals. In Chicago, for example, where the movement had some of its most notable successes, the child-savers included Louise Bowen and Ellen Henrotin who were both married to bankers;[30] Mrs. Potter Palmer, whose husband owned vast amounts of land and property, was an ardent child-saver when not involved in the exclusive Fortnightly Club, the elite Chicago Women's Club or the Board of Lady Managers of the World's Fair;[31] another child-saver in Chicago, Mrs Perry Smith, was married to the vice-president of the Chicago and Northwestern Railroad. Even the more radically-minded child-savers came from upper-class backgrounds. The fathers of Jane Addams and Julia Lathrop, for example, were both lawyers and Republican senators in the Illinois legislature. Jane Addams' father was one of the richest men in northern Illinois, and her stepbrother, Harry Haldeman, was a socialite from Baltimore who later amassed a large fortune in Kansas City.[32]

The child-saving movement was not simply a humanistic enterprise on behalf of the lower classes against the established order. On the contrary, its impetus came primarily from the middle and upper classes who were instrumental in devising new forms of social control to protect their privileged positions in American society. The child-saving movement was not an isolated phenomenon but rather reflected massive changes in productive relationships, from laissez-faire to monopoly capitalism, and in strategies of social control, from inefficient repression to welfare state benevolence.[33] This reconstruction of economic and social institutions, which was not achieved without conflict within the ruling class, represented a victory for the more 'enlightened' wing of corporate leaders who advocated strategic alliances with urban reformers and support of liberal reforms.[34]

Many large corporations and business leaders, for example, supported federal regulation of the economy in order to protect their own investments and stabilize the marketplace. Business leaders and political spokesmen were often in basic agreement about fundamental economic issues. 'There was no conspiracy during the Progressive Era,' notes Gabriel Kólko. 'There was basic agreement among political and business leaders as to what was the public good, and no one had to be cajoled in a sinister manner.'[35] In his analysis of liberal ideology in the Progressive era, James Weinstein similarly argues that 'few reforms were enacted without the tacit approval, if not the guidance, of the large corporate interests.' For the corporation executives, liberalism meant 'the responsibility of all classes to maintain and increase the efficiency of the existing social order.'[36]

Progressivism was in part a businessmen's movement and big business played a central role in the Progressive coalition's support of welfare reforms. Child labor legislation in New York, for example, was supported by several groups, including upper-class industrialists who did not depend on cheap child labor. According to Jeremy Felt's history of that movement, 'the abolition of child labor could be viewed as a means of driving out marginal manufacturers and tenement operators, hence increasing the consolidation and efficiency of business.'[37] The rise of compulsory education, another welfare state reform, was also closely tied to the changing forms of industrial production and social control. Charles Loring Brace, writing in the mid-nineteenth century, anticipated the use of education as preparation for industrial discipline when, 'in the interests of public order, of liberty, of property, for the sake of our own safety and the endurance of free institutions here,' he advocated 'a strict and careful law, which shall compel every minor to learn to read and write, under severe penalties in case of disobedience.'[38] By the end of the century, the working class had had imposed upon them a sterile and authoritarian educational system which mirrored the ethos of the corporate workplace and was designed to provide 'an increasingly refined training and selection mechanism for the labor force.'[39]

While the child-saving movement was supported and financed by corporate liberals, the day-to-day work of lobbying, public education and organizing was undertaken by middle-class urban reformers, professionals and special interest groups. The more moderate and conservative sectors of the feminist movement were especially active in anti-delinquency reforms.[40] Their successful participation derived in part from public stereotypes of women as the 'natural caretakers' of 'wayward children.' Women's claim to the public care of children had precedent during the nineteenth century and their role in child rearing was paramount. Women, generally regarded as better teachers than men, were more influential in child-training and discipline at home. The fact that public education also came more under the direction of women teachers in the schools served to legitimize the predominance of women in other areas of 'child-saving.'[41]

The child-saving movement attracted women from a variety of political and class backgrounds, though it was dominated by the daughters of the old landed gentry and wives of the upper-class nouveau riche. Career women and society philanthropists, elite women's clubs and settlement houses, and political and civic organizations worked together on the problems of child care, education and juvenile delinquency. Professional and political women's groups regarded child-saving as a problem of women's rights, whereas their opponents seized upon it as an opportunity to keep women in their 'proper place.' Child-saving became a reputable task for any woman who wanted to extend her 'housekeeping' functions into the community without denying anti-feminist stereotypes of woman's nature and place.[42]

For traditionally educated women and daughters of the landed and industrial genty, the child-saving movement presented an opportunity for pursuing socially acceptable public roles and for restoring some of the authority and spiritual influence which many women felt they had lost through the urbanization of family life. Their traditional functions were dramatically threatened by the weakening of domestic roles and the specialized rearrangement of the family.[43] The child-savers were aware that their championship of social outsiders such as immigrants, the poor and children, was not wholly motivated by disinterested ideals of justice and equality. Philanthropic work filled a void in their own lives, a void which was created in part by the decline of traditional religion, increased leisure and boredom, the rise of public education, and the breakdown of communal life in large, crowded cities. 'By simplifying dress and amusements, by cutting off a little here and there from our luxuries,' wrote one child-saver, 'we may change the whole current of many human lives.'[44] Women were exhorted to make their lives useful by participating in welfare programs, by volunteering their time and services, and by getting acquainted with less privileged groups. They were also encouraged to seek work in institutions which were 'like family-life with its many-sided development and varied interests and occupations, and where the woman-element shall pervade the house and soften its social atmosphere with motherly tenderness.'[45]

While the child-saving movement can be partly understood as a 'symbolic crusade'[46] which served ceremonial and status functions for many women, it was by no means a reactionary and romantic movement, nor was it supported only by women and members of the old gentry. Child-saving also had considerable instrumental significance for legitimizing new career openings for women. The new role of social worker combined elements of an old and partly fictitious role – defender of family life – and elements of a new role – social servant. Social work and professional child-saving provided new opportunities for career-minded women who found the traditional professions dominated and controlled by men.[47] These child-savers were members of the emerging bourgeoisie created by the new industrial order.

It is not surprising that the professions also supported the child-saving movement, for they were capable of reaping enormous economic and status rewards from the changes taking place. The clergy had nothing to lose (but more of their rapidly declining constituency) and everything to gain by incorporating social services into traditional religion. Lawyers were needed for their technical expertise and to administer new institutions. And academics discovered a new market which paid them as consultants, elevated them to positions of national prestige and furnished endless materials for books, articles and conferences. As Richard Hofstadter has noted:

> The development of regulative and humane legislation required the skills of lawyers and economists, sociologists and political scientists, in the writing of laws and in the staffing of administrative and regulative bodies. Controversy over such issues created a new market for the books and magazine articles of the experts and engendered a new respect for their specialized knowledge. Reform brought with it the brain trust.[48]

While the rank and file reformers in the child-saving movement worked closely with corporate liberals, it would be inaccurate to simply characterize them as lackeys of big business. Many were principled and genuinely concerned about alleviating human misery and improving the lives of the poor. Moreover, many women who participated in the movement were able to free themselves from male domination and participate more fully in society. But for the most part, the child-savers and other Progressive reformers defended capitalism and rejected socialist alternatives. Most reformers accepted the structure of the new industrial order and sought to moderate its cruder inequities and reduce inharmonies in the existing system.[49] Though many child-savers were 'socialists of the heart' and ardent critics of society, their programs were typically reformist and did not alter basic economic inequalities.[50] Rhetoric and righteous indignation were more prevalent than programs of radical action.

The intellectual and professional communities did little to criticize Progressive reforms, partly because so many benefited from their new role as government consultants and experts, and partly because their conception of social change was limited and elitist. As Jackson Wilson observed, many intellectuals in the Progressive movement were 'interested in creating a system of government which would allow the people to rule only at a carefully kept distance and at infrequent intervals, reserving most real power and planning to a corps of experts and professionals.'[51] Those few reformers who had a genuine concern for liberating the lives of the poor by considering socialist alternatives were either coopted by their allies, betrayed by their own class interests, or became the prisoners of social and economic forces beyond their control.[52]

IMAGES OF CRIME AND DELINQUENCY

The child-saving reformers were part of a much larger movement to readjust institutions to conform to the requirements of corporate capitalism and the modern welfare state. As the country emerged from the depressions and industrial violence of the late nineteenth century, efforts were made to rescue and regulate capitalism through developing a new political economy, designed to stabilize production and profits. The stability and smooth functioning of this new order depended heavily on the capacity of welfare state institutions, especially the schools, to achieve cultural hegemony and guarantee loyalty to the State. As William Appleman Williams has commented, 'it is almost impossible to overemphasize the importance of the very general – yet dynamic and powerful – concept that the country faced a fateful choice between order and chaos.'[53] In order to develop support for and legitimize the corporate liberal State, a new ideology was promoted in which chaos was equated with crime and violence, and salvation was to be found in the development of new and more extensive forms of social control.

The child-savers viewed the 'criminal classes' with a mixture of contempt and benevolence. Crime was portrayed as rising from the 'lowest orders' and threatening to engulf 'respectable' society like a virulent disease. Charles Loring Brace, a leading child-saver, typified popular and professional views about crime and delinquency:

> As Christian men, we cannot look upon this great multitude of unhappy, deserted, and degraded boys and girls without feeling our responsibility to God for them. The class increases: immigration is pouring in its multitudes of poor foreigners who leave these young outcasts everywhere in our midst. These boys and girls ... will soon form the great lower class of our city. They will influence elections; they may shape the policy of the city; they will assuredly, if unreclaimed, poison society all around them. They will help to form the great multitude of robbers, thieves, and vagrants, who are now such a burden upon the law-respecting community....[54]

This attitude of contempt derived from a view of criminals as less-than-human, a perspective which was strongly influenced and aggravated by nativist and racist ideologies.[55] The 'criminal class' was variously described as 'creatures' living in 'burrows,' 'dens,' and 'slime'; as 'little Arabs' and 'foreign childhood that floats along the streets and docks of the city – vagabondish, thievish, familiar with the vicious ways and places of the town';[56] and as 'ignorant,' 'shiftless,' 'indolent,' and 'dissipated.'[57]

The child-savers were alarmed and frightened by the 'dangerous classes' whose 'very number makes one stand aghast,' noted the urban reformer Jacob Riis.[58] Law and order were widely demanded:

> The 'dangerous classes' of New York are mainly American-born, but the children of Irish and German immigrants. They are as ignorant as London flashmen or costermongers. They are far more brutal than the peasantry from whom they descend, and they are much banded together, in associations, such as 'Dead Rabbit,' 'Plug-ugly,' and various target companies. They are our *enfant perdus*, grown up to young manhood.... They are ready for any offense or crime, however degraded or bloody.... Let but Law lift its hand from them for a season, or let the civilizing influences of American life fail to reach them, and, if the opportunity offered, we should see an explosion from this class which might leave this city in ashes and blood.[59]

These views derived considerable legitimacy from prevailing theories of social and reform Darwinism which, *inter alia,* proposed that criminals were a dangerous and atavistic class, standing outside the boundaries of morally regulated relationships. Herbert Spencer's writings had a major impact on American intellectuals and Cesare Lombroso, perhaps the most significant figure in nineteenth century criminology, looked for recognition in the United States when he felt that his experiments on the 'criminal type' had been neglected in Europe.[60]

Although Lombroso's theoretical and experimental studies were not translated into English until 1911, his findings were known by American academics in the early 1890s, and their popularity, like that of Spencer's works, was based on the fact that they confirmed widely-held stereotypes about the biological basis and inferior character of a 'criminal class.' A typical view was expressed by Nathan Allen in 1878 at the National Conference of Charities and Correction: 'If our object is to prevent crime in a large scale, we must direct attention to its main sources – to the materials that make criminals; the springs must be dried up; the supplies must be cut off.'[61] This was to be achieved, if necessary, by birth control and eugenics. Similar views were expressed by Hamilton Wey, an influential physician at Elmira Reformatory, who argued before the National Prison Association in 1881 that criminals had to be treated as a 'distinct type of human species.'[62]

Literature on 'social degradation' was extremely popular during the 1870s and 1880s, though most such 'studies' were little more than crude and racist polemics, padded with moralistic epithets and preconceived value judgements. Richard Dugdale's series of papers on the Jukes family, which became a model for the case-study approach to social problems, was distorted almost beyond recognition by anti-intellectual supporters of hereditary theories of crime.[63] Confronted by the evidence of Darwin, Galton, Dugdale, Caldwell and many other disciples of the biological image of behavior, many child-savers were compelled to admit that 'a large proportion of the unfortunate children that go to make up the great army of criminals are not born right.'[64] Reformers adopted and modified the rhetoric of social Darwinism in order to emphasize the urgent need for confronting the 'crime problem' before it got completely out of hand. A popular proposal, for example, was the 'methodized registration and training' of potential criminals, 'or these failing, their early and entire withdrawal from the community.'[65]

Although some child-savers advocated drastic methods of crime control – including birth control through sterilization, cruel punishments, and life-long incarceration – more moderate views prevailed. This victory for moderation was related to the recognition by many Progressive reformers that short-range repression was counter-productive as well as cruel and that long-range planning and amelioration were required to achieve economic and political stability. The rise of more benevolent strategies of social control occurred at about the same time that influential capitalists were realizing that existing economic arrangements could not be successfully main-tained only through the use of private police and government troops.[66] While the child-savers justified their reforms as humanitarian, it is clear that this humanitarian-ism reflected their class background and elitist conceptions of human potentiality. The child-savers shared the view of more conservative professionals that 'criminals' were a distinct and dangerous class, indigenous to working-class culture, and a threat to 'civilized' society. They differed mainly in the procedures by which the 'criminal class' should be controlled or neutralized.

Gradually, a more 'enlightened' view about strategies of control prevailed among the leading representatives of professional associations. Correctional workers, for example, did not want to think of themselves merely as the custodians of a pariah class. The self-image of penal reformers as 'doctors' rather than 'guards,' and the medical domination of criminological research in the United States at that time facili-tated the acceptance of 'therapeutic' strategies in prisons and reformatories.[67] Physicians gradually provided the official rhetoric of penal reform, replacing cruder concepts of social Darwinism with a new optimism. Admittedly, the criminal was 'pathological' and 'diseased,' but medical science offered the possibility of miraculous cures. Although there was a popular belief in the existence of a 'criminal class' sepa-rated from the rest of humanity by a 'vague boundary line,' there was no good reason why this class could not be identified, diagnosed, segregated, changed and incorporated back into society.[68]

By the late 1890s, most child-savers agreed that hereditary theories of crime were overfatalistic. The superintendent of the Kentucky Industrial School of Reform, for example, told delegates to a national conference on corrections that heredity is 'unjus-tifiably made a bugaboo to discourage efforts at rescue. We know that physical here-dity tendencies can be neutralized and often nullified by proper counteracting precautions.'[69] E.R.L. Gould, a sociologist at the University of Chicago, similarly criti-cized biological theories of crime as unconvincing and sentimental. 'Is it not better,' he said, 'to postulate freedom of choice than to preach the doctrine of the unfettered will, and so elevate criminality into a propitiary sacrifice?'[70]

Charles Cooley, writing in 1896, was one of the first American sociologists to observe that criminal behavior depended as much upon social and economic circum-stances as it did upon the inheritance of biological traits. 'The criminal class,' he observed, 'is largely the result of society's bad workmanship upon fairly good material.' In support of this argument, he noted that there was a 'large and fairly trustworthy body of evidence' to suggest that many 'degenerates' could be converted into 'useful citizens by rational treatment.'[71]

Although there was a wide difference of opinion among experts as to the precipitating causes of crime, it was generally agreed that criminals were abnormally conditioned by a multitude of biological and environmental forces, some of which were permanent and irreversible. Strictly biological theories of crime were modified to incorporate a developmental view of human behavior. If, as it was believed, criminals are conditioned by biological heritage and brutish living conditions, then prophylactic measures must be taken early in life. 'We must get hold of the little waifs that grow up to form the criminal element just as early in life as possible,' exhorted an influential child-saver. 'Hunt up the children of poverty, of crime, and of brutality, just as soon as they can be reached.'[72] Efforts were needed to reach the criminals of future generations. 'They are born to crime,' wrote the penologist Enoch Wines, 'brought up for it. They must be saved.'[73] New institutions and new programs were required to meet this challenge.

JUVENILE COURT AND THE REFORMATORY SYSTEM

The essential preoccupation of the child-saving movement was the recognition and control of youthful deviance. It brought attention to, and thus 'invented', new categories of youthful misbehavior which had been hitherto unappreciated. The efforts of the child-savers were institutionally expressed in the juvenile court which, despite recent legislative and constitutional reforms, is generally acknowledged as their most significant contribution to progressive penology. There is some dispute about which state first created a special tribunal for children. Massachusetts and New York passed laws, in 1874 and 1892 respectively, providing for the trials of minors apart from adults charged with crimes. Ben Lindsey, a renowned judge and reformer, also claimed this distinction for Colorado where a juvenile court was, in effect, established through an educational law of 1899. However, most authorities agree that the Juvenile Court Act, passed by the Illinois legislature in the same year, was the first official enactment to be recognized as a model statute by other states and countries.[74] By 1917, juvenile court legislation had been passed in all but three states and by 1932 there were over 600 independent juvenile courts throughout the United States.[75]

The juvenile court system was part of a general movement directed towards developing a specialized labor market and industrial discipline under corporate capitalism by creating new programs of adjudication and control for 'delinquent,' 'dependent' and 'neglected' youth. This in turn was related to augmenting the family and enforcing compulsory education in order to guarantee the proper reproduction of the labor force. For example, underlying the juvenile court system was the concept of *parens patriae* by which the courts were authorized to handle with wide discretion the problems of 'its least fortunate junior citizens.'[76] The administration of juvenile justice, which differed in many important respects from the criminal court system, was delegated extensive powers of control over youth. A child was not accused of a crime but offered assistance and guidance; intervention in the lives of 'delinquents' was not supposed to carry the stigma of criminal guilt. Judicial records were not generally available to the press or public, and juvenile hearings were typically conducted in private. Court procedures were informal and inquisitorial, not requiring the presence of a defense attorney. Specific criminal safeguards of due process were not applicable because juvenile proceedings were defined by statute as civil in character.[77]

The judges of the new court were empowered to investigate the character and social background of 'predelinquent' as well as delinquent children; they concerned themselves with motivation rather than intent, seeking to identify the moral reputation of problematic children. The requirements of preventive penology and child-saving further justified the court's intervention in cases where no offense had actually been committed, but where, for example, a child was posing problems for some person in authority, such as a parent or teacher or social worker.

The role model for juvenile court judges was doctor-counselor rather than lawyer. 'Judicial therapists' were expected to establish a one-to-one relationship with 'delinquents' in the same way that a country doctor might give his time and attention to a favorite patient. Juvenile courtrooms were often arranged like a clinic and the vocabulary of its participants was largely composed of medical metaphors. 'We do not know the child without a thorough examination,' wrote Judge Julian Mack. 'We must reach into the soul-life of the child.'[78] Another judge from Los Angeles suggested that the juvenile court should be a 'laboratory of human behavior' and its judges trained as 'specialists in the art of human relations.' It was the judge's task to 'get the whole truth about a child' in the same way that a 'physician searches for every detail that bears on the condition of the patient.'[79] Similarly, the judges of the Boston juvenile court liked to think of themselves as 'physicians in a dispensary.'[80]

The unique character of the child-saving movement was its concerns for pre-delinquent offenders – 'children who occupy the debatable ground between criminality and innocence' – and its claim that it could transform potential criminals into respectable citizens by training them in 'habits of industry, self-control and obedience to law.'[81] This policy justified the diminishing of traditional procedures and allowed police, judges, probation officers and truant officers to work together without legal hindrance. If children were to be rescued, it was important that the rescuers be free to pursue their mission without the interference of defense lawyers and due process. Delinquents had to be saved, transformed and reconstituted. 'There is no essential difference,' noted a prominent child-saver, 'between a criminal and any other sinner. The means and methods of restoration are the same for both.'[82]

The juvenile court legislation enabled the state to investigate and control a wide variety of behaviors. As Joel Handler has observed, 'the critical philosophical position of the reform movement was that no formal, legal distinctions should be made between the delinquent and the dependent or neglected.'[83] Statutory definitions of 'delinquency' encompassed (1) acts that would be criminal if committed by adults; (2) acts that violated county, town, or municipal ordinances; and (3) violations of vaguely worded catch-alls – such as 'vicious or immoral behavior,' 'incorrigibility,' and 'truancy' – which 'seem to express the notion that the adolescent, if allowed to continue, will engage in more serious conduct.'[84]

The juvenile court movement went far beyond a concern for special treatment of adolescent offenders. It brought within the ambit of governmental control a set of youthful activities that had been previously ignored or dealt with on an informal basis. It was not by accident that the behavior subject to penalties – drinking, sexual 'license,' roaming the streets, begging, frequenting dance halls and movies, fighting, and being seen in public late at night – was especially characteristic of the children of working-class and immigrant families. Once arrested and adjudicated, these 'delinquents' became wards of the court and eligible for salvation.

It was through the reformatory system that the child-savers hoped to demonstrate that delinquents were capable of being converted into law-abiding citizens. Though the reformatory was initially developed in the United States during the middle of the nineteenth century as a special form of prison discipline for adolescents and young adults, its underlying principles were formulated in Britain by Matthew Davenport Hill, Alexander Maconochie, Walter Crofton and Mary Carpenter. If the United States did not have any great penal theorists, it at least had energetic administrators – like Enoch Wines, Zebulon Brockway and Frank Sanborn – who were prepared to experiment with new programs.

The reformatory was distinguished from the traditional penitentiary in several ways: it adopted a policy of indeterminate sentencing; it emphasized the importance of a countryside location; and it typically was organized on the 'cottage' plan as opposed to the traditional congregate housing found in penitentiaries. The ultimate aim of the reformatory was reformation of the criminal, which could only be achieved 'by placing the prisoner's fate, as far as possible, in his own hand, by enabling him, through industry and good conduct to raise himself, step by step, to a position of less restraint....'[85]

Based on a crude theory of rewards and punishments, the 'new penology' set itself the task of re-socializing the 'dangerous classes.' The typical resident of a reformatory, according to one child-saver, had been 'cradled in infamy, imbibing with its earliest natural nourishment the germs of a depraved appetite, and reared in the midst of people whose lives are an atrocious crime against natural and divine law and the rights of society.' In order to correct and reform such a person, the reformatory plan was designed to teach the value of adjustment, private enterprise, thrift and self-reliance. 'To make a good boy out of this bundle of perversities, his entire being must be revolutionized. He must be taught self-control, industry, respect for himself and the rights of others.'[86] The real test of reformation in a delinquent, as William Letchworth told the National Conference of Charities and Correction in 1886, was his uncomplaining adjustment to his former environment. 'If he is truly reformed in the midst of adverse influences,' said Letchworth, 'he gains that moral strength which makes his reform permanent.'[87] Moreover, reformed delinquents were given every opportunity to rise 'far above the class from which they sprang,' especially if they were 'patient' and 'self-denying.'[88]

Reformation of delinquents was to be achieved in a number of different ways. The trend from congregate housing to group living represented a significant change in the organization of penal institutions. The 'cottage' plan was designed to provide more intensive supervision and to reproduce, symbolically at least, an atmosphere of family life conducive to the re-socialization of youth. The 'new penology' also urged the benefits of a rural location, partly in order to teach agricultural skills, but mainly in order to guarantee a totally controlled environment. This was justified by appealing to the romantic theory that corrupt delinquents would be spiritually regenerated by their contact with unspoiled nature.[89]

Education was stressed as the main form of industrial and moral training in reformatories. According to Michael Katz, in his study on nineteenth-century education, the reformatory provided 'the first form of compulsory schooling in the United States.'[90] The prominence of education as a technique of reform reflected the widespread emphasis on socialization and assimilation instead of cruder methods of social control. But as Georg Rusche and Otto Kirchheimer observed in their study of the relationship between economic and penal policies, the rise of 'rehabilitative' and educational programs was 'largely the result of opposition on the part of free workers,' for 'wherever working-class organizations were powerful enough to influence state politics, they succeeded in obtaining complete abolition of all forms of prison labor (Pennsylvania in 1897, for example), causing much suffering to the prisoners, or at least in obtaining very considerable limitations, such as work without modern machinery, conventional rather than modern types of prison industry, or work for the government instead of for the free market.'[91]

Although the reformatory system, as envisioned by urban reformers, suffered in practice from overcrowding, mismanagement, inadequate financing and staff hiring problems, its basic ideology was still tough-minded and uncompromising. As the American Friends Service Committee noted, 'if the reformers were naive, the managers of the correctional establishment were not. Under the leadership of Zebulon R. Brockway of the Elmira Reformatory, by the latter part of the nineteenth century they had co-opted the reformers and consolidated their leadership and control of indeterminate sentence reform.'[92] The child-savers were not averse to using corporal punishment and other severe disciplinary measures when inmates were recalcitrant. Brockway, for example, regarded his task as 'socialization of the anti-social by scientific training while under completest governmental control.'[93] To achieve this goal, Brockway's reformatory became 'like a garrison of a thousand prisoner soldiers' and 'every incipient disintegration was promptly checked and disinclination of individual prisoners to conform was overcome.'[94] Child-saving was a job for resolute professionals who realized that 'sickly sentimentalism' had no place in their work.[95]

'Criminals shall either be cured,' Brockway told the National Prison Congress in 1870, 'or kept under such continued restraint as gives guarantee of safety from further depredations.'[96] Restraint and discipline were an integral part of the 'treatment' program and not merely expediencies of administration. Military drill, 'training of the will,' and long hours of tedious labor were the essence of the reformatory system and the indeterminate sentencing policy guaranteed its smooth operation. 'Nothing can tend more certainly to secure the most hardened and desperate criminals than the present system of short sentences,' wrote the reformer Bradford Kinney Peirce in 1869.[97] Several years later, Enoch Wines was able to report that 'the sentences of young offenders are wisely regulated for their amendment; they are not absurdly shortened as if they signified only so much endurance of vindictive suffering.'[98]

Since the child-savers professed to be seeking the 'best interests' of their 'wards' on the basis of corporate liberal values, there was no need to formulate legal regulation of the right and duty to 'treat' in the same way that the right and duty to punish had been previously regulated. The adversary system, therefore, ceased to exist for youth, even as a legal fiction.[99] The myth of the child-saving movement as a humanitarian enterprise is based partly on a superficial interpretation of the child-savers' rhetoric of rehabilitation and partly on a misconception of how the child-savers viewed punishment. While it is true that the child-savers advocated minimal use of corporal punishment, considerable evidence suggests that this recommendation was based on managerial rather than moral considerations. William Letchworth reported that 'corporal punishment is rarely inflicted' at the State Industrial School in Rochester because 'most of the boys consider the lowering of their standing the severest punishment that is inflicted.'[100] Mrs. Glendower Evans, commenting on the decline of whippings at a reform school in Massachusetts, concluded that 'when boys do not feel themselves imprisoned and are treated as responsible moral agents, they can be trusted with their freedom to a surprising degree.'[101] Officials at another state industrial school for girls also reported that 'hysterics and fits of screaming and of noisy disobedience, have of late years become unknown....'[102]

The decline in the use of corporal punishment was due to the fact that indeterminate sentencing, the 'mark' or 'stage' system of rewards and punishments, and other techniques of 'organized persuasion' were far more effective in maintaining order and compliance than cruder methods of control. The chief virtue of the 'stage' system, a graduated system of punishments and privileges, was its capacity to keep prisoners disciplined and submissive.[103] The child-savers had learned from industrialists that persuasive benevolence backed up by force was a far more effective device of social control than arbitrary displays of terrorism. Like an earlier generation of penal reformers in France and Italy, the child-savers stressed the efficacy of new and indirect forms of social control as a 'practical measure of defense against social revolution as well as against individual acts.'[104]

Although the child-saving movement had far-reaching consequences for the organization and administration of the juvenile justice system, its overall impact was conservative in both spirit and achievement. The child-savers' reforms were generally aimed at imposing sanctions on conduct unbecoming 'youth' and disqualifying youth from the benefit of adult privileges. The child-savers were prohibitionists, in a general sense, who believed that social progress depended on efficient law enforcement, strict supervision of children's leisure and recreation, and enforced education. They were primarily concerned with regulating social behavior, eliminating 'foreign' and radical ideologies, and preparing youth as a disciplined and devoted work force. The austerity of the criminal law and penal institutions was only of incidental concern; their central interest was in the normative outlook of youth and they were most successful in their efforts to extend governmental control over a whole range of youthful activities which had previously been handled locally and informally. In this sense, their reforms were aimed at defining, rationalizing and regulating the dependent status of youth.[105] Although the child-savers' attitudes to youth were often paternalistic and romantic, their commands were backed up by force and an abiding faith in the benevolence of government.

The child-saving movement had its most direct impact on the children of the urban poor. The fact that 'troublesome' adolescents were depicted as 'sick' or 'pathological,' imprisoned 'for their own good,' addressed in paternalistic vocabulary, and exempted from criminal law processes, did not alter the subjective experiences of control, restraint and punishment. It is ironic, as Philippe Ariès observed in his historical study of European family life, that the obsessive solicitude of family, church, moralists and administrators for child welfare served to deprive children of the freedoms which they had previously shared with adults and to deny their capacity for initiative, responsibility and autonomy.[106]

The child-savers' rhetoric of benevolence should not be mistaken for popular, democratic programs. Paternalism was a typical ingredient of most reforms in the Progressive era, legitimizing imperialism in foreign policy and extensive state control at home. Even the corporate rich, according to William Appleman Williams, 'revealed a strikingly firm conception of a benevolent feudal approach to the firm and its workers' and 'were willing to extend – to provide in the manner of traditional beneficence – such things as new housing, old age pensions, death payments, wage and job schedules, and bureaus charged with responsibility for welfare, safety, and sanitation.'[107] But when benevolence failed – in domestic institutions such as schools and courts or in economic policies abroad – government officials and industrial leaders were quick to resort to massive and overwhelming force.[108]

This is not to suggest that the child-savers and other Progressive movements did not achieve significant reforms. They did in fact create major changes. In the arena of criminal justice they were responsible for developing important new institutions which transformed the character of the administration of juvenile justice. But these reforms, to use André Gorz's distinctions, were 'reformist' rather than 'structural':

> [S]tructural reform ... does not mean a reform which rationalizes the existing system while leaving intact the existing distribution of powers; this does not mean to delegate to the (capitalist) State the task of improving the system. Structural reform is by definition a reform implemented or controlled by those who demand it. Be it in agriculture, the university, property relations, the region, the administration, the economy, etc., a structural reform *always* requires the creation of new centers of democratic power. Whether it be at the level of companies, schools, municipalities, regions, or of the national Plan, etc., structural reform always requires a *decentralization* of the decision making power, a *restriction on the powers of State or Capital,* an *extension of popular power,* that is to say, a victory of democracy over the dictatorship of profit.

By this definition, then, the child-saving movement was a 'reformist reform.' It was not controlled by those whom it was supposed to benefit; it did not create new centers of democratic power; it extended and consolidated the powers of the state; and it helped to preserve existing economic and political relationships.

[...]

NOTES AND REFERENCES

1 See, for example, The President's Commission on Law Enforcement and Administration of Justice, *Juvenile Delinquency and Youth Crime* (Washington D.C.: U.S. Government Priniting Office, 1967), pp. 2–4.
2 Charles L. Chute, 'The Juvenile Court in Retrospect,' 13 *Federal Probation* (September, 1949), p. 7; Harrison A. Dobbs, 'In Defense of Juvenile Court,' *Ibid.,* p. 29.
3 Charles L. Chute, 'Fifty Years of the Juvenile Court,' *National Probation and Parole Association Yearbook* (1949), p. 1.
4 George H. Mead, 'The Psychology of Punitive Justice,' 23 *American Journal of Sociology* (March, 1918), pp. 577–602; August Aichhorn, 'The Juvenile Court: Is It a Solution?', in *Delinquency and Child Guidance: Selected Papers* (New York: International Universities Press, 1964), pp. 55–79.
5 Murray Levine and Adeline Levine, *A Social History of Helping Services: Clinic, Court, School, and Community* (New York: Appleton-Century-Crofts, 1970), p. 156.

6 Gerhard O.W. Mueller, *History of American Criminal Law Scholarship* (New York: Walter E. Meyer Research Institute of Law, 1962), p. 113.

7 See, for example, Herbert H. Lou, *Juvenile Courts in the United States* (Chapel Hill: University of North Carolina Press, 1927); Negley K. Teeters and John Otto Reinmann, *The Challenge of Delinquency* (New York: Prentice-Hall, 1950); and Ola Nyquist, *Juvenile Justice* (London: Macmillan, 1960).

8 Robert S. Pickett, *House of Refuge: Origins of Juvenile Reform in New York State, 1815–1857* (Syracuse: Syracuse University Press, 1969), p. 188.

9 See, for example, Arthur M. Schlesinger, *The American as Reformer* (Cambridge: Harvard University Press, 1950).

10 See, for example, Richard Hofstadter, *The Age of Reform* (New York: Vintage Books, 1955) and Joseph R. Gusfield, *Symbolic Crusade: Status Politics and the American Temperance Movement* (Urbana: University of Illinois Press, 1963).

11 R. Jackson Wilson (ed.) *Reform, Crisis, and Confusion, 1900–1929* (New York: Random House, 1970), especially pp. 3–6.

12 Arthur M. Schlesinger, Jr., *The Age of Jackson* (Boston: Little, Brown, 1946), p. 505.

13 Louis Hartz, *The Liberal Tradition in America* (New York: Harcourt, Brace & World, 1955), p. 228.

14 Hofstadter, *op. cit.,* Chapter IV.

15 *Ibid.,* p. 18.

16 The President's Commission on Law Enforcement and Administration of Justice, *op. cit.,* pp. 7, 8.

17 Hofstadter, *op. cit.,* p. 16.

18 The President's Commission on Law Enforcement and Administration of Justice, *op. cit.,* p. 7.

19 For discussions of earlier reform movements, see Pickett, *loc. cit.* and Sanford J. Fox, 'Juvenile Justice Reform: An Historical Perspective,' 22 *Stanford Law Review* (June, 1970), pp. 1187–239.

20 The child-saving movement was broad and diverse, including reformers interested in child welfare, education, reformatories, labor and other related issues. This paper is limited primarily to child-savers involved in anti-delinquency reforms and should not be interpreted as characterizing the child-saving movement in general.

21 William P. Letchworth, 'Children of the State,' National Conference of Charities and Correction, *Proceedings* (St Paul, Minnesota, 1886), p. 138.

22 Hill, R.W. 'The Children of Shinbone Alley,' National Conference of Charities and Correction, *Proceedings* (Omaha, 1887), p. 231.

23 William Appleman Williams, *The Contours of American History* (Chicago: Quadrangle Books, 1966), especially pp. 345–412.

24 Pickett, *op. cit.,* pp. 50–5.

25 Committee on the History of Child-Saving Work, *History of Child-Saving in the United States* (National Conference of Charities and Correction, 1893), p. 5.

26 Charles Loring Brace, *The Dangerous Classes of New York and Twenty Years' Work Among Them* (New York: Wynkoop and Hallenbeck, 1880), pp. 282–83.

27 Committee on the History of Child-Saving Work, *op. cit.,* pp. 70–73.

28 *Ibid.,* pp. 80–81.

29 *Ibid.,* p. 270.

30 For more about these child-savers, see Anthony Platt, *The Child-Savers: The Invention of Delinquency* (Chicago: University of Chicago Press, 1969), pp. 75–100.

31 Louise C. Wade, *Graham Taylor: Pioneer for Social Justice, 1851–1938* (Chicago: University of Chicago Press, 1964), p. 59.

32 G. William Domhoff, *The Higher Circles: The Governing Class in America* (New York: Random House, 1970), p. 48 and Platt, *op. cit.,* pp. 92–98.

33 'The transformation in penal systems cannot be explained only from changing needs of the war against crime, although this struggle does play a part. Every system of production tends to discover punishments which correspond to its productive relationships. It is thus necessary to investigate the origin and fate of penal systems, the use or avoidance of specific punishments, and the intensity of penal practices as they are determined by social forces, above all by economic and then fiscal forces.' Georg Rusche and Otto Kirchheimer, *Punishment and Social Structure* (New York: Russell & Russell, 1968), p. 5.

34 See, for example, Gabriel Kolko, *The Triumph of Conservatism: A Reinterpretation of American History, 1900–1916* (Chicago: Quandrangle Books, 1967); James Weinstein, *The Corporate Ideal in the Liberal State, 1900–1918* (Boston: Beacon Press, 1969); Samuel Haber, *Efficiency and Uplift: Scientific Management in the Progressive Era, 1890–1920* (Chicago: University of Chicago Press, 1964); and Robert H. Wiebe, *Businessmen and Reform: A Study of the Progressive Movement* (Cambridge: Harvard University Press, 1962).

35 Kolko, *op. cit.,* p. 282.

36 Weinstein, *op. cit.,* pp. ix, xi.

37 Jeremy P. Felt, *Hostages of Fortune: Child Labor Reform in New York State* (Syracuse: Syracuse University Press, 1965), p. 45.

38 Brace, *op. cit.,* p. 352.

39 David K. Cohen and Marvin Lazerson, 'Education and the Corporate Order,' 8 *Socialist Revolution* (March–April, 1972), p. 50. See, also, Michael B. Katz, *The Irony of Early School Reform: Educational Innovation in Mid-Nineteenth Century Massachusetts* (Cambridge: Harvard University Press, 1968), and Lawrence A. Cremin, *The Transfromation of the School: Progressivism in American Education, 1876–1957* (New York: Vintage, 1961).

40 It should be emphasized that child-saving reforms were predominantly supported by more privileged sectors of the feminist movement, especially those who had an interest in developing professional careers in education, social work and probation. In recent years, radical feminists have emphasized that 'we must include the oppression of children in any program for feminist revolution or we will be subject to the same failing of which we have so often accused men: of not having gone deep enough in our analysis, of having missed an important substratum of oppression merely because it didn't directly concern *us*.' Shulamith Firestone, *The Dialectic of Sex: The Case for Feminist Evolution* (New York: Bantam, 1971), p. 104.

41 Robert Sunley, 'Early Nineteenth Century American Literature on Child-Rearing,' in Margaret Mead and Martha Wolfenstein (eds), *Childhood in Contemporary Cultures* (Chicago: University of Chicago Press, 1955), p. 152: see, also, Orville G. Brim, *Education for Child-Rearing* (New York: Free Press, 1965), pp. 321–49.

42 For an extended discussion of this issue, See Platt, *loc. cit.* and Christopher Lash, *The New Radicalism in America, 1889–1963: The Intellectual as a Social Type,* (New York: Alfred A. Knopf, 1965), pp. 3–68.

43 Talcott Parsons and Robert F. Bales, *Family, Socialization and Interaction Process* (Glencoe, Illinois: Free Press, 1955), pp. 3–33.

44 Clara T. Leonard, 'Family Homes for Pauper and Dependent Children,' Annual Conference of Charities, *Proceedings* (Chicago, 1879), p. 175.

45 Lynde, W.P. 'Prevention in Some of its Aspects,' *Ibid.,* pp. 165–66.

46 Joseph R. Gusfield, *Symbolic Crusade, loc. cit.*

47 See, generally, Roy Lubove, *The Professional Altruist: The Emergence of Social Work as a Career, 1880–1930* (Cambridge: Harvard University Press, 1965).

48 Hofstadter, *op. cit.,* p. 155.

49 Williams, *op. cit.,* p. 373 and Weinstein, *op. cit.,* p. 254.

50 Williams, *op. cit.,* pp. 374, 395–402.

51 R. Jackson Wilson, 'United States: the Reassessment of Liberalism,' *Journal of Contemporary History* (January, 1967), p. 96.
52 Ralph Miliband, *The State in Capitalist Society* (New York: Basic Books, 1969), pp. 265–277.
53 Williams, *op. cit.*, p. 356.
54 Committee on the History of Child-Saving Work, *op. cit.*, p. 3.
55 See, generally, John Higham, *Strangers in the Land: Patterns of American Nativism, 1860–1925* (New York: Atheneum, 1965).
56 Brace, *op. cit.*, pp. 30, 49; Bradford Kinney Peirce, *A Half Century with Juvenile Delinquents* (Montclair, New Jersey: Patterson Smith, 1969, originally published 1869), p. 253.
57 Nathan Allen, 'Prevention of Crime and Pauperism,' Annual Conference of Charities, *Proceedings* (Cincinnati, 1878), pp. 111–24.
58 Jacob A. Riis, *How the Other Half Lives* (New York: Hill and Wang, 1957, originally published in 1890), p. 134.
59 Brace, *op. cit.*, pp. 27, 29.
60 See, for example, Lombroso's comments in the Introduction to Arthur MacDonald, *Criminology* (New York: Funk and Wagnalls, 1893).
61 Allen, *loc. cit.*
62 Hamilton D. Wey, 'A Plea for Physical Training of Youthful Criminals,' National Prison Association, *Proceedings* (Boston, 1888), pp. 181–93. For further discussion of this issue, see Platt, *op. cit.*, pp. 18–28 and Arthur E. Fink, *Causes of Crime: Biological Theories in the United States, 1800–1915* (New York: A.S. Barnes, 1962).
63 Richard L. Dugdale, *The Jukes: A Study in Crime, Pauperism, Disease, and Heredity* (New York: G.P. Putnam's Sons, 1877).
64 Sarah B. Cooper, 'The Kindergarten as Child-Saving Work,' National Conference of Charities and Correction, *Proceedings* (Madison, 1883), pp. 130–38.
65 Kerlin, I.N. 'The Moral Imbecile,' National Conference of Charities and Correction, *Proceedings* (Baltimore, 1890), pp. 244–50.
66 Williams, *op. cit.*, p. 354.
67 Fink, *op. cit.*, p. 247.
68 See, for example, Illinois Board of State Commissioners of Public Charities, *Second Biennial Report* (Springfield: State Journal Steam Print, 1873), pp. 195–96.
69 Peter Caldwell, 'The Duty of the State to Delinquent Children,' National Conference of Charities and Correction, *Proceedings* (New York, 1898), pp. 404–10.
70 Gould, F.R.L. 'The Statistical Study of Hereditary Criminality,' National Conference of Charities and Correction, *Proceedings* (New Haven, 1895), pp. 134–43.
71 Charles H. Cooley, ' "Nature" *v.* "Nurture" in the Making of Social Careers,' National Conference of Charities and Correction, *Proceedings* (Grand Rapids, 1896), pp. 399–405.
72 Committee on the History of Child-Saving Work, *op. cit.*, p. 90.
73 Enoch C. Wines, *The State of Prisons and of Child-Saving Institutions in the Civilized World* (Cambridge: Harvard University Press, 1880).
74 Helen Page Bates, 'Digest of Statutes Relating to Juvenile Courts and Probation Systems,' 13 *Charities* (January, 1905), pp. 329–36.
75 Joel F. Handler, 'The Juvenile Court and the Adversary System: Problems of Function and Form,' 1965 *Wisconsin Law Review* (1965), pp. 7–51.
76 Gustav L. Schramm, 'The Juvenile Court Idea,' 13 *Federal Probation* (September, 1949), p. 21.
77 Monrad G. Paulsen, 'Fairness to the Juvenile Offender,' 41 *Minnesota Law Review* (1957), pp. 547–67.
78 Julian W. Mack, 'The Chancery Procedure in the Juvenile Court,' in Jane Addams (ed.), *The Child, the Clinic and the Court* (New York: New Republic, 1925), p. 315.

79 Miriam Van Waters, 'The Socialization of Juvenile Court Procedure,' 21 *Journal of Criminal Law and Criminology* (1922), pp. 61, 69.

80 Harvey H. Baker, 'Procedure of the Boston Juvenile Court,' 23 *Survey* (February, 1910), p. 646.

81 Illinois Board of State Commissioners of Public Charities, *Sixth Biennial Report* (Springfield: H.W. Rokker, 1880), p. 104.

82 Frederick H. Wines, 'Reformation as an End in Prison Discipline,' National Conference of Charities and Correction, *Proceedings* (Buffalo, 1888), p. 198.

83 Joel F. Handler, *op. cit.,* p. 9.

84 Joel F. Handler and Margaret K. Rosenheim, 'Privacy and Welfare: Public Assistance and Juvenile Justice,' 31 *Law and Contemporary Problems* (1966), pp. 377–412.

85 From a report by Enoch Wines and Theodore Dwight to the New York legislature in 1867, quoted by Max Grünhut, *Penal Reform* (Oxford: Clarendon Press, 1948), p. 90.

86 Peter Caldwell, 'The Reform School Problem,' National Conference of Charities and Correction, *Proceedings* (St. Paul, 1886), pp. 71–76.

87 Letchworth, *op. cit.,* p. 152.

88 Committee on the History of Child-Saving Work, *op. cit.,* p. 20.

89 See Platt, *op. cit.,* pp. 55–66.

90 Katz, *op. cit.,* p. 187.

91 Rusche and Kirchheimer, *op. cit.,* pp. 131–132.

92 American Friends Service Committee, *op. cit.,* p. 28.

93 Zebulon R. Brockway, *Fifty Years of Prison Service* (New York: Charities Publication Committee, 1912), p. 393.

94 *Ibid.,* pp. 310, 421.

95 *Ibid.,* pp. 389–408.

96 *Ibid.*

97 Peirce, *op. cit.,* p. 312.

98 Enoch Wines, *op. cit.,* p. 81.

99 On informal cooperation in the criminal courts, see Jerome H. Skolnick, 'Social Control in the Adversary System,' 11 *Journal of Conflict Resolution* (March, 1967), pp. 52–70.

100 Committee on the History of Child-Saving Work, *op. cit.,* p. 20.

101 *Ibid.,* p. 237.

102 *Ibid.,* p. 237.

103 *Ibid.,* p. 251.

104 Rusche and Kirchheimer, *op. cit.,* pp. 155–156.

105 *Ibid.,* p. 76. For a similar point, see American Friends Service Committee, *op. cit.,* p. 33.

106 See, generally, Frank Musgrove, *Youth and the Social Order* (London: Routledge and Kegan Paul, 1964).

107 Philippe Ariès, *Centuries of Childhood: A Social History of Family Life* (New York: Vintage Books, 1965).

108 Williams, *op. cit.,* p. 382.
    On benevolence and repression in foreign policy, see Felix Greene, *The Enemy; What Every American Should Know about Imperialism* (New York: Vintage Books, 1971). For examples of domestic repression, see William Preston, Jr., *Aliens and Dissenters: Federal Suppression of Radicals, 1903–1933* (New York: Harper Torchbooks, 1966) and Jacobus ten Brock, Edward N. Barnhart and Floyd W. Matson, *Prejudice, War and the Constitution* (Berkeley: University of California Press, 1968).

13

Penal strategies in a welfare state

David Garland

THE RECONSTITUTED SOCIAL REALM

[…]

The crucial feature of the social policies implemented by the Liberal reforms of
the 1900s was the establishment of mechanisms of security and integration, which
could overlay and reorganise the effects of the labour market while maintaining its
basic capitalistic terms. The provision of pensions, state-subsidised insurance, labour
exchanges, school meals and so on ensured that the harshest consequences of the
market system were tempered, and the inequalities of its distributional effects modified. The degree of risk and insecurity encountered by the worker or his family was
significantly reduced for those encompassed by the new schemes, and at the same
time a small measure of equalisation took place. Although much was made of the progressive taxation of Lloyd-George's 1909 budget, this equalisation was not *between*
classes, but rather between the various employed and unemployed, old and young,
sick and healthy individuals, *within* the labouring class. But the importance of this
new rhetoric of equalisation was that it talked not of classes, but of *citizens*, in which
regard all were to be treated alike. Members of the lower classes, like their better-
placed brethren, became: 'individuals within a population which is now treated
for this purpose as though it were one class' (Marshall, 1963: 107). In this way, the
new social policies added an image of 'equality of status' to the 'political equality'
that had followed the expansion of the franchise. The social message of these new
provisions was that workers were no longer to be viewed merely as commodities in
the market, to be used or discarded according to the desires of capital, the moralism
of charity and the repression of the poor law. In place of these vagaries and hazards
were substituted a measure of material provision and a new form of social status and
recognition.

Taken together, these measures of security and equalisation of status were
designed to bring about a 're-admission of the outcast' (Jones, 1971) and the formation of a solidarity that would unite the nation. Thus Churchill in 1909:

SOURCE: This chapter is taken from *Punishment and Welfare: A History of
Penal Strategies*, Aldershot, Gower, pp. 231–63 (abridged).

> The idea is to increase the stability of our institutions by giving the mass of the industrial workers a distinct interest in maintaining them. With a 'stake in the country' in the form of insurances against evil days these workers will pay no attention to the vague promises of revolutionary socialism. (Quoted in the *Daily Mail,* August 1909 and in Harris, 1972)

and a Liberal Party pamphlet of 1912:

> all the poor and the working classes have acquired a new and a vast stake in the country. Instead of being used when useful and cast aside when no longer useful, they have become the children of the State ... not a Socialistic State but a Social State. (Rea, 1912)

In this new domain of security and solidarity, the institution of insurance is the key technology that supports the rest. It ensures a *redistribution,* 'spreading the costs involved in compensating ... invalidity to all the social partners' (Donzelot, 1979b: 81) and a form of *integration,* allowing 'the passage of subjects from a merely individual level to that of joint interests' (Procacci, 1978: 70), giving all citizens a stake in the nation, and ensuring the allegiance of a lifetime of regular contributions. But it does so in a manner which brilliantly avoids statism and any challenge to the system of free enterprise, individuation and inequality. Through insurance, the state certainly extended its influence, but it did so by setting up a regulatory technology that does not depend upon statism so much as a beneficial relation established between the individual and a state-sponsored scheme. It enlists the individual's self-interest and desires for security and promotion, rather than simply providing his needs. Likewise, its legislators were careful to preserve the image and form of a *contract* (albeit an obligatory one) and the entitlement to which it gives rise, rather than admitting the principle of non-contributory social provision which alternative schemes would have done. Insurance thus establishes a social field of individual contracts and claims, suppressing the notion of social rights and any competing forms of social solidarity.

As Donzelot (1979a: 64) says, 'need was made to operate as a means of social integration and no longer as a cause of insurrection', but it must be stressed that this integration took a very definite form. Like the vote – that other great mechanism of integration, which was expanding during this period – insurance promoted a form of social solidarity that none the less retained the primacy of the category of the individual within it.

To the new technology of regulatory controls (labour exchanges, public works, minimum conditions, etc.), the new strategy added an insurance-based safety net, which reduced the risks of those within the labour market, along with a set of auxiliary provisions (pensions, school meals, health care, etc.) for those who had either retired from their labours or else had yet to begin them. Together, these promoted a market that was more efficient and better organised, and a workforce that was 'engaged' on a long-term basis, not just by individual employers, but also by the new agencies of the state. The rewards, support and security that benefited the worker were thus made to operate simultaneously to the benefit of his employers and the system as a whole, by reducing waste and conflict and at the same time increasing individual commitment and regularity.

Similarly, the apparatus of insurance and pensions used the worker's self-interest and desire for security in both positive and negative ways. These interests first of all drew him into the system, winning his allegiance and commitment to it in the name of his own and his family's future. But once committed, these same interests operated to ensure that the worker observed the attached conditions of benefit – that is, was regular, stable, worked 'according to his ability', was of good character, avoided prison, and so on. The apparatus thus ensured that the worker was policed and regulated by a manipulation and utilisation of his own self-interest.

THE NEW PENAL REALM

If this elaborate apparatus of provision and state-induced self-control could be trusted to succeed for the majority of the population, and for the 'normal' individual, it was nevertheless supported by a more compelling back-up mechanism for the recalcitrant minority of deviant and marginal cases. [...] [T]his back-up was supplied by the newly assembled range of penal practices and institutions which, because of their shared reliance upon a number of common techniques, images and principles, could articulate easily and effectively with the new social complex. The institutions of penality thus came to support and extend those of the social realm in the following ways.

(1) It is already clear that the rewards, provisions and benefits of the social are conditional upon certain norms of conduct, some of which are specified in regulations, while others are merely implied or assumed. Penality negatively reinforces these terms by threatening to deal coercively with those who refuse them. This threat comes into play whenever the positive inducements of normal socialisation are experienced as being weak or difficult to attain.
(2) Penality relieves the social realm of its 'failures', subjecting them to a series of normalising, corrective or segregative institutions which will either return the individual to the normal social sphere or else will remove him from it permanently. It thus sets up a series of exchanges and transfers (of knowledge, records, individuals, etc.) between the normal institutions of socialisation and their penal adjuncts.
(3) The new penal complex provides extensive measures of state control, which serve to police such a system in the absence of the traditional mechanisms of repression and exclusion [...] Moreover it does so in a form that appears to be neither statist (cf. the important mediation of voluntary agencies) nor repressive (cf. the new insistence upon 'abnormality' and its 'correction').
(4) Finally, in representational terms, penality extends and completes the positive character of the state's new self-image. This new kind of social state is 'bent on generating forces, making them grow, and ordering them' (Foucault, 1981: 136), and the reformative character of the new penal practices reinforces this crucial image: 'the old idea of penal discipline was to crush and break, the modern idea is to fortify and build up force of character' (Blagg and Wilson, 1912: 5).

This new field of penality has a function and constitution that are quite different from those of the Victorian system [...] Although it retains a deterrent aspect, it is by no means confined to this, being committed also to various forms of correction and normalisation, care and improvement. In accordance with these revised objectives, it now displays a new structure and overall form. What was once a hierarchy of severity has now become a much more differentiated and diverse grid of dispositions, the vertical axis of Victorian punishment being tilted increasingly towards the horizontal.

As we shall see, the new aspects of this grid may be analysed in terms of the three major sectors that compose it, each one containing a number of institutions and agencies. These 'normalising', 'corrective' and 'segregative' sectors are positioned at increasing distances from the normal institutions of the social realm, and movement from the first sector towards the last entails increased measures of control and a deepening penal involvement. As well as the exchanges between social and penal spheres, a definite system of transfers from better to worse, worse to better, is established *within* the penal network, which follows the insistence of numerous reports that each line of institutions should have at its end-point a coercive state-run terminus. This system of grades and transfers between institutions precisely parallels the new system of discipline that came to operate *within* institutions, where the old systems of punishments were replaced by a more positive structure of rewards, privileges and their withdrawal. And both of these, in turn, are local examples of a more general mechanism of promotion and demotion, which runs the whole length of the new social-penal complex.

SANCTIONING CRITERIA AND FORMS OF ALLOCATION

Before describing these sectors in more detail, it is necessary to say something about the criteria of allocation and the forms of administration which preside over this new penal network and direct its functioning.

[...] [T]he Victorian system was inscribed almost exclusively within the terms of legal discourse, being regulated by criteria of guilt, responsibility, legal evidence and proportionate punishment. In the new penal complex, the terms of this legal discourse are undercut and redefined by the introduction of other discourses and considerations. 'Guilt', for example, is no longer the founding principle of legal intervention in this sphere. [...] [N]ew legislation on children, inebriacy, habituals, etc. allowed interventions to be triggered without the necessity of offence behaviour and to be justified on quite other grounds than the guilt of the subject. Besides 'guilt', intervention can now be premised upon a 'condition', a 'character' or a mode of life', which indicates a failure to meet one's social obligations or else an inability to do so. 'Responsibility', too, is subjected to a serious revision in its scope and usage. Although it is [...] retained as 'the normal case', the increasing number of exceptions, modifications and deviations from this rule ensure that it can no longer be simply assumed. There is consequently something of a movement from rationalism to empiricism, whereby 'responsibility' ceases to be an *a priori* which is universally presumed and instead becomes subject to the test of empirical investigation in an increasing number of cases.

What these detailed changes described is a more general movement away from the traditional laying down of *laws* towards an increasing resort to the mobilisation of *norms*, a movement which has the effect of extending and revising the operations of the judicial power. As Foucault points out:

[This] does not mean to say that the law fades into the background or that the institutions of justice tend to disappear, but rather that the law operates more and more as a norm, and that the judicial institution is increasingly incorporated into a continuum of apparatuses (medical, administrative and so on) whose functions are for the most part regulatory. (Foucault, 1981: 144)

The sense and importance of this distinction between 'law' and 'norm', and the revision of one by the other, can be gathered from the following demarcations. The protocols of the law (ideally) require publicly specified offences, guilt and responsibility, publicly proven according to the specified conventions of evidence, fact and law. They involve an open adversarial trial, definite safeguards and limitations with regard to evidence, and the availability of review and appeal procedures. In contrast, the norm which comes to supplement the law in cases of juveniles, children, the feeble-minded, etc. operates according to quite different criteria. It bases itself upon expert decisions (certified by doctors, psychiatrists, social workers, etc.) regarding the normality or pathology of 'characters', 'mental or moral states' and 'modes of life'. These decisions, which need not be publicly explained, are based upon an expertise in the 'human sciences' that is not widely shared nor easily challenged. According to this logic, sentencing becomes less a matter of justice and more a question of proper administration and diagnosis. The norms of the human sciences become a new kind of *raison d'état*, whose demands justify serious departures from the usual terms of the law.

Much more than with traditional law, the new system of laws-plus-norms requires a thoroughgoing knowledge of the case before it. This knowledge does not concern itself merely with the 'immediate facts' and the legal provisions that apply, but also with the background, history, character and corrigibility of the individual concerned. At the same time there is a subtle shift in the role of the judge, who becomes not just the arbiter of adversaries, but also the ultimate interlocutor of various confessionals and processes of investigation. This shift is most clearly visible in the new juvenile court:

> it is always helpful to get from him, or her, a statement of the reasons for being brought into court. It is the direct and natural method of approach.... The child should be interviewed outside the hearing of any other person.... The important thing is to get the truth from the child. (Hall, 1926: 63)

But also from the parents, the school, the investigating officer and all the other potential sources of useful information.

[...] [T]his requirement of knowledge gives rise to a whole apparatus of investigation and inquiry that reaches far beyond the forensic inquiries of the police, and supplements the various forms of inspection and inquiry entailed within the new network of social institutions. Through the services of the various voluntary agencies, probation officers, after-care agents, etc., the range of knowledge available to the authorities is extended to encompass not only the offender, but also his family and his home. As one manual of investigation put it:

> It is in the home and its immediate associations that the most powerful environmental influences are found, and it is from the home, therefore, that the most important information will be obtained. (LeMesurier, 1935: 91)

At the same time, the depth of penetration of this inquiry is increased in order to peer into the character and history of the offender, producing a knowledge which goes beyond immediate appearances, and even beyond the understanding of the offender himself:

> It may be said that, in general, any reason given for commission of an offence will be more in the nature of an excuse than an explanation. It should be accepted as such, and the probation officer should not, at this stage, attempt to probe deeper. In all probability the offender does not know the reasons which induced him to offend, and it is only after a consideration of all the factors in the offender's life that the probation officer can venture to suggest any explanation. (Le Mesurier, 1935: 96)

With the aid of various techniques borrowed from the repertoire of charity and social work ('the circular approach', 'separate and contradictory questioning', 'practical verification of the family's way of life', 'the surprise visit' and so on), the inquiries of the law are transformed in their scope and their form.

In his 1908 account of the new 'social politics' Kirkman Gray commented that: 'Inspection is undergoing an interesting development which may be described as a movement from the inspection of *things* to the inspection of *persons*' (Kirkman Gray, 1908: 267) [...] He went on to argue that these same channels of inquiry and inspection serve not just to gain knowledge, but also – in the reverse direction – to relay advice and directions for conduct in a form and depth previously unattainable:

> This giving of advice represents a new function the importance of which may easily be overlooked, but can hardly be exaggerated. At first there is only an inspector of *things* empowered to demand the observance of certain rules. Action in regard to things is limited in extent, and it might be possible for the legislator to foresee all that should need to be done. But action in regard to persons is illimitable in range and infinitely delicate. It would be absurd to limit the function of the inspectors of infants to any statutory schedule. Two women and a baby are beyond the philosophy of the Parlimentary draftsman. The real business is not so much to tell the mother what she *must* do as to advise her as to what she *can* and *should* do. (Kirkman Gray, 1908: 268)

These important insights of Kirkman Gray's apply just as well to the new normalising style that followed the shift from the enforcement of laws to the implantation of norms. Kirkman Gray recognises, as others have done since, how this new mode of inquiry opened up a new field of intervention – its new supplies of knowledge implying a new scope for power. For the new system of normalisation, with its capacity to prise open and enter into the intimate details of the individual's life, allows a measure of penetration and subtlety, which was altogether new to the forces of the criminal law.

I shall now proceed to examine the various apparatuses that were committed to this dual function of inquiry and normalisation, along with the other institutions that make up the new penal complex.

THE PENAL COMPLEX AND ITS MODES OF OPERATION

If we examine the new penal complex as a whole, it is possible to discern a number of distinct modes of operation, which underpin and organise the various sanctions and institutions that make up its diverse network. On this basis it is possible to distinguish three major sectors – *the normalising, the corrective* and *the segregative.*

The normalising sector

The new, state-sponsored practices of probation, after-care and licensed supervision [...] share a common commitment to a mode of operation which might be termed *normalisation.* Each of these practices is concerned not just to prevent law-breaking, but also to inculcate specific norms and attitudes. By means of the personal influence of the probation or after-care officer, they attempt to straighten out characters and to reform the personality of their clients in accordance with the requirements of 'good citizenship'. Of the three sectors mentioned, this one is closest to the normal or primary institutions of socialisation – the family, the school, the workplace, etc. It is physically close, in so far as these are community-based sanctions which do not remove the offender from his or her work or home. It is close in the sense that it is the 'shallow end' of penality, used for those who are not yet fully criminalised or else are returning to normal life after a period of Borstal, reformatory school, etc. Finally, it is functionally close, in so far as it uses the normal mechanisms of socialisation such as personal influence, friendly persuasion, teaching, etc., with the important difference that it does so with the backing of the court's coercive powers.

The establishment of this sector as an organised and extensive apparatus of official penality was perhaps the most important innovation in the new penal strategy, and one which had distinct repercussions throughout the rest of the complex. We have already discussed the effect of those normalising agencies in the provision of detailed knowledge and means of inquiry, but in addition to this, they brought about two major effects in terms of sanctioning practice. The first of these – hinted at already – was the *extension of the judicial power* which this 'entering into the lives and homes' of offenders facilitated (Report of the Prison Commissioners, 1913/14: 24). The range of this power – its capacity to effect and influence those it contacts – is thus extended beyond the offender to include his parents and his family. As Herbert Samuel (Chairman of the 1909 Departmental Commission of Probation) commented, 'the home is put under probation' (Report on Probation, 1909, p. 1087).

Probation, supervision, after-care – all of these represent an extension and multiplication of the judicial gaze, and of the consequent range of intervention. The 1909 reports states:

> the cardinal principle in this probation work is that the court is always cognisant of the actions of the probationer through the probation officer. (p. 365)

> Securing for him a respectful hearing, and furnishing a motive for the acceptance of his counsels, there is always in the background the sanction of the penal law – the knowledge that the probation officer is the eye of the magistrate; that misbehaviour will be reported to the court, and will bring its penalty. (p. 2)

At the same time, the depth and penetration of this power to intervene are extended. The 'personal touch' of the supervising officer actually does touch the person of the offender, engaging his personality, attitudes, beliefs and working upon them in a way that was previously beyond the scope of official penality. Moreover since the goal is 'normality' and good citizenship, the aim of this intervention goes much deeper than mere crime prevention. And, since 'there can be no such thing as the completely normal child ...' – or adult for that matter – it is less easily satisfied.

The other major effect of this normalising sector was one of *refinement*. The Victorian system [...] was fairly crude in its operations, with a tendency to be either too harsh – spiralling individuals downwards into the criminal class – or else ineffective, leaving those ineligible for prison completely 'beyond control'. This new apparatus was discreet, humane and relaxed by comparison, but promised at the same time to be more effective in operation. To begin with, normalisation could exercise its control without disrupting those disciplines already provided by the home, the school, the workplace, etc.:

> The sentence of probation, whilst it formally places the child under the control of the probation officer, allows him at the same time to return to his home and family. In this way parental authority is respected and parental responsibility maintained. (Morrison, 1896: 191)

And as with the child and his parents, so too with the adult and his family, his workplace, and so on. Indeed, far from disrupting these 'normal' controls, the supervising agent seeks to support them, to prop and augment them with his or her own influence. As Kirkman Gray points out:

> A co-partnership has been established over the [working class] home. The partners are the parents and the State.... The result is not a breaking up, but a consolidation of home. The incursion is not really the incursion of a stranger, but the entrance of a member. The hearth is empty, but the representative of society is found there. (Kirkman Gray, 1908: 39; cf. Donzelot, 1979a)

Of course, if the discipline of the home and the family is entirely inadequate, then probation or licensed release would not be deployed, but there are cases where 'the parents are as much to blame as the children', whereupon the agent must turn his attention to improving *their* conduct and protecting his ward from their infelicities. In such cases:

> The parents quite as much as the children are 'put on probation'. Working through the family and the home, the system gives the unfortunate a strong friend from the outside who can provide education and training and employment. (Blagg and Wilson, 1912: 19)

At the same time:

> The parent is advised and watched over by the probation officer ... and ... the child is protected against the weakness or unworthiness of the parent. (Morrison, 1896: 191)

In all such cases, the agent seeks to extend his powers of influence and to continue them in his absence by enlisting the aid of other agencies of improvement:

> One of the principal things the probation officer has to do is to make use of existing social agencies. The officer knows that in the offender's life he is but a passing agent, not a permanent one. His endeavour, therefore, is to put his charges in touch with such permanent social and religious agencies as are appropriate to their individual need; his purpose of

course being that these agencies shall continue to influence the offenders' lives long after the probationary period terminates. (Leeson, 1914: 124; see also Russell and Rigby, 1908: 253 and Hall, 1926: 25)

All of this, if it goes well, is efficient as well as economical and discreet. But it should also be experienced by the offender and the public as less negative and repressive than the prison, the fine or corporal punishment. It appears as a positive and humane means of 'building up' offenders and their families, *adding* to the social welfare rather than reducing it:

> It is better than prison from the economic as well as from the humane point of view, for the offender is not removed from work in the outside world, so need not be maintained by the State, nor is the wage earner's family thrown upon the Poor Law. There is no criminal taint, no loss of status, no association with other offenders, on the contrary in the most successful cases the whole tone of the home is raised. The system aims at making both the unit and the family more useful to society. (Blagg and Wilson, 1912: 19)

The correctional sector

If we turn now to the next sector, one stage further into the penal complex, we can identify another series of institutions sharing a common mode of operation and a common position in the network. The various Borstals, reformatory schools, industrial schools and privately-run retreats and reformatories for the inebriate and the weak-minded together constitute what might be termed the *correctional* sector, part of which was entirely new, the rest being continued from the previous system in a somewhat augmented form.

Each of these elements centred upon a mode of operation that was institutionally based, but distinctly correctional or reformative in design. These correctional features – which may or may not have reformed offenders – were actually intrinsic to their mode of operation, rather than mere imagery or rhetoric. Each institution was to be allocated only particular types of offender, selected in terms of their corrigibility, youth, character, etc.; indeed they had the power to refuse those who appeared to them to be incorrigible. Each one was run on a basis of indeterminate non-proportionate sentences, which could be terminated at the discretion of the institution's staff, release being subject to further supervision and specified as depending upon criteria of correction and reform. Similarly, each one was statutorily obliged to provide a regime of corrective training, education and reform, though the details of such regimes were never thoroughly specified, depending largely upon the initiative of the governors, superintendents and voluntary workers who ran the various institutions.

This correctional sector is functionally adjacent to the normalising sector and exhibits a number of links and continuities with it. It is next in line after the failure of the normalising apparatus, or in those cases where the character of the offender or his or her background make that first sector inappropriate. Similarly, it depends upon the investigations of probation and after-care agencies for the information required to make the original assessment and allocation, the subsequent classification by character, and the eventual decision as to release. Finally, the correctional institutions utilise the services of these other agencies to conduct the supervision and after-care that is an integral feature of the correctional operation; and to feed back information about the offenders' progress, the need for recall, the success of the training, etc.

The effect of the legislation that consolidated this correctional sector in the 1900s was thus once again to extend the duration and effectivity of penal control – through the longer reformative sentences, the additional periods of supervision, etc. – and to represent penality with a positive public image of correction and reform. At the same time, as we shall see, it established an intermediary sector, which played a crucial role in firmly ushering offenders back into the social fold or else placing them squarely within the sphere of penal control.

The segregative sector

The third and 'final' area of the penal complex – furthest removed from the realm of normal social life and containing those who have refused or have been unable to submit to the disciplines of the dominant social order – might best be termed the *segregative* sector. The institutions that compose this sector include the various state reformatories for the inebriate and the feeble-minded, the preventive-detention institutions and, to a great extent, the ordinary prisons throughout the country.

It is important to note that although such segregation existed in the institutions of Victorian penality, the formation of the new complex served to demarcate this sector much more clearly, augmenting it with new institutions, specialising its tasks and distinguishing them from the correctional and normalising sectors. It is also important to realise that this segregative mode of operation, though firmly established, was rarely represented in such negative terms.

If we take these institutions one by one, we can see how this sectoral specialisation took place and also demonstrate the segregative nature of each of them. [...] The new preventive-detention regime, established by the 1908 Act, was designed to deal with those habitual offenders who were deemed to be incorrigible. Its lengthy sentences were oriented towards the incapacitation of the habitual and the protection of the public through simple segregation, rather than towards punishment or reform: 'All that is wanted is that they should be under discipline and compulsorily segregated from the outside world' (Confidential Memorandum, in PRO file on Habitual Offenders, P. Com. 7. 286). Similarly, the state-run reformatories for inebriates and defectives were deliberately designed to form a warehouse that would contain the failures and disruptive elements of the private institutions, thereby allowing these other places to carry out their reformative functions. As Ruggles-Brise admitted:

> The value of the State reformatory will not consist in the production of actual results, but its existence will permit of certified institutions carrying on a work of reformation otherwise impossible. (Ruggles-Brise, 1921)

The most controversial element of my argument here is in regard to the prison, which [...] was never presented in primarily negative, segregative terms. And yet if we analyse the effects of the various penal changes upon the role of the prison, we find that they have definitely displaced it away from correction and towards segregation, despite an official rhetoric which claimed the reverse. In the years between 1895 and 1914, the population of the prison was reconstituted by the removal of a whole series of categories to specialist institutions or else non-custodial measures. But those removed included not just the habituals and the mentally ill who were beyond reform, but also all of the reformable, hopeful categories – the children, the juveniles, the first offenders – and even the mildly inebriate and feeble-minded, who might be expected to respond well to treatment. In consequence, the prisons were left with all those persons whose offences were serious or frequent enough to warrant not correction or normalisation, but the punishment of imprisonment. The reduction of the frequency of short sentences (through legislation on fine instalments, for example) only served to compound this segregative trend. Moreover despite claims that the prison regime was to become more reformative in orientation, there was no introduction of the fundamental techniques of correction such as indeterminacy, release on licence, and so on. The paradoxical effect of the post-Gladstone reforms upon the prison was thus to render it *less*, rather than more likely to have a reformative effect.

This segregative sector, then, operated as the coercive terminus for the whole penal network, in just the same way that the penal complex as a whole supplied the coercive back-up for the institutions of the social realm. It formed the 'deep end' of the complex, which functioned as a sanction of last resort, supporting the others by its threatening presence. As an article of 1912 pointed out:

> The reflex effect of the segregation of the defectives on the larger number of responsible prisoners is not to be overlooked.... The knowledge that their fortunes are not at the lowest ebb, that there is a place to which irresponsible offenders are committed indefinitely can but act as a deterrent. (Fernald, 1912/13: 874)

As we shall see in a moment, this segregative sector plays an important negative role in the overall strategic operation of the penal complex. But given this, we should again note the significance of the fact that the public rhetoric of officials and ministers insisted, and still insists, upon giving this negative function a positive gloss – whether by calling preventive detention a reformative regime or by referring to incarceration as 'positive custody'. [...] It would appear that negativity, in its various forms, is deeply antithetical to the modern state's self-image.

Their interrelations

The three sectors I have identified interrelate by means of a series of strategic connections and exchanges. The deeper, more repressive measures supply a lever of deterrent force which allows the normalising agents to operate in a way that is both relaxed and yet ultimately forceful, being both within and without repression. At the same time, the more severe sectors relieve the milder ones of their dangerous or unruly cases, allowing them to function without any unnecessary use of force. The other side of this transferral mechanism is, of course, the incentive of promotion which exists in the other direction, holding out the promise of more lenient institutions for those who follow orders and show signs of improvement. Finally, the existence of the milder institutions ensures that the existence of repressive ones appears justified and necessary. Having done 'all we can', the only resort for those who refuse such offers of help must be a positive and humane custody, to be quickly terminated on any sign of reform. This complex of balances and leverage, promotion and demotion, the offer of provision followed by the penalty for refusal, as well as the circle of legitimation that it sets in motion, is the strategic formation of modern penal welfare. And if one recalls the operations of the social realm, set out at the beginning of this chapter, it will be clear that the penal welfare strategy is in many respects a miniaturised version of the social strategy that it underpins.

[...] [T]he social engineering proposals of the various programmes set up a kind of grid of possibilities, ranging through public to private, and from population to individual in its subjective and objective co-ordinates. Each of the programmes favoured a different line on this grid, some proposing that private 'subjects' should act upon individuals, others proposing that the object of intervention should be the population and its subject the state. From our discussion of the social and penal strategies that were actually established, it should be clear that they combined state *and* private agencies as the new subjects of social intervention, with the latter usually regulated by, but formally independent of, the former. At the same time, the objects that were addressed by these strategies included populations *and* individuals – frequently with one being addressed through the other, or else both being addressed through the *family* as an intermediary relay of norms and values. The overall effect of this eclecticism was not to choose one line of intervention at the cost of another, but rather to merge the whole range of possibilities in a strategic network that ranged across the whole grid, simultaneously exploiting all of its potential.

NEW STRATEGIES AND PROBLEMS OF SOCIAL REGULATION

The problem of provision

It will be recalled that the transformations that have been described, and the strategies that they constructed, were in fact concerted attempts to deal with the political repercussions of a social and penal crisis. If we remind ourselves of the central elements of this crisis, and the political problems that they posed, it will become clear that the new strategies did in fact address and alleviate these problems in a direct, but always subtle manner.

To take the social crisis first, and simply mentioning the basic co-ordinates of a complex and overdetermined network of problems, we can recall the following. A revised and more interventionist economic policy was made desirable by a long-term change in the relations of production and market forces, but also by the perceived need to promote efficiency at the level of market institutions and at the level of the population which supplied the nation's labouring and military forces. At the same time, new policies were demanded to avert the growing threat of socialist agitation, to stabilise the political effects of the market upon the lower orders, and to win the allegiance of a newly extended electorate, which appeared volatile and increasingly militant. Moreover some means was required to modify the repressive and exclusory operations of the institutions and ideologies through which the lower orders were addressed.

As we have seen, the new institutions of 'the social' effected a definite reorganisation of the market, an improvement of its functioning and efficiency, and an extended range of interventionist techniques more in keeping with the post-*laissez-faire* nature of the economic terrain. At the same time, these and other institutions improved the provision of health care, housing and nourishment, and sought generally to promote the physical efficiency of the working population. The political claim of this spate of reforms was to have given the working class 'a stake in the country', creating a unified and extended nation to replace the divided and class-based society that preceded them. Through pensions, insurance benefits, school meals and labour exchanges a definite material improvement was accorded to large sectors of the population; and the consequent alterations in poor law practice, and the treatment of the unemployed provided a strategic response to the 'legitimate grievances' of the poorer classes.

Perhaps more importantly, the new strategy involved a significant transformation in the *mode of address* officially deployed towards the working classes and their disadvantaged sectors. The repressive language of moral distinction, 'desert' and 'worth', and the odious 'testing' of the destitute by further destitution were replaced by an administrative machinery and discourse quite separate from those of the hated poor law institutions. Pensions were to be distributed through the Post Office; school meals, health care and insurance benefits provided without disenfranchisement; and if the worker was still forced to be responsible, regular and stable, then this force was discreetly contained in automatic administrative decisions, not revealed in the mouths of 'philanthropists' and poor law officials. On the basis of this ideological initiative, the Liberal government hoped to win for itself the class loyalty of workers and their votes, and, for the system, the lifelong allegiance of regular, contributing individuals.

As some recent writers have pointed out, the very structure of this new machinery involved an ideological effect of its own, achieving a depoliticisation or 'deconflictualisation' of the social field within which it operated:

> This shift entailed, or was intended to entail, a definite reduction in the general social and political consequences of economic events – industrial conflict, unemployment and so forth – by ensuring that, whether working or not, citizens were, in effect, employees of society. Attention was thus switched from the analysis of the structure of the social and economic relations within which unemployment, sickness and so forth are produced, to a consideration of the consequences of the various technical and actuarial options entailed in the calculation and distribution of allowances and benefits. (Rose, 1980: 123)

At the same time, it promoted the forms of passive solidarity and individual integration in the social, which I have already noted, as well as the beginnings of an institutional incorporation or 'corporatism' which Marshall, the Barnetts and others had advocated, and which the Industrial Conciliation Act (1896), the Industrial Council (1911) and the poor law franchise reforms of 1900 began to set in motion.

The sublety of these measures, and the basis of their political plausibility at the time, lay in the fact that they comprehensively reorganised the network of social and political relations without disturbing the underlying distributions of wealth or the basic relations of power and production. [...] [T]he redistributions that occurred were primarily intra-class, while the new insurance scheme served to underwrite market relations rather than undermine them. As Churchill pointed out (in the *Nation*, 7 March 1908), the essence of the social reforms was the establishment of 'that minimum standard below which competition cannot be allowed, but above which it may continue healthy and free'. Thus despite the ideological revision already discussed the new framework of social security preserved within itself the basic tenets of an individualistic ideology. It preserved notions of individual responsibility, thrift, self-help, freedom from state collectivism, and the earned, contractual basis of individual rights or entitlements. As Beveridge argued later, endorsing these same principles as the basis of the 'Welfare State':

> The plan for Britain is based on the contributory principle of giving not free allowances to all from the State but giving benefits as of right in virtue of contributions made by the insured persons themselves. (Beveridge, quoted in Gilbert, 1966)

Which is to say, of course, that such rights are not social rights at all, but merely the individual entitlements that arise from a contractual relation.

This retention of the contractual within the collectivist, the individual in the social, is well illustrated by the insurance principle. Although the notion of a contributory insurance provided a means of financing benefits without a major resort to (progressive) taxation, this insurance principle was hardly an actuarial reality. Not only was it state-subsidised from the start, but as Rose points out:

> it differs from ordinary insurance practices in a variety of ways: there is no adjustment of premium to risk, nor are premiums accumulated separately to provide for future benefits, as is done in pension funds or Friendly Societies – indeed if they were they would be by no means sufficient to meet obligations. (Rose, 1980: 124)

The insurance principle, with its apparent basis in normal financial contracts, is in this sense, mythical:

> In fact, an appearance is constructed of some logical relation between contributions and benefits for reasons which may be termed 'moral' – that is to say, in terms of the psychological effect which such a relation is considered to have on those caught up within it. It was these moral effects of the principle of insurance – its reinforcement of the notion of contractual obligation, its encouragement of thrift, the distinctions it maintains between earned and unearned benefits – which formed one of the major objectives of the advocates of this system rather than the other 'universal' schemes which were considered. (Rose, 1980: 124)

By means of such measures the political effects of the social problem were deflected and its forces reoriented. In place of an untrammelled market and a repressive policing mechanism was substituted an apparatus that could regulate population, restore efficiency and enforce responsibility, but could also present itself as merely the combined outcome of a nation of contracting individuals.

The problem of disciplinary regulation

[...] [T]he penal realm of the 1890s was also marked by a series of crises and disruptions, involving the failure of the prison, the chronic problem of recidivism, an over-severity which was often ineffective, and a corresponding crisis of popular legitimacy, manifested in frequent scandals and public outcries.

The political repercussions of these problems were compounded by the coming of 'advanced democracy', which made it important to discover a means of policing the population that would accord with the new political and ideological relations of the social state. In the new democracy, where citizenship and security extended to all classes, discipline could no longer function through repression and exclusion.

Henceforth its modalities would have to be more refined and discreet. Yet at the same time they would require to be more systematic and penetrating, more thorough in their effects. Their task was to ensure that the new and permanent threat posed to the system of class domination by the workers' vote, their mass trade unions and their collective political existence was counterbalanced by an equally extensive and thoroughgoing regulation and discipline, reducing the 'risks' that democracy entailed, ensuring that new citizens were good citizens.

Enough has already been said to show that the main co-ordinates of this crisis were indeed addressed by the new penal strategy which, as we have seen, repaired the deficiencies of the 1890s and created a more extensive and refined network of control. But again it is crucial to realise that along with this institutional change went a definite alteration of the ideological mode of address implicit in penal practice.

The categories and practices of the new complex did not employ the openly repressive terms of the old prison-based system, nor even the explicit signs of the labour colony and its social segregation. In their place it deployed a new language of reform, correction and normalisation, supporting the inadequate, protecting the irresponsible, and restoring the morally deficient to the fullness of good citizenship.

In the language of the new complex, the deviant was no longer represented as wicked or worthless – punishable because of the moral choices for which he was responsible. Instead, the deviant appears as *deficient* – mentally, morally or physically – his actions appearing as 'incompetent' (Pearson, 1975: 69) rather than intended. The function of penality is to restore him to an elusive normality by means of training and treatment, substituting new values and norms for defective old ones, supplying a discipline previously lacking, or a physical training to counteract degeneracy and neglect. As Ruggles-Brise clearly saw:

> Penal law is, through its prohibitions, the expression of the social standard of life in the country. Where the standard was high [and it was rising all the time] there must be a residuum of individuals whose mental and physical state does not enable them to live up to that standard. (Preface to Goring, 1913: vi)

Penality's task was to intervene to address such deficiencies. The various sectors of the penal complex were to restore absent virtues and capacities, correct vices and abnormalities, or else, in the case of those whose incapacities were chronic, simply segregate in humane conditions for the protection of society and the individuals themselves.

This shift in the basis of penality's logic is what has been hailed as the liberalisation of punishment. It appears again and again in the texts of the 1900s and of today as the transformation that took punishment into its present civilised era, an era in which repression has become reform, and the 'reversionary rights' (Ruggles-Brise, 1921) of every citizen are recognised and provided for:

> It is in harmony with what one may perhaps call the *modern* growth of social consciousness that society becomes more and more concerned with the problem of treatment of those of its members who fall below the accepted normal standard. The submerged tenth, the insane, the degenerate, the criminal, the problem of the abnormal factors of the social organism becomes more and more insistent with the advance in that order which is the expression of a higher consciousness – social in its inception, humanitarian in its activity. (Heath, 1909: 233)

And yet, if we look closer, a less worthy operation is simultaneously taking place here. This drastic revision of penality's logic occurs precisely at the historical moment when the political franchise is being extended to include the mass of the (male) working class within its terms for the very first time. At this moment the legal basis for full participatory political citizenship begins to change fundamentally from a question of economic substance to one of straightforward adult status (Marshall, 1963: 81). But at precisely the same time a whole series of institutions and regulations are put in place which are designed to identify all those legal citizens (or prospective legal citizens) who lack the normative capacity to participate and exercise their new-found rights responsibly. Once identified, these deviants are subjected to a work of normalisation, correction or segregation, which ensures one of two things. Either they become responsible, conforming subjects, whose regularity, political stability and industrious performance deems them capable of entering into institutions of representative democracy; or they are supervised and segregated from the normal social realm in a manner that minimises (and individualises) any 'damage' they can do.

So in fact the sweep of the franchise and the social realm is indeed widened, but at the same time the conditions for participation in social life are made more rigorous, more contingent upon behaviour and character. Participation in the political domain is thus extended along one axis, only to be restricted along another. The political reliability of citizens can no longer be assumed on account of their economic substance, so a certain caution is adopted in regard to the conditions of entry of the new classes. Just as the extending vote argued in favour of an educational provision for all, it also promoted the 'remedial education' of penality and its practices:

> The right of the state to subject the transgressor to an education which makes him fit to fulfil the elementary conditions of social life with others in an orderly society rests essentially on the same basis as the right to provide for the education and the instruction of children. In both cases the state sets up the level below which its members must not sink and tries to help those up who have not yet reached it or who have sunk down below it. (Hoffding, 1911/12: 694)

This new and more subtle form of exclusion served to remove deviants *physically* from the domain of full and independent citizenship (where the extending franchise had placed them) and to remove *symbolically* the apparent rationality of all such deviance by ensuring that its perpetuators were deemed irresponsible, less-than-rational, less-than-citizens. At the same time, it ensured that fewer groups were left 'beyond control', having redefined as pathological all those individuals who might fail to be deterred by the old system of punishments. Failure to be deterred thus became a mark of individual pathology, rather than a mark of the failure of penal institutions. Not for the first time, the institutions of penality preferred to change the nature of man himself, rather than question the political principles of their practice.

It was through this new version of citizenship and its necessary attributes that the new penal notions of abnormality and irresponsibility were articulated on to the strategies of the social field. And of course the corresponding ideology of beneficial provision to help those citizens-who-lacked was achieved without reference to the political transformation of 'citizenship', and the extension of state control, which it undoubtedly involved. Instead, it was represented as an (apolitical) moral duty to help those whom modern science had recognised as being in need of care and control: a moral duty previously left to voluntary philanthropy, but now supported and ensured by a benevolent charitable state.

As we saw earlier, this depoliticisation was achieved as a result of the state–voluntary alliance and the mediation of the evangelical penal reform groups in the reception of criminological innovations. This alliance (which took place in the social as well as the penal realm) allowed probation officers, social workers and supervisors eventually to become professionalised and to represent their ministrations not as class-based moralising, but instead as the provision of expert counselling and advice. At the same time this new concern with reform tends to undercut resistance, both from the offender/client, whose rights are displaced by his needs, leaving him unable to appeal to justice or even to know his own interests, *and* from the public, which sees only benevolence and compassion where once was cruelty.

Finally, we should notice that this new extended strategy of intervention is not expressed in the traditional terms of the criminal law, which would involve declaring numerous minor irregularities as crimes carrying serious and lengthy sentences. Nor is it 'totalitarian' in establishing a state apparatus which constantly and universally intervenes in the lives and homes of all its subjects. Instead the strategy functions by stating a series of normative expectations and standards, and at the same time establishing a number of authorities and expert bodies to ensure these norms are met. These normative requirements are stated not just by law, but also by schools, labour exchanges, housing authorities, health boards, poor law institutions and so on, and the onus is placed upon individuals and families to recognise these norms and comply with them. Those who succeed remain 'free' – within these terms – and undisturbed by the incursions of state agencies. Those who fail thereby express their inadequacy, and their deviant behaviour, failure to meet requirements, or claims for special provision function to trigger intervention accordingly:

> It is through the *failures and deficiencies* of families that the State and public powers find the means and the cause to intervene. Parental deficiency and juvenile delinquency provide routes for intervention, pretexts under the liberal order whereby children can be removed from families or families placed under supervision.
>
> The autonomy of the family comes to depend not on law or proprietorial right but on *competence*. It enjoys a loosely supervised freedom to the extent that it meets social norms. (Hirst, 1981: 73–4)

Or as one contemporary observed as early as 1915, in a chapter entitled 'The administered child':

> A consistent policy of acquiescence keeps a parent out of reach of official and voluntary interference in his home. But if he does not acquiesce, his case becomes abnormal and he is likely to feel the official weight. (Pepler, 1915)

The penal and social agencies thus used such 'failures' as their points of entry in a more subtle and systematic repetition of the old philanthropic rescue – although 'failure' was now measured in relation to the normative institutions of the social realm and not, as previously, to the labour market itself. This strategy involves no violation of the liberal ideology of an equal law for all, nor yet any entry into a totalitarian statism. Instead, certain categories of person are identified (or identify themselves) on the basis of a 'failure' that can only appear to lie with themselves, since so much in the way of education, security and support has already been provided. Consequently this failure or deficiency requires that they be removed from the politico-judicial sphere to the technical-administrative realm of penal welfare. And so once more the deficiencies of the (modified) market system are displaced on to those most disadvantaged by it. On this basis a systematic, but always discreet distinction can be made between the bourgeois family, which may freely conform to norms made in its image and for its benefit, and a lower-class family, which is subjected to supervision and intervention in the name of a normative order that is not its own.

[···]

REFERENCES

Blagg, H. and Wilson, C. (1912) *Women and Prisons*, Fabian Tract No. 163, London: Fabian Society.

Donzelot, J. (1979a) *The Policing of Families*, London: Hutchinson.

Donzelot, J. (1979b) 'The poverty of political culture', *Ideology and Consciousness*, no. 5.

Fernald, G.G. (1912/13) 'The recidivist', *Journal of the American Institute of Criminal Law and Criminology*, vol. 3.

Gilbert, B.B. (1966) *The Evolution of National Insurance in Great Britain: The Origins of the Welfare State*, London: Joseph.

Foucault, M. (1981) *The History of Sexuality,* Vol. One, Harmondsworth: Penguin.

Goring, C. (1913) *The English Convict*, Prison Commission.

Hall, W. Clarke (1926) *Children's Courts*, London: Allen & Unwin.

Harris, J. (1972) *Unemployment and Politics: A Study in English Social Policy, 1886–1914*, Oxford: Clarendon Press.

Heath, C. (1909) 'Crime and social responsibility', *International Journal of Ethics*, vol. 19.

Hirst, P. (1981) 'The genesis of the social', in *Politics and Power*, vol. 3, London: Routledge & Kegan Paul.

Hoffding, H. (1911/12) 'The state's authority to punish crime', *Journal of the American Institute of Criminal Law and Criminology*, vol. 2.

Jones, G. Stedman (1971) *Outcast London: A Study in the Relationship between Classes in Victorian Society*, Oxford: Clarendon Press.

Kirkman Gray, B. (1908) *Philanthropy and the State, or Social Politics*, London: P.S. King.

Leeson, C. (1914) *The Probation System*, London: P.S. King.

Le Mesurier, L. (1935) *A Handbook of Probation and Social Work for the Courts*, National Association of Probation Officers.

Marshall, T.H. (1963) 'Citizenship and social class', in *Sociology at the Crossroads and Other Essays*, London: Heinemann.

Morrison, W.D. (1896) *Juvenile Offenders,* London: T. Fisher Unwin.

Pearson, G. (1975) *The Deviant Imagination,* London: Macmillan.

Pepler, H.D. (1915) *Justice and the Child,* London: Constable.

Procacci, P. (1978) 'Social economy and the government of poverty', *Ideology and Consciousness,* no. 4.

Rea, R. (1912) 'Social reform versus socialism', in the collection of *Liberal Party pamphlets,* National Library of Scotland.

Report of the Departmental Committee on Probation (1909) *PP,* 1910, XLV.

Report of the Prison Commissioners (1913/14) *PP,* 1914, XLV.

Rose, N. (1980) 'Socialism and social policy: the problems of inequality', *Politics and Power,* no. 2, London: Routledge & Kegan Paul.

Ruggles-Brise, E. (1921) *The English Prison System,* London: Macmillan.

Russell, C.E.B. and Rigby, L.M. (1908) *Working Lads' Clubs,* London: Macmillan.

14

On the decriminalisation of English juvenile courts

Anthony Bottoms

In 1969 the United Kingdom Parliament passed the Children and Young Persons Act, relating to juvenile justice in England and Wales. If it is ever fully implemented, this Act will have, *inter alia,* the following effects:

(i) It will be impossible to prosecute any child under fourteen for a criminal offence (excluding homicide); and it will also be impossible for compulsory civil care measures to be applied to an offender of this age unless the court is satisfied not only that he has committed an offence but also that 'he is in need of care or control which he is unlikely to receive unless the court makes an order' (Section 1 (2)).

(ii) As a corollary of (i), wherever possible children should not have to go to court when they have committed an offence, but treatment should be voluntarily agreed between parents and social workers (unless it is to be residential treatment, which should only be permitted with a formal court order).

(iii) Young persons (aged 14 and under 17) may be prosecuted in certain specified cases, but the non-criminal 'care proceedings' (see (i)) will be available as an alternative, and should be preferred in most cases, with voluntary agreements (see (ii)) an even more desirable possibility.

(iv) Two main 'disposals' will be available for persons successfully prosecuted or found in need of compulsory care, i.e. the 'care order' and the 'supervision order'. In both, supervising social workers will have a significant element of discretionary power which is not subject to court review or scrutiny.

Although the Act leaves the formal composition and constitution of the English juvenile courts virtually unchanged,[1] it is clear that the jurisdiction of these courts is intended to be radically altered by the provisions. There is a substantial move towards either voluntary agreements or civil proceedings rather than criminal proceedings; hence it is correct to speak of the Act as a decriminalizing Act, though

SOURCE: This chapter is taken from R. Hood (ed.) *Crime, Criminology and Public Policy*, London, Heinemann, 1974 (abridged).

in the rather special sense of 'substitutory decriminalization', i.e. 'substituting one kind of formal control for another kind of formal social control'.[2] The Act is also quite clearly a move towards a more explicitly 'welfare' oriented jurisdiction, and is in large part based on classical social work concepts. In particular, it enshrines two major assumptions:

(i) That delinquency is to be understood, as in psychoanalytic thought, as a pre-senting symptom of some deeper maladjustment; hence the problems of delin-quents are similar to the problems of other children in need, and the two should be dealt with together and not separated by the accident of whether the symp-tom calling attention to the need happened to be an offence or (say) truancy or persistent bedwetting.
(ii) That court appearances, especially on a criminal prosecution, cause stigma and should be avoided wherever possible in favour of more informal treatment deci-sions by professional social workers.

CHANGING THE JUVENILE COURTS: A DECADE OF DEBATE

The essential core of the explanation of the English Act lies, it is submitted, in a conjunction of interests and ideology between the British Labour Party and those in key positions in British social work. However, although this is a necessary kernel of the explanation, it is not a sufficient explanation, since this conjunction existed (though perhaps in a different context) both at the time of the failure of 1965–6 and in the later success of 1968–9. The additional elements of the explanation can only be understood in the light of the social history of the various debates preceding the legislation, to which we now turn.

The history begins with the setting up in 1956, quietly and almost as a matter of post-war routine enquiry, of a Departmental Committee under Viscount Ingleby, with strangely bifurcated terms of reference: to enquire into the working of the law on juvenile courts in all its aspects, *and* 'whether local authorities should be given new powers to prevent or forestall the suffering of children through neglect in their own homes'. The committee was of fairly unadventurous composition: apart from the distinguished child psychiatrist Peter Scott, it was composed entirely of lawyers, administrators, and magistrates – in particular, it should be noticed, there were no social workers. It reported in 1960, and declared that the juvenile courts should be retained and that, with very minor exceptions, the then existing range of treatment orders and treatment facilities was adequate.[3] The committee was clear that the answer to the second question referred to it was in the affirmative, but thought that any question of the reorganization of the social services to meet this need lay 'well outside our terms of reference', although important for 'further study'. In these respects it was by no means unfair for Donnison to describe the general tenor of the report as 'respectable and cautious'.[4]

Nevertheless, the committee did unearth one major 'weakness' in the juvenile court system, and what it considered to be the logic of this situation led it to its most radical proposal. The 'weakness' was the discrepancy between the expectation of 'just deserts' raised by the forms of a *criminal* trial, which were adhered to in the juvenile court up to the time guilt was proved or admitted; and the subsequent specific direction that in considering treatment, it was the duty of the court to 'have regard for the welfare of the child or young person'.[5] In a now famous passage, the committee pointed out that (para. 66):

> It results, for example in a child being charged with a petty theft or other wrongful act for which most people would say that no great penalty should be imposed, and the case apparently ending in a disproportionate sentence. For when the court causes enquiries to be made ... the court may determine that the welfare of the child requires some very substantial interference which may amount to taking the child away from his home for a prolonged period. It is common to come across bitter complaints that a child has been sent away from home because he has committed some particular offence which in itself was not at all serious.

To get around this logical difficulty, however, there was no suggestion that the 'welfare' ethic at the sentencing stage should be abandoned, as many would now certainly demand. Rather, it was thought that in 'offence' cases, one should move away from a criminal-type jurisdiction for younger children, so that the inappropriate expectations aroused by a criminal trial should be lessened. Hence the solution propounded was that the age of criminal responsibility should be raised from eight to twelve immediately, and perhaps to fourteen eventually; below that age, only civil 'welfare' proceedings could be brought, but a child would be proved to be in need of protection or discipline under these if he had acted 'in a manner which would render a person over that age liable to be found guilty of an offence'.

Whether this is a solution to the problem posed by the committee is doubtful on intellectual grounds.[6] Of more interest to this essay, however, is the way the committee related its proposed procedures to its assumptions about delinquency. These, set out fully in its paras. 107–8, are that responsibility for crime in juveniles is shared between the child and 'those responsible for his upbringing'. By and large, children come to court because those responsible for their upbringing (i.e. parents, school and general community) have 'been unable in different degrees and for various reasons to bring the child up in the way he should go. They have been unable ... to teach him to behave in an acceptable manner'. For the younger child, most of the responsibility lies 'squarely' with the upbringers; but later on 'the child must learn to stand on his own feet and accept greater responsibility for his actions'. In other words, the model was, in crude terms, one of social pathology for the younger child, but more classical assumptions about choice of evil for the older child; and these models were to be reflected in the differing procedures – civil proceedings for the younger child and criminal for the older.

Duster has pointed out a central problem in the way Western societies typically deal with the offender: he is treated as a 'rational being' in the early stages of police processing and the determination of guilt by the court, but in later stages, notably in prison and probation treatments, the emphasis is on pathology or psychic disturbance.[7] Taking this idea further, one can see that in the adult court, where sentencing to prison, fine or whatever is in the majority of cases carried out on retributive and deterrent principles, the potential clash between the ideology of the first stage of court proceedings (the trial) and the second stage (the sentence) is a manageable one. But in the juvenile court, with its much greater typical emphasis on 'treatment' or 'the welfare of the child' at the dispositional stage, the conflict of two incompatible ideological models within one courtroom case may appear acute. This, one suspects, lies at the heart of the 'problem of the juvenile court', and is the reason why the rôle of the juvenile court or its equivalent raises so much controversy in so many countries. The Ingleby committee perceived the problem: their solution was, in effect, to inject the pathological model into the *whole* of the court proceedings for younger children, and for older children to reduce the force of the conflict by stressing moral responsibility for crime and thus minimize the pathological model at the sentencing stage.

This point has been spelt out in some detail because it is related to the varying reaction to the Ingleby report. The Conservative Party, then in power, and at the time busy dealing with the aftermath of serious disturbances at an approved school,[8] as well as warding off the strong pressure of its grass-roots supporters for the reintroduction of corporal punishment for juvenile delinquents,[9] was in no mood to minimize the moral seriousness of juvenile crime. Hence its reaction to the Ingleby proposal to raise the age of criminal responsibility was a distinctly cool one; in November 1961 the Home Secretary (R.A. Butler) made it clear that he did not intend to raise the age, and, although the Government was subsequently forced to compromise and raise the age to ten, it did so with noticeable reluctance. This type of reaction, stressing the seriousness of much juvenile crime and the moral responsibility of offenders, was a typical one in subsequent Conservative attitudes throughout the ensuing years of debate.

The Labour Party's reaction to Ingleby was very different. It thought the report far too timid, as evidenced in speeches in Parliament and in a special critical Fabian Society pamphlet on the report.[10] The proposal to raise the age of criminal responsibility was generally welcomed, but this was not thought sufficient, and two main additional points were stressed.

The first of these was that, though Ingleby had located the family as an important source of delinquency, too little had been suggested to help the family: 'there is no doubt that the Ingleby committee's recommendations were a great disappointment, [and] those who hoped to find the outline of a statutory service of help to the family in need looked in vain'.[11] The background to this was that during the 1950s, significant elements in Labour thinking began to regret some of the philosophy of the Labour administration of 1945–51 which had largely created the apparatus of the Welfare State in Britain. At that earlier time 'it was clear that social workers would be needed to do various jobs in the big [new] specialist statutory services, but many people assumed that old-fashioned general social work, or family casework, would gradually wither away'.[12] Now an opposing movement had gained force, partly due to the typical plight of the problem family with multiple needs, knocking on the doors of one specialist agency after another; and partly influenced by emerging notions among social workers of so-called 'generic social work', which had emerged from the common psychoanalytic base of social work practice in the 1950s, and was increasingly affecting social work training. But, though pressed to do so by evidence from Labour organizations, the Ingleby committee had given no lead to the creation of a unified 'family service'.

The second Labour criticism of Ingleby rested on a version of stigma theory. It was argued that the committee, despite its endorsement of special statutory powers of prevention, was not sufficiently concerned about keeping children out of courts altogether. As Miss Alice Bacon, leading for the Opposition in a 1963 debate put it:[13]

> I want to ensure not only that young children are not charged with having committed a crime – which is important – but that as far as possible we shall keep young children out of the courts altogether. This is the important thing. It is not just the nature of the charge made in court; it is the appearance in court which can do so much damage to a young child.

These two strands of Labour thinking, the 'family service' concept and stigma theory, were both to be of central importance in the next stage of proposals. It is important to note, however, that although Ingleby was attacked for its timidity, the Labour stress was not for a more pathological view of the deviant than Ingleby's, but rather if anything a modification of Ingleby's social-pathological concept towards a broader view of the delinquent in relation to the wider society – or, in Duster's terms, the delinquent as a 'victim of external forces' rather than as 'psychically inadequate'. For example, Labour accounts of the family indicated the difficulties of the family unit in coping with problems of accommodation in the private rented sector and of stress caused by conflicting policies of different social agencies.[14] Nevertheless, the Labour view did not stress the view of the offender as morally evil, and, particularly in view of the emphasis on the family, its ideology allowed much greater possibilities of conjunction to Ingleby's notion of social pathology – and subsequently, to more social work-based notions of individual and family maladjustment – than did the Conservative ideology. This was to remain the position for the rest of the decade.

In retrospect, then, we can see the Ingleby Report as important in identifying an apparent anomaly in the juvenile court system, and as having to some extent polarized the position of the two political parties vis-à-vis the juvenile justice issue. Although the most controversial Ingleby proposal did not become law, to ignore the symbolic importance of the Ingleby debates in relation to subsequent events would be a serious mistake.[15]

By 1964, the Labour Party was confidently girding itself for power after the forthcoming election. In readiness for it, a private party committee on criminal policy was set up under the chairmanship of Lord Longford (subsequently a Cabinet minister), with a very strong membership including the future Lord Chancellor and seven other future Ministers as well as two criminologists, Terence Morris and T.C.N. Gibbens. As with Ingleby, however, the committee contained no professional social worker.

The committee's report[16] was very wide-ranging, but certainly one of its major proposals was for the total abolition of juvenile courts, based on the philosophy that 'no child in early adolescence should have to face criminal proceedings: these children should receive the kind of treatment they need, without any stigma'. Instead, non-judicial and entirely informal consultations between the child, his parents, and a new Family Service were envisaged: proposals as to treatment would be put by the social worker, and only if no agreement could be reached (or in certain other serious cases aged over thirteen referred by the Family Service) would the matter go to court. If it did go to court, this would be to a new 'Family Court', the establishment of which for many kinds of family problems was held by the committee to be of the 'highest importance'.

In considering these proposals, the two characteristic strands of Labour thinking in the response to Ingleby are again very evident. The second of them, stigma theory, was reinforced in this committee by Lady Wootton, who according to Lord Longford was a witness who powerfully and decisively influenced the committee and who previously and subsequently made very strong statements about the stigma of court appearances.

The receptivity of Labour politicians to these ideas perhaps needs a little elaboration, though it is readily understandable. Especially on the strong trade union wing of the party, there has always been a deep suspicion of courts and lawyers, based on a justifiable feeling that in English industrial history, lawyers had always been on the side of the property owners and industrialists. At the same time, the egalitarian orientation of the party made it very aware that, as the Longford Report put it, 'the machinery of the law is reserved mainly for working class children who more often than not are also handicapped by being taught in too big classes in unsatisfactory school buildings', while middle-class parents often managed to cloak their sons' delinquency and have it dealt with elsewhere. As for the Family Service concept [...] this appealed not only to the paternalism of upper-class Socialists like Lord Longford, but also to the strong lower-middle-class/nonconformist traditions of family solidarity, which are often very influential in Labour politics.

It is important to see, however, that the Longford Report does not bear any strong imprint of 'pure' social work ideas – there is for example no hint of the later view of delinquency being merely a symptom of deeper maladjustment – but rather is the expression of a general social democratic ideology. Nevertheless, social workers were not slow to appreciate how the tenor of the report chimed in with their own ideology. This, based on psychoanalytic concepts, stressed particularly the 'presenting symptom' theory, and the consequent adoption of a medical-treatment analogy in considering delinquency prevention. It was also critical of courts and lawyers, partly on the basis of a stigma theory very similar to Labour's, and partly on the grounds that lawyers operated with over-rationalistic concepts of human behaviour. These ideas had, at that time, come closest to official recognition in the Kilbrandon Report for Scotland.[17] A typical social work reaction to Longford stressed the extent to which it had come close to these notions: 'the ideas expressed by the (Longford) group, although not exactly identical with the Kilbrandon Committee's ... had at least this much in common with them: avoidance of criminal proceedings for young offenders, and, instead, merging the treatment of young offenders with that of other school age children who require specialized provisions.[18] Social workers, with the exception of probation officers (discussed further below) were therefore glad to be able to use the Longford proposals to press their own case, and certainly found Longford much more congenial than Ingleby.

Labour gained power, albeit with a precarious Parliamentary majority, four months after the publication of the Longford report. Ten months later came the famous but abortive White Paper, *The Child, The Family and the Young Offender,*[19] in which the Government published 'provisional proposals' subject to 'discussion'.

The White Paper substantially reproduced the Longford proposals on the abolition of the juvenile courts, except that the purely informal consultations with the Family Service proposed in the earlier document were to be replaced by a formal 'Family Council' in each area, consisting of 'social workers of the children's service and other persons selected for their understanding and experience of children'. This change, however, hardly affected the major issue of abolishing juvenile courts, and few people found the difference important enough to affect their overall attitude to the two reports. Nevertheless, the change is possibly symptomatic of a slightly greater direct social work influence in the concepts of this report as against Longford, another sign of which is a stronger stress on the family and the absence of comment as to the class-biased clientele of the juvenile courts.

The Longford Report had attracted some criticism in professional and academic circles, but its reception was quietness itself compared with the flood of criticism which now descended upon the new White Paper. In retrospect, it is difficult to recall the heat of the battles in those days, though a rereading of, for example, the special issue of the *British Journal of Criminology* (April 1966) shows the bitterness of the struggle seeping out behind the intellectual debating points. This greater degree of controversy reflects not so much the detailed differences between the two reports, as the fact that the second contained Government proposals which seemed likely to lead to imminent legislation, especially after the Queen's Speech in October 1965 when it was announced that the Government would 'promote the provision of improved services for the family [and] the development of new means of dealing with young persons who come before the courts'.

The main opposition came from lawyers, magistrates, and probation officers. The last group is of particular interest, as they shared much of the psychoanalytic ideology of other social workers; but they also had a long tradition of independence of local authorities, and of service to courts, and it was from this standpoint that their critique was made.[20] On the other side of the debate, the main supporters of the proposals were other social workers, particularly members of the child care service, and many of these talked openly of their gaining through the proposals much more professional prestige and recognition for their service which was still less than twenty years old.[21]

Eventually the opponents of the paper triumphed, and the proposals were withdrawn. Since, as has been seen above, they appealed to significant strands in Labour ideology, it is important to ask why the campaign of resistance was successful, especially as the abandonment was by no means immediate. Although no certain answer can be given, the probability seems to be that there were two main reasons: the strength of the opposition, and a change of Home Secretary.

In gauging the effect of opposition, one has to bear in mind the general political difficulties of the Government. Until the General Election of spring 1966, it had only a hair's breadth majority of three in the House of Commons, and was no doubt not anxious to risk defeat on matters not central to its political programme – as this was not. After the election, it very quickly ran into very great economic difficulties which for some time were a major preoccupation. More generally, the Government must have been aware that the strong opposition of the legal lobby and the probation officers would cause some of its own supporters to waver, and it may have been especially important that on this issue the specialists engaged in the detailed controversy were able to appeal to a wider constituency which in general was prepared to uphold the value of courts as defenders of individual rights.

Speculatively, one might also suggest that the civil servants within the Home Office were less than wholeheartedly sympathetic to the proposals. In the nature of the case, there is no firm evidence to support this; but the inference may perhaps be drawn from the facts that (i) the original proposals in Longford were drawn up without civil service advice, and (ii) that the proposals which emerged three years later, which were demonstrably much influenced by civil servants, were of a rather different nature. If this speculation is correct, it could have been of considerable importance in view of the known importance of the civil service in modifying Government policy on certain occasions.

An additional factor of some importance was almost certainly the change of Home Secretary in December 1965. For Mr Roy Jenkins, who took over the post from the ailing Sir Frank Soskice, is not the kind of Socialist to whom any of the arguments against courts or for a Family Service make a strong emotional appeal. Rather, as has been said in an assessment of other aspects of his Home Secretaryship, he is a 'technocrat Socialist, seeking cures for economic malaise by efficient achievement' and believing in a 'civilized bourgeois socialism', with a 'concern for the individual and his place vis-à-vis the bureaucracy'.[22] In the field of penal policy, these concerns were manifested in his strong drive for greater police efficiency through amalgamations of forces, better equipment, etc. and in his liberal reforms in the Criminal Justice Act 1967, such as the parole system and (in intention though not in practice) the suspended sentence. The juvenile court reforms do not loom large in such a perspective, and no doubt the intellectual in Jenkins was also deterred by the frankly rather poor and simplistic general level of the argument in the 1965 White Paper, and in the Longford Report before it.

The 1965–6 reform movement, then, was unsuccessful. But two to three years later, in April 1968, the Government produced a second White Paper *Children in Trouble*[23] which, with minor modifications, became law as the 1969 Children and Young Persons Act (for the main provisions, see the introduction to this paper). The problems raised by *Children in Trouble* are (i) why did it emerge, after the abandonment of the earlier proposals; (ii) why was it not successfully opposed, as the previous paper had been?

A clue to the first problem lies, perhaps, in a careful reading of the paper itself in comparison with the 1965 predecessor. Undoubtedly the level of the argument presented is higher, whatever one may think of its substantive merits. But more importantly, the argument has much more of the influence of professional social work thinking than of the Fabian politico-social thinking, which tended to characterize the earlier Labour papers, especially Longford. This seems to reflect the growth to power in the three-year interim of a very strong team of civil servants at the top of the Children's Department of the Home Office. This group, led by the late D.H. Morrell and Miss Joan Cooper, was committed to a 'child care' view of delinquency in a strong form. The published works of Morrell and Cooper make this very clear:[24] for them, delinquency is a presenting symptom of a deeper maladjustment; children will grow up deviant if they are denied the advantage of early social work intervention at crisis periods; and residential institutions, they maintained, should take the form of therapeutic communities. A comparison of the *treatment* proposals of the 1965 and 1968 White Papers is especially instructive in seeing how a more consistently professional social work approach has in the intervening years been applied to various aspects of the proposed reorganizations. For example, though both papers intended to replace the approved school order with the care order (giving parental rights to the local authority), only in 1968 had a systematic plan for 'community homes' and their philosophy been evolved;[25] or again, the 1965 White Paper intended to retain both attendance centres and detention centres, whereas by 1968 the intention was to phase these out because of their punitive connotations, and to bring replacements within the concept of 'intermediate treatment' – which, however, would be solely in the discretion of the social worker.

Of course, some aspects of the 1968 proposals were allied closely to the earlier Labour philosophy, in particular the proposal to avoid court proceedings and prefer voluntary agreements wherever possible, aimed at eliminating the effects of stigma. But the section of the Act by which courts were empowered to explore the possibility of a voluntary agreement (section 1(2)) could be and was attacked on the grounds that it was class-biased against the working-class boy.[26] By a deep irony, it was the *Conservatives* in parliament who raised this objection: not surprisingly, Labour spokesmen never seemed very comfortable in dealing with it. The irony can be explained as the result of the greater social work influence of 1968: from a classical social-work position, the section can be defended much more easily than from a typical Labour position, though why the Labour Government allowed itself to adopt the clause must remain a matter of difficulty.

The apparently strong influence of the Home Office Children's Department in the formation of the Act requires some further comment. For it is unlikely that this group would have had either the influence or the confidence which it had, were it not for some parallel developments in English social work.

Throughout the 1960s, many social workers in England and Wales were pressing for two goals which they saw as closely related: (i) the unification of various statutory local authority social services into a single Social Services Department for each authority; (ii) the creation of a unified professional body for social workers, instead of the then existing multiplicity of organizations (Association of Child Care Officers, Association of Psychiatric Social Workers, National Association of Probation Officers, etc.). At the time of Longford and the 1965 White Paper, both these aims seemed relatively remote, for although the professional organizations had taken a crucial step in 1963 by coming together into a consultative group (Standing Conference of Organizations of Social Work), this still essentially reflected an ideological, pre-organizational, stage of development. By 1968–9, however, all was different. In 1968, a major Inter-Departmental Committee report was published, urging the creation of unified local authority departments,[27] and this became law in the Local Authority Social Services Act of 1970, though the probation service has remained separate from the new departments. Also in 1970, the professional social work organization was finally achieved in the form of the British Association of Social Work, and it had been clear for some little time previously that this would be the result. These twin developments, it can be argued, probably crucially assisted the institutionalization of professional social work concepts within the Home Office at the relevant time. They also, and perhaps just as importantly, debilitated the National Association of Probation Officers, which throughout the period 1966–70 was fighting a severe internal battle as to whether or not it should merge itself into the proposed B.A.S.W. Those probation officers in favour of unification tended to be very critical of those who opposed the 1965 and 1968 White Papers too vigorously, in case other social workers thought probation officers too reactionary and too much on the side of lawyers. This was more important in 1968 than 1965, since the influence of this group was then stronger; and N.A.P.O. was no doubt thankful that the retention of courts in the 1968 proposals allowed it, consistently with its earlier position, to give a much greater welcome to *Children in Trouble* than to its predecessor. Nevertheless it still was unhappy about some aspects of the proposals, but arguably had less influence precisely because its own internal squabbles had partly deprived it of external credibility.

One other irony deserves comment. The social work concepts employed in the 1969 Act were what I have described as the 'classical' ones, derived from the strong dependence of British social work on psychoanalytic theory in the 1950s and early 1960s. This common conceptual base was also one of the major origins of the suggestion to merge professional organizations. But from the vantage point of the early 1970s, we can see that in the late 1960s those ideas were beginning to change rapidly at a grass roots level, towards a more sociological stance; though in 1968 the challenges which this involved were all at a non-institutionalized and hence powerless level in the professional orgnization of social work. The interaction between social work conceptions of knowledge, professional reorganization, and legislative activity for juvenile offenders in the 1960s is certainly a highly complex one which is deserving of further study.

But we have not yet shown why the 1968 White Paper succeeded where the 1965 one failed. Certainly, the strong commitment of civil servants of the Home Office Children's Department, not present at least to the same extent in 1965, must be considered a factor; and in this case a further change of Home Secretary a few months before publication of the White Paper does not seem to have been a decisive event. An additional factor was no doubt the Government's insistence that some legislation on the subject must be carried: it is embarrassing to a Government to withdraw proposed legislation on a subject twice in one term of office.

The decisive difference appears to have been the lesser degree of opposition to the new proposals. It is true that the Magistrates' Association again took a very critical stance, but their opposition, together with that of some lawyers and probation officers, had much of the sting taken from it by the retention of the juvenile court, the proposed abolition of which had caused so much opposition in 1965. It is much easier to appeal to a wider constituency with opposition to the abolition of a court than with opposition to some of the more technical matters the 1969 opposers were fighting. Indeed, the retention of the court, while radically altering the jurisdiction and conceptual basis of the court's operation, seems in retrospect a masterly manoeuvre by the Home Office. At the grass roots level if not at the level of the Magistrates' Association, juvenile justices seem to have thought they had won a victory in 1969 with the retention of the court. But after the Act had been implemented in part in 1971 a serious magisterial revolt took place. Major conflicts with the local authority social workers[28] led to the almost unprecedented step of a full-scale conference of interested groups with the responsible Government Minister in January 1973. The main ingredient in this dispute was, by common consent, the different operating philosophies of magistrates and social workers: yet this conflict had not led to really sustained pressure by magistrates against the 1968 White Paper. Almost certainly, the reason for this is that the symbolic retention of the court in the 1968 proposals meant that magistrates had failed to realize how far the traditional functions and operating philosophy of the juvenile court were being eroded by the details of the new framework.

To sum up then: it is submitted that the main framework of an explanation of the English Act is approximately as follows. The Ingleby committee brought to the fore a central anomaly in juvenile justice, and helped to polarize the political positions of the two major parties on the issue. From different but conjoining standpoints, both the Labour party and social workers wanted a more welfare-oriented juvenile justice system. The first attempt was put forward by Labour, relatively unassisted by professional social workers but strongly backed by them. This attempt failed, due to the strength of the opposition, the wider issues it was able to raise, the political difficulties of the Government, and a change of Home Secretary. The second attempt was – aside from the retention of the court – much more by professional social work ideas, but was still backed by Labour because of the conjunction of concepts. The emergence of this attempt can be mainly traced to a very influential group of social-work oriented civil servants, but they in turn would not have been so influential but for parallel developments towards professional and organizational unity in British social work. The success of the attempt as against the failure of the earlier attempt is attributable to a number of technical matters, but particularly to the retention of the juvenile courts in the second White Paper, which deprived the opposition of its most evocative symbol. This outline is tentative, and certainly in need of further research, but I believe its main thrust is likely to be correct.

NOTES AND REFERENCES

1 The courts are composed of part-time unpaid magistrates, sitting in an informal atmosphere, in private, and with restrictions on press reporting: see generally W.E. Cavenagh, *Juvenile Courts: The Child and the Law*, Harmondsworth, Pelican Books, 1967. The 1969 Act alters this only by giving the Lord Chancellor greater power over appointments to the juvenile bench.
2 See I. Anttila, 'Conservative and Radical Criminal Policy in the Nordic Countries', *Scandinavian Studies in Criminology*, 1971, 3, 9–21.
3 *Report of the Committee on Children and Young Persons*, Cmd. 1191, London, HMSO, 1960.
4 D. Donnison, 'Social Services for the Family' in *The Ingleby Report: Three Critical Essays*, London, Fabian Research Pamphlet No. 231, 1962.
5 Children and Young Persons Act 1933, section 44.
6 See Cavenagh, op. cit., pp. 261–2; Barbara Wootton, 'The Juvenile Courts', *Criminal Law Review* [1961], 669–77 at 673–5.
7 Troy Duster, *The Legislation of Morality*, Glencoe, Ill., Free Press, 1970.
8 *Disturbances at the Carlton Approved School: Report of Inquiry by Mr. Victor Durand, Q.C.*, Cmd. 937, London, HMSO, 1960.
9 Advisory Council on the Treatment of Offenders, *Corporal Punishment*, London, HMSO, 1960. The then Home Secretary, R.A. Butler, subsequently commented after his retirement that this was one of the most difficult campaigns with which he had to deal in his political career.
10 D. Donnison, P. Jay and M. Stewart, *The Ingleby Report: Three Critical Essays*, London, Fabian Research Pamphlet No. 231, 1962.
11 Peggy Jay, 'A Plan for Family Bureaux', in Donnison *et al.*, op. cit.
12 Donnison, op. cit.
13 H.C. Deb. vol. 672 col. 1288.
14 Jay, op. cit.
15 Nevertheless, some of the Ingleby recommendations did become law in the Children and Young Persons Act 1963, notably the proposal to empower local authorities to carry our preventive work with juveniles. As a consequence of this, the following year the Conservative Government issued a circular to police forces (Home Office circular 20/1964) asking them to consult with local authority children's departments before prosecuting children under twelve. These arrangements were supported by the Labour party, and there was thus in these respects a consensus on certain steps to keep some younger children out of courts altogether.
16 *Crime: A Challenge to Us All*: Report of the Labour Party's Study Group, London, 1964.
17 *Children and Young Persons: Scotland*, Cmd. 2306, Edinburgh, HMSO, 1964.
18 Peter Boss, *Social Policy and the Young Delinquent*, London, Routledge and Kegan Paul, 1967, p. 86. Even here, note that Boss has elevated to a major place the concept

of treating delinquents and non-delinquents together, while in Longford (p. 30) the idea is implied but not stressed.

19 Cmd. 2742, 1965.

20 See, e.g. the statement by the National Association of Probation Officers, 'The Child, The Family and the Young Offender: Observations by N.A.P.O.', *Probation*, 1965, 11, 83–91 at p. 84: 'no action should be taken to interfere with the liberty of an individual on grounds of his conduct, or with the rights of parents on allegations of their failings, except as the result of a judicial assessment'.

21 The local authority children's departments were set up in 1948 to deal with deprived children, leaving probation officers to deal with delinquents. Inevitably there was always some overlap, and inter-service rivalry as to their relative professional competence in handling child delinquents. For a children's officer's view of the 1965 White Paper see B.J. Kahan, 'The Child, The Family and the Young Offender: Revolutionary or Evolutionary?', *British Journal of Criminology*, 1966, 6, 159–69.

22 E.J.B. Rose *et al.*, *Colour and Citizenship: A Report on British Race Relations*, London, Oxford University Press, 1969, pp. 513–14.

23 Cmd. 3601, 1968.

24 D.H. Morrell, 'The Educational Role of the Approved Schools', in *The Residential Treatment of Disturbed and Delinquent Boys*, ed. R.F. Sparks and R.G. Hood, Cambridge Institute of Criminology, 1968; J. Cooper, 'Social Disadvantage and Social Help', *Approved Schools Gazette*, 1969, 643–5; J. Cooper, 'Social Care and Social Control', *Probation*, 1970, 15, 22–5.

25 Morrell, op. cit., Home Office, *Care and Treatment in a Planned Environment*, op. cit.

26 The wording of the section is, in part, 'and also that he is in need of care or control which he is unlikely to receive unless the court makes an order'. It was argued that it would be easier to prove this to mainly middle-class magistrates against a working-class than against a middle-class boy; since for under-14's no intervention could be made unless this matter were proved, the result could be no action against one child and a major intervention against another, arising out of the same offence incident. See D.R. May, 'Delinquency Control and the Treatment Model: Some Implications of Recent Legislation', *British Journal of Criminology*, 1971, 11, 359–70, at pp. 364–5.

27 *Report of the Committee on Local Authority and Allied Personal Social Services*, Cmd. 3703, London, HMSO, 1968 (Seebohm Report).

28 See Brian Harris, 'Children's Act in Trouble: An Appreciation of the Children and Young Persons Act 1969 in Operation', *Criminal Law Review* [1972], 670–84; G. Smith, 'The Children Act: What is Going Wrong?' *New Society*, 1972, 22, 681–3.

15

Children's hearings and children in trouble

Janice McGhee, Lorraine Waterhouse and Bill Whyte

BACKGROUND TO THE HEARINGS SYSTEM

The Children's Hearings System in Scotland was established under the Social Work (Scotland) Act 1968 and came into operation on 15 April 1971. This innovation in dealing with children in trouble was a direct result of the deliberations of the Kilbrandon Committee, who sought to find solutions to the rise in the rate of juvenile delinquency in post-war Scotland. Evidence gathered at the time indicated the triviality of most of the offences dealt with in the juvenile courts where 37 per cent of disposals in 1962 were either subject to absolute discharge or admonition. It was further found that in 95 per cent of cases there were no disputes as to the facts alleged and only 5 per cent were guilty pleas (Cooper, 1983).

The committee found that the legal distinction between juvenile offenders and children in need of care and protection was not a meaningful distinction when the underlying circumstances and needs of the children were examined. This has remained the central philosophy of the system where 'needs' rather than 'deeds' are the basis for decision making and intervention.

Kilbrandon saw the desirability of a national machinery to deal with children where services should be coordinated for children in difficulty. He envisaged a new 'social education department' located within education authorities to be responsible for providing services to deprived and delinquent children. This would include both field and residential services and would exercise the duties which probation officers (and subsequently social services departments) carried out in England in regard to child offenders.

There were concerns, however, from social work professionals both about their role in the proposed new 'social education departments' and the lack of emphasis on social measures to resolve child and family difficulties. The lack of flexibility within Scottish education at that time, with its emphasis on parental responsibility for the

SOURCE: This chapter is taken from S. Asquith (ed.) *Children and Young People in Conflict with the Law*, London, Jessica Langley, 1996, pp. 56–72 (adridged).

child's behaviour, was seen as thwarting the emphasis within social work on the need to assess all the factors (social, environmental, and individual) which influence a child's development. Education alone was seen as providing too narrow a focus for the wide-ranging, complex needs of children in trouble.

The outcome of debate and lobbying by social work associations and academics led to the creation of the social work departments as we know them today. In Scotland there is no separate probation service; social work services carry out the duties associated with probation in England and Wales, these duties having been integrated into their remit alongside responsibility for child care. This was a surprising development considering the punitive attitudes towards adult offenders in Scotland.

This enlightened system has also attracted criticisms both nationally and internationally which have focused on the tension between justice and welfare (Adler, 1985). Since its inception the Children's Hearings System has given rise to debate about the balance to be struck between justice, the rights of children, their parents and the welfare of children. This debate was brought into public focus by the Orkney (Scottish Office 1992a) and Fife (Scottish Office 1992b) inquiries, and the recent case of O v. Rae 1992 SCLR 318 has drawn further attention to this argument whereby the children's hearing was able to make decisions using information which could have founded a condition of referral but had not been tested before a sheriff.

This tension is particularly stark in child protection cases where the interests of parents may be in conflict with the child. Since 1985 the chairperson of a hearing and also the sheriff have been able to appoint a safeguarder in situations where there is a conflict between the interests of a child and his/her parents. Most recent Scottish Office figures (Scottish Office, 1993) indicate that safeguarders were appointed in 1.6 per cent of cases in 9646 disposals in 1988, compared with 3.6 per cent of 8449 disposals in 1993. Safeguarders are more likely to be appointed for children attending a hearing referred on non-offence grounds (5.9 per cent of 4484 cases in 1993) than children referred on offence grounds (0.7 per cent of 3106 cases in 1993). Nonetheless, there has been continuing disquiet about the ability of lay panels to address the complex nature of these cases and to arbitrate between the potentially conflicting interests and rights.

Despite the controversy over this system there has been a dearth of social research into the operation of the system, decision making at all levels, and child care outcomes. The major empirical study was that by Martin, Fox and Murray which reported in 1981 on information relating to the period 1978–79. Other major writing about the system has largely been about the philosophical (Adler, 1985) or legal functioning of the system (Kearney, 1987). Other research has focused on limited aspects of the system (see for example, Bruce and Spencer (1976) on the initial implementation of the system; Lockyer (1988) on the relationship between social work recommendations to hearings and the decisions taken; and Finlayson (1993) on Reporters' accountability).

In view of this, the Scottish Office has commissioned a study of the operation of the Children's Hearings System in two parts. The first concerns the processes of decision making within the Hearings System; the second is a national study of the characteristics and outcomes for children who are referred to the Reporter and followed up over three years. These studies should highlight the rationale for decisions taken and provide a picture of the social backgrounds and experiences of children within the Hearings System. It is also expected that any progression to the adult criminal justice system will be examined.

As Kilbrandon intended, the Children's Hearings System separated the functions of looking at the needs of children from establishing guilt. The courts were only to be involved where the facts were disputed, for appeals and dealing with more serious offences. Children under 16 years of age can only be prosecuted in the criminal courts at the instructions of the Lord Advocate. It remains an early intervention system for those children who would benefit from compulsory measures of care and protection. It is not a court but a tribunal serviced by lay people drawn from the community of the child with knowledge of children and family life. Each local authority has a Children's Panel Advisory Committee which has the responsibility for recruiting and training lay panel members and ensuring members carry out their duties satisfactorily. Many more people apply than are accepted, which may suggest popular support for and understanding of the system.

Each region currently has a department of the Reporter to the Children's Panel and whilst the Reporter is employed by the local authority s/he is independent and can only be removed by the Secretary of State for Scotland. The Reporter is the 'lynch-pin' (Thomson, 1991) of the system, s/he receives all referrals and decides if there is sufficient evidence to establish a condition of referral and whether a child may be in need of compulsory measures of care which include protection, control, guidance and treatment. The Reporter's options include the decision to take no further action, to refer to the social work department for voluntary measures of care or to arrange a children's hearing.

Reporters come from a range of disciplinary backgrounds although law, social work and to a lesser extent education dominate. The separation of departments has led to differing local practices both in decision making and response to referrals. This has given rise to concern and with the Local Government (Scotland) Act 1994 a new centralised service will be introduced with the advent of local government reform in Scotland in April 1996. There will be a Principal Reporter and a Children's Hearings Administration responsible for a national service. This may ensure the development of more standardised procedures and decision making.

THE PROCESS OF THE HEARING

A children's hearing involves three lay members of the panel (one of whom chairs the meeting), the parents or guardians of a child, the child in the majority of cases, representatives from the social work department, and the Reporter who provides legal advice to the hearing but does not take part in the proceedings. There is provision for parent(s) and/or the child to bring a representative, who may be a friend or a legal adviser, although legal aid is not available at this stage. The chair has the responsibility for the formal aspects of the proceedings and puts the grounds of referral to the child and his/her family. If the child and/or parent/guardian do not accept the grounds, or the child is too young, or is unable to understand the grounds, then the proceedings stop. The chair asks the Reporter to refer the matter to the sheriff and a formal court hearing will be heard in chambers to establish if the conditions for the grounds are met. Legal aid is available at this stage. If the child has been offended against the abuser does not have to be named, unlike in a criminal prosecution, and proceedings do not have to await the outcome of any criminal prosecution.

If the grounds are established the case is remitted back to the children's hearing for disposal; if the grounds are not upheld the case is discharged. For those cases which proceed to a hearing where a supervision requirement is made there is a system of review to establish progress and ensure that compulsory measures of care continue to be required. Review is annual unless requested earlier by the child and/or parent(s) or social work department.

The social work department provides reports and is responsible for the care and supervision of the child. A recent European Court of Human Rights decision has criticised the UK for refusing to giving parents the right to see any written reports provided by professionals. While it is certainly accepted social work practice to allow family members the opportunity to read reports this remains discretionary. The Children's (Scotland) Bill 1994 included proposals to allow increased access to professional reports.

STATISTICAL TRENDS

In 1993 24,304 children were referred to the Reporters' Departments of which 15,622 were boys and the remainder girls. This reflects a steady increase in the number of girls referred under 16 years. The pattern for boys continues to decrease although the overall rate per 1000 of the population for boys is higher than the comparable figure for 1972 (the first year of the operation of the Children's Hearings System). The increase in the number of referrals for girls is likely to be associated with the overall increase in care and protection grounds while for boys the decrease is associated with a reduction in offence grounds. In 1993 there was a 7 per cent decrease in the number of offence grounds from 1992.

The official statistics highlight the changing pattern of referrals to the children's hearings system. Martin, Fox and Murray (1981), in a study completed soon after the inception of the hearings system, drew attention to the predominance of offence referrals. They found of 678 cases 73 per cent of first grounds of referral were for offences, while only 5 per cent were related to parental neglect or an offence committed against a child. This trend has changed dramatically in the intervening 15 years. Most recent Scottish Office statistics (Scottish Office, 1994) show for the first time the rate of children referred to reporters on non-offence grounds exceeded those of offence grounds with a non-offence rate of 13.5 in 1993 compared with an offence rate of 11.9 in 1993. The grounds of referral to a Children's Hearing are set out in s. 32(2) Social Work (Scotland) Act 1968.

GENDER DIFFERENCES IN REFERRAL

The last ten years have seen a steady increase in the rate of non-offence grounds from 5.0 in 1983 to 13.5 in 1993. The most common ground of referral for both girls and boys was ground (d) where the child was a victim of neglect, assault or ill-treatment. However there was a clear gender difference, as of all referrals on this ground 40 per cent related to girls compared to 33 per cent for boys. This contrasts with ground (c), lack of parental care, where boys and girls were equally affected in 1993, constituting about one-fifth of all referrals.

It is also interesting to note that referrals for ground (f), non-attendance at school, increased by 9 per cent in 1993 for girls but only 4 per cent for boys. This has worrying implications for the educational attainments of children, especially girls, who may already be disadvantaged within educational settings. It has also been found that children in public care suffer from disruptions in their educational experience which may account for their subsequently poor performance on standardised examinations (Milham *et al.*, 1986).

Loss of schooling in children who are already facing adversity appears to have further negative consequences for later life chances. Rutter and Quinton (1988), looking at outcomes for young people raised in institutions, have shown the importance of positive school experiences in mediating adverse adult outcomes where home circumstances were characterised by poor relationships. Schooling is of central importance to children who come from already difficult backgrounds whilst for children from ordinary backgrounds good experiences at school make little difference to how they fare. This would seem to support Kilbrandon's early formulation of an emphasis on 'social education' for children.

This is particularly relevant for girls where research has shown that choice of partner is likely to reflect their own circumstances of disadvantage and to further limit their horizons (Rutter and Quinton, 1988). Girls who come from backgrounds of family discord and experience institutional care are more likely to select deviant partners perhaps as a well-intentioned but misguided escape from discordant relationships at home. Positive educational experience can in effect widen the choice of partner, research having shown that a supportive marital relationship is a protective factor against stressful experiences (Brown and Harris, 1978) and may support reasonable child rearing practice (Rutter and Quinton, 1988).

This serves to illustrate the double jeopardy which girls in our society are currently facing, where not only are they more likely to be the victim of an offence – Dobash, Carnie and Waterhouse (1993) found girls were significantly over-represented as victims of sexual offences – but they also face an increased likelihood of missing out on educational experiences which may be vital to their future well-being.

Martin, Fox and Murray (1981) found the peak age for referral to a Reporter for both boys and girls was 12–15-year-olds with 10,699 out of a total of 13,566 boys and 2791 out of a total of 3742 girls referred in that year (p. 38, table 3.5). This finding is further reflected in the 1993 statistics which show a similar gradual rise in referrals to the Reporter for both boys and girls for the ages 12–15.

There has been a fluctuating but slightly decreasing rate of referral on offence grounds from 13.2 in 1983, through 14.6 in 1987 to 11.9 in 1993, 15 years remaining the peak age for both boys and girls for alleged offending. Compared to children aged 8–11 years the rate of referral for both boys and girls is similar for non-offence grounds but boys are over-represented for offence related grounds with 1507 boys compared to 173 girls referred to Reporters for alleged offences in 1993. The comparable figures for boys and girls on non-offence grounds are 1499 for boys and 1245 for girls.

It is not clear whether the increased offence referrals for boys in this group reflect a real increase in offending behaviour or are an artefact of legal definitions with similar behaviours being redefined as offending but previously categorised under care and protection. The age of criminal responsibility in Scotland is 8 years. It remains unclear how children who enter the Hearings System under offence grounds fare in the longer term both in relation to subsequent criminality and later social functioning compared to those who enter under non-offence grounds. Nor is it clear what proportion of children move between these two categories throughout their childhood. How many children who enter the Hearings System on care and protection grounds at an early age subsequently re-enter at a later stage on offence-related grounds?

Although Kilbrandon strove to place the emphasis on needs rather than deeds the continuing differentiation between offenders and non-offenders has always remained and is reflected in the different standards of legal proof. Children who are offended against require grounds to be established on the civil standard of proof (the balance of probability) while for offenders the criminal standard (beyond reasonable doubt) has been retained.

[···]

SOURCES OF REFERRAL

Law enforcement agencies continue to dominate as key sources of referral to Reporters. Martin, Fox and Murray (1981) found that nearly 80 per cent of all referrals came from law enforcement agencies (that is, police (65 per cent), courts (1 per cent) and Procurators Fiscal (13 per cent). This pattern has remained remarkably consistent from 1983 to 1993 at around 78 per cent (Scottish Office, 1994). Similarly, Martin *et al.* (1981) found that alleged offence grounds constituted 73 per cent of all referrals to Reporters while in 1993 Scottish Office statistics showed this figure to have had a small but steady decline from 74 per cent in 1989 to 67 per cent in 1993.

Social work and education departments contributed 19 per cent of all referrals in Martin *et al.* (1981) study and have remained consistently at this level throughout the past 10 years. This pattern has been found in other child care research. For example, Packman (1986) and Vernon and Fruin (1986) found the influence of law enforcement agencies was central in the identification of children who may be in need of social work intervention. Their influence in the decision whether to admit to public care was critical, but if we look at the Hearings System Martin *et al.* (1981) found the opposite effect in that a referral from the school or social work department was much more likely to result in a subsequent referral to a children's hearing than if the source of referral was one of the law enforcement agencies.

There are no comparable statistics available for 1993 but Harvey (1994), in an unpublished report, noted that a higher proportion of non-offence referrals proceed to hearings. She found in 1991 42 per cent of cases referred to a hearing were on non-offence grounds compared with 31 per cent on offence grounds. This may give some support to the pattern found by Martin *et al.* (1981) remaining the same, as police are the most common source of offence referrals.

Parental referral to the Reporter has remained at exactly the same level of 1 per cent found by Martin *et al.* (1981) throughout the past 10 years (Scottish Office, 1993). This is perhaps surprising when the original idea was to encourage families to come forward for help to a universally available social service comparable to health and education.

Kilbrandon had predicted that in the main the offences committed by children would not be of a serious nature. Martin *et al.* (1981) examined the seriousness of alleged offences and found that of the 514 offences allegedly committed theft (40 per cent) and housebreaking (19 per cent) were the most common. Violence only accounted for 3 per cent and public order and property damage was (17 per cent) (table 5.3, p. 67). Current statistics do not routinely report the seriousness of offences alleged and therefore direct comparison is not possible. However in cases involving children under 16 referred to the court in 1992, most resulted in admonition, discharge, supervision or fine, which would suggest that they were not considered serious offenders (Scottish Office, 1993, p. 19).

VARIATIONS IN REPORTER'S PRACTICE

The Children's Hearings System includes a diversionary element demonstrated in the discretion afforded to Reporters in their decision making. Martin *et al.* (1981) highlight a range of influences on this decision making including personal conviction, group norms and departmental practice. Variation in decision making was reduced by regionalisation but still exists both between and within districts in Regions.

There is recognition that decision making should reflect local concerns and interest. Scottish Office statistics reflect this continuing variation with, for example, Strathclyde referring 37 per cent of all referrals to children's hearings in 1993 compared to Central with only 17 per cent. However, this disguises a general reduction in the percentage of referrals which went to hearings between 1990 and 1993 (Scottish Office, 1994). Shetland is an outstanding example of this trend, with 29 per cent of referrals going to hearings in 1990 rising to 36 per cent in 1991 and dropping to 12 per cent in 1993. Most other Regions have had a small but steady decline and this may reflect a greater emphasis on the diversionary aspects of the system which may be further amplified with the institution of a National Reporters Administration. The number of children referred to a hearing on non-offence grounds has remained consistently higher than referrals on offence grounds throughout.

DECISIONS OF HEARINGS

The most frequent disposal by hearings is a non-residential supervision requirement accounting for 85 per cent of all disposals by hearings in 1993 (Scottish Office, 1994). This pattern of disposal varies by grounds of referral but not apparently gender. Of the children who were not currently under supervision when referred to a hearing 55 per cent of boys and 54 per cent of girls referred on offence grounds were placed on supervision while for children referred on non-offence grounds the comparable figures are much larger for both boys and girls with 80 per cent and 79 per cent respectively. Over all age groups the use of supervision is increasing although this is most marked for the youngest children. Since 1983 the rate per 1000 of children under 5 years subject to a supervision requirement has consistently increased up until 1991, since when there has been a small decrease. Even taking into account this recent decrease the rate in 1993 is still nearly twice that of 1983.

DISCUSSION

The original philosophy of Kilbrandon to focus on 'needs not deeds' attempted to emphasise the similarity between children in need of care and protection and those who primarily came to the attention of the authorities because of their offending. The individual welfare of both groups of children was seen as the common focus for decision making and intervention. While on one level both these groups appear to face similar adverse social and family circumstances the apparent lack of direct attention towards offending behaviour may have served to undermine confidence in the system to deal with persistent offenders.

Similar concern is reflected in other jurisdictions which have moved towards different solutions for children who offend compared to those in need of care. This is exemplified in England and Wales where there are plans to introduce secure training units for persistent offenders. This reflects a growing punitive approach towards juveniles in trouble with an emphasis on mandatory sentencing of increasing length and a preference for adult models, which risk dissolving the important distinction between adult and juvenile justice. If this trend were to develop in Scotland then the Children's Hearings System will either have to alter their approach to juveniles in trouble or face a declining role in decisions about their future.

Nearly 25 years later the gap Kilbrandon tried to close between the needs of children in trouble with the law and children in need of care is beginning to open. As Cleland (1995) suggests, this change in outlook is reflected both in the United Kingdom and abroad and is likely to pose a serious challenge to the philosophy which lies behind the Children's Hearings System. She argues increased public pressure to make children accountable for wrongdoing, plus a growing concentration on the needs of victims, have contributed to the public focus shifting from the welfare of the child to offending behaviour and its consequences.

As outlined earlier Kilbrandon found the majority of offences committed by children were not serious in nature. Although there are no recent comparable statistics for children under 16 years, young people 16 years and over referred to the adult court have tended to receive minor sentences for what are therefore likely to be minor offences. Kilbrandon may have underestimated the problems posed to the system by children who persistently offend, but Hagel and Newburn's (1994) research affirms the adversity of their personal and social backgrounds in comparison to other children who offend.

Policy appears to be shifting from a concern with the social and personal needs of juvenile offenders to the frequency and nature of their offences. These are not necessarily mutually exclusive but a balance needs to be struck between addressing offending behaviour and responding to the needs of children in trouble.

These arguments are reflected in child protection policy and practice within the United Kingdom, where an increased emphasis is given to investigation and surveillance and less on the welfare of the child through provision of universally available child care resources. There is a similar danger that focusing on offending behaviour alone will hinder the development of wider social and educational resources necessary for all children especially those who are disadvantaged. Hallett (1993), comparing European and UK practices in relation to child protection, stresses the need to strike a balance between the paramountcy of the welfare of the child and the notion of justice within the wider community. This struggle is also played out in relation to children who offend. The law and social work practice have attempted to balance these competing claims against a growing background of public policy which seeks to isolate the young offender for the protection of the community.

[...]

The current desire to remove young offenders from child care decision making to a justice model risks stepping back into failed past experiments rather than addressing the social and family conditions which may contribute towards offending behaviour.

REFERENCES

Adler, R. (1985) *Taking Juvenile Justice Seriously*. Edinburgh: Scottish Academic Press.

Anderson, L., Kinsey, R. and Smith, C. (1993) *Cautionary Tales, A Study of Young People and Crime in Edinburgh*. Edinburgh: Criminal Research Unit, Scottish Office.

Brown, G.W. and Harris, T.O. (1978) *Social Origins of Depression: A Study of Psychiatric Disorder in Women*. London: Tavistock Publications, New York: Free Press.

Bruce, N. and Spencer, J. (1976) *Face to Face with Families. A Report on the Children's Panels in Scotland*. Loanhead: Macdonald Publishers.

Cleland, A. (1995) Legal solutions for children: comparing Scots Law with other jurisdictions. *Scottish Affairs* 10, winter, 6–24.

Cooper, J. (1983) *The Creation of the British Personal Social Services 1962–74*. London: Heinemann Education Books.

Dobash, R., Carnie, J. and Waterhouse, L. (1993) Child sexual abusers: recognition and response. In L. Waterhouse (ed.) *Child Abuse and Child Abusers: Protection and Prevention*. London: Jessica Kingsley Publishers.

Farrington, D. (1993) Juvenile delinquency. In J. Coleman (ed.) *The School Years*. London: Routledge.

Farrington, D. and Hawkins, J. (1991) Predicting participation, early onset, and later persistence in officially recorded offending. *Criminal Behaviour and Mental Health 1*, 1–33.

Finlayson, A. (1993) *Reporters to Children's Panels. Their Role, Function and Accountability*. Edinburgh: Social Work Services Group, Scottish Office, HMSO.

Gendreau, P. and Ross, R. (1987) Revivification or rehabilitation: evidence from the 1980s. *Justice Quarterly* 4, 349–407.

Hagel, A. and Newburn, T. (1994) *The Persistent Offender*. London: Policy Studies Institute.

Hallet, C. (1993) Child protection in Europe: convergence or divergence? *Adoption and Fostering* 17, 4, 27–32.

Harvey, J. (1994) The Children's Hearings system in Scotland: key issues for research. Unpublished manuscript. Edinburgh: Scottish Office.

Kearney, B. (1987) *Children's Hearings and the Sheriff Court*. Edinburgh: Butterworths/The Law Society of Scotland.

Kennedy, R. and McIvor, G. (1992) Young offenders in the Children's Hearing and criminal justice systems: a comparative analysis. Unpublished report for Tayside Regional Council.

Kilbrandon, L. (1964) *Children and Young Persons, Scotland*. Cm 2306. Edinburgh: Scottish Home and Health Department.

Lipsey, W. (1990) Juvenile delinquency treatment: a meta-analytic enquiry into the viability of effects. In T. Cook *et al.* (eds) *Meta-Analysis for Explanation.* New York: Sage.

Lockyer, A. (1988) *Study of Children's Hearings Disposals in Relation to Resources. Children's Panel Chairman's Group.* Edinburgh: Macdonald Lindsay.

Martin, F.M., Fox, S.J. and Murray, K. (1981) *Children Out of Court.* Edinburgh: Scottish Academic Press.

Millham, S., Bulock, R., Hosie, K. and Haak, M. (1986) *Children Lost in Care. The Family Contact of Children in Care.* Aldershot: Gower.

Murray, K. (1983) Children's Hearings. In J. English and F. Martin (eds) *Social Services in Scotland.* Edinburgh: Scottish Academic Press.

Packman, J., Randall, J. and Jacques, N. (1986) *Who Needs Care? Social Work Decisions about Children.* Oxford: Basil Blackwell.

Pease, J. and Barlow, G. (1989) *Contradictions Inherent in the Children's Hearing System.* Edinburgh: Scottish Child and Family Alliance (now Children in Scotland).

Rutter, M. and Quinton, D. (1988) *Parenting Breakdown. The Making and Breaking of Intergenerational Links.* Aldershot: Avebury.

Save the Children (1992) *16 and 17 Year Olds at the Interface between the Children's Hearings System and the Criminal Justice System.* Glasgow: Save the Children.

Scottish Office (1992a) *The Report of the Inquiry into the Removal of Children from Orkney in February 1991.* Edinburgh: HMSO.

Scottish Office (1992b) *Inquiry into Child Care Policies in Fife.* Edinburgh: HMSO.

Scottish Office (1990, 1991, 1993) *Statistical Bulletins: Criminal Proceedings in Scottish Courts.* Edinburgh: Government Statistical Service.

Scottish Office (1994) *Statistical Bulletin, Social Work Series. Referrals of Children to Reporters and Children's Hearings 1993.* Edinburgh: Government Statistical Service.

Thomson, J.M. (1991) *Family Law in Scotland.* 2nd ed. Edinburgh: Butterworths/The Law Society of Scotland.

Vernon, J. and Fruin, D. (1986) *In Care: A Study of Social Work Decision Making.* London: National Children's Bureau.

16

Restorative youth justice

The last vestiges of welfare?

Loraine Gelsthorpe and Allison Morris

A number of commentators on youth justice systems have outlined a significant departure from welfare-based principles and practice in recent years (see, for example, Gelsthorpe and Morris, 1994; Goldson, 1999; Muncie, 1999a). While the preceding chapters in Part III tell a story of the increasing importance (although perhaps never dominance) of child saving, decriminalization and welfarism in the late nineteenth century and up to the 1960s, the 1970s, 1980s and 1990s were largely characterized by other principles. Indeed, in the English and Welsh context, we have seen instead an increasing tendency to rely on the principles and practices of crime control, although the Scottish youth justice system perhaps survived some of the rigours of the 1980s and 1990s with more of its welfare principles intact (Kearney, 1987; Young and Young, 1996; Lockyer and Stone, 1998; Duff and Hutton, 1999). In the late 1990s and into the new millennium other approaches began to emerge: many of these reflect restorative justice principles and there is evidence of engagement with such ideas in England, Northern Ireland and Scotland. This chapter concentrates on the situation in England and Wales, but following a major review of youth justice policy and practice in Northern Ireland there has been conscious movement towards a restorative justice model following years of 'crime control' (see O'Mahony and Deazley, 2000, for further details). In Scotland too, a reassessment of the Children's Hearing System suggests that at least some procedural elements of restorative justice are already in place (Hallett *et al.*, 1998).

We begin with a brief overview of developments since the 1960s to indicate the apparent, if partial, eclipse of welfare principles in the English and Welsh context. But the main purpose of the chapter is to examine recent developments in youth justice and in particular to assess engagement with restorative justice principles as indicative of a re-enchantment with social welfare ideas.

SOURCE: Commissioned for this volume. Loraine Gelsthorpe is Senior Lecturer in Criminology, Institute of Criminology, University of Cambridge, UK. Allison Morris is former Director of the Institute of Criminology and Professor of Criminology, Victoria University, Wellington, New Zealand.

JUVENILE JUSTICE IN THE 1960S

The 1960s saw a period of intense activity in England and Wales culminating in the 1969 Children and Young Persons Act. The Labour Party promoted ideas to blur the distinction between the deprived and the depraved child and to deal with young offenders by way of care and protection rather than criminal proceedings. The general aim was to divert young offenders from the youth justice system or, where it was absolutely necessary, to send them to court, to 'care for' and 'treat' young offenders rather than punish them (Gelsthorpe and Morris, 1994; Muncie, 1999a). However, the 1969 Act proved to be a high-water mark and there was a quick retreat from some of its key principles. A Conservative government replaced Labour in 1970 and the Conservatives made it clear that they would not fully implement the Act – particularly Labour's proposals to raise the age of criminal responsibility to fourteen and to abolish custody for the under-seventeens. When the Labour Party was re-elected in 1974 it was no longer politically or popularly viable to implement the Act in full. Thus some new welfare measures were added on to, but did not replace, the old punitive ones; further, other welfare initiatives (such as care proceedings) never got off the ground (Gelsthorpe and Morris, 1994; Muncie, 1999a).

JUVENILE JUSTICE IN THE 1970S

The new theme was essentially that the appropriate response to the delinquent in the court room was correction through discipline and punishment. Indeed, the use of custody for juveniles under both Conservative and Labour governments in the 1970s increased. A second paradoxical trend also occurred – a decline in the use of welfare-oriented dispositions (care orders, for example) despite the intentions underlying the 1969 Act (Gelsthorpe and Morris, 1994). This can be at least partially explained by the impact of diversion (cautioning) practices, by the increased use of fines and compensation, by the emerging intermediate treatment provision (Bottoms et al., 1990), by the introduction of criteria to restrict the use of custody and by the increased legal representation of young offenders which led to a reduction in the use of custody (Gelsthorpe and Morris, 1994).

JUVENILE JUSTICE IN THE 1980S: TOWARDS CRIME CONTROL

In the 1980s in England and Wales, as elsewhere, there was an explicit revival of traditional criminal justice crime control values. It is no accident that this coincided with and was fuelled by the electoral campaigns and eventual election of a Conservative government in 1979 with a large majority. The 'need to stand firm against crime' was especially apparent in the electoral campaigns of the Conservative Party in 1979, where it presented itself as the party which *could* and *would* take a strong stand against crime, in contrast to the Labour Party, which was presented as excusing crime and as being too sympathetic towards offenders.

The campaign message focused on the need to protect victims from offenders, and the need to reduce the high level of recorded crime and the alleged increased seriousness of crime, particularly among juveniles. Specifically, the political rhetoric referred to 'young thugs' who were to be sent to detention centres for a 'short, sharp shock', to increasing the number of secure places for juveniles, and to expanding the number of attendance centres. After they had won the election, the Conservative government's Criminal Justice Act 1982 saw the reintroduction of traditional criminal justice values, policies and practices which hit at the root of the social welfare perspective underlying the 1969 Act, although there was some endorsement of the expansion of diversion (cautioning) and a reduction in the minimum period of custody for which a boy could be held in a detention centre. There was also a move towards the notion of personal responsibility, punishment and parental responsibility. In brief, the 1982 Act made available to magistrates three new powers of disposal: youth custody, care orders with certain residential requirements and community service. The 1980s was arguably a period of 'law and order' and 'crime control', with policies which were designed to reassert the virtue and necessity of authority, order and discipline (Muncie, 1999a).

YOUTH JUSTICE IN THE 1990S: TOWARDS REFORM

The first significant events of the 1990s were the implementation of the 1989 Children Act and the introduction of the 1991 Criminal Justice Act, which had the combined effect of separating the systems for dealing with children perceived to be in need of care (to be dealt with in the family courts) and those charged with criminal offences (to be dealt with in the newly named Youth Court). The most important change in this context perhaps was the cessation of the use of the care order (an established symbol of welfare) as a disposal available to the court in criminal proceedings, and the removal of the offence condition in proceedings justifying state intervention in the life of a family. This change at once recognized the enormous decline in the use made of the care order, the seeming inappropriateness of a care order in criminal proceedings, the principle of determinacy in sentencing, and the importance that the government attached to parental responsibility.

Concern about increases in juvenile crime in the 1990s was fuelled by such things as joyriding incidents in deprived areas, increased publicity about persistent young offenders and the murder of James Bulger by two ten-year-old boys (Gelsthorpe and Kemp, 2002). As a result, the need to be seen to be 'tough on crime' prompted new thinking in the main political parties. The use of cautions and warnings was heavily criticized as being ineffective and routine, and was actively discouraged. The Criminal Justice and Public Order Act 1994 introduced secure training orders for twelve to fourteen-year-olds, and longer custodial sentences. The Conservative government also considered the introduction of 'high impact incarceration programmes' – more commonly referred to as 'boot camps' (military-style camps). The idea was that a tougher, more physically demanding regime might have an impact on young offenders' criminal propensities (Mackenzie and Souryal, 1994; Farrington et al., 2000).

As a result of court cases in 1994 and 1995 (most notably the case of the two boys tried for killing two-year-old James Bulger), the principles governing the criminal responsibility of children between the ages of ten and thirteen were also reviewed (Bandalli, 1998). The age of criminal responsibility in England and Wales is ten years, and children under that age cannot be found guilty of a criminal offence. Children between ten and thirteen were presumed in law to be *doli incapax* (incapable of criminal intent) and this presumption had to be rebutted by the prosecution before they could be convicted. In order to rebut the presumption, the prosecution had to show beyond all reasonable doubt that the child appreciated that what he or she did was 'seriously wrong' as opposed to merely naughty or mischievous. Nevertheless, following the review, the principle of *doli incapax* was upheld on the grounds that there is wisdom in protecting young children against the full rigour of the criminal law because of the need to acknowledge varying rates of child development and maturity. The age of criminal responsibility in England and Wales is unusually low in comparison with most countries of western Europe, where offenders under fourteen are dealt with by civil court proceedings. The principle of *doli incapax* arguably provided some recognition that children of this age should not be considered as fully criminally responsible as adults.

Despite all these efforts to ensure the control of crime by young people, both the youth courts and custodial institutions involved came to be perceived as ineffective (Audit Commission, 1996, 1998). Thus the stage was set for major reform in the next phase of development under a new government.

THE CRIME AND DISORDER ACT 1998

Throughout its opposition years from 1979 to 1997 the Labour Party argued that youth crime and youth justice would be a priority of the next Labour government. Having produced a paper, *Tackling Youth Crime, Reforming Youth Justice* (Home Office, 1997a), as it contemplated the ballot box, the newly elected government (in May 1997) was quick to produce further proposals (Home Office, 1997b, c). The general tenor of these proposals was to suggest that there must be an effort 'to improve the effectiveness of the Youth Justice system in preventing, deterring and punishing youth crime' (Home Office, 1997d, p. 2). The White Paper containing the main framework of the legislation was published in November 1997, its title giving a telling clue to what lay within: *No More Excuses* (Home Office, 1997d). The Crime and Disorder Act 1998 which followed was described as a 'comprehensive and wide-ranging reform programme' (Home Office, 1997b, p. 1). Many of its provisions were explicitly aimed not only at young offenders, but at young people more generally. However, one of the key questions for us in this chapter concerns how far the government returned to the welfarist principles which Labour had championed in the 1960s. In many ways the legislation largely appeared to favour punishment to signal society's disapproval of criminal acts and deter offending. But crucially, some would say, the government remained faithful to its commitment to be 'tough on crime, tough on the causes of crime' by referring at various times to the social factors which contribute to crime and by proposing orders to prevent reoffending through an interventionist, welfare approach reminiscent of interventions in the 1960s. Importantly, the Act also contains provisions which underline support for the government's belief in restorative justice principles, the central tenet of which is that crime should be seen primarily as a matter concerning the offender and victim and their immediate families and thus should be resolved by them through constructive effort (reparative measures) to put right the harm that has been done.

Details of the Crime and Disorder Act 1998 are described elsewhere (Fionda, 1999; Muncie, 1999b; Gelsthorpe and Morris, 1999; Ball, 2000). Suffice it to say here that, with the concomitant Youth Justice and Criminal Evidence Act 1999, there are new measures to ensure the effective functioning of the system through, for example, the introduction of

- A national Youth Justice Board – to give strategic direction, set standards for and measure the performance of the youth justice system as a whole.
- Local youth offending teams.
- Various measures to speed up the punishment process.

Notwithstanding previous support for the *doli incapax* rule, that rebuttable presumption was repealed by Section 34 of the Crime and Disorder Act 1998 (Bandalli, 2000). There are also fresh measures in this Act to ensure that offenders address their offending behaviour and reduce their risk to the community (through, for example, warnings – which trigger intervention from youth offending teams – action plan orders, and drug treatment and testing orders), and measures to ensure the protection of the community (through, for example, antisocial behaviour orders) (see NACRO, 2000, for details). There are measures too which involve taking anticipatory action on the basis of the probability of offending (such as child safety orders which involve curfews on individual children; for details see Gelsthorpe and Morris, 1999; Goldson, 1999). In the same Act local curfew orders may apply to all children under the age of ten in a specific area and prevent them meeting in specified public places between 9.00 p.m. and 6.00 a.m. unless accompanied by a parent or responsible adult. Local authorities can impose these curfews on the basis that such children are 'at risk' of committing offences. Parenting orders (which involve guidance or counselling sessions once a week for up to twelve weeks) can also be imposed on parents whose children are on a child safety order, an antisocial behaviour order or a sex offender order (see NACRO, 2000, for details) – and *have* to be imposed where magistrates believe that a child under sixteen may reoffend unless the parents are instructed in how to take greater responsibility for their offspring's behaviour (Gelsthorpe and Morris, 1999; Drakeford and McCarthy, 2000). But the key issue to explore here is whether or not the new youth justice agenda contains seeds of 'welfarism'. But first, an apparent digression: why would we want to retain welfarism, given the severe critique of it in the 1970s? (See Morris *et al.*, 1980.)

For some time it has been recognized that minor offences are characteristic of a certain stage of adolescence, in both boys and girls. However, it is also recognized that a significant proportion of offences are committed by a very small group of offenders, whose offending is unrelated to age (Graham and Bowling, 1995). These persistent offenders are seemingly characterized by an early onset of offending and chaotic lives in which poverty, violence, neglect, abuse and school failure play a large part (Farrington, 1997). As Andrew Rutherford (1992) has claimed, however, knowledge of the needs of young offenders does not necessarily require a return to the unsatisfactory welfare-based solutions of the 1960s. A renewed interest in welfare involves encouraging young offenders to accept responsibility and increasing accountability to victims, as well as dealing more explicitly with the needs of young offenders. Much of this comes under the heading of 'restorative justice'. Significantly, the White Paper *No More Excuses* (Home Office, 1997d) acknowledged the need 'to reshape the criminal justice system in England and Wales to produce more constructive outcomes with young offenders' and referred to the need to build on three concepts: *responsibility*, *restoration* and *reintegration* (para. 9.21) (our emphasis).

RESTORATIVE JUSTICE

Restorative justice has come into prominence in Western societies only since the mid-1980s, though the concept is far from new. Consedine (1995) links it with the traditions of the Celts, Maori and Samoans and other indigenous peoples, as well as placing its roots in various religious communities.

Restorative justice means rather different things to different people, however; it has been equated, among other suggestions, with victim–offender mediation, compensation and community service (Marshall, 1999). There are certainly overlaps, but restorative justice is arguably about more than a particular forum for decision making or a particular set of outcomes (Haines, 2000). It is about a particular set of values which underpin and impact on both processes and outcomes and which take priority over competing values (Braithwaite, 1999; Morris and Young, 2000).

Restorative justice involves restoring responsibility to offenders for their offending and its consequences, certainly, but it is also about taking charge of the need to make amends for what they have done and restoring a belief in them that the process in which they are involved, and the outcomes reached, are fair and just. The offender's inclusion in the process and in determining the outcome, therefore, is crucial. This means that, in restorative processes, offenders *themselves* speak about their offending and matters associated with it, rather than through some third party (for example, through a lawyer), and thereby accept responsibility for it. It means that they interact directly with any victim(s) present, express their remorse about what has occurred, apologize for what they have done and attempt to make amends for it. And it also means that they contribute to and agree with decisions about eventual outcomes rather than having decisions made for and about them by others and then imposed on them. From all this, it is assumed that offenders will have a better understanding of their offending and its consequences, and that, as a result of increased understanding, the offender will be less likely to reoffend. But it is also acknowledged that some steps have to be made to put right, where possible, the circumstances which led to the offending in the first place (for example, by addressing drug and alcohol abuse), and to include the offender in future social life (for example, by offering training or exploring job options).

The inclusion of victims is also a core value of restorative justice. They too can directly participate in the process if they so wish or, if they prefer, indirectly through a representative; they can speak about the effects of their experience on them, their family, their friends and, perhaps, their community; they can interact with the offender, hear the offender explain what happened and ask questions of him or her; they can contribute to decisions about eventual outcomes; and they can accept an apology, if one is offered, for what has been done. From all this, victims too will have a better understanding of their experience: why it happened to them and what the chances are of it happening again. Thus 'restoration' is not simply about reparation, but about seeking to restore the victim's security, safety, self-respect, dignity and, most important, sense of control. Where possible, here too some steps have to be taken to put right the consequences of the offending (for example, by providing the victim with direct service or practical help) and to include the victim in future social life (for instance, by offering the victim counselling to deal with the aftermath of the offence and to enable him or her to move on).

In essence, then, restoring justice is about putting right the wrong to the extent that it is possible for *both* victim and offender. This means, as the White Paper (Home Office, 1997d) recognized, a stress on responsibility, restoration and reintegration.

Restorative justice in practice

Various jurisdictions have attempted to introduce restorative justice practices into their youth justice systems. Probably the most advanced are some Australian states and New Zealand. The systems there differ markedly from the youth justice system in England and Wales and so, before examining the extent to which England and Wales reflect restorative justice processes and practices, we outline developments in Australia and New Zealand.

Australia and New Zealand

In the main, restorative justice processes and practices in Australia and New Zealand are set out in statutes as part of a coherent response to young offenders. New South Wales, the Northern Territory, Queensland, South Australia, Tasmania, Western Australia and New Zealand all have statutory systems of conferencing. (The Australian Capital Territory – ACT – and Victoria also use conferencing, but it is not statutorily based.) Except in Queensland, these statutory schemes apply to all young offenders throughout the jurisdiction and not just in certain areas. And the aim in all jurisdictions is to deal with young offenders as much as possible without reliance on formal court processes. Daly (2001) estimated that just under 6,000 young people a year took part in restorative conferences in Australia. The number is much the same in New Zealand. The rest of this section describes family group conferences in New Zealand.

Family group conferences, introduced in New Zealand in 1989, directly involve those most affected by the offending – specifically the offender, the victim and their families – in determining appropriate responses to it. The aim of conferences is to hold offenders accountable for their actions and to take into account the interests of the victim. The most usual outcomes are apologies and community work (see Maxwell and Morris, 1993).

Conferences are held in two situations in New Zealand: in the first situation, where the police decide not to warn or otherwise divert the young person and want him or her dealt with by a judge in court, the young person will normally appear in court, but the judge cannot sentence without first referring the offender to a conference which will then make a recommendation to the judge about how the offender should be dealt with. Most judges follow these recommendations. In the second situation, where the police have arrested the young person, he or she will be referred to court only if the conference decides that it cannot otherwise deal with the offending. Most of these cases do not proceed to court (Maxwell and Morris, 1993).

Research on family group conferences in New Zealand has shown that they can meet restorative justice expectations. In brief, they have shown that offenders can be held accountable for their offending in meaningful ways; that the voices of victims can be heard; that victims can feel better as a result of their participation; and that outcomes which address both victims' and offenders' needs or interests can be reached (Morris and Maxwell, 2000). Research has also shown that conferences can impact on reoffending (Maxwell and Morris, 1999).

Of particular interest here are the restorative justice factors which distinguished the non-reconvicted from the reconvicted: the young person still remembering the conference at the time of the re-interview (some six years later), the young person completing the tasks agreed to, the young person saying they felt sorry about the offending, showing it and feeling that she or he had repaired the damage, the young person not being made to feel a bad person, the young person feeling involved in the decision making, the young person agreeing with the conference outcome and the young person meeting the victim and apologizing were all significantly related to no reconviction. Also influential in preventing reoffending were a number of factors indicative of reintegration into the community, such as gaining educational qualifications and vocational skills, developing close and positive relations with family, friends and partners, and settling into a stable lifestyle. In brief, they pointed to the importance of strategies to effect social inclusion.

England and Wales

The use of mediation and reparation between offenders and victims in England and Wales (embodying some restorative principles) began in an *ad hoc* way in the 1970s. More recent examples include the police-led restorative conferencing scheme in the Thames Valley Police force (Pollard, 1999; Young and Goold, 1999), the Milton Keynes retail theft initiative, the multi-agency Northamptonshire Diversion Unit and the Kent Intensive Support and Supervision Programme for persistent offenders (Akester, 2000). There are other less publicized examples of conferencing in operation in other parts of England and Wales, but the number of cases dealt with has been small and the type of offending being dealt with seems minor (Marsh, 1996; Marsh and Crow, 1998; Dignan and Marsh, 2001). The Hampshire youth justice family group conference project, for example, was set up for repeat offenders who were deemed unlikely to respond to further cautioning (Jackson, 1998). One of the main characteristics of all these developments, of course, was that they were peripheral to the mainstream youth justice system, operated without statutory authority, and depended to a large extent on local initiative and energy. In contrast, the Crime and Disorder Act 1998 in England and Wales and the Youth Justice and Criminal Evidence Act 1999 together formally introduced elements of restorative justice as a supposedly mainstream response to youth offending in a number of different ways:

- Diversionary measures which trigger referral to local multi-agency youth offending teams (YOTs) and involve rehabilitation or 'change' programmes linked with final warnings. Reparative measures may include: letters of apology from the offender, direct reparative activities performed for the victim, direct or indirect mediation, family group or restorative conferencing, reparation to the community at large, victim awareness exercises (including the use of surrogate victims), for instance.
- Court referrals to youth offender panels for those coming before the court for the first time who plead guilty, with the aim of agreeing a contract (a programme of behaviour designed to emphasize responsibility for offending and thus prevent reoffending, make reparation and achieve reintegration into the community). The referrals are mandatory unless either an absolute discharge or a custodial sentence is considered appropriate. The panels, established by local youth offending teams, consist of three members – one from the youth offending team and two from a pool of community volunteers with different skills and experience, as well as a parent or guardian, the young offender and the victim. The youth offender panel is perceived as potentially a major mechanism for introducing elements of a

restorative justice approach. Significantly, such a referral constitutes the only sentence that may be imposed for the relevant offence(s) and the offender can be taken back to court only if he or she fails to comply with the agreed contract. As Dignan and Marsh (2001) note, this move to a community conference model of decision making marks a significant change from decision making in the court room.

- Court-ordered reparation or action plan orders. In the White Paper *No More Excuses*, which preceded the 1998 and 1999 legislative reforms, it was suggested that reparation would be a 'valuable way of making young offenders face the consequences of their actions and see the harm they have caused' (Home Office, 1997d, para. 4, p. 13). It was described there as a 'catalyst for reform and rehabilitation' and as also benefiting victims. The reparation order was introduced in courts (from April 2000) for offenders aged ten and older, and requires them to make some sort of reparation to their victims (if they consent) or to the community at large. Reparation orders can vary in length up to twenty-four hours and occupy a place in the sentencing tariff equivalent to the conditional discharge; it is envisaged that they will be the main entry-level penalty for less serious offenders. The action plan order, designed to be the first option for young people whose offending behaviour is serious enough to warrant a community sentence, is described as a central plank of the youth justice provisions contained in the 1998 Act and is depicted by Dignan as having 'a strong restorative justice component to it' (Dignan, 1999, p. 53). The orders are applicable to ten to seventeen-year-olds, last three months and involve a short, intensive programme of community intervention. Before making an order the court has to obtain a report from a probation officer, social worker or YOT worker which indicates the requirements to be included in the order and their likely benefits. (It is also worth noting that reparation can be included as a requirement in a supervision order.)
- Provision for victims to be consulted before any reparative intervention is organized and for their views to be relayed to the court. Offenders can be ordered to make direct reparation only where the victim agrees. Victims are also allowed to participate in youth offender panels.

Thus the range of reparative interventions is available at both the pre-court and post-court stages. (For further details of legislative provision see Leng *et al.*, 1998; Birch and Leng, 1999.)

The prospects for restorative justice and welfare in England and Wales

Possible 'pitfalls on the path to restorative justice' were acknowledged early on (Dignan, 1999). These include: the failure of the government to address the spiralling prison population, the continuing 'tough talk' on crime, and other provisions of the Crime and Disorder Act which express objectives in conflict with restorative justice (Morris and Gelsthorpe, 2000). There are many elements of the legislation which prop up the pivotal role of custody in the panoply of provisions, for example. The idea of a generic custodial sentence – the detention and training order – at once blurs the boundaries between the secure training orders for twelve to fourteen-year-olds established in the Crime and Disorder Act 1994, local authority secure care orders and pre-existing orders for detention in a young offenders' institution, and paves the way to increased use of custody (Fionda, 1999; Muncie, 1999b; Gelsthorpe and Morris, 1999). In this respect, children aged ten and above are now treated like adults. English and Welsh children are almost alone in Europe in being regarded as criminals at the age of ten. They are also 'punished'/subject to intervention measures below that age under the child safety order in unique fashion. In our view, collectively, these 'pitfalls' are such as to suggest little likelihood of the true potential of restorative justice being realized.

Ian Brownlee's (1998) analysis lends support to this view. He provides a searching critique of New Labour's 'new penology' as reflected in the 1998 legislation (and implicitly in the 1999 Act too) by noting the continuing tendency to locate the causes of crime at the level of individual failure and the continuing punitive discourse.

In addition to the possibility of restorative principles being *diluted* within a newly devised system which reflects competing ideological values, a number of specific concerns about the framing of restorative values have been voiced. There have been questions about whether restorative justice principles can work when reparation orders are *imposed* on offenders without their consent, for example (Morris and Gelsthorpe, 2000). Further, there have been questions about what it means when victim–offender mediation is only a *possibility* as part of a reparation order but not an integral part of it (Morris and Gelsthorpe, 2000). Such provisions seem to be at odds with restorative values which see the offender and the victim as key decision makers (Maxwell and Morris, 1993). As Dignan himself speculated in anticipation of the 1998 Act, the compulsory nature of reparation may 'undermine the salutary and therapeutic benefits for offenders that have been associated with voluntary schemes' (Dignan, 1999, p. 55). Under the Act the courts can *direct* personal apologies. This may lead to grudging or insolent attitudes being displayed when young offenders meet their victims. Victims too may perceive their involvement in reparation schemes less favourably if they do not feel *fully* involved in the decision. Also, despite optimism that there is a shift to community-based decision making (Dignan and Marsh, 2001), it is argued by some that the reformed youth justice system confirms the court as the central part of the system (Akester, 2000). Finally, the mandatory referral order introduced under the 1999 Act may prove to be difficult to operate because of uncertainties about the membership and powers of youth offender panels, the muddled nature of the 'contract' based on a programme of behaviour drawn up between the offender and the panel (that it will not be entirely 'freely negotiated': Wonnacott, 1999) and the lack of recognition of the resource implications for local authorities and other agencies meant to be involved in tackling the causes of crime alongside the structural changes in the youth justice system itself (Ball, 2000).

The main tenor of Labour criminal justice legislation since the party came to power perhaps mirrors Labour's sympathetic thinking of the 1960s about 'children in trouble', and so on, but in practice indicates a melting pot of contradictions, ideas and ideologies which may militate against each other rather than serving the notion of clear and consistent sentencing (Fionda, 1999). From consideration of the recent changes in the youth justice system it is more possible to conceive of an ideological shift in favour of punishment and crime control reminiscent of Cohen's 'punitive city' (Cohen, 1985) in which more and more people, including children, are brought into the criminal justice system for an ever expanding range of 'criminal' or 'troublesome' behaviour (Gelsthorpe and Morris, 1999) than to discern 'some elements of the restorative approach as part of the mainstream response to offending behaviour by young people', or to see the current political climate as having 'done so much to transform the prospects for a restorative justice approach to take root and flourish as an integral part of the criminal justice system' (Dignan, 1999). In contrast, it is possible to see restorative justice as just *one* theme in a somewhat punitive and controlling piece of legislation. Given these strands in the new legislation, it is hard to have much confidence in those elements of restorative justice which we suggested may signal a new 'welfare' perspective.

This is confirmed by examination of the implementation of the legislation thus far. There are a number of key findings resulting from the evaluation of the pilot areas that are worth noting here (Holdaway *et al.*, 2001). First, not all youth offending teams are offering the full range of restorative interventions. Also, there appear to be significant differences in the delivery of these interventions. The issue of consultation with victims is sometimes overridden by the need for speedy justice, and, whilst voluntary involvement by offenders has been central to the philosophies of victim–offender reparation schemes and restorative conferencing in other countries, the compulsory nature of reparation under the 1998 Act means that reparation has become 'routine' rather than 'meaningful', with letters of apology being rehearsed by hard-pressed YOT workers anxious to get young people through the activities (Williams, 2001). The nature of some of the activities organized as part of reparation orders has also raised some disquiet. Holdaway *et al.* (2001) found a strong emphasis on practical tasks such as litter collection or conservation work. Whilst such activities may have their place in the repertoire of activities, it is hard to see how they are restorative or reintegrative. Some of those interviewed for the evaluation of the pilot reparation projects described such activities as 'a form of junior community service with minimal reparative benefits' (Dignan, 2000, p. 24). Overall, the researchers evaluating the pilot areas reported wide variation in the form and delivery of specified activities in the orders – including the reparative elements. The researchers also noted that there is little to distinguish these elements from reparative elements in warning programmes and supervision orders (Holdaway *et al.*, 2001).

Victims in restorative justice practices in New Zealand have, as we noted earlier, the right to be present and to give their views on appropriate outcomes and, in some jurisdictions, they have a veto on whether or not the matter should be dealt with through the courts rather than through restorative processes. This is a key point because research suggests that involvement in these restorative processes is as important as, if not more important than, restorative outcomes (see Maxwell and Morris, 1993). Many of the points raised as emerging from practice with regard to restorative justice through the 1998 Act are seemingly at odds with traditional restorative values which see the offender and the victim as key decision makers for the reasons outlined earlier in this chapter. Indeed, it seems that the ethos of restorative justice is quite limited in certain sections of the new youth justice system (Holdaway *et al.*, 2001; and see Chapter 31 of this volume).

CONCLUSION

The practices which are part of the 'restorative package' introduced in the Crime and Disorder Act 1998 and Youth Justice and Criminal Evidence Act 1999 do not seem set to deliver the promise of radical change in the way in which we respond to young people who offend. It seems that restorative practices are developing in a somewhat *ad hoc* fashion at numerous decision points in the youth justice system, but at no point are the key participants in all of this – offenders, victims and their families – actually able to take charge. Victims are no longer marginalized in quite the way they have been, but their involvement is arguably hardly significant. Offenders may be coerced into reparation, yet nothing in the research literature suggests that this will be likely to prevent reoffending. The critical question is whether or not restorative justice is sufficiently powerful to revitalize youth justice in England and Wales.

There are a number of points to note here which distinguish the restorative justice aspirations in the Crime and Disorder Act in England and Wales from the restorative justice practices in Australasia. First, the power of professionals to make decisions is curtailed by conferencing in Australasia and, second, the role of the courts is quite marginal. Importantly also, although conferences are held for only about 20 per cent of young offenders in New Zealand, it is the 20 per cent who have committed medium–serious and serious offences (the only offences excluded are murder and manslaughter) or who have offended persistently. Thus conferences are held for young people who have committed burglary, robbery, rape, arson, and so on (Morris and Maxwell, 2000). This is indicative of the mainstream role of restorative justice.

It seems to us that, despite the good intentions and enthusiasm of many politicians, policy makers and practitioners, the hold of restorative justice in England and Wales will remain tenuous unless the competing and contradictory values running through criminal and youth justice policy in general, and the new youth justice legislation in particular, concede more space. The aim of using restorative justice principles to promote accountability, victim satisfaction and prevent reoffending is laudable, but key findings following the introduction of reforms suggests that the way restorative justice principles are being implemented may well limit achievements here.

It is certainly the case that the government is concerned to 'get tough on the causes of crime'. The Social Exclusion Unit and the Community Development Foundation have created programmes to facilitate greater access for young people to the employment market and encouraged social improvement in socially deprived areas (Carpenter *et al.*, 2000). But whether or not these activities signal a return to the policies first introduced in the Children and Young Persons Act 1969, which aimed to recast the offender as a victim of social deprivation, is highly questionable. Moreover, it is difficult to see how they will be funded, given Labour's well rehearsed commitment to reduce public spending (Joyce, 1999).

Whilst there is little space to enlarge on it here, what appears to have happened is that the social welfare agenda of the 1960s has been replaced by a moral agenda in the late 1990s. Restorative justice in the English and Welsh system sits alongside detention and training orders, antisocial behaviour orders, parenting orders and other more punitive orders to signal a 'remoralization initiative' (Day Sclater and Piper, 2001). Daly (2001) has speculated on why Australia and New Zealand have been at the forefront of the restorative justice movement; she suggests that 'compared to the United States, Canada, and England and Wales, Australia and New Zealand continue to be more ideologically committed to policies that emphasize social welfare and crime prevention' (Daly, 2001, pp. 60–1). She also refers to these developments as 'reflecting something positive about the conditions of life and modes of governance in these countries, where there is an openness to addressing social problems and to redressing inequalities' (Daly, 2001, p. 61). It is our view that only a new emphasis on such problems and a rebalancing of responsibility, restoration and reintegration, both within and beyond the youth justice system, would truly signify a turn to welfare considerations.

REFERENCES

Akester, K. (2000) *Restoring Youth Justice: New Directions in Domestic and International Law and Practice*, London, Justice.

Audit Commission (1996) *Misspent Youth: Young People and Crime*, London, Audit Commission.

Audit Commission (1998) *Misspent Youth 1998: The Challenge for Youth Justice*, London, Audit Commission.

Ball, C. (2000) 'The Youth Justice and Criminal Evidence Act 1999', Part I 'A significant move towards restorative justice, or a recipe for unintended consequences?', *Criminal Law Review*, April, pp. 211–21.

Bandalli, S. (1998) 'Abolition of the presumption of *doli incapax* and the criminalisation of children', *Howard Journal*, vol. 37, no. 2, pp. 114–23.

Bandalli, S. (2000) 'Children, responsibility and the new youth justice' in B. Goldson (ed.) *The New Youth Justice*, Lyme Regis, Russell House.

Birch, D. and Leng, R. (1999) *Blackstone's Guide to the Youth Justice and Criminal Evidence Act 1999*, London, Blackstone Press.

Bottoms, A.E., Brown, P., McWilliams, B., McWilliams, W. and Nellis, M. (1990) *Intermediate Treatment and Juvenile Justice*, London, HMSO.

Braithwaite, J. (1999) 'Restorative justice: assessing optimistic and pessimistic accounts' in M. Tonry (ed.) *Crime and Justice: A Review of Research*, vol. 25, Chicago IL, University of Chicago Press.

Brownlee, I. (1998) 'New Labour – new penology? Punitive rhetoric and the limits of managerialism in criminal justice policy', *Journal of Law and Society*, vol. 25, no. 3, pp. 313–35.

Carpenter, A., Nicolson, R. and Robinson, D. (eds) (2000) *What If? Fifteen Visions of Change for Britain's Inner Cities*, London, Community Links.

Cohen, S. (1985) *Visions of Social Control: Crime, Punishment and Classification*, Cambridge, Polity Press.

Consedine, J. (1995) *Restorative Justice: Healing the Effects of Crime*, Lyttelton NZ, Ploughshare Publications.

Daly, K. (2001) 'Conferencing in Australia and New Zealand: variations, research findings, and prospects' in Morris and Maxwell (eds) *Restorative Justice for Juveniles*.

Day Sclater, S. and Piper, C. (2000) 'Re-moralising the family? family policy, family law and youth justice', *Child and Family Law Quarterly*, vol. 12, no. 2, pp. 135–51.

Dignan, J. (1999) 'The Crime and Disorder Act and the prospects for restorative justice', *Criminal Law Review*, January, pp. 48–60.

Dignan, J. (2000) *Youth Justice Pilots Evaluation*, Interim Report on Reparative Work and Youth Offending Teams, Department of Law, University of Sheffield.

Dignan, J. and Marsh, P. (2001) 'Restorative justice and family group conferences in England: current state and future prospects' in Morris and Maxwell (eds) *Restorative Justice for Juveniles.*

Drakeford, M. and McCarthy, K. (2000) 'Parents, responsibility and the new youth justice' in B. Goldson (ed.) *The New Youth Justice*, Lyme Regis, Russell House.

Duff, P. and Hutton, N. (eds) (1999) *Criminal Justice in Scotland*, Aldershot, Ashgate/Dartmouth.

Farrington, D. (1997) 'Human development and criminal careers' in M. Maguire, R. Morgan and R. Reiner (eds) *The Oxford Handbook of Criminology* (2nd edn), Oxford, Clarendon Press.

Farrington, D., Hancock, G., Livingston, M., Painter, K. and Towl, G. (2000) *Evaluation of Intensive Regimes for Young Offenders*, Research Findings no. 121, Home Office Research, Development and Statistics Directorate, London, HMSO.

Fionda, J. (1999) 'New Labour, old hat: youth justice and the Crime and Disorder Act 1998', *Criminal Law Review*, January, pp. 36–47.

Gelsthorpe, L. (1999) 'Youth crime and parental responsibility' in A. Bainham, S. Day Sclater and M. Richards (eds) *What is a Parent?* Oxford, Hart Publishing.

Gelsthorpe, L. and Kemp, V. (2002) 'Comparative juvenile justice: England and Wales' in J. Winterdyk (ed.) *Comparative Juvenile Justice*, Toronto, Canadian Scholars' Press.

Gelsthorpe, L. and Morris, A. (1994) 'Juvenile justice 1945–1992' in M. Maguire, R. Morgan and R. Reiner (eds) *The Oxford Handbook of Criminology*, Oxford, Clarendon Press.

Gelsthorpe, L. and Morris, A. (1999) 'Much ado about nothing: a critical comment on key provisions relating to children in the Crime and Disorder Act 1998', *Child and Family Law Quarterly*, vol. 11, no. 3, pp. 209–21.

Goldson, B. (1999) 'Youth (in)justice: contemporary developments in policy and practice' in B. Goldson (ed.) *Youth Justice: Contemporary Policy and Practice*, Aldershot, Ashgate.

Graham, J. and Bowling, B. (1995) *Young People and Crime*, Home Office Research Study no. 145, London, HMSO.

Haines, K. (2000) 'Referral orders and youth offender panels: restorative approaches and the new youth justice' in B. Goldson (ed.) *The New Youth Justice*, Lyme Regis, Russell House.

Hallett, C., Murray, C., Jamieson, J. and Veitch, B. (1998) *The Evaluation of Children's Hearings in Scotland*, Edinburgh, Scottish Office Central Research Unit.

Holdaway, S., Davidson, N., Dignan, J., Hammersley, R., Hine, J. and Marsh, P. (2001) *New Strategies to Address Youth Offending: The National Evaluation of the Pilot Youth Offending Teams*, Home Office Research, Development and Statistics Directorate Occasional Paper no. 69, London, HMSO.

Home Office (1997a) *Tackling Youth Crime, Reforming Youth Justice*, consultation paper, London, HMSO.

Home Office (1997b) *Tackling Delays in the Youth Justice System*, consultation paper, London, HMSO.

Home Office (1997c) *New National and Local Focus on Youth Crime*, consultation paper, London, HMSO.

Home Office (1997d) *No More Excuses: A New Approach to Tackling Youth Crime in England and Wales*, Cm 3809, London, HMSO.

Jackson, S. (1998) *Family Justice? An Evaluation of the Hampshire Youth Justice Family Group Conference Pilot Project*, University of Southampton paper.

Joyce, P. (1999) *Law, Order and the Judiciary*, London, Hodder & Stoughton.

Kearney, B. (1987) *Children's Hearings and the Sheriff Court*, London, Butterworth.

Leng, R., Taylor, R. and Wasik, M. (1998) *Blackstone's Guide to the Crime and Disorder Act*, London, Blackstone Press.

Lockyer, A. and Stone, F.H. (eds) (1998) *Juvenile Justice in Scotland: Twenty-five Years of the Welfare Approach*, Edinburgh, Clark.

Mackenzie, D. and Souryal, C. (1994) *Multi-site Evaluation of Shock in Incarceration*, Washington DC, National Institute of Justice.

Marsh, P. (1996) 'The development of FGCs: an overview' in K. Morris and J. Tunnard (eds) *Family Group Conferences: Message from UK Practice and Research*, London, Family Rights Group.

Marsh, P. and Crow, G. (1998) *Family Group Conferences in Child Welfare*, Oxford, Blackwell.

Marshall, T. (1999) *Restorative Justice: An Overview*, London, Home Office Research, Development and Statistics Directorate.

Maxwell, G. and Morris, A. (1993) *Family, Victims and Culture: Youth Justice in New Zealand*, Wellington, Social Policy Agency and Victoria University of Wellington.

Maxwell, G. and Morris, A. (1999) *Reducing Reoffending*, Wellington, Institute of Criminology, Victoria University of Wellington.

Morris, A. and Gelsthorpe, L. (2000) 'Something old, something borrowed, something blue, but something new? A comment on the prospects for restorative justice under the Crime and Disorder Act 1998', *Criminal Law Review*, January, pp. 18–30.

Morris, A. and Maxwell, G. (2000) 'The practice of family group conferences in New Zealand: assessing the place, potential and pitfalls of restorative justice' in A. Crawford and J. Goodey (eds) *Integrating a Victim Perspective within Criminal Justice*, Aldershot, Ashgate.

Morris, A. and Maxwell, G. (eds) (2001) *Restorative Justice for Juveniles: Conferencing, Mediation and Circles*, Oxford, Hart Publishing.

Morris, A. and Young, W. (2000) 'Reforming criminal justice: the potential of restorative justice' in H. Strang and J. Braithwaite (eds) *Restorative Justice: From Philosophy to Practice*, Aldershot, Ashgate.

Morris, A., Giller, H., Geach, H. and Szwed, E. (1980) *Justice for Children*, London, Macmillan.

Muncie, J. (1999a) *Youth and Crime: A Critical Introduction*, London, Sage.

Muncie, J. (1999b) 'Institutionalized intolerance: youth justice and the 1998 Crime and Disorder Act', *Critical Social Policy*, vol. 19, no. 2, pp. 147–75.

NACRO (2000) *Crime and Disorder Act 1998*, Briefing, London, National Association for the Care and Resettlement of Offenders.

O'Mahony, D. and Deazley, R. (2000) *Juvenile Crime and Justice, Review of the Criminal Justice System for Northern Ireland*, Research Report no. 17, Belfast, Northern Ireland Office.

Pollard, C. (1999) 'Victims and the criminal justice system: a new vision', *Criminal Law Review*, January, pp. 5–17.

Rutherford, A. (1992) *Growing out of Crime: The New Era*, Winchester, Waterside Press.

Williams, B. (2001) 'Reparation orders for young offenders: coerced apologies?' *Relational Justice*, no. 9, p. 8.

Wonnacott, C. (1999) 'The counterfeit contract: reform, pretence and muddled principles in the new referral order', *Child and Family Law Quarterly*, vol. 11, no. 3, pp. 271–87.

Young, P. and Young, M. (1996) *Crime and Criminal Justice in Scotland*, Edinburgh, Scottish Office.

Young, R. (2001) 'Just cops doing "shameful" business? Police-led restorative justice and the lessons of research' in Morris and Maxwell (eds) *Restorative Justice for Juveniles*.

Young, R. and Goold, B. (1999) 'Restorative police cautioning in Aylesbury: from degrading to reintegrative shaming ceremonies', *Criminal Law Review*, February, pp. 126–38.

Part IV

Justice, diversion and rights

Justice for children and young people has been expressed in a number of divergent ways. Part IV explores the degree to which youth is afforded justice by the recognition of young people's basic need for protection, by ensuring that they are treated fairly through the due process of the law and by securing not only their civil but also their socio-economic rights.

Procedures designed to avoid the stigma of formal adult-style court processing and incarceration have long been one of the hallmarks of youth justice, whether this is conceived as crime prevention (diversion from crime), cautioning (diversion from prosecution) or community correction (diversion from custody). Diversion emerged as a dominant trend in youth justice in the 1960s with a number of initiatives designed to keep young people out of court, custody and residential care. In Chapter 17 James Austin and Barry Krisberg present a critical analysis of the intended and unintended consequences of such reform movements in the United States. They find that the movement to divert may have secured many alternative community-based means of dealing with young people but, paradoxically, has drawn more rather than fewer into the remit of state intervention. Moreover the expansion of prevention initiatives has brought successively younger populations into the net of formal control. Similarly, experiments in due process, just deserts, decarceration and decriminalization have tended to harden attitudes to young offenders and encouraged the development of new and strengthened 'nets'. Again, paradoxically, when such 'liberal' reforms have been perceived as soft options they have also fuelled the fire of those advocating a 'return' to overtly deterrent sanctions.

In a parallel debate, as revealed in Chapter 18 by Stewart Asquith, diversion was a key element of the movement to get 'back to justice' that proliferated in many Western systems of youth justice in the 1970s and 1980s. Liberal lawyers, radical social workers and civil libertarians became increasingly critical of the principles of welfare and rehabilitative sentencing. They argued that the 'need for treatment' acted as a spurious justification for placing excessive restrictions on individual liberty, particularly for young women, which were out of proportion either to the seriousness of the offence or to the realities of being in 'need of care and protection'. Indeterminate sentencing schemes, for example, could mean that minor offenders could serve longer sentences than those convicted of more serious offences. Probation, social work and welfare judgements were viewed as a form of arbitrary and discretional power. Many offenders, it was argued, were subjected to apparently non-accountable state procedures and their liberty was often unjustifiably denied.

In the field of youth justice it was similarly argued that the investigation of social background was an imposition: that social work involvement not only pre-served explanations of individual pathology, but also undermined the young person's right to natural justice. Young people were placed in double jeopardy – sentenced for their background as well as for their offence – and as a result their movement up the sentencing tariff was often accelerated. In the wake of these criticisms a new justice-based model of youth corrections emerged. It sought an end to indeterminate, treatment-oriented sentences; to judicial, professional and administrative discretion; and to disparities in sentencing. In turn, it was proposed that proportionality of punishment to fit the crime, determinate sentencing and the protection of rights through due process should be reinstated at the centre of youth criminal justice practice. But here again we are faced with a series of ambiguities and paradoxes. Asquith details how the justice model may have had progressive intentions, but also brought with it a renewed focus on the doctrines of individual responsibility and personal accountability. Minimal intervention may have been the goal, but retribution was the outcome. Moreover Asquith queries the extent to which justice can be provided simply through the powers of formal justice and legalism. Policies which ignore 'structural injustices' and which are divorced from the reality of social and economic disadvantage may 'promote children's rights procedurally but fail to realize them substantively'.

Much of this is echoed in Chapter 19 in which John Clarke also makes the important point that laws and their application are not separate from but part of structures of material inequalities. He also notes how critiques of welfare and social work readily coalesce with the concerns of traditional retributivists that rehabilitation is a 'soft option'. The staking out of 'justice' as a strategy for reform is always liable to allow proponents of law and order to recruit the arguments of 'natural justice' to their own ends, although the former is more concerned with retribution and the latter with judicial equality and consistency. In the political climate of the 1980s the language of 'justice and rights' was indeed appropriated by one of 'self responsibility and obligation'. For Clarke, what is required is less focus on legal accountability and more commitment to securing the means of political accountability. In hindsight, the 'back to justice' movements, despite being able to claim some short-lived success in the late 1980s, particularly in implementing 'custody-free zones', have in the long term facilitated the onslaught of a renewed retributivism.

The flaws involved in the pursuit either of welfare or of justice are brought into sharp focus by Annie Hudson's analysis of the treatment of 'troublesome girls'. In Chapter 20 Hudson argues that both tend to adjudi-cate as much on questions of emotionality, sexuality and appropriate femi-ninity as they do on matters of guilt and innocence. In considering alternative policies Hudson moves some way towards a welfare-based rights agenda in which recognition of needs and personal autonomy, coupled with the right to participate in decision making, are viewed as central. In the short term, she argues, this might be best pursued by the development of a separatist strategy in which a social and political space can be created to take young women's concerns seriously.

The final chapter, by Phil Scraton and Deena Haydon, continues to make the case for a move away from a narrow 'welfare or justice' debate in youth justice. For them the key issue is the pursuit of 'positive rights' through the advocacy of a rights-based welfare approach involving protection as well as participation, decriminalization, proportionality, review, transparency and accountability. In this endeavour the UN Convention on the Rights of the Child may be taken as a starting point. Full compliance with the Convention would, on its own, place on the political agenda such issues as raising the age of criminal responsibility, decarceration and the formulation of child-centred policies. It would also provide an initial means of breaking away from the child demonization discourses and repressive youth justice policies that have prevailed in countries such as England and Wales since the late 1990s and into the early twenty-first century.

17

Wider, stronger and different nets: the dialectics of criminal justice reform

James Austin and Barry Krisberg

[···]

The criminal justice system can be conceptualized as a net or series of nets functioning to regulate and control personal behavior. Each component of the justice system (police, public, defenders, prosecutors, sheriffs, judges, probation officers, and correctional agencies) is authorized by the state to intervene in our personal lives. Theoretically, this power will be used only when our behavior exceeds legally prescribed norms. Thus, police are authorized to arrest us if we exhibit behaviors that violate criminal laws passed by local and federal legislatures. Judges can place us in punitive or therapeutic settings, and correctional administrators can detain us in prisons or jails until such time as we become 'well' or their authority for state intervention expires.

Criminal justice agencies are in a constant state of change. Laws are passed which change their authority, new theories of social control are promoted and funded, budgets expand or contract. Administrators are forced to decide which activities will be emphasized, terminated, or begun anew. As justice system agencies change, so do the nets. This is not to say that the social control system is shaped exclusively by subordinate organizational factors. Instead, social control – and organizational change – must also be understood as part of changes in the political and social milieu. Reform strategies that ignore powerful ideological and economic forces will fail or have unintended consequences.

The following pages review the relative effects, on the state's ability to intervene, of efforts related to diversion, decarceration, due process, decriminalization, deterrence, and just deserts. Each reform movement is analyzed to determine whether it has (intentionally or unintentionally) strengthened or expanded control nets, or created new ones. For purposes of this paper, three types of changes in social control nets are defined as follows:

SOURCE: This chapter is taken from *Journal of Research in Crime and Delinquency*, Vol. 18, No. 1, 1981, pp. 165–96 (abridged).

1   *Wider nets:* Reforms that increase the proportion of subgroups in society (differentiated by such factors as age, sex, class, and ethnicity) whose behavior is regulated and controlled by the state.
2   *Stronger nets:* Reforms that increase the state's capacity to control individuals through intensifying state intervention.
3   *New nets:* Reforms that transfer intervention authority or jurisdiction from one agency or control system to another.

DIVERSION

Since 1967, when the President's Commission on Law Enforcement issued its report recommending use of diversion in criminal justice, there have been extensive diversionary efforts undertaken within the adult and juvenile justice systems. During the past decade, the federal government, through LEAA, has funded over 1,200 adult and juvenile diversion programs at an estimated cost of $112 million.

Diversion has been implemented through the addition, by criminal justice agencies, of new programs and new resources to the existing system. The programs are administered by police, probation officers, or prosecutors at the pretrial level and ostensibly serve to divert 'offenders' from the stigma associated with court conviction and incarceration. Advocates of diversion hoped that divertees would be less susceptible to the phenomenon of secondary deviance (Lemert, 1951, 1967), crime would decrease, court congestion and costs would be reduced, and prison and jail populations would drop. It was assumed that criminal justice was a closed and linear process in which reduced intervention at the front end, which presumably could be easily achieved, would cause associated reductions in more severe forms of intervention later on in the process (e.g., imprisonment). Reducing the net at the points of arrest and prosecution would result in similar reductions in jail and prison populations.

Research completed thus far shows these assumptions to be incorrect. The pretrial criminal justice process is much more an 'open' system, in which agencies compete and conflict with one another and in which various and diverse decision makers exert considerable discretionary powers (Feeley, 1979; Austin, 1980). Desired changes in organizational practices at one or more points in the system are frequently circumvented by more powerful agencies in opposition to the reform objectives and ideologies. Placed under the control of the criminal justice system, diversion programs have been transformed into a means for extending the net, making it stronger, and creating new nets.

Rovner-Pieczenik (1974), in her critical review of several adult pretrial intervention projects, observed that in many cases pretrial diversion was reserved for defendants whom the district attorney was unwilling to prosecute or would be unable to prosecute successfully. Consequently, such diversion programs functioned to allow the court to extend jurisdiction over cases which ordinarily would have been dismissed or barely punished for a three- to six-month period of supervision.

Mintz and Fagan (1975) conducted a feasibility study for San Francisco on whether to institute a pretrial diversion program for misdemeanant defendants. Based on their analysis of typical court dispositions from the preceding year, they concluded that such a program would have minimal impact on reducing court congestion and would probably increase rather than reduce the jurisdiction of the court. They also recommended that no 'new' criminal justice agencies be created until existing shortcomings of police, probation, and the courts were corrected.

Klein (1975), in his evaluation of police diversion projects for juveniles in Los Angeles, found that divertees were typically youths whom the police would have ignored or dismissed had diversion programs not existed. Duxbury (1973) found the same phenomenon in her analysis of California's Youth Service Bureaus, noting that most referrals were not from criminal justice agencies. Gibbons and Blake (1975) and Dickover (1976) also found indications of over-extension by law enforcement agencies via the diversion process.

One survey (Palmer, 1978) of eleven California juvenile diversion programs found that 51 percent of the clients were diverted from traditional court dispositions. The remainder were subjected to more intensive forms of processing than would otherwise have been the case. A similar phenomenon of expanding the net and making it stronger was found in British police juvenile liaison programs, where diversion became a third control option available to police, supplementing formal processing and the decision to screen and release (Morris, 1975).

Two studies (Austin, 1980; Hillsman-Baker, 1979) of adult diversion programs used randomized experimental and control populations to test diversion's impact on offenders' recidivism, costs of intervention, and level of social control. Both found diversion to have an insignificant effect on recidivism and to have actually increased the costs of dealing with and the level of supervision of defendants. Both studies concluded that diversion's failure could be attributed to the selection of defendants with non-serious charges – persons who, in lieu of diversion, would have had their cases dismissed or received minimal sanctions (fines, informal probation, one to three days in jail).

Diversion programs also serve to strengthen the net and to create new nets by formalizing previously informal organizational practices and by creating practices where none had existed. Diversion programs have also been severely criticized for the failure to accord divertees the rights of due process. The response to such criticism among program administrators has been to establish formal contractual agreements with diversion participants – agreements listing conditions of supervision and services, certifying the waiver of constitutional rights to a speedy trial, and so on. In some instances, divertee participation is conditioned upon a formal admission of guilt, which can later be used in court should the divertee fail to complete the agreed-upon conditions. These developments represent an increasing elaboration of rules, procedures, and policies governing potential clients (youths and adults) – often before any determination of guilt has been made. As such, diversion programs represent an erosion of due process and increased formal intervention by the state. Instead of justice, there is diversion.

DECARCERATION

Administrative, legal, and programmatic means have been used in attempts to reduce the rate of imprisonment in this country. In Massachusetts, the Division of Youth Services closed most of the state's training schools by using existing administrative powers (Coates et al., 1978; Rutherford, 1978). Legislation recently was passed in California (A.B. 3121) that curtails the detention of status offenders and children classified as dependent and neglected. Finally, bail release, work release, and deinstitutionalization of status offender programs have been set in place to encourage administrative use of 'community correctional alternatives' to incarceration.

All three strategies have had mixed results and unintended consequences. In Massachusetts, the population of incarcerated juveniles was reported to have been successfully reduced and then transferred to community correctional settings (Coates *et al.*, 1978). However, recent evidence raises questions about these early results. One study has found that rates of temporary juvenile detention have increased as long-term institutional placements have declined (Massachusetts Advocacy Center, 1980). Similar results are noted by Lemert and Dill (1978) and Lerman (1975), with respect to the California Probation Subsidy. In this instance, legislation was passed providing economic incentives for local jurisdictions to reduce the number of youths and adults committed to the state correctional facilities. Initially, a significant decrease in the populations incarcerated in state prisons and training schools was observed. However, two ways in which the net was strengthened were also noted. Lerman found that the length of incarceration for those committed to the California Youth Authority increased as the numbers incarcerated decreased. Officials reasoned that because the less serious cases were being diverted, youths remaining in state institutions were the tougher cases, requiring longer periods of incarceration. Yet statistical evidence on the institutionalized population showed that this was no different from the population incarcerated before the probation subsidy. Lemert and Dill (1978) and Lerman (1975) also found instances of net expansion at the juvenile hall and in police detention. That is, police and probation departments opposing the probation subsidy law sought to circumvent its intent by increasing their discretionary powers of temporary detention. Lemert and Dill (1978) observed, moreover, that some counties used subsidy funds to construct local detention and correctional facilities. In recent years, the original subsidy legislation has been significantly amended, with less emphasis placed on counties' meeting fixed commitment quotas. The probation subsidy program has evolved from a decarceration reform movement into a revenue-sharing program for local juvenile justice agencies (Little, 1980).

The federal government, through the LEAA Office of Juvenile Justice and Delinquency Prevention, recently sponsored a national program to remove status offenders from secure facilities. The reform strategy assumed that probation agencies, when given substantial funds, could create alternatives to detention in secure facilities for controlling and servicing status offenders. The national evaluation of this program found that such programs had minimal impact on recidivism and did little to change youths' attitudes. It also described a relabeling process that was occurring: Youths previously defined by police and the court as status offenders were being labeled delinquents (Klein and Kobrin, 1980). This change in definition allowed police and probation authorities to detain the 'new delinquents,' since the status offender label no longer applied. The overall effect was a strengthening of the net for the status offender, who was now elevated to juvenile criminal offender status; and the net was expanded to a new class of status offenders, who filled the void created by the relabeling.

A similar relabeling phenomenon was noted in relation to California's A.B. 3121 legislative reform, which mandated that status offenders not be placed in secure facilities for longer than forty-eight hours. Police and probation intake officials saw little value in arresting and processing status offenders, who could not be controlled through incarceration intake centers. Austin *et al.* (1978) and Little (1980) found evidence of increasing arrests and detention of delinquent youths, compensating for the 'losses' in the status offender market. In order to continue to control wayward youths, police and probation selected the more serious delinquent charges (those carrying the most serious criminal sanctions) for purposes of realizing their crime control and treatment objectives. Before the legislation, law enforcement would often select for intervention youths committing less serious, status, offenses (e.g., running away, curfew violation); these cases were easier to establish in juvenile court and law enforcement's powers of intervention were not restricted.

Decarceration reforms can also create new nets. One example is the deinstitutionalization of mental patients, a movement which began in the 1950s because of a decline in the state's fiscal resources, which made the construction of additional and expensive institutions economically unfeasible (O'Conner, 1973; Scull, 1977), and new developments in drug research, which made it possible to control mental patients in community centers through medication. As the mental patients were pushed out of mental institutions, there was an accompanying rise in jail populations. And increasingly, those jailed were persons with histories of placement in mental institutions. With referral to mental hospitals of marginal 'criminal' cases – persons apprehended for disorderly conduct, indecent exposure, drunkenness, or miscellaneous property offenses (e.g., vandalism, petty theft) – no longer possible, this population was transferred to a new net, with fewer mental health resources.

New nets also have been created within the criminal justice system as adjuncts to the prison system. Under the label *community correction*, these reforms are an attempt to decarcerate prisoners through halfway houses, civil commitment drug treatment programs, work release programs, expansion of parole and probation, and restitution programs.

Hylton (1980) used time series data on the Canadian province of Saskatchewan to determine the effects of community correctional programs introduced from 1962 to 1979. He found that these programs had no impact on the prison population and actually tripled the proportion of persons under state control.

> When the use of community programs was expanded in Saskatchewan, no corresponding decrease in the use of correctional facilities could be observed. Rather, the utilization of correctional facilities, whether measured in terms of daily counts or admissions, increased steadily. It appeared, however, that community programs permitted the correctional system to expand at a tremendous rate, with the result that an even larger proportion of the population was under some form of supervision by the state (p. 16).

Miller applied a similar analysis to California and Massachusetts data. He provides convincing data to show that new programs frequently are new alternatives for old alternatives (1980: 327); that is, persons charged with minor offenses, who previously would have been placed on probation, become the best candidates for the new programs.

DUE PROCESS

Reforms aimed at expanding juvenile and adult defendants' constitutional rights to defend themselves against unwarranted criminal charges are a popular strategy for shrinking the criminal justice net. Due process advocates share the assumption that police and the courts often abuse their discretionary powers and infrequently act in the best interest of the defendants. Control agencies are described as preoccupied with a crime control ideology emphasizing efficient case disposition, informal plea negotiation, and presumption of guilt. Due process advocates emphasize an adjudicative model incorporating presumption of innocence and formal procedural rules to protect the defendant's rights (Packer, 1968; Skolnick, 1966; Feeley, 1978; Cole, 1972).

Due process reforms stem largely from appellate and supreme court interpretation of existing law and from the passage of new legislation. Two examples of United States Supreme Court interpretation (*Gault* and *Miranda*) and one example of legislation (1961 California Juvenile Court Act) are reviewed here. In all three cases, the objective was to provide defendants with greater adversarial procedural rights during the pretrial stage of the criminal justice process. Although defendants have benefited from these changes, evidence suggests that the reforms have also had harmful effects, effects that have made the net stronger.

In the *Gault* decision the Court ruled that youths brought before the juvenile court were entitled to basic procedural protection, including the right to counsel, right to notice, right to cross-examination, and safeguards against self-incrimination. Theoretically, this would prevent youths from being unfairly processed through the juvenile court. However, such procedural rights, which conflicted with the juvenile court's parens patriae ideology, threatened to impede the work of the courts. As a result, many juvenile courts have developed ways to counter the intended effects of *Gault* as well as other higher court rulings (e.g., *In re Kent, In re Winship*). An example of the countermoves is the court's encouragement of waivers of the juveniles' rights to cross-examine witnesses and to counsel. As the present authors noted,

> Soon after the Supreme Court's decision in the *Gault* case, many states rushed to develop ways of encouraging youths to voluntarily forfeit procedural safeguards, thereby bypassing the intended effect of the U.S. Supreme Court ruling. To be effective, reform of the juvenile court must be rooted in principles of social justice for children, not merely in easily circumvented procedural safeguards (Krisberg and Austin, 1978: 68).

Another observer of the post-*Gault* court has written,

> We are now in the ninth year of the post-Gault era and, in my view, have lagged severely in implementing both the letter and the spirit of that mandate, particularly as to the right of counsel. Despite the obvious conflict of interest, juvenile courts still allow the parents of a status offender to waive the child's right to counsel. Juvenile courts in many communities still actively discourage youth from exercising their right to counsel through a variety of approaches and with a variety of motivations (Rubin, 1977: 5).

In the *Miranda* decision, the United States Supreme Court sought to give adult defendants greater protection and more safeguards at the point of arrest. The Court's intent was to prohibit police from obtaining involuntary and coerced confessions. Here, again, legal action was intended to prevent police and the courts from making unwarranted interventions. Lewis and Allen (1977) documented a psychological technique used by police agencies to subvert this intent, calling it the 'participating Miranda.' Briefly, police using this technique read the rights of the accused gradually, over a long period of interrogation, instead of immediately and fully beforehand. This allows the police to elicit confessions that might not have been made if the defendants had been fully apprised of all their rights at the point of arrest.

[T]he police have successfully subverted the *Miranda* rules and obtained an apparently voluntary confession (in the traditional sense); the defendant has pled guilty to the substantive charge or a reduced charge and has been sentenced to prison.... [T]he police are pleased that another 'dangerous criminal' is off the streets: the defense attorney and prosecutor 'believe' that the defendant was given his full *Miranda* warnings; the sentencing judge is officially unaware that the defendant was subjected to *participating Miranda*: and in most jurisdictions, an appellate court will not review collateral issues attending a guilty plea. All participants are 'satisfied' that justice has been served (Lewis and Allen, 1977: 79–80).

In studying juvenile court reforms legislation in California, Lemert (1967, 1971) found evidence that new laws had affected organizational behavior and were successful in establishing a more formalized and adversarial process of juvenile justice.

The evidence is impressive that representation by counsel more often secures a favorable outcome of the case than where there is no counsel. Proportionately, dismissals were ordered nearly three times as frequently in attorney as in non-attorney cases (1967: 442).

However, Lemert qualified the success of the new legislation, noting that counsel was present in 17 percent of the dispositions. Sixty percent of the cases in which counsel appeared were ones in which the charge centered on unfit parents or an inadequate home life; such cases had little impact on representation of youths charged with delinquency (1971: 194). Lemert also noted, in one California county studied, that juveniles without attorneys were less likely to be detained while awaiting trial (1967: 443).

DECRIMINALIZATION

This reform movement seeks to shrink the net legislatively by removing certain behaviors from the jurisdiction of the criminal justice system. It is argued that by decriminalizing such behaviors as drug abuse, abortion, prostitution, and homosexual acts among consenting adults, justice system activity will, more appropriately, be focused on serious crime. It is assumed that decriminalization will not significantly increase the frequency of 'victimless' crimes; in fact, proponents argue that by decriminalizing these behaviors, other related crimes (e.g., burglaries by addicts, manslaughter by illegal abortionists) will be prevented.

Decriminalization has been attempted most frequently for drug use, abortion, and homosexuality. Public support for removing these offenses from criminal codes has grown as the acceptance and visibility of these behaviors within the middle and upper socioeconomic classes have increased. For example, with respect to marijuana, several groups (e.g., National Organization to Reform Marijuana Laws) have formally organized to push for decriminalization or a significant reduction in the penalties for use, possession, and cultivation. Some law enforcement agencies tolerate or ignore drug use, especially those in rural communities where the marijuana business is an important part of the community's economy.

In July 1975, the California Legislature passed S.B. 95. which made possession of one ounce or less of marijuana a citable misdemeanor instead of a possible felony. A study of this limited attempt at decriminalization found that this change had minimal impact on private use of the drug (Narcotics and Drug Abuse Office, 1977).

Predictably, arrests, prosecutions, and sentences for marijuana-related offenses also decreased significantly. Law enforcement agencies quickly learned that strict enforcement of laws related to marijuana would have little public support and that such cases would be treated lightly by the courts.

But what was the effect of the law on the rest of the criminal justice net? Most criminal justice officials favored decriminalization, claiming that it allows them to concentrate on the more serious criminal behaviors that remain under their jurisdiction. Following enactment of S.B. 95, the Narcotics and Drug Abuse State Office (1977) found an associated increase in arrests of heroin addicts and persons committing other drug-related offenses. In this example, decriminalization successfully reduced the net with respect to one offense but may have had a corresponding effect of widening and toughening the net in other areas of law enforcement.

Similar dynamic and elastic effects of the criminal justice net can be seen in attempts to decriminalize homosexual acts among consenting adults. Geis *et al.* (1976) surveyed the effects in seven states of decriminalizing homosexuality. Similar to the findings related to marijuana use, Geis's findings were that decriminalization had no effect on increasing the frequency of forced homosexual acts (rape), participation of homosexuals in non-sex related crimes, or homosexual involvement with minors. Prosecutors and police reported that the new laws gave them more time and resources to devote to more serious crimes. Although Geis does not present actual arrest and conviction data, these responses suggest that decriminalization may temporarily shrink the net but ultimately result in a shifting to and refocusing upon other behaviors labeled criminal, resulting here in a more intensively and more severely controlled situation for the more 'serious' offenses.

Attempts to legalize (rather than decriminalize) prostitution present an example of replacing the old net with a new one. Prostitution is illegal in every state except Nevada, where it is permitted in certain counties. Bills have been introduced in many state legislatures that would transfer the control and regulation of prostitution from the criminal justice system to other state agencies (Women Endorsing Decriminalization, 1973; Bryant, 1977; PPWGO, 1975). These legislative reforms have been resisted by organizations of prostitutes and feminist groups, who argue that legalization will only perpetuate and not solve the problem. The licensing and regulation involved in legalization would likely represent an invasion of privacy and create a new but equally exploitive structure controlled by those licensing and regulation the brothels (WED, 1973; PPWGO, 1975).

> Legalized prostitution would lead to the further oppression of women prostitutes. As long as sexism and economic oppression persist, the supply and demand for prostitution will continue. Decriminalization will not eliminate prostitution, but it will remove the burden of guilt and the fear of jail from women as we struggle to destroy the social and economic roots of prostitution and the degradation that all women in our society share (WED, 1973: 161).

Here we see the dilemma of decriminalization versus legalization, where the effects of legalization may be harmful to the presumed beneficiaries. Of course, should decriminalization take place, there is no assurance that an unregulated marketplace would be more humane and less oppressive than a tightly controlled state operation.

Similarly, with respect to abortion, the decriminalization movement has met with extremely well-organized resistance, resulting in undesirable consequences. Critics of abortion have successfully blocked the use of public funds for abortion. Thus, while well-to-do women may freely seek abortions, the poor must prove that the abortion is a medical necessity to qualify for public subsidies. An illegal market providing medically substandard abortions for the poor is one obvious result of these political restrictions on federal assistance in obtaining medical care.

DETERRENCE

Deterrence differs dramatically from the other reform strategies. Instead of shrinking the net, deterrence reforms work to expand and toughen it. This is accomplished by increasing the presence of law enforcement and adding to court resources for prosecution, sentencing, and pretrial detention. Deterrence reforms also seek to increase the certainty and severity of punishment through mandatory sentencing structures. Clearly, the assumption here is that potential offenders are aware of the probable 'costs' of criminal acts. It is alleged that potential criminals rationally evaluate the costs and certainty of punishment versus the benefits of crime. When the costs clearly exceed the benefits, individuals choose to refrain from crime.

Deterrence also implies increasing the capacity of the net to incapacitate by isolating offenders from society. This has two effects: prevention of crimes that would otherwise have been committed on nonprison populations and possible deterrence of crimes after the offenders' release. In postulating the latter effect, proponents assume that the experience of imprisonment teaches the offender about the cost of crime.

Deterrence reforms have become increasingly popular during the past decade. Frustrated by the impotence of rehabilitation and increasing crime rates, states have worked to increase the length of prison sentences through mandatory sentencing provisions. In the juvenile system, legislation is being passed to encourage waivers of juveniles committing serious crimes to adult courts, where longer prison sentences can be imposed. The public appears to support these conservative trends (Hindelang, 1974; NCCD, 1980; Duffee and Ritti, 1977), despite the high cost of imprisonment and the fact that the United States already ranks third in the world – behind the Soviet Union and South Africa – in its use of incarceration (Nagel, 1979).

Several studies have examined various policy experiments in deterrence, experiments ranging from crackdowns on drunken drivers to capital punishment. The results of these studies are mixed. In a comprehensive review of general deterrence, the National Research Council (NRC) concluded that the evidence on deterrence is insufficient to warrant deterrence-based policy changes (Blumstein et al., 1987: 7). The NRC found that in removing from society persons likely to continue in their criminal activities, incapacitation of identified offenders did have a preventive effect. However, the studies reviewed (Clarke, 1974; Greenberg, 1975; Ehrlich, 1974) all concluded that the effect of incapacitation is minimal (Blumstein et al., 1978: 209–10) and that a dramatic increase in prison populations would be needed to bring about a small decrease in crime rates (Blumstein et al., 1978: 225). This weak relationship between imprisonment and crime rates is further questioned by Nagel (1977), who found a positive relationship between prison expansion and crime rates in a cross-state comparison. The expansion of prisons in seen by deterrence advocates as only temporary: Once the public learns of the certainty of punishment, crime and the need for prisons should diminish. However, Rutherford et al. (1977) found that the best prediction of prison populations is the availability of prison beds and not crime rate trends.

The limitations in studies of deterrence policy experiments have been noted elsewhere (see e.g., Zimring, 1978) – for example, their frequent use of faulty designs, the inadequate analytic and measurement procedures, lack of theory, and failure to account for the process-related dynamics of the reform experiment.

[...]

Other studies (e.g., Wolfgang *et al.*, 1972; Elliott, 1978; Petersilia *et al.*, 1978), noting the episodic and transitory nature of many crimes, have suggested limited prospects for deterrence strategies. The absence of 'rational' or linear criminal careers and the importance of external socioeconomic variables in crime rates are important constraints on deterrence policy reforms – regardless of how well executed the reforms may be.

JUST DESERTS

Strategies emphasizing just deserts reflect an odd mixture of several other reform ideologies, making the task of assessing the intended and unintended effects of this approach more difficult. Included in this evaluation is an array of works by lawyers, criminologists, economists, civil libertarians, and prisoner's rights groups. Although the proponents of just deserts share no single perspective or set of objectives, they reject both the model of rehabilitation and the belief that criminal behavior can be deterred simply by increasing the presence and power of control agencies. They see value in swift and certain punishment and assert that due process is an important component of the goal of eliminating the criminal justice system's subjective, informal, and arbitrary discretionary processes (especially at the levels of sentencing and prison release). Some proponents, like von Hirsch (1976) and especially Fogel (1975), believe many inmates could be diverted out of prisons into nonprison settings. Others (Wilson, 1975; Dershowitz, 1976) argue that more criminals should be sent to prison, but for shorter periods of time.

The principal policy experiment related to just deserts is determinate sentencing. Initially advocated by liberals and prisoner's rights groups (American Friends Service Committee, 1971), determinate sentencing was proposed as a cure for the arbitrariness of indeterminate sentencing and parole decisions, one that would create a more equitable net. Advocates also hoped that the control net would shrink, since the sentences served by some offenders would be shorter than under the previous system, and unnecessary imprisonment would be minimized by the standardization of sentencing decisions and elimination of long periods of parole supervision.

During the past several years, a number of states (e.g., California, Illinois, Indiana, Maine, and Pennsylvania) have enacted and implemented determinate sentencing structures. Obviously, the final results of these policy experiments will not be known for some time. However, two preliminary findings are worth noting. First, determinate sentencing as implemented has significantly increased the number and the length of many prison sentences (NCCD, 1980; Clear *et al.*, 1978; Little, 1980). In California, persons previously placed on probation or in jail are now more likely to be sent to the state prison (Little, 1980: v). It has been projected that Indiana's sentencing structure will increase the prison terms of first-time felony offenders by almost 50 percent (Clear *et al.*, 1978: 443). The most immediate result of determinate sentencing has been severe prison overcrowding and reduced discretionary release power to relieve the situation via parole. Although determinate sentencing may not be the sole contributor to prison overcrowding, it has encouraged the state's reliance on imprisonment.

Second, determinate sentencing has not eliminated discretion. Instead, it has shifted discretion to different points in the system. A number of studies (NCCD, 1980: 271; Little, 1980: vii; Clear *et al.*, 1978: 435–439) have concluded that prosecutorial discretion has been enhanced in Indiana and California. Although the states' laws specify that, under specific conditions, certain offenses must be punished by imprisonment, prosecutors and the court may 'ignore' aggravating circumstances (e.g., use of a weapon, aggravated violence) in exchange for a guilty plea. Little (1980) found a significant increase in guilty pleas after the adoption of determinate sentencing in California. Clear *et al.* (1978) also found the discretion of correctional administrators to have shifted from parole to the decisions surrounding allocation of good-time credits. Parole release decisions are no longer made in Indiana, but correctional officers have greater control over awarding good-time credits that directly affect the length of incarceration. Thus despite the intentions of the reformers, discretion has not been removed and the severity of imprisonment has increased. The net is wider and stronger.

How did this happen? Several observers (Messinger and Johnson, 1978; Greenberg and Humphries, 1980; Clear *et al.*, 1978) of California, Illinois, and Indiana have concluded that determinate sentencing, as originally promoted by liberals and prisoners' rights groups, was later transformed and coopted by the politically more powerful law enforcement organizations, which desired greater certainty and severity of punishment. These later goals were accomplished by increasing sentence lengths, adding mandatory provisions, and ensuring a presumption of imprisonment – all under the aegis of determinate sentencing reforms.

> Determinate sentencing reform legislation has commonly been introduced by liberal legislators in response to the criticism of discretionary sentencing generated by justice model proponents. However, the constituencies expected on the basis of the AFSC Working Party analysis to support these revisions either have not done so or have not been politically strong enough to carry through the legislation. Instead, politicians have responded to pressure from voters who are more concerned with their safety than with doing justice, and from the law enforcement lobby seeking stiffer penalties for reasons relating to occupational ideology and interests (Greenberg and Humphries, 1980: 223).

It was not the concept of determinacy that failed, but rather the ways in which the just deserts position was manipulated by conservative groups.

[…]

CONCLUSIONS

[…]

'Widening the net' describes the nightmare of the benevolent state gone haywire. This horror has already been vividly portrayed in Orwell's *1984*, Solzhenitsyn's *Cancer Ward*, Kesey's *One Flew Over the Cuckoo's Nest*, and Burgess's *Clockwork Orange*.

Social scientists and criminologists have just caught up with the humanists. Now it is the urgent task of social theory and research to explain how the widened net can be reduced immediately and avoided in the future.

To respond in socially constructive ways to crime without widening the net is a dilemma. [...] Achieving *criminal justice* in an unjust society may be a contradiction in terms. As C. Wright Mills observed, 'Know that many personal troubles cannot be solved merely as troubles, but must be understood in terms of public issues and in terms of the problem of history making' (1959: 226).

New reform programs must include detailed analyses of the current political-economic system as well as the interconnections of that system and the social control apparatus.

Contemporary reformers must confront a political-economic system that is becoming increasingly dysfunctional. Economic trends indicate that the class of permanently unemployed will grow even larger (see Wilhelm, 1970). Chronically high rates of unemployment and uncontrollable inflation are heightening pressures bearing on physical survival, and the increased social costs of the political economy are placing greater demands on public funds to control the casualties of that system (O'Connor, 1973). Thus, the state is experiencing a fiscal crisis making very real the need to develop less costly, community-based control devices (Scull, 1977); yet, the negative reactions among the public to the new types of community-based control have produced calls for increased punishment of criminals. The economic trends are complicated further by political malaise: In the post-Watergate age, the benevolent state has lost most of its legitimacy. The task of enforcing laws and reforming offenders is becoming ever more difficult.

Given this grim portrayal of the immediate future of our society, one should not be surprised at the bleak visions being presented by social scientists. At stake may be the construction of a whole new political-economic structure. Many will argue that the goal of broad social and economic change is impractical. Yet, we must consider that the nightmare of the widening net may require more radical remedies than the current menu of criminal justice reforms.

REFERENCES

American Friends Service Committee (1971) *Struggle for Justice.* New York: Hill & Wang.

Austin, J. (1980) 'Instead of Justice: Diversion.' Ph.D. diss. Davis. Calif.: University of California.

Austin, J., Krisberg, B. and Lawrence, W. (1978) *Open Space. Community Detention, Pittsburgh–Antioch Diversion (AB 312): Diverting the Status Offender.* San Francisco: Research Center West, National Council on Crime and Delinquency.

Barak, G. (1974) 'In Defense of the Poor: The Emergence of the Public Defender System in the United States (1900–1920).' Ph.D. diss. Berkeley: University of California.

Blumstein, A., Cohen, J. and Nagin, D. (eds) (1978) *Deterrence and Incapacitation: Estimating the Effects of Criminal Sanctions on Crime Rates.* Washington, D.C.: National Academy of Sciences.

Boostrom, R.E. (1974) 'The Personalization of Evil: The Emergence of American Criminology 1865–1910.' Ph.D. diss. Berkeley: University of California.

Bremner, R.H., *et al.* (eds) (1970) *Children and Youth in America: A Documentary History*. Cambridge, Mass.: Harvard University Press.

Bryant, M.A. (1977) 'Prostitution and the Criminal Justice System.' *Journal of Police Science and Administration*, 5 (4): 379–389.

Burgess, A. (1962) *Clockwork Orange*. London, England: Heinemann.

Cicourel, A.V. (1968) *The Social Organization of Juvenile Justice*. New York: John Wiley.

Clarke, S.H. (1974) 'Getting 'Em Out of Circulation: Does Incarceration of Juvenile Offenders Reduce Crime?' *Journal of Criminal Law and Criminology*, 65 (4): 528–535.

Clear, T.R., Hewitt, J.D. and Regoli, R.M. (1978) 'Discretion and Determinate Sentence: Its Distribution, Control, and Effect on Time Served.' *Crime & Delinquency*, 24 (4): 428–445.

Cloward, R., and Piven, F. (1971) *Regulating the Poor*. New York: Pantheon.

Coates, R.B., Miller, A.D. and Ohlin, L.E. (1978) *Diversity in a Youth Correctional System: Handling Delinquents in Massachusetts*. Cambridge, Mass.: Ballinger.

Cohen, S. (1979) 'The Punitive City: Notes on the Dispersal of Social Control.' *Contemporary Crises*, 3 (4): 339–363.

Cole, G.F. (1972) *Criminal Justice: Law and Politics*. Belmont, Calif.: Duxbury Press.

Coles, R. (1967) *Children of Crises: A Study of Courage and Fear*. Boston: Little Brown.

Currie, E. (1973) 'Managing the Minds of Men: The Reformatory Movement, 1865–1920.' Ph.D. diss. Berkeley: University of California.

Dershowitz, A.M. (1976) Fair and Certain Punishment. New York: McGraw-Hill.

Dickover, R. (1976) *Evaluation of Adult Diversion Projects: CBCEP Report, Part One*. Sacramento: California Department of Corrections.

Doleschal, E. (1980a) '1965–1976 Comparison of National Correctional Caseloads.' Unpub. Hackensack, N.J.: National Council on Crime and Delinquency.

Doleschal, E. (1980b) 'Crime Trends – Uniform Crime Reports Compared with Victimization Surveys.' Unpub. Hackensack, N.J.: National Council on Crime and Delinquency.

Duffee, D. and Ritti, R.R. (1977) 'Correctional Policy and Public Values.' *Criminology*, 14 (4): 449–460.

Duxbury, E. (1973) *Evaluation of Youth Service Bureaus*. Sacramento: California Youth Authority.

Ehrlich, I. (1974) 'Participation in Illegitimate Activities: An Economic Analysis.' In *Essays in the Economics of Crime and Punishment*. G.S. Becker and W.M. Landes, eds. New York: Columbia University Press, pp. 68–134.

Ehrlich, I. (1975) 'Deterrence: Evidence and Inference.' *Yale Law Journal*, 85 (2): 209–227.

Elliott, D.S., *et al.* (1978) *Diversion – A Study of Alternative Processing Practices: An Overview of Initial Study Findings*. Boulder. Colo.: Behavioral Research Institute.

Feeley, M.M. (1978) 'The New Haven Redirection Center.' In *Innovations and Implementation in Public Organizations*, R.R. Nelson and D. Yates (eds). Lexington. Mass.: Lexington Books, pp. 39–67.

Feeley, M.M. (1979) *The Process Is the Punishment*. New York: Russell Sage Foundation.

Flacks, R. (1971) *Youth and Social Change*. Chicago: Rand McNally.

Fogel, R. (1975) '*... We Are the Living Proof ...*': *The Justice Model for Corrections* Cincinnati: Anderson.

Foucault, M. (1979) *Discipline and Punish: The Birth of the Prison*. New York: Vintage.

Fox. S.J. (1974) 'The Reform of Juvenile Justice: The Child's Right to Punishment.' *Juvenile Justice*, 25 (2): 2–9.

Gaylin, W., *et al.* (1976) *Doing Good: The Limits of Benevolence*. New York: Pantheon.

Geis, G., *et al.* (1976) 'Reported Consequences of Decriminalization of Consensual Adult Homosexuality in seven American States.' *Journal of Homosexuality*, 1 (4): 419–426.

Gibbons, D.C. and Blake, G.F. (1975) *Evaluating the Impact of Juvenile Diversion Programs*. Portland, Ore.: National Criminal Justice Education Project, Portland State University.

Gossett, T. (1965) *Race: The History of an Idea in America*. New York: Schocken.

Greenberg, D.F. (1975) 'Problems in Community Corrections.' *Issues in Criminology*, 10 (1): 2–11.

Greenberg, D.F. and Humphries, D. (1980) 'The Cooptation of Fixed Sentencing Reform.' *Crime & Delinquency*, 26 (2): 206–225.

Gusfield, J. (1963) *Symbolic Crusade: Status Politics and the American Temperence Movement*. Urbana: University of Illinois Press.

Handlin, O. (1959) *The Newcomers*. New York: Doubleday.

Hanis, D. (1969) *Justice*. New York: Dutton.

Hillsman-Baker, S. (1979) *Court Employment Program Evaluation: A Summary of Findings*. New York: Vera Institute of Justice.

Hindelang, M.J. (1974) 'Public Opinion Regarding Crime, Criminal Justice, and Related Topics.' *Journal of Research in Crime and Delinquency*, 11 (2): 101–116.

Hylton, J.H. (1980) *Community Corrections and Social Control: A Canadian Perspective*. Regina, Canada: University of Regina.

Joint Committee on New York Drug Law Evaluation (1977) *The Nation's Toughest Drug Law: Evaluating the New York Experience*. New York: Association of the Bar of the City of New York.

Kesey, K. (1962) *One Flew Over the Cuckoo's Nest*. New York: Viking.

Klein, M. (1975) *Pivotal Ingredients of Police Diversion Programs*. Washington, D.C.: National Institute for Juvenile Justice and Delinquency Prevention, Law Enforcement Assistance Administration.

Klein, M., and Kobrin, S. (1980) *National Evaluation of the Deinstitutionalization of Status Offender Programs: Executive Summary*. Los Angeles: Social Science Research Institute.

Krisberg, B., and Austin, J. (1978) *The Children of Ishmael: Critical Perspectives on Juvenile Justice*. Palo Alto, Calif.: Mayfield Press.

Lagoy, S.P., Hussey, F.A. and Kramer, J.H. (1978) 'A Comparative Assessment of Determinate Sentencing in the Four Pioneer States.' *Crime & Delinquency*, 24 (4): 385–400.

Lemert, E. (1951) *Social Pathology*. New York: McGraw-Hill.

Lemert, E. (1967) 'Legislating Change in the Juvenile Court.' *Wisconsin Law Review*: 421–428.

Lemert, E. (1970) *Social Action and Legal Change: Revolution within the Juvenile Court*. Chicago: Aldine.

Lemert, E. (1971) *Instead of Court: Diversion in Juvenile Justice*. Rockville, Md.: National Institute of Mental Health.

Lemert, E. and Dill, F. (1978) *Offenders in the Community: The Probation Subsidy in California*. Lexington, Mass.: Lexington Books.

Lerman, P. (1975) *Community Treatment and Social Control: A Critical Analysis of Juvenile Correctional Policy*. Chicago: University of Chicago Press.

Lewis, P.W., and Allen, H.E. (1977) 'Participating Miranda.' *Crime & Delinquency*, 23 (1): 75–80.

Lipton, D., Martinson, R. and Wilks, J. (1975) *The Effectiveness of Correctional Treatment*. New York: Praeger.

Little, A.D., Inc. (1979) *Evaluation of the County Justice System Subvention Program. First Annual Report*. San Francisco: Arthur D. Little.

Little, A.D., Inc. (1980) *Determinate and Indeterminate Sentence Law Comparisons Study: Feasibility of Adapting Law to Sentencing Commission – Guideline Approach*. San Francisco: Arthur D. Little.

Martinson, R. (1974) 'What Works? – Questions and Answers about Prison Reform.' *Public Interest*, 55 (Spring): 22–54.

Massachusetts Advocacy Center (1980) *Delinquent Detention*. Boston: Massachusetts Advocacy Center.

Mennel, R.M. (1973) *Thorns and Thistles*. Hanover, N.H.: University Press of New England.

Messinger, S.L. and Johnson, P.D. (1978) *California Determinate Sentencing Statute: History and Issues*. Proceedings of the Special Conference on Determinate Sentencing. Washington, D.C.: Govt. Printing Office.

Miller, D. (1980) 'Alternatives to Incarceration: From Total Institutions to Total Systems.' Ph.D. diss. Berkeley: University of California.

Mills, C.W. (1959) *The Sociological Imagination*. New York: Oxford University Press.

Mintz, R., and Fagan, J. (1975) *The Feasibility of Pre-Trial Diversion for Misdemeanant Defendants in San Francisco*. San Francisco: Northern California League.

Morris, N. (1975) *The Future of Imprisonment*. Chicago: University of Chicago Press.

Moynihan, D.P. (1969) *Maximum Feasible Misunderstanding*. New York: Free Press.

Nagel, W.G. (1977) 'On Behalf of a Moratorium on Prison Construction.' *Crime & Delinquency*, 23 (2): 154–172.

Nagel, W.G. (1979) 'Prisonia – America's Growing Sprawling Megalopolis.' Paper presented at the Brookings Institution's Seminar for State Legislators on Alternatives to New Prison Construction, Washington, D.C.

Narcotics and Drug Abuse Office (1977) *A First Report of the Impact of California's New Marijuana Law (SB 95).* Sacramento: California State Office of Narcotics and Drug Abuse.

National Council on Crime and Delinquency (1980) *A New Correctional Policy for California: Developing Alternatives to Prison.* San Francisco: NCCD Research Center West.

O'Connor, J. (1973) *The Fiscal Crisis of the State.* New York: St Martin's Press.

Orwell, G. (1949) *1984.* New York: Harcourt Brace.

Packer, H.L. (1968) *The Limits of the Criminal Sanction.* Stanford, Calif.: Stanford University Press.

Palmer, T., Bohnstedt, M. and Lewis, R. (1978) *The Evaluation of Juvenile Diversion Projects: Final Report.* Sacramento: California Youth Authority.

Pennsylvania Program for Women and Girl Offenders, Inc. (1975) *The Decriminalization of Prostitution.* Philadelphia.

Petersilia, J., Greenwood, P.W. and Lavin, M. (1978) *Criminal Careers of Habitual Felons.* Washington, D.C.: Govt. Printing Office.

Platt, A. (1968) *The Child Savers – The Invention of Delinquency.* Chicago: University of Chicago Press.

Pound, R. (1942a) *An Introduction to the Philosophy of Law.* New Haven: Yale University Press.

Pound, R. (1942b) *Social Control through Law.* New Haven: Yale University Press.

Pound, R. (1943) 'A Survey of Social Interests.' *Harvard Law Review,* 57 (1): 1–39.

Quinney, R. (1974) *Critique of Legal Order.* Boston: Little, Brown.

Rothman, D.J. (1971) *The Discovery of the Asylum.* Boston: Little, Brown.

Rovner-Pieczenik, R. (1974) *Pretrial Intervention Strategies: An Evaluation of Policy Related Research and Policymaker Perceptions.* Washington, D.C.: American Bar Association.

Rubin, T. (1977) 'The Juvenile Court's Search for Identity and Responsibility.' *Crime & Delinquency,* 23 (1): 1–13.

Rusche, G. and Kirchheimer, O. (1968) *Punishment and Social Structure.* New York: Russell and Russell.

Rutherford, A. (1978) 'The Dissolution of the Training Schools in Massachusetts.' In *The Children of Ishmael.* B. Krisberg and J. Austin, eds. Palo Alto, Calif.: Mayfield, pp. 515–534.

Rutherford, A., *et al.* (1977) *Prison Population and Policy Choices.* Volume I: *Preliminary Report to Congress.* Washington, D.C.: U.S. Department of Justice, Law Enforcement Assistance Administration.

Scull, A.T. (1977) *Decarceration.* Englewood Cliffs, N.J.: Prentice-Hall.

Skolnick, J. (1966) *Justice without Trial.* New York: John Wiley.

Skolnick, J. (1967) 'Social Control in the Adversary System.' *Journal of Conflict Resolution* II: 52–70.

Solzhenitsyn, A. (1968) *Cancer Ward,* New York: Dial Press.

U.S. National Commission on Law Observance and Enforcement (1931) *Reports.* 15 vol. Washington, D.C.: Govt. Printing Office.

Van Den Haag, E. (1975) *Punishing Criminals.* New York: Basic Books.

Von Hirsch, A. (1976) *Doing Justice.* New York: Hill & Wang.

Ward, L. (1883) *Applied Sociology*. Boston: Atheneum Press.

Ward, L. (1896) *Dynamic Sociology*. Boston: Atheneum Press.

Wilhelm, S. (1970) *Who Needs the Negro?* Cambridge, Mass.: Schenkman.

Williams, W.A. (1973) *The Contours of American History*. New York: New Viewpoints.

Wilson, J.Q. (1975) *Thinking about Crime*. New York: Basic Books.

Wolfgang, M.E., Figlio, R.M. and Sellin, T. (1972) *Delinquency in a Birth Cohort*. Chicago: University of Chicago Press.

Women Endorsing Decriminalization (1973) 'Prostitution: A Non-Victim Crime?' *Issues in Criminology*, 8 (2): 137–162.

18

Justice, retribution and children

Stewart Asquith

> It is not enough ... for a system of law to comply with the formal attributes of justice even though tempered with a spirit of equity. For in addition, law needs to possess a just content, and this can only mean that its actual rules must themselves by their provisions aim at and endeavour to conform to some criteria of rightness which repose on values exterior to justice itself in the sense that no merely formal idea of justice can dictate to us the basis upon which we are to prefer one set of values to another. (Lloyd, 1964, 133)

Some time ago whilst participating as a member of the now legendary Brains Trust, Professor Joad, a philosopher, achieved some notoriety by beginning many of his replies to questions with the phrase 'It all depends on what you mean by ...'. Since justice is what Gallie (1964) calls a 'contestable concept' it is subject to a variety of often conflicting interpretations which have to be analysed. And, depending on what meaning is given to the concept, proposals purporting to provide justice may in fact be unjust. This will depend on the crucial distinction drawn between formal and material justice referred to above by Lloyd and in this essay I will elaborate on the importance of this distinction and address three areas: the relationship between the concept of justice and retributivism; the appropriateness of retributivism in the context of the material conditions which characterize modern social life; and the difference between dealing with adults who commit offences and children who commit offences.

The provision of justice for children is necessarily a political enterprise which has to be informed by a comprehensive theory of social relationships in which the status of children and any rights they may possess are clearly identified.

RETRIBUTIVISM AND JUSTICE

The current attack on what might be termed a welfare philosophy as the basis for systems of juvenile justice is composed of two main elements, both conceptually linked.

SOURCE: This chapter is taken from A. Morris and H. Giller (eds) *Providing Criminal Justice for Children*, London, Edward Arnold, 1983, pp. 7–18.

The first is that children's rights receive insufficient protection in systems based on welfarism for a number of reasons. *Theoretically,* the critics argue (Morris and McIsaac, 1978; Morris *et al.,* 1980) that welfarism is based on philosophically unsound principles insomuch as it is not possible to identify criteria which can either be employed to explain delinquent behaviour or to inform the measures to which children are subjected in their 'best interests'. In short, if we do not really know what we are doing with children we should not pretend to be employing the rhetoric of therapy when what is being exercised is a very subtle form of social control. Semantic and linguistic devices too readily conceal the ambiguity and confusion which is seen to be at the very root of welfarism. *Practically,* the justice movement deplores the absence of sufficient legal and judicial safeguards in a system of control based on welfare principles and in that respect their claims are reminiscent of the arguments made in relation to the infamous Gault and Kent cases which fostered a policy of constitutional revisionism in the United States in the 1960s (see, for example, Faust and Brantingham, 1974). The 'return to justice' movement as currently conceived then includes arguments in favour of a court hearing, judicial review of decisions and legal representation. Only in this way, it is said, can children avail themselves of the safeguards commonly available to adults caught up in the criminal justice system. It is no surprise to find that the Scottish system of juvenile justice in which hearings take the form of administrative tribunals comes in for particular comment and criticism along these lines. Indeed, there has more recently been empirical evidence to the effect that even the minimal statutory requirements which should govern children's hearings in Scotland are in practice often being ignored (Martin *et al.,* 1981, and see Chapter 15 of this volume).

The second argument is that measures imposed on children should be offence- (rather than child-) oriented and that children can, therefore, be legitimately punished for what they have done. Advocacy of children's rights and of punishment is, within the terms of a justice approach, conceptually linked: only in a system in which children are punished for what they have done can their rights best be protected. Within a welfare philosophy children can be subjected to measures which are indeterminate and which may appear inconsistent with the measures inflicted on children who have committed *prima facie* similar offences. Accordingly, the main proponents of the justice movement include amongst their main principles the proposal that measures should be determinate, proportional (to the offence) and consistent (with other offences). Needless to say these in themselves provide for a decision-making process that is, in theory at least, more structured and restrictive than that manifested in a welfare system in which wide discretionary powers are available to decision-making personnel. A retributively oriented philosophy underpinning a legally and judicially constituted form of decision-making is seen as the most appropriate and most just basis for a system of juvenile justice.

What is particularly interesting about such arguments is the extent to which they are currently being voiced in a number of countries. Very similar arguments are contained in proposals made by the ABA/IJA Standards Project (1977) in the USA, the Black Committee (1979) for Northern Ireland, Morris *et al.* (1980) for England and Wales and Joutsen (1981) in the republic of Ireland. There are a number of differences in the recommendations made by these different bodies and individuals but what they have in common is the commitment to punishment (as opposed to welfarism) as *the* means of dealing with children who offend and to judicial proceedings (as opposed to what are seen to be wide discretionary powers available within administrative forms of decision making).

In the attempt to clarify when and in what circumstances an individual may be justly punished one of the most important debates in moral and political philosophy is encountered: the extent to which moral autonomy can be reconciled with legitimate political authority. Indeed the question of authority to punish is inextricably linked with definitions of punishment. Flew (1954), and later Watson (1976), offer a number of conditions that must be satisfied before the word punishment can be applied. They suggest that punishment must be an *intended* unpleasantness to the subject; punishment must be for an *offence*; punishment must be of an *offender* and punishment must be imposed by virtue of some special authority. There is a problem with this and one which may, I believe, be reflected in philosophies advocating a return to justice.

Though these conditions *may* be entailed in the definition of punishment they are not themselves *sufficient* to form a means of determining under what circumstances and to what degree punishment may be inflicted. In the justification of punishment, definitional statements of necessity have to be supplemented by moral arguments. It is the lack of an essentially *moral* justification for a system of punishment that may render the notion of 'justice' open to criticism. The suggestion that 'welfarism' is basically unjust, supposing that to be the case, must be supplemented by arguments which justify punishment as being *the* form of institutional control. It is not enough to assert that a system of punishment, subject to judicial control, constitutes a more 'just' system in which the rights of children are protected. The success of these arguments depends on the conception of justice employed.

There are two elements to the concept of justice – formal and what is often referred to as material or substantial. Formal justice is traditionally associated with judicial proceedings and means little more than treating like cases alike and in this way relates very closely to the principles of equal treatment of similar cases and to the demand for consistency advocated by Morris *et al.* (1980). For the retributivists, an offender is punished because he has done something to deserve his punishment, but punishment somehow has to fit the offence and ought not to be decided upon simply with atonement in mind. A limit then has to be imposed on the severity of the sanction and the infliction of retributive sanctions can further be limited by relating the punishment to the offence. The obvious difficulty here is in deciding on the criteria to be employed in relating offences and sanctions; the retributivist principle of proportionality offers little help in general though it may contribute to the maintenance of balance in the sanctions employed for different types of offences. Moreover, in terms of limiting retributivism, the importance of the moral culpability of the offender is further signified by Walker (1969, 31) in the principle that 'society has no right to apply an unpleasant measure to someone against his will unless he has done something prohibited'. Thus, only those who behave responsibly can be justly punished and here retributivism and formal justice parallel each other: the justice of the sanction has to be determined in relation to the culpability of the offender and with reference to the treatment meted out to those who commit similar offences. That is, like cases have to be treated alike. It is precisely because of this that Mundle (1954) argued that retributivism is a logical not a moral doctrine since it allows us to determine *who* can be punished and how much.

Similarly, formal justice means something like the application of the law impartially and fairly with all individuals treated equally before the law. What formal justice and retributivism share is the notion of the individual as a juridic person, equal before the law and punishable by virtue of his capacity as a morally autonomous being. However, this tells us little about what is meant by cases being alike and it is in this context that the material content of justice is to be articulated. Though formal justice may mean that rules have to be applied equally to cases alike in nature, the very content of the rules and the categories employed to define 'likeness' of cases have to be established and these raise questions of material, not formal, justice. Formal justice may allow us to determine the application of punishment in *particular* cases but it is only through the concept of material justice that the institution of punishment may be morally justified. This is the distinction drawn by Rawls (1955) between the justi-fication of a rule or practice on the one hand and the justification of a particular action on the other. To my mind, both concern the moral justification of punishment but one refers to the morality of the institution or the practice as a whole whereas the other refers to the moral appropriateness in a particular instance of the application of punishment within that practice. A number of points have to be made here.

First, the concept of justice employed by many of the proponents of a justice approach reflects concern with the procedural injustices which may arise within systems of delinquency control espousing a commitment to welfare. As such, proposals for change, even in the advocacy of retributive sanctions, are primarily directed at promot-ing greater procedural justice *within* systems of control and there is often little discus-sion of how these are, or ought to be, related to the material conditions of social life.

Second, in the pursuit of greater protection for children within systems of control, further consideration has to be given to the distinction between dealing with children and dealing with adults and, consequently, between children's rights and adults' rights. The perception of the offender in retributive thinking is rational and respon-sible and this poses particular problems for any social institution dealing with those whose status as morally autonomous agents needs careful consideration. The extent to which children can be considered criminally or morally responsible or both is a crucial question. The mental capacity of the individual has always been singled out as a prime factor to be taken into account in determining the character of retributive sanctions. Walker (1969, 23), for example, argues that 'the amount and therefore the severity of the penalty should be governed by the offender's intentions and not by the actual result'. In this respect, the issues involved in dealing with juveniles parallel very closely the debates about the punishment of the mentally ill since both involve questions of moral agency and moral competency.

RETRIBUTIVISM AND INJUSTICE

The criterion of 'likeness' employed by the proponents of 'justice for children' seems determined by the offence committed and the moral culpability of the offender. Indeed, both are required since no one who was not morally culpable could be justifi-ably punished. Further, for those following Kantian orthodoxy, only retributivism recognizes, in punishment, human dignity, self-realization and moral autonomy. In theory, the status of the person who can justly be punished is closely connected with the right of the state to punish and with a particular conception of social relation-ships. According to Murphy (1973) the state has a right to pursue retributive objectives only if certain conditions are satisfied. First, all men have to be considered as rational and autonomous beings; only then can they justifiably be punished. Secondly, all men have to be seen as participating equally and fully in a social system in which they experience mutually beneficial relationships and enjoy similar social, political and economic opportunities. Only in this way can the state derive the right to punish since all men can participate in deciding who can be punished and for what reason. In a sense, argues Murphy, the decision to punish an individual is one in which the offender, as a participating member of the social system, has himself participated.

It could be argued that such a social system is a purely abstract form and can be criticized on much the same grounds as theories of society employing metaphysical notions such as Social Contract or General Will. However, it indicates two things. One is that retributivist theories of punishment cannot simply be presented on the grounds of increased procedural justice alone but require an elaborate social and political theory by means of which any justification offered can be given material content. The use of force in the pursuit of retributivist objectives and the threat it poses to individual liberty and autonomy has to be promoted within a theory of society and social relationships in which men participate as equal individuals. As Murphy (1973) puts it, retributivism depends on a political philosophy of reciprocity. Only in this way can it be seen as containing any semblance of material justice.

The other is that, put quite simply, where men do not share equally in social and economic opportunities, retributivism is *materially* inadequate. In Murphy's words:

> The theories of moral, social, political and legal philosophy presuppose certain empirical propositions about man and society. If these propositions are false, then the theory (even if coherent or formally correct) is materially defective and practically inapplicable. (1973, 73)

Though Murphy is addressing the relationship between Marxism and retribution, I am not suggesting that a Marxist stance has to be taken. My argument is simpler. Retributivist philosophies do contain a degree of internal coherence or logic. Their relevance for modern societies, however, which are characterized by gross social inequality, must be seriously considered. The danger is that in constructing a social institution, such as a criminal justice system, which satisfies the demands of formal justice one may compound basic social and structural injustices.

This means that, in accepting a retributivist philosophy and the notion of a responsible offender, the advocates of a justice approach must articulate what part social, economic and environmental circumstances play in the production of crime. In practice, they tend to suggest that these circumstances are relevant but that they are not resolvable within a criminal justice system. The difficulty this presents is that, as Murphy (1973) explicitly points out, there may well be a theoretical gap between the assumptions and principles employed in philosophies of crime causation and those embodied in philosophies of crime control.

The second problem in adopting a retributive stance towards dealing with children rests on the difficulty of establishing to what extent, under what circumstances and at what age children can be held responsible. The question is whether or not there is or can be any retributivist justification for dealing with children differently from adults.

CHILDREN AND RETRIBUTION

The central problem for retributivist justifications of punishment for children is that they rest on notions which are complicated because of the status of childhood. If one relies on equal treatment of offenders in accordance with such principles as consistency and proportionality with what the offender has done, there appears to be little reason, *prima facie,* for differentiating between child and adult offenders. Indeed, a major thrust of current developments in social policy for delinquents is to erode any distinction which may exist in juvenile and criminal justice systems. In Canada, for example, recent proposals include the fingerprinting of children, open courts and judicial inquiry; in Finland, recent arguments for a court-based system include the demand for a reduction in the age of criminal responsibility (this is in itself a logical consequence of the acceptance of retributive sanctions for child offenders since punishment of children who are not criminally responsible would not only be not morally justifiable but also presumably illegal); and in Northern Ireland, proposals for a punishment system with fixed penalties for particular offences are accompanied by the suggestion that there should be two types of court – a welfare court and a criminal court, a recommendation very similar to that made by Morris *et al.* (1980). All these proposals derive, it would appear, from the commitment to offer children protections in a juvenile justice system which are afforded to adults in the criminal justice system.

It could be argued that children's rights do indeed demand greater procedural and administrative protection in *both* a punishment and a welfare system. One of the great sources of debate about the Scottish system of Children's Hearings, for example, is how best to offer such protection in an administrative tribunal. However, increased procedural protection does not *ipso facto* mean that children should be treated in substantive terms as adults. Though a philosophy of delinquency control which concentrates on relating sanctions to what has been done would appear to require that those who commit similar offences are dealt with in like fashion, whether children or adults, this is not necessarily so. Clearly, in a retributivist approach only those who are responsible for an offence can be punished and it has generally been accepted that children may not always be the subject of punishment since they do not necessarily have the same mental capacity and moral competence as adults. This much has been recognized in the criminal law with the rebuttable and irrebuttable presumption of responsibility and also in the fact that there is a line below which (the age of criminal responsibility) children are not considered capable of truly criminal behaviour because they are incapable of the requisite moral and cognitive processes. In short, even the traditionally espoused tenets of retributivism allow that children may not be punished as readily as adults since there are factors related to their status *qua* children which may be employed to absolve them from punishment. That is, there are criteria which can be employed on children's behalf as excusing conditions which are not available to adults (perhaps with the exception of the mentally ill). Children do not occupy the same status as adults in what Schrag refers to as the 'moral order' (1977).

A number of points can be considered in relation to this:

Welfarism

A welfare philosophy as a basis for dealing with offenders is seen by the proponents of a justice approach as *theoretically* shaky (we do not know what the needs of children are nor do we know how to meet them) and *practically* unjust. If welfarism is to be totally rejected on the grounds that we do not really know what we are doing, a particular problem arises. The advocates of a *justice* system do not deny that children have needs. What they are saying is that the needs of children should be met in other contexts – families, schools, social and medical services – and not in the courts. The problem though is that such informal and formal approaches to caring for children are required to and *do* operate on the assumption that children's needs can be met. Morris *et al.* (1980) themselves argue that even a justice-oriented system could 'provide the offender with guidance, supervision and other assistance in coping with any difficulties *he* may feel he has met' (p. 65, emphasis original). And the Black Report (1979), whilst advocating a system of fixed penalties determined by judicial inquiry, asserts that child offenders may have needs but that these could best he served by a welfare court. In both cases, questions about what to do with an offender, whether in the course of, or as a supplement to, judicial inquiry, require assessment and plans involving criteria other than offence considerations (see also Borowski, 1981 and Adler, 1981).

Children, justice and rights

In terms of Murphy's (1973) analysis, children do not participate equally with adults in social and political systems; they are not members of a 'gentleman's club' of social relationships and for that reason, where formal state intervention operates in accordance with principles of equality and notions such as the juridic person, the justice of such intervention has to be made out. The pertinence of this rests on the fact that the issue of children's rights has to be seen as inextricably linked to questions about their status as persons in society and the amount of freedom or liberty they are allowed to have (see Schrag, 1977). A difficulty arises when we try to reconcile offering children as much liberty and freedom as possible and promoting their interests to the utmost of our ability. It is in this respect that any move to get justice for children must be accompanied by a clearly stated theory of rights. The conflict between promoting children's interests and offering them as much freedom as possible is perhaps best epitomized by the literature on rights.

It is generally recognized that there are two predominant types of 'rights' theories. These are what McCormick (1976) calls (a) 'interest' theories (referred to by Freeman (1981) as 'nurturance' theories) and (b) 'will' theories (referred to by Freeman (1981) as 'self-determination' theories). 'Interest' theories mean those theories of rights which are designed to promote the interests of the individuals concerned, in this discussion, children. Individuals have a right to have their interests advanced and these rights impose obligations and duties on others such as parents, teachers and the state to meet them. 'Will' theories mean those theories which maintain that individuals have a right to maintain and exercise control over their own lives in accordance with *their* will. The problem in dealing with children, of course, is that there is considerable disagreement as to just how much freedom of decision-making they should have. Few would deny that children ought to have some say in what happens in or to their lives and the recent trend to employ contracts in child care and custody proceedings in which the child states his point of view or participates fully in negotiations about his future reflect this. Proponents of the justice approach endorse these in arguing that children should be encouraged to take responsibility for what they have done. However, concern with children's interests is also evident inasmuch as legal representation and judicial scrutiny are seen to be appropriate means of serving children's interests. Children, the argument goes, have a right to legal representation, a right to be heard in court and even, according to some commentators, a right to punishment. However, to repeat much of what has been said above, the pursuit of justice and the promotion of children's rights are directed more at the procedures adopted in the decision-making process and are less concerned with the substantive rights of children *qua* children in terms of the provision of welfare or the meeting of their needs. The furtherance of children's interests demands more than the development of procedural safeguards. If we are genuinely concerned about the life opportunities and life chances of children in modern society then more positive measures will be required to ensure that the rights and interests of the young are promoted.

The promotion of children's rights, if it is to be a genuine attempt to promote justice for children, has to involve more than just tinkering with the legal system since children who are formally processed tend, as a matter of historical contingency, to come from less well-off areas and less well-off families and are by virtue of their status *qua* children in a position of subordination and dependency. In much the same way that the pursuit of equality and justice for women involved major political innovations, the pursuit of justice for children is an essentially political affair requiring examination of the roles allotted to children in social and legal relationships. Rights imply duties and the rights that children have impose duties on individuals such as parents and on the state to guarantee that these rights are realized.

TWO-WAY PENDULUM

In the course of this essay, a rather simple point has been made: any attempt to promote justice for children has to be premised on some understanding of the roles that children, particularly those caught up in formal systems of control, occupy in our society. My concern has not been to attack punishment and retribution *per se* but to suggest that any theory of control whether based on welfare or punishment principles must not simply be logically coherent and internally consistent but must also bear some relationship to the material conditions of social life. The current trend to retribution and judicial proceedings no doubt anticipates a swing back to some form of liberalism. Developments in juvenile justice, as in criminal policy, have generally displayed pendulum like movements swinging between welfarism and punishment. As a consequence, formal policy statements and the systems premised thereon are all too often riven with ambiguity, an almost inevitable result of trying to reconcile philosophies of control that are in the abstract based upon very different principles. The danger of continuing to formulate policies in this way is that the institutions of control, though they may bear the hallmarks of formal justice, can themselves become unjust and constitute one means of perpetuating what Harris (1973) calls 'structural injustices'. Providing justice for children will not be possible without analysing the way in which life opportunities and experiences are socially distributed. This is essentially a *political* exercise.

Policies which ignore the social and economic realities in which children find themselves, while promoting greater equality and justice within formal systems of control, may not only ignore but may compound the structural and material inequalities which have been historically associated with criminal behaviour. The provision of justice for children will require a fundamental reappraisal of the social distribution of life opportunities offered to children. Increased protection within systems of control may promote children's rights procedurally but may fail to realize them substantively. It may also enable the abrogation of our responsibility to meet those rights. To do so would be unjust.

REFERENCES

Adler, R. (1981) Black on young offenders: Policy without principles or no policy at all? *Scolag*, August.

Black Report, The (1979) *Report of the children and young persons review group*. Belfast: HMSO.

Borowski, E.J. (1981) Looking glass justice. *The Hearing*, February.

Faust, F. and Brantingham, P. (eds) (1974) *Juvenile justice philosophy*. St Paul, Minnesota: West Pub. Co.

Flew, A. (1954) The justification of punishment, *Philosophy*, XIXX (3), October.

Freeman, M.D.A. (1981) The rights of children who do 'wrong'. *British Journal of Criminology*, 21 (3).

Gallie, W.B. (1964) *Philosophy and the historical understanding*. London: Chatto & Windus.

Harris, R. (1973) Structural Injustice. *Philosophy and Public Affairs*, 3, Spring.

Harrison, B. (1971) Violence and the rule of law. In Shaffer, J. (ed.), *Violence*, quoted in Murphy (1973).

Joutsen, M. (1981) The rationale for intervention. Paper presented to the IVth International Conference on Comparative Studies in Juvenile Justice, May.

King, M. (1981) Welfare and justice. In King, M. (ed.), *Childhood, welfare and justice*. London: Batsford.

Lloyd, D. (1964) *The idea of law*. Harmondsworth: Pelican.

Martin, F., Fox, S. and Murray, K. (1981) *Children out of court*, Edinburgh: Scottish Academic Press.

McCormick, D.N. (1976) Children's rights: a test-case for theories of right. *Archiv für Rechts and Sozial Philosophie*, LX (11/3).

Morris, A., Giller, H., Szwed, E. and Geach, H. (1980) *Justice for children*. London: Macmillan.

Morris, A. and McIsaac, M. (1978) *Juvenile justice?* London: Heinemann.

Mundle, C.W.K. (1954) Punishment and Desert. *Philosophical Quarterly*, IV (16).

Murphy, J.G. (1973) Marxism and retribution. *Philosophy and Public Affairs*, 3, Spring.

Rawls, J. (1955) Two concepts of rules. *Philosophical Review*, LXIV.

Schrag, F. (1977) The child in the moral order. *Philosophy*, 52.

Walker, N. (1969) *Sentencing in a rational society*. Harmondsworth: Penguin.

Watson, D. (1976) The underlying principles. In Martin, F. and Murray, K. (eds), *Children's hearings* (Edinburgh: Scottish Academic Press).

Wootton, B. (1959) *Social science and social pathology*. London: Allen & Unwin.

19

Whose justice? The politics of juvenile control

John Clarke

[...]

Recently, there have been a number of arguments that a revival of 'justice' principles provides the basis for a progressive politics of juvenile justice. Such arguments have criticised the discretionary powers which the welfare orientation of the 1969 Children and Young Persons Act established in England and Wales. This article takes issue with the claim that a 'justice' approach provides the basis of a progressive strategy, and argues that the presentation of juvenile justice as the site of an opposition between the principles of justice and welfare is ill-conceived, and leads to potentially dangerous political consequences.

The starting point for these arguments must necessarily be the 1969 Children and Young Persons Act. For the proponents of 'justice', this Act provides the focal point for their discussion of the consequences of discretionary control of juveniles. It installed local authority social work in a central role in the process of juvenile justice, provided social workers with control over the 'treatment' of juveniles, and extended the scope of control to 'pre-delinquents' by the introduction of intermediate treatment provisions. [But] In my view, the equation of the 1969 Act with the principles of welfarism and discretionary powers has been overstated in these arguments.

[...]

LIVING WITH THE CONSEQUENCES: THE 1969 ACT IN PRACTICE

The consequences of the 1969 Act are now well and extensively documented. [See Chapter 14 of this volume.] The operation of the Act has seen increasing numbers of juveniles cautioned by the police and appearing before the court. It has seen increasing numbers of juveniles being incarcerated through one disposal route or another. It has seen an increasing willingness on the part of social workers to recommend forms

SOURCE: This chapter is taken from *International Journal of the Sociology of Law*, Vol. 13, No. 4, 1985, pp. 407–21.

of institutional 'care' in SERs. Finally, it has seen the expansion of intermediate treatment to the 'pre-delinquent', pulling more juveniles into the orbit of the state.

The accumulated evidence is incontrovertible. What seems more problematic is interpreting the causes of those consequences. For the proponents of justice, the expanded role of unaccountable discretionary decision-making has been the central force. In particular, local authority social work is accused of using the absence of proper legal controls to subject growing numbers of juveniles to social control. Professional imperialism has advanced by claiming a monopoly of knowledge of the 'best interests of the child'.

Both 'progressive' and 'reactionary' expositions of the need to restore justice share this view of social work as the agency responsible for the consequences of the Act. Giller & Morris argue that:

> Increasingly, as the mechanisms of these processes are researched and investigated, the traditional ascriptions of responsibility for these results to an unsympathetic magistracy or judiciary cannot be substantiated ... A fuller picture suggests that the benign and helping agencies can and do (often unwittingly) contribute to the production of punitive juvenile justice (Giller & Morris, 1983, pp. 151–2).

Morgan argues:

> It is part of the progressive folklore typified in the *Guardian* and *New Society* that responsibility for the expansion of secure places or 'intensive care' is to be laid at the door of the public's and the magistrates' intolerance of dangerous, repeated or serious delinquents. Both are accused of converting the care order into an instrument of punishment and public protection. However, this ignores the fact that transferral within the care system is completely dependent upon the evaluations and decisions of its own staff. (Morgan, 1981, p. 57).

Although there are disagreements about other aspects of juvenile justice policy, the 'justice' arguments centre on the necessity of re-establishing the formal process of justice in counterpoint to the growth of discretion:

> By restricting the powers of the juvenile court and limiting intervention so that it is proportionate to the offences children commit, it is argued that a more rational disposition process will emerge and that justice for children will be provided (Giller & Convington, 1983, p. 146).

Morgan, discussing welfarist discretion, says:

> Clearly, all this must undercut principles of fairness or equality before the law, where standard procedures and sentences are applied to particular cases. And, whatever else they may be, *disposals are inherently unjust* when they are applied on consideration of future welfare and in accordance with personal criteria. Given this, it is hardly remarkable that rehabilitation aims have a tendency to undermine those features of the law which traditionally safeguarded fairness, such as public proceedings, adversarial practice and appeal (Morgan, 1981, p. 63).

These themes form the centre piece of the revival of justice. The safeguards of the process have been undermined by the rise of personalised treatment. The certainties of legal punishment, and the countervailing forces of legal rights, have become lost in the morass of discretionary powers and rehabilitative vagueness. In what follows, I want to question both the diagnosis of the troubles of the juvenile justice system, and the recommended treatment prescribed by the justice movement.

THE 1969 ACT: PRINCIPLES AND PRACTICE

It seems that in the continuing court room drama of Justice *v.* Welfare, some basic analytic questions are being put to one side. Both Giller & Morris, and Morgan, in their targeting of social work's 'responsibility' seem over-hasty in writing other agencies out of the analysis. It is true that research studies have revealed social work collusion in the extension of control, but that is hardly all that they have shown. In both the extracts reproduced above, there are rather shaky ascriptions of responsibility to social work. Giller & Morris argue against the 'ascription of responsibility to an unsympathetic magistracy', but only suggest that helping agencies '*contribute to*' punitive juvenile justice. Morgan equally narrows the target of attack, moving from 'responsibility for the expansion of secure places' to social work's responsibility for 'transferral within the care system'. There are suppressions of argument in these shifts, and they are precisely suppressions of issues about the role of non-welfare agencies involved in the production of juvenile justice.

These other agencies have played a substantial role in shaping the juvenile justice system, and practice within it. The partial implementation of the Act by the Conservative government of 1970 owed much to pressure from magistrates and the police to limit the 'damage' being done by the Act's 'welfarism'. Since its introduction, these agencies (and others such as the Magistrates' Clerks Association, and the Society of Conservative Lawyers) have mounted attacks on the Act's 'permissiveness' and the softness of social work. As Morris & Giller argued in an earlier article, this pressure has had its success:

> By pressing for the introduction of secure care orders, the Right (magistrates/the police/the Conservative Party) continues to present its stereotype of juvenile offenders across the *whole machinery* of the juvenile justice system. Its aim now seems to be to ensure that social service resources become more obviously mechanisms of social control (Morris & Giller, 1979, p. 27).

In the practice of the Act, these agencies have systematically worked to produce juvenile justice of a distinctive sort. The rising rate of prosecutions for young offenders has been one effect of the police reaction to the supposed 'diversionary' intent of the Act. Similarly, magistrates (in spite of their complaints) did continue to exercise decision-making power in the juvenile court, in particular over disposals. Both in principle and in practice, then, the system of juvenile justice created by the 1969 Act is hardly one of pure welfarist principles. David Thorpe and his colleagues have argued that what the 1969 Act produced was a system of 'vertical integration':

> What happens when a system that is intended as a replacement is simply grafted on to its predecessor and run in parallel with it ... Considered abstractly there are two possibilities, of which the first is intense conflict and abrasion. While there has indeed been a great deal of conflict at the ideological level ... this simply has not happened in practice. The other possibility is that the two systems come to some form of accommodation, an implicit set of demarcation agreements and neutral zones, and that the sector served by the old system

simply expands in order to make room for the newcomer. It is in this direction that all the available evidence points in the case of the 1969 CYPA. The two systems have in effect, become vertically integrated and an additional population of customer-clients has been identified in order to ensure that they both have plenty of work to do. (Thorpe *et al.*, 1980, Chapter 22, p. 3)

Here we are getting closer to a structural understanding of how social work has come to 'contribute to a punitive juvenile justice': not the replacement of 'justice' by 'welfare', but the articulation of two different systems, sets of powers and ideologies. Thorpe *et al.* identify a precise structural location for social work within juvenile justice, which allows them to explore the concessions, compromises and collusion through which social work sought a role within this system. It is perhaps worth noting that the Lancaster study has become widely known for its detailed research on care orders, while relatively little has been said about its analysis of the structural context within which the care order operates. It is this structure, and the subordination of social work to pre-existing pattens of juvenile justice, which has been played down in the attention given to social work's powers.

MEET ON THE LEDGE: PROGRESSIVISM AND THE RULE OF LAW

Ten years ago, E.P. Thompson reflected, in the conclusion to his study of the 'Black Acts', on the role of law in class struggle. He argued against those who would see the law as merely as an instrument of class rule and oppression:

> It is inherent in the especial character of law, as a body of rules and procedures, that it shall apply logical criteria with reference to standards of universality and equality ... The essential precondition for the effectiveness of law, in its functions as an ideology, is that it shall display an independence from gross manipulation and shall seem to be just.

> ... there is a difference between arbitrary power and the rule of law. We ought to expose the shams and inequities which may be concealed beneath this law. But the rule of law itself, the imposing of effective inhibitions upon power and the defence of the citizen from power's all-intrusive claims, seems to me to be an unqualified human good (Thompson, 1975, pp. 262–3, 266).

In this conclusion, Thompson describes the position he presents through the metaphor of 'standing on a narrow ledge'. That ledge is now becoming crowded as well as narrow. The 'back to justice' movement embodies some of Thompson's argument in defending the legal rights of the child citizen against the 'intrusive' and unregulated power of welfare bureaucracies. Arguments from the juvenile justice debates echo some of the concerns expressed in Thompson's defence of the rule of law:

> The tools of tyranny are ages old, and lie in the perversion of the due process of law by secrecy, discretion, vaguely defined offences and seemingly arbitrary and disproportionate penalties (Morgan, 1981, p. 44).

The positions here are not identical. Where Thompson stresses the class contradictions of the law as a basis for arguing its political importance, Morgan draws more directly on the traditions of bourgeois individualism revived in the New Right's embracing of the Rule of Law as a central political theme. They are not identical, but there are overlaps. They do indeed meet on Thompson's ledge, and this meeting provides cause for political concern about its outcome. As Thompson's own work demonstrates, justice and the Rule of Law are the subjects of political conflicts, and the current balance of political forces makes me, at least, uneasy about the political consequences of reviving 'justice', as the basis of a progressive strategy.

That political concern is one to which I shall return. Before that, though, I want to explore what the Rule of Law involves. The main attention – from Thompson and the 'back to justice' movement – has been focused on the Law as a set of abstract, and universally applicable, principles and procedures. I think that the Law has to be explored as a more complex set of processes than this in assessing the implications of justice for juveniles. In doing so, I will suggest that at least three different aspects of Law need to be distinguished.

(1) Law as due process

This is the level at which most discussions of the Rule of Law and justice are pitched: the abstract principles which guide the practical operation of the Law. It is here that one discovers the 'juridical subject' defined in terms of rights, access to the law, expectations of just treatment and the subject of due process. It is here that equality before the Law and the expectation of impersonalised justice for the citizen are established. 'Juridical subjects' are de-personalised citizens, stripped of their specific social characteristics, confronted by the impersonal process of Law.

This terrain of formal equality of citizens under the Law is often contrasted in critical commentaries, with the prevailing material or substantive inequalities of social structure:

> ... proposals for change, even in the advocacy of retributive sanctions, are primarily directed at promoting greater procedural justice *within* systems of control and there is often little discussion of how these are, or ought to be, related to the material conditions of social life (Asquith, 1983, p. 11).

While I in no sense want to wish away this issue of material inequalities, I do nevertheless think there is a danger in treating the issue of 'justice' as if it poses a tension between the Law (embodying procedural justice and formal equality) and Society (embodying social injustice and material inequality). That is the tension which emerges if we only consider Law as an abstract set of principles, but the Rule of Law involves more than this.

(2) The law as specific prohibitions

In addition to the procedural rules and principles, the Law is composed of specific laws, prohibiting and censuring particular social acts. These prohibitions are socially *motivated* and socially *targeted*. Their origins lie not only in the decision of which *acts* to prescribe, but in social judgements which link acts to particular social groups whose behaviour is deemed worthy of regulation. The Law-as-specific-prohibitions is socially selective. For example, David Dixon's study of the 1906 Street Betting Act indicates the class selectivity of the act in terms of the types of gambling (predominantly working-class) which it sought to prescribe, and those (upper-class) forms of gambling which it left unregulated (Dixon, 1981).

Similarly, the array of national and local laws which have been used to regulate conduct in 'public space' have historically targeted the (male) working class as the group who occupied public space in ways thought to be at least disorderly, if not potentially dangerous. Here, one can see the interrelationship between material inequalities in 'society' (the unequal access to *private* space) and material inequalities in the Law (the regulation of conduct in public space). Conflicts over public order laws (e.g. the use of 'sus' under the 1834 Act, and 'stop and search' powers) are not merely generated by police 'abuse', but are inscribed in the set of laws which govern public space.

Thus, the Law needs to be seen as the combination of formal principles with specific prohibitions. The combination is a complex one, since these specific prohibitions are produced in the language of those formal principles. Even where their targets are socially precise, they do not address specific social groups or individuals, but formal 'juridical' subjects – the legal person. The 1906 Gambling Act did not proscribe working-class gambling, but 'persons' who gambled in this or that manner. Specific prohibitions are spoken in the language of the Law:

> But once the state has become an independent power vis-à-vis society, it produces forthwith a further ideology. It is indeed among professional politicians, theorists of public law and jurists of private law that the connection with economic facts gets lost for fair. Since in each particular case the economic facts must assume the form of juristic motives in order to receive legal sanction, and since, in doing so, consideration has been given to the whole legal system in operation, the juristic form is, in consequence, made everything, and the economic content nothing (Engels, 1968, p. 617).

(3) Law as social process

There is one further aspect of the Law which needs to be taken into account, in which specific censures are applied, by the agencies of Law, to specific, socially located, individuals. For juveniles, the process of Law begins with the police and only subsequently involves the courts, magistrates and social workers. The 'discretion' which they encounter is not only the discretionary powers of local authority social work departments, but also police discretion – to ignore, caution or recommend for prosecution. Here, as endless studies of police–juvenile interaction have shown, the specific prohibitions of Law are applied through discretionary decision-making embedded in the 'knowledges' of police practice. Before the juvenile becomes a 'juridical subject', she/he is first encountered by the police as a social individual, bearing the signs of a social place (class, race, gender, locality, reputation, etc.), and 'discretion' employs all that information alongside the formal issue of law-breaking.

Even when the formal processes of Law begin, the social individual continues to coexist uncomfortably with the juridical subject. The social characteristics of the individual do not simply fall away as she/he enters the courtroom, but become part of the intangible evidence weighed in the scales of justice. 'Welfarism' in juvenile justice *highlights* the social character of the individual by allocating it an explicit and central role in the decision-making process. It would, however, be a gross error to assume that 'justice' is as blind to social character as its inconography would have us believe. The constitutional purity of Law as a formal process needs to be assessed alongside the impurities of Law as a social process.

Wherever the 'justice movement' recognises the problem of class inequalities, it takes the issues up in a rather peculiar way. Several contributors to Geach and Szwed's *Providing Civil Justice for Children* (1983) discuss 'class bias', but attribute the focusing of state attention on working-class children to the middle-class values of social workers. The reduction of class inequalities in the care process to the subjective domain of social workers' class and/or professional values is a little worrying. It leaves out of account the structural context of social work's relationship to 'family life'. From its origins in the mid-nineteenth century, social work has had a structural relationship to the working-class household as a source of 'social problems' (Jones, 1983), and its attention to the 'problem family' is inseparable from the class forces in which social work is embedded. To reduce this issue to the domain of class and professional values of *social workers,* rather than the structural position of social work, allows the 'justice movement' to shift questions of class power to questions of subjective bias.

KEEPING BAD COMPANY: THE POLITICAL IMPLICATION OF JUSTICE

I wish to turn these observations into two, more general, propositions about the justice movement. First, I find their analysis of the problems of juvenile justice intellectually unconvincing. Their over-attention to the discretionary power of social workers (and the values which may influence the exercise of that discretion) involves a substantial oversimplification of the social process of juvenile justice. In particular, it underplays both the structural vulnerability of working-class youth to the process of law, and the central positions still occupied by non-welfarist agencies (police, magistracy) in those processes. Secondly, those analytic failures add further impetus to my political concern about the staking out of 'justice' as a progressive strategy of reform.

This second point concerns the overlapping of would-be progressive and clearly reactionary arguments in favour of the return to justice. It is an issue to which the 'progressive' proponents of justice have addressed themselves. Acknowledging criticisms of 'justice' strategies which have pointed out their reactionary potential, Giller & Morris argue:

> Such strategies should not be automatically rejected on the basis that in other places and at other times they have been manipulated for repressive ends (Giller & Morris, 1983, p. 153).

I agree wholeheartedly. Reforms rarely have a single, clear-cut, political character, and the enthusiasm of the New Right for something cannot be *automatic* grounds for its rejection. But neither is this a satisfactory case for the adoption of a reforming strategy. Automatic rejection can be ruled out, but that should mean the establishment of some basis for non-automatic rejection or acceptance. I do not find in the justice arguments a political case established for why they should be adopted. There is, by contrast, a case to be made about why they should be rejected – or, at least, viewed with great scepticism.

To make such a case must involve an attempt to assess the balance of political forces and strategies around the issue of juvenile justice, and I do not believe that this gives much basis for progressive optimism about 'justice'. Let me identify two problems associated with the return to justice.

First, its over-constitutionalist conception of Law as due process makes it inattentive to the class (and other) inequalities in Law as specific prohibitions and Law as a social process. By itself, a more 'just' system of legal processing through courts and post-court disposals fails to engage with the profoundly unequal decisions which determine offences and 'discover' offenders. [See Chapter 18 of this volume.] [...]

I would want to insist that laws and their application (the processes of criminalisation) *must* be understood as an integral part of the 'structural and material inequalities ... associated with criminal behaviour'.

Secondly, and more importantly for the contemporary political assessment, the justice movement is simultaneously an anti-welfare argument. In debates surrounding the 1969 Children and Young Persons Act since its inception, anti-welfarism, and anti-social work arguments, have been a constant theme. They have been the almost exclusive property of the constituencies of the Right. The police, the magistracy, magistrates' clerks, Conservative lawers, have systematically attacked the 1969 Act for conceding power to social workers. In doing so, they have consistently linked the attack on welfarism with demands for the restoration of *their* powers and for the restoration of punishment in place of treatment.

The attempt to create a progressive justice movement does not appear on an empty stage, but one which is already peopled with political actors. 'Justice' is not waiting to be taken up: it has already been politically mobilised. One consequence is that the research studies and arguments at the core of the justice movement have already been recruited in service of the New Right's anti-welfarism. Patricia Morgan's defence of justice and punishment draws on the same bibliography of studies and proposals as do the 'progressives', even though the 'justice' that she wishes to reassert intends a rather different impact on its beneficiaries.

Those of us who criticise social work face a difficult political problem. Attacks on social work-as social control, on its biases, and on its 'abuses of power' take place in a political context where anti-welfarism is the political property of the New Right, and where that anti-welfarism has already had very material consequences for the welfare state (including social work) in Britain. Patricia Morgan's article on juvenile justice appears in a pamphlet in the Social Affairs Unit's appropriately titled series, *Cases for Contraction?*

The political consequences of 'back to justice' are two-fold. On the one hand, it appears as a support to more dominant propositions linking justice and punishment:

> The re-examination of the nature and purpose of the criminal law characterised as the 'back to justice' movement, has shown how punishment is inseparable both from the notion of justice *and* the concept of crime itself. Crime without punishment is a nonsense, since it implies that it does not matter if rules are broken. And, should it not matter what anybody does, the basis of human society as moral order is denied (Morgan, 1981, pp. 64–5).

On the other hand, 'back to justice' provides some of the supporting evidence for the New Right's anti-welfarism. I am *not* arguing that the 'back to justice' movement is intrinsically or necessarily reactionary. I am suggesting that it has tried to occupy a political arena where 'justice' and 'anti-welfarism' are already well established and already colonised by the New Right. It is not clear how the justice movement believes that this arena can be politically reorganised to turn 'justice' around to a progressive strategy.

BACK TO JUSTICE: A VIEW FROM THE SIDELINES

I want to make it clear that this is not intended as a defence of welfarism, social work and discretionary power. If positions are not to be automatically rejected because of the radical Right's enthusiasm for them, no more are they to be adopted simply because the Right is opposed. The criticisms of social work within the 1969 Children and Young Persons Act are well founded, even if the political conclusions drawn from them are erroneous. So my response to the 'back to justice' argument is not merely a restatement of the virtues of welfarism. Having said that, I do think there are some virtues there which the justice movement has been too hasty in rejecting.

'Welfarism', in the guise of the 1969 Act, contained two elements which I believe are still worthy of consideration. One was the anti-institutionalist or decarcerationist pressure to remove juveniles from state institutions (be they repressive, rehabilitative or therapeutic). While the practice of the 1969 Act has contradicted this intention, I do not think it should be lost sight of in an over-general condemnation of welfarism. The other was that the planning which led to the 1969 Act did recognise (though in a very distorted way) something of the class inequalities of juvenile justice which led to the overrepresentation of working-class youth in its processing. Even this (mis-)recognition, and the consequences of enforced treatment which followed from it, seem to me to be a political step ahead of the justice movement's conception of equality through formal procedures.

Nevertheless, I think something more than a restatement of some 'virtues' of welfarism is needed as a response to the justice movement. The problem is that the way in which the debate about juvenile justice has been framed makes the development of such arguments rather difficult. Giller & Covington have established a powerful moral and political imperative:

> If the left is to do anything other than stand as critical commentators on the sidelines of the slide into repression, there is a need to participate in and contribute in a tangible way to the current policy debate (Giller & Covington, 1938, p. 148).

It seems churlish to resist such a powerful imperative, but I do wish to linger on the sidelines a little longer because there are some problems associated with this demand for participating in the current policy debate. One central problem is the debate itself.

As the 'sidelines' metaphor suggests, the debate is conceived of as taking place between two teams. It is a debate between justice and welfare, viewed as principles for the organisation of juvenile justice. I am not convinced that the current juvenile justice is a war between these two abstract principles. Rather it needs to be seen as a system which criminalises working-class youth, and manages the delinquent using a patchwork of processes and disposals which draw upon justice, retribution, rehabilitation and welfarism. The fact that a Home Secretary can describe the extension of the 'short, sharp, shock regime' to all detention centres as 'therapeutic' (*Observer*, 3 March 1984) is not just an indication of his mental confusion, but also of how deeply enmeshed justice, welfare and punishment are as principles and practices in the current system. [See Chapter 22 of this volume.]

Secondly, while I cannot quarrel with Giller & Covington's description of the contemporary state of Britain as being on a 'slide into repression', I am less convinced that welfarist-influenced discretion in juvenile justice is at its heart. Taking juvenile justice alone for the moment, I want to insist on the role of the police in initiating prosecutions; the role of the magistracy in pressing for 'secure' institutions; the role of the Conservative party in developing the afore-mentioned 'short, sharp, shock'; and the role of all these in developing a campaign about the liberal 'softness' of the 1969 Act and the need for *punishment* for young offenders as being the core of contemporary authoritarianism.

Beyond juvenile justice, the spread of authoritarianism is equally strongly located in the appropriation of the 'Rule of Law' by the New Right. In industrial relations law, in the proposed new police powers, in prosecutions for social security fraud, etc., the Law and its 'firmer' application has been at the forefront of repression. And while discretionary powers have played a part in some of these areas (e.g. 'counselling out' social security claims), and while the system of legal and quasi-legal rights and appeals has seen occasional successes in limiting repression, the Law is constantly being remade in content and practice so that the Right have it 'on their side'.

So, although there may be merit in defending due process, it does not seem to me that it can be the centre piece of a socialist resistance to repression. Such resistance is already visible, not around the Rule of Law, but around the refusal of specific *laws* (stop and search powers, the Police and Criminal Evidence Bill) and their application in practice (the nature of policing). The struggles of various groups over the last few years have focused on issues of laws and policing (black communities and 'sus'; the women's movement and sexual harassment; mining communities and the policing of public order). While these do not form a natural and harmonious 'socialist strategy', they do highlight issues about the Law, inequality and repression which are marginalised by the justice movement's concern with formal equality.

ACCOUNTABILITY: THE MISSING LINK?

In order to find a way off the sidelines, let me return to one of the central themes of the justice movement's attack on discretionary powers. They argue that one key problem of 'discretion' is its lack of accountability. The 'disappearance' of decisions into the internal structures of social work departments, the absence of public criteria, legal representation and appeal are at the core of discretionary power.

In challenging discretion, the justice movement has reasserted 'due process' as the means of making decisions public, subject to commensurable criteria, and subject to forms of challenge and redress. From this view, accountability is equated with legal accountability, the formal guarantees of rights within the due process of Law. This is, indeed, one model of accountability, though its horizons are relatively limited. The agencies and agents of 'justice' are themselves only subject to the countervailing force of other agencies of justice. The police and magistrates are susceptible to challenge only in the name of the Law.

In framing accountability in specific legal terms, the justice movement has excluded other conceptions of accountability – in particular, accountability as a political rather than legal relationship. Over the last five years, there has been a growing concern about making policing subject to local political accountability, and one clear impetus to this has been the way young people have been policed. At the same time, there has been a growing interest in decentralising welfare services and establishing greater responsiveness to local needs and demands as a way of undercutting the complex of bureaucratic and professional powers in social work. In this context, it is rather surprising to find the justice movement equating accountability with the legal form of due process and ignoring the political form of democratic representation.

As I have argued elsewhere (Clarke, 1983), I do not think that democracy is *inherently* socialist, nor the inevitable guarantor of progressive policies. It is politically unstable, and in the form of local representation highly dependent on local social composition and political organisation. It is, to put it crudely, very messy. Nevertheless, the argument is not between the impurities of democratic control and the purity of due process, but between the instability of democratic processes and the inequalities of law as a social process.

Conceived of in this way, I would rather argue for the whole process of juvenile justice to be subjected to political rather than legal accountability for two reasons. Scrutiny of the whole array of agencies (police, magistracy, social work) seems preferable to a dependence on legal checks and balances on some (primarily social work). Secondly, representative accountability provides the ground on which arguments about juvenile strategies can be fought out. Where the justice model confines debate within the state, political accountability offers the possibility of opening up the state.

My conclusion (such as it is) is therefore that we should avoid being trapped into a constant recycling of the justice *v.* welfare principles. That debate is a misconception of the politics of juvenile justice, and offers us only the choice of which form of oppression is preferable. In contrast, we should be looking to politicise both the legal and welfare agencies involved in the process of juvenile justice as the basis for progressive strategies. In that sense, I am only willing to leave the sidelines (and stop being a commentator) if we can play a different game.

REFERENCES

Asquith, S. (1983) Justice, retribution and children. In Morris, A. and Giller, H., eds.

Clarke, J. (1983) Taking politics seriously: Thatcherism, Marxism and the welfare state. *Crime and Social Justice*.

Dixon, D. (1981) Gambling and the Law: the Street Betting Act, 1906, as an attack on working-class culture. In *Leisure and Social Control* (Tomlinson, A., ed.) Brighton Polytechnic/Chelsea School of Human Movement (mimeo).

Engels, F. (1968) Ludwig Feuerbach and the end of Classical German Philosophy. In *Marx and Engels: Selected Works*. Lawrence and Wishart: London.

Geach, H. and Szwed, E. (eds) (1983) *Providing Civil Justice for Children*. Edward Arnold: London.

Giller, H. and Covington, C. (1983) Structuring discretion: question or answer? In *Providing Criminal Justice for Children* (Giller, H. and Morris, A. eds). Edward Arnold: London.

Jones, C. (1983) *State social work and the working class,* Macmillan: London.

Morgan, P. (1981) The Children's Act: sacrificing justice to social workers' needs? In *Criminal Welfare on Trial* (Brewer, C. *et al.,* ed.) Social Affairs Unit.

Morris, A. and Giller, H. (1979) Juvenile justice and social work, In *Social Work and the Courts* (Parker, H., ed.). Edward Arnold: London.

Morris, A. *et al.* (1980) *Justice for Children,* Macmillan: London.

Thompson, E.P. (1975) *Whigs and Hunters.* Allen Lane.

Thorpe, D. *et al.* (1980) *Out of Care,* Allen and Unwin: London.

20

'Troublesome girls': towards alternative definitions and policies

Annie Hudson

> She is a very promiscuous girl and, if all that she tells the other girls is to be believed, *then no young man is safe*. (Residential Social Worker, my emphasis)

Embedded at the heart of contemporary British welfare practice with adolescent girls is an almost psychic fear of a predatory female sexuality. The irony of this should be obvious: it is men who rape and the sexual abuse of children is almost entirely perpetrated by men. Yet, perhaps highest on the professional agenda is the assumption (and concomitant practices) that girls in trouble fundamentally have problems with *their* sexuality. Whilst welfare professionals frequently legitimate their intervention with girls as 'for their protection', the quote from the social worker above (made in a report for a case conference) prises open the complexity of the 'welfare as protector' discourse. It suggests that, hidden beneath, lies an almost inarticulated but profound fear of the young woman who is sexually active, sexually explicit, and who is not actually possessed by any one male. This conceptualization of adolescent girls as 'property' (of men, of the family, of the dominant social order) will be a key thread to much of this discussion. It helps explain why some girls are defined as 'troublesome'; it is also a crucial component of any attempt to conceptualize different welfare strategies for responding to their needs.

This chapter focuses on girls who are seen, often very generally and vaguely, as manifesting some kind of social or emotional trouble. The apparently loose concept of 'troublesome girls' allows for a discussion of girls who are not necessarily delinquent (in the sense of committing criminal offences). Statistics (DHSS, 1986) suggest that the majority of girls do not get drawn into the complex web of the British personal social services because they have committed offences. It is more likely to be because of concerns about their perceived sexual behaviour and/or because they are seen to be 'at risk' of 'offending' against social codes of adolescent femininity.

Work with girls in trouble has, in terms of explicit policy, been marginalized and rendered almost invisible. Because girls do not so publicly resist the normative order (McRobbie and Garber, 1976) because there is not much political capital to be gained

SOURCE: This chapter was originally published in M. Cain (ed.) *Growing up Good*, London, Sage, 1989, pp. 197–219 (abridged).

by developing strategies for responding differently to their modes of rule-breaking, and because it has been assumed that girls' deviant behaviour will be normally dealt with from within the boundaries of the family, policies have been *ad hoc*, framed in vague and diffuse language and lacking in imagination. This, of course, does not mean that the net result has had any less of an impact upon the experience of girls deemed to require state intervention, whether controlling or apparently benign. In fact, the reverse has often been true; the assumption that extant policies and practice are 'in their best interests' adeptly conceals a complex fabric of control and subordination (for example, see Casburn, 1979; Campbell, 1981).

[···]

REDRAFTING THE AGENDA: WHOSE TROUBLES, WHOSE DEFINITIONS?

The somewhat skewed triangular relationship between adolescent girls, their families and welfare professionals forms the axis around which definitions, policies and practices have evolved. In prizing open some of the implicit assumptions and ideologies embedded in such definitions, we can begin to redraft a somewhat different agenda for policy and practice.

Social historians such as Weeks (1981) have suggested that the 1880s were a particularly significant moment when the dichotomy between the private/decent and the public/unrespectable was firmly established. But whilst women and girls are supposed to keep to the former area, men are free to travel between the two without fear of social sanction. Moreover, in their zeal to protect working-class girls from prostitution, late nineteenth-century reformers created new objects for control. Simultaneously they also established an explanatory code that portrays girls as passive and in need of protection, but also as potentially socially dangerous if they do not conform to codes of sexual respectability and domesticity. Such codes are clearly still firmly entrenched (Hutter and Williams, 1981). But it is girls from specific social groups who are particularly vulnerable to state intervention. Working-class and black girls have to walk a particularly shaky tightrope between demonstrating both their respectability and their sexual attractiveness. Black girls for example may be perceived as contesting not only codes of femininity but also white norms; they may thus be on the receiving end of a double dose of disapproval. One residential social worker commented about a Rastafarian girl in a report in my study: 'Her hair is the one thing which she resents us criticizing and it is this which spoils her otherwise attractive appearance.'

The overt moral tone of the late Victorian era was gradually eroded by the ascendancy and increasing attachment to psychoanalytic paradigms which meant that an apparently plausible veneer of scientism could occlude latent values. Girls who got into trouble (criminal or otherwise) could be confidently defined as 'neurotic', 'hysteria prone' and so on. Such scientism continues to legitimize welfare professionals' assessments not just about current behaviour but, more significantly, about anticipated future behaviour. Such persistence in maintaining the validity and viability of 'the tutelary complex' (Donzelot, 1979) in such a full-blown form is perhaps particularly striking when we consider that welfare's management of boys in trouble has increasingly been subjected to scepticism about the capacity (let alone the morality) of making judgements about future conduct.

[...]

Four key precepts form the kernel of the discussion that follows and provide the basis for the alternative practices suggested in the final section:

1 girls as the 'property' of the family: is the home so safe?
2 adolescent female sexuality as a barometer of 'womanhood': the need to problematize gender relations;
3 'troublesome girls' as victims of psychological inadequacies: reclaiming emotionality;
4 normalizing girls' troublesome behaviour: collective similarities and differences.

Girls as the 'property' of the family: is the home so safe?

There is more than a note of truth in the assumption that girls' troubles are often related to family problems and their position in the family. However, such 'family problems' have been viewed in an apolitical way: the power dynamics between parents and daughters (most crucially those between fathers and daughters), and those between women and men in the family have been completely obscured by traditional commentators. Yet it is the family which is one of the key sources of the social control of women (Barrett and McIntosh, 1982; Segal, 1983). The under-reporting of child sexual abuse together with the blaming of mothers for such abuse is obviously one of the most blatant ways in which the politics of family life is pushed aside as 'irrelevant' (Ward, 1984). Moreover, whilst the Cleveland child sexual abuse 'crisis' provoked an enhanced consciousness of the extensiveness of child sexual abuse, the terms in which that debate is developing suggest that there continues to be a reluctance both to acknowledge that child sexual abuse occurs in otherwise seemingly 'normal' families and that it is predominantly a crime perpetrated by adult men towards children whom they know and are supposed to protect. (For an excellent discussion of the Cleveland 'crisis', see Campbell, 1988.) Child sexual abuse is thus a powerful mechanism by which girls and young women are maintained within the institution of the family. Physical violence and threats from abusers that disclosure will lead to 'breaking up the family' added to girls' internalized feelings that they are guilty and responsible for the crimes of adult men ensure that the costs of disclosure of abuse frequently seem greater than the benefits.

However, in other more subtle ways, girls are subjected to an unspoken but relentless subordination. For daughters, like their mothers, are essentially seen as the 'property' of 'the family'. Adolescent girls are controlled by the idea that they 'belong' to the home, unlike their brothers whose rights to be 'on the street' are unquestioned. Girls are expected to act like 'little housewives' and to service the family (and particularly their fathers and brothers) both emotionally and materially (Griffin, 1985). Such beliefs affect families as much as welfare professionals. When the family's regulation of girls seems to be breaking down parents can easily construe that their daughters are 'beyond their control' and demand that 'something is done'; over a quarter of the cases in my study fell into this category. What is perhaps of equal significance is that it was usually the mother who was most active in expressing such concerns to welfare agencies. This reflects, I suggest, the role of mothers as 'emotional housekeepers' which demands that they nurture and cosset the family's emotional life. If conflicts arise, they are expected to act to resolve and smooth them over.

Like their daughters, mothers are in a double bind; they are vested with a duty and responsibility to be concerned about their daughters' behaviour, to be worried if they do not return at night or when they seem depressed. But they also frequently get blamed when things go wrong inside the family. Given the lack of emotional support from fathers in many families it is perhaps not surprising that some mothers turn to welfare agencies for help and support. Blaming mothers for their daughters' problems leaves unchallenged the inequitable division of emotional labour in families.

It is important to point out here that girls themselves (unlike the majority of boys who are referred to the personal social services) often request to be taken into care. The emotional (and sometimes physical) struggle for survival at home becomes too much for some girls to cope with. They have few accessible or legitimate 'escape' routes and so care may be viewed as a preferable, if not ideal, alternative. Sometimes therefore welfare agencies do need to offer girls a refuge from the family; such provision, however, needs to be based around different assumptions and methods of practice than residential care is at present.

The constant sexualizing of the 'troublesome' behaviour of girls by welfare professionals has meant that they have often avoided looking at a further contradiction of familialism: the extensiveness of sexual abuse of girls in their families. In a fifth of the cases I studied the girl had been sexually abused by her father or stepfather, but in only a small percentage had this been a factor influencing the decision to take her into care. It was normally only much later that the abuse had come to light.

In refusing to recognize the deeply entrenched power inequalities between male and female members of families, social workers have thus colluded with the assumption that 'the home is a safe place' (Hudson, A., 1985). When girls are 'signalling' that they are being abused (for example by constantly running away or by taking overdoses) their behaviour is reinterpreted as evidence of their 'uncontrollability' and of their pathology, rather than as a manifestation of the results of their father's abuse of power and trust. Moreover, in tacitly accepting a variety of myths, for example that girls are 'seductive', social workers have thereby reinforced the moral and emotional guilt felt by girls who have been sexually abused.

The girl as property of the family ideology is carried on into the workings of welfare establishments. For not only are girls' residential establishments often based around the objective of re-establishing femininity (Ackland, 1982), but if girls in care do become pregnant then this is often viewed in a positive light. It is as if pregnancy symbolically represents a girl's return to 'the family' and her apparent acceptance of traditional femininity. This is somewhat ironic given that fears of unmarried teenage motherhood are usually high on the list of the perceived risks of adolescent girls becoming 'beyond control'.

When girls reject or refuse to take on their responsibilities as 'dutiful daughters' they are viewed as problematic and 'disloyal'; in short, they are not 'good little girls'. As long as welfare policies collude with such definitions there will be little possibility of diminishing the unequal power differentials in families; as long as they remain, adolescent girls are the losers.

Adolescent female sexuality as a barometer of 'womanhood': the need to problematize gender relations

The development of a more critical and feminist influenced analysis of young women's deviance (see, for example, Casburn, 1979; Heidensohn, 1985; Smart, 1976) has demonstrated how girls who appear before the juvenile court for criminal offences are subject to a 'double penalty'. They are punished both for the offence itself and for the 'social' crime of contravening normative expectations of 'appropriate' female conduct via 'promiscuity', 'wayward' behaviour, 'unfeminine' dress and so on. Similarly, my study found that the most common cause of anxiety at the point of referral was that the girl was 'beyond control' and/or at risk morally. The centrality of sexuality in welfare's definitions of 'troublesome' girls reflects three key taken-for-granted assumptions.

First, it is assumed that girls' sexuality, once 'unleashed', is uncontrollable and not bound by any sense of self-responsibility or self-control. As Bland (1983) has argued, the instincts of woman have traditionally been viewed as focused on her reproductive capacity, on her potential for maternity. The prostitute or the adolescent girl whose behaviour is interpreted as potentially like that of a prostitute is seen as representative of an active female sexuality, of a sexuality which may threaten the girl's interest and capacity to be a 'good wife' and mother and therefore her future 'womanliness'.

Secondly, a girl's apparent sexual behaviour is seen as a barometer for testing her capacity to learn the appropriate codes of social (but particularly sexual) conduct with men (Lees, 1986). One of the contradictions of the double standard revealed time and time again in this volume is that it implies that boys need to have access to different sexual experiences; yet the girls who presumably are supposed to 'meet' such needs are stigmatized and punished.

As long as boys' sexual behaviour is heterosexual their sexuality remains unproblematic; it is 'natural' and thus does not merit attention. But my own research highlighted how a girl's sexual 'reputation' is often a determining factor in shaping her career through the personal social services. In over a quarter of the cases examined, social workers acknowledged that their decision making was a function of what other people (particularly the police and parents) were alleging. Moreover, once an opinion had been formed, it was easy for the label of 'promiscuity' or 'being on the game' to stick, with all the negative connotations that such labels imply. Labels based on shifting and unsubstantiated opinions are particularly hard to shed; as one social worker commented about one of her young female clients: 'Once (she) had developed a 'reputation' (for sexual activity), it became very easy to say that she was actually involved in prostitution.' Once created, such reputations, with all their attendant anxieties, seem to have pushed many of the social workers in my study (if sometimes quite reluctantly) to regard many of their adolescent female clients as in need of the 'protective' care and attention of a residential placement. This was despite the fact that many social workers acknowledged that care is hardly an effective contraceptive.

There was also evidence that the police similarly act on a girl's 'reputation' in this way. They were involved in almost half of the referrals in my study and in more than half of these they obtained place of safety orders (these give police or social workers the power to remove children and young people). Police involvement in these situations was only very rarely because a girl had committed a criminal offence. Moreover, there were disproportionately more police place of safety orders taken on girls living in an area with a significant Afro-Caribbean population and also with a local 'reputation' as a 'red-light district'. The other area studied was comparable in terms of many indices of social disadvantage but did not have such a reputation; the Afro-Caribbean population was also much smaller. This suggests that the level of police (and possibly social work) control may increase according to the social composition and 'reputation' of the neighbourhood. Although as yet not empirically tested, it would seem that certain groups of black adolescent girls (most particularly Afro-Caribbean girls) are especially vulnerable to perceptions by the police and possibly social workers that their behaviour warrants special scrutiny and policing.

The research also highlighted other ways in which racist stereotypes can affect police and welfare practice. One social worker said of her white adolescent female client, who had run away from home and was detained by the police on a place of safety order: 'People think that as she has got black boyfriends, she must be promiscuous, she must be on the game, or she is being used'. The association in some people's eyes between black men and 'unrespectable' sexuality suggests that the fears of racial miscegenation which were so prevalent in the 1950s and 1960s in the UK (Gilroy, 1987) continue to have purchase on the relationship between working-class white girls and welfare agencies. In short, white girls' relationships with black male youth may conjure up images of the potential 'descent of white womanhood' (Gilroy, 1987: 80) and thereby further 'legitimate' the intensification of state intervention.

Whilst it is increasingly accepted that girls (like adult women) are informally disciplined through concepts of acceptable sexuality, what is undoubtedly more contentious is what should be done. It would be naive to suggest that girls are not vulnerable to male sexual exploitation but balancing 'here and now' realities with visions of what the future could and should be like poses acute problems. To date the problem has always been framed as a problem of and for women; male power and responsibility barely enter the discussion. Bringing gender relations on to the agenda allows us instead to see cultural definitions of male sexuality as problematic.

We must take seriously girls' rights as well as their responsibilities and the risks to which they are subject. One such right must surely be to informed contraceptive advice and practice; there is, moreover, as yet little evidence that AIDS health education programmes are altering young male heterosexual practices. Another right should be to an adequate understanding of gender and familial relations. Finally, there are issues concerning girls' rights to choose their sexual identity. Social work agencies should be more conscious of the extent to which policy and practice is predicated upon an assumption of heterosexuality as both the norm and as the most 'desirable' form of sexual expression. The option of lesbianism is almost invariably closed off in discussions between welfare professionals and adolescent girls. If it is part of the discussion it is invariably cloaked with negative connotations. Some girls may want to choose lesbianism as their preferred sexual identity; to deny them this as an option is once more to misrecognize and render invisible the real needs of individual girls.

We need also to unlatch the association of adolescent female sexuality from its connotation of potentially sullying a girl's prospects of a 'happy and satisfying' womanhood. There is no reason why either having had several or no sexual partners in adolescence should prejudice a girl's enjoyment of adult life. Her enjoyment and satisfaction as an adult woman is much more likely to be related to other factors such as decent housing, employment, and adequate child-care provision.

At a more concrete level, the influence of girls' reputations in the decision-making processes affecting them should be critically monitored. Welfare professionals need to take a much stronger stand, *vis-à-vis* the police, their own organizations and girls' families, in seeking out actual evidence of the risks which a girl is alleged to be under. Similarly, court reports and case conference discussions should be more thoroughly scrutinized as a way of beginning to minimize the power of the 'give a dog a bad name' process that clearly operates against the interests of many girls.

'Troublesome girls' as victims of psychological inadequacies: reclaiming emotionality

The dominance of psychopathological paradigms in welfare professionals' assessments of the needs of adolescent girls has been emphasized elsewhere (Hudson, B., 1984b; Campbell, 1981). The persistence, in my study, of such explanations as 'bizarre family relationships', 'missing out on affection' and 'insufficient parental control' testifies to the continued adherence to a family pathology model.

I would not want to contest unequivocally the notion that girls manifest some of the social contradictions of adolescent femininity in emotional ways; many girls referred to welfare agencies often do feel depressed, suicidal and have very poor self-images. But the assumption that emotional expression is intrinsically negative and that emotional responses are unaffected by social and material processes has to be challenged. Perhaps it is rather the lack of overt emotionality amongst boys and men which should be problematized. The rational, masculinist British culture generally denigrates emotional expression as a sign of weakness; moreover, whilst British culture rewards men for certain forms of emotionality (aggression is the most obvious example), it punishes girls for the same kind of behaviour.

The emotionality of 'troublesome girls' is usually problematized and even feared. Certainly, many social workers take for granted the assumption that girls are 'more difficult to work with'; their apparent mood swings, non-rationality, outbursts of aggression and internalization of emotional discontents often act to make welfare professionals feel impotent, uncertain of their skills and at a loss for what to do. So when girls step outside the bounds of expectation that they should be self-controlled and passive, it is not wholly surprising that they meet with panic, disapproval, and assessments that they need 'treatment'. For, after all, they are implicitly challenging normative codes of emotional conduct. Two shifts in thinking are required. First, adolescent girls' emotional responses need to be seen as a form of resistance or struggle against 'the inner hold' of their oppressive circumstances. Their responses should be legitimated as not 'unnatural' but as quite rational ways of surviving. To psychopathologize their emotions is to perpetuate the belief (one that is often internalized by girls themselves) that their troubles are their fault. Secondly, emotionality as a means of social communication and expression should be seen not as a sign of a deficient personality but rather as a positive resource. It is only by affirming girls' emotional responses as a comprehensible and positive means of coping with their experience of social injustice that they are likely to begin to feel any sense of autonomy in their lives. As long as they are effectively told that their emotional responses are 'crazy' their confidence in their right to express themselves will be undermined.

Normalizing girls' troublesome behaviour: collective similarities and differences

It has become obvious that the dominant definitions and assumptions of troublesome girls are essentially social constructs. What is also striking is how many of these 'troubles' are experienced, in some way or other, by the majority of adolescent girls. Certainly one of the most constant characteristics of my personal contact with girls 'in trouble' is how very many of their dilemmas, problems and needs connect with my own memories of growing up 'to be a woman'.

This leads to the central imperative, in addressing alternative definitions and policies for 'troublesome girls', of developing a framework which normalizes their behaviour. Linked to this is the parallel urgency to analyse and act towards girls' troubles from a perspective which actively acknowledges the cultural, ideological and material pressures on adolescent girls, and most particularly those which black and working-class girls face. The bifurcation of adolescent girls into the 'respectable and decent' and the 'promiscuous and dangerous' creates socially constructed categories which are both rigid and ambiguous. They deny the fact that most girls experience the need to demonstrate respectability and sexual attractiveness. Such a dichoto-mizing of young women also denies that girls might be interested in things other than the opposite sex, such as work, politics, music, female friends, social adventure and excitement.

My own experience of working with adolescent girls has consistently highlighted how they are invariably extremely aware (in both a personal and political sense) of many of the contradictions of adolescent femininity. Whilst some girls cope with such contradictions and injustices in an overtly rebellious and public way, others inter-nalize them as 'their fault'. Still other girls accept their 'lot' apparently stoically and fatalistically but recognizing, at the same time, that there are personal costs (for example, 'tolerating' violence from boyfriends because 'I love him'). Girls who have particularly restricted access to society's material and social 'goodies' (employment, education, decent housing and so on) perhaps have less to lose by their active resistance than their more privileged counterparts.

The principle of defining girls' needs, problems and resources in collective terms could facilitate a depathologizing of their particular predicaments, whether those be as survivors of sexual abuse, arguments with parents or delinquency. It could also encourage a recognition of the possibility of girls providing more effective support to one another than huge armies of professional 'helpers'. The concern with collective consciousness raising in the contemporary women's movement evolved out of the need to enable women to name more publicly what were previously private experi-ences. Certainly, welfare agencies could learn much from the work of feminist groups such as Women's Aid and Rape Crisis Centres in asserting the possibility of the support and concrete action that can emerge out of challenging traditional maxims about how people are best 'helped' (Pahl, 1985).

Alternative approaches to welfare practice with adolescent girls must thus be based upon an active acknowledgement both of their socially constructed similarities and of the differences mediated by class, race and sexual identity. The hegemony of casework in social work has inhibited the possibility of recognizing similarities which, whilst mediated through individuals, are none the less socially and culturally constructed. There are, however, certain inherent dangers in shifting from an individualistic paradigm to one which places 'blame' on external social forces. Very few radical perspectives on social relations have explored the ways in which social circumstances distort and appropriate the individual's needs and capacities. In contrast, feminists have politicized subjectivity and highlighted the reciprocal relationship between individual identity and the material world (see, for example, the work of Eichenbaum and Orbach, 1984). Girls' apparently personal troubles should be viewed through a perspective which recognizes that girls' experiences are both unique and linked inextricably to their status as young women.

TOWARDS ALTERNATIVE POLICIES AND PRACTICE

Welfare tasks in the UK, as elsewhere in northern Europe at least, tend to be boxed into supposedly linked, but in reality often isolated, compartments such as health, housing, education and personal social services. Needs and problems are seen as 'belonging' to a particular agency's sphere of responsibility. For example, 'problem' young people in the school system are referred to 'disruptive units' or to the personal social services, thereby inhibiting a critique of the school's deficiencies and failure to cope with non-conforming youngsters. Only by looking at welfare's management of girls in trouble from within a systems perspective can alternative policies be effectively implemented. Although any of these services could provide a starting point, I shall concentrate here on the personal social services.

The development of equal opportunities policies in many British local authorities could be a useful lever in getting the needs of 'troublesome' girls on policy agendas. But services for 'troublesome' adolescent girls continue to be marginalized and undebated. Generally, only front-line workers are actively questioning how policy definitions are put into operation. However, their capacity to influence decision making is circumscribed by the structures of the organizations in which they work. Policy makers (elected members and senior officers) should take positive action in initiating more equitable and comprehensive strategies for intervention with girls in trouble. Of equal importance is the need to begin to develop anti-sexist strategies for work with boys and young men in trouble. For to concentrate concerns about gender solely on girls and young women is to imply that the male half of the population is unaffected by sexism. Yet as we have seen only by problematizing gender relations generally is it likely that welfare agencies can begin to respond to the needs of adolescent girls in trouble in a sensitive and equitable manner. Male welfare professionals have a particular responsibility to scrutinize critically the ways in which masculinist assumptions shape their work with boys in trouble (Hudson, A., 1988).

But what do we mean by 'alternative policies' and how can these evolve so that 'top down' definitions are not perpetuated? Social policies generally have tended to be constructed around the needs of the economy; such needs focus on the relations between labour and capital rather than on relations in the family and the community (Coote, 1984). No doubt this is one of the reasons why male delinquency is seen to warrant the attention and resources it commands (young males being viewed as the future army of waged labour). It is perhaps not surprising that social policies relating to 'troublesome girls' have failed to acknowledge how family and community relations shape both the 'problems' girls present and the welfare responses which they precipitate.

In considering some concrete proposals for policy and practice with girls in trouble, there are three key and interrelated issues:

1 empowerment and participation;
2 welfare or justice: is least always best?
3 a separatist strategy: possibilities and problems.

Empowerment and participation

A fundamental prerequisite of any attempt to grapple with the complex task of evolving alternative policies for girls in trouble (criminal or otherwise) is to eradicate the victimology which underpins the *status quo*. Rowbotham *et al.* (1979) have reminded us of the importance of seeing disadvantaged groups not as 'passive victims' but as people who do have the means and wherewithal for generating the power which all groups create as a means of survival and resistance. Girls are no more passive victims of their oppressive circumstances than are waged labourers, battered women or black youth.

'Empowerment' and 'participation' can, however, be deceptively simple slogans. What they might mean in practice is much more difficult to articulate; not least because girls and welfare professionals alike have been socialized to assume that 'adults know best'. Certainly the educational system disinclines us to contemplate young people as active contributors to their own learning.

A very basic way of beginning to give girls in trouble some power is to involve them more readily in defining their needs. Whilst, for example, girls (like boys) are now more likely to be allowed access to case conferences, anyone who has attended such meetings will testify to the frequent marginalization of their voices: 'Yes, dear, but you know you do really need to learn to be more self-controlled/less aggressive/more mature before …' Such patronizing of girls in trouble denies that they might have any conception of what they want and need. As long as girls expect their needs and strengths to be misinterpreted or denied they are unlikely to feel that it is worthwhile discussing them with professionals.

The emphasis here on girls' capacities is important. Because social work deals with society's 'problem' groups, modes of intervention have focused on remedying deficits rather than building on the resources of such groups. The professional–client relationship reinforces the idea of the 'expert' having something to offer with the client as the passive recipient of the 'goodies'.

None the less some positive developments have recently been taking place in the corners of some welfare agencies. Drawing upon a social education model some social workers have taken creative initiatives in working collectively with girls in trouble. Empowering young women and giving them the confidence to participate are central tenets of such schemes (Mountain, 1988). As one social worker has commented:

> Our agenda is to provide an opportunity for young women to explore issues that are important to them, to provide a forum whereby they can develop some confidence in their own power and to act as facilitators in the group, taking action on their own behalf.
> (National Association of Youth Clubs, 1985: 13)

That girls do indeed want to talk about and do something about the issues affecting their lives (family, school, friendships, experiences of male violence) has been similarly underlined by my contact with other, similar schemes in social services departments. Giving girls access not only to different activities but also to different roles and assumptions about femininity can give girls an opportunity to work out, with girls in a similar situation, everyday strategies for coping with sexism.

Yet there are certain in-built difficulties. Women's Aid has been able to challenge the 'traditional charitable relationship of helped and helper' (Hanmer, 1977) in part because of its relative autonomy from the State and also because adult women are involved. But State welfare agencies endeavouring to implement even a very watered-down empowerment philosophy are likely to be doubly constrained, first, by their statutory roles (which can inhibit a sense of safety and confidentiality for any girls who are involved) and, secondly, by legal and social considerations of the rights and capacities of adolescent girls 'to have a say'. Whilst the work of the National Association of Young People in Care (Stein, 1983) has undoubtedly forced some agencies to reconsider their assumption that they 'know what's best', the reluctance to give young people any rights remains firmly entrenched.

This points us to another important aspect of empowerment oriented policies: girls in trouble could be encouraged to have closer contact with non-statutory women and girls' groups and organizations. Girls in residential care are particularly likely to be 'cordoned off' not only from their 'normal' peers but also from women and girls' groups and organizations which might be able to help them increase their confidence. There could also be greater collaboration with some of the more constructive policies and practices in youth work (see Yeung, 1985, for a 'route map' of such work with girls). The fears of 'contamination' which continue to perpetuate many statutory-based agencies and which mean that much youth provision is still effectively for 'good' girls (and boys) are, however, likely to brake such possibilities.

Fears of 'contamination' also work the other way around; feminist influenced organizations are not infrequently seen by welfare professionals as potentially 'damaging' for their female clients. There is still a widespread belief that women-only and girls-only groups will be used to reinforce their clients' 'distrust' and 'hatred' of men and, moreover, that feminists will use such groups to further their own philosophies. Apart from this being a gross misunderstanding of the objectives of feminism, such fantasies also inhibit women and girls from having the opportunity to enhance their sense of personal worth and confidence with women who may have been through similar experiences, such as sexual abuse.

Given that welfare professionals are likely to resist the viability and desirability of 'empowerment' philosophies, *their* education should perhaps be highest on the agenda. Perhaps because so many welfare professionals (at least in the lower ranks) are female, there has been no wholesale commitment to tackle the endemic sexism of welfare practice. Indeed suggestions that there is a problem are frequently met with denial or patronizing humour. Social workers who are committed to developing more gender-sensitive perspectives and skills for working with girls in trouble are therefore marginalized and isolated. Support from management, in terms of resources and supervision, is usually, at best, non-existent, or, at worst, quite hostile.

Managers and practitioners alike should be forced to look at their attitudes, assumptions and values in this sphere of welfare practice. The allocation of resources demands critical scrutiny but so too should recruitment policies be reviewed. This latter point is especially important for residential-based posts where the power of managers to determine the regimes of their establishments is relatively unfettered.

Welfare or justice

In many respects the re-ascendancy of a justice model for the management of juvenile delinquency can be responded to quite positively. For it has redressed some of the excesses of a 'welfarist' paradigm whereby social work's 'needology' has pulled an increasing number of male and female juveniles into the system through definitions of their need for 'treatment' (Thorpe, 1978). However, the fact that the critique of welfarism has coalesced around an uneasy alliance of the left (who see it as an erosion of civil liberties) and the right (who view it as 'soft and ineffective') should make us more hesitant before accepting the justice orientation, lock stock and barrel. In the current political climate the latter perspective is likely to have a more powerful purchase.

Barbara Hudson has pointed to some of the endemic problems of transferring girls to a pure justice model; they would still be subjected to 'the double condemnation as offenders and as flouting the values of femininity' (Hudson, B., 1985: 16). She argues that only a change in social attitudes will give girls any real chance of justice. This is undoubtedly the case. However, it is worth considering ways in which we might begin to loosen the grip of the assumption that girls become criminal because of welfare problems. The current muddling of welfare and justice needs pushes girls up the tariff, in many cases, more quickly and for more trivial offences than boys (Harris and Webb, 1987). The writing of court reports gives social workers a not inconsiderable power to influence the courts in disposing of offenders. They should desist from using girls' appearances on criminal offences to justify supervision or care for welfare needs and instead use the tariff in stricter, justice terms. This might lead to more civil proceedings (for supervision and care) under the Children and Young Persons Act 1969. But at least there would be a greater degree of clarity and honesty about the objectives of welfare intervention rather than the double messages and standards which now prevail.

Perhaps 'least is best' as far as criminal justice considerations are concerned (not least because the vast majority of juveniles 'grow out of' offending). But such a principle is more problematic when considering the majority of girls who come into care essentially for 'welfare' reasons (in 1983 only 24 per cent of girls who came into care on a statutory order were there under criminal offence clauses of the 1969 Act; this contrasts with 67 per cent of boys). We have already seen how the politics of family life renders girls vulnerable to exploitation. Some girls want and have a right to an alternative to the home. When kith and kin are not available or willing to provide such an alternative, welfare agencies may need to step in. For girls who have had to run away from home to escape the abuse of their fathers, care will be preferable to sexual molestation.

Moreover, when families are rejecting their daughters some form of interim 'breathing space' provision is required. Once in care it is often difficult for girls to be extricated not least because behaviour in care can be used to rationalize the original decision to receive her into care ('she's running away and aggressive and obviously "out of control"'). Smaller neighbourhood-based and explicitly 'transitional' units could do much to provide the 'breathing space' that girls and their families may need. Finally, the structures and workings of many residential establishments are based on familial ideas about the gender division of labour; indeed many attempt explicitly to offer 'alternative families'. They are certainly not often organized to encourage adolescent girls' personal autonomy and rights to participate in the decisions affecting them. They are often large institutions, situated away from the girl's community; generally they are very second-rate alternatives. A range of provision that is both less stigmatizing and more flexible is undoubtedly required, as well as provision that does not idealize a specific cultural form of domestic and familial arrangements by a self-conscious and self-proclaimed 'second bestness' to it.

A separatist strategy

Social work, in common with most other welfare professions, has always been reluctant to acknowledge, in its methods of work, the collective similarities between some of its individual clients. The deeply enshrined principle of 'individualizing the client' has kept sociological contributions at the threshold of intervention. Moreover, social work's liberal democratic origins and self-image has always enabled it to rebuff charges of discrimination: taken-for-granted principles of 'client self-determination' and 'objectivity' have prompted the rhetoric that 'we respond to clients on the basis of individual need'. The needs of social minorities such as black people and girls have thus been denied.

Those involved with girls in trouble could usefully learn from the experiences of some women youth workers who have fought (sometimes quite successfully) for the establishment of girls' projects (Yeung, 1985). A similar separatist strategy is also warranted inside personal social service agencies; it could begin to reduce the marginality of work with girls in trouble and support those who are endeavouring to work in different ways. Many of those social workers (mostly women) who are endeavouring to establish work with girls as a legitimate 'specialism' undoubtedly do have a clear commitment to challenge the *status quo*; they are also well aware of the invisibility and misrecognition of girls' needs by the agency in which they work. However, many still feel at a considerable loss as to how to proceed; in contrast with their relative confidence when working with boys they often feel uncertain as to the kind of approach and activities which girls will both enjoy and find useful.

Reference has been made throughout this chapter to the differences as well as the similarities of the needs of girls in trouble. The needs of black and Asian girls particularly are currently denied and misinterpreted. Workers involved in working with girls in trouble thus need to have a more critical understanding of exactly how the system currently responds to the needs of girls from minority groups. The negative evaluation of black and Asian family structures means, for example, that assessments are loaded not only with sexist but also racist stereotypes (Bryan *et al.*, 1985). White feminists, in particular, may need to examine the extent to which they frame the predicaments of Afro-Caribbean and Asian girls as emanating from sexism within their cultures rather than as emerging out of the culture of racism in Britain. Such perspectives implicitly affirm the superiority of Western social arrangements where girls are concerned (Ahmed, 1986). Only if resources are specifically allocated both for the training of workers and for need-responsive services will the complexity of the differences between girls' needs and their 'careers' through welfare agencies develop with any principled and strategic rigour.

Some will protest that a separatist strategy will either further ghettoize adolescent girls or that it will prevent girls from becoming more confident and assertive with boys and men; the assumption presumably being that you need boys or men to increase your assertive powers. Such arguments can be countered by pointing to the necessity of creating a social and political space in which work with girls can develop. Managers must be persuaded of the legitimacy of creating such a space. Whilst there is a risk that a separatist strategy might encourage 'endogenous' system expansion, carefully constructed, it would at least amount to putting girls in trouble on to a social policy agenda. Until that task is tackled, girls in trouble will continue to be at the receiving end of a system imbued with values which render it dubiously able to cope with their needs.

REFERENCES

Ackland, J. (1982) *Girls in Care*. Aldershot: Gower.

Ahmed, S. (1986) 'Cultural racism with Asian women and girls', in S. Ahmed, J. Cheetham and J. Small (eds) *Social Work with Black Children and their Families*. London: Batsford.

Barrett, M. and McIntosh, M. (1982) *The Anti-Social Family*. London: Verso.

Bland, L. (1983) 'Purity, motherhood, pleasure or threat', in S. Cartledge and J. Ryan (eds) *Sex and Love*. London: Women's Press.

Bryan, B., Dadzie, S. and Scafe, S. (1985) *The Heart of the Race: Black Women's Lives in Britain*. London: Virago.

Campbell, A. (1981) *Delinquent Girls*. Oxford: Basil Blackwell.

Campbell, B. (1988) *Unofficial Secrets: Child Sexual Abuse – the Cleveland Case*. London: Virago.

Casburn, M. (1979) *Girls will be Girls: Sexism and Juvenile Justice in a London Borough*. London: Women's Research and Resources Centre.

Coote, A. (1984) 'A new starting point', in J. Curran (ed.), *The Future of the Left*. London: Polity Press and New Socialist.

Eichenbaum, L. and Orbach, S. (1984) *What do Women Want?* London: Fontana.

Gilroy, P. (1987) *There ain't No Black in the Union Jack*. London: Hutchinson.

Griffin, C. (1985) *Typical Girls?* London: Routledge & Kegan Paul.

Hanmer, J. (1977) 'Community action, women's aid and the women's liberation movement', in M. Mayo (ed.) *Women in the Community*. London: Routledge & Kegan Paul.

Harris, R. and Webb, D. (1987) *Welfare, Power and Juvenile Justice*. London: Tavistock.

Heidensohn, F. (1985) *Women and Crime*. London: Macmillan.

Hudson, A. (1985) 'Feminism and social work: resistance or dialogue?', *British Journal of Social Work*, 15: 635–55.

Hudson, A. (1988) 'Boys will be boys: masculinism and the juvenile justice system', *Critical Social Policy*, 21 (Spring): 30–48.

Hudson, B. (1984) 'Adolescence and femininity', in A. McRobbie and M. Nava (eds) *Gender and Generation*. London: Macmillan.

Hudson, B. (1985) 'Sugar and spice and all things nice?', *Community Care*, 4 April: 14–17.

Hutter, B. and Williams, G. (eds) (1981) *Controlling Women: the Normal and the Deviant*. Bromley: Croom Helm.

Lees, S. (1986) *Losing Out: Sexuality and Adolescent Girls.* London: Hutchinson.

McRobbie, A. and Garber, J. (1976) 'Girls and subcultures', in S. Hall and T. Jefferson (eds) *Resistance through Rituals.* London: Hutchinson.

Mountain, A. (1988) *Womanpower: a Handbook for Women Working with Young Women in Trouble.* Leicester: National Youth Bureau.

National Association of Youth Clubs (NAYC) (1985) 'Feedback', *Working with Girls Newsletter, 29.*

Pahl, J. (1985) 'Refuges for battered women: ideology and action', *Feminist Review,* 19: 25–43.

Rowbotham, S., Segal, L. and Wainwright, H. (1979) *Beyond the Fragments.* London: Merlin.

Segal, L. (ed.) (1983) *What is to be Done about the Family?* Harmondsworth: Penguin.

Smart, C. (1976) *Women, Crime and Criminology: a Feminist Critique.* London: Routledge & Kegan Paul.

Stein, M. (1983) 'Protest in care', in B. Jordan and N. Parton (eds) *The Political Dimensions of Social Work.* Oxford: Basil Blackwell.

Thorpe, D. (1978) 'Intermediate treatment: problems of theory and practice', in R. Bailey and P. Lee (eds) *Theory and Practice in Social Work.* Oxford: Basil Blackwell.

Ward, E. (1984) *Father–Daughter Rape.* London: Women's Press.

Weeks, J. (1981) *Sex, Politics and Society.* Harlow: Longman.

Yeung, K. (1985) *Working with Girls: a Reader's Route Map.* Leicester: National Youth Bureau.

21

Challenging the criminalization of children and young people

Securing a rights-based agenda

Phil Scraton and Deena Haydon

The recent history of youth justice theory-into-practice reveals a tension between – and integration of – 'welfare' and 'justice' approaches. With justification, the application of the criminal law to children and young people is controversial. In the United Kingdom an unusually low age of criminal responsibility (ten in England and Wales; eight in Scotland) assumes that young children are as criminally responsible as adults. Yet the welfarist approach was initiated to divert children from the criminal justice system – away from punishment and retribution and towards adaptive 'treatment' programmes. Its positive characterization is that it recognizes and provides for the 'best interests' of the child, intervening through state-funded programmes of care and protection while challenging punishment and incarceration (see Chapter 13 of this volume). Critics, however, argue that welfarism abandons legal and judicial safeguards, leaving children to the discretionary, permissive powers of professionals while subjecting them to indeterminate measures without recourse to review or accountability.

The 'justice' or 'just deserts' approach advocates informed and transparent decisions through the due process of the law, in courts whose powers are adapted to recognize and accommodate children's status and where criminal justice safeguards applied to adults are extended to children. Punishment is portrayed as rational, consistent and determinate: 'fitting' the crime while protecting the child against disproportionate or arbitrary punitive measures masked as 'treatment'. The tension between welfare and justice approaches is not confined to limiting professional discretion or

SOURCE: Commissioned for this volume. Phil Scraton is Professor of Criminology and Director of the Centre for Studies in Crime and Social Justice, Edge Hill University College, UK. Deena Haydon is a Principal Officer for Research and Development, Barnardo's, UK, and Research Fellow at the Centre for Studies in Crime and Social Justice.

treatment versus punishment outcomes. It is concerned fundamentally with children's rights and the application of criminal justice in the broader, structural context of social injustice. This chapter addresses these issues, exploring the relationship between rights and the administration of justice in the context of the 1989 UN Convention on the Rights of the Child (UNCRC), the barriers to its implementation in the United Kingdom and the potential of a rights-based agenda for reversing the spiralling criminalization and incarceration of children and young people.

THE SIGNIFICANCE OF RIGHTS

In established, 'mature' democracies the conceptualization, definition, and formulation of commonly held and institutionally applied rights would seem straightforward. At the heart of internationally agreed conventions, supported by international law, regarding human rights is the recognition that 'the state is obliged not only to refrain from committing certain acts against the individual but also to carry out certain duties of an affirmative nature' (Méndez, 1997, p. 5). The language of rights is instructive. They are 'fundamental', 'inalienable', 'universal'. It is a language of certainty which presents rights as obvious and as absolutes. In principle, at least, human rights extend beyond the borders of sovereign states, universally declared and shared, internationally convened and agreed. Their implementation becomes a significant yardstick through which the progress of states in transition to democracy is monitored. Thus the legal and judicial procedures of rights implementation are derived in the political processes of rights affirmation.

Yet rights discourses are complex – reflecting a long history of contestation. Rights can be defensive or negative in proclaiming the 'right' not to be on the receiving end of the actions of others (e.g. the 'right to life'). Also, they can be proactive or positive – Méndez uses the term 'affirmative' – providing the right to something (e.g. information or consultation). Taken together, an inventory of rights, whether conceptualized as defensive or affirmative, whether socio-economic or civil-political, represents a statement of minimally acceptable standards applied within and across sovereign states. Freeden (1991, p. 11) proposed that a 'satisfactory theory of basic rights' has to meet three key criteria. First, 'rational and logical standards' (philosophical); second, 'terms that are emotionally and culturally attractive' (ideological); third, 'translatable into codes of enforceable action' (legal).

On the second and third criteria the internationalization of rights raises political and ideological issues concerning sovereignty. In the United Kingdom, for example, there has been significant 'emotional' and 'cultural' resistance to what has been perceived and represented as interference with the rule of law. Yet, importantly, internationalization secures the protection of citizens from rights violations *within* their states. In those circumstances, such as the European Convention on Human Rights, where a rights agreement is accompanied by a higher court through which domestic rulings can be reversed, the formalizing of internationally agreed rights is associated with the formalizing of internationally agreed justice. Articles of a convention not only become the conduit through which certain actions are policed and specified freedoms guaranteed, but also they provide mechanisms through which culpability is established and redress delivered. For it is in international courts and tribunals that member states are found wanting in failing to protect the substantive interests and liberties of their citizens.

Rights take on particular significance where the protection of the 'weak', the 'vulnerable', the 'oppressed' or the 'minority interest' is concerned. Central to the cultural imperialism and arrogance of Western democracies is the assumption that their children and young people are the beneficiaries of political and legal processes which identify and safeguard their rights and 'best interests'. Yet abuse, degradation and exclusion of children by adults are global issues. It is important to recognize different social, cultural and political contexts and to guard against crude universalism. But the suffering of children through the words and actions of adults – their helplessness in the face of adult power – is not restricted by class, culture, gender, religion, state or industry. The extent and depth of personal harm, physical and sexual abuse and violence, intimidation and harassment, economic exploitation and poverty, political and social marginalization endured by children in advanced democratic societies is pervasive. It is, like so many forms of oppression, a power relation that silences as well as exploits.

The Children's Rights Office (1995, p. 8) provides a litany of serious problems endured by children in the United Kingdom: 'growing inequality, increased poverty, drug abuse, teenage pregnancy, high levels of violence ... sexual abuse, child prostitution, homelessness ... suicide and mental illness, a deteriorating environment and alienation from the political process'. Without voting rights children 'can only experience change through the actions of others' (AMA, 1995, p. 11). Consequently, children and young people experience 'adult mediation in all matters ... ranging from physical punishment in the home, in childcare or in schools ... to accessing contraception and abortion advice' on the basis of adult definitions of 'competence' (Scraton, 1997, p. 180). Yet, to all intents and purposes, the rights of children are prescribed and protected by the UNCRC, ratified by the UK government in December 1991. The UNCRC comprises over fifty articles, the main aims being to establish the right of children to adequate and appropriate care and protection, to provide services and facilities appropriate to their basic needs and to encourage institutional arrangements which enable effective participation in their society. Binding in international law, the expectation is that states will initiate legal and policy reform and develop formal interventionist practices within the UNCRC's articles. These protect rights and indicate duties across the social and community spectrum; providing a directional framework for all state institutionally based policies and practices and recognizing the role of the state in supporting families and carers in the development, socialization and welfare of children.

That the UNCRC was effective in identifying, codifying and protecting children's rights was brought seriously into question in 1993 following the killing of two-year-old James Bulger by Robert Thompson and Jon Venables, both aged ten. Nine months after their arrest, having been kept in custody without recourse to psychological support or counselling, they were tried for murder in an adult court with little concession to their status as children. They experienced the full glare of the international media and, having been found guilty, their identities and photographs were made public – unleashing an unprecedented media-hyped public campaign of hate against them (see Hay, 1995; Franklin and Petley, 1996; Davis and Bourhill, 1997; Haydon and Scraton, 2000). Despite judicial recommendations that the boys should serve eight years (the trial judge) or ten years (the Lord Chief Justice) the then Home Secretary, Michael Howard, intervened and, bowing to the public campaign, established the minimum period of incarceration at fifteen years. Eventually Howard's decision was overturned by the House of Lords and his action drew severe criticism in the European Court of Human Rights, where the UK government was ruled to have violated the European Convention on Human Rights on three counts (fair trial; fixing sentence; periodic review of sentence). Minority opinions within the court were scathing about the UK government's retributive and vengeful prosecution of the boys (Haydon and Scraton, 2000, p. 439).

Further, Dame Butler-Sloss, in the High Court, ruled that on release the identities of both young men should remain undisclosed because of the 'real possibility of serious physical harm and possible death from vengeful members of the public or from the Bulger family' (Butler-Sloss, 2001, p. 44). In taking this decision Butler-Sloss placed the principle of the right to life, enshrined in the European Convention and adopted in the 1998 Human Rights Act, above the right to freedom of expression. What this case demonstrates, from the prosecution through to the release of Robert Thompson and Jon Venables, is that debates over rights and justice do not happen in a social or political vacuum. They are informed, mediated and – to an extent – regulated by the historical and contemporary contexts in which they arise.

RIGHTS AND JUSTICE IN A CLIMATE OF RETRIBUTION

The abduction and killing of James Bulger did not, of themselves, generate the policy and legislative clamp-down on children and young people which began with the 1994 Criminal Justice and Public Order Act and culminated in the 1998 Crime and Disorder Act. It was an exceptional tragedy conveniently exploited to illustrate the most serious end of a continuum of children's criminality and antisocial behaviour. It reflected a 'fermenting body of opinion that juvenile justice in particular and penal liberalism in general had gone too far' (Goldson, 1997, p. 129). The law-and-order rhetoric of the early 1990s was directed towards children and young people as 'joyriders', 'persistent young offenders', 'bail bandits' and 'thugs'. Blackbird Leys (Oxford), Ely (Cardiff), Meadowell (north Tyneside), and other estates in Blackburn, Birmingham and Merseyside, were portrayed as police 'no go' areas where children and youths had free rein, intimidating and bullying residents through fear of violence. The James Bulger case took the debate over childhood indiscipline and lawlessness to a different level. While authors such as Campbell (1993) put forward a more reasoned, critical analysis of the broader context of antisocial, harassing and violent behaviour on the part of boy children and young men, more reactionary perspectives used it as a catalyst to criticize the ineffectiveness of 'liberal', community-based youth justice initiatives.

The velocity and intensity of media coverage and political opportunism regarding a 'crisis' in 'childhood' were so great that the amplification spiral – used by criminologists as an analytical metaphor – became almost tangible. 'New Right' theorists located the 'crisis' within an underclass created by an uncomplicated mix of welfarism, fecklessness and individual pathology (Murray, 1990, 1994). Self-styled 'ethical socialists' shared a version of underclass theory in locating high crime rates, antisocial behaviour and personal irresponsibility in the 'dismembered family' (Dennis, 1993; Dennis and Erdos, 1992). What united these analyses, reflecting the hard-line responses of police organizations, was the assumption that diversionary and decriminalizing interventions within youth justice indicated a state which had 'gone soft' on crime. This was clear in the all-party condemnation of social workers and youth justice professionals in the immediate aftermath of James Bulger's tragic death.

What evolved was a generic process of child demonization. Children had lost all sense of decency, discipline and morality; their 'innocence' had been 'corrupted'. They were claimed to be 'inherently evil', 'barbaric' and 'lawless'; the inevitable progeny of hedonistic, 'broken' homes, excused by 'soft' juvenile justice and abandoned by ineffectual, progressive schooling. What was demanded was the reconstitution of adult authority (see Chapter 26 of this volume). In this, legitimacy is claimed for adult power solely on the basis that adults are adults; their authority prevails whether in the family or state institution and is imposed rather then negotiated. It imposes surveillance disguised as prevention, subservience disguised as discipline and punishment disguised as correction. The 'crisis' in 'childhood', fuelled by the media and seized upon by politicians, carries the 'ideological whiff of child-hate'; a manifestation of power and subordination akin to race-hate, mysogyny or homophobia (Haydon and Scraton, 2000, p. 447). It represents the harsh end of a politics of adultism 'legitimated, reinforced and reproduced through professional discourses' and 'expressed via a language of exclusion and denial; confirming children and young people as outsiders, the "other" to adult essentialism' (*ibid.*, p. 448).

The struggle within criminal justice theory and policy remains locked in the debate over welfarism and care as the most appropriate route to rehabilitation and just deserts and punishment as the fairest and least discretionary means of establishing a universally applied form of justice. While the full persuasive force of righteous indignation demands exemplary punishment for persistent young offenders as a deterrent, and institutionalized leniency is promoted as the primary reason for repeat offending, the 'new retributivists' or 'deserts theorists' defend the principle of proportionality. In his critique of punishment theories Christie (1994, p. 138) argues that deserts theorists establish an unambiguous relation 'between the concrete act and the punishment', the latter reflecting the 'blameworthiness' of a specific act. Put another way, punishment is 'derived from the seriousness of the offence and from the culpability of the offender' (Hudson, 1996, p. 41).

This process aims to achieve the diminution, if not elimination, of social mitigation. Deserts theory proposes that social factors 'obfuscate the clear and supposedly justly deserved punishment resulting from the evil act' and, as a simple and objective mechanism, it 'becomes a most useful theory for fast justice and depersonalization of the offender ...' (Christie, 1994, p. 138). The system becomes tightened. Values other than 'the question of the gravity of the act' are eliminated. In 'matching the gravity of a crime with a portion of pain' the established 'system of justice is converted into a system of crime control' (*ibid.*, p. 175).

Setting tariffs as 'just measures of pain' within crime control systems presumes and demands a calculation which matches the seriousness of crime to the severity of punishment – proportionality. Seemingly rational and progressive, challenging the discretionary and often arbitrarily applied powers of the welfare model, such a measured calculation also prevents the intrinsic injustice of deterrent sentencing and exemplary punishment administered at the height of a moral panic. What this 'gain' has to be balanced against, however, is the 'loss' to offenders of relevant mitigating circumstances. It is a significant loss, given the consequences inherent in the determining contexts of class, 'race', gender, sexuality and age inequalities. Returning to the James Bulger case, surely age in itself mediated, if not mitigated, the circumstances in which the boys acted.

Most recent UK criminal justice policy embodies proportionality in so far as it prescribes the seriousness of offences. Hudson (1996, p. 55) notes that 'getting tough' on crime, a persistent and influential ideological construction directed particularly at children, has encouraged policies which suggest that 'deserved retribution' is not the only priority in Western democracies. Others include 'protection from dangerous or persistent offenders' and 'strong action against kinds of offending that become suddenly prevalent'. Elsewhere she argues that 'in popular and political discourse' justice has become 'endangered' through its now inextricable ties with vengeance and punishment. Consequently, justice 'is now very much less important than "risk" as a preoccupation of criminal justice/law and order policy' (Hudson, 2001, pp. 104–5).

According to Christie (1994, p. 24) this 'reactive framework' is the context in which what then happens is placed 'solidly on the person who commits the crime'. It unleashes a 'new situation, with an unlimited reservoir of acts that can be defined as crimes ... unlimited possibilities for warfare against all sorts of unwanted acts'. While the protection of the personal and the material (from, for example, violence and robbery) is essential, there have to be what Christie defines as 'reflections on limits' to criminalization and the formal mechanisms of crime control. For, if the 'reservoir of acts' is tapped relentlessly, and antisocial behaviour of all kind is recast as crimes, the expansion of incarceration is reconstructed as 'destiny, not choice' (*ibid.*, p. 34).

Yet, as Hudson (2001, p. 145) notes, finding 'an adequate definition' of justice which moves beyond criminalization, vengeance and retribution is both 'difficult and inconclusive'. The underlying tension evident throughout the socio-legal and penal debates is the relationship between securing consistency in the administration and distribution of justice where victims have been harmed or wronged and accepting that all actions are, to an extent, unique and mediated by particular circumstances and structural contexts. Taking this last point to its logical conclusion, de Haan (1991, p. 210) calls for a politics of redress via a conceptual and administrative framework inviting 'open discussion about how an unfortunate event should be viewed and what the appropriate response ought to be'. Criminal justice discourse, locked into the negative, reactive and reactionary manifestations of crime and punishment, would then give way to Christie's (1994, p. 11) call for a 'real dialogue'.

Programmes based on principles of redress, restitution or reparation have become increasingly familiar – offering community-related alternatives for achieving just solutions to real problems. They are premised on the establishment of procedures and mechanisms for conflict resolution and interpersonal reconciliation which are not only rational but also prescriptive towards a more tolerant, understanding and diverse social order. Resting on the pillars of negotiation, mediation and arbitration, the 'aim is compensation rather than retaliation; reconciliation rather than blame allocation' (de Haan, 1991, p. 212). The latter is less problematic than the former. Reparation and redress are not imprinted on a clean slate; they are invariably attempted in a reactive context of crime and punishment. Further, the harm done cannot be erased, since reconciliation for the victim/survivor does not mean recovery. Also, the seriousness of the act does matter. So how is an appropriate level of compensation to be set which is not infected by the notion of a 'just measure of pain'? Finally, and crucially, there is the problem of power.

Restorative justice implies a transaction, personal or material or both, between the victim/survivor and offender through which the harm caused and endured through the act can be overcome (see Chapter 16 of this volume). It trades punishment for reparation and, accordingly, addresses the residual fear left with the victim/survivor. But does it? When Muncie comments that a 'conception of crime without a conception of power is meaningless' he is undoubtedly correct. He is also optimistic that the 'redefining of crime as harm opens up the possibility of dealing with pain, suffering and injury as conflicts and troubles deserving negotiation, mediation and arbitration rather than as criminal events deserving guilt, punishment and exclusion' (Muncie, 2000, pp. 221–3). This provides a discourse 'less concerned with controlling, preventing and punishing and more with enabling and empowering'.

Yet naming power does not challenge its legitimacy or authority. Apart from the major social and ideological transition involved in shifting collective consciousness from one in which most UK citizens would vote for an immediate reinstatement of capital punishment and would consider prisons (even for children) too lenient, the big issue of power remains. Power centres of production, patriarchy, neo-colonialism and age – their inherent structural inequalities wrapped in legal frameworks – persist, as does their currency of exploitation, subjugation and oppression. Corporate negligence, corruption, pollution, state-sanctioned violence, inhuman and degrading treatment, child abuse, neglect, harm and human rights violations remain endemic in advanced capitalist political economies. In this context Hudson's (2001, p. 166) argument for the promotion of 'substantive justice' through 'the development of a rights-based approach which is predicated on difference, on conflicts of rights that will be generated by individual cases' seems apposite. She considers, however, that 'universal statements of rights ... and attempts to interpret them as a practical guide to governance' should be viewed as 'starting points' which could and should 'lead to the development of a jurisprudence of rights geared to deciding conflicts and upholding rights in specific cases'.

FORMALIZING CHILDREN'S RIGHTS: INTERNATIONAL CONVENTIONS AND RECOMMENDATIONS

Cohen (2001, p. 139) comments: 'Historical skeletons are put in cupboards because of the political need to be innocent of a troubling recognition; they remain hidden because of the political absence of an inquiring mind.' Regarding the history of genocide, atrocity, torture and state repression this powerful comment is demonstrable. Yet an 'inquiring mind', even if used as a collective metaphor, requires process and procedure to facilitate redress and, if possible, some form of reconciliation. Politically, as stated earlier, this is found in a discourse of rights made concrete by a framework of rights implementation. While, in Hudson's terms, the UNCRC provided a 'starting point', it is also 'the fullest legal statement of children's rights to be found anywhere' (Freeman, 2000, p. 277). It provides the basis, then, for the unpacking of 'troubling recognition' of child abuse, exploitation and marginalization by the 'inquiring mind' while also establishing a framework through which a 'jurisprudence of rights' can emerge via specific cases.

The UNCRC established a framework of principles and minimum standards for legislation, policy and practice concerning children and young people. Ratification by states implies a commitment to the general principles underpinning the UNCRC and specific articles concerning youth justice. Other complementary international instruments (such as the UN Rules for the Protection of Juveniles deprived of their Liberty, 1990; UN Standard Minimum Rules for the Administration of Juvenile Justice – the Beijing rules, 1985; UN Guidelines for the Prevention of Juvenile

Delinquency – the Riyadh guidelines, 1990; UN Standard Minimum Rules for Non-custodial Measures – the Tokyo rules, 1990) also relate to the planning and implementation of youth justice programmes.

Several key articles identify general principles informing policy and practice for all children in any circumstances. For example, rights established by the UNCRC should be respected and ensured 'without discrimination of any kind ... irrespective of the child's ... race, colour, sex, language, religion, political or other opinion, national, ethnic or social origin, property, disability, birth or other status' (Article 2.1). In all actions concerning children, 'the best interests of the child shall be a primary consideration' (Article 3.1), and 'the institutions, services and facilities responsible for the care or protection of children shall conform with the standards established by competent authorities'; particularly regarding safety, health, the number and suitability of staff and competent supervision (Article 3.3).

States are expected to 'ensure to the maximum extent possible the survival and development of the child' (Article 6.2). While in the care of parents, legal guardians or any other person, 'all appropriate legislative, administrative, social and educational measures' should be taken 'to protect the child from all forms of physical or mental violence, injury or abuse, neglect or negligent treatment, maltreatment or exploitation, including sexual abuse' (Article 19.1). Such measures should include, as appropriate, 'effective procedures for the establishment of social programmes to provide necessary support for the child and for those who have the care of the child', as well as for 'other forms of prevention' and the 'identification, reporting, referral, investigation, treatment and follow-up of instances of child maltreatment' (Article 19.2).

Crucially, Article 12.1 states: 'the child who is capable of forming his or her own views' should be assured of 'the right to express those views freely in all matters affecting the child', its views 'being given due weight in accordance with the age and maturity of the child'. As well as assuring the child's right of expression, this obliges adults to hear and take children's views seriously. In particular, the child should be 'provided the opportunity to be heard in any judicial and administrative proceedings affecting the child', either directly or through a representative/appropriate body (Article 12.2).

Regarding youth justice, states should 'seek to promote the establishment of laws, procedures, authorities and institutions specifically applicable to children alleged as, accused of, or recognized as having infringed the penal law' (Article 40.3). They should also establish 'a minimum age below which children shall be presumed not to have the capacity to infringe the penal law' (Article 40.3a). The UNCRC defines a child as 'every human being below the age of eighteen years unless ... majority is attained earlier' (Article 1). The *Manual on Human Rights Reporting* refers to eighteen as a 'general upper benchmark', which should be 'used by States Parties as a rule and a reference for the establishment of any other particular age for any specific purpose or activity' (cited in Hodgkin and Newell, 1998, p. 4). Accordingly, states should ensure special protection to every child below this limit.

While international instruments do not specify an appropriate 'age of criminal responsibility', the Beijing rules suggest that it should 'not be fixed at too low an age level, bearing in mind the facts of emotional, mental and intellectual maturity' (Rule 4). The important consideration is 'whether a child, by virtue of his or her individual discernment and understanding, can be held responsible for essentially anti-social behaviour'. Contextually, the rule recognizes the 'close relationship between the notion of responsibility for delinquent or criminal behaviour and other social rights and responsibilities (such as marital status, civil majority)'.

Under the UNCRC 'the arrest, detention or imprisonment of a child ... shall be used only as a measure of last resort and for the shortest appropriate period of time' (Article 37b). All children should be entitled to a number of guarantees, including the presumption of innocence 'until proven guilty according to the law' (Article 40.2b; see also Universal Declaration of Human Rights, Article 11; International Covenant on Civil and Political Rights, Article 14.2). Culpability should be 'determined without delay by a competent, independent and impartial authority or judicial body in a fair hearing ... in the presence of legal and other appropriate assistance and ... in particular, taking into account his or her age or situation ...' The child should 'not ... be compelled to give testimony or to confess guilt' (see also Universal Declaration of Human Rights, Article 11; International Covenant on Civil and Political Rights, Article 14.3g). The child should also 'have his or her privacy fully respected at all stages of the proceedings'. If considered to have infringed the law, 'this decision and any measures imposed in consequence' should be 'reviewed by a higher competent, independent and impartial authority or judicial body'.

Throughout the prosecution process, children should be 'treated in a manner consistent with the promotion of the child's sense of dignity and worth'. While reinforcing the child's respect for the human rights and freedom of others, formal responses should take into account the child's age and the desirability of promoting reintegration (Article 40.1). The Beijing rules (Rule 17, Commentary) imply that 'strictly punitive approaches are not appropriate'. Although it is recognized that just deserts and retributive sanctions may have merit in adult cases, or when young people have committed serious offences, such considerations 'should always be outweighed by the interest of safeguarding the well-being and the future of the young person'.

A 'variety of dispositions, such as care, guidance and supervision orders; counselling; probation; foster care; educational and vocational training programmes and other alternatives to institutional care' should be available to ensure that 'children are dealt with in a manner appropriate to their well-being and proportionate both to their circumstances and the offence' (Article 40.4). The Beijing rules (Rule 17.1a) confirm that action taken in criminal cases should be proportionate not only to the 'circumstances and the gravity' of the offence, but essentially to the 'circumstances and the needs of the juvenile'. The use of custodial sentences for children and young people is strongly opposed. In addition to existing 'alternative' sanctions, the Beijing rules encourage the development of 'new alternative sanctions' (Rule 17, Commentary). Finally, the UNCRC states that every child deprived of liberty should: 'be treated with humanity and respect ... and in a manner which takes into account the needs of persons of his or her age'; 'be separated from adults unless it is considered in the child's best interest not to do so'; and 'have the right to maintain contact with his or her family through correspondence and visits' (Article 37c).

In 1994 the UK government submitted its initial report to the UN Committee on the Rights of the Child concerning progress towards implementation of the UNCRC. In its response the committee (UN Committee on the Rights of the Child, 1995) raised a number of concerns. It questioned whether sufficient consideration had been given to the establishment of mechanisms to co-ordinate and monitor the implementation of children's rights. The insufficiency of measures ensuring implementation of the UNCRC's general principles, in particular the 'best interests of the child', was noted.

It indicated that the low age of criminal responsibility and national legislation relating to the administration of juvenile justice were incompatible with Articles 37 and 40. Of particular concern was the ethos of guidelines for establishing and administering secure training centres, which emphasized incarceration and punishment. The committee was concerned that children placed in care under the social welfare system might be diverted to such centres.

Consequently a range of recommendations was made. The UN committee encouraged the UK government to review its reservations to the UNCRC with a view to withdrawing them (UK government, 1999). It suggested the establishment of a permanent mechanism for monitoring implementation of the 1989 Children Act and the UNCRC throughout the United Kingdom, with regular and closer co-operation between the government and the non-governmental community. It proposed that the general principles of the UNCRC, particularly those relating to the best interests of the child, should guide the determination of central and local government policy making. It recommended appropriate measures for disseminating the principles and provisions of the UNCRC to adults and children, with children's rights incorporated into the training curricula of professionals working with or for children (such as the police, judges, social workers and personnel in care and detention institutions).

In addition to giving greater priority to the general principles of the UNCRC (especially Articles 3 and 12) in legislative and administrative measures, the committee recommended legal reform to ensure that the system of administration of juvenile justice was child-oriented. It recommended that serious consideration should be given to raising the age of criminal responsibility throughout the United Kingdom, and that the 1994 Criminal Justice and Public Order Act should be monitored to ensure full respect for, and compatibility with, the UNCRC. Of specific concern were provisions in this Act allowing the placement of secure training orders on twelve to fourteen-year-olds, indeterminate detention and the doubling of sentences on fifteen to seventeen-year-olds. The committee emphasized the development of programmes and strategies to ensure appropriate measures promoting the physical and psychological recovery and social reintegration of children in the youth justice system.

BARRIERS TO THE IMPLEMENTATION OF THE UN CONVENTION

In November 1996 the Audit Commission (1996) heavily criticized the youth justice system as expensive, inefficient, inconsistent and ineffective. Its controller, Andrew Foster, called for a 'systematic overhaul' to end 'the cycle of antisocial behaviour that has become a day-to-day activity' (*Guardian*, 21 November 1996). Following the 1997 election victory, the Labour government's Home Secretary, Jack Straw, announced a 'root and branch' reform of youth justice. This culminated in the rushed passage of the 1998 Crime and Disorder Act, which not only overhauled youth justice but also introduced: reparation orders; antisocial behaviour orders; parenting orders; child safety orders; local child curfew schemes; final warning schemes; action plan orders and detention and training orders. It abolished the presumption of *doli incapax* for ten to fourteen-year-olds and affirmed a commitment to secure custody for serious or repeat offenders. For Muncie (1999, p. 154), the Act is: 'an amalgam of "get tough" authoritarian measures with elements of paternalism, pragmatism, communitarianism, responsibilization and remoralization whose new depth and legal powers might be best described as "coercive corporatism"'.

A year later the UK government (1999, p. 179) submitted its second report to the UN committee, claiming that measures directed at children and young people in the 1998 Act would 'be effective in further implementing' the UNCRC. Using a discourse of 'rights' and 'responsibilities', the punitive potential of the Act is reconstructed as enabling, supportive welfare intervention. In an ironic interpretation of Article 3, the report states: 'It is in the interests of children and young people themselves to recognize and accept responsibility, and to receive assistance in tackling criminal behaviour'. The government argued that the welfare of the child is only one factor to be taken into account by courts dealing with children or young people, rather than a factor of 'primary consideration'. Reflecting political priorities and demands for visible accountability on the part of offenders, the others include punishment, risk and public confidence in the system (Howard League, 1999, p. 12). The law consequently focuses on legal priorities – establishing intent, proving guilt and applying punishment – at the expense of welfare. Regarding practice, there is evidence that children have been moved from local authority secure units to young offenders' institutions when, in the opinion of professionals, it has been considered detrimental to the interests of the child (Howard League, 1999, p. 13).

Responding to the UN committee's concern about the introduction of privately managed Secure Training Centres (STCs), the government claims that the committee 'may have misunderstood the purpose and ethos of these institutions, and the circumstances in which young people might be sent there' (UK government, 1999, p. 184). Despite assurances that 'the primary purpose of STCs is not penal', a Social Services inspection of the first STC found excessive use of force; unsatisfactory educational provision; inexperienced and incompetent staff who had not been adequately trained; lack of effective and experienced managers; failure of programmes designed to tackle offending behaviour; virtually no access to fresh air and exercise for some children, left in an enclosed environment for twenty-four hours a day (Howard League, 1999, p. 11).

Having stated that the government intends to abandon custodial remand for fifteen and sixteen-year-olds, the report continues 'but there is currently insufficient provision elsewhere' (UK government, 1999, p. 190). Consequently, the government retains its reservation to Article 37c. Additionally, a child receiving a long sentence will be accommodated initially in a welfare-oriented secure unit and then transferred to a young offenders' institution (run by the prison service for fifteen to twenty-one-year-olds) for completion. The duty of the prison service to 'look after ... young offenders with humanity and help them lead constructive lives while in custody and prepare them for a law-abiding life on release' is affirmed in the report. Yet serious concerns have been raised about the general state of young offenders' institutions (see Howard League, 1995; Goldson and Peters, 2000) and, in his review of young offenders' institutions, the Chief Inspector of Prisons concludes that the prison service is 'neither structured nor equipped to deal with children'. Conditions 'in many cases ... are far below the minimum conditions in Social Services Department secure units required by the Children Act 1989 and the UN Convention on the Rights of the Child' (Ramsbotham, cited in Howard League, 1999, p. 9).

Abolition of the rebuttable presumption of *doli incapax* for ten to fourteen-year-olds in England and Wales means that, from the age of ten, children are treated as having the same criminal intent and maturity as an adult when a court decides on guilt or innocence. In addition, there is no longer a mechanism for the court to establish whether a child is capable of criminal intent, understands the criminal proceedings or is capable of giving instructions to legal representatives. The government justifies this change by suggesting that it will ensure that courts are 'able to address the offending behaviour by children between the ages of 10 and 14 at the earliest possible opportunity, and so nip that offending behaviour in the bud' (UK government, 1999, p. 177).

Courts will be allowed to draw inferences from the failure of an accused child to give evidence or answer questions at trial, 'thereby ensuring that all juveniles are treated in the same way in court' (*ibid.*, p. 177). This is also intended to 'contribute to the right of children appearing there [in court] to develop responsibility for themselves' (*ibid.*, p. 180). While children remain protected by the court's discretion not to draw inferences from silence if the court considers the child's mental or physical state makes this undesirable, the government justifies these changes as 'common sense to expect a child who has an innocent explanation for his or her conduct to provide that explanation, rather than to deprive him of her of that responsibility' (*ibid.*, p. 180).

Ignoring the UN committee's recommendation that the age of criminal responsibility should be raised, the government confirms the age of ten (in England and Wales) as 'an appropriate level, reflecting the need to protect the welfare of the youngest'. The priorities of the government's youth justice reform are evident in the report: 'if children aged 10 or older start to behave in a criminal or anti-social way, the Government considers that we do them no favours to overlook this behaviour' (*ibid.*, p. 180). Considering the relationship between the age of criminal responsibility and moral competence, the government maintains that in

> today's sophisticated society, it is not unjust or unreasonable to assume that a child aged 10 or older can understand the difference between serious wrong and simple naughtiness, and is therefore able to respond to intervention designed to tackle offending behaviour. If for some reason a child is lacking in this most basic moral understanding, it is all the more imperative that appropriate intervention and rehabilitation should begin as soon as possible.
>
> (*Ibid.*)

It argues that the changes 'will not have the effect of treating children in the same way as adults as far as the criminal justice system is concerned', with the emphasis 'firmly placed not on criminalizing children, but on helping them to recognize and accept responsibility for their actions where this is appropriate, and on enabling them to receive help to change their offending behaviour' (*ibid.*). Given the existence of 'an entirely different set of sentences, graduated by age, for juvenile offenders', a court would be able to 'reflect a young offender's age and level of maturity at the point of sentence' (*ibid.*). However, the then Home Secretary, Jack Straw, was unambiguous in resolving that, from the age of ten, children accused of serious offences should continue to be tried as adults in Crown courts because 'if justice is not open, it cannot be seen to be fair' (Hansard, col. 21, 13 March 2000).

In the administration of youth justice generally, discriminatory practice has been well documented. For example, African-Caribbeans are markedly more likely to be stopped by the police and to be remanded in custody before trial. They are over represented in the prison population and serve a disproportionately large number of long sentences (CRDU, 1994, p. 215). Significant differences in how females and males are treated within criminal justice mean that a higher proportion of girls are likely to be placed in secure accommodation because of concern about their welfare or behaviour rather than for reasons directly associated with offending (see Goldson, 1999). Youth justice work within local authorities has not been afforded a high priority and significant cuts in youth service budgets have affected provision. Schemes such as drink and drug programmes, off-site school units and innovative youth justice initiatives have been reduced. Preventive measures intended to strengthen social support, ensure the provision of appropriate housing, employment and leisure opportunities are not sufficiently widely available (CRDU, 1994, p. 214).

SECURING A POSITIVE RIGHTS AGENDA

Rights politics in general, and children's rights campaigns in particular, have received criticism across the political spectrum. Scepticism concerning the political opportunism regularly associated with popular discourse around the defence and implementation of rights is well founded. The previous section demonstrates the ease with which draconian measures consolidating the incarceration and exclusion of children and young people can be inverted through a liberal veneer of welfarism and equality of opportunity. As Fionda (1999, p. 46) concludes, the 1998 Crime and Disorder Act reforms amounted to a 'melting pot of principles and ideologies', mixing 'punishment and welfare approaches'.

'Rights' and 'rights discourses' may be criticized for being no more than symbolic gesturing rather than vehicles of effective structural change. This is a significant point, given that it is possible to establish and ratify a convention based on defensive and proactive statements of rights while persisting with, even reinforcing, structural inequalities, pursuing harsh policies and maintaining punitive institutional regimes against the marginalized. Further, and from distinct and different political positions, rights discourses have been portrayed as: too permissive or emancipatory; failing to confront individuals with their social responsibilities; undermining established and significant cultural conventions; over-reliant on the rule of law to redress complex wrongs derived in difficult circumstances; diminishing broader political and collective responsibility through excessive individualism. Despite such wide-ranging criticisms and the 'chasm between the [UN] Convention and practice', Freeman (2000, pp. 279–80) asserts that a 'regime of rights is one of the weak's greatest resources'.

Clearly, UNCRC implementation should be grounded in a welfare approach, its three core principles having significant implications for youth justice. First, children's status requires discrete recognition and different responses from adult status, while taking account of individual experiences and capacities. Second, children's welfare should be prioritized. This implies treatment, support and guidance based on individual needs rather than punishment, retribution and deterrence. Third, children should participate fully in decisions affecting their lives, having had opportunities to gain confidence, explore issues of importance to them, learn the skills required to actively participate, and take action on their own behalf. Freeman (ibid., p. 282) notes the irony of developing a convention which establishes the 'right to participation' while failing to consult children during its formulation. Not only should children's voices be heard, but the existing recognition of differences between children should be extended. Extension should be based around 'inclusion' as proactive in addition to the more reactive conceptualization of 'non-discrimination', emphasizing needs specific to children's circumstances. As Freeman suggests, the 'future of children's rights requires us to build upon the Convention by concentrating on neglected groups of children, by revising, reforming and innovating the rights with which we wish to endow children, and by strengthening implementation mechanisms' (*ibid.*, p. 290).

As discussed earlier in this chapter, a positive rights-based agenda both protects and promotes the interests of people within and between states. In protecting, it establishes the rights of all – strong and weak – not to be harmed, intimidated, degraded or abused. In promoting, it provides safeguards for the vulnerable while prioritizing and meeting their identified needs. Children require protective (defensive) and promotional (proactive) rights. Within youth justice a positive rights-based agenda requires a critical rethink of the appropriateness of the justice or just deserts approach. While incorporating some progressive principles regarding locally based crime strategies, multi-agency integrated interventions and anti-discriminatory practices, in effect the 1998 Crime and Disorder Act criminalizes children, young people and their parents. Politically it was mobilized in response to the public clamour for criminalization and punishment. Further, its implementation, far from being consistent and universally applied, remains arbitrary and uneven. This extends to the multi-agency initiatives directed at children and their parents once civil injunctions are applied.

Yet the government's defence of the justice approach relies on the presumption, stated unambiguously to the UN Committee on the Rights of the Child (UK government, 1999), that from the age of ten children's offending and/or antisocial behaviour will be addressed via the 'open', 'visible' and recorded procedures of courts. It is maintained that through their representatives, legal or otherwise, children can participate fully in preparing their defence and in following the progress of their case. This suggests that the justice approach minimizes, if not eliminates, adult discretion in defining the nature and circumstances of the offence, the degree of culpability and proportionality in passing sentence. It reinforces the classical proposition that the courts offer the only appropriate mechanism for establishing and calibrating a 'just measure' of punishment corresponding to the quantifiable seriousness of the crime. Clearly, these claims cannot be sustained – the administration of 'justice' being mediated by a range of social, institutional and structural factors and contexts.

Applying a justice approach to children, whatever the 'welfare' interventions built into the process, denies the status of childhood embodied in all internationally agreed conventions and guidelines. Far from safeguarding or promoting 'rights' and 'responsibilities', the arbitrary use of civil injunctions and the extension of child custody are two examples of adult-oriented justice responses in breach of the UNCRC. As this chapter emphasizes, children's knowledge and understanding – moral, social, cultural – are defined and restricted by their socially and politically imposed status as children and by their life experiences. Given that the social construction and structural location of childhood are unlikely to change significantly, institutional responses to offending or antisocial behaviour must recognize and reflect the complexity of the transition from childhood to adulthood.

Dealing with such complexity does not require the moral certainty, inflexibility and universalism of a renewed justice model, but the adaptability of a rights-based welfare approach. To move away from a 'justice' or just deserts approach, however modified or rationalized, to a more radical welfare approach does not necessarily mean a return to hidden, arbitrary and discretionary punitive welfare interventions. Proportionality, protection, review, transparency and accountability can be built into professional practice, as can safeguards against net widening. Of course, widespread revelations of institutionalized physical, emotional and sexual abuse of children in residential care demonstrate how adults responsible for the care and protection of children can abuse their power. Such revelations, however, reinforce arguments for reforming welfare interventionism rather than further extending the criminal justice system. As recent studies demonstrate, young offenders' institutions do not inspire confidence regarding the good health and well-being of children in custody (see Chapter 26 of this volume).

The real potential of a positive rights-based welfare approach is its challenge to constructions of children as innocent, vulnerable and weak through promoting their right to information, expression of views and their participation in decision-making. Such an approach prioritizes children's accounts and experiences, the meaning they invest in their acts and their active participation in the process. It also expects full transparency of formal procedures and practices while constructing effective political and professional accountability measures for all interventions. This represents a profound change, extending the promotion of social justice beyond childhood, thus also requiring a radical overhaul of the criminal justice system for adults. A priority here is the necessary challenge to the ever-expanding 'reservoir of acts' defined under new legislation as 'crimes'. Against this tide, the focus should be decriminalization, decarceration and diversion into welfare-based programmes sensitive to the contexts in which individuals live.

For children and young people, the age of criminal responsibility should be raised to sixteen, in line with other social responsibilities within UK legislation. The detention and training orders introduced by the 1998 Crime and Disorder Act should be abolished and an end to youth custody in young offenders' institutions and prison for children under eighteen should be key objectives of a positive rights-based agenda. This reflects not only the UNCRC commitment to incarceration as a 'last resort' but also the damning indictment of young offenders' institutions by the Chief Inspector of Prisons. In opposition to the prevailing ideological (emotional and cultural) discourses in the United Kingdom, the development of a rights-based welfare approach would end the imposition of youth justice via prosecution, sentencing and incarceration for children and young people aged ten to sixteen. This would require a range of welfare-based, multi-agency interventions involving young people in defining their needs. It would acknowledge that young people's 'offensive' or 'offending' acts may be ways of coping with, or reacting to, their experience of social injustice rather than pathological symptoms of a deficient personality or dysfunctional family. It would define acts currently labelled 'crimes' or 'offences' as outside the criminal justice process if committed by children or young people under sixteen, redefining such acts as inappropriate or causing harm. Rather than a punitive response, such acts would lead to social welfare intervention. While recognizing the circumstances in which such acts are committed, welfare-based intervention would help young people appreciate the seriousness of the act, focusing on changing their behaviour through acceptance of responsibility for their actions. In the context of rights, this process would acknowledge the status of children while recognizing their specific needs, promoting their best interests and ensuring active participation.

The debate over rights, as discussed earlier, is not without structural context. Children's offending and antisocial behaviour, like their other life experiences and personal opportunities, are located within powerful, structural determining contexts.

Through unemployment, poverty and differential opportunities class impacts significantly on communities, families and children. The politics of reproduction, in the context of patriarchy, creates quite different possibilities – and probabilities – for girls and young women in both the private and the public spheres. Sexuality remains forbidden territory until puberty, when gendered ideologies reinforce femininity, hegemonic masculinity and heterosexism. Finally, racism – within the politics of neo-colonialism – remains a formidable barrier to equality of opportunity for any child defined as 'ethnic minority'. While each individual's experiences are distinctively mediated, these are powerful ideological as well as material determinants. Yet they remain 'determining contexts' rather than mechanisms of total determination. Formally and informally, attitudinal and institutionalized ideologies and practices have been contested and, at all levels, some significant social and political changes have been effected. Despite the resistance and achievements of individuals and the excellent work done by children's rights organizations and children's advocates across professions, the advancement of a positive rights agenda remains limited. The success of creating and implementing such an agenda depends on a more fundamental shift in the structural relations and determining contexts of power which marginalize and exclude children and young people from effective participation in their destinies.

REFERENCES

AMA (1994) *Checklist for Children: Local Authorities and the UN Convention on the Rights of the Child,* London, Association of Metropolitan Authorities.

Audit Commission (1996) *Misspent Youth: Young People and Crime,* London, Audit Commission.

Butler-Sloss, Dame P. (2001) *Judgement: Between Jon Venables, Robert Thompson and News Group Newspapers Ltd, Associated Newspapers Ltd, MGM Ltd,* High Court of Justice, QBD, 8 January 2001.

Campbell, B. (1993) *Goliath: Britain's Dangerous Places,* London, Methuen.

CRDU (1994) *UK Agenda for Children,* London, Children's Rights Development Unit.

Children's Rights Office (1995) *Making the Convention Work for Children,* London, Children's Rights Office.

Christie, N. (1994) *Crime Control as Industry: Towards Gulags Western Style* (2nd edn), London, Routledge.

Cohen, S. (2001) *States of Denial: Knowing about Atrocities and Suffering,* Cambridge, Polity Press.

Davis, H. and Bourhill, M. (1997) '"Crisis": the demonization of children and young people' in P. Scraton (ed.) *'Childhood' in 'Crisis'?,* London, UCL Press.

de Haan, W. (1991) 'Abolitionism and crime control: a contradiction in terms' in K. Stenson and D. Cowell (eds) *The Politics of Crime Control,* London, Sage.

Dennis, N. (1993) *Rising Crime and the Dismembered Family: How Conformist Intellectuals have Campaigned against Common Sense,* London, Institute of Economic Affairs.

Dennis, N. and Erdos, G. (1992) *Families without Fatherhood,* London, Institute of Economic Affairs.

Fionda, J. (1999) 'New Labour, old hat: youth justice and the Crime and Disorder Act 1998', *Criminal Law Review*, January, pp. 36–47.

Franklin, B. and Petley, J. (1996) 'Killing the age of innocence: newspaper reporting and the death of James Bulger' in J. Pilcher and S. Wagg (eds) *Thatcher's Children? Politics, Childhood and Society in the 1980s and 1990s*, London, Falmer Press.

Freeden, M. (1991) *Rights*, Milton Keynes, Open University Press.

Freeman, M. (2000) 'The future of children's rights', *Children and Society*, vol. 14 (3), pp. 277–93.

Goldson, B. (1997) 'Children in trouble: state responses to juvenile crime' in P. Scraton (ed.) *'Childhood' in 'Crisis'?*, London, UCL Press.

Goldson, B. (1999) *Youth Justice: Contemporary Policy and Practice*, Aldershot, Ashgate.

Goldson, B. and Peters (2000) *Tough Justice: Responding to Children in Trouble*, London, Children's Society.

Hay, C. (1995) 'Mobilization through interpellation: James Bulger, juvenile crime and the construction of a moral panic', *Social and Legal Studies*, vol. 4, no. 2, pp. 197–223.

Haydon, D. and Scraton, P. (2000) '"Condemn a little more, understand a little less": the political context and rights implications of the domestic and European rulings in the Venables–Thompson case', *Journal of Law and Society*, vol. 27, no. 3, pp. 416–48.

Hodgkin, R. and Newell, P. (1998) *Implementation Handbook for the Convention on the Rights of the Child*, New York, United Nations Children's Fund (UNICEF).

Howard League for Penal Reform (1995) *Banged Up, Beaten Up, Cutting Up*, London, Howard League for Penal Reform.

Howard League for Penal Reform (1999) *Protecting the Rights of Children*, briefing paper, London, Howard League for Penal Reform.

Hudson, B. (1996) *Understanding Justice: An Introduction to Ideas, Perspectives and Controversies in Modern Penal Theory*, Milton Keynes, Open University Press.

Hudson, B. (2001) 'Punishment, rights and difference: defending justice in the risk society' in K. Stenson and R. Sullivan (eds) *Crime, Risk and Justice: The Politics of Crime Control in Liberal Democracies*, Cullompton, Willan.

Méndez, J.E. (1997) 'In defence of transitional justice' in A.J. McAdams (ed.) *Transitional Justice and the Rule of Law in New Democracies*, Notre Dame IN, University of Notre Dame Press.

Muncie, J. (1999) 'Institutionalized intolerance: youth justice and the 1998 Crime and Disorder Act', *Critical Social Policy*, vol. 19. no. 2. pp. 147–75.

Muncie, J. (2000) 'Decriminalizing criminology' in G. Lewis, S. Gewirtz and J. Clarke (eds) *Rethinking Social Policy*, London, Sage.

Murray, C. (1990) *The Emerging British Underclass*, London, Institute of Economic Affairs.

Murray, C. (1994) *Underclass: The Crisis Deepens*, London, Institute of Economic Affairs.

Scraton, P. (1997) 'Whose "childhood"? What "crisis"?' in P. Scraton (ed.) *'Childhood' in 'Crisis'?*, London, UCL Press.

UK government (1999) *Convention on the Rights of the Child: Second Report to the UN Committee on the Rights of the Child by the United Kingdom,* London, HMSO.

UN Committee on the Rights of the Child (1995) *Concluding Observations of the Committee on the Rights of the Child: United Kingdom of Great Britain and Northern Ireland,* CRC/C/14, Add. 34 (15 February 1995).

Part V

Detention and retribution

In the prevailing dominant discourse about 'the crime problem', things are seemingly simple and straightforward in terms both of the causes of crime and, equally, of what is to be done about the criminal. Crime is a crime and the criminal deserves to be caught and punished. Within this discourse an ideology of 'popular punitiveness' holds sway, emphasizing the importance of punishing offenders for their wrongdoing in the name of retribution, chiefly by means of custodial detention. The moral justification of punishment is that the offender deserves it. In the 1990s this strategy of crime control was most clearly articulated in the political soundbite 'prison works'. In some respects it might be assumed that 'popular punitiveness' has less purchase in the field of youth justice than in the punishment of adult offenders, given the historical ascendancy of the combined logics of welfare and justice throughout the twentieth century. However, it is contended in contributions to this part of the volume that detention and retributive punishment have always occupied a crucial place in the routine control of the 'youth problem' across most modern societies.

Part V opens with John Muncie's critical history of the detention centre in the post-war United Kingdom. He traces the emergence of the 'experiment' of the detention centre, beginning in 1948, when young offenders aged between fourteen and twenty-one were sent into custody for a short period and exposed to an explicitly punitive regime. Muncie clearly shows that recurrent appeals to custodial 'short, sharp shocks' by politicians and policy makers in the field of youth justice were not based on any rational, 'evidence-led' understanding. Detention centres have consistently failed in their primary purpose of deterring their 'subjects' from reoffending. Rather, the continued attraction of custodial detention to politicians is shown to reside in its emotive and popular appeal in the context of law-and-order politics. Echoing the French historian Michel Foucault's aphorism regarding the history of the modern prison, Muncie notes that 'failure never matters' in the punitive detention of young offenders. The populist political need to be seen to be 'acting tough' on youthful crime by means of repressive penal policy outweighs logical, rational arguments from criminology, research and practical experience.

Chapter 23 by Jonathan Simon focuses on developments in youth crime control in the United States since the Second World War as a means of exploring a much larger sociological question – namely, whether we are witnessing a new era in the history of modern punishment. He follows the long sociological tradition, from the work of Durkheim and Elias to that of Foucault and Garland, in arguing that exploring developments in punishment is important for exploring the 'self-understanding' of societies more generally.

Simon is widely known for his work with Malcolm Feeley in which they argue that the old penology of correctionalism and rehabilitation has been increasingly undermined by the rise of a new, pragmatic, risk management-oriented discourse of actuarial justice (as discussed in Part VI of this volume). In Chapter 23 Simon uses the emergence of the punitive experiment of the 'boot camp' in the United States in the mid-1990s to illustrate his thesis that 'emotive', authoritarian discourses overlap with the new actuarialism. In part, such experiments in custodial detention have been justified as cheaper alternatives to the prison. It is claimed by their proponents that short and intense periods of retributive punishment can be successful in transforming and reforming offenders (and thus in reducing recidivism). However, Simon finds no sign yet of success on these fronts. Echoing Muncie's reference to 'failure never matters' in the punitive detention of young offenders, Simon argues that the secret of the popularity of boot camps lies in the political and cultural message they offer the population. For Simon, the boot camp is an exercise in 'wilful nostalgia', acting as a form of compensation for the anxieties generated by present uncertainties. The essential political and populist attraction of this penal innovation would appear to reside in its promise of a rapid transformation of the young delinquent's 'soul'. Experiments in crime control in the United States have, of course, been massively influential in affecting policy and practice internationally. One of the lessons to be drawn from Simon's account is that the influence of vindictiveness and nostalgia for the 'good old days' cannot be discounted in contemporary strategies of youth justice and crime control.

Chapter 24 by Andrew Rutherford and Chapter 25 Thomas Mathiesen again offer us critiques of the logic of penal incapacitation. However, they differ in emphasis from the chapters by Muncie and Simon in two important ways. First, neither Rutherford nor Mathiesen is explicitly concerned with youth justice *per se*; instead, the focus is on the broader issues of retributive punishment and the crisis of the prison. Second, both of these writers move beyond mere critique of the existing, dominant strategy by developing alternative policy, political and cultural agendas for reform. Rutherford is a famous penal reform campaigner as well as an academic, who is most associated with the promotion of an 'alternatives to custody' discourse. Having noted the contemporary expansion of prison systems, in Chapter 24 Rutherford outlines what he terms a 'reductionist agenda' of penal reform. In particular, he argues against the dominant 'common sense' by maintaining that policy choice on prison population size does exist and that such choices need to be made. He puts forward nine items on a realistic 'wish list' for the reduction of prison populations, ending with the most challenging item, namely that the scope of the criminal law should be narrowed and that of civil law approaches to dispute resolution and redress increased.

Chapter 25 from the Norwegian abolitionist Thomas Mathiesen shares many of these concerns. Mathiesen also prioritizes the importance of recognizing the possibilities of change and the existence of political choices. Drawing on historical evidence, he goes on to outline four major possibilities for addressing the recurrent crisis of the prison: penal systems could be 'frozen in size'; they could be 'reduced in size'; they could be 'partially abolished', or they could be 'fully abolished'. As a leading exponent of abolitionism, Mathiesen argues that we need to do away with punitive responses to criminalized problems. We also need to reimagine the possibilities and potential for social change. In support of this argument, he cites the movement for the abolition of slavery in the nineteenth century as a seemingly utopian and unrealistic campaign that nonetheless helped radically transform power relations and the sources of human misery in the modern world. Some 'short-term' concrete steps could be taken in order to transform existing penal policy, through both legislation and what Mathiesen terms 'policy preparation'. In conclusion, Mathiesen moves beyond Rutherford's reformist and reductionist agenda in calling for a fuller 'long-term' restructuring of our thinking about crime, to the extent that we might be able to abandon – or abolish – the very concept of crime and replace it with the notion of 'problematic situations'.

The final chapter in this part, by Barry Goldson, analyses the resurgent appeal, particularly since the 1990s, of a custodial and punitive response to troubled and troublesome children and young people. Goldson clearly shows that the punitive incarceration of children is not a new phenomenon in the United Kingdom. Echoing Muncie's argument, Goldson views the history of child incarceration as a story of political expediency and incompetence, producing in its wake human suffering and human rights abuses. Of particular concern is the highly charged re-emergence of 'popular punitiveness', first under Conservative administrations in the 1990s and subsequently developed by New Labour administrations into the twenty-first century. Overall, Goldson concludes that we are witnessing an intensified thirst for harsher punishments for children and young people, aided and abetted by the strategy of responsibilization and the atavistic appeal of popular vengeance. The depressing but realistic conclusion reached by Goldson is that authoritarian policies of child incarceration will continue to remain both abiding and growing features on the contemporary landscape of youth justice in the United Kingdom, not least as a result of the emulation of punitive lessons from the United States.

22

Failure never matters: detention centres and the politics of deterrence

John Muncie

On the 1st of October 1988 a landmark was reached in post-war penal policy. Legislation within the Criminal Justice Act of that year officially ended an 'experiment' with the treatment of young offenders that had lasted exactly 40 years. Detention centre orders, popularly renowned as regimes of short, sharp shock, were merged with youth custody orders into a single sentence of 'detention in a young offender institution'. Whether this means that the particular regimes of short, sharp shock, based on military drill and strict discipline, have been phased out in all institutions is debatable, but their foreclosure, at least in name, revealed the government's acknowledgement that the 'experiment' had come to an end. It does however, remain possible, for the Prison Service to send young male offenders aged 14 to 21 to custodial institutions tailor-made to deal with those on short sentences. Indeed the Prison Service clearly do not view the move to a combined sentence as earmarking a fundamental change in regimes. A 'brisk induction period' remains a key element particularly for those on sentences of four months or less (*Prison Service College Briefing* no. 2, 1988). The new institutions retain the same staff and facilities and are detention centres and youth custody centres in all but name. But as the term 'detention centre' fades out of public view it is apposite to recall how a regime described variously as 'brutal, brutalising and pointless' (Children's Legal Centre, 1985) and as 'creating in young criminals a wholesome dread of punishment' (Butler, Conservative Home Secretary, 1958) managed to survive forty years of controversy and failure.

'A SHORT, BUT SHARP REMINDER'

> There is a type of offender to whom it appears necessary to give a short but sharp reminder that he is getting into ways that will inevitably land him in disaster ... their ('detention centres') regime will consist of harsh discipline and hard work. (*Hansard*, 1947, vol. 44)

SOURCE: This chapter is taken from *Critical Social Policy*, No. 28, 1990, pp. 53–66.

These are not the words of William Whitelaw, Leon Brittan or some other Conservative spokesperson of the Thatcher administration, but rather part of a speech by Chuter Ede, the then Labour Home Secretary, introducing to Parliament in 1947 his Government's Criminal Justice Bill.

The earliest reference to the need for a short custodial sentence for young offenders can be found in the views expressed by a number of witnesses to the Departmental Committee on the treatment of young offenders who reported in 1927 that 'on all grounds we should like to see an alternative to prison ... It may be suggested that in some cases a short period of detention would serve an effective purpose in breaking up bad companionships which have contributed towards delinquency'[1] (Home Office, 1927).

Strong appeals were made at this time that the practice of sending boys under 21 to prison be curtailed, as this resulted in 'contamination of young minds' and the manufacture of criminality. Magistrates could sentence young offenders to six months' borstal, but in effect this meant committing them to prison, since every borstal trainee spent up to three months in Wormwood Scrubs whilst awaiting allocation to an appropriate institution. However, the idea of setting up an alternative to prison was rejected on the grounds that it would interrupt schooling and did not allow sufficient time for rehabilitative training.

The idea did not surface again until 1938 when the Cadogan committee concluded its report on the abolition of birching. It noted that magisterial use of corporal punishment had declined steadily since 1900 and that the juvenile courts lacked a penalty to deal with minor offenders whose criminality was due, in the main, to 'nothing more than a misguided sense of adventure'. What was required, in its view, was some form of 'short, sharp punishment which will pull him up and give him the lesson which he needs'; an institution where offenders would 'hate the place sufficiently to determine them never to return and furthermore to tell other members of their gang about its unpleasantness' (Home Office, 1938, para. 31).

These early debates on the efficacy of a short, punitive sentence were thus cloaked in the discourse of deterrence but also of liberal reform. The key concern was to implement a system in which neither prison nor corporal punishment played a part in the treatment of minor offenders. Indeed the Criminal Justice Bill of 1938 whilst including the committee's recommendations on the abolition of corporal punishment, made no provision for special places of detention. Instead, it recommended the use of Saturday Attendance centres and Howard Houses.[2] The establishment of detention centres may have ended there and then, but the onset of the Second World War prevented the Bill from reaching the statute [book].

After the war a different moral and political climate was prevalent. During the period of the war, there had been a large increase in recorded offending by the young. The number of recorded offenders aged 17 to 21 had increased by nearly 50 per cent (Land, 1975, p. 318). It is also clear that the war-time experience of the military detention centre or 'glasshouse' had some impact on those who were looking for alternatives to imprisonment and corporal punishment. Whilst the idea of short-term detention had existed for some 20 years, its precise form, as formulated after the war, undoubtedly owed much to the experience of dealing with absconders in the war years[3] (see Choppen, 1970 and Crow, 1979).

Against this background of higher crime rates and a magistracy that seemed intent on introducing some form of short-term custody, it became clear that if the government still wanted to abolish corporal punishment then it would have to be seen to be replacing it with other severe measures. As a result the Criminal Justice Act of 1948 enabled the courts to make a detention centre order for three (or exceptionally six) months for offenders aged from 14 to 21 who had committed an offence for which a term of imprisonment could have been imposed and who had not previously served a borstal or prison sentence, and where the court had considered every other method and had concluded that none were appropriate. The proposed detention centres were split between those for juniors (14 to 16) and seniors (17 to 21). Both forms were to be administered by the Prisons Commission.[4] The passage of the 1948 Act through the Commons evoked surprisingly little interest (Dunlop and McCabe, 1965, p. 2). MPs who might have wished to retain corporal punishment seemed satisfied with variations on the theme of short and sharp punishment, whilst those who were concerned that the centres would merely replicate prisons for young people could only await events, given the vagueness of the government proposals.[5] Very little information was given on what kind of institution a detention centre would be in practice or on the characteristics of those who might populate it (Land, 1975, p. 324). The Home Secretary excused the vagueness of the proposals on the grounds that the centres were an 'experiment'. Whilst this proved an effective tactic for getting the legislation through Parliament, it also helped obscure the character of detention centres and gave the Prisons Commission almost total discretion in constructing their regimes.

This is a recurring theme in the history of detention centres. Any subsequent perceived failure or lack of precise definition of purpose has been passed over as temporary and thus retrievable. Given that detention centres were continually in an 'experimental stage', opposition was circumvented. Such a political tactic also allowed its proponents to remain vague about the actual regimes involved and preclude any real debate.

Such vagaries were generated because detention centres were at one and the same time promoted as a liberal alternative to prison *and* as a harsh deterrent, depending on the political persuasion of the audience. From the outset the detention centre was legitimated through the contradictory notion that those sentenced to the regime should be punished, but also treated and, hopefully, cured of their offending behaviour.

'DE-TEDDYFYING THE TEDDY BOYS'

Although on the statute in 1948, the first detention centre did not open until 1952. Their early development was affected by problems of finding suitable locations, buildings, staff and financial resources. The Prison Commission's report for 1951 announced that a 'pilot' junior detention centre at Campsfield House (a converted workhouse) in Oxfordshire would be opened in the following year. Its regime promised to deliver a 'short, sharp shock' and 'from the start a boy must do as he is told' (Home Office, 1953). However the warden of Campsfield House also insisted that whilst detention centres should be first and foremost punitive, he intended to introduce reformative and educational influences. Indeed Grunhut's (1955) study of the first 100 receptions described a regime of medium security in which boys were expected to work largely in gardening and in the laundry and if of school age to attend education classes in the morning and afternoon. The regime appeared to differ from borstal only in the respects that physical training and the degree of supervision were more prominent. A majority were committed for three months; 9 per cent had no previous convictions, 75 per cent had up to three previous convictions and 15 per cent were described as having serious criminal experience (such classification may be questioned: this latter category included one boy who took a motor car, whilst on probation). Twenty one per cent were reconvicted within the first six months after their release. Grunhut (1955, p. 208) concluded that a short custodial sentence was more likely to succeed with those who had not previously experienced any strict institutional discipline (as in an approved school or remand home) and that release should be followed by a considerable period of probation and after-care.

The success of detention centres and in particular the question of who should populate them was from the start, characterised by inconsistency and uncertainty. Magistrates were reluctant to commit first offenders to what was considered a severe punishment, yet Grunhut's research appeared to show that it was with this section that 'success' was more likely.[6]

The emphasis on physical training also highlighted some of the contradictions of the detention centre philosophy. The warden of Blantyre House (the first senior centre opened in 1954) explained how physical training was mainly responsible for the 'fresh and healthy outlook on life' that was achieved. However, if the regime was meant to be so unpleasant that the offender would not want to return, then once inmates began to enjoy their physical training, this objective was defeated (Land, 1975, p. 339). The 1955 Report of the Prison Commission in some contradiction, noted with approval that physical training had engendered a corporate spirit among inmates, providing an interest in personal progress and pride in achievement.[7]

Despite these dilemmas, the numbers of detention centres first rose cautiously to two for juniors and two for seniors by 1957, but then more rapidly to a total of twelve by 1963. The reasons for this initial expansion are not to be found in any newly defined statement of purpose or in any proven deterrent effect, but in consideration of the prevailing mood of the politics of punishment.

Butler, appointed Home Secretary in 1957, looked forward to developing penal establishments as places of rehabilitation and training, rather than as places of punishment. However, whatever innovative policies he had in mind were soon subdued under increased pressure from his own party, the Magistracy and the Prison Commission to increase detention centre provision. Between 1955 and 1957 the official statistics showed a dramatic increase in the crime rate, particularly for 17 to 21 year olds, and magistrates had responded by sending more boys to prison for a period of six months or less. In 1958 magistrates expressed their dissatisfaction at the lack of detention centre places and Butler was obliged to instigate a review because 'the system has been subjected to severe strains as a result of the great increases in crime in this age group' (Home Office, 1959). Grunhut's (1959–60) sequel to his 1955 study was referred to by the Prisons Commission to substantiate further expansion, because although he now recorded reconviction rates of 45 per cent for juniors and 56 per cent for seniors within two years of release, he still maintained that the institution worked for the 'good risks' who had few previous convictions. He also remained at pains to applaud its reformative potential.

The demands for increasing places of short detention also took place against media outrage of the rising crime rate in which it was suggested that the problem lay in loosening family relationships and the cure in imposing discipline and restraint. At the Conservative Party Conference in 1958 delegates advocating a return to corporal punishment as the only response to 'a society dominated by young thugs' received 'cheers of applause'. Butler announced to conference that he wanted 'to create in young criminals a wholesome dread of punishment, but was opposed to flogging or birching. Rather 'some new method was needed of dealing with the young criminal ... the new detention centre. The object is de-Teddyfying the Teddy Boys and that is having a deterrent effect' (The *Times* 10 October, 1958). In the absence of any alternative which would appease the punishment lobby, short of reintroducing corporal punishment, the 1961 Criminal Justice Act opened the way for detention centres to replace short-term imprisonment as the standard custodial disposal for young offenders.

As a result the numbers of young men passing through detention centre each year steadily increased from less than 2000 at the end of the 1950s, to 6000 in the middle 1960s and to over 10,000 in the middle 1970s. In 1962 the regime at Send detention centre was described as

> typical in its austerity and no concessions are made to relaxation and comfort ... Reveille is at 6.10 ... and movement is ceaseless until tea at 5 o'clock. Time is occupied by parades, drills and physical training, outside work on the centre's market garden, cleaning and general duties and by frequent changes of clothes. Lights are out by 9.30. The emphasis is on strict discipline, hard work, appearance and deportment, cleanliness and respect for staff and other inmates. (*Justice of Peace Review* vol cxxvi, 8 September 1962).

Nevertheless the Home Office continued to justify their existence as 'part of a constructive reformative system in which the staff would make a real effort to find out what was wrong with a boy and put it right' (Home Office, 1959).[8]

Indeed a sole emphasis on punishment came under increasing fire during the 1960s. Prison officers, especially, found it difficult to sustain a solely negative approach and, unhappy with the exclusively 'punisher' role, attempted, with varying degrees of failure, to temper this with more positive elements. In this they were to some degree supported by a developing liberal consensus which informed would-be penal reformers throughout the 1960s. The rehabilitative ideal emanating from the growth of welfare professionalism filtered down towards the detention centre. The 1961 Act, on the advice of Grunhut, introduced the compulsory after-care of detainees and by 1967 the Home Office drew attention to the importance of 'establishing relationships between individual members of staff and boys' in order to effect 'an element of individual treatment' (Home Office, 1967). This period of welfare treatment optimism culminated in the 1969 Children and Young Persons Act which advocated the phasing out of junior centres altogether and the Home Office's report on detention centres in 1970 applauded the move from the 'short, sharp shock' to 'a more positive approach' (Home Office, 1970, para. 2). How much of this official discourse was actually present in day-to-day practice remains open to question. For example although the 1969 Act promised abolition, the use of detention centres positively burgeoned during the 1970s. The treatment focus of juvenile justice was circumvented by a new Conservative government, supported by the magistracy and the Advisory Council on the penal system. Instead of replacing custodial measures with community-based disposals, the treatment measures were used simply to expand the system to include a younger and less delinquent population.

Much of this was due to a sustained and purposeful campaign waged by magistrates who believed that full implementation of the 1969 Act would transfer their power into the hands of social workers. As a result by 1981 it could be stated that 'the number of juveniles sent to detention centre and borstal has risen fivefold since 1965. Less than one fifth of the rise relates directly to increased offending, the remainder is caused by an increased tendency to give custodial sentences for almost all types of offence' (DHSS, 1981, quoted in Muncie, 1984, p. 154). The fact that reconviction rates had, by 1974, risen to 73 per cent of juniors and 50 per cent of seniors was of little importance. By then a new category of the 'hard core and persistent offender' had been created in the wake of the systems expansion. Whilst treatment was offered to offenders at the newly created 'soft end', those sections who had always occupied custodial institutions were now seen as 'tough and sophisticated criminals' and thus disqualified from the more 'lenient' measures, even though their offending history was no worse than those inmates of the 1960s (Pratt, 1983, p. 26). The fact of their reconviction merely helped secure the popular impression that they were also 'intractable' and 'not affected by any penalty'.

Speaking in a wide ranging debate on law and order in the House of Commons in February 1978 Whitelaw, the then Conservative Opposition Spokesperson on Home affairs, stated that the only possible solution was to

> set up an experimental project with severe discipline providing short, sharp, shock treatment ... to promote public confidence in our whole penal system by saying that we are prepared to try and deal with the small minority of young thugs who thumb their noses up at authority and laugh at all the present penal arrangements (*Hansard*, vol. 95, 1978).

Once again the imagery of a 'short, sharp shock' was evoked to bolster the impression that a new and untried initiative was being introduced into penal policy. Once more the practice of introducing overtly deterrent measures was legitimised by calling them an 'experiment'.

'THESE WILL BE NO HOLIDAY CAMPS'

During the 1970s a succession of moral panics about football hooliganism, juvenile delinquency, mugging, trade unions, immigration, international terrorism and sexual permissiveness were identified as evidence of a growing moral degeneration and a crisis of authority in Britain. Consequently, the Conservative Party conducted their entire general election campaign of 1979 around the themes of law and order and the rule of law. The result of the election demonstrated that such issues indeed touched a popular nerve and marked a dramatic shift away from social democratic ideologies to those of an authoritarian populism (Holt, 1985, p. 28).

In the field of juvenile justice, this new authoritarianism was duly expressed in a 'new' get tough approach to offenders. At conference in October 1979 the newly appointed Home Secretary William Whitelaw announced that detention centres were to be reformed so that

> life will be conducted at a brisk tempo. Much greater emphasis will be put on hard and constructive activities, on discipline and tidiness, on self-respect and respect for those in authority ... These will be no holiday camps and those who attend them will not ever want to go back (Thornton *et al.*, 1984, para. 1).

The denigration of existing detention centres as 'holiday camps', however dubious, heralded a new onslaught on the rehabilitative ideal and a shift towards an ideology based on punishment and an obsession with vindictiveness (Pitts, 1988, pp. 40–59).

A pilot project, which had been officially described as an 'experiment' in the 1979 election manifesto, was established in April 1980 at New Hall – a senior detention centre – and at Send – a junior detention centre. The new short, sharp shock regimes included increased emphasis on a more sustained pace in carrying out tasks, hard physical work, more physical education, fewer privileges, less association, an earlier time for lights out and an increase in the number of parades, inspections and drill sessions (Home Office, 1984). At New Hall, the Construction Industry Training Course, which gave young offenders some work experience, was closed on the grounds that it was inappropriate to the tougher regime (NACRO, 1984). The 'experiment' was to be evaluated by the Home Office's Young Offender Psychology Unit; its brief being to assess whether young offenders can be effectively deterred from committing further offences by spending a period of weeks in a detention centre with a more vigorous and demanding regime. The results of the evaluation should have been (and probably were) already known by the Home Office. The Prison Department, in their evidence to a sub-committee of the House of Commons Expenditure Committee had noted in 1978 that all available evidence suggested that alterations in prison regimes were irrelevant as far as reconviction rates were concerned. It had already urged 'extreme caution' in proceeding with the tougher regimes project. Indeed when he first raised the idea, Whitelaw had confessed that he did not think that 'this scheme will necessarily work' (*Hansard* vol. 945, 1978) and when the experiment was announced the message from the Home Office was that 'Whitelaw himself had no faith in the regime he had introduced' (Shaw, 1985, p. 2). However he was in no doubt as to the experiment's political popularity and its ability to act as a punitive, enduring and strong symbol of social order. Moreover at the time of the announcement Whitelaw also had to deal with the mounting problem of prison overcrowding. His solution – an early release scheme for adult prisoners – could only be accepted politically if he was not seen to be going soft in other areas. It was significant then that the experiment was suddenly extended to two more detention centres in 1981, before the results of the evaluation were known and just one month before Whitelaw, unsuccessfully, attempted to convince the Conservative Party Conference of the need for an early release scheme.

The government showed no great hurry to publish the results of the evaluation of the experiment. Official forecasts of the publication date drifted from late 1982 until the report finally appeared in July 1984. In evaluating the primary purpose of the experiment, the researchers investigated several aspects including trainee characteristics and reactions, staff reactions and reconviction rates. They concluded that 'the introduction of the pilot project had no discernible effect on the rate at which trainees were reconvicted' (Thornton *et al.*, 1984, para. 8.21). The actual reconviction rates 12 months after release from Send were 57 per cent both before and after the experiment; at New Hall the rate rose from 46 per cent to 48 per cent. Moreover when the crime figures for the Pilot Project catchment areas were examined, it was not possible to show that the new regimes had any effect on the general levels of recorded crime; leading the researchers to conclude that there was no evidence that the Pilot Regimes had any general deterrent effect (Thornton *et al.*, 1984, para. 7.6).

Doubt was also expressed as to whether the new regimes were experienced by trainees as more rigorous and demanding. Indeed some of the activities on which strong emphasis was placed, such as drill and physical education were comparatively popular; more so than the continuous chore of a humdrum work party which they replaced (Thornton *et al.*, 1984, para. 3.142).

Two years after the introduction of the experiment, the Prison Officers' Association had already reported that they believed the extra drill 'to be a waste of time, a boring and demoralizing activity' (Shaw, 1985, p. 3). The Chief Inspector of Prisons had also noted that the level of staff morale had 'undoubtedly slipped during the period since the regime had first been applied' (quoted in NACRO, 1984).

Despite such findings, Whitelaw's successor, Leon Brittan, formally announced in a written reply to a question at the Commons that the tougher regimes would not be abandoned, but would be *extended* to all detention centres. Once again the enduring qualities of 'short, sharp shock' were to be grounded in political expediency, rather than in its real practical effects, established by the Home Office's own sponsored research.

In February 1985 a new consistent regime was authorised throughout the detention centre system. However those activities such as physical education that had been enjoyed by inmates were reduced to a minimum, whilst those activities which were least liked, such as scrubbing and cleaning, were extended.

The political need for a repressive penal policy again overshadowed logical argument. The 'new supertough' philosophy merely activated minor shifts in the style of the deterrence, rather than altered the logic of existing penal philosophy. This was not a difficult feat to achieve. As Harris (1982, p. 248) argued: 'punitive and liberal legislation are judged by different criteria, the latter being immediately at risk when it fails to reduce recidivism, but the former, however ineffective appearing to a society in which to punish wrongdoing seems natural, to contain an intrinsic logic'.

Without too much difficulty then, Brittan was able to shift the debate away from the failure of the experiment to produce lower reconviction rates towards the need to establish 'a positive and well defined regime'. He continued:

> the new detention centre regime will be a marked improvement over the regime which was in operation before the tougher regimes experiment was introduced in 1980. In incorporating much of the experimental regime on a permanent basis, it will provide a penalty to which the courts can turn with confidence when dealing with an offender for whom a short period in custody is necessary.

> (Brittan quoted in *Childright* no. 10, 1984)

'HUMILIATED, ISOLATED AND WORTHLESS'

Brittan's initiative, designed to restore the 'courts' confidence' was, however, to misfire, largely through the unintended consequences of his government's own legislation.

Before the 1982 Criminal Justice Act, magistrates had a vested interest in expanding the detention centre network. The detention centre was their main custodial resource, with the three month detention centre order one of their most concrete and secure powers. However, the 1982 Act substantially increased their power and discretion throughout the sentencing tariff. For example, magistrates in the juvenile court could now commit offenders directly to youth custody centres (previously borstals), whereas previously they were limited to making recommendations for borstal training to be reconsidered by the higher court. The Act also stipulated that detention centre orders could be made for three weeks and up to a maximum of four months.

In practice magistrates used these powers not to expand the very short sentence population, but to give many more youth custody orders. So, for example, between July 1984 and June 1985, 6 per cent fewer 17–21 year olds were sentenced to detention centres than in 1982, and youth custody receptions of 15 and 16 year olds increased by 41 per cent, compared to borstal receptions in 1982. It was apparent that substantial numbers of young offenders, who might formerly have been received into a detention centre, were received under a youth custody order; a shift which also represents a tendency of magistrates to sentence higher up the sentencing tariff.[9] Recurring stories of magistrates sentencing offenders for four months and one day to ensure youth custody entry revealed that the practice was not isolated (Shaw, 1985, p. 4). Clearly magistrates were more interested in delivering longer sentences, and were not to be distracted by the style of the new short deterrent.

This phenomenon had a devastating effect on the Prison Department. In January 1985 occupancy levels at detention centres were 59 per cent of total capacity, whilst youth custody centres were overflowing. From March 1985 to August 1987 eight detention centres – including the two used for the Tougher Regimes Experiment – were either closed or converted to help ease overcrowding in other parts of the prison system. By 1988 only 10 (of a 1982 maximum of 20) detention centres remained open.

From the instigation of Brittan's 'new sense of purpose', detention centres had come under fire from all quarters. In 1984 the Monday Club argued that the policy was 'based on gimmickry' and that little could be achieved with young offenders 'by shouting at them, giving them meaningless tasks and trying to make them feel as humiliated, isolated and worthless as possible'. The new regime was considered a 'trivial but potentially damaging intervention' (Monday Club, 1984). In 1986 Brittan's successor, Douglas Hurd, rejected the need for an independent review but admitted that the short, sharp shock was under utilised and was 'poor value for money' (quoted in Bottomley and Fielding, 1986, p. 280).[10] The 1984 Evaluation report had concluded that a majority of detention centre inmates were not the so-called 'hardcore', but comprised many 'unhappy individuals' with long histories of residential care and contacts with psychiatrists and psychologists (Thornton *et al.*, 1984, Tables 2.5 and 2.6).[11] The Children's Legal Centre (1984, 1985, 1986a, b, c, 1987) had also publicised a series of major scandals in detention centres concerning incidents of alleged ill-treatment and prison officer behaviour which was contrary to the 1983 Detention Centre Rules. The following is indicative: (from *Childright* no. 10, 1984)

> I am 16 years old ... It was very difficult being in Send. What I remember most of all is getting beat up by the screws – about five or six times ... They thought that I'd fight back but I never did. (Inmate)

> 'An officer in dealing with an inmate shall not use force unnecessarily.' (Rule 46)

In April 1985 police were called to Aldington Detention Centre to investigate allegations of brutality revealed anonymously by probation officers. In May 1986 The Inspectorate of Prisons cited incidents at Usk Detention Centre where Prison Officers behaved towards inmates 'in a way which could only be construed as humiliating and intimidating' (cited by Bottomly and Fielding, 1986, p. 280). By 1986 the Children's Legal Centre reported that nine prison officers had been dismissed and twenty-three suspended for 'a range of managerial reasons', since 1981. The trauma of detention centre on its inmates also resulted in 175 known cases of deliberate self injury between 1979 and April 1988 (*Childright*, no. 57, 1989); and two suicides in the detention centre unit at the Glenochil penal complex in Scotland (Scraton and Chadwick, 1985; Killeen, 1986; Pitts, 1988, pp. 57–9). In 1986 the Prison Officers' Association admitted that it was 'still not happy with the short, sharp shock syndrome' and added that it was concerned about the rising level of complaints (*Guardian*, 24 November, 1986). Not surprisingly probation officers, directors of social services, the Prison Reform Trust, NACRO and the Howard League for Penal Reform also added their own critical voices. Significantly though the Magistrates' Association also lent its support partly as a reaction to the cynicism of the government's insistence to extend the 'short, sharp shock' despite its reported failure (Rutherford, 1989). Faced with such opposition the government formally abolished the detention centre order in 1988. However it still remains the case that a regime of short, sharp, shock exists within some young offender institutions under the direction of the Prison Department.

'FAILURE NEVER MATTERS'

In 1975 Land had concluded her review of the history of detention centres by stating that they were 'an experiment which could not be allowed to fail' (Land, 1975, p. 344). Perhaps a more apposite epitaph in the late 1980s would be Foucault's lesson that 'failure never matters'. Land's conclusion refers to the fact that detention centres were established and expanded as the political price for the abolition of corporal punishment and for keeping young people out of adult prisons. Their development depended little on whether they were judged to be a success or failure.

The short, sharp shock persisted for 40 years with, despite the rhetoric, only superficial changes being made to its regime. The drift towards treatment in the 1960s was arguably little more than a public relations exercise and the tougher regimes' philosophy of the 1980s more a matter of words, than deeds. Detention centres have always operated a strict, brisk, tough and unpleasant regime. The case against the detention centre – that it has consistently failed in its primary objective of deterring from reoffending – is easy to make. Indeed the Home Office's handbook for courts advises that the perceived severity of penalties has little effect on deterring potential offenders (Home Office, 1986, para. 3.4). In fact in the history of detention centres reconviction rates, which from the start were 'disappointing', have steadily grown worse.

Since 1948, the shifts in detention centre policy identified above have depended less on responding to research evaluations or practical experience or indeed common criminological knowledge, but more to the political purchase of the slogan 'short, sharp shock'. At one time the policy could be sold on progressive grounds, as an alternative to prison, at others on punitive grounds, as a tough alternative to corporal punishment and as a legitimate punishment for the 'hard core'.

It is a history which reveals how political expediency has consistently taken precedence over rational argument in the formulation of post-war penal policy. In the 1990s, the detention centre, despite its demise, may well continue this process. The apparent lack of an overtly punitive sanction will doubtless be referred to as the Thatcher administration moves forward in its attempt to supplement custodial institutions with additional forms of 'punishment in the community'.

NOTES

1. Ward (1981) notes that the term 'short, sharp shock' may be derived from Gilbert and Sullivan's *Mikado*, where it referred to decapitation.
2. Significantly, the initial justification for Attendance centres was that they would provide a short and sharp punishment.
3. One writer, with 20 years' military experience, concluded, after observing one detention centre in the 1980s, that it would do most military camps credit (Etherton, quoted by Cain, 1988).
4. The Prisons Commission was responsible for all penal institutions and enjoyed a good deal of autonomy. It was dissolved in 1963 when its functions were transferred to the Home Office (Land, 1975, p. 313).
5. Whilst the 1948 Act abolished corporal punishment as a sentence, corporal punishment *within* penal establishments was not abolished until 1967.
6. Crow's research (1979) almost a quarter of a century later noted the same dilemma of the unjustifiable nature of giving a custodial sentence to first offenders, but also the ineffectiveness of detention centres to prevent the reoffending of the habitual offender.
7. This contradiction came to the fore again in 1984 when the Home Office noted that the presumed punitive aspects of physical training, in fact was that aspect of the regime most positively enjoyed and appreciated by its inmates.
8. The discourse of detention centre policy was, and remains, male dominated. Despite significant opposition a detention centre for girls was opened at Moor Court, near Stoke-on-Trent in 1962. It was closed seven years later, arguably because the practice of military drill and physical education was not considered appropriate in the 'training' of young women.
9. NACRO (1989b) notes how this trend has disproportionately affected young black offenders. They are imprisoned with fewer convictions than young white offenders and less likely to receive bail or non-custodial penalties. In 1987 12 per cent of the young male sentenced population and almost 20 per cent of the remand population were from ethnic minorities, even though they only made up some 5 per cent of the general population. However because of the tendency to give longer sentences a majority of these are contained within youth custody centres. For example on 30 June 1987 young offenders of West Indian or Indian origin made up some 7 per cent of the detention centre population, but some 14 per cent of those in the youth custody population who had been sentenced to over 18 months.
10. In the financial year 1985/5 the average cost per week of keeping a young person in a detention centre was £334 (*Childright* no. 24, 1986).
11. The notion of 'hard core' is also undermined by examining offender histories. In 1986 44 per cent of juveniles received into detention centre had been convicted of burglary, 25 per cent theft, handling stolen goods, fraud and forgery, 4 per cent robbery, 1 per cent sexual offences and 13 per cent violence against the person. Seventeen per cent had no previous convictions, 36 per cent had one or two convictions. (NACRO, 1988a.)

REFERENCES

Baldock, J.C. (1980) 'Why the prison population has grown larger and younger', *Howard Journal,* vol. 19.

Bottomley, K. and Fielding, N. (1986) *Howard Journal*, vol. 25, Penal Policy File no. 23.

Bottoms, A.E. (1977) 'Reflections on the Renaissance of dangerousness', *Howard Journal*, vol. 16.

Brittan, L. (1985) 'A new sense of purpose', *Community Care*, 2 May.

Cain, M.G. (1988) The History of the Detention Centre, MA Social Work thesis (unpublished), University of Leicester.

Children's Legal Centre (1984) 'Mr Brittan's blind confidence', *Childright*, no. 10.

Children's Legal Centre (1985) 'A brutal, brutalizing and pointless regime', *Childright*, no. 19.

Children's Legal Centre (1986a) 'The most terrible time you have had in your life', *Childright*, no. 29.

Children's Legal Centre (1986b) 'DC assault allegations dropped', *Childright*, no. 31.

Children's Legal Centre (1986c) 'Assault and abuse at DCs', *Childright*, no. 32.

Children's Legal Centre (1987) 'Short, sharp, shock can slide into unacceptable practices', *Childright*, no. 35.

Choppen, V. (1970) 'The origins of the philosophy of detention centres', *British Journal of Criminology*, vol. 10.

Cohen, S. (1985) *Visions of Social Control*, Cambridge, Polity.

Crow, I. (1979) *The Detention Centre Experiment: A Review*, NACRO.

Dunlop, A. and McCabe, S. (1965) *Young Men in Detention Centres,* Routledge.

Field, E. (1969) 'Research into detention centres', *British Journal of Criminology*, vol. 9.

Foucault, M. (1977) *Discipline and Punish: The Birth of the Prison*, Allen Lane.

Grunhut, M. (1955) 'Juvenile delinquents under punitive detention', *British Journal of Delinquency*, vol. 5.

Grunhut, M. (1959–60) 'After effects of punitive detention', *British Journal of Delinquency*, vol. 10.

Harris, R.J. (1982) 'Institutionalized ambivalence: social work and the Children and Young Persons Act 1969', *British Journal of Social Work*, vol. 12.

Holt, J. (1985) *No Holiday Camps: Custody, Juvenile Justice and the Politics of Law and Order*, Leicester, Association for Juvenile Justice.

Home Office (1927) *Report of the Departmental Committee on the Treatment of Young Offenders*, Cmnd. 2831, HMSO.

Home Office (1938) *Report of the Departmental Committee on Corporal Punishment*, Cmnd 5684, HMSO.

Home Office (1953) *Report of the Prison Commissioners for 1952*, Cmnd. 8948, HMSO.

Home Office (1959) *Penal Policy in a Changing Society*, Cmnd. 645, HMSO.

Home Office (1967) *Report on the Work of the Prison Department 1966*, Cmnd. 3088, HMSO.

Home Office (1970) *Detention Centre Report of the Advisory Council on the Penal System,* HMSO.

Home Office (1984) *Regimes in Detention Centres*, circular 9/1985.

Home Office (1986) *The Sentence of the Court*, HMSO.

Hudson, B. (1987) *Justice Through Punishment*, Macmillan.

Killeen, D. (1986) 'Short, sharp death', *New Society*, 15 August.

Land, H. (1975) 'Detention centres: the experiment which could not fail' in Hall, P. et al., *Change Choice and Conflict in Social Policy*, Heinemann.

Monday Club (1984) 'Juvenile crime, institutions for young offenders', Policy paper, December.

Muncie, J. (1984) *The Trouble With Kids Today: Youth and Crime in Post-war Britain*, Hutchinson.

Muncie, J. (1987) 'The juvenile criminal justice system', *Crime, Justice and Society* (D310) Block 3 Part 4, Open University.

NACRO (1984) *Tougher Regimes in Detention Centres*, NACRO.

NACRO (1985a) *Tougher Regimes in Detention Centres: The Evaluation Report*, NACRO.

NACRO (1985b) *Detention Centres*, NACRO.

NACRO (1988a) *Some Facts About Juvenile Crime*, NACRO.

NACRO (1988b) *Detention in a Young Offender Institution*, NACRO.

NACRO (1989a) *Imprisonment in the 1980s: Some Facts and Figures*, NACRO.

NACRO (1989b) *Some Facts and Findings about Black People in the Criminal Justice System*, NACRO.

NACRO (1989c) *The Cost of Penal Measures*, NACRO.

Perry, T. (1989) 'After the short, sharp shock', *Adjust*, no. 20.

Pitts, J. (1988) *The Politics of Juvenile Crime*, Sage.

Pratt, J. (1983) 'Intermediate treatment and the normalization crisis', *Howard Journal*, vol. 22.

Rutherford, A. (1986) *Growing Out of Crime*, Penguin.

Rutherford, A. (1989) 'The mood and temper of penal policy. Curious happenings in England during the 1980s', *Youth and Policy*, no. 27.

Shaw, S. (1985) 'Reflections on short, sharp shock', *Youth and Policy*, no. 13.

Thornton, D. et al. (1984) *Tougher Regimes in Detention Centres*, Home Office, HMSO.

Scraton, P. and Chadwick, K. (1985) 'The experiment that went wrong', *Abolitionist*, no. 20.

Ward, T. (1981) 'Short, sharp shocks and the politics of punishment', *Christian Action Journal*, Autumn.

23

The boot camp and the limits of modern penality

Jonathan Simon

INTRODUCTION: ARE WE POSTMODERN?

A number of scholars have begun to suggest that a significant rupture has occurred or is occurring in our practices of punishment and social control (Cohen, 1994; Feeley and Simon, 1992, 1994; Simon, 1993a; Brodeur, 1994; Garland, 1994; Nelken, 1994; Dumm, 1994). At their broadest, these analyses amount to the claim that modernity in punishment, which has been predominant since the end of the 18th century (and has traces going back centuries further), is coming to an end. The term 'postmodern' is deliberately tentative. It suggests that something is over, but does not describe what has begun. As Jean-Paul Brodeur (1994: 3) points out, the question of postmodernity is really two questions.

> The first question is *historical* and it relates to fact: is the situation now or that shortly will be prevailing in the field of penal practice discontinuous with what we have been experiencing for the last two centuries or is it the consolidation of a program that was expressed over the last two centuries and is now becoming self-conscious and self-critical? The second question is *theoretical*. Is the sociology of modernity an adequate framework in which to consider the present developments in penology?

Most of those engaged in the discussion of these questions share the sense that they cannot be resolved at the abstract level of theory. Terms like modern and postmodern are at best gross homogenizations of complex and contextually specific processes. They are useful primarily as 'grids' that we use to make historical sense of practices and discourses that surround us.

To some, no doubt, this entire debate is rather peripheral. It does not help us answer the pressing questions of policy formation. Nor does it develop (yet, at any rate) novel purposes or approaches to exercising or abolishing the power to punish,

SOURCE: This chapter is taken from *Social Justice*, vol. 22, No. 2, 1995, pp. 25–48 (abridged).

which has been so central to state formation in Western societies. For the moment, the question of whether current forms of punishment are postmodern turns on evidence of longer-term historical change. The specific tendencies of contemporary punishment may not provide a clear indication. For example, the rapid growth of imprisonment over the last two decades in the United States and to a lesser extent in the United Kingdom neither confirms nor denies the thesis that modern punishment is being fundamentally changed. Indeed, the growth of the system may indicate either the vigor of modern penal strategies or the dangerous distending of a system that is no longer functionally regulated by its internal processes or external environment. In short, we need to develop much richer middle-range accounts of penal strategies and practices before we can really answer questions about the fate of modern punishment.

Still, awareness of these larger questions seems relevant for two reasons. First, our major ways of thinking and talking about punishment and social control are modern. Hence our ability to recognize change, and ultimately to discuss even conjunctural events, is to some extent dependent on the continued validity of this modern understanding. Second, students of punishment and modernity (Foucault, 1977; Elias, 1978; Garland, 1990) have seen punishment as a leading sector of the modernization process in society as a whole. The break-up of modern penal strategies and understandings, if it is indeed occurring, may be significant for the self-understanding of these societies more generally.

The present article offers more grist for this mill by examining a new and remarkably popular penal innovation in the United States that offers hints to the robustness of penal modernity. Penal 'boot camps,' also known as 'shock incarceration programs,' have proliferated rapidly since they were first introduced in Georgia and Oklahoma in 1983 (Osler, 1991: 35). As of 1993, programs of various specifications approximating the boot-camp model had been set up by 30 states, 10 local jurisdictions, and the federal government (MacKenzie, 1993). The Violent Crime Control and Law Enforcement Act of 1994, enacted by the United States Congress in the fall, calls for appropriations of $150 million for grants to states to fund alternatives to traditional incarceration, specifically including boot camps. In addition, the Juvenile Justice and Delinquency Prevention Act of 1993 called for the conversion of up to 10 closed military bases into boot camps for state youth offenders.

The basic element of each of these programs is a reproduction in appearance and tone of military basic training of the type familiar throughout much of the 20th century and known colloquially as 'boot camp.' The new penal boot camps typically include military-style drilling and quartering, ceremonies at entrance and exit, harsh verbal evaluations from correctional officers trained to act like drill sergeants, and summary punishments for disciplinary infractions in the form of physically taxing exercises. In some places, officers and inmates are dressed in approximations of military uniforms and use terms derived from boot-camp lore.

Penal boot camps have, up to now, primarily targeted juveniles or young adult offenders. Most programs are limited to nonviolent first offenses. Most are of short duration, lasting only 90 to 120 days, followed by a period of supervised release in the community. From this basic core of military-style discipline and drilling, state penal programs have branched out to incorporate in varying degrees almost every significant move in the history of modern penality. All involve harsh manual work, with little training. All involve some variant of drug treatment. Some incorporate education, '12-step'-style substance abuse programs, and a therapeutic community (*Ibid.*). Increasingly, the programs include an 'aftercare' portion in which the improved habits presumably inculcated by the camp tactics are preserved by intensive parole supervision.

Programs also differ considerably in the procedures through which inmates are selected (Mackenzie and Piquero, 1994). In some, a judge chooses whether to send a person to boot camp. In others, a person already sent to prison by a judge may be diverted to a boot camp at the discretion of prison authorities. Recent studies suggest that the mode of selection influences whether the boot camp is filled with people who would otherwise be occupying prison beds or whether it draws in people who would otherwise be on probation, and thus influences whether it saves money over regular sentencing strategies (Mackenzie, 1994; Parent, 1994).

The most common official goals of boot-camp programs are to reduce recidivism and costs (*Ibid.*). Preliminary findings suggest that recidivism differences are marginal and that costs are saved only where selection procedures limit access to the prison bound (MacKenzie, 1994). (Even then, the savings are counterbalanced by any tendency to return boot-camp graduates to prison for violations at a higher rate than other offenders.) Hopes that the rigors of boot-camp life, with its emphasis on self-discipline coupled with rehabilitative education or training, would result in a better success rate after release to the community have yet to be borne out by the data (Parent, 1994).

Hints of failure, still provisional, have done little to dampen the boot camp's popularity. During a period of massive public concern with crime, when many policy matters have set criminal justice officials against politicians and the public against both, the boot camp has been one of the few initiatives that seems to resonate with all three. Penal administrators have recognized the need to improve their public profile at a time when the public expresses little confidence in the penal system (even as they support longer sentences). As Norval Morris (1993: 834–835) recently noted:

> Many prison administrators support the boot camp movement, not because they think that the short, sharp shock of military-style discipline will reform the criminal, but because that idea appeals politically, and to the public, and will allow a shortening of the prison term and a movement to a follow-up period of community-based treatment for drug abusers so sentenced.

Politicians have also recognized the boot camp as a chance to identify themselves with the 'values' of the public. Boot-camp scenes of young, usually African American men, dressed in humbling uniforms (no metals and epaulets here) and forced to stand or march in ranks, have become standard fare in campaign advertising. Once elected, public officials are drawn to promises of reduced costs associated with the shorter sentences and barracks-like structures.

Public commentators in the media and policy centers have also shown considerable enthusiasm for boot camps. Conservatives find in the boot camp confirmation of the philosophy that the collapse of personal discipline is behind the crime problem. Liberals applaud the rhetoric of transformation. The appeal is based, in part, on the fact that many adult males in the United States have actually been through basic training (Nix, 1993: 18). For many others, the absence of personal experience is easily filled by images in the popular culture that associate the boot camp with the most triumphant and affluent period for U.S. society, from its entry into World War II (1942) through at least its withdrawal from Vietnam (1973).

Whatever its merits as a policy choice, the boot camp and its popularity present an empirical focus for the discussion of modern penality and its limits. There is much about the boot camp that signals the continuity of the modern in punishment. Indeed, we find in the range of practices and discourses being deployed in boot camps most of the major themes of modern punishment, including discipline, proportionality, rehabilitation, training in work habits, education, treatment, and aftercare.

One way of interpreting this development is that it shows the robustness of modern penal strategies and understandings (Garland, 1994). As Foucault (1977: 264–265) noted, the discourses of modern punishment have been highly repetitive from the start:

> In a very strange way, the history of imprisonment does not obey a chronology in which one sees, in orderly succession, the establishment of a penality of detention; then a recognition of its failure; then the slow rise of projects of reform, seeming to culminate in the more or less coherent definition of penitentiary technique; then the implementation of this project; lastly, the recognition of its success or its failure. There was in fact a telescoping or in any case a different distribution of these elements.

An alternative interpretation is that the boot camp evidences an end game of penal modernity. Although the forms of modern penality had their referents in real forces of social control available in modern society, the boot camp has as its referent the forms of modern penality themselves. Along with other recent developments, including the death penalty and the rebirth of curfew laws and community policing, the boot camp is an exercise in what some scholars have called 'willful nostalgia,' a sensibility that is a crucial marker of postmodernization in a variety of social fields (Stauth and Turner, 1988; Turner, 1987). Indeed, the boot camp's main appeal may be precisely the ease with which it projects a host of associations with minimal practical interference. As Mark Osler (1991: 34) perceptively puts it:

> The lure of shock sentences is particularly acute in an age in which the primary medium of mass communication has become the sound bite. Video images of drill instructors 2 inches from an inmate's face, a team of inmates clearing brush, and reveille at 4 a.m. cater to 'popular desires' for a quick fix to crime through harsh punishment, discipline, and deterrence.

[...]

The military as a model for modernity

Clearly, in one sense the boot camp is a renewal of military elements that have long been around modern penal strategy (Morash and Rucker, 1990: 207). According to Foucault (1977: 209), the military was an early site for the development of new disciplinary strategies aimed at exercising power over individuals. The well-disciplined citizen armies like those of Napoleon or Frederick the Great proved that large masses of unskilled people could produce great amounts of efficient force on the battle field if subjected to rigorous training in coordinating the individual movement to the mass action. These new armies drew on the lower classes of society and proved themselves capable of organizing these elements into highly productive forces.

Not surprisingly, penal reformers throughout the modern period have looked at the military as a possible model for punishment (Morash and Rucker, 1990: 207).

Barracks, rigorous training of the body, methods of tight organizational control over command and performance – all of these provided general and specific technologies that those charged with containing large numbers of presumptively recalcitrant individuals could use. The Auburn penitentiary, progenitor of the 'congregate' model in which prisoners worked together rather than separated in individual cell work-shops, turned to military-style drilling as a way of maintaining greater control over individuals who, thrown together, were capable of much more resistance. In the 1880s, the famed penologist Zebulon Brockway developed a regime for juvenile offenders at his Elmira Reformatory, which explicitly borrowed military ranks, uniforms, and drilling (Osler, 1991; Smith, 1988; Rothman, 1980).

The appeal of the military model to those faced with governing large numbers of confined criminals is obvious. Indeed, it may be surprising that it was not more influential. In part this may reflect the more democratic and capitalistic spirit of these societies (Huntington, 1957). It may also reflect the enduring aspects of honor ethos associated with the military, which would be endangered by too great an association with punishment. In the United States and Western Europe (Foucault, 1977; Ignatieff, 1978; Melossi and Pavarini, 1981), this model lost out to another that combined many of the same disciplinary technologies of the military barracks with a less prob-lematic ideology, i.e., the factory. Industrial manufacturing was also a leader in developing social technologies to make the unskilled masses highly productive while controlling the potential dangers of concentrating groups of an urban working class that remained highly contentious together with machinery capable of carnage (Simon, 1993b). It also offered an ethos conducive to attaining the effective consent of a mass of recalcitrant men. While military discipline referenced the danger of combat, factory discipline had a plausible link to personal satisfaction through wages and consumption.

In the early years of this century, a successful (understudied) movement consisting of both labor and employers compelled most states to move away from the fully effective deployment of industrial labor in prisons. Since then, work, when available, has consisted mainly of internal service labor (cleaning, building, and repairing prison structures, etc.) along with some industrial production for state use, such as office equipment and license plates. Industrial discipline remained important to the penal model through the parole system, which attempted to place prisoners in employment and keep them there as a condition for release from imprisonment (Simon, 1993a).

[...]

World War II marked a high point of the military-industrial model. Thousands of prisoners were released directly into defense factories and into the army, and millions of potential offenders found themselves preventively detained in both settings. A con-tinuing decline in the demand for industrial labor has troubled corrections (Simon, 1993a: 66). From the 1940s to the 1970s, a psychologically oriented rehabilitation program was one way of maintaining the normative framework of modern punish-ment in the face of a declining industrial community (*Ibid.*). Since the 1970s, it has been difficult to identify any model behind penal strategies other than that kind of antimodel described by fiscal considerations and managerialism (Simon, 1993a; Feeley and Simon, 1992, 1994).

The return of the military model

Does the rising interest in the penal boot camp signal a reversal of fortune for the military model? If so, we might conclude that this development marks the stability of penal modernity. Indeed, if one of the strongest arguments for penal postmodernity has been the increasingly reflexive nature of a penal system driven largely by internal performance parameters (Heydebrand and Serron, 1990; Feeley and Simon, 1992; Simon, 1993b), then the boot camp suggests that the basic normative orientation toward transformation and reintegration of offenders remains in modern punishment. This view seems plausible on the surface, but a number of anomalies suggest that something else is going on.

1 The penal boot camp is not a direct transfer from the military boot camp

One of the most significant facts about the current penal boot camp practice is that it has few direct institutional links to the military at all. The real sources lie in both personal memory and the collective forms of memory provided by popular culture. Many programs have sought to hire officers with experience as training instructors in the military (a process made easier by the large number of former military personnel who enter corrections). Indeed, the originators of the penal boot camp idea were corrections officials in the South, many of whom had doubtless been in the military, but who were not acting as agents of, or directly borrowing from, contemporary military practice. There is an important distinction between borrowing images and borrowing technologies, however. The military shows up in the boot camp not as functional structure with application to the penal realm, but as a meaning-laden fragment of memory of the sort we see in nostalgia films (more on that later).

2 The military is moving away from the boot camp

Studies conducted by the military itself since the 1970s have suggested overwhelmingly that the classic boot camp model is counterproductive for many of the military's own goals (Morash and Rucker, 1990: 210–211). The new training model emphasizes such things as health and stress reduction (Baker, 1990). Thus, the military – the model for the boot camp – is a remembered military.

3 There is no evidence that military-style discipline is becoming a more general social qualification

It is true that the resonance of the boot-camp metaphor is not limited solely to the penal realm. In a recent resolution of the Senate Education Committee, the administration's national service program was praised as providing 'the kind of "boot camp" experience that will help them [youth] mature and better understand the value of hard work so they will make better adults.' The boot camp has also been an attractive metaphor for some private-sector ventures, including Ross Perot's Electronic Data Systems Corporation, a tennis school, and a Japanese managers' training school (Morash and Rucker, 1990: 217).

The bigger picture of labor deployment, as sketched by thinkers as diverse as current House Speaker Newt Gingrich (1984) and Labor Secretary Robert Reich (1983), is one quite different from the military model. In a work force organized for maximum global competitiveness, with an open flow of both capital and labor across borders, loyalty is less valued than individual initiative. Rote obedience is denigrated in favor of flexible authority lines and encouragement of innovation at all levels of enterprise. Indeed, while the military model might have fit the classical industrial economy, where corporations promised lifetime employment and generous benefits, it is about the least viable model imaginable for the new flexible accumulation/ just-on-time-production model that emphasizes constant change and individual responsibility (Piore and Sabel, 1984).

Critics have noted ruefully that it seems peculiar to take a device intended for the introductory transition into a more prolonged experience of military duty and to use it on a population destined only for return to the same communities where they operated as criminals. They are correct to note that the penal boot camp lacks a functional relationship with the sources of social control in the community. Yet the lack of fit is even more profound. The penal boot camp is lacking in any real-world referents. Indeed, what referents it does have are self-consciously fabricated images of the past that characterize the mode of willful nostalgia. [...]

THE BOOT CAMP AS NOSTALGIA

The return of military gestures in contemporary penal practices is an exercise in nostalgia. That does not mean, of course, that it does not serve practical needs. If the United States continues to maintain the historically high incarceration rates it has in the past decade, it will undoubtedly need to develop forms of lower-cost custody. The custodial facilities being created through boot-camp programs represent an effective, and possibly cheaper, form of custody. This goal of lowered costs sets a limit on how far the boot-camp program can be stretched before it becomes more expensive than prison. Beyond that, cost considerations have little direct relationship to the boot-camp program. Instead, these facilities are engaged in an invocation of the past.

Deco nostalgia: the awareness of artifice

One of the essential distinctions between willful nostalgia and its classical forms is the self-consciousness of the former. The crowd watching Reagan ride off into the sunset knows that it is in fact not a re-creation of the sunset, but a re-creation of a cinematic re-creation of a sunset that is involved. Indeed, that is the source of the pleasure they take in it as participants. Fredric Jameson (1991: 288) refers to this as 'deco nostalgia,' the nostalgia of the collector, of one who seeks to achieve a lifestyle, not a way of life.

Likewise, much of the appeal of the boot camp lies not in its reference to a real set of social practices, i.e., the military, labor, or education, but in its reference to modern penality's reference to these external forces. In fact, all these institutions are themselves in crisis. It is difficult to imagine a penal manager today looking at the decrepit public schools, the downsizing military, or the dismal unskilled labor market and seeing there answers to how to deal with offenders. To an unprecedented degree, penal managers are conscious of this transposition. The State of Louisiana, for one, describes as one of the goals of its boot camp: 'To promote a positive image of corrections and, in general, to enhance public relations' (quoted in MacKenzie, Shaw, and Gowdy, 1993: 1).

The preeminence of the military metaphor does not necessarily reflect even the relative superiority of the military to other bad models for the penal process. Instead, it reflects the relative standing of the military as a rich source of nostalgia for modernity. The boot camp is not only a general gesture toward this tradition, but also a reference to World War II, the defining moment of high modernity (at least for the United States). It was during that era that all the country's modernizing systems, driven by the war economy, achieved a kind of apotheosis. Some 50 years later, World War II carries an increasing currency of nostalgia that grows as the events themselves (with their real privations) become distant and the sense of loss associated with the relative certainties of postwar politics and economics grows.

It is not the real war, but its cinematic images that draw the nostalgia of current generations. The World War II movie genre, which saturated first the cinema and later the television screen from the war years until the 1970s, may be the most salient machinery of memory on this score. Starting immediately after the U.S. declaration of war, Hollywood produced a bevy of movies that focused not so much on war as on the preparation for it. The productions were generally light-hearted and low-budget, with titles like *I Wanted Wings, Dive Bomber, Flight Command, Navy Blues, Buck Private, Tanks a Million,* and *D.I.* (Koppes and Black, 1987: 36). These movies portrayed the foibles of young men yanked from their disparate lives and subjected to dramatic transformation at the command of the federal government. Whatever the central plot, usually nonsensical, the films almost always portrayed some examples of stereotypical American 'outsiders', including urban toughs, upper-class twits, small-town innocents, and rural hayseeds, who are at first crushed by the system, but are ultimately remade as normal American men.

A leading study of the genre argues that the point of these movies was not to militarize the nation, but to reassure it (*Ibid.*):

> Many such pictures had no explicit propaganda message, but the application of movie glamour and its repetition probably helped create a favorable impression of the armed forces.... These humorous treatments may have helped 'humanize and trivialize' the experience and hence, perhaps, eased the anxieties of potential draftees and their families.

Sentiment against entering the European war remained high in the United States after World War I. Military service and its consequences were viewed in a highly skeptical light. Throughout the 1920s, popular writers like F. Scott Fitzgerald and John Dos Passos held the images of honor and glory to scathing review. Thus, Hollywood's transformation of basic training from a short trip to a foreign grave into a low-budget rite of passage was a tremendous achievement of cultural work.

The potency of this genre is negatively reflected in its invocation in one of the most powerful antiwar movies to come out of the Vietnam War experience, Stanley Kubrick's *Full Metal Jacket* (Warner Bros., 1987). The movie, especially its first half, is as much a play on the images of the boot-camp genre film as it is about war generally or Vietnam in particular. The drill sergeant is vicious but human and with paternal intent. The protagonist and his more normal buddies confirm their self-confidence, but learn humility. Most importantly, an outsider, here a fat recruit with little confidence or self-control, is put through a crushing humiliation and then what appears to be the utterly predictable rise to normality. Yet this meticulous re-creation of one of our most comforting cinematic images only sets the viewer up for a harder shock when the traditional post-*oedipal* reconciliation between drill sergeant and the fat recruit is replaced by a burst of parricidal and then suicidal gunfire.

Kubrick seems to warn us that the Vietnam experience places our seemingly robust sense of personal and collective security at risk by destabilizing our most comforting metaphors for power. The renewed popularity of the boot camp as a model for punishment and other functions suggests that even if Kubrick is correct, the process of recognition is a complicated one. For the moment, at any rate, the distancing of the memories of Vietnam allows the penal boot camp to effectively transfer the legitimacy and meaning that remains laden, not in modernity's artifacts, but in popular culture representations of these artifacts.

The meaning of meaningfulness

The other feature of willful nostalgia that distinguishes it from the classical form is that it recovers the possibility of meaningfulness rather than a particular meaning. The penal boot camp suggests this by its relentless drive to incorporate not only the images of military discipline, but also virtually every gesture and cliché in the history of modern penality, including education, work, therapy, and moralization.

The problem is that this nostalgic appropriation of modernism's artifacts is rapid and insatiable, giving rise to a kind of breathlessness. This is visible in the sentiments expressed by prosecutor Carole Ann Nix as she describes her visit to Michigan's Camp Sauble.

> The one day I spent at Camp Sauble in Freesoil, Michigan, was an unforgettable experience. Something important was happening at Camp Sauble. I could sense it. Former young street punks were engaged in a transformation process. The probationers were clean, healthy, and exhibited more self-discipline, self-esteem, and motivation than any of the thousands of criminal defendants I have seen in court during my ten plus years in prosecution. I was impressed....
>
> Probationers who complete the program develop a strong sense of loyalty to the program. They also become loyal to each other as individuals. They realize that the staff cares about them. Most of these offenders have never experienced this kind of care before. Staff members push them to their very best, to give 100 percent of what they are able. Pride grows. A person changes as he accepts the program. I heard a staff member describe the probationer who finally accepts the program as one who walks straight, holds his head up high, and has a glisten in his eye (Nix, 1993: 20).

Willful nostalgia has a kind of exhilarating quality for its consumers that may help give corrections a short-term jump in popular confidence. Yet its stimulus comes from its very concentration of the memory and experience of past ways of life into a fleeting evocation. How long will the fad for basic training last?

The boot camp and the temporal structure of nostalgia

This interpretation of the penal boot camp as an exercise in willful nostalgia is strengthened as we move from the content of the boot camp, its regnant images, to its underlying temporal structure. Scholars of modern culture emphasize the unique temporal structure of modernity and the profound social struggles that went into producing it. The historian E.P. Thompson (1967) argued that the creation of a modern industrial work force required a massive reconstruction of the way ordinary people conceived of time. The matrix of clock and calendar time was a strange imposition in the lives of early modern workers. Those workers, even the ones involved in manufacturing, were used to producing on their own schedule. They often violently resisted the imposition of strict time disciplines. Indeed, many forms that we take as foundational to the modern, like the factory, were designed in large part to accommodate the techniques of power necessary to make this new temporal order enforceable.

Modern penality was rooted in this kind of modern time (Rothman, 1978). The first great innovation of modern punishment, the ideal of a rational penal code promulgated by Beccaria (1738–1794) and his many followers, envisioned a transparent equivalence between crime and punishment that would be effortlessly communicated by the penal code itself. Although Beccaria himself thought of metaphoric punishments, the regimes that began implementing the Beccarian idea at the turn of the 19th century turned to the new calendar and clock time as the preferred medium of sanction. The idea that the benefits of crime could be counterbalanced by the threatened loss of a certain quantity of time, i.e., deterrence, formed an enduring logic of economic rationality in punishment.

The penitentiary practice that grew up around this seizure of time established its own kind of temporality, one in which goals of normalization rather than accountability established the duration of confinement. David Rothman described this as 'therapeutic time' (Rothman, 1978: 131), which he saw exemplified in the indeterminate sentence system that prevailed for much of the 20th century.

There are important tensions between deterrent time and therapeutic time, the time of the code and the time of the penitentiary, that have manifested themselves continually in the history of sentencing policy. Indeterminate sentencing schemes, which were the hot innovation of the late 19th century, were attacked on the basis that they undermined deterrence by making it difficult for potential criminals to engage in a rational calculus about the costs and benefits of crime. Determinate sentencing schemes, popular since the 1970s, can be criticized for undermining rehabilitation and incapacitation by removing the ability to individualize sanctions. Despite these kinds of differences, most modern penal practices share an orientation toward a linear and progressive structure of time as manifested in terms of proportionality and recidivism. So long as the kinds of concerns summarized by those terms can be intelligibly expressed, an argument can be made that we remain definably modern in our penal mentality.

The boot camp has features that evoke both poles, but its actual temporal organization is difficult to fit into either. The penal boot camp program incorporates rehabilitative techniques, but it does not embrace anything like the 'therapeutic time' that such techniques require. As Osler (1991: 40) points out:

> The supposedly therapeutic boot camp ... abandons the idea of therapeutic time while simultaneously embracing the therapeutic idea. The type of firmly structured, mandatory therapy the boot camp offers (vocational training, education, relaxation therapy, etc.) beyond the

normal prison offerings is undermined by the other unique element of the boot camp: its short duration. Ninety to 180 days are insufficient to complete such programs of therapy.

The boot camp is a composite of strong but inconsistent references to modern time. It invokes images of inmates awakened before dawn to be run through a precisely timed schedule of drills and drill-like tasks whose only *metier* is time: images of inmates engaged in physically punishing exercises that make the shorter time of boot-camp sentences worth far more in some penal economy of deterrence. Yet these images come apart all too easily. No evidence of heightened deterrence values has emerged from carefully controlled studies. The incredible level of violence in prisons and poverty-ridden inner-city communities suggests that the 'hardness' of boot-camp time is a completely ideological quality more likely to excite its middle-class television audience than to intimidate its actual underclass subjects.

Observers of the boot camp have expressed dismay that its effects, if beneficial, are difficult to sustain once inmates 'graduate'. As Osler (1991: 39) remarks:

> They [boot camps] strip down a person through regimentation, then send the offender home to an environment that is the exact opposite of the boot camp – formally unstructured and often lacking commanding directives for positive behavior.

Yet this surprise demonstrates how much the temporal structure of modern punishment continues to influence our expectations. The boot camp's lack of 'fit' is only troubling if one assumes that it should fit in a logic where past, present, and future are linked in a linear and transparent way.

The essential feature of the boot camp's temporal structure is brevity. Although some states have tinkered with lengthening the program (and many have tacked on aftercare), it is clear that real changes cannot be made in its temporality without undermining some or all of the key reasons that make the boot camp popular. First, administrators and politicians (for somewhat different reasons) favor boot camps because they promise to provide real punishment at a much lower cost. Lengthening the boot camp experience and aftercare is certain to add not only direct costs, but also the indirect costs of increasing the likelihood that a new sanctionable offense will be committed and detected, thus generating further custody costs.

Second, the boot camp's brevity is the key to the nostalgic satisfaction it brings to its public audience. Rapid and total transformation was the key cultural theme that Hollywood linked to the boot camp. The hoodlum or hayseed is transformed into a worthy vessel of American manhood in a period of some weeks. Once unbound from brevity and from the promise of dramatic transformation, the boot camp image blurs into that of camps for displaced persons, such as the sort set up for refugees after World War II and since. I suspect that image remains far less comforting (although I fear a day not far off when it may be a matter of indifference).

[···]

REFERENCES

Baker, Ross K. (1990) 'Back to Basics.' *American Demographics* (March): 64.
Brodeur, Jean-Paul (1994) 'Penal Saturation.' Paper presented at the American Society of Criminology, Annual Meeting (November).

Cohen, Stanley (1994) 'Social Control and the Politics of Reconstruction.' David Nelken (ed.) *The Futures of Criminology*. London: Sage.

Doane, Janice and Devon Hodges (1987) *Nostalgia and Sexual Difference: The Resistance to Contemporary Feminism*. London: Methuen.

Duke, Steven (1993) 'Clinton and Crime.' *Yale Journal on Regulation*, 10: 575–587.

Dumm, Thomas L. (1994) 'The Penitentiary in Ruins.' Paper presented at the Annual Meeting of the American Political Science Association, New York (August 31 to September 4).

Elias, Nobert (1978) *The Civilizing Process*. Translated by Edmund Jepthcott. New York: Urizen Books.

Ermath, Elizabeth (1990) *Sequel to History: Postmodernism and the Crisis of Representational Time*. Princeton, N.J.: Princeton University Press.

Feeley, Malcolm M. and Jonathan Simon (1994) 'Actuarial Justice: Power/Knowledge in Contemporary Criminal Justice.' David Nelken (ed.) *The Futures of Criminology*. London: Sage: 173–201.

Feeley, Malcolm M. and Jonathan Simon (1992) 'The New Penology: Notes on the Emerging Strategy of Corrections and Its Implications.' *Criminology*, 30: 449–474.

Foucault, Michel (1977) *Discipline and Punish: The Birth of the Prison*. Translated by Alan Sheridan. New York: Random House.

Garland, David (1994) 'Penal Modernism and Postmodernism.' Unpublished manuscript.

Garland, David (1990) *Punishment and Modern Society: A Study in Social Theory*. Chicago: University of Chicago Press.

Gingrich, Newt, with David Drake and Marianne Gingrich (1984) *Window of Opportunity: A Blueprint for the Future*. New York: Doherety Associates in Association with Baien Enterprises.

Gordon, Collin (1991) 'Governmental Rationality: An Introduction.' Graham Burchell, Collin Gordon, and Peter Miller (eds) *The Foucault Effect: Studies in Governmentality*. Chicago: University of Chicago Press: 1–52.

Hall, Stuart, Chas Critcher, Tony Jefferson, John Clarke, and Brian Roberts (1979) *Policing the Crisis: Mugging, the State, and Law and Order*. London: Macmillan.

Heydebrand, Wolf and Carrol Seron (1990) *Rationalizing Justice: The Political Economy of Federal District Courts*. Albany, N.Y.: State University of New York Press.

Huntington, Samuel P. (1957) *The Soldier and the State: The Theory and Politics of Civil–Military Relations*. Cambridge, Mass: Harvard University Press.

Ignatieff, Michael (1978) *A Just Measure of Pain*. London: Penguin Books.

Jahoda, M., P.F. Lazarsfeld, H. Ziesel (1972) *Marienthal: The Sociography of an Unemployed Community*. London: Tavistock Publications (original 1933).

Jameson, Fredric (1991) *Postmodernism or the Cultural Logic of Late Capitalism*. Durham, N.C.: Duke University Press.

Koppes, Clayton and Gregory Black (1987) *Hollywood Goes to War: How Politics, Profits, and Propaganda Shaped World War II Movies*. N.Y.: Free Press.

Lamb, David (1993) 'Last Shot to Salvage Their Lives: First-Time, Nonviolent Offenders Get a Chance at Redemption by Going Through Paramilitary Boot Camps. Clinton Has Embraced "Shock Incarceration," But Its Effectiveness Is Unclear.' *L.A. Times* (January 17): A1.

MacKenzie, Doris Layton (1994) 'Boot Camps: A National Assessment.' *Overcrowded Times*, 5: 1.

MacKenzie, Doris Layton (1993) 'Boot Camp Prisons in 1993.' *National Institute of Justice Journal* 227 (November): 21–24.

Mackenzie, Doris Layton and Alex Piquero (1994) 'The Impact of Shock Incarceration Programs on Prison Crowding.' *Crime and Delinquency*, 40: 222–249.

Mackenzie, Doris L., James W. Shaw, and Voncile B. Gowdy (1993) *An Evaluation of Shock Incarceration in Louisiana*. NIJ: Research in Brief (June).

Melossi, Dario and Massimo Pavarini (1981) *The Prison and the Factory: Origins of the Penitentiary System*. Totowa, N.J.: Macmillan Press.

Morash, Merry and Lila Rucker (1990) 'A Critical Look at the Idea of Boot Camp as a Correctional Reform.' *Crime and Delinquency*, 36: 204–222.

Morris, Norval (1993) 'Comments to Franklin E. Zimring. Drug Treatment as a Criminal Sanction.' 64 *U. Colo. L. Rev.* 831, 835.

Nance, Sheryl (1991) 'Group Urges Wider Use of Shock Incarceration.' *New York Law Journal* (March 29): 1.

Nelken, David (1994) 'Reflexive Criminology?' David Nelken (ed.) *The Futures of Criminology*. London: Sage: 7–42.

New York Times (1994) 'Editorial: Mr. Clinton's Future and the G.O.P.' *New York Times* (Tuesday, December 6): National Edition.

Nix, Carol Ann (1993) 'Boot Camp/Shock Incarceration – An Alternative to Prison for Young, Nonviolent Offenders in the United States.' *The Prosecutor*, 28: 15–24.

O'Malley, Pat (1994) 'Penalising Crime in Advanced Liberalism.' Paper presented at the American Society of Criminology, Annual Meeting (November).

Osler, Mark W. (1991) 'Shock Incarceration: Hard Realities and Real Possibilities.' *Federal Probation* (March): 34–42.

Parent, D. (1994) 'Boot Camps Failing to Achieve Goals.' *Overcrowded Times*, 5: 1.

Parent, D. (1989) *Shock Incarceration: An Overview of Existing Programs*. NIJ.

Piore, Michale J. and Charles F. Sabel (1984) *The Second Industrial Divide: Possibilities for Prosperity*. New York: Basic Books.

Reich, Robert B. (1983) *The Next American Frontier*. New York: Times Books.

Robertson, Roland (1990) 'After Nostalgia? Willful Nostalgia and the Phases of Globalization.' Bryan S. Turner (ed.) *Theories of Modernity and Postmodernity*. London: Sage.

Rorty, Richard (1989) *Contingency, Irony, and Solidarity*. New York: Cambridge University Press.

Rothman, David J. (1980) *Conscience and Convenience: The Asylum and Its Alternatives in Progressive America*. Toronto: Little Brown.

Rothman, David J. (1978) 'Doing Time.' *International Journal of Comparative Sociology* 19.

Rothman, David J. (1971) *The Discovery of the Asylum: Social Order and Disorder in the New Republic*. Toronto: Little Brown.

Scheingold, Stuart A. (1991) *The Politics of Street Crime: Criminal Process and Cultural Obsession*. Philadelphia: Temple University Press.

Shearing, Clifford and Phillip Stenning (1984) 'From the Panopticon to Disney World: The Development of Discipline.' Anthony Doob and Allen Greenspan (eds) *Perspectives in Criminal Law*. Toronto: Aurora.

Simon, Jonathan (1994) 'Reflections in Krome: Punishment and Social Structure in Global City.' Unpublished manuscript.

Simon, Jonathan (1993a) *Poor Discipline: Parole and the Social Control of the Underclass, 1890–1990.* Chicago: University of Chicago Press.

Simon, Jonathan (1993b) 'For the Government of Its Servants: Law and Disciplinary Power in the Work Place, 1870–1906.' *Studies in Law, Politics, and Society*, 13: 105–136.

Skogan, Wesley G. (1990) *Disorder and Decline: Crime and the Spiral of Decay in American Neighborhoods.* New York: Free Press.

Smith, Beverly A. (1988) 'Military Training at New York's Elmira Reformatory.' *Federal Probation*, 52: 33.

Stauth, Georg and Bryan S. Turner (1988) 'Nostalgia, Postmodernism, and the Critique of Mass Culture.' *Theory, Culture and Society*, 52–53: 509–526.

Stewart, Kathleen (1992) 'Nostalgia – A Polemic.' George Marcus (ed.) *Rereading Cultural Anthropology*. Durham, N.C.: Duke University Press.

Texas Lawyer (1991) 'Bustin' Loose.' *Texas Lawyer* (April 8): 2.

Thompson, E.P. (1967) 'Time, Work Discipline, and Industrial Capitalism.' *Past and Present*, 38: 56–97.

Turner, Bryan (1987) 'A Note on Nostalgia.' *Theory, Culture and Society*, 22: 147–156.

Walker, Samuel (1993) *Taming the System: The Control of Discretion in Criminal Justice, 1950–1990*. New York, Oxford University Press.

24

The reductionist agenda

Andrew Rutherford

Most contemporary prison systems are expanding through a combination of drift and design. Criminal justice administrators perpetuate the myth that the prison system is swept along by forces beyond their control or influence. The convenient conclusion is announced that, given increased rates of reported crime and court workloads, it inevitably follows that there is no alternative other than for the prison system to expand further. Strategies which might shield the prison system from increases in persons processed by criminal justice have been disregarded and administrators have preferred to proceed as though policy choices do not exist. In large part, criminal justice administrators are the architects of the crisis with which they are now confronted.

Reductionist policy has as its underlying premise that the prison system should deal only with persons sentenced or remanded in connection with serious crime. As a starting point, reductionist policy recognizes that most prison systems are bogged down in dealing with relatively minor offenders. Indeed minor offenders are the staple fodder from which the expanding prison system feeds. The reductionist alternative seeks strategies aimed at barring the entry of minor offenders from the prison system and, if such persons do enter, of effecting their expeditious removal.

Some prison systems are proactively expanionist and pursue growth by design. Most typically, expansion occurs in the absence of coherent policy and takes a reactive stance to perceived demands made by other segments of the criminal justice process or by various interest groups. In England since the early 1980s prison system policy has followed an expansionist course and has displayed both reactive and proactive elements. The view that an alternative policy direction is urgently required has been expressed in a series of reports by Parliamentary and other committees.[1] Most of these reports, however, have proposed what amounts to standstill policy. For example, although the Home Affairs Committee of the House of Commons concluded that the public interest would not suffer from a diminished use of imprisonment and went on to recommend a number of strategies by which the size of the English prison population might be reduced, its report remained firmly within the standstill frame of reference. 'We would emphasize that we do not regard the provision of additional

SOURCE: This chapter is taken from *Prisons and the Process of Justice*, London, Heinemann, 1984, pp. 171–186 (abridged).

resources for the prison system and the reduction of the prison system as alternatives: the two are complementary, and both are necessary to a resolution of the present crisis.'[2]

This viewpoint echoes the official theme, articulated by prison system administrators, of aligning the supply of resources and the demand for prison places. Standstill policy is not in the long term a viable alternative to expanding prison systems: at best short-term relief from population pressures is provided. Furthermore, standstill policy fails to take account of the extent to which the size of the prison population is determined by the capacity of the prison system and of the criminal justice process as a whole. A supply-led view of the criminal justice process should be accompanied by profound caution before resources are increased to match actual or forecasted increases in crime.

Crises which would undermine the foundations of most other orgnizations tend, instead, to generate yet further resources for the prison system. In the mid-1960s the English prison system was gravely shaken by embarrasing lapses of security. The result of the Mountbatten Inquiry was the injection of greatly increased manpower and capital resources. Twelve years later there were signs indicating that management had lost control of English prisons to local branches of the Prison Officers' Association. The result was a recommendation by the May Committee to further escalate prison system expenditure. Just as rationales change for increasing resources for the prison system so do the justifications for imprisonment. Notions of general deterrence gave way to those of rehabilitation which, in turn, have been superseded by the language of selective incapacitation and individual deterrence. The new expansionist phase in England leans most heavily upon two justifications: the incapacitation of serious offenders and individual deterrence for minor offenders. This dualistic approach to prison purposes, if given full expression in penal practice, will ensure prison population growth in excess of that forecasted by the Home Office.

By the early 1980s, standstill policy regarding the English prison system had been abandoned for reactive expansionism. The Home Secretary declared, to the applause of his political colleagues, that room would be found in the prison system for all persons whom the courts wished to send. Home Office forecasts of prison population during the 1980s were revised upwards to take account of modified assumptions about 'demand'. For example, the forecast published in March 1982 concerning the size of the English prison population in 1984 increased by ten per cent the projection made a year before. The anticipated total of 47,000 prisoners first published by the Home Office in 1978 for 1987 had by 1982 been brought forward to 1984.[3]

Forecasting prison population size does not occur in a political vacuum and is usually closely related to the allocation of public funds.[4] Prison population forecasting plays a crucial part in expansionist policy-making, and it is insufficiently appreciated that it is not possible to forecast prison population size accurately, even over the short-term. A forecasted prison population is no more than a set of assumptions, particularly in relation to prosecution and sentencing practice. If the forecast turns out to be accurate, it may well be by chance. In England, as in America, where expansionist prison system policies reign, the forecasting method is to present a single scenario of the future. Single scenario forecasting assumes that the size of the population is determined by external forces and that these are largely beyond regulation.[5] Although caveats may be made as to reliability, especially with reference to long-term forecasts, the multiple scenario method is eschewed. Multiple scenarios of the future highlight the point which expansionist administrators prefer to obscure, namely that policy choices on prison population size exist and need to be made.

[···]

The reductionist approach to the prison system inevitably and necessarily overlaps with broader aspects of social and economic policy. In particular, policy and practice concerning education, mental health and the extent and distribution of poverty impinge upon directions set for the prison system. [...] The reductionist agenda consists of nine items. While these items are reviewed primarily with reference to the situation in England, the general principles apply to expansionist systems elsewhere from Scotland to Texas. Although the items are not listed in a strict sequential order, there is merit in the view that action should commence with the prison system itself. The prison represents the deepest end of criminal justice, and strategies which restrict the availability of custody produce a ripple effect through other parts of the process. The classic example of criminal justice reform which focused at the deep-end was the abrupt closure in the early 1970s of most of the youth institutions in Massachusetts. This event had the consequence of forcing the development of procedures to ensure the highly selective allocation of the few available secure settings and also encouraging a wide range of alternative programmes in the community.[6]

The nine items on the reductionist agenda are as follows:

- The physical capacity of the prison system should be substantially reduced.
- There should be a precise statement of minimum standards as to the physical conditions of imprisonment and these should be legally enforceable.
- The optimal prison system staff-to-prisoner ratio should be determined and implemented.
- The prison system should have at its disposal early release mechanisms and use these to avoid overcrowding.
- Certain categories of persons sentenced to imprisonment should, if space be not immediately available, wait until called-up by the prison system.
- Sentencing discretion should be structured towards use of the least restrictive sanction.
- Breach or default of non-custodial sanctions should only exceptionally be dealt with by imprisonment.
- The range of non-imprisonable offences should be widened to include certain categories of theft.
- The scope of criminal law should be considerably narrowed.

The physical capacity of the prison system should be substantially reduced

If the prison population in England is to be reduced to about 20,000, the required capacity, allowing a five per cent margin, would be 21,000. With reference to the existing penal estate, this implies a reduction in capacity of 18,000 places or about 45 per cent. The reduction of capacity has three central components:

A freeze on new prison construction In England this would mean cancellation of the prison building programme which in 1982 envisaged 5,000 new places by the end of the 1980s. The freeze would include so-called replacement prisons, which are more than likely to result in supplementation of the existing prison system. Even rebuilding projects on the existing site carries risks of this sort, as is evident at Holloway, the women's prison in London. The new Holloway prison is planned to have almost twice the certified accommodation of the original facility.

A phased programme of prison closures, amounting in England to, say, 12,500 places In England only five institutions, all open prisons and borstals, with a total capacity of about 800 have been closed since 1945.[7] There have been no closures of Victorian prisons during this period which, in the words of one Home Office official, are 'collapsing around our ears'.[8] The Home Office estimated in 1978 that four institutions with a total of 1,000 places were in such poor condition that they were not worth retaining for another decade.[9] Expansionist prison systems are highly resistant to closing prisons regardless of their physical conditions. In October 1979, the May Committee wrote of Dartmoor prison, '... what was permissible in a convict prison for the rigours of penal servitude on the reoccupied Napoleonic site of the 1850s, is nowadays simply against nature'.[10] On the day the May Report was published the Member of Parliament for the constituency which includes the prison within its boundaries expressed alarm in the House of Commons at '... the possible closure of Dartmoor prison which would have very serious social implications for Princetown'. His fears were quickly put at rest. The Home Secretary replied that, in the present conditions of overcrowding, '... there is no question of closing down Dartmoor'.[11]

A refurbishment programme carried out in remaining prisons which will further reduce capacity The Home Office has estimated that provision of integral sanitation would eliminate 5,500 cells.[12] As noted in the next section, in the absence of further construction, adherence to minimum physical standards is likely to result in substantial reductions in total capacity.

There should be a precise statement of minimum standards governing the physical conditions of prison systems, and these standards should be legally enforceable

A central plank of reductionist policy is the articulation of and adherence to minimum standards. Minimum standards provide a basic floor, below which conditions should not be permitted to sink and should be differentiated from standards which are essentially aspirational in character. It is partly for this reason that some commentators prefer the concept of 'humane containment' to the elusive rhetoric of 'treatment and training'. King and Morgan have argued that '... the goal of humane containment is capable of being defined in ways which enable staff (and the public) to know when they are achieving it or when they are falling short'.[13]

There is, however, a reluctance within most prison systems to articulate basic standards. Officials prefer to be guided by lofty aspirations rather than measurable minimum standards. The former speak to good intentions which may remain beyond the grasp of the prison administrators who, claiming perseverance, remain absolved from blame. Measurable minimum standards provide criteria against which the prison administrator can be held accountable. Standards regarding physical space provide a linchpin of reductionist policy on the prison system. Minimum standards bring together the three strands of prison policy, namely population size, the level of capacity and the quality of conditions.[14]

In 1982 unsuccessful attempts were made to incorporate precise standards regarding prison accommodation into the Criminal Justice Bill. One amendment proposed no enforced cell sharing and a minimum of 60 square feet per person in dormitories when confined for ten hours or less per day, and a minimum of 80 square feet when confined for more than ten hours per day. [...] [T]he Netherlands and West Germany have given statutory expression to some minimum standards. In the United States, although the Supreme Court has ruled in the contrary direction, lower courts have continued to find overcrowded conditions to be a crucial component in breaches of the cruel and unusual punishment provision of the Eighth Amendment. These considerations have prompted courts to order reductions of prison and jail populations.

By contrast, gross overcrowding continues to be tolerated in England. In 1973, the United Kingdom signed the Standard Minimum Rules for the Treatment of Prisoners, Rule 5(3), which sets forth the basic principle that: 'Deprivation of liberty shall be effected in material and conditions which ensure respect for human dignity.' As the Chief Inspector of Prisons has commented, conditions in English prisons certainly fall short of this standard. Unfortunately, the language of the European Rules lacks precision with respect to space and cell-sharing. Furthermore, while the Rules carry some moral force, they are not mandatory and lack enforcement machinery. The European Convention on Human Rights, on the other hand, does provide redress through the European Commission on Human Rights and the European Court. The key provision is Article 3 – 'No one should be subject to torture or inhuman or degrading treatment or punishment.' It is surprising that the European Court had not by the early 1980s been asked whether Article 3 is breached when three persons are crowded into a cell designed for one person, with no integral sanitation.[15] Eventually, pressure from the European Court may encourage British courts to take a more active position on this issue and the rights of prisoners generally. One legal commentator has written: 'To exempt from judicial control an administrative activity of the scale and importance of the prison system can have no justification either in principle or on grounds of expediency.'[16]

From the standpoint of reductionist policy, it is important that the penal scene does not become swamped with competing sets of standards, which is one of the difficulties facing reformers in the United States. What is required are a few tightly articulated central minimum standards which set the direction for action and provide a measure of its efficacy. It is also important to recognize the danger that minimum standards may also be used to secure increased resources and enhance expansionist policies. From the reductionist standpoint, minimum standards have the intrinsic virtue of imposing a population ceiling on existing prison system accommodation.

The optimal staff-to-prisoner ratio within the prison system should be determined and implemented

Serious problems arise for the prison system if there are too few or too many staff. Most expansionist prison systems are characterized by considerable increases in manpower, often accompanied by extensive restrictive practices and huge amounts of overtime. Under these circumstances, manpower costs are likely to be met at the expense of conditions within the prison. Too many staff may be counterproductive in terms of effective control of prisoners but on the other hand some prison systems, notably in the United States, have rapidly expanded their prison populations while retaining low manpower levels. In these prison systems, control problems of alarming dimensions are commonplace. Despite the high financial costs of staffing, little is known about what constitutes appropriate manning levels and optimal staff-to-prisoner ratios. The crude nature of the staff-to-prisoner ratio has not been refined to take account of considerations such as the security level of the prison, the extent to which prisoners are confined to their cells, staff tasks away from the prison, and the amount of overtime worked. Closely related to the optimal ratio is the important question of the morale of prison staff and the satisfaction they derive from their work.

The implications of reductionist policy for manpower needs vary according to the levels of staff to prisoners and the particular tasks of the prison. The experience in Japan and the Netherlands was that substantial reductions in prison populations were not accompanied by a decline in the number of custodial staff. In Japan, the number of prison officers remained static, whereas in the Netherlands manpower increased despite the decline in prison population. A fifty per cent reduction in the English prison population and no change in manpower would result in a prison officer-to-prisoner ratio of 1:1. This ratio is already achieved in English dispersal prisons and by the prison system of the Netherlands. Clearly formulated manning levels are an essential aspect of reductionist policy, and negotiations involving staff associations would need to take account of the interests of all grades of staff.

The prison system should have at its disposal early release mechanisms, and use these to avoid overcrowding

Most prison systems are responsible for the use of remission or 'good-time' and, where parole exists, exercise at least some degree of influence on parole decisions.[17] In addition to these general powers, a prison system should have at its disposal various schemes of temporary and early release. Temporary release usually takes the form of home leave or other furloughs and is especially important in Sweden and West Germany. In West Germany following the Prison Act of 1976, the number of furloughs has more than doubled.[18] Early release can take various forms. The Republic of Ireland has since 1960 developed a scheme of 'full temporary release', under which selected short-term offenders (serving sentences of 12 months or less) are released, often shortly after committal, to serve their sentences in the community.[19] Intensive supervision is provided by the probation services, with the ratio of releases to probation officers being about eight to one. The full temporary release scheme is occasionally used directly as a means of regulating prison population size. When numbers in the prisons become high, short-term offenders are granted full temporary release without supervision.[20]

Another method of early release is the amnesty. Amnesties are used fairly regularly to regulate prison population size in France, Israel and elsewhere.[21] While the amnesty provides reductions in prison population only over the short term, it is a useful tool for avoiding overcrowding. Powers exist under the Criminal Justice Act of 1982 to release specified categories of prisoners during the last six months of their sentence.[22]

*Certain categories of persons sentenced to
imprisonment should, if no space is immediately
available, wait until called-up by the prison system*

In Continental law countries, where the person sentenced to prison is on bail at
the time of sentence, or in other specified situations, a common procedure is for the
person to await call-up by the prison system. For example, in the Netherlands at any
one time, there are some 10,000 persons waiting for a prison place to become vacant.
From the standpoint of the person sentenced to imprisonment the procedure, while
not free from anxiety, does allow time for personal affairs to be attended to and perhaps flexibility as to when custody commences; from the standpoint of the prison
system the call-up procedure permits an unhurried decision to be taken as to where
the sentence will be served, and in particular forestalls overcrowded conditions. Of
special importance, when there are increased demands on prison capacity, the procedure ensures that the pressure point is located outside rather than inside the
prison system. A scheme along the Dutch lines was recommended by the Home
Affairs Committee of the House of Commons in 1981 only to be rejected by the
Government.[23]

*Sentencing discretion should be structured towards
use of the least restrictive sanction*

The legislature should establish a commission with the task of determining sentencing
guidelines. The purpose of these guidelines would be to structure sentencing decisions
so that custody is regarded as the sanction of last resort. To the sentencing commission would be delegated the immensely complex task of weighing the value questions
concerning offence types as well as directing attention to aggravating and mitigating
circumstances. The guidelines would in particular address the decision to impose
custody in addition to formulating a jurisprudence governing the use of non-custodial
sanctions. Experience in England and elsewhere has amply demonstrated that exhor-
tations to sentencers by the legislative and executive branches of government to be
more sparing in the use of custody are likely to go unheeded. While the Court of
Appeal has provided some guidance on the length of prison sentences, it has made
very little progress in fashioning a coherent jurisprudence as to when imprisonment
is appropriate.

The Sentencing Guidelines Commission in Minnesota [...] is characterized by a
gradual and evolutionary development. It is certainly to be expected that such a commission would vary in structure and style from one jurisdiction to another. A model
for England was proposed in 1982 by Andrew Ashworth, not, it might be noted, to
resounding cheers from either the Home Office or the judiciary.[24] Opposition to
efforts to structure sentencing in part arise from constitutional conventions regarding
the independence of the judiciary. As Andrew Ashworth comments: 'The judiciary
seems to believe that it has the right to determine sentencing policy, and for that
there is neither constitutional or pragmatic justification.'[25] The prerogative resides
with the legislature which may decide to entrust the detailed work to a commission.
Sentencing guidelines address both the decision on whether to imprison and the length

of any custodial sentence that is imposed. The important consideration with respect to sentence length is less the maximum allowed by statute than the actual decision reached by the sentencer.[26] As to statutory maxima, the task of effecting reductions may be a political minefield. When in 1978 the Advisory Council on the Penal System sensibly proposed reductions to maximum terms of imprisonment, the report was howled down in derision by much of the popular press.[27]

The more viable reform strategy is to structure sentence length by means of a combination of guidelines and appelate review. The danger must always be guarded against that any reduction in sentence length may result in an increase in the total number of custodial sentences. When this occurs, the use of custody is likely to replace non-custodial sanctions. Sentencers may be impressed by opportunities to use the prison system to provide a taste of custody, since after allowance is made for remission and for time remanded in custody, the length of time to be served may be very brief. The personal consequences, however, are likely to be similar regardless of the period in custody. In particular, the individual has to deal with having a record of being in prison, the stigma of which is not reduced by reference to duration. Custody should be a sanction of last resort regardless of length of time to be served.

The Criminal Justice Act of 1982 provided courts with more rather than fewer opportunities to impose brief tastes of custody. In sentencing adults, the availability of the partly suspended sentence poses this danger.[28] Of greater significance, the new minimum three week detention centre sentence, which becomes two weeks after allowing for remission, promises a fourfold escalation of numbers of young men aged 14–20 passing through detention centres.[29] These considerations underline the crucial importance of structuring sentencing decisions with respect to the use of custody regardless of sentence length.

Breach of default of non-custodial sanctions should only very exceptionally be dealt with by imprisonment

The prison system should not, as a general rule, be available for persons in breach of non-custodial sanctions. The problem remains of fine defaulters coming into the English prison system despite a series of statutes intended to curb this practice. In fact, fine defaulters represent the most rapidly growing category of prison receptions, accounting in 1981 for 21,000 persons, or one in every four sentenced persons entering the English prison system.[30] Very exceptional circumstances might be specified where custody be considered but generally other means of enforcement would be pursued. Resort to imprisonment often occurs because courts have not obtained adequate information about the individual and as a result of poorly developed enforcement procedures.

Existing legislation in England needs to be strengthened to ensure that courts satisfy specified conditions regarding information and enforcement procedures before prison for default can be considered.[31] [...] [L]ittle advantage is gained from making an offence non-imprisonable if, as is the case with respect to the offence of being drunk and disorderly, imprisonment remains an option in the event of non-payment of a fine. When prison is regarded as inappropriate for the original offence it should not, in general, be available to enforce compliance with a lesser sanction.

The range of non-imprisonable offences should be widened to include certain categories of theft

Imprisonment is qualitatively different from non-custodial sanctions and should be used only when any lesser punishment would depreciate the seriousness of the offence. Few reformers of the penal system have urged the total abolition of the prison system and most would agree that prison be retained as the 'detestable solution' in dealing with persons convicted of serious offences. However, expanding prison systems have much to do with persons who are not serious offenders. From its earliest history, the prison system has served as a depository for persons involved in petty crime, much of which is little more than a social nuisance. While the prison system continues to provide this residual function, alternative means of responding to this type of behaviour are unlikely to emerge. The criminal justice process in general and the prison system in particular should not be a substitute for the delivery of welfare.[32]

The Criminal Justice Act of 1982 made one or two offences, such as sleeping rough and begging, non-imprisonable. Amendments to make other trivial offences non-imprisonable were defeated. Welcome as these proposals were, the arena for legislative action has to be considerably more ambitious. On pragmatic grounds, the impact on the size of the prison population will be very slight unless the reform thrust is extended to include at least some categories of theft and other property offences. Beyond these pragmatic considerations, however, there is the fundamental question of whether it is right to imprison persons for other than serious offences. On economic and philosophic grounds, property offences where the amount involved is less than, say £100, should be non-imprisonable. This approach is consistent with Andrew Ashworth's proposal for a rigorous ceiling, 'so that an offender who commits a modest theft for the fifth, tenth or fifteenth time should not be at risk of a custodial sentence'.[33] There may be more public support for avoiding imprisonment for property offenders, including burglary, than is sometimes supposed. An English public opinion poll on attitudes to crime and punishment found that more than half the respondents favoured a non-custodial sentence for burglary.[34]

Prosecutorial discretion should be structured towards restricting entry into the criminal justice process

Prosecutorial decision-making remains largely uncharted territory, and the significance of decisions by prosecutors for prison systems cannot be overestimated. In the Netherlands and Japan, both countries with centrally administered systems of prosecution, discretion exercised not to prosecute has played a crucial part in the reduction of prison population size. Elsewhere, prosecutors have contributed to the mounting pressures on the courts and ultimately the prison system. Diversion by prosecutors is not without its dangers as a large body of research literature, mostly in the United States, has testified.[35] Unless the diversion strategy is pointed outside the criminal justice process, the probability exists that the scope of the criminal justice net will be widened and not narrowed. In England the complex task of structuring prosecutorial discretion is compounded by the absence of prosecuting agencies which are independent of the police. A preliminary step would be the establishment of Crown Prosecutors as recommended by the Royal Commission on Criminal Procedure.[36] Accepted in principle by the government in 1982 this proposal is a crucial component of coherent criminal justice policy. Efforts to structure decision-making in this area must take account of the inter-related nature of prosecution and sentencing. As attempts are made to formulate sentencing policy in a reductionist direction the probability exists that progress made will be counteracted by prosecutors. In Minnesota and other jurisdictions where sentencing guidelines are in use, attention is now being directed at decision-making which occurs earlier in the criminal justice process.

The scope of the criminal law should be narrowed

The criminal law extends across a broad and highly diverse canvas of events. In England more than seven thousand events are defined as criminal.[37] More than half these offences are of strict liability with no account taken of the individual's motivation. Compared to other forms of social control the administration of the criminal law is often slow, cumbersome and inefficient. For this and other reasons civil proceedings are often preferred. The Inland Revenue, for example, invokes informal rather than criminal procedures in virtually all cases of tax evasion, even when very large sums are involved. Most decriminalization has taken the *de facto* route, and this offers the most promising means to cutting back the scope of criminal justice.

Selective non-enforcement of the criminal law, however, carries dangers of serious inequities and disrespect for the rule of law. Legislative action is required on two fronts. Firstly, the temptation should be resisted to further widen the scope of criminal law. Wherever possible the legislature should be persuaded to provide for civil rather than criminal redress. This outcome, for example, was achieved in the area of racial discrimination following amendments to the Race Relations Bill.[38] Secondly, vigorous efforts should be made to achieve decriminalization by statute.[39] Louk Hulsman has urged the replacement of criminal by civil proceedings across a variety of problematic situations. Hulsman argues that the key question is how to promote better ways of tackling the very divergent problems labelled crime. By 'civilization', Hulsman refers to approaches by which the compensatory model of civil law replaces the blunt instrument of criminal law. Furthermore, Hulsman and others are finding growing support for the view that state resources should be directed primarily to the family, the school, the work setting and the neighbourhood, and that wherever possible the control of conflict and mediation be left to them.[40]

Existing policy and practice in many countries are geared for further massive expansion in prison systems throughout the remainder of the century. The myths of Great Expectations for criminal justice persist despite extensive knowledge regarding its inefficiency as a means of social control. The prison system represents the crude deep-end of society's control apparatus and growth by the prison system ultimately threatens the freedom of everyone. Unless expansionist policies are halted and reversed, the legacy for the twenty-first century will be a prison system archipelago of monstrous proportions. Reductionist policy options are available at each of the various stages of the criminal justice process. The starting point, however, must be the prison system itself. The urgent requirement is not for tentative steps at the margins, but for bold, decisive and sustained action at the penal epicentre.

NOTES AND REFERENCES

1 See, e.g. Fifteenth Report from the Expenditure Committee, Session 1977–8, vol. 1. Report, *The Reduction of Pressure on the Prison System,* HC 662–1, HMSO, 1978, pp. xxxviii–xlix; Parliamentary All-Party Penal Affairs Group, *Too Many Prisoners, An Examination of Ways of Reducing the Prison Population,* Chichester and London: Barry Rose, 1980; Fourth Report from the Home Affairs Committee, session 1980/81. *The Prison Service,* vol. 1, House of Commons Paper 412–1, 1981, pp. xv–xxxix; Parliamentary All-Party Penal Affairs Group, *Still Too Many Prisoners, An Assessment of the Government's Response to the Report 'Too Many Prisoners' since June 1980,* 1981; see also 'Prisons', Labour Party Discussion Document, London, 1982, pp. 6–7; and *A Time For Justice, A report on crime, prison and punishment,* Abingdon: Catholic Social Welfare Commission, 1982, pp. 17–19.
2 Fourth Report of the Home Affairs Committee, op. cit., p. xv.
3 At the request of the May Committee, the Home Office made available to them a longer-range forecast which the May Report summarizes in graphic form only. The chart indicates a growth in average daily population commencing about 1985 and reaching 47,000 by 1987. No supportive documentation was provided by the Home Office for the long-range forecast. The May Committee commented: 'As the Home Office has pointed out to us, even the short-term forecasts are not precise and have a margin of error which increases the further ahead the forecast is being made. Indeed such considerations have led the Home Office to confine itself to publishing five-year forecasts only and not making – including initially also to us – the ten-year forecasts available publicly'. *Report of the Inquiry into the United Kingdom Prison Services,* Chairman Mr Justice May, Cmnd 7673, London: HMSO, 1979, p. 43.
4 For a description of the Home Office approach to prison population forecasting, see Memorandum submitted by the Home Office to the Home Affairs Committee, 'Projections of the Prison Population', Minutes of Evidence, 16 March 1981, pp. 217–18.
5 See generally, Andrew Rutherford *et al., Prison Population and Policy Choices,* vol. 1, Preliminary Report to Congress, Washington D.C.: National Institute of Law Enforcement and Criminal Justice, 1977, pp. 131–245.
6 See Andrew Rutherford, 'Decarceration of Young Offenders in Massachusetts, The Events and their Aftermath', in N. Tutt (ed.), *Alternative Strategies for Coping With Crime,* Oxford: Blackwell, 1978, pp. 103–19.
7 Additionally, one other prison was closed in 1974, but reopened the following year with its capacity reduced by 230.
8 Home Affairs Committee, Minutes of Evidence, H.C. 412–2, 1981, p. 17.
9 May Report, op.cit., note 3, p. 143. In 1981 the Home Office provided the Home Affairs Committee with a list of twelve prisons which it wished to close. Home Affairs Committee, Minutes of Evidence, H.C. 412–2, 1981, p. 219.
10 May Report, op. cit., note 3, p. 125.
11 *H.C. Deb.,* vol. 972, col. 1239, 31 October 1979.
12 May Report, op. cit., note 3, p. 143.
13 Roy King and Rod Morgan, *The Future of the Prison System,* Farnborough: Gower, 1980, p. 27.
14 Minimum standards address a very much wider arena than physical space. In England, only very tentative steps have been taken to what these might be, and Home Office drafts of a white paper set forth some ideas for going some way further forward than existing Prison Rules. The Chief Inspector of prisons has drawn attention to particular parts of the European Standard Minimum Rules, for example on work (Rule 72(3)) and on education and training (Rules 66 and 67).

15 See, e.g. Michael Zander, Home Office Bicentenary Lecture, 1982, p. 14. The European Commission has had an impact in other areas, especially prisoners' rights regarding correspondence. See, e.g., *Silver and others against the United Kingdom, Report of the Commission*, Strasbourg, 11 October 1980. The Commission found that the English prison system had violated three Articles of the European Convention on Human Rights. This ruling led to the revision and publication of Standing Orders on communications in June 1981.

16 Graham Zellick, 'Prison Rules', *Criminal Law Review*, 1981, p. 616.

17 Parole was introduced in England in 1967 partly as a device for reducing prison population size. The extent to which parole has this effect depends upon whether sentencers compensate for parole when determining sentence length. There has been no research on whether the 'penal credibility gap' influences sentencers in this way. In 1975, parole procedures were modified so as to increase the rate of parole. See generally, Howard League for Penal Reform, *Freedom On Licence, The Development of Parole and Proposals for Reform*, Sunbury: Quartermaine, 1981, esp, pp. 15–31. For estimates of the effect on prison population of various early release mechanisms, see NACRO, 'Attempts to reduce the prison population and their estimated effect.' Additional information submitted to the Home Affairs Committee, vol. 2, Minutes of Evidence, H.C. 412–2, 1981, pp. 275–6.

18 Johannes B. Feest, *Imprisonment and the Criminal Justice System in the Federal Republic of Germany*, University of Bremen, 1982, pp. 26–7.

19 Some prisoners serving longer terms are released under this scheme after completing one third of their sentence.

20 *Criminal Justice Act of 1960*, Section 2(1): 'The Minister may make rules providing for the temporary release, subject to such conditions (if any) as may be imposed in each particular case of persons serving a sentence of penal servitude or imprisonment'. While the total so released was 891 in 1980 and 441 in 1981, the number released at any one time is small, rarely exceeding ten. The practice of unplanned release is only resorted to when all institutions are full and '... has been considered preferable to large-scale doubling or trebling of offenders in cells that were designed for one occupant only'. Personal communication from the Irish Department of Justice, 27/3/82; see *Annual Report on Prisons and Places of Detention for 1980*.

21 There have been seven amnesties of prisoners in France since 1945. When President Mitterand took office in 1981, he extended the amnesty to cover sentences of up to six months (previous amnesties had included sentences of up to three months), and released 7,000 persons. The French prison population fell by 28 per cent from 43,000 to 31,000 between April and September 1981. In Israel amnesties take three forms: Presidential amnesties (usually involves about 120 prisoners), special amnesties (e.g. in 1967 when 501 persons were released, and in 1982 when 440 persons were released; the prison administration wanted 800 but the police objected), and routine amnesties, available after half sentence is completed and have to be signed by Minister of Justice, usually involves 80–120 persons per year. Personal communication from Professor Menachem Amir of the Hebrew University of Jerusalem. See also Leslie Sebba 'Amnesty – A Quasi-Experiment', *British Journal of Criminology*, 19, 1979, pp. 5–30.

22 Provision for early release was first made available under the Imprisonment (Temporary Provisions) Act of 1980, emergency legislation enacted during the Prison Officers' industrial dispute but was not brought into effect. In December 1981, a minister at the Home Office suggested that powers contained in the Criminal Justice Act of 1982 would not be used. *H.C. Debs* 2 December 1981. The Michigan Prison Overcrowding Emergency Act of 1980 does appear to have succeeded in keeping the state prison population from rising. In 1981 Michigan was the only state prison system where the prison population fell. *Detroit Free Press*, 3 May 1982.

23 Fourth Report from the Home Affairs Committee, *The Prison Service,* House of Commons Paper 412–1, July 1981; para. 104 and the Government's Reply to the Fourth Report, Cmnd 8446, London: HMSO, December 1981, p. 20.

24 Andrew Ashworth, 'Reducing the Prison Population in the 1980s: The Need for Sentencing Reform', lecture to NACRO, 1982, draft pp. 17–21.

25 *Ibid.,* p. 14.

26 Reductions in sentence length may significantly reduce prison population. For example, the Home Office have calculated that if sentences of up to four years imposed on non-violent offenders had been halved, the effect would have been a reduction in total prison population size of about 20 per cent. Home Affairs Committee, vol. 2, Minutes of Evidence, H.C. 412–2, 1981, pp. 218–19.

27 Advisory Council on the Penal System, *Sentences of Imprisonment: A Review of Maximum Penalties,* London: HMSO, 1978; see also Marjorie Jones, *Crime, Punishment and the Press,* London: NACRO, 1980, pp. 9–20.

28 The partly suspended sentence, under Section 47 of the Criminal Law Act of 1977 came into operation on 29 March 1982. The Criminal Justice Act of 1982 attempts to restrict its use. See D. A. Thomas, 'The Partly Suspended Sentence', *Criminal Law Review,* May 1982, pp. 288–95; and *R. v. Clarke, Criminal Law Review,* 1982, pp. 464–7.

29 In 1981, 13,600 young men were sentenced to detention centres. The minimum length of stay, with full remission was 6½ weeks for 14–16 year olds and eight weeks for 16–20 year olds. Under the provisions of the Criminal Justice Act of 1982 with remission of one-third for both age groups, the minimum sentence (making no allowance for time spent in custody or remand) becomes two weeks. The number of receptions into detention centres could by the mid-1980s increase to about 54,000 per year.

30 *Prison Statistics for 1981,* London: HMSO, 1982, p. 19.

31 The Magistrates' Courts Act 1980, Section 88 specifies conditions but these require to be extended and tightened. The Howe Committee on Fine Default observed: 'We are disturbed by indications that a number of people without the means to pay do, nevertheless, end up in prison for fine default'. *Fine Default,* Report of a NACRO Working Party, London: NACRO, 1981, p. 20. The report provides a comprehensive review of fine enforcement problems and possibilities. See also, P. Softley, *A Survey of Fine Enforcement,* Home Office Research Unit, London: HMSO, 1973.

32 See Susan Fairhead and Tony F. Marshall, 'Dealing with the Petty Persistent Offender: an account of the current Home Office Research Unit Studies', in *The Petty Persistent Offender,* London: NACRO, 1979, pp. 1–9.

33 Andrew Ashworth, op. cit., note 34, p. 17. In 1981, 34 per cent of all persons received on sentence (excluding fine defaulters) were convicted of theft or related offences. *Prison Department Statistics, 1981,* 1982. Remarkably little research has been conducted on the composition of prison populations. There has been no general prison population census in England, and the only detailed study was carried out in 1972 and based upon a ten per cent sample in the South East Region. This research found that 30 per cent of the sample of sentenced adult men could be described as petty or minor offenders. See 'A Survey of the South East Prison Population', *Home Office Research Unit Bulletin,* No. 5, 1978, pp. 12–24.

34 Stephen Shaw, *The People's Justice, A Major Poll of Public Attitudes on Crime and Punishment,* London: Prison Reform Trust, 1982, p. 18. While 47 per cent of the respondents favoured immediate imprisonment, seven per cent of those in favour of an alternative sentence advocated corporal punishment.

35 See, e.g., Elizabeth and James Vorenberg, 'Early Diversion from the Criminal Justice System', in *Prisoners in America,* ed. Lloyd Ohlin, New York: Prentice Hall, 1973. See also the extract from the statement by Daniel J. Freed to the Subcommittee of the Committee on the Judiciary of the House of Representatives in 1974, contained in

Diversion from Criminal Justice in an English Context. Report of a NACRO Working Party, Chairman, Michael Zander, Chichester and London: Barry Rose, 1975, pp. 41–4.

36 *Report of Royal Commission on Criminal Procedure,* Chairman, Sir Cyril Philips, Cmnd 8092, London: HMSO, 1981, pp. 144–70.

37 Justice, *Breaking the Rules,* London: Justice, 1980.

38 Anthony Lester and Geoffrey Bird, *Race and the Law,* London: Penguin, 1972, pp. 98–120.

39 See, for example, David Tench, *Towards a Middle System of Law,* London: Consumers' Association, 1981.

40 See especially Louk Hulsman, 'Penal Reform in the Netherlands: Part 1, Bringing the Criminal Justice System Under Control', *Howard Journal,* vol. 20, 1981, pp. 150–9; and Part II in vol. 21, 1982, pp. 35–47; see also Nils Christie, 'Conflicts as property', *British Journal of Criminology,* 17, 1977, pp. 1–15.

Hulsman was a central influence on the Council of Europe's comprehensive and far-reaching report on decriminalization. See European Committee on Crime Problems, *Report on Decriminalisation,* Strasbourg, Council of Europe, 1980. See also Fifteenth Criminological Research Conference, *Sexual Behaviour and Attitudes and their implications for Criminal Law, Conclusions and Recommendations,* Strasbourg, 25 November 1982.

25

The future of imprisonment

Thomas Mathiesen

[···]

When we are situated in the context of the present, that present easily appears unchangeable and permanent.

Yet, when situating ourselves outside the context of the present, we know that the present becomes past, and that present and prior present, past, may differ. In fact, we know that with time, the prior present, or past, may and frequently does differ drastically from the present. There is continuity in history. But there is also change.

There is abundant evidence of this in the area of penal policy, over shorter as well as longer periods of time. Concretely, there is empirical evidence from history showing that major penal systems have been *frozen* in size, *reduced* in size, *partially abolished,* and *fully abolished.*

All four possibilities exist because the development of penal systems, and the size of the populations in them, is not an automatic reflection of external changes such as simple alterations in the crime rate but determined by political choices – however conditioned these choices may be by structures and processes in the environment.

Let us look briefly at material showing the viability of the four possibilities.

In 1985, the notion of a *freeze* on prison construction was introduced in a plenary sub-session of the VIIIth United Nations' Congress on the Prevention of Crime and the Treatment of Offenders (Mathiesen, 1985). The background was the mounting prison figures, and huge construction projects, in many countries. The need for a halt and a rethink was emphasized. The reaction among the delegates was telling. No proposals or recommendations came out of the initiative, but there was widespread interest and, unusual in the UN context, applause. Perhaps the applause came from the younger parts of the delegations. In any case, a straightforward proposal for a freeze on construction appeared to be received as something of a relief in the bureaucratic context of the United Nations. A number of delegates asked for more information. And information could be given.

SOURCE: This chapter is taken from *Prison on Trial*, London, Sage, 1990, pp. 137–68 (abridged).

[...] Sweden in practice froze its prison population in 1983 by introducing half time parole for the large bulk of the country's prisoners. And this happened [...] without any serious detriment to the population. It implied that through several years in the 1980s, the Swedish prison population remained below its size in 1982. [...] The reform created a debate and may, on rather invalid grounds, be reversed. And it should be emphasized that in early 1989, prison figures are again exceeding figures from 1982. This, however, does not detract from the fact that in practice, it was possible to institute something like a freeze for some years.

Denmark has a similar experience, using different methods. In 1982, Denmark introduced maximum punishments for a number of property crimes in addition to reducing the minimum time for release on parole and liberalizing the rules concerning drunken driving. The reduced maximum sentences for property crimes were intended to reduce the general sentencing level by one-third. The total daily average number of prisoners, which had been increasing since 1977, fell in 1982 and stabilized at the new level during the following year. It did not last – the new rules concerning sentencing levels still left much discretion to decision-making bodies, and figures are again rising. But the fact that a stabilization could occur is suggestive, showing concretely that relatively undramatic measures may make a difference to the prison population.

The details of the Swedish and Danish experiences mentioned here suggest that with a little more stamina in given proposals, and with a somewhat greater emphasis on mandatory rather than discretionary rules, it might have been possible to stabilize given prison populations for a longer period, or at least stabilize or control their increase.

Notable examples suggest that major *reductions* of prison populations, over long periods of time, are possible.

In an important contribution entitled *Prisons and the Process of Justice*, Andrew Rutherford has examined three historical instances of major reductions (Rutherford, 1986) – England 1908–1938, Japan 1950–1975 and the Netherlands 1950–1975 [see Chapter 24 of this volume].

In all three countries during the relevant periods, prison populations were significantly reduced and sustained at a new low level. In Rutherford's analysis, two general explanatory conditions emerge. First, in all three countries, 'key decision-makers shared a profound scepticism as to what benefits, if any, derive from imprisonment' (Rutherford, 1986: 145). A detailed review of this scepticism and questioning is provided for all three countries. For England, an intriguing account of Winston Churchill's particular role is given. Secondly, 'the responses to crime by officials engaged throughout the criminal justice process' (Rutherford, 1986: 146) were important. In the Netherlands and Japan, the courts were insulated from the impact of increasing numbers of offenders due to actions taken by the public prosecutors, notably their tendency to dismiss charges. In addition came a widespread intolerance of overcrowding. In England, on the other hand, the critical intervening tactic was the movement away from custody in sentencing practice by the courts. Thus, different personnel sectors were involved. But the role of personnel engaged in practice throughout the system was a common denominator.

We may speculate whether the *combination* of scepticism on the part of top level decision-makers and activities at the grass roots of the system was important.

Sustained reduction was perhaps made possible by the fact that the two levels functioned in the same direction. Perhaps top level scepticism alone is rather easily followed by reductions or standstills which are temporary, while sustained reduction requires that the two levels function in an integrated fashion.

Notable historical examples also exist of *partial abolitions* of penal systems. Two such examples may be mentioned briefly.

The first is the abolition of forced labour in Norway (for details, see Mathiesen, 1974: 90–97). [...] Forced labour, introduced by the so-called vagrancy act of 1900 which criminalized public drunkenness, was primarily used against vagrant alcoholics, and implied that alcoholics could spend years in institutions within the prison system. Though the latter part of the 1960s was generally characterized by rather conservative trends in criminal policy, the period saw a mounting criticism, from a spectrum of professional quarters such as medicine, law and criminology, of the forced labour system. It was characterized as unjust as well as ineffective. The Norwegian prisoners' organization was rather efficient in collecting and channelling this criticism, which penetrated into political decision-making bodies as well as the practising grass roots of the criminal justice system. In 1970, a unanimous Storting (Parliament) decided to abolish the system, a decision which at the time implied a major reduction of the prison population (250 out of the country's 2000 prisoners). And though the abolition was neutralized later in terms of total prison figures, this particular category of people – particularly impoverished, destitute, homeless alcoholics – *never came back to the system*. In the present context, this is a significant conclusion.

An important feature emerges from the relative success of the Norwegian vagrancy act example. An abolition of this part of the system required not only scepticism towards the system at the top level, and not only agreement at the grass roots within the system, but, additionally, widespread support of and strong pressure for change from professional groups outside the system. In the climate created through the interaction between those three corners, abolition succeeded. But it should also be noted that the pressure for change came primarily from the professions. The wider lay community was not as intensely involved. We shall return to this point later.

Norway is a small country, with a small-scale system. The second example refers to a large country with a large system – the dissolution of the training schools for youthful offenders in Massachusetts. The story has been told before, and is well known (Rutherford, 1974; see also Rutherford, 1986: 121). Building on a prior period of strong criticism of the training schools or youth prisons, a particular commissioner of the Department of Youth Services – Jerome Miller – closed the schools of the state in the course of 1972, and was able to show an important and sustained reduction in institutional populations. From the example some patterns emerge which resemble those characterizing the abolition of the Norwegian vagrancy statutes. The strong prior criticism in the environment is one of them. Furthermore, somewhat like the vagrancy example, Jerome Miller apparently had political backing from above, and was able to communicate and channel his message through important mass media. Contextual aspects of the situation as well as political relationships favoured the commissioner's abrupt abolition.

We have referred to freeze or standstill, reduction, and partial abolitions. Are there, finally, examples of full abolition, in which total penal or sanctioning systems have been abolished? There are, and we see them if we distance ourselves a little more from our own present.

In an intriguing piece on the memories of abolitionist victories of the past, the German criminologist Sebastian Scheerer reminds us that 'there has never been a major social transformation in the history of mankind that had not been looked upon as unrealistic, idiotic, or utopian by the large majority of experts even a few years before the unthinkable became reality' (Scheerer, 1986: 7). He points to how magnificent the extension of the Roman empire was, and how victoriously its armed forces fought the Huns, twenty-five years before its fall. 'And when', Scheerer writes, 'in August 476, the last of the West Roman emperors was quietly ordered to retire, there were no dramatic changes in everyday life, even though this was the end of an empire that had lasted for more than a millennium, and that had been believed to be invincible' (Scheerer, 1986: 7). Who, in their own present, could see that this was happening?

Scheerer goes on with another example, closer to our issue: the same holds true, he argues, for modern slavery. An estimated 15 million Africans were brought to the New World between the fifteenth and the nineteenth centuries. Slavery became an indispensable feature of world trade. In the early 1800s, only a few decades before the formal abolition of slavery (in the US in 1865), 'abolitionists were still few in number and widely regarded as awkward customers' (Scheerer, 1986: 7). Slavery had succeeded in looking extremely stable almost until the day it collapsed. Who would have thought, at the time, that it was going to fall completely? The conditions which advanced the abolition of slavery are complex and probably not fully unravelled, but we certainly know that political choice and decisions were deeply involved.

A third example to be added here is that of the European witch hunts. Who would have believed, in 1487, when Heinrich Institor Krämer and Jakob Spränger published their major theological and legal dogmatic work on witches, *Malleus Maleficarum* (or *The Witch Hammer*), that the institution of witch hunts would some day disappear, as in fact would the Inquisition itself?

In contrast to the examples of the Roman empire and slavery we are, with Krämer and Spränger, in the early phase of the period in question. Before writing their important work, they had used all their enthusiasm and energy to have as many witches as possible taken to the stake, but had met much resistance, partly to the claim that it was necessary to liquidate so many witches, and partly against their own competence as judges. The two inquisitors even had to swallow that secular authorities sometimes protected witches (Alver, 1971: 25). And to cut a long story short, in their embarrassment they turned to Rome, where Pope Innocent VIII resided, to complain, and on 5 December 1484 Innocent issued his papal bull on witches, *Summis Desiderantes Affectibus,* which provided the decisive churchly sanction to the witch hunts. With the bull as basic authority, the two inquisitors wrote *The Witch Hammer,* which essentially was a handbook on witch hunting. The work contained a dogmatic argument for and proof of the existence of witches (including a counter-proof of the popely *Canon Episcopi* from the 1100s, which had expressed the view that a belief in nightly travel with and to demons was imagination), a detailed treatment of the desecrating acts committed by witches, and, thirdly, a legal manual on witch hunting. Within a period of thirty years the work was printed in fourteen editions (the second edition including a reprint of Pope Innocent's bull), and it became profoundly important as a theological–legal basis for the subsequent witch hunts in Europe. Who would have thought, at the time, that all of this would one day wither and be gone?

And even towards the end of the witch hunts, the institution's demise must have been difficult or impossible to imagine by many, partly because the popular belief in witches remained strong. In a major work the Danish historian Gustav Henningsen has described and analysed the beginning of the end of the witch hunts in the region of Northern Spain in the early 1600s (Henningsen, 1981; see also Henningsen, 1984; Lea, 1906/1966, vol. IV, Ch. IX).

The beginning of the end came 100 years earlier in this region than in the rest of Europe. The Inquisition, first established in the 1200s as a special force to combat heresy, and organized in Spain during the late 1400s, was at the height of its power. With a point of departure in Navarra in Northern Spain, Henningsen describes the Spanish branch of the special force as a huge spider with a wide net of intelligence services, secret police forces, sentencing authorities and arrests, organized in nineteen (later twenty-one) tribunals throughout the enormous Spanish empire. The tribunals entered a network of definite and bureaucratic communication lines to the super spider in Madrid, *la Suprema*, the Inquisition Council. The beginning of the end came, in fact, among the bureaucrats within this enormous organization.

When the members of the local tribunal agreed, *la Suprema* rarely intervened. But when there was disagreement, extensive communication with the central authority would ensue. Henningsen describes in detail how liberal inquisitors in Northern Spain in the early 1600s, notably a certain inquisitor Alonso de Salazar Frias, began to doubt certain aspects of the witch crazes, the frenzied waves of persecution of witches. The background was an auto-da-fé in Logrono in 1610, which also Salazar had set his name to, where eleven witches had been burnt during the presence of 30,000 spectators. Following the auto-da-fé, and at the initiative of *la Suprema*, Salazar and his aides undertook a major empirical investigation of Basque witches, interviewing over 1800 individuals. To Salazar the question of proof was central, and he found no proof whatsoever of witchcraft. Rather, he found that the best weapon against the appearance of large numbers of witches in fact was *silence* ('I deduce the importance of silence and reserve from the experience that there were neither witches nor bewitched until they were talked and written about'; Salazar as quoted in Lea, 1906/1966, vol. IV: 234). But the other members of the local tribunal did not agree, and the dissensus necessitated communication with *la Suprema*. *La Suprema* had a long tradition in restraint in terms of sentencing witches (as did, in fact, the Italian Inquisition – the major European persecutions predominantly came in areas outside the jurisdiction of the Inquisition), with a practice of pardoning those sentenced to the stake by the local tribunals. Liberal views thus had a sounding board in *La Suprema*, and generalized doubt was beginning to be cast over the issue. In the end, *la Suprema* decided to follow Salazar's recommendation to suspend the witch cases, asking him to prepare a new set of instructions for the handling of witches. The instructions were adopted, with almost no changes, by *la Suprema* in 1614. A liberal inquisitor with support from above thus became instrumental in the subsequent abolition of witch burning and, indeed, hunts, in a way interestingly reminiscent of the professionals involved in the prison reductions and abolitions of more modern times mentioned earlier in this chapter.

Obviously, major social forces outside individual liberal inquisitors were essential in preparing for abolition. We do not know enough about these forces (Henningsen, 1984: 37), which worked differently from parallel forces in the late 1400s. Much greater research effort should be placed on scrutinizing the social conditions fostering such abolitions. It would add importantly to our stock of knowledge about how to achieve results today. The important point here, however, is that political choice and action again was part of the process, and that the vanishing of the witch hunts (and, as I have said, of the Inquisition itself, finally abolished in Spain in 1820), indicates the *realism* contained even in the total abolition of major and whole penal and sanctioning systems.

But, before closing this section: though the Roman empire has disappeared, is it not true that new empires have emerged? Though slavery has vanished, does not discrimination and repression exist? And though the old witch hunts are gone, have not new ones developed?

Undeniably so. Functional equivalents to patterns which are gone have come about. Though on a much larger scale, this is a bit like the return to new trends of imprisonment, perhaps of other groups, in the more limited examples of freeze, reduction and partial abolition of prisons referred to above. Three points, however, should be made.

First, there are degrees of difference between the old and the new witch hunts. There is a degree of difference between being burnt at the stake in the Europe of the 1500s and being politically persecuted for leftist sympathies in the Europe of the 1980s. In our own present, such degrees may not constitute an important part of our phenomenology, but if we place ourselves a little outside, we see them. This is not meant to be taken as a unilinear improvement theory. The Europe of the mid-1900s suggests how problematic such a theory would be. But it is meant to propose the taking of degrees of difference as something important.

Secondly, in so far as equivalents to patterns abolished develop, I would suggest that this is part of the historical process and thereby of the political struggle as an unending activity. Political struggle consists of hard work oriented towards victory and change, but not towards finality. Victory and change later abated or for that matter neutralized do not invite despair but new political struggles on a new level.

Thirdly, perhaps more may be done to prevent return to prior conditions. Perhaps, in fact, this is also one of the lessons of history. We shall return to this possibility shortly.

Through what steps?

Backed by history as a major source of knowledge and inspiration about the viability of another course, we may finally ask: what concrete steps should be taken to attain a different course?

It probably depends somewhat on the particular course. Andrew Rutherford is probably right in saying that a freeze or standstill policy is not in the long term a viable alternative in expanding prison systems, but more of a short-term relief from population pressures (Rutherford, 1986: 172). [...] Partly for this reason, the course should be more radical. In 1986 Rutherford proposed a 50 per cent reduction as the target for the English prison population by 1990. The three examples of successful prison shrinkage which Rutherford analysed (see above), accomplished such a reduction. It would have brought the number of English prisoners per 100,000 inhabitants down to the range of 35 (Rutherford, 1986: 174). The wide variations which exist between different European countries in terms of numbers of prisoners *per capita*, with several countries certainly having under 50 prisoners per 100,000 population, make such a goal entirely practical. I have recently targeted a close to full abolition of the Norwegian prison system by 2010, the year when our neighbouring Swedes have decided to close down their last nuclear power plants (Mathiesen, 1987). This target is less practical, in view of the counterforces, but in principle it is attainable. In any case, the goal for socialists and social democrats in countries like Britain, Norway and Sweden could well be set to *a contraction of two-thirds of the prison population* within our century.

The steps with which to reach such a goal may be discussed on two levels, the level of legislation and the level of what may be called policy preparation. Policy preparation presents the most complex issues, and will demand most of our attention.

Legislation

Concrete legislation would have to depend on the country concerned, and its legal and penal context. But a *widening of the range of non-imprisonable offences* on the one hand, and a *narrowing of the scope of the criminal law,* providing for a civil rather than a criminal solution and redress, on the other, are two essential and supplementary legislative roads. The former is frequently referred to as 'depenalization', the latter as 'decriminalization'. Rutherford has called attention to the former (Rutherford, 1986: 182–3), the Dutch criminologist Louk Hulsman very forcefully to the latter (Hulsman, 1986; see also Rutherford, 1986: 183–4).

In addition to these major legislative ways, legal measures such as a lowering of maximum sentences, an increase of early release measures, and a strict programme of prison closure, would be important supplementary methods. Prison closure would be vitally important in order to prevent returns to prior prison policies. One particularly important danger should be kept in mind – the tendency for legislation to have unintended consequences. In particular, there is considerable evidence suggesting that the introduction of so-called 'alternatives to prison' may actually have a 'net-widening' effect: rather than bringing very many people out of the prisons, they may actually bring new people into a wider control system [see Chapter 17 of this volume]. The process is hardly inevitable, and recent reassessments of, among others, Canadian data suggest moderations of the general conclusion (McMahon, 1988). But the danger should be kept clearly in mind. It suggests that the attack on the prisons should come *before* rather than after the alternatives, alternatives to prison should be *preceded* by depenalization and/or decriminalization. As Rutherford has pointed out, this reverses conventional wisdom regarding alternative sanctions 'which is that when these are made available, less use will be made of custody' (Rutherford, 1986: 168). It may be noted that in both of the major partial abolitions referred to earlier in this book, the abolition of the Norwegian forced labour system and of the Massachusetts training schools, this 'deep-end strategy', attacking the prison solution first, was explicitly followed. Indirect evidence suggests that other major abolitions in history have followed a similar course (Henningsen, 1981).

Policy preparation

Policy preparation comprises the social and political preparation of the wider community or society for the change in question. The more radical the target change is, the more vital is policy preparation. Without it, the necessary legislation will remain wishful thinking, only follow haphazardly, or follow but create a change which will not last.

The lack of long-term permanence in major reductions or abolitions of earlier times is partly explainable in terms of lack of policy preparation of the wider societal context. As we have seen, several of them (apparently even the abolition of the Spanish witch hunts), were initiated 'from above' by key professionals and professional levels, without major and systematic attempts to prepare the community. The implication of policy preparation is to move the issue, in a preparatory way, beyond the initiated professional circles into the community. This may partially be done by attitude preparation, but, most significantly, also by introducing measures which in a better way satisfy relevant needs in the community.

When discussing policy preparation, I envisage a socialist/social democratic government in power, in charge of the considerable resources necessary for preparatory work. This is not the situation in Britain today, but it is the situation in Sweden and has recently been so in Norway, and it is obviously a possible option in the British future. The reader may feel that in the light of today's political situation, and of how social democracy is developing at least in Sweden and Norway, I am demanding quite a bit of such a government. But we should demand quite a bit, and are entitled to do so.

Policy preparation has to go back to *the ideology of prison* and to *the socialist ideology,* discussed as basic and conflicting ideological frameworks in the opening part of this chapter, and take cognizance of their full significance. Briefly put, the ideology of prison has to be *countered,* while the socialist ideology has to be *built.*

The ideology of prison contains, as we have said, a supportive component in the form of a series of ideological functions which the prison fills, and a negating component in the form of a series of denials in various public spheres of the fiasco of prison.

The two major components of the ideology point to the necessity of two types of work to counter the ideology – 'counter-functional work' and 'counter-denial work'.

First a few words about *counter-functional work.* The expurgatory, power-draining, diverting, symbolic and action-signifying functions of prison are functions in the public sphere. This is the implication of their being ideological. They are, in a sense, a series of impression managements: without them, those we wish to be purged of would be visible to us, they would be more vocal, we would not be as easily diverted from the real dangers in society, we would not be as able to see ourselves as white, and we would not be as falsely relieved that something is being done about crime. Counter-functional work would imply massive allocation of resources to information and attitude campaigns concerning the existence and dubiousness of these unauthorized functions: the dubiousness of segregating people under conditions which only increase their propensity to crime, the dubiousness of not giving them a voice, of seeing them as the major danger, of seeing ourselves as falsely white, and of being falsely relieved that something is done.

Easy to communicate? Obviously not. From communication research we know that mass media communication – which would have to be extensively used – is more efficient in confirming than in changing existing attitudes (Klapper, 1960; Mathiesen, 1986). But we also know that attitudes *may* be changed. This is a viable possibility if mass media communication is intensely supplemented by interpersonal communications – at the workplace, in the neighbourhood, in the schools. The labour unions, as part of the socialist and social democratic cause and as builders of the ideology, would have to be called upon. Extensive resources would have to be spent on communication at this level.

Essential in the communication effort would be the task of *making the prisoners visible to us* [...] [N]earness creates nuances, nearness makes for understanding. It is the invisibility of the prisoner which makes it possible to maintain the ideological functions of the prison. Visibility is the Achilles' heel of the functions.

Counter-denial work is also work in the public sphere. It would imply that the range of denial mechanisms – non-recognition, pretence and disregard concerning the fiasco of the prison – would have to be effectively countered. The information and attitude campaigns suggested above would also have to include this task. Counter-denial work would have to contain two major components.

First, exposure of *the denial,* whereby the mechanisms of denial would have to be made known, would be necessary. Such exposure might be painful to those actively participating in non-recognition, pretence and (perhaps especially) disregard of the fiasco of prison. One would have to be prepared for political conflict.

Secondly, and as a parallel, exposure of *the actual fiasco* of prison would be essential. Something has already been done in this respect. The rehabilitative fiasco of prison has probably already been effectively exposed, at least in the Scandinavian countries. The deep problems and fiascos contained in general prevention, incapacitation and justice are certainly less widely known. It is in these respects that denial in its various forms is particularly forceful. Exposure would have to take place in the wide variety of communication contexts mentioned earlier. Again, major resources would have to be allotted to the task.

Not only would counter-functional work and counter-denial work have to be integrated. Both would in turn have to merge with the second major feature of policy preparation – that of building the socialist ideology in this area.

As we have said, the socialist ideology, broadly speaking, also comprises two major components, those of solidarity and compensation. Compensation refers to methods of practising solidarity.

The building of solidarity through compensation is vitally important. The countering of the prison ideology through counter-functional work and counter-denial work negates the prison, says 'no' to it. Standing alone, the negation is unlikely to succeed. Supplemented by the construction of solidarity and compensation, the negation has a chance to succeed, because in sharp contrast to the prison solution, it will give something important to both of the major parties – victim and perpetrator – in the conflict. Both parties are vitally in need of solidarity and compensation, because both are, as we have seen, politically and socially weak. Two generalized types of work emanate from this – 'victim' work and 'offender' work.

Victim work may be oriented to 'current' and 'potential' victims, as current victim work and potential victim work.

In the Scandinavian countries, there has been some movement in the direction of added resources for individual victims, especially in the form of economic compensation for certain types of crime. But the movement has been very slow and small-scale. Three major kinds of solidary compensation to current victims may be envisaged.

For one thing, automatic and full material compensation – automatic in the sense that it should be released immediately, and full in the sense that it should be used to the fullest extent across the spectrum of offences. In view of the poverty of the offenders, such compensation would have to be the duty of the state. It is actually fantastic that advanced social-democratic states like Norway and Sweden have not long ago intro-duced automatic insurance, from birth, against crime, but has left the question of insurance to the individual's private initiative. Very modest fees, as part of a taxation package, would be enough to cover the costs.

Furthermore, symbolic compensation is needed – new rituals of sorrow and grief, resources for processing or going over what has happened, new ways of conferring what may be called status compensation, that is to say compensation for lost dignity.

Finally, social support-network establishments around victims, sometimes physical shelters, the latter perhaps modelled on women's crisis centres in the Scandinavian countries, are required.

A number of victims will want little more than economic compensation. Some will want a great deal of symbolic compensation and social support, for example in the forms suggested here. Socialists and social democrats have so far used far too little of their imagination on developing compensatory solidarity in these respects.

Two major kinds of solidarity with potential victims may be envisaged, the first in a broad sense paralleling material compensation to current victims, the second paralleling symbolic compensation and social support.

For one thing, what may be called 'vulnerability relief' should be emphasized. Though the average statistical chance of becoming a victim is very small for street crime in general, some population groups are more vulnerable than others. Vulner-ability may be relieved through a series of material arrangements, community organi-sation measures and similar street level innovations. This would be tantamount to work oriented towards crime prevention at the street level. It would take the place of ineffective general prevention and incapacitation on the part of prisons. But in line with socialist ideology, the work would have to have a structural sociological rather than a policing profile.

Furthermore, what may be called 'anxiety relief' would be of the utmost impor-tance. Anxiety over crime has become a major welfare problem, perhaps especially in some groups which are not highly vulnerable. At the back of it lies selective depen-dence on current mass media images, lack of alternative channels of communication, and flare-ups of moral panics around concrete events, revolving around kernels of truth. The kernels of truth are meant to be met by the vulnerability relief suggested above. Socialists and social democrats have done almost nothing with the irrational-ities – the task of anxiety relief. It may be provided through some of the same com-munication mechanisms and types of measures as may current victim work and vulnerability relief for potential victims.

So much, here, about victim work. Like victim work, *offender work* may also be oriented to 'current' and 'potential' offenders; current offender work and potential offender work.

Current offenders ending up in prisons, which are our focus of attention here, tend to show signs of extreme poverty in three generalized respects, parallel to the dimen-sions of poverty among victims.

Their material situation is regularly acute, and coupled with illness, drug addiction and distress. Their symbolic standing, in their own eyes and in the eyes of others, is the lowest possible. And their social situation is characterized by isolation and cultural poverty.

It is especially with a background in the extreme and general poverty among a large majority of those caught and imprisoned that the so-called 'new realists' call for intensified policing as the only or main method of combating crime becomes cool and empty of compassion.

The material standing of these people may be fundamentally changed through relatively simple and fairly modest material inputs. Their symbolic standing and social situation requires more imagination. But rituals may be envisaged which confer new standing and status in early and middle, as well as late phases of the individual's development. One small example: the Norwegian chaplain Leer-Salvesen suggests, in a study of Norwegian murderers (Leer-Salvesen, 1988), that the usual radical isolation of murderers during the protracted remand phase is probably the most detrimental thing which can be done to an individual in acute need of working through sorrow and refinding status. This is an example from within the prison. Outside the prison, which is our focus of attention, rituals conferring standing and status may range from reorganized and non-bureaucratic interaction patterns with state and municipal agencies to the establishment of networks conferring new status to specific individuals in need of it.

What would potential offender work consist of? A great deal of stored knowledge exists concerning the sociological correlates to intensive criminal behaviour. [...] [T]here is research evidence strongly suggesting that a relatively small group of juveniles with a wide range of serious social and socio-personal problems are responsible for a sizeable proportion of the more serious juvenile delinquency (Balvig, 1984). This evidence would constitute an important point of departure. The task of introducing compensatory mechanisms with a view towards cancelling out the correlates on the community level would be near at hand for socialists and social democrats. This would involve a new housing policy, a new educational policy, a new youth policy, to mention a few examples.

Another approach would be intensified policing. This would imply intensified proactive police control: control before crime occurs. While few people would object to having police officers in an ordinary way patrolling the streets, a policy of intensified proactive police control as major strategy would run counter to basic principles of legal security also cherished in modern socialist thinking, and counter to – and creating conflict with – important parts of the community. It is the structure of the community, and its material and social foundations, which are in need of change.

Correlates are not necessarily causes. It should openly be admitted that we do not know enough about the effects of the sociological correlates on behaviour defined as crime, and about the effects of altering the correlates. But altering them contains a welfare value of its own – in itself important to socialists and social democrats. And the whole weight of the evidence suggests that intensified police control solves little. The sensible policy is therefore to begin with the alternative.

[...]

The kinds of policy preparation suggested above, meant to prepare a major contraction of the prison system within a few years, would have to *move alongside and contextualize* the contraction, and be stepped up as the contraction gained momentum through concrete legislation.

It would cost money. But there would also be savings ahead. The prison business is extremely costly. In the financial year 1985/86, the budget for the Norwegian penal system was 498 million Norwegian crowns. The parallel budget for the British penal system was £822 million (Sim, 1986: 41). Cut by two-thirds during the 1990s, roughly 330 million 1986 crowns, or £540 million 1986, would be saved *per year*, and could be spent on countering the ideology of prison and on building the ideology of socialism – on counter-functional work, counter-denial work, victim work and offender work.

In the beginning of the period, more money would have to be spent than saved, because prisons would not yet be closed down (and also to allow a period for pensioning of staff). Towards the end of the period the budget might – with one important exception – well balance. The exception would be potential offender work. This work, which would involve whole new policies in housing, education, and so on, would be costly. But it would be a part of a generalized socialist policy, and as I have said have a value of its own, over and above crime prevention.

CLOSING: THE NEAR AND THE DISTANT FUTURE

Above we have been discussing the near future – the rest of our century.

Let us for the last time draw on history, and recall once more that major repressive systems have succeeded in looking extremely stable almost until the day they have collapsed. With this in mind, the thought that policy preparation in the near future may trigger further effects in a future more distant, may be more than wishful thinking. Victim work and offender work will certainly prove far more satisfactory than prison, and we may envisage further contraction, possibly abolition.

This would be congruent with the whole weight of the evidence on prisons. In actual fact, anything else is tantamount to acceding to irrationality. But full abolition would perhaps require that we stretch even further, towards an even fuller restructuring of our thinking about crime.

[...] In this chapter, I have used the concept of crime, and I have assumed the continued existence of criminalization, although much more narrowly drawn. But it may be argued that for prison fully to lose its irrational grip, the very concept of 'crime' has to be abandoned as a tool.

There are, as Louk Hulsman says, problematic situations, which today are criminalized. These problematic situations have an aetiology and a course of development. And they may be handled in a wide variety of much more civilized ways than today.

This, obviously, is still only on the drawing board. But the exercise of thinking away crime as a conceptual tool, and of opening up for imaginative rethinking of the whole handling of problematic situations, should be intriguing to social scientists.

And challenging to politicians.

REFERENCES

Alver, Bente Gullvåg (1971) *Heksetro og trolldom* (Witch Faith and Witch Craft). Oslo: Universitetsforlaget.

Balvig, Flemming (1984) *Ungdomskriminalitet i en forstadskommune* (Juvenile Delinquency in a Surburban Community). Copenhagen: Det kriminalpræventive råd.

Henningsen, Gustav (1981) *Heksenes advokat* (The Witches' Advocate). Copenhagen: Delta. Rev. ed. of Gustav Henningsen (1980) *The Witches'*

Advocate. Basque Witchcraft and the Spanish Inquisition (1609–1614). Reno: University of Nevada Press.

Henningsen, Gustav (1984) *Fra heksejagt til heksekult 1484–1984* (From Witch Craft to Witch Cult 1484–1984). Copenhagen: Gyldendal.

Hulsman, Louk (1986) 'Critical criminology and the concept of crime', *Contemporary Crises,* 10: 63–80.

Klapper, Joseph (1960) *The Effects of Mass Communication.* New York: Free Press.

Lea, Henry Charles (1906) *A History of the Inquisition of Spain.* New York: AMS Press, Inc., vol. IV. 2nd ed., 1966.

Leer-Salvesen, Paul (1988) *Etter drapet. Samtaler om skyld og soning* (After the Murder Conversations about Guilt and Atonement). Oslo: Universitetsforlaget.

McMahon, Maeve W. (1988) 'Changing penal trends. Imprisonment and Alternatives in Ontario 1951–1984.' PhD dissertation. Toronto: University of Toronto.

Mathiesen, Thomas (1974) *The Politics of Abolition. Essays in Political Action Theory.* Oxford: Martin Robertson.

Mathiesen, Thomas (1985) 'The arguments against building more prisons', in N. Bishop (ed.) *Scandinavian Criminal Policy and Criminology 1980–1985,* Copenhagen: Scandinavian Research Council for Criminology, pp. 89–98; presented on the occasion of the VIIIth UN Congress on the Prevention of Crime and the Treatment of Offenders.

Mathiesen, Thomas (1986) *Makt og medier. En innføring i mediesosiologi* (Power and Media. An Introduction to Media Sociology). Oslo: Pax.

Mathiesen, Thomas (1987) *Kan fengsel forsvares?* (Prison: Does it Have a Defence?). Oslo: Pax.

Rutherford, Andrew (1974) *The Dissolution of the Training Schools in Massachusetts.* Columbus: Academy for Contemporary Problems.

Rutherford, Andrew (1986) *Prisons and the Process of Justice.* Oxford: Oxford University Press.

Scheerer, Sebastian (1986) 'Towards abolitionism', *Contemporary Crises,* 10: 5–20.

Sim, Joe (1986) 'Working for the clampdown. Prison and politics in England and Wales', in B. Rolston and M. Tomlinson (eds) *The Expansion of European Prison Systems.* Working Papers in European Criminology No. 7, Belfast: The European Group for the Study of Deviance and Social Control, pp. 41–62.

26

New punitiveness

The politics of child incarceration[1]

Barry Goldson

> One can understand the self-evident character that prison punishment very soon
> assumed ... It seemed to have no alternative, as if carried along by the very movement
> of history ... We are aware of all the inconveniences of prison, and that it is dangerous
> when it is not useless. And yet one cannot 'see' how to replace it. It is the detestable
> solution, which one seems unable to do without.
>
> (Foucault, 1991, p. 232)

> ... I am a child. They should understand that when they're sending us all to prison.
>
> (cited in Lyon *et al.*, 2000, p. 32)

There is little doubt that punitive imperatives have shaped contemporary policy
responses to child 'offenders' in England and Wales (Goldson, 1999, 2000; Muncie,
1999a; Pitts, 2001). Equally, there is ample evidence to confirm that such punitiveness is frequently expressed through practices of institutional containment. Ruxton
(1996, p. 313), for example, has observed that 'although the figures are far from
complete, they suggest, nevertheless, that the countries of the United Kingdom ...
send a vastly greater proportion of young people to prison than any other state in the
EU'. Moreover, child incarceration expanded and consolidated in the 1990s and there
are no immediate signs to suggest that the trend is due to be reversed. There is good
reason to be troubled by such developments but, in some senses at least, they are not
exactly new.

Indeed, the practice of child incarceration is well established in England and Wales
and it casts its shadow over the best part of two centuries. Since the establishment of
the first penal institution exclusively for children at Parkhurst Prison for Boys in 1838
an array of policy initiatives, legal developments and carceral experiments have
created and sustained a panoply of institutional forms. The Youthful Offenders Act
1854 provided the *Reformatory*; the Industrial Schools Act 1857 introduced the

SOURCE: Commissioned for this volume. Barry Goldson is a Lecturer in the
Department of Sociology, Social Policy and Social Work Studies at the
University of Liverpool, UK.

Industrial School; the Prevention of Crime Act 1908 ushered in *Borstals*; the Children and Young Persons Act 1933 served to replace the Reformatory and the Industrial School with the *Approved School*; the Criminal Justice Act 1948 established *Remand Centres* and *Detention Centres*; the Children and Young Persons Act 1969 replaced Approved Schools with *Community Homes with Education*; the Criminal Justice Act 1982 set up *Youth Custody Centres*; the Criminal Justice Act 1988 replaced both the Detention and Youth Custody Centres with *Young Offender Institutions*; the Criminal Justice and Public Order Act 1994 prefaced the opening of *Secure Training Centres* and the Crime and Disorder Act 1998 served to 'modernize' the 'juvenile secure estate' by rebadging the Young Offender Institutions and the Secure Training Centres as *Detention and Training Centres.*

Incarcerative institutions for children, therefore, are hardly new at all. Nor is the source of their political and professional legitimacy (variously, and often incongruously, underpinned both by care/welfare priorities and by punitive/retributive objectives); the associated rehabilitative and correctional claims that are made for them (equally diverse in nature); or the scandals, abuses, failings and miseries that are routinely produced and reproduced through their operational practices. Indeed, the history of institutional experimentation and child incarceration is a history of political expedience; constant invention, reinvention and cosmetic reform; human suffering; and quite spectacular incompetence when measured in terms of its own claims to restore and rehabilitate its young charges. As Miller so astutely puts it:

> Reformers come and reformers go. State institutions carry on. Nothing in their history suggests that they can sustain reform, no matter what money, staff, and programs are pumped into them. The same crises that have plagued them for 150 years intrude today. Though the casts may change, the players go on producing failure.
>
> (Miller, 1991, p. 18)

So why, given such a long history of failure and inhumanity, does the state, and its criminal justice organs, continue to plough the incarcerative furrow? Why, given the contemporary emphasis on 'evidenced-based' approaches, 'what works' imperatives and 'best-value' priorities, does state policy continue to court expensive failure? Why are the messages from research evidence and practical experience consistently ignored (Goldson, 2001a)? Why is the punitive mood, and the concomitant practice of child incarceration, currently re-energized and so highly charged? These questions and related concerns will be considered in this chapter. First, however, a final review of history, albeit of more recent times, during which the 'reductionist agenda' (see Chapter 24 of this volume) and the prospect of an incarcerative 'freeze' (see Chapter 25 of this volume) appeared to signal the future direction of policy responses to child 'offenders'.

DECARCERATION AS TRANSIENCE: A 'PROGRESSIVE' MIRAGE

> ... it is doubtful whether the extensive use of incarceration has any real influence on the actual or future incidence of crime.
>
> (Conservative Party Study Group, 1988, cited in Stern, 1989, p. 19)

> Imprisonment is likely to add to the difficulty which offenders find in living a normal and law abiding life.
>
> (Home Office, 1988, p. 2)

The practice of child incarceration has a long history to which it was widely expected that the election of a Conservative government in 1979, under the leadership of Margaret Thatcher, would add a particularly punitive and expansionist chapter. Newburn (1997, p. 642) describes the 1979 Conservative manifesto as 'the most avowedly 'law and order' manifesto in British political history ... [it] promised, among many other measures, to strengthen sentencing powers with respect to juveniles'. Indeed, the 1980 White Paper *Young Offenders* promoted Detention Centres with tough regimes designed to deliver a 'short, sharp, shock' and William Whitelaw, the Home Secretary, warned that the children and young people 'who attend them will not ever want to go back' (see Chapter 22 of this volume).

Paradoxically however, it was against this punitive backdrop that support developed for an approach to juvenile crime derived in decarcerative imperatives and which comprised, in the words of Rutherford (1995, p. 57), 'one of the most remarkably progressive periods of juvenile justice policy'. The legitimacy for this 'new orthodoxy' was rooted in the coalescence of four otherwise disparate influences. First, key messages from academic research, particularly those that confirmed that institutional and/or custodial responses to children and young people were harmful, expensive and counterproductive. Second, professional developments within juvenile justice practice which (by drawing on previous experience and informed by the academy) emphasized diversionary, decriminalizing and decarcerative priorities. Third, specific policy objectives of Thatcherite Conservatism, particularly with regard to relieving the Treasury of some of its more onerous public spending commitments. As Pratt (1987, p. 429) noted: 'to reduce the custodial population on the grounds of cost effectiveness ... led to a general support for alternatives to custody initiatives'. Fourth, it became increasingly difficult to sanction child incarceration by appealing to the stated imperative of the police and the courts, to reduce the incidence of juvenile crime, in the light of compelling contra-evidence from research and practice and diminishing political support. Each of these influences combined to form a delicately balanced consensus which was to guide decarcerative juvenile justice policy and practice through the decade of the 1980s and into the 1990s (for a fuller discussion see Goldson, 1997a, pp. 124–9, 1999, pp. 4–7). Indeed, the apparently well founded fear that Thatcherite Conservatism would produce a sharp rise in child imprisonment was never realized. In fact developments in law and policy at this time had quite the opposite effect.

The Criminal Justice Act 1982 introduced 'criteria for custody' which served to impose restrictions on the courts' powers to make custodial disposals. The Act also replaced the indeterminate nature of the Borstal Training Order with the determinate sentence of Youth Custody and introduced the Specified Activities Order as a direct alternative to custody. Partly in response to the 'specified activity' provisions of the 1982 Act, the Department of Health and Social Security in 1983 made £15 million available in order to support the development of alternatives to custody projects. A hundred and ten such projects were established by voluntary organizations in partnership with sixty-two local authority Social Services Departments in England and Wales (NACRO, 1992, p. 3; see also Chapter 28 of this volume). Home Office circulars in 1985 (14/1985) and 1990 (59/1990) provided unequivocal support (if not encouragement) for the development of cautioning initiatives in order to divert children from the formal criminal justice process (Goldson, 2000, pp. 35–45). The Prosecution of Offences Act 1985 established the Crown Prosecution Service, which meant that all areas had a specialist Crown Prosecutor for juveniles. Moreover the Code for Crown Prosecutors specified that children should be prosecuted only as a 'last resort' and when it was clearly in the public interest. The Criminal Justice Act 1988 tightened the criteria for custody further and created a unified sentence of detention in a Young Offender Institution to replace the separate disposals of Detention Centre and Youth Custody. The Children Act 1989 established that 'the welfare of the child is the court's paramount concern' and imposed on local authorities the duty to make arrangements for the diversion from prosecution of child 'offenders'. Finally, the Criminal Justice Act 1991 tightened the criteria for custody further still, abolished the sentence of detention in a Young Offender Institution for fourteen-year-old boys and contained provisions, to be implemented at a future time, for the similar abolition of prison remands for all fifteen to seventeen-year-olds. The combined diversionary and decarcerative effect of such a policy change was not insignificant.

By 1990 70 per cent of boys and 86 per cent of girls aged between fourteen years and sixteen years who offended were being cautioned and thus diverted from prosecution. Similarly, the decarcerative emphasis produced a substantial decrease in the number of custodial sentences imposed on children, which fell from 7,900 in 1981 to 1,700 in 1990 (cited in Goldson, 1997a, pp. 127–8). Such was the confidence in the decarcerative thrust of policy and practice that penal reform organizations referred to 'diverting juveniles from custody', 'phasing out prison department custody for juvenile offenders', and 'replacing custody' (NACRO, 1987, 1989a, b), and Moore (2000, p. 116) reflected that 'in the early 1990s it was not inconceivable to suppose that the wholesale imprisonment of children might be abolished before the end of the century'. Support for the progressive policy and practice of decarceration was always conditional, however, and its fortunes ultimately depended upon the extent to which it continued to suit wider political imperatives.

Traditionally, the Conservative Party cherished its reputation as the party of 'law and order', the monopolistic guardian of disciplinary ideology, and it routinely caricatured Labour as being 'soft on crime'. However, the strength of the Conservatives' electoral mandate throughout the 1980s was such that the party was both able and prepared to relax its long-established attachment to punitive 'law and orderism' (read imprisonment) to enable it to bankroll tax cuts and finance its commitment to economic libertarianism. Between 1989 and 1992, however, Britain experienced a major economic recession which indirectly, but no less dramatically, served to subvert the decarcerative emphasis. Downes (2001, p. 69) observes that 'with male unemployment rising to 15 per cent; a prison population falling from 50,000 to 42,000; and a crime rate that rose by almost 50 per cent … the Conservative lead over Labour as the party best able to guarantee law and order' was seriously threatened 'for the first time in over 30 years'. The arrogant triumphalism of Thatcherism was finally waning, opinion polls indicated that public confidence in the Conservatives was abating, and the party reacted. John Major was installed to lead the Conservative Party and, along with senior colleagues (and the support of the Association of Chief Police Officers), he set about restoring its traditional 'law and order' mantle.

For its part the Labour Party detected the political vulnerability of the Conservatives and inevitably attempted to exploit it. Labour too digressed from its traditional position, which had tended to connect criminal justice with social justice, and to conceive fluctuations in rates of crime as manifestations of broader patterns of economic inequality and social polarization. However, the restyled New Labour project which was emerging under the increasing influence of Tony Blair chose a different tack and 'pressed home [its] advantage not by emphasizing the links between economic factors and rising crime but by stressing the leniency of sentencing' (Downes, 2001, p. 69). The political air soon filled with punitive rhetoric and before long each party would turn to the child in order to flex its authoritarian and disciplinary muscle. The decarcerative experiment was over.

RETURN THE PUNITIVE POLITIC: FEAR AND LOATHING AND LOTS OF VAGUENESS

> The process of switching between these contradictory rationalities, of moving from one discursive register to another, is very much a *political* process. It is governed not by any criminological logic but instead by ... political actors and the exigencies, political calculations and short-term interests that provide their motivations. In its detailed configuration, with all its incoherence and contradictions, the field is thus a product of the decidedly aleatory history of political manoeuvres and calculations.
>
> (Garland, 2001, p. 191, original emphasis)

The policy of diversion and decarceration was not only effective in terms of reducing the number of criminal prosecutions being brought against children and moderating the practice of child incarceration but also, according to David Faulkner, the head of the Home Office Crime Department between 1982 and 1990, it was 'successful in the visible reduction of known juvenile offending' (cited in Goldson, 1997b, p. 79). However, once political priorities shifted, the combined effect of economic efficiency, humanity and practical effectiveness was not enough to sustain the decarcerative approach.

During the early 1990s there emerged a fermenting body of opinion that juvenile crime policy in particular, and penal liberalism in general, had gone 'too far'. Both the media and the police drew attention to car crime, youth disorder, children offending whilst on court bail, and those whom they described as 'persistent young offenders', with increasing regularity and developing force. Such phenomena were shrouded in vagueness and there was minimal effort to distinguish, and thus account for, the specificities of the various forms of 'antisocial behaviour' and the different 'types' of child 'offender'. Similar imprecision applied to the actual extent of juvenile crime but the vagueness itself was used to energize burgeoning public concern: every troublesome child was portrayed as 'out of control' and a 'menace to society'; all of childhood was in 'crisis' (Scraton, 1997). An emotive ferocity characterized the moment as myth and 'fantasy began to replace objectivity and detachment and conjure monsters that seem to lurk behind the gloss and glitter of everyday life' (Pratt, 2000, p. 431). Troublesome children were 'essentialized as other' (Young, 1999) and an 'ecology of fear' (Davis, 1998) was awakened and mobilized. Indeed, within a context in which 'the ideological whiff of child-hate' (Haydon and Scraton, 2000, p. 447) was discernible, a punitive spectacle unfolded as the two major political parties competed to demonstrate who could be 'toughest' on child crime. More detailed accounts of the general processes of moral panic, 'folk devilling' and demonization (Young, 1971; Cohen, 1972; Hall *et al.*, 1978; Pearson, 1983; see also Chapters 3 and 4 of this volume), together with the specifics of this particular moment (Hay, 1995; Franklin and Petley, 1996; Davis and Bourhill, 1997; Goldson, 1997a, 2001a; Muncie, 1999a), can be found elsewhere and do not bear repeating here. However, some reflection upon related, but rather broader, issues is warranted.

The (re)emergence of punitiveness, and ultimately a return to practices of incapacitation and incarceration following a decade of effective decarcerative policy in juvenile justice, connected with broader shifts in penological relations. Garland detects:

> a new relationship between politicians, the public and penal experts ... in which politicians are more directive, penal experts are less influential, and public opinion becomes a key reference point for evaluating options. Criminal justice is now more vulnerable to shifts of public mood and political reaction ... The populist current in contemporary crime policy is, to some extent, a political posture or tactic, adopted for short term electoral advantage ... Almost inevitably the demand is for more effective penal control ... What this amounts to is a kind of retaliatory law-making, acting out the punitive urges and controlling anxieties of expressive justice. Its chief aims are to assuage popular outrage, reassure the public, and restore 'credibility' of the system, all of which are political rather than penological concerns.
>
> (Garland, 2001a, pp. 172–3)

Thus political priorities and 'electoral anxieties' (Pitts, 2000) come to exercise greater influence over policy formation than criminological expertise and the proven effectiveness (or otherwise) of various forms of practice. Within this context the currency of populist authoritarianism and the punitive urges that apparently characterize modern times begin to exercise significant purchase. Indeed, although the findings from 'the most extensive analysis to date of British attitudes towards sentencing and related criminal justice issues' (Hough and Roberts, 1998, p. 43) are (at least partially) equivocal, the elements which reveal a thirst for harsher punishments are significant. Moreover, such thirst appears to be intensifying and is not necessarily quenched by the increasing flow of the punitive tap. On the basis of the International Crime Victimization Survey therefore, the proportion of the public favouring tougher penalties has risen rather than fallen since 1992, precisely at a time when the use of imprisonment has been growing rapidly (Mayhew and van Dijk, 1997). Furthermore, the apparent punitive turn in public attitudes is particularly evident in relation to child 'offenders'. The 1998 British Crime Survey, for example, reveals that 'three out of four respondents [think] that the police and courts are too lenient in their treatment of juvenile offenders' and '40 per cent [think] that they were 'much too lenient' (Mattinson and Mirrlees-Black, 2000, p. ix). Conversely, only 2 per cent of respondents appear to believe that policy and practice responses to child 'offenders' are 'too tough' (*ibid.*, pp. 18–19). Each of these surveys draws attention to widespread public 'ignorance' and the consistent tendency for 'ordinary people' to substantially overestimate both children's involvement in crime and their own risk of victimization. Notwithstanding its groundless nature, however, fear of children, and concomitant antipathy to them, apparently pervades public consciousness. Moreover, the punitive response that such fear induces, and the political legitimacy that it provides, have serious repercussions.

The manufacture and political exploitation of such fear derives from long-established, but recently replenished, adult ambivalence towards children and childhood (Scraton, 1997; Goldson, 2001b; see also Chapter 21 of this volume). How else could children and young people be regarded as the second most common public concern, trumped only by 'litter and dog mess' (Audit Commission, 1999, p. 29)? How else could senior politicians confidently refer to children as 'nasty little juveniles' and 'vermin' (cited in Goldson, 1997a, pp. 130–1)? How else indeed, could John Major as Conservative Prime Minister in 1993 proclaim that the time had come to 'condemn a little more and understand a little less', and Tony Blair as Labour Prime Minister in 1997 state that there should be 'no more excuses'?

Such fear and loathing also connects with a broader tendency within criminal justice policy in particular, and social/welfare policy more generally. Here the emphasis seeks to moralize and responsibilize at the level of individual agency and to negate the significance of structural context. In this way the everyday lived reality of the 'offender' becomes an abstraction and her/his 'offence' is dematerialized and decontextualized. In other words, material circumstance is impatiently dismissed as an excusing distraction within a crude anti-intellectual aetiology rooted as it is in spurious constructions of morality and individual responsibility. When this is applied to child 'offenders' a further layer of condemnatory responsibilization is evident. The very status of 'childhood', the actual child self, is denied. Levels of responsibility ordinarily reserved for adults are randomly applied to children as young as ten: they are 'adulterized' and in many senses their unique claim to childhood is taken from them. The combined effect of the processes of dematerialization, responsibilization and adulterization therefore, comprises a formidable conceptual rubric and underpins what Muncie (1999a) has called 'institutionalized intolerance'. Thus it no longer actually matters that child poverty has cut deep into the national socio-economic fabric and that most child 'offenders' are the victims of such poverty. It is no longer significant that punitive responses to such children are neither effective nor appropriate. Nor does it matter that any reasonable conceptualization of justice might insist that children should be guaranteed certain age-determined legal safeguards and allowances (see Chapter 21 of this volume). Indeed, when political interests are at stake the profound relevance of such phenomena is rendered irrelevant, and the seductive simplicity of populist 'common sense' alone is enough to sanction the power to punish.

THE 'DETESTABLE SOLUTION'? THE INTENSIFICATION AND DIVERSIFICATION OF CHILD INCARCERATION

> ... however many official reports and critical books are written, what can the Prison Service do when ... a Home Secretary prioritizes prison above all other considerations? ... In such circumstances, it creates a sledgehammer – a penal instrument which smashes at the already-smashed and which, in its penal ferocity, is a disgrace to a civilized society.
>
> (Carlen, 1998, p. viii)

Once the political project is reduced to responding to, or indeed offering, various 'gestures of popular vengeance' (Simon, 2000, p. 303; see also Chapter 23 of this volume) a return to incarceration is inevitable. Imprisonment comprises the most 'emotive and ostentatious' form of punishment, and it is at this very political juncture that the state 'is prepared to revisit the possibilities of punishing that give out more obvious signs of unpleasantness to offenders and reassurance to the public' (Pratt, 2000, p. 431).

The irrationality of such punitiveness is a secondary concern. It scarcely matters that the rate of youth crime has apparently fallen in recent years (NCH, 2000, p. 280), or that over three-quarters of the prison population have been convicted of non-violent offences (Wilson and Ashton, 1998, p. 26). Of less significance still are the substantial costs of child incarceration and the miserable failure of custodial responses.

In 1993 NACRO estimated that it cost £190 million per year to keep children and young people in prison (NACRO, 1993). Since that time unit costs have certainly inflated but so too have the numbers of children and young people locked up. Estimated expenditure on the prison service *per se* for 1997–98 amounted to £1,257 million (Home Office, 1998, p. 112); Wilson and Ashton (1998, p. 27) note that each new prison costs something in the region of £90 million; and the most recent Home Office research puts the average annual *per capita* cost of imprisonment at £25,965 (Cullen and Minchin, 2000). The costs of locking children up are inevitably higher than this, and the costs attributable to the incarceration of children in privately run institutions (a practice which has become more common and is set to become more common still) are considerably higher again. Nathan (2000, p. 6) has reported that the capital costs involved in the construction of a forty-bed Secure Training Centre (a private children's jail) reach the order of £10 million and according to a recent report from Prison Privatization International it costs £4,800 per week to keep each child locked up in such an institution (cited in Wilson and Ashton, 1998, p. 60). Stern raises sobering questions in this regard. 'How much imprisonment can a society afford? What shall we have to go without in order to have such a large percentage of people made dependent on state funding?' (Stern, 1998, p. xxi).

The financial investment in child incarceration is even more problematic when it is set alongside the spectacular failure of custodial institutions, what Mathieson (see Chapter 25 of this volume) chooses to call 'the rehabilitative fiasco of prison'. Indeed, Miller observes:

> The hard truth is that ... juvenile penal institutions have minimal impact on crime. If most prisons were closed tomorrow, the rise in crime would be negligible ... incapacitation as the major tenet of crime control is a questionable social policy.
>
> (Miller, 1991, pp. 181–2)

Indeed, reconviction rates for children and young people discharged from custodial settings have always been high. Eighty-eight per cent of fourteen to fifteen-year-olds released from prison in 1995 for example, were reconvicted within two years (NACRO, 2000). Moreover, research in respect of the most expensive form of child custody, for example, is far from encouraging in this respect. Indeed, a third of children released from Medway Secure Training Centre (the first of a new group of private jails) committed criminal offences leading to arrest within one month of their release and 67 per cent had similarly offended within a period of twenty weeks (Hagell *et al.*, 2000). Such is the failure of incarceration in terms of crime control that it has been estimated that a 25 per cent increase in the prison population of England and Wales would be necessary in order to achieve a 1 per cent fall in crime (Home Office, 1998, p. 131). However, despite the weight of evidence which confirms the extraordinary costs and the minuscule benefits of child incarceration recent cross-party policy development has extended its scope, intensified its application and diversified its institutional form.

Section 1 of the Criminal Justice and Public Order Act 1994, introduced by the Conservative Party, created a new custodial sentence – a Secure Training Order – allowing the incarceration of children between the ages of twelve and fourteen years in new privately run Secure Training Centres. This effectively reversed a decarcerative trend in youth justice policy in respect of children of this age which dated back to the Children Act 1908. The Labour Party, whilst opposing various aspects of the Criminal Justice and Public Order Bill in its committee stages, abstained on the final vote (Howard League, 1995a, p. 3). It effectively colluded with the diversification of the penal estate by acceding to the introduction of the new child jails. Moreover, within months of coming to power in 1997 the New Labour government introduced an extraordinarily wide-ranging Crime and Disorder Bill which received Royal Assent in July 1998. Whilst the Crime and Disorder Act 1998 served to abolish the Secure Training Order (previously available for twelve to fourteen-year-old children) it replaced it with the Detention and Training Order (which also replaced the sentence of detention in a Young Offender Institution previously reserved for those children aged fifteen to seventeen years). Thus the courts' power to lock up children between the ages of twelve and seventeen years for non-grave offences is now provided within the remit of a single custodial sentence, and there is provision in the Crime and Disorder Act 1998 to allow the Home Secretary to further extend the powers of the court to encompass children aged ten and eleven years. Furthermore, the Detention and Training Order increases the power of the courts to impose longer sentences on children aged fifteen to seventeen years and relaxes the criteria for the imposition of custody on children aged twelve to fourteen years.

New Labour faces both ways with its Detention and Training Order. On the one hand the order consolidates and extends punitive imperatives as outlined above. On the other, the emphasis on 'training' softens the carceral edge and promises to provide a more benign and meaningful experience for children during periods of detention. Indeed, the Youth Justice Board for England and Wales is ostensibly keen to 'raise standards', promote 'constructive custody' and apparently has no doubt that the Detention and Training Order is 'a better sentence for young offenders' (Youth Justice Board, 2000, p. 1). New Labour double-speak is thus applied to the practices of child incarceration in such a way that it can switch interchangeably between 'tough' punitive authoritarianism and a more 'modernized' benign child-centredness in order to suit the political moment. The modernizing project no longer relies ultimately upon the *prison system* but is modelled instead around a *'juvenile secure estate'*. Stern once observed:

> Prisons for children and young people are given a variety of names ... the names are intended to show that these are not prisons, but places of good intent, where the previous bad influences of the young people's lives will be corrected by caring people.
>
> (Stern, 1998, p. 157)

The New Labour position is a perfect example of this, but it is deeply problematic on at least four counts.

First, it resonates with what Cohen (1985, p. 273) so perceptively calls the 'anaesthetic function of political language' and is thus tantamount to 'structured bad faith [which] allows indefensible forms of control to look more defensible'. This is not only ethically suspect but also has a significant practical impact. Indeed, 'it is by making the system appear less harsh, that people are encouraged to use it more often' (*ibid.*, p. 98). This can have only one effect: the intensification of child incarceration, of which there is ample evidence in England and Wales (Goldson and Peters, 2000; Moore, 2000). Second, it serves to conceal the inappropriate regimes (and not infrequently the brutalizing conditions) to which children are routinely exposed in locked institutions (Children's Legal Centre, 1993; Howard League, 1995b; HM Inspectorate of Prisons, 1997; Social Services Inspectorate, 1999; Goldson and Peters, 2000; Moore, 2000; see also Chapter 22 of this volume). Third, the packaging of child incarceration (at least in part) as a courtesy to children deflects attention from the institutionalized injustices of the 'justice' process. Custodial institutions primarily serve to incapacitate the children of the poor, with racialized and gendered patterns of injustice interacting with class inequality to produce a skewed population of incarcerated children (Howard League, 1997; Goldson and Chigwada-Bailey, 1999; Worrall, 1999; Goldson and Peters, 2000). It is less likely that such injustice will be foregrounded and accordingly problematized if the overall experience of custody is thought to be 'constructive' as distinct from the opposite. Fourth, New Labour's auspicious temperance and pseudo-congeniality are not an alternative to new punitiveness but a peculiar expression of it. Indeed, when the political moment demands, such as a general election campaign, the raw edge of such punitiveness is once again fully exposed. In this way, just months before the country was due to go to the polls in 2001, the Home Secretary had no hesitation in announcing:

> new proposals ... to give the courts additional powers to deal with juvenile offenders ... the measures, tabled as amendments to the Criminal Justice and Police Bill will strengthen the powers of the courts by allowing them to [target] ... young offenders who 'thumb their noses' at the law ... It is simply not acceptable that the courts have no powers to remand those juvenile offenders to custody.
>
> (Home Office, 2001, pp. 1–2)

The 'offenders' to whom the Home Secretary refers are twelve to sixteen-year-old children. Similarly, New Labour's election manifesto proclaims:

> We need a new approach to catch, convict, punish and rehabilitate more of them. Youth Offending Teams will track up to 2,500 of the most persistent young offenders 24 hours a day, seven days a week ... persistent offending should lead to increased punishment ... firmer measures will be taken ... our proposals are based on a simple principle: stay straight or you will stay supervised or go inside.
>
> (Labour Party, 2001, p. 33)

Such statements are not simply hollow sound bites. The New Labour government is investing substantial financial resources in correctional facilities and the Youth Justice Board announced a further expansion of the 'juvenile secure estate' with the purchase of an additional '400 new places in the independent sector' (Youth Justice Board, 2001, p. 3). There are no signs of immediate relief in terms of child incarceration. The penal estate continues to expand and diversify, welcoming as it does the steadily consolidating influence of the private sector.

END NOTE: LESSONS FROM AMERICA?

Michael Howard, speaking as Home Secretary in 1993, made an extraordinary statement when he confidently announced that 'prison works' (cited in Goldson, 1997a, p. 131). Three years later, with similar assurance, Howard reported that 'I am not simply copying what has been done there, I am putting in place some very carefully targeted measures which learn from the experience of the United States' (*Guardian Outlook*, 25 May 1996, p. 1). Three days after returning from the United States, in January 1993, Tony Blair, as shadow Home Secretary, coined his now famous sound bite 'Tough on crime, tough on the causes of crime' and in 1998, following the landslide electoral success of New Labour, the Home Secretary, Jack Straw (commenting on the 'special relationship' between the United Kingdom and the United States), confirmed that 'the two governments are learning more from one another all the time, there is now a deep ideological relationship' (cited in Pitts, 2000, p. 3). The youth justice policy continuities which extend across the Conservative–New Labour relation are ultimately informed and influenced by the United States. Within this context incarceration takes centre stage.

In the United States the number of people incarcerated increased by 300 per cent, from 500,000 to 2 million, between 1980 and 2000, and in 1998 nearly 6 million people were under some form of correctional supervision. 'These developments are not primarily the consequence of rising crime rates, but rather of "get tough" policies' (Beckett and Western, 2001, pp. 43–4). In England and Wales precisely the same patterns are evident. There was a 28 per cent increase in imprisonment between 1995 and 1999 and the *per capita* rate is the second highest in western Europe (Barclay *et al.*, 2001, p. 6). Additionally, as we noted above, 2,500 children and young people are about to be subjected to round-the-clock surveillance in the 'community'. Nor is this a direct consequence of recorded crime rates, which fell by 10 per cent during exactly the same period that imprisonment increased by 28 per cent (*ibid.*, p. 2).

In the United States leading criminological commentators now refer to 'mass imprisonment' (Garland, 2001b, p. 5); 'carceral hyperinflation' (Miller, 2001, p. 158) and 'hyper-incarceration' (Simon, 2000, p. 285). It is a place where a 'society of captives' (*ibid.*, p. 285) occupy the 'new iron cage' (Garland, 2001c, p. 197), and it is also the very same place 'which invented the juvenile court but is now executing juveniles' (Downes, 2001, p. 75). Shall there be an alternative to pernicious transatlantic punitive emulation or could child execution be a forthcoming chapter in our 'special relationship'?

NOTE

1 I am deliberately emphasizing the constructs of 'child', 'children' and 'childhood' throughout this chapter in accordance with the definition provided by Article 1 of the UN Convention on the Rights of the Child: 'a child means every human being below the age of eighteen years'. Whilst the terms 'young person' or 'youth' may occasionally be used interchangeably with 'child', the emphasis tends towards the latter, not least to stress the particular incivility of *child* incarceration.

REFERENCES

Audit Commission (1999) *Safety in Numbers: Promoting Community Safety*, London, Audit Commission.

Barclay, G., Tavares, C. and Siddique, A. (2001) *International Comparisons of Criminal Justice Statistics 1999*, London, HMSO.

Beckett, K. and Western, B. (2001) 'Governing social marginality: welfare, incarceration and the transformation of state policy', *Punishment and Society*, vol. 3, no. 1, pp. 43–59.

Carlen, P. (1998) *Sledgehammer: Women's Imprisonment at the Millennium*, Basingstoke, Macmillan.

Children's Legal Centre (1993) *Treated with Humanity and Respect? Conditions for Young People in Custody*, London, Children's Legal Centre.

Cohen, S. (1972) *Folk Devils and Moral Panics: The Creation of the Mods and Rockers*, New York, St Martin's Press.

Cohen, S. (1985) *Visions of Social Control*, Cambridge, Polity Press.

Cullen, C. and Minchin, M. (2000) *The Prison Population in 1999: A Statistical Review*, Home Office Research Findings no. 18, London, HMSO.

Davis, M. (1998) *Ecology of Fear: Los Angeles and the Imagination of Disaster*, New York, Metropolitan Press.

Davis, H. and Bourhill, M. (1997) '"Crisis": the demonization of children and young people' in Scraton (ed.) *'Childhood' in 'Crisis'?*

Downes, D. (2001) 'The macho penal economy: mass incarceration in the United States – a European perspective', *Punishment and Society*, vol. 3, no. 1, pp. 61–80.

Foucault, M. (1991) *Discipline and Punish: The Birth of the Prison*, London, Penguin.

Franklin, B. and Petley, J. (1996) 'Killing the age of innocence: newspaper reporting of the death of James Bulger' in J. Pilcher and S. Wagg (eds) *Thatcher's Children? Politics, Childhood and Society in the 1980s and 1990s*, London, Falmer Press.

Garland, D. (2001a) *The Culture of Control*, Oxford, Oxford University Press.

Garland, D. (2001b) 'Introduction: the meaning of mass imprisonment', *Punishment and Society*, vol. 3, no. 1, pp. 5–7.

Garland, D. (2001c) 'Epilogue: the new iron cage', *Punishment and Society*, vol. 3, no. 1, pp. 197–9.

Goldson, B. (1997a) 'Children in trouble: state responses to juvenile crime' in Scraton (ed.) *'Childhood' in 'Crisis'?*

Goldson, B. (1997b) 'Children, crime, policy and practice: neither welfare nor justice', *Children and Society*, vol. 11, no. 2, pp. 77–88.

Goldson, B. (1999) 'Youth (in)justice: contemporary developments in policy and practice' in B. Goldson (ed.) *Youth Justice: Contemporary Policy and Practice*, Aldershot, Ashgate.

Goldson, B. (2000) 'Whither diversion? Interventionism and the new youth justice' in Goldson, B. (ed.) *The New Youth Justice*, Lyme Regis, Russell House.

Goldson, B. (2001a) 'A rational youth justice? Some critical reflections on the research, policy and practice relation', *Probation Journal*, vol. 48, no. 2, pp. 76–85.

Goldson, B. (2001b) 'The demonization of children: from the symbolic to the institutional' in P. Foley, J. Roche and S. Tucker (eds) *Children in Society: Contemporary Theory, Policy and Practice*, Basingstoke, Palgrave.

Goldson, B. and Chigwada-Bailey, R. (1999) '(What) justice for black children and young people?' in B. Goldson (ed.) *Youth Justice: Contemporary Policy and Practice*, Aldershot, Ashgate.

Goldson, B. and Peters, E. (2000) *Tough Justice: Responding to Children in Trouble*, London, Children's Society.

Hagell, A., Hazel, N. and Shaw, C. (2000) *Evaluation of Medway Secure Training Centre*, London, HMSO.

Hall, S., Critcher, C., Jefferson, T., Clarke, J. and Roberts, B. (1978) *Policing the Crisis: Mugging, the State and Law and Order*, London, Macmillan.

Hay, C. (1995) 'Mobilisation through interpellation: James Bulger, juvenile crime and the construction of a moral panic', *Social and Legal Studies*, vol. 4, no. 2. pp. 197–223.

Haydon, D. and Scraton, P. (2000) 'Condemn a little more, understand a little less? The political context and rights implications of the domestic and European rulings in the Venables–Thompson case', *Journal of Law and Society*, vol. 27, no. 3, pp. 416–48.

HM Inspectorate of Prisons (1997) *Young Prisoners: A Thematic Review by HM Chief Inspector of Prisons for England and Wales*, London, HM Inspectorate of Prisons.

Home Office (1988) *Punishment, Custody and the Community*, London, HMSO.

Home Office (1998) *Reducing Offending: An Assessment of Research Evidence on Ways of Dealing with Offending Behaviour*, London, HMSO.

Home Office (2001) *Persistent Juvenile Offenders: Courts to get New Powers*, news release, 27 February, London, HMSO.

Hough, M. and Roberts, J. (1998) *Attitudes to Punishment: Findings from the British Crime Survey*, London, Home Office.

Howard League (1995a) *Secure Training Centres: Repeating Past Failures*, briefing paper, London, Howard League for Penal Reform.

Howard League (1995b) *Banged Up, Beaten Up and Cutting Up*, London, Howard League for Penal Reform.

Howard League (1997) *Lost Inside: The Imprisonment of Teenage Girls*, London, Howard League for Penal Reform.

Labour Party (2001) *Ambitions for Britain: Labour's Manifesto 2001*, London, Labour Party.

Lyon, J., Dennison, C. and Wilson, A. (2000) *'Tell them so they listen': Messages from Young People in Custody*, London, HMSO.

Mattinson, J. and Mirrlees-Black, A. (2000) *Attitudes to Crime and Criminal Justice: Findings from the 1998 British Crime Survey*, London, HMSO.

Mayhew, P. and van Dijk, J.J.M. (1997) *Criminal Victimisation in Eleven Industrial Countries*, The Hague, Research and Documentation Centre.

Miller, J. (1991) *Last One over the Wall: The Massachusetts Experiment in Closing Reform Schools*, Columbus OH, Ohio State University Press.

Miller, J. (2001) 'Bringing the individual back in: a commentary on Wacquant and Anderson', *Punishment and Society*, vol. 3, no. 1, pp. 153–60.

Moore, S. (2000) 'Child incarceration and the new youth justice', in Goldson (ed.) *The New Youth Justice.*

Muncie, J. (1999a) 'Institutionalised intolerance: youth justice and the 1998 Crime and Disorder Act', *Critical Social Policy,* vol. 19, no. 2, pp. 147–75.

Muncie, J. (1999b) *Youth and Crime: A Critical Introduction,* London, Sage.

NACRO (1987) *Diverting Juveniles from Custody: Findings from the Fourth Census of Projects funded under the DHSS IT Initiative,* London, NACRO.

NACRO (1989a) *Phasing out Prison Department Custody for Juvenile Offenders,* London, NACRO.

NACRO (1989b) *Replacing Custody: Findings from Two Census Surveys of Schemes for Juvenile Offenders funded under the DHSS Intermediate Treatment Initiative covering the Period January to December 1987,* London, NACRO.

NACRO (1992) *Briefing: Trends in the Custodial Sentencing of Juvenile Offenders,* London, NACRO.

NACRO (1993) *New Approaches to Youth Crime: Creating More Criminals,* London, NACRO.

NACRO (2000) *Unlocking Potential: Reducing the Incarceration of Children in England and Wales,* London, NACRO.

Nathan, S. (2000) 'Detention and training orders: further experimentation in juvenile incarceration', *Youth Justice Matters,* June, pp. 3–11.

NCH (2000) *Factfile 2000,* London, NCH Action for Children.

Newburn, T. (1997) 'Youth, crime and justice' in M. Maguire, R. Morgan and R. Reiner (eds) *The Oxford Handbook of Criminology* (2nd edn), Oxford, Clarendon Press.

Pearson, G. (1983) *Hooligan: A History of Respectable Fears,* Basingstoke, Macmillan.

Pitts, J. (2000) 'The new youth justice and the politics of electoral anxiety' in Goldson (ed.) *The New Youth Justice.*

Pitts, J. (2001) *The New Politics of Youth Crime: Discipline or Solidarity,* London, Palgrave.

Pratt, J. (1987) 'A revisionist history of intermediate treatment', *British Journal of Social Work,* vol. 17, pp. 417–436.

Pratt, J. (2000) 'Emotive and ostentatious punishment: its decline and resurgence in modern society', *Punishment and Society,* vol. 2, no. 4, pp. 417–39.

Rutherford, A. (1995) 'Signposting the future of juvenile justice policy in England and Wales' in Howard League for Penal Reform, *Child Offenders: UK and International Practice,* London, Howard League for Penal Reform.

Ruxton, S. (1996) *Children in Europe,* London, NCH Action for Children.

Scraton, P. (ed.) (1997) *'Childhood' in 'Crisis'?,* London, UCL Press.

Simon, J. (2000) 'The "society of captives" in the era of hyper-incarceration', *Theoretical Criminology,* vol. 4, no. 3, pp. 285–308.

Social Services Inspectorate (1999) *Inspection of Medway Secure Training Centre,* London, Department of Health.

Stern, V. (1989) *Imprisoned by our Prisons: What needs to be Done?,* London, Unwin Hyman.

Stern, V. (1998) *A Sin against the Future: Imprisonment in the World,* London, Penguin.

Wilson, D. and Ashton, J. (1998) *What Everyone in Britain should know about Crime and Punishment*, London, Blackstone Press.

Worrall, A. (1999) 'Troubled or troublesome? Justice for girls and young women' in B. Goldson (ed.) *Youth Justice: Contemporary Policy and Practice*, Aldershot, Ashgate.

Young, J. (1971) *The Drugtakers*, London, Paladin.

Young, J. (1999) *The Exclusive Society*, London, Sage.

Youth Justice Board (2000) *Youth Justice Board News*, no. 4, London, Youth Justice Board for England and Wales.

Youth Justice Board (2001) *Reform of the Juvenile Secure Estate: A Four Year Plan by the Youth Justice Board*, London, Youth Justice Board for England and Wales.

Part VI

Risk management and prevention

The emergence of the terms 'risk management' and 'prevention' in the field of youth justice is related to the broader shifts in crime control that occurred in the last decades of the twentieth century. In particular, they reflect the growing importance of what has been termed a new penology of actuarial justice (derived from the term 'actuary', an expert in statistical risk calculation). According to its proponents, this radical shift took place initially in the United States in the 1980s in response to demands for greater accountability and rationality in correctional policy. Since then, it is claimed, traditional goals of individual rehabilitation have been increasingly replaced by the rather less transformative goals of risk assessment and risk management. The shift from treating individuals to targeting and managing specific categories of people is crucial to this penal sea change. Strategies of risk management and prevention tend to result in the displacement of individually based justice by decision making based on the statistical probability of reoffending. However, critics of the new penology suggest that the thesis may be prone to exaggeration regarding its pervasive influence on the practice of crime control. Part VI addresses many of the crucial questions raised by this new penological paradigm – for example, to what extent do risk calculation and managerial techniques underpin correctional policies in contemporary youth justice? Are the techniques of risk management and crime prevention an inclusive 'foil' to the exclusive practices of 'popular punitiveness'?

Chapter 27 by John Pratt represents one of the first attempts to theorize the shift in youth justice from welfare/justice to a pragmatic and managerialist model of 'corporatism'. Pratt argues that such a shift first came to the fore in the routine workings of youth justice via the strategies of multi-agency 'diversion' that emerged in the United Kingdom in the 1980s. He contextualizes these local shifts in delinquency management and corporate governance in terms of wider changes in the state and the economy. Diversion implies 'defining deviance down' that is, adapting to high crime rates and to increased case loads for practitioners, alongside a recognition that penal custody does not work in reducing reoffending. It also accords with practical moves towards the rationalization of resources and the establishment of an efficient crime management apparatus. Pratt focuses in particular on the dangers this new instrumentalist corporatism may pose to the delivery of just and accountable services for young people. His work echoes the net-widening concerns articulated by Stanley Cohen in his path-breaking book *Visions of Social Control* (1985; see also Chapter 17 of this volume). Pratt's concerns in this reading, published in 1989, articulate and presage many of the concerns which have since come to the fore in debates about actuarial justice and the logic of risk management in youth justice. He argues that corporatist strategies were distanced from wider philosophical and moral arguments of both welfare and punishment and instead simply promoted cost-effective and efficient ways of managing the delinquent population.

In Chapter 28 John Pitts echoes some of these concerns in his broad critique of the 'justice model' that emerged in the United Kingdom in the 1980s. Much of his analysis rests on misgivings over the political use of 'justice' by a neo-liberal Conservative government (see also Chapter 19 of this volume). The rise to prominence of a 'something works' doctrine is viewed as legitimating the goal of cost-effective management of delinquent bodies. Furthermore, Pitts fears that an ideology of 'technical rationality' may also turn practitioners, such as probation officers, into politically prescribed technicians of social control, rather than professionals concerned with the humane treatment of often vulnerable clients.

David Farrington is the leading proponent globally of the theory and practice of youth criminality prevention, focusing on the risk factors at play in the aetiology of delinquency. In Chapter 29 Farrington provides a brief overview of his work in this growth area of crime prevention. Perhaps the greatest appeal of the risk factor paradigm lies in its simplicity and its overtly practical orientation for identifying the interrelated factors associated with antisocial behaviour and managing the 'problem' by means of specific targeted techniques. This preventive approach combines the actuarial calculation of risk with a continuing commitment to positive intervention in the lives of young people and their families/communities. At its core is the claim that the approach is 'evidence-led' and predicated upon the credo of 'what works'. Farrington's work, and that of the burgeoning industry of psychological risk profiling, is not narrowly or purely 'actuarial' in character. Instead it is indicative of much theory and practice in youth crime prevention which combine the techniques of risk calculation with a continuing 'rehabilitative' commitment to 'changing people'. Nevertheless, one of the major concerns expressed by critics of this body of work is that it may lead to premature 'labelling' of the most vulnerable and poorest children and young people, thereby reinforcing their criminalization and exclusion.

In Chapter 30 Kimberley Kempf-Leonard and Elicka Peterson present an overview of developments in youth justice in the United States at the end of the twentieth century. Crucial to their analysis is a critical engagement with the claim that new forms of youth justice are indeed increasingly governed by the principles of risk management. Their reading provides us with a valuable exposition of the main features of this expanding realm of youth penology and the related claim that it amounts to a paradigmatic shift in the treatment of young offenders. In plotting this expanded realm of actuarial youth justice, Kempf-Leonard and Peterson suggest that its major political attraction lies in its capacity to manage large numbers of 'unwanted people' in a way that does not attract hostile public reaction. However, they also crucially question the thesis that actuarial justice and the logic of risk management are all-pervasive, by pointing to the continuing diversity of institutional settings and treatment options. As is evident in Chapter 29 by Farrington, it would be premature to speak of the total demise of rehabilitation in the realm of youth justice (see also Chapter 16 of this volume). Managerial and preventive strategies, alongside authoritarian intervention based on detention and retribution (discussed in Part V of this volume), now represent key features of the constellation of policies in youth justice which in turn challenge the previously influential strategy of penal welfarism. But we need to be wary of assuming that there has been a total transformation and break with old times. The contributions form Farrington and Kempf-Leonard and Peterson, for example, confirm the continued presence and redeployment of some traditional values and practices around rehabilitative intervention.

In the final chapter Tim Newburn provides a broad overview of current trends in youth crime prevention in the United Kingdom. Newburn pays particular attention to the shape that youth crime prevention appears to be taking and the direction in which it seems to be heading. In the course of painting this broad picture he argues that the changing nature of youth justice and crime prevention under New Labour defies easy characterization. Not least, he suggests that there appears to be some disparity between a rhetoric of punitive populism and what is realized in practice. Newburn is also at pains not to overemphasize the seeming dominance of an actuarial and managerial 'new penology'. Alongside the managerialist strand are continuing attempts to incorporate restorative justice elements within the youth justice system. In particular, Newburn draws attention to the emergence of referral orders as both the latest and the most significant attempt to draw on such principles. In conclusion, he suggests that there are both important continuities and important discontinuities between New Labour and previous Conservative administrations. The appeal to a rhetoric of punitive populism speaks to the present continuities with previous 'tough' politics of youth justice. On the other hand, the rise to prominence of a 'what works' paradigm and a centralizing managerialist discourse marks something of a distinct, and potentially positive, break with the past.

27

Corporatism: the third model of juvenile justice

John Pratt

[···]

There can be no denying that justice-model talk and ideas have assumed an *ideological* dominance over those of welfare. However, there has been no corresponding shift towards a fully blown justice-model legal form which puts into operation all this talk and these ideas. Against some of the prerequisites of this model, such as certainty, due process, visibility, accountability, least restrictive intervention, we see instead an increase in administrative decision-making, greater sentencing diversity, centralization of authority and co-ordination of policy, growing involvement of non-juridical agencies, and high levels of containment and control in some sentencing programmes.

For the proponents of justice, such features will no doubt be written off as unintended consequences of their ideas, or as ironic anomalies: Conservative governments provide LAC3 monies to encourage private and voluntary sector initiatives, which has the effect of feeding money to social work activities with offenders despite the suspicions and hostilities that government representatives had expressed in relation to this (see Holt, 1984).

However, these trends can also be seen as *necessary* and *essential* features of a third model of juvenile justice: *corporatism*. This sociological concept refers to the tendencies to be found in advanced welfare societies whereby the capacity for conflict and disruption is reduced by means of the centralization of policy, increased government intervention, and the co-operation of various professional and interest groups into a collective whole with homogeneous aims and objectives (Unger, 1976). Corporatist tendencies must be understood as part of a historical process. The shift away from a nineteenth-century state form (where a free market economy and *Gesellschaft* legal process were essential and complementary features) to a welfare state pattern of intervention, regulation, and planning also saw crucial changes in the legal form.

SOURCE: This chapter is taken from *British Journal of Criminology*, Vol. 29, No. 3, 1989, pp. 236–54 (abridged).

The first type of effect is the rapid expansion of the use of open ended standards and general clauses in legislation, administration and adjudication ...

The second major impact of the welfare state on law is the turn from formalistic to purposive or policy oriented styles of legal reasoning and from concerns with formal justice to an interest in procedural and substantive justice. (ibid. 194; see also Prosser, 1982)

In effect, this constitutes a major shift from uniformity and general rules with universal validity to policy-ordered decision-making and legal reasoning. But of course, the welfare state itself is not a static entity (Mishra, 1984). These trends come to be exemplified in the advanced form of the welfare state, which takes on the characteristics of corporatism. This entails

the effacement both in organisation and in consciousness of the boundary between state and society and therefore between the public and the private realm. As the state reaches into society, society itself generates institutions that rival the state in their power and take on many attributes formerly associated with public bodies. (Unger, 1976: 201)

And in contrast to the typology of *Gesellschaft* law, the legal process now assumes the form of *bureaucratic–administrative* law, where

the presupposition and concern is neither an organic human community nor an atomic individual; the presupposition and concern is a non-human abstracted ruling interest, public policy or on-going activity of which human beings and individuals are subordinates, functionaries or carriers ... [such] regulations ... take for their object ... the efficient execution of tasks and attainment of goals and norms ... which are set by the authorities, or the 'community', or the bureaucracy as its representative. (Kamenka and Tay, 1975: 138)

This is not to say that corporatism is an *exclusive* phenomenon. Some of the features of this model have been in existence during the hegemony of different legal forms. It should thus be of no surprise that some developments *do* correspond to features of the *Gesellschaft* ideal type (see Garland and Young, 1983). Futhermore, corporatism in the juvenile justice section is not reflective of a general phenomenon now taking place in civil society. In this respect, I am following Panitch's (1980: 161) argument that corporatism in a 'partial structure', as opposed to the 'increasingly common tendency to see these particular corporatist structures not as representing new *partial* elements *within* the existing economic and political system, but as corporatist ideologues once claimed they would be, new political and/or economic systems in their own right' (emphasis in original).

Indeed, given that most analyses of corporatism have been set at the level of changes in the state formation and have usually drawn empirically on economic and industrial relations policies (Winckler, 1975; Panitch, 1981), it would seem to be a highly problematic concept to apply right across British society post-1979 with the advent of Thatcherism. The subsequent break-up of the political consensus of the post-war years, the commitment, in varying degrees to free-market rather than state-managed economic policies, the reduction of union power, the willingness to tolerate high levels of unemployment – all seem to be pointing the way to or are features of a 'post-corporate' state formation (Lewis and Wiles, 1984). As part of this process, it may be that these same shifts away from corporatism in the areas of industrial relations, economic policy, and so on necessitate a shift *towards* corporatist intervention and regulation in the penal spectrum (see also Bottoms, 1983; O'Malley, 1983). More starkly, free-market economic policies that generate high levels of unemployment, *particularly among the young*, necessitate extended and increased forms of social policing. Corporatism provides the mechanics and machinery for this. However, the detail of such a hypothesis must be the matter of a separate paper. The task here, and to which I shall now turn, is to sustain the argument that corporatism has become the predominant trend in juvenile justice.

In this respect, let us first consider the increase in administrative discretion that diversion programmes and the like encouraged. As argued earlier, the pre-court tribunal has replaced the juvenile court as the main site for the dispensation of juvenile justice. In addition, referral to programmes (diversion from court or alternative to custody) is likely to be subject to the discretion of some other decision-making committee. For example:

> Prior to the preparation of the Social Enquiry Report the Social Worker or Probation Officer would negotiate with the young person, his parents, with [the project] and with other involved parties.
>
> Subsequently the applications would be brought before an Admission Panel consisting of Programme Workers, [the project] Manager, and an independent permanent Chair Person. The School will be asked to send a representative if appropriate.
>
> For the successful applicant a contract will be drawn up. This will identify a programme of Intermediate Treatment and will also include details about what will be expected of the young person ... (Halton Intermediate Treatment Scheme, n.d.: 2)

If such developments contradict the dictates of the justice model, they none the less support the corporatist argument. Reliance on the formal processes of law and due process can lead to inefficiency and delay, which hinders policy implementation – hence the *importance* of administrative decision-making to this model (Winckler, 1975). The increase in discretion is not just an unintended consequence of the supposed move 'back to justice', but is *central to the functioning of the corporatist model*. Delays and costs can be avoided in this way. Equally, instead of relying on breach procedures for every failure to report to the alternative-to-custody intermediate treatment centre, let power be given to social workers to impose sanctions. If not, cases might be brought back into the formal legal system, resulting in a sanction (custody) that the state is anxious to avoid wherever possible. Consequently, many projects now have their own built-in sanctions, which can be applied and administered without recourse to courtroom approval, as in the following example:

> Minor breaches or problems will be dealt with by counselling and/or restriction of privileges etc. If these should continue, or when serious violations occur, the young person will be recalled to the residential unit and a conference held, in order to discuss reasons for the action, and to outline new objectives as necessary, with return to the community in mind. (Coventry PACE, n.d.: 3)

The 'hard core' will still be locked up: but a delinquency management service is now provided in the community for that troublesome segment of the youth population not dangerous enough to lock away but too disruptive to ignore. Hence the concentration of resources here to the exclusion of those with more welfare-based problems: so long as the latter remain just a threat to themselves they do not warrant further attention. But social workers are not merely co-opted into the adjudication and decision-making processes: they may be involved in constructing and devising the penalty itself. Raynor (1985: 204) describes a sanction put together by a probation officer, made up of a number of smaller penalties and administrative dictates, the intention being that it would then operate as an alternative to custody:

> This programme ... involved the active participation of the defendant: the court, his parents, the other members of the intermediate treatment group; the beneficiaries of the community service work; the victim; the volunteers who supervised the work; the police, the Careers Officer; and the psychiatrist, in addition of course to the [Probation] Officer himself ... it offers an interesting illustration, not of some vague notion of 'community involvement' but of the purposeful mobilisation of community resources to resolve a criminal justice problem in a fair and helpful way.

Second, in place of a reassertion of the *judicial* determination of crime and punishment (which the justice model requires) we find the 'blurring of the boundaries' (Unger, 1976; Cohen, 1979) between the private and public realm, as with the LAC3 initiative; between the courts and other decision-making bodies, and between various criminal justice agencies whose positions and responsibilities become increasingly amorphous in the inter-agency co-operation ventures, whether this be to administer punishment or prevent crime (HOC 8/84). The blurring of the boundaries at an agency level is taken to its ultimate form in the model of the Northampton Juvenile Liaison Bureau. Designed to act as a body that will divert cases from court and deliver a form of administrative justice, it was constituted by a wholesale merger of the various juvenile justice agencies and

> employs full time a social worker, probation officer, youth worker, teacher and police officer and is administered by a management team consisting of local managers of the represented agencies [who] undertake the consultation process involving all the parent agencies ... and possibly some others as well, for example, the education welfare service and child guidance clinic. (Northamptonshire CC, 1982)

Such developments are again essential to the corporatist model of juvenile justice. Importantly, they allow potential conflict to be negotiated, managed, and thus diffused: adversarial proceedings may again be expensive and inefficient, and may ultimately hinder the implementation of policy. Far better to work out in advance what kind of penalty will be acceptable in each case.

> Magistrates need to be satisfied that each youth will receive proper supervision from social workers or probation officers and that a programme of school attendance, youth training or work experience is available. Some of the young people attend day centres where they receive special training. In addition, more intensive levels of community service work are often prescribed such as helping with meals on wheels, running youth clubs, or repairing toys for the children's ward of a local hospital. (Tutt, 1984)

Furthermore, a recourse to privatization does not mean that the government is contracting out of or giving up on its responsibilities, For reasons of fiscal policy, the government *does* have a vested interest in ensuring that the LAC3 initiative, like other aspects of its deinstitutionalization programme, is successful. As such, privatization enables central government to intervene *much more directly* in the framework of local policy. Recourse to the private sector ensures that social service bureaucracies (which might be able to subvert policy) are bypassed, and that negotiations take place with individuals who are likely to have a commitment to the success of the policy.

Third, instead of an emphasis on 'rights', what we find in practice at nearly all levels of decision-making is this overarching emphasis on policy. To ensure policy objectives, the personal autonomy of social workers and the judiciary is reduced. Furthermore, the rights of the client come to be conflated with the objectives of policy. This can be seen in the justification for the introduction of the Northampton Juvenile Liaison Bureau:

> The delays inherent in the [previous] system which lacked a co-ordinated approach by the various agencies, together with the enormous number of cases being processed through the courts, meant that the juvenile court was extremely busy sitting some six half-day courts each week, with all the attendant costs and problems that this entailed. (Bowden and Stevens, 1986: 326)

Fourth, the issue of punishment. The justice model maintains a philosophical commitment to the imposition of punishment, alongside its administrative principles of due process and so on. However, although many alternatives to custody projects do maintain high levels of punishment, they do *not* represent a return to the punishment principles of classicism (and as re-presented in the justice model). Outside of the custodial sector, we are not seeing a resurgence of a kind of retributive moral enforcement wherein punishment is measured in exactitude to the amount of harm done, is awarded exclusively by the judiciary for a set and known period, and so on. Instead, what we find is an emphasis on the development of penalties that provide for a form of behavioural containment (O'Malley, 1983). This can be behaviour *modification* in the community, as with the Church of England PACE project:

> Its prime objective is to enable the young person to learn to live within his family and community without major conflict or risk to himself or others and without needing to resort to delinquent or other forms of anti-social behaviour. This will be achieved by working to a plan tailored to each individual need and circumstance, in order to help the young person to recognise and accept responsibility for himself and his own actions, as well as to acknowledge and deal with the reality of his everyday situation …
>
> The underlying philosophy of the scheme is the conviction that to establish an intense, positive supportive one to one relationship and to provide a powerful alternative adult model is the most effective means of producing positive changes in behaviour and attitudes. (Coventry PACE, n.d.: 2)

Alternatively, there is behaviour *surveillance*: schemes such as 'tracking', which offer precisely this. Thus the Nottinghamshire 'linking' programme:

> In one scheme the linker lived with the family every weekend for a month and was responsible for the linkee form Friday at 4.30 p.m. until Monday at 8.30 a.m. The linkee in question had been involved in the commission of offences during the weekend period for some considerable time and this input over a relatively short period is effective and gives time for other less intensive alternatives to be worked out between the linkee, his/her family and the linker and caseholder. (A. Thorpe, 1983: 2)

This 'new behaviourism' (Cohen, 1985) is more in keeping with the objectives of corporatism than the justice model in that it provides a logical response to the aims of keeping offenders out of courts and institutions. Restriction of behaviour opportunities, or programmes that induce changes in behaviour, clearly offers far more in terms of policy implementation than the punishment 'pure and simple' of the justice model (unlikely to have any consequences on future behaviour); and offers more than the treatment-based practices of the welfare model (ineffective and inefficient).

A fifth factor is the expanding dialogue on delinquency that emanates from all the inter-agency meetings and discussions. It had been the hope that the justice model would minimize the delinquency problem, after the excesses of welfare. Yet we now find the maximization of delinquency as a crucial social issue, magnified by the production of more flow charts, community profiles, and so on, which become the products of each new inter-agency venture. For example:

> Local authority departments in particular are likely to be useful sources both of information directly about crime, such as vandalism of school buildings and on housing estates, and of the social and demographic data necessary to place crime in its local context. Such data might, for example include information about housing stock, population characteristics, and perhaps transport and recreational facilities in areas noted for high levels of crime. (HOC 8/84: 3)

This, again, is essential to corporatism: the increasing range of agencies involved in the administration of juvenile justice necessitates more efficient and detailed use of resources. 'What is being proposed is not additional, unproductive work, but a more systematic use of available statistics' (*ibid.*).

As such, the juvenile justice specialists have a far more enlarged role than would have been possible under the strict application of a justice model format which minimized such social work intervention. Instead, the specialists are at the hub of the juvenile justice system itself; they have become the socio-technical experts of corporatism – instrumental in policy implementation within their own organizations, crucial figures in promoting inter-agency dialogue. In effect, the post-war social democratic faith in social planning (the subject of so much criticism in areas such as health, social security, and housing in the political climate of the 1970s and 1980s) has been given a fresh lease of life in this particular sector of the welfare state.

> There is an opportunity here for social workers and their managers to get away from the generally *ad hoc* planning decisions of the 1970s and use the new technology not to replace case files and administrative registers, but to provide a detailed analysis of local policy and practices which will enable the broadest discussion of policy objectives and more rational and economic deployment of resources to meet those objectives. (D. Thorpe, 1981: 21)

A RECONSIDERATION OF THE WELFARE–JUSTICE ARGUMENT

The specific characteristics and attributes to the corporatist model of juvenile justice can now be seen in contrast to those of welfare and justice (see Table 27.1). If, then, the whole debate about welfare and justice has been something of a sideshow while centre stage a very different play has been performed, why is it that this has not been recognized? Why is it that the emergence of corporatism has gone largely unnoticed?

Table 27.1 *Three Models of Juvenile Justice*

Parameter	Welfare	Justice	Corporatism
Characteristics	Informality	Due process	Administrative decision-making
	Generic referrals	Offending	Offending
	Individualized sentencing	Least restrictive alternative	Diversion from court/ custody
	Indeterminate sentencing	Determinate sentences	Alternative to care/custody programmes
Key personnel	Child care experts	Lawyers	Juvenile justice specialists
Key agency	Social work	Law	Inter-agency structure
Tasks	Diagnosis	Punishment	Systems intervention
Understanding of client behaviour	Pathological	Individual responsibility	Unsocialized
Purpose of intervention	Provide treatment	Sanction behaviour	Retrain
Objectives	Respond to individual needs	Respect individual rights	Implementation of policy

Certainly, the justice critique repudiated many of the previous ideas that had informed the history of juvenile justice; and in its rise to ideological dominance contributed a new form of penological language that has been popularized among social work professionals. Phrases such as 'least restrictive intervention', 'diversion from court', and 'alternatives to custody' have become part of the contemporary discourse of juvenile justice specialists, as indeed they have become signifiers of government policy (Hudson, 1987). However, there simply has not been a shift towards the exclusively adversarial process that the justice model dictates: indeed, most trends are away from this. Meanwhile, support for other justice objectives in relation to sentencing and punishment initiatives has come mainly from members of social work organizations, whose administrative powers over the offending population have increased during the course of their espousal of the justice model, and about whom its initial architects had been so critical.

Thus, notwithstanding the commitment to these new objectives and new ventures in social work with offenders, it is clear that much of the ideology and discourse of social work in the welfare era has not disappeared – not that it ever could have been simply effaced from memory. Instead, it has been refurbished, brought up to date, remodelled–and then set down in new domains and locations. Here a link is maintained with the helping and caring tradition of social work intervention. The new programmes are not so far removed from social work that they will alienate and deter support from within the profession. Indeed, they are seen as new steps in social work, an innovative way forward. For example, 'an appropriate definition of [intermediate treatment] might be 'A method of social work with children which adds a new dimension to improve the quality of life through community based opportunities for personal growth and development' (East Sussex County Council, n.d.: 3). In this way support for these policies can be galvanized and sustained from *within* social work and traditional oppositions maintained (for example, to Conservative governments), while at the same time ensuring effective alliances with welfare critics and the policy objectives of governments.

What we find, then, is a replication of some of the mistakes made during the welfare era. The 'best interests' tradition facilitates the growth and extension of new control systems. Yet the apparatus of these systems, their technology, their talk, and so on, are indicators of future developments and trends. There can be 'no return to rehabilitation' (Hudson, 1987; Matthews, 1987), as if all that we now see represents some kind of temporary aberration, ready to be swept aside. Not only is this to misunderstand the reality of power and its operation, but the concept of rehabilitation has anyway been updated and informs the 'new behaviourism'. At the same time, there can be no going back to a non-technologized past. It will be within this system of the future that we will variously find advantages and disadvantages, points of resistance and new initiatives of control.

Having said this, then clearly one of the main functions of the justice rhetoric and the humanitarian ideals it is intended to address has been to mask, disguise, and/or justify developments that seem to be the opposite of its rubric (Cohen, 1984, 1985). Instead of a concern for the protection of individual rights, we find instead an emphasis on efficiency and the primacy of policy objectives. Instead of a shift from the inhumanities and injustices of the institution, we find these features of the carceral system now being reproduced in the community – in those projects that are supposed to be *alternatives* to the institution. *This is not to say that such developments are inevitably and always unhealthy.* But what we should try to separate out are humane objectives from their inhumane effects – which, in the current context, allegiance to justice-model rhetoric helps to obscure.

REFERENCES

Bottoms, A. (1983) 'Neglected Features of Contemporary Penal Systems', in *The Power to Punish*, D. Garland and P. Young, (eds), 166–202. London: Heinemann.

Bowden, J. and Stevens, M. (1986) 'Justice for Juveniles: A Corporate Strategy in Northampton', *Justice of the Peace*, 326–9, 345–7.

Cohen, S. (1979) 'The Punitive City: Notes on the Dispersal of Social Control', *Contemporary Crises*, 3: 339–64.

Cohen, S. (1984) 'The Deeper Structures of the Law, or 'Beware of the Rulers Bearing Justice': A Review Essay', *Contemporary Crises*, 8: 83–93.

Cohen, S. (1985) *Visions of Social Control*. Cambridge: Polity Press.

Coventry, PACE (n.d.) *Intensive Intermediate Treatment Project*. Church of England Children's Society.

East Sussex County Council (n.d.), *Intensive Intermediate Treatment Report*.

Garland, D. and Young, P. (1983) 'Towards a Social Analysis of Penalty', in D. Garland and P. Young, eds., *The Power to Punish*, 1–36. London: Heinemann.

Halton Intermediate Treatment Scheme (n.d.) *Alternatives to Care and Custody Programme*. Cheshire Social Services.

Holt, J. (1984) *No Holiday Camps*. Leicester: Association of Juvenile Justice.

Hudson, B. (1987) *Justice through Punishment*. London: Macmillan.

Kamenka, E. and Tay, A.E-S. (1975) 'Beyond Bourgeois Individualism', in E. Kamenka and R. Neale (eds), *Feudalism, Capitalism and Beyond*, 126–44. London: Edward Arnold.

Lewis, N. and Wiles, P. (1984) 'The Post-Corporatist State', *Journal of Law and Society*, 11: 65–89.

Matthews, R. (1987) Taking Realist Criminology Seriously', *Contemporary Crises*, 11: 371–402.

Mishra, R. (1984) *The Welfare State in Crisis*. Brighton: Wheatsheaf.

Northamptonshire County Council (1982) *Juvenile Liaison Bureau Information Handout*. Wellingborough.

O'Malley, P. (1983) *Law, Capitalism and Democracy*. Sydney: Allen & Unwin.

Panitch, L. (1980) 'Recent Theorization of Corporatism', *British Journal of Sociology*, 31: 159–87.

Prosser, T. (1982) 'Towards a Critical Public Law', *Journal of Law and Society*, 5: 1–11.

Raynor, P. (1985) *Social Work, Justice and Control*. Oxford: Basil Blackwell.

Thorpe, A. (1983) *Linking: One Year Review*. Leicester: National Youth Bureau.

Thorpe, D. (1981) 'Diverting Delinquents', *Community Care*, 25 June.

Tutt, N. (1984) 'Short, Sharp and Ineffective', *Observer*, 7 October.

Unger, R. (1976) *Law and Modern Society*. London: Macmillan.

Winckler, J. (1975) 'Law, State and Economy: The Industry Act 1975 in Context', *British Journal of Law and Society*, 2: 103–28.

28

The end of an era

John Pitts

I fail to comprehend how the discourse of criminology has been able to go on at this level. One has the impression that it is of such utility, is needed so urgently and rendered so vital to the working of the system, that it does not even need to seek a theoretical justification for itself, or even simply a coherent framework. It is entirely utilitarian. (Michel Foucault, 1980, p. 47)

In Spring 1991 the Home Office announced an unprecendented 17.4 per cent rise in recorded crime in England and Wales. At the same time, and in marked contrast, a conference entitled 'What Works: Effective Methods to Reduce Re-offending' was announced. The advertisement expressed the belief, one which is gaining currency among criminologists and sections of the probation service, that:

> The 'Nothing Works' doctrine is dead. A large and growing body of evidence shows that re-offending can be systematically reduced.

The former event, the increase in crime, may prove to have historic significance but the latter has the feel of history in the making; the end of an era. 'Nothing Works' is dead, long live 'Something Works'. Putting to one side the question of whether there is such 'a large and growing body of evidence', this statement offers us an important insight into the discontinuous and doctrinaire nature of accepted wisdom in the sphere of work with offenders. Beyond this, it begs the question of whether we may not, in fact, be witnessing the replacement of a 'Nothing Works' *doctrine* with a 'Something Works' *doctrine*.

THE DECLINE OF THE REHABILITATIVE IDEAL

It was not so long ago that most probation officers, criminologists and penal reformers appeared to subscribe to the idea that:

SOURCE: This chapter is taken from *The Howard Journal of Criminal Justice*, Vol. 31, No. 2, 1992, pp. 133–49 (abridged).

> It does not seem to matter what form of treatment in the correctional system is attempted, whether vocational training or academic education; whether counselling inmates individually, in groups or not at all; whether therapy is administered by social workers or psychiatrists; whether the institutional context of the treatment is custodial or benign; whether the sentences are short or long; whether the person is placed on probation or released on parole; or whether the treatment takes place in the community or in institutions. (Wilson, 1975, p. 169)

This sombre assessment, based on Martinson's (1974) survey of 231 research studies, has been underscored by many subsequent investigations which have drawn similarly pessimistic conclusions (Hood, 1971; Wilkins, 1969; Sinclair, 1971; Davies, 1969, 1974; Dunlop, 1974; Millham *et al.*, 1975; Cornish and Clarke, 1975; Folkard, Smith and Smith, 1976; Bottoms and McWilliams, 1979; Thorpe *et al.*, 1980). Indeed, it was on the basis of such evidence that in the mid-1970s, criminologists reluctantly announced 'the decline of the rehabilitative ideal' (Preston, 1980). Over the next decade and a half a broad political consensus emerged to support the view that the best we could hope for in our work with offenders was to minimise the negative impact of prosecution, imprisonment and social work intervention on their lives (Bottoms and McWilliams, 1979; Thorpe *et al.*, 1980; Morris *et al.*, 1980).

THE RENAISSANCE OF OPTIMISM

Yet now, apparently, 'Something Works' and a previously discredited 'correctional-ism' is being exhumed. In 1989 the Home Office initiated a research programme aimed at identifying those components of an, as yet undefined, *Intensive Probation* which would 'work' (Mair, 1989). Meanwhile, criminologists are returning to the data upon which their belief that 'Nothing Works' was based:

> ... the outcome research of the early 1970s was capable of being interpreted in other ways than 'Nothing works'.... This has recently led some writers, for example Ken Pease, who worked at the Home Office Research Unit in the 1970s to argue that the pessimistic conclusions drawn from this research were not necessarily justified. (Blagg and Smith, 1989, p. 86)

In this they are no doubt correct since the 'Nothing Works' doctrine, based as it was on a global analysis of reconviction rates, failed to pinpoint those individuals, projects and institutions whose endeavours did, in fact, 'work'. While such localised data does not undermine the thesis that rehabilitative *methods* tend, by and large, not to rehabilitate; it does suggest that sometimes, with some people, in some circumstances, for some reason, some things 'work'.

Blagg and Smith argue that the pessimistic interpretation of the data might be explained in terms of its acceptability to a government committed to minimising state intervention in the lives of citizens and hostile to both the values of the welfare state and social work's claims to professionalism. There is, after all, a remarkable comple-mentarity between the governmental commitment to cutbacks in welfare provision which characterised this period and much contemporary research in the spheres of penology and social work which, by default or design, identified those services and institutions which were expendable (Schur, 1974; Folkard, Smith and Smith, 1976;

Thorpe *et al.*, 1980). We might also add to this explanation the tendency of research conducted in an established 'Nothing Works' paradigm to produce 'Nothing Works' results and to ignore contrary evidence (Kuhn, 1962).

Yet, while these factors may account for the abandonment of the quest for effective forms of rehabilitation in the late 1970s, they do not explain the resumption of that quest in the 1990s. They fail to tell us why a widely accepted 'fact' has been turned on its head. To find the origins of this conceptual *volte face* it is necessary to return to the ideas developed in the juvenile justice system in the mid-1980s.

COST-EFFECTIVE JUSTICE

At a conference on intermediate treatment in 1979 Patrick Mayhew, a Minister of State at the Home Office, borrowing a phrase from the Duke of Edinburgh, bemoaned 'the rising tide of anarchy and violence threatening to engulf our shores' (DHSS, 1979). In the same year, James Anderton called for labour camps for young thugs and William Whitelaw, the Home Secretary, promised to provide them, and in doing so, give previously unprecedented numbers of 'hooligans' a 'short, sharp, shock' (see Chapter 22 of this volume).

In 1991, by contrast, Kenneth Baker, the Home Secretary, responded to the unprecedented increase in recorded crime by accusing its victims of not taking proper care of their property.

Clearly, in the twelve years which separate these utterances, both the message, and the language in which the message is couched, have changed substantially. Arguably, the rhetorical flourishes of early Thatcherism had three main functions. They aimed to placate the vocal right wing which had been swept into parliament by the Thatcher landslide; they served as a demonstration of toughness to an electorate which had been wooed with promises of safe streets, and they were an attempt to divert attention from a faltering economy. In retrospect, the bloodcurdling rhetoric of the early Thatcher years appears less like the announcement of a new, pugnacious law and order era and more like the last gasp of the Tory hangers-and-floggers.

From the mid-1980s, the government attempted to fashion a rational, cost-effective justice system. In doing so it adopted the radical, 'scientific' managerial style pioneered in Westminster and Wandsworth; describing its mission in terms of 'targets', 'minimum standards' and 'performance indicators'. It set itself against restrictive practices in the police, the law and the prison service and within a very short space of time these groups, which had previously regarded Conservative governments as their ally, were talking of betrayal. It told probation officers that if they felt that, in conscience, they would be unable to comply with government plans, the government would find somebody in the private sector who would. It was anti-union, anti-professional and pro-privatisation. It was full-blown Thatcherism.

It is therefore particularly ironic that, having alienated and enraged most of the established professional groupings in the justice system, the government established, what was in effect, an alliance with a previously marginal group of radical juvenile justice professionals in the voluntary and statutory sectors through the DHSS Intermediate Treatment (IT) Initiative (1983) (Pitts, 1988; Nellis, 1989; Pratt, 1989 and see Chapter 27 of this volume).

THE DHSS INTERMEDIATE TREATMENT INITIATIVE

Between 1981 and 1989 the numbers of juveniles imprisoned in England and Wales fell from 7,900 to 2,200. Although the period from 1979 to 1989 witnessed a 25 per cent decrease in the numbers of children and young people in the age range there was a reduction in juvenile imprisonment of approximately 68 per cent. The projects developed within the DHSS Intermediate Treatment Initiative were a key factor in this reduction.

'Initiative' projects provided some diversion-from-prosecution schemes in co-operation with the police but their major contribution to the reduction of youth imprisonment was the provision of alternative-to-custody programmes which relied on the co-operation of the magistrates (Bottoms *et al.*, 1990). What commended the 'Initiative' to the government and has persuaded it to develop a similar strategy for young adult offenders was the apparent ability of workers in 'Initiative' projects to co-operate with, and influence the sentencing decisions of, magistrates. The development of similar skills by probation officers, is seen by the government to hold the key to the resolution of the penal crisis (Home Office, 1990; Patten, 1991). Central to the success of the 'Initiative' was the development of what came to be called the 'Justice Model'.

THE JUSTICE MODEL

At the inception of the 'Initiative', project workers attempted to establish working relationships with all the agencies and individuals comprising the local juvenile justice system. Their objective was to create joint policies for diverting young people from prosecution or custody. The projects developed a range of 'programmes' or 'packages' designed, in consultation with magistrates, to serve as alternatives to custody for ajudicated 'high-tariff' offenders. These programmes, characteristically, included an element, variously entitled 'offending workshops' or the 'correctional curriculum', in which the offender was required to address, with staff, and sometimes with other offenders, the criminal act/s which had brought them to the project. The duration of programmes reflected the duration of the custodial sentence the young person might otherwise have attracted. Additional elements like intensive supervision through 'tracking' and a requirement to spend time away from home at an outdoor activities centre were options available for use with 'high tariff' offenders in some programmes (Curtis, 1989).

This mode of work, described by its adherents as the 'Justice Model' is said to have a number of clear advantages over the 'Welfare' model which it superceded.

These advantages are claimed to be:

1 Everybody knows what it is. The magistrate, the worker and the young offender all know that participation in the programme is a direct result of a penalty imposed on the young offender by the court for a crime s/he has committed; they are getting their 'just deserts'.
2 Everybody knows where they are. The magistrate knows that s/he must impose one of a number of specified penalities if the young offender fails to comply with the conditions of their order. The workers knows the programme that s/he must

put the young offender through and the sanctions they must impose if they fail to comply with it. The young offender, and often their parents as well, sign a contract which specifies the conditions of the court order, details of the programme to be pursued and the sanctions that will be invoked for non-compliance.
3   Everybody is talking the same language. There is a shared culture in which the talk is of offending, punishment and reparation. The techniques adopted focus on offending. There is no talk of 'need' or 'deprivation' since, within the justice model, no link is made between the personal or social circumstances of the young offender and the crime/s they have committed.

It is no accident of course that this is precisely the new language and culture which John Patten, the Home Office minister responsible for restructuring the probation service, is attempting to promote:

> (I want) to promote a cultural change not just in the probation service, but among the sentencing classes ... The punishing classes and the helping classes are now talking to each other in a way they never did before. (*The Guardian*, 12 April 1991, p. 4)

THE 'JUSTICE MODEL' AND COMMON SENSE

The major 'achievement' of the IT Initiative was to get the 'punishing classes' and the 'helping classes' to 'talk to each other' in this way. It was an attempt to develop a 'common sense', between the agents and agencies which constitute local juvenile justice systems, about the problem of, and the most efficacious response to, juvenile offending. The creation of just such a 'common sense' between probation officers, magistrates, judges, the police and voluntary organisations is the objective of the new Criminal Justice Act [1991] and many of the recent developments in the probation service have been geared towards this.

In the attempt to achieve such a 'common sense', the integration of legal and social scientific perspectives plays a crucial role. In King's (1991) view the primary role of law is the organisation of expectations. It is concerned first and foremost with what 'the reasonable man' might reasonably be expected to do, or might reasonably expect from others. To that extent, law serves to reinforce and underpin a common sense to which we are all able to subscribe.

The social sciences, those disciplines which have provided the theoretical underpinnings for the practice of social work and probation, as well as the rationale for their claim to professional status, can offer no such reassurance. Their stock in trade is irony. They delight in pointing out the discrepancy between what we believe to be the case and what is. To that extent, social science subverts both common sense and the type of 'common sense' developed in the 'Initiative' and suggested by the 'new way of talking' commended to the probation service by John Patten. Rather than a shared language, it creates a multiplicity of languages in which events in the world might be discussed and a diversity of perspectives from which they might be viewed (Rorty, 1989).

When, in a period in which explanations of the world offered by law and laywers have greater political import and greater social impact than those offered by social science and social workers, they both make claims upon the same terrain, as was the case in the 'Initiative' projects, continues to be the case in the sphere of child protection and is increasingly the case in probation, the law tends to win. King (1991), points to 'the law's propensity to "enslave" other discourses or produce hybrid or bastard discourses of dubious validity'. (p. 8) As a result of this 'enslavement' it is only those bits of social science which echo the common-sense individualism of law which are assimilated into the hybrid discourse. In this regard, it is interesting to note that the 'Justice Model' developed in the 'Initiative' projects has tended to absorb only those elements of social scientific theory which support time-limited, individualised, interventions with an exclusive focus on offending. Those perspectives which address the personal, cultural, social, economic and racial factors which may increase the vulnerability of young people to involvement in crime or heightened surveillance by the police are not admitted. Nor are those which address the absence of educational and vocational opportunity which are often associated with high levels of juvenile crime (Cloward and Ohlin, 1960; Lea and Young, 1984). The same may be said of many of the working methods currently being developed in the probation service.

The problem with a hybrid discourse of the type described here is that it must inevitably be conceptually bankrupt. Those elements of theory which are enslaved will be appropriated because they address the same object, in the same uncritical manner, as the legal/common-sense discourse which has enslaved them.

Yet, the veracity or integrity of the position notwithstanding, the 'Justice Model' might still be defended if it can be shown to have worked and, therefore, to hold the promise of working again in the adult system.

DID IT WORK? WILL IT WORK AGAIN?

The 'Initiative' aimed, explicitly and implicitly, to do four things:

1   To reduce the incarceration of children and young people.
2   To thereby reduce the disabling and criminogenic effects of incarceration.
3   To prevent crime.
4   To reduce re-offending amongst participants.

1 Reducing incarceration

The Initiative was a factor, and probably the most important factor, in diverting many custody-prone young people in England and Wales from prison in the period 1984 to 1989. Its primary objective was to effect change in the functioning of the local juvenile justice system in general and the sentencing decisions of juvenile court magistrates in particular. To this end projects adopted Systems Management strategies of the type developed by Information Systems Lancaster and NACRO.

The key factor in the success of the 'Initiative' projects was the plausibility of their 'common sense' correctional techniques in the eyes of magistrates. Bottoms *et al.* (1990) have demonstrated that the confidence of juvenile court magistrates was the single most important factor determining whether they used alternatives to custody or not. That there was never any evidence that these techniques had a greater impact on offending than other forms of social intervention appears to have done nothing to shake this confidence.

This result was obviously heartening for a government attempting to manage a penal crisis fuelled, in no small part, by the readiness of the adult courts to imprison young adult offenders (NACRO, 1990). They reasoned that if the probation service could be made to develop the same kind of relationships with the bench that the juvenile justice workers had, reductions in the incarceration of young adults would follow. The problem was that the relationship between the probation service and the adult bench was a well established one, and according to some magistrates, had turned somewhat sour. There was, it seemed, little confidence in the ability of the probation service to offer a serious alternative to imprisonment. As Mair (1989) observes:

> The Green Paper too notes that 'not every sentencer or member of the public has full confidence in the present orders which leave offenders in the community'. And the Chairman of the council of the Magistrates' Association has expressed 'sadness and worry' that 'many magistrates and members of the public have lost the unquestioning confidence and trust which they had formerly had in the probation service'. (pp. 6–7)

Beyond this, many people involved with the IT 'Initiative' maintain that a significant element in its success was an acceptance on the part of sentencers that young offenders, by dint of age and immaturity, would simply 'grow out of crime' (Rutherford, 1986). Whether, therefore, the same strategies can be used to divert older offenders from custody remains an open question:

> Unlike juveniles, young adult offenders suffer from unemployment and homelessness, they may be married, have children, and are more likely to be involved in drug use. Factors such as this mean that juvenile justice initiatives cannot be replicated unproblematically with respect to 17–20 year old offenders. (Mair, 1989, p. 8)

It is not at all clear how the view, apparently widespread amongst magistrates, that young adult offenders are more culpable, intractable and deserving of punishment than juveniles, will be changed. Parker *et al.* (1989) have observed, that magistrates distinguish between those cases in which they will impose custodial sentences and those about which there can be some negotiation. This distinction is drawn on the basis of the seriousness of the offence and beliefs about the culpability of the offender. A major factor determining perceptions of culpability is, of course, age.

The 1970s witnessed a dramatic reduction in intervention with, and the institutionalisation of, juvenile offenders aged 10–14. The 1980s saw a similar de-escalation in respect of 14–17 year olds. In both cases the moral map was redrawn in order to represent these young people as less culpable and more deserving of our assistance than our wrath. The major justification for this metamorphosis was that they would 'grow out of it'. The question facing the Home Office and the probation service at the moment is whether such an ideological transformation can be effected with people who are already 'grown up' or whether they will have to be content with slipping a few 18 year olds under the wire into the juvenile justice system.

2 Reducing the effects of incarceration

To the extent that the 'Initiative' diverted young people from prison it is probably true that it averted the problems identified by Gallo and Ruggerio (1991) in their aptly titled *Custody as a Factory for the Manufacture of Handicaps*. Any attempt to replicate strategies devised in the 'Initiative' will mean that the potential clientele is far more likely to have had a taste of imprisonment already. This will make them far harder to work with and pose problems of containment and control on a significantly different scale from those encountered in the 'Initiative'.

3 Preventing crime

A senior police officer recently remarked that to expect the police to prevent crime was like expecting the staff of a hospital emergency ward to stop road accidents. With a clear-up rate of less than 20 per cent and a rate of recorded crime which understates its actual incidence by at least 100 per cent, it would be remarkable if anything that the police, the courts or social workers and probation officers did with, for or to, those few apprehended offenders they meet had much impact on the phenomenon of crime. At the moment, of all the agencies charged with crime prevention only the police have acknowledged such limitations. The probation service remains wedded to the task of 'Protecting the Public' (Home Office, 1990).

Some enthusiastic commentators have cited reductions in levels of recorded juvenile crime in the period 1979 to 1989 as evidence of the impact of alternatives to custody. Yet it is completely implausible that the 17.4 per cent increase in recorded crime, noted above, is an exclusively adult phenomenon. It is more likely that the reduction in recorded juvenile crime is a product of a growing reluctance on the part of the police to proceed against 10–14 year olds and the 25 per cent drop in the numbers in the age range.

While there is evidence that significant reductions in crime can be achieved in previously high-crime neighbourhoods they are not achieved by a strategy which aims only to manage the local justice system more cost-effectively (Bright and Petterson, 1984; King, 1988; NACRO Youth Activities Unit, 1988). As such, this gives a somewhat hollow ring to the suggestion, implicit in the White Paper *Crime Justice and Protecting the Public,* that the introduction of tougher and more flexible probation orders will in some way protect the public from criminal victimisation.

4 Reducing offending

What little evidence we have suggests that about 60 per cent of participants in Initiative projects were reconvicted within two years. Clearly, this is a better outcome than might have been expected if the young people had been imprisoned but one which is roughly similar to what might have been expected if they had simply been left to their own devices.

It is at least likely that if the techniques developed in the 'Initiative' are applied to an older age group with a deeper commitment to more serious offending, reconviction rates will be higher.

Thus, the claim that a new form of rehabilitative work with offenders called the 'Justice Model' or 'Confronting Offending Behaviour', which has a significantly greater impact on the behaviour of individual offenders than the techniques which came to serve as evidence to support the 'Nothing Works' doctrine, is not proven. We are therefore driven to the conclusion that what we are in fact witnessing is the emergence not of something which works but of a 'Something Works' *doctrine.*

THE ROLE OF A 'SOMETHING WORKS' DOCTRINE

The political role of a 'Something Works' doctrine is to offer legitimacy to the government's attempts to promote an alternative, non-custodial, sentencing tariff. The audiences from whom such legitimacy must be evoked are the government's own back benchers, the media, the sentencers and, very occasionally, the electorate. If such legitimacy is established, the government may then be able to realise its goal of the cost-effective management of delinquent bodies.

However, such legitimacy cannot be achieved by the deployment of political rhetoric alone. The rehabilitative or correctional technology must also be seen either to be effective, or subject to the type of 'objective' or 'scientific' testing which will, in the fullness of time, demonstrate its effectiveness. The need for such legitimacy is all the more pressing when the repertoire of techniques available to workers has been reduced, by administrative fiat, to one 'trick'.

To this end, the government must institute a plausible research and monitoring strategy (cf. Mair, 1989). For their part, the people who operate the correctional technology must appear to be similarly 'competent', 'objective' and 'disinterested'. For this to be achieved, their professional knowledge base must be 'proceduralised' (Habermas, 1976). In this process, professional education is reoriented towards the acquisition of a limited range of specific 'competencies' rather than a broader range of 'value-laden', and potentially critical, concepts (cf. Coleman, 1989).

Thus it is, that by putting an 'objective' gloss on to pragmatic political endeavours an ideology of technical rationality comes to provide a 'scientific' legitimation for what 'reasonable men' knew all along.

The major role of this ideology is, however, to move the official discourse of crime, justice and victimisation out of the politial arena and into a depoliticised, and hence uncontentious, scientific/technical realm (Habermas, 1968).

Alongside, and in response to these political developments, we see the emergence of a professional and academic style which we might characterise as 'macho-correctionalism'. It is adopted by those professionals and social work academics who wish to distance themselves from their, unfashionable, social work roots. Instead, they emphasise their personal hard-headedness and the efficacy of the correctional technology (Davies, 1982; Davies and Wright, 1989). Like the government, they simultaneously repudiate the values and methods of a traditional, psycho-dynamically based social work and theoretical and political perspectives which locate the origins of crime, poverty and inequality beyond the individual.

However, other social workers and probation officers are concerned that the abandonment of a social and political perspective and the deprofessionalisation inherent in the new orthodoxy is too high a price to pay for popularity with the present government.

DEPROFESSIONALISATION

Clearly, the government wishes to transform the probation service into a more precise instrument of its criminal justice policy and the introduction of the 'Justice Model' into the adult justice system provides the means whereby this is to be achieved. As we have seen, however, the success of the model is dependent upon the proceduralisation of knowledge, the repudiation of contrary or critical theoretical or political perspectives and the surrender of professional autonomy. As such, the justice model could probably be operated more effectively by technicians than professionals.

A professional has a hand in defining the problem and determining the response that will be made to that problem. A technician, by contrast, applies techniques devised by somebody else to problems defined by somebody else. Professionals and technicians must both develop skills and techniques but professionals carry an additional responsibility to exert judgement and discernment. It is for this reason that, in defending their actions, professionals can never claim that they were 'only following orders'.

If this is the distinguishing feature of professionalism then we may argue that a consequence, if not the intention, of recent developments in the probation service has been the deprofessionalisation of probation officers.

Whereas the 'IT Initiative' and the 'Justice Model' served as a vehicle to carry juvenile justice workers from the margins to the centre of the juvenile justice system, probation officers fact a future in which their power and centrality within the system will be further eroded.

It appears that in the future the court will specify which standardised 'correctional' 'package' is to be 'delivered' to an offender and the probation officer will 'deliver' it. The vacuous rhetoric of correctional 'newspeak' inevitably evokes the image of Postman Pat going about his uncontentious, and socially useful job, with a smile on his face and a cheery word for everyone. This, one imagines, is what John Patten (1991) had in mind when he said that: 'The punishing classes and the helping classes are now talking to each other in a way they never did before.'

[...]

REFERENCES

Bateman, T. *et al.* (1991) 'Towards a policy for effective work with young people in crisis', in: J. Dennington and J. Pitts (eds) *Developing Services for Young People in Crisis*, London: Longman.

Becker, H. (1963) *Outsiders: Studies in the Sociology of Deviance*, New York: Free Press.

Blagg, H. and Smith, D. (1989) *Crime, Penal Policy and Social Work*, London: Longman.

Bottoms, A., *et al.* (1990) *Intermediate Treatment and Juvenile Justice. Implications and Findings from a Survey of Intermediate Treatment Policy and Practice Evaluation Project, Final Report*, London: HMSO.

Bottoms, A. and McWilliams, W. (1979) 'A non-treatment paradigm for probation practice', *British Journal of Social Work*, 9 (2), 159–202.

Bright, J. and Petterson, G. (1984) *Safe Neighbourhoods*, London: NACRO.

Cloward, R. and Ohlin, L. (1960) *Delinquency and Opportunity*, New York: Routledge and Kegan Paul.

Coleman, D.A. (1989) *Home Office Review of Probation Training, Final Report*, London: Home Office.

Cornish, D. and Clarke, R. (1975) *Residential Treatment and its Effects on Delinquency* (Home Office Research Study No. 32), London: HMSO.

Curtis, S. (1989) *Juvenile Delinquency: Prevention through Intermediate Treatment,* London: Batsford.

Davis, M. (1969) *Probationers in their Social Environment* (Home Office Research Study No. 2), London: HMSO.

Davies, M. (1974) *Prisoners of Society,* London: Routledge and Kegan Paul.

Davies, M. (1982) 'Community based alternatives to custody: the right place for the probation service' (address to conference of chief probation officers, unpublished).

Davies, M. and Wright, A. (1989) *The Changing Face of Probation, Skills Knowledge and Qualities* (Social Work Monographs), Norwich: University of East Anglia.

DHSS (1979) *Getting on with Intermediate Treatment,* London: DHSS.

Dunlop, A. (1974) *The Approved School Experience* (Home Office Research Study No. 25), London: HMSO.

Folkard, M., Smith, D. and Smith, D. (1976) *IMPACT* Vol II (Home Office Research Study No. 36), London: HMSO.

Foucault, M. (1980) (Colin Gordon ed.) *Power/Knowledge,* Brighton: Harvester.

Gallo, E. and Ruggerio, V. (1991) *Custody as a Factory for the Manufacture of Handicaps,* Enfield: Middlesex Centre for Criminology.

Gunn, J. (1991) *Meeting the Need,* London: Home Office.

Habermas, J. (1968) *Towards a Rational Society,* London: Heinemann.

Habermas, J. (1976) *Legitimation Crisis,* London: Heinemann.

Harding, J. (ed.) (1987) *Probation and the Community,* London: Tavistock.

Home Office (1990) *Crime, Justice and Protecting the Public,* Cm. 965.

Hood, R.G. (1971) 'Research on the effectiveness of punishments and treatments', in: L. Radzinowicz and M. Wolfgang (eds), *Crime and Justice,* New York: Basic Books.

ILPS (1991) *Demonstration Unit Data on Addiction Amongst Probation Clients,* London: ILPS.

Jones, A., Kroll, B., Pitts, J., Smith, P. and Weiss, J. (1992) *A Probation Handbook,* London: Longman.

King, M. (1988) *How to Make Social Crime Prevention Work: The French Experience,* London: NACRO.

King, M. (1991) *How the Law Thinks about Children,* London: Tavistock.

Kuhn, T. (1962) *The Structure of Scientific Revolutions,* Chicago: University of Chicago Press.

Lea, J. and Young, J. (1984) *What is to be Done about Law and Order,* Harmondsworth: Penguin.

Mair, G. (1989) 'Intensive probation in England and Wales: origins and outlook', (paper presented to the British Criminology Conference, Bristol, 17–20 July, unpublished).

Martinson, R. (1974) 'What Works? – Questions and Answers about Prison Reform,' *The Public Interest,* Spring, 22–54.

Millham, S., Bullock, R. and Cherrett, P. (1975) *After Grace, Teeth,* London: Chaucer.

Morris, A., Giller, H., Szued, M. and Geech, H. (1980) *Justice for Children,* London: Macmillan.

NACRO (1990) *Young Adult Offenders* (NACRO briefing), London: NACRO.

NACRO (1991) *The Role of Juvenile Justice Workers in Crime Prevention,* London: NACRO.

NACRO Youth Activities Unit (1988) *Golf Links Youth Project,* London: NACRO.

Nellis, M. (1989) 'Juvenile justice and the voluntary sector', in: R. Matthews (ed.), *Privatising Criminal Justice,* London: Sage.

Parker, H., Sumner, M. and Jarvis, G. (1989) *Unmasking the Magistrates,* Milton Keynes: Open University Press.

Parker, V. and Kilfeather, J. (1991) 'Creating choices. Working with long term solvent abusers', in: J. Dennington and J. Pitts (eds), *Developing Services for Young People in Crisis,* London: Longman.

Patten, J. (1991) 'Making the punishment fit the frame', *Guardian,* 20 February.

Pitts, J. (1988) *The Politics of Juvenile Crime,* London: Sage.

Pitts, J. (1991) 'Less harm or more good: politics, policy and practice with young people in crisis', in: J. Dennington and J. Pitts (eds), *Developing Services for Young People in Crisis,* London: Longman.

Pratt, J. (1989) 'Corporatism, the third model of juvenile justice', *British Journal of Criminology,* 29, 236–54.

Preston, R. (1980) 'Social theology and penal theory and practice: the collapse of the rehabilitative ideal and the search for an alternative', in: A.E. Bottoms and R.H. Preston (eds), *The Coming Penal Crisis,* Edinburgh: Scottish Academic Press.

Rorty, R. (1989) *Contingency, Irony and Solidarity,* Cambridge: Cambridge University Press.

Rutherford, A. (1986) *Growing out of Crime,* Harmondsworth: Penguin.

Schur, E. (1974) *Radical Non-Intervention,* New York: Prentice Hall.

Sinclair, I. (1971) *Hostels for Probationers* (Home Office Research Study No. 6), London: HMSO.

Thorpe, D., Smith, D., Green, C. and Paley, J. (1980) *Out of Care,* London: Allen and Unwin.

Wilkins, L.T. (1969) *Evaluation of Penal Measures,* New York: Random House.

Wilson, J.Q. (1975) *Thinking about Crime,* New York: Basic Books.

29

Understanding and preventing youth crime

David Farrington

YOUTH CRIME

The number of young people found guilty by the juvenile courts or formally cautioned by police has fallen in England and Wales during the past 15 years. For example, between 1983 and 1993 the proportion of 10- to 13-year-old boys who were found guilty or cautioned for more serious 'indictable' offences dropped by 42 per cent, with a corresponding 15 per cent decline among 14- to 17-year-olds.

However, the apparent decrease is almost certainly an illusion. Police-recorded crime statistics and national surveys of the victims of crime both agree that the types of offence most often committed by young people – such as burglary and taking vehicles – have risen dramatically over the same period.

Procedural changes appear to account for the discrepancy, especially a growing reluctance to take juveniles to court and an increasing tendency on the part of police to issue unrecorded warnings rather than formal cautions. The House of Commons Home Affairs Committee suggested in 1993 that one explanation for a higher crime rate and a lower number of juvenile offenders might be an increase in the number of persistent young offenders responsible for a disproportionate volume of crime. But there is no evidence to support this suggestion.

CRIMINAL CAREERS

The life-time likelihood of acquiring at least one criminal conviction is greater than commonly realised. More than four out of ten males and one in ten females are likely to be found guilty or cautioned for an indictable offence at some point during their lives. However, it is also true that a comparatively small proportion of the population – about 5 per cent of males – are chronic offenders who account for about half of all known offending.

Official records and 'self-report' studies also show that individuals more often break the law when they are young. The 'peak' ages at which they are most likely to

SOURCE: This chapter is taken from *Social Policy Research Findings*, No. 93, 1996. York, Joseph Rowntree Foundation.

be found guilty or cautioned are between 15 and 19. Criminal involvement typically starts before the age of 15, but declines markedly once young people reach their 20s. However, young people who become involved in crime at the earliest ages – before they are 14 – tend to become the most persistent offenders, with longer criminal careers.

Young offenders tend to be versatile and rarely specialise in particular types of crime, including violence. Longitudinal research has identified features in the childhood and adult lives of violent offenders and non-violent persistent offenders that are very similar, suggesting that violent offenders are essentially frequent offenders. Studies have also found that young offenders are versatile in committing other types of antisocial behaviour, including heavy drinking, drug-taking, dangerous driving and promiscuous sex. Delinquency is, therefore, only one element in a much larger syndrome of antisocial behaviour.

Interviews with young offenders, meanwhile, suggest that their crimes are most commonly committed for material gain. However, a minority of offences, especially vandalism and taking vehicles without the owner's consent, are committed for excitement, enjoyment or to relieve boredom.

RISK FACTORS

Research concerned with the backgrounds, circumstances and attitudes of future offenders has identified thousands of factors that point to an increased risk that children and young people will become criminally involved in the future. The major risk factors for juvenile offending are:

- *Prenatal and perinatal*: early child-bearing increases the risks of such undesirable outcomes for children as low school attainment, antisocial behaviour, substance use and early sexual activity. An increased risk of offending among children of teenage mothers is associated with low income, poor housing, absent fathers and poor child-rearing methods.
- *Personality*: impulsiveness, hyperactivity, restlessness and limited ability to concentrate are associated with low attainment in school and a poor ability to foresee the consequences of offending.
- *Intelligence and attainment*: low intelligence and poor performance in school, although important statistical predictors of offending, are difficult to disentangle from each other. One plausible explanation of the link between low intelligence and crime is its association with a poor ability to manipulate abstract concepts and to appreciate the feelings of victims.
- *Parental supervision and discipline*: harsh or erratic parental discipline and cold or rejecting parental attitudes have been linked to delinquency and are associated with children's lack of internal inhibitions against offending. Physical abuse by parents has been associated with an increased risk of the children themselves becoming violent offenders in later life.
- *Parental conflict and separation*: living in a home affected by separation or divorce is more strongly related to delinquency than when the disruption has been caused

by the death of one parent. However, it may not be a 'broken home' that creates an increased risk of offending so much as the parental conflict that led to the separation.

- *Socio-economic status*: social and economic deprivation are important predictors of antisocial behaviour and crime, but low family income and poor housing are better measurements than the prestige of parents' occupations.
- *Delinquent friends*: delinquents tend to have delinquent friends. But it is not certain whether membership of a delinquent peer group leads to offending or whether delinquents simply gravitate towards each other's company (or both). Breaking up with delinquent friends often coincides with desisting from crime.
- *School influences*: the prevalence of offending by pupils varies widely between secondary schools. But it is not clear how far schools themselves have an effect on delinquency (for example, by paying insufficient attention to bullying or providing too much punishment and too little praise), or whether it is simply that troublesome children tend to go to high delinquency-rate schools.
- *Community influences*: the risks of becoming criminally involved are higher for young people raised in disorganised inner city areas, characterised by physical deterioration, overcrowded households, publicly-subsidised renting and high residential mobility. It is not clear, however, whether this is due to a direct influence on children, or whether environmental stress causes family adversities which in turn cause delinquency.

One difficulty in explaining the development of offending is that most risk factors coincide and are interrelated. For example, adolescents living in physically deteriorated and social disorganised neighbourhoods tend, disproportionately, to come from families with poor parental supervision and erratic discipline, and to display a high level of impulsiveness and low intelligence.

Moreover, while a great deal is known about risk factors, comparatively little attention has been paid to factors that may protect young people, especially those from high-risk backgrounds, against offending. Those factors that are known include having: a resilient temperament; a warm, affectionate relationship with at least one parent; parents who provide effective supervision, pro-social beliefs and consistent discipline; and parents who maintain a strong interest in their children's education. An understanding of how to build on the positive features influencing individuals, their families and communities can be used to increase the effectiveness of prevention strategies.

PREVENTION TECHNIQUES

Strategies for preventing crime, drug misuse and other antisocial behaviour among young people should be designed to counter specific risk factors and, where possible, to enhance known protective factors. A combination of interventions may be more effective than a single method. On the basis of well-designed experimental research – mostly conducted in the United States and Canada – the most hopeful methods of preventing youth crime are outlined below.

- *Frequent home visiting* by health professionals to women during pregnancy and infancy provide advice about prenatal and postnatal care of the child, infant development, proper nutrition, and avoiding smoking, drinking and drug use in pregnancy. Studies suggest that this can lead to a reduction in child abuse by parents as well as a longer term reduction in delinquency among the children concerned.
- *Pre-school 'intellectual enrichment' programmes* are designed to stimulate thinking and reasoning ability in young children, and hence to increase their school success. The High/Scope Perry Preschool Programme in Michigan provided high quality nursery education for an experimental group of children in a disadvantaged African American community, including a curriculum that encouraged children to plan, implement and review their play activities. A long-term follow-up of former participants at age 27 found that they were less likely to have been arrested than a control group of similar children, and more likely to have completed their secondary education, to have reasonably well-paid jobs and to own their homes.
- *Parenting education programmes* encourage parents to notice what their children are doing, to praise good behaviour, to state house rules clearly, and to make rewards and punishments contingent on children's behaviour. A number of programmes have demonstrated success in reducing children's antisocial behaviour, although reductions in stealing and other delinquent activities have in some instances proved short-lived.
- *Cognitive and social skills training* teaches children to stop and think before acting, to consider the consequences of antisocial behaviour, to understand other people's feelings, and to solve interpersonal problems by negotiation rather than aggression. Some of these techniques, intended to strengthen children's own inhibitions against antisocial behaviour, have also been used to reduce re-offending among juvenile offenders.
- *Peer influence strategies* offer young people advice on how to resist pressure from friends to engage in antisocial behaviour ranging from under-age drinking and smoking to drug abuse and other crimes. Research suggests that advice is most likely to be heeded when given by specially trained, high-status peers rather than by parents or teachers.
- *Classroom management* and other training can help teachers to communicate clear instructions and expectations, to notice and reward children for socially desirable behaviour and to be consistent in their use of discipline.
- *Anti-bullying initiatives in schools* include implementing explicit rules that encourage children to report bullying incidents and offer help to the victims. Playground monitoring and supervision may also need to be improved. Programmes in Norway and Britain have demonstrated success in reducing bullying, which is itself associated with an increased risk of delinquency.

Efforts to modify the risk factors associated with delinquency have also included community crime prevention programmes, with a focus on achieving physical improvements in disadvantaged neighbourhoods and providing recreational facilities for young people. Unfortunately, there is a shortage of convincing evidence for the effectiveness of these programmes. Crime prevention in the United Kingdom has, meanwhile, tended to emphasise measures designed to reduce the opportunities for crime in particular situations. Techniques include increased surveillance by closed circuit cameras, improving physical security, and protecting individuals against re-victimisation. The major difficulty with such programmes is that they may merely displace crime to other places or victims rather than preventing it altogether.

PRIORITIES FOR RESEARCH AND DEVELOPMENT

The most important knowledge about the causes and development of offending in the United Kingdom derives from rather old longitudinal data. New follow-up studies are needed to investigate the development of antisocial behaviour from childhood into the teenage years, and from the teenage years into adulthood. Such research should be closely concerned with protective as well as risk factors.

Although well-designed evaluations of preventive projects have been carried out in America, there is an urgent need to evaluate the replicability and effectiveness of such strategies in the United Kingdom. The available evidence suggests that prevention programmes are best implemented as elements of a larger programme targeted geographically on high crime areas. The aim should be to carry out a systematic assessment of the main risk factors in a community and to adopt effective strategies for reducing or eliminating them. A programme should also identify protective factors and other strengths within a community with a view to enhancing them.

COMMUNITIES THAT CARE

The *Communities that Care* programme for reducing antisocial behaviour among young people has been devised by researchers at the University of Washington, Seattle and is one of the most promising strategies to emerge in America. Its combination of flexibility and a systematic approach would lend itself to adaptation in the United Kingdom. Described as 'a risk and protection focused programme', it is based on a social development strategy that can be tailored to the specific needs of a neighbourhood, district or city. Its main features are:

- *Community mobilisation*: key leaders are brought together and a management board set up consisting of representatives from local agencies and the community. The board's task is to arrange a detailed assessment of local risks and resources and to agree an action plan.
- *Implementation*: prevention plans address the priority risk and protection factors by implementing techniques from a menu of strategies that research has shown to be effective.
- *Evaluation*: detailed monitoring is carried out to ensure that the programme's progress and effectiveness can be evaluated.

CONCLUSIONS

The time is now ripe to mount a large-scale community-based programme against crime that adopts the most promising prevention strategies to tackle risk factors that are problematic within particular communities. Such an approach would have similarities with public health programmes that seek to reduce illnesses such as coronary heart disease by tackling the known risk factors (smoking, a high-fat diet and lack of exercise, for instance). The programme's aim should be to promote community safety, pro-social behaviour and healthy development as well as to prevent drug misuse and crime.

30

Expanding realms of the new penology: the advent of actuarial justice for juveniles

Kimberly Kempf-Leonard and Elicka Peterson

Juvenile justice has begun to feel the effects of a paradigm shift inherited from criminal justice. This shift, originally called the new penology, was identified by Malcolm Feeley and Jonathan Simon in 1992 as a set of contemporary correctional policies aimed at efficient custody and control, without embracing traditional penal objectives of rehabilitation or punishment (Feeley and Simon, 1992). Feeley and Simon then refined and expanded their original observations, renamed the phenomenon actuarial justice, and offered their explanation for its evolution in criminal justice (Feeley and Simon, 1994). They characterized actuarial justice as a set of techniques and objectives de-emphasizing the offender:

> It is actuarial. It is concerned with techniques for identifying, classifying, and managing groups assorted by levels of dangerousness. It takes crime for granted. It accepts deviance as normal. It is skeptical that liberal interventionist crime control strategies do or can make a difference. Thus its aim is not to intervene in individuals' lives for the purpose of ascertaining responsibility, making the guilty 'pay for their crime' or changing them. Rather it seeks to regulate groups as part of a strategy of managing danger. (Feeley and Simon, 1994: 173)

More recently, Simon and Feeley (1995: 174) contend that 'the new penology is not a fixed entity but an evolving formation of knowledge and power.' They argue that 'while the new penology is formally neutral as to the specific objectives of the criminal process, its tendency to translate all issues into system flow questions ultimately influences the normative effects of penalty' (Simon and Feeley, 1995: 172). They also note that although the new penology produces representations of the system that facilitate objectives like deterrence and incapacitation, it not only has trouble recognizing the

SOURCE: This chapter is taken from *Punishment and Society*, Vol. 2, No. 1, 2000, pp. 66–97 (abridged).

cultural investment in the figure of the criminal, it has trouble with the concept of *humanity* (Simon and Feeley, 1995: 172, 174).

In short, actuarial justice presents a theoretical model of criminal justice processing in which the pursuit of efficiency and techniques that streamline case processing and offender supervision replace traditional goals of rehabilitation, punishment, deterrence, and incapacitation, and the focus on due process or crime control procedures (Packer, 1968). Feeley and Simon are not alone in noting this paradigm shift, other researchers, such as Garland (1996) have noticed this changing emphasis as well: 'The promise to deliver "law and order" and security for all citizens is now increasingly replaced by a promise to process complaints or apply punishments in a just, efficient and cost-effective way' (1996: 459). This theoretical model is unique, however, in having its *sole* objective that of a cost-saving entrepreneur; *justice,* however conceived, is not imperative. This efficiency objective is somewhat difficult to discern because it has advanced – actually free ridden, under the shadow of current themes associated with punishment. This is particularly true when a just deserts orientation is present, because its goal is making offenses and punishments commensurate and the current statistical techniques often used to determine this equity also make measurement of each more clear and routine. These statistical techniques are fundamental to actuarial justice. As these techniques for measurement improve and the routines become more accepted and established, the independent effect of actuarial justice should become easier to observe. But we should not wait until observation is easy and the techniques of actuarial justice are fully institutionalized, because intervention will be much more difficult, if not impossible, to achieve once actuarial justice is firmly established. The actuarial objective that justice systems should be efficient, devoid of the traditional treatment, deterrence, punishment, or even incapacitation, should give us cause for concern about formal mechanisms of social control now.

[...]

More importantly, what has not yet been appreciated fully, and the reason this new theory is significant, is that it argues that these actuarial instruments are beginning to take on a life of their own. Garland (1996) highlights this point in asserting that the 'new performance indicators tend to measure "outputs" rather than "outcomes," what the organization *does,* rather than what, if anything, it *achieves*' (1996: 458). Indeed, these techniques are not merely vehicles for more effective implementation of policy, rather, they are becoming the actual objectives of policy. If the means have become the end, then there is reason for concern.

Although public and scholarly attention has continued to center on the relative merits of prevention, rehabilitation, deterrence, and just deserts, those who administer justice systems have been gravitating toward techniques associated with actuarial justice and the convenience they offer. Simon and Feeley argue that:

> unlike earlier eras in which they took an active role in articulating and shaping public opinion on crime policy, criminal justice professionals are now on the fringes. Their discourse – expressed in varying degrees in terms of the new penology – has barely penetrated and has not even begun to shape public debate. (1995: 154)

The appeal of actuarialism for criminal justice personnel is probably a reaction to feelings of frustration and pessimism that arise from working in an overcrowded,

---

High influence

Pre-hearing detention
Private institutionalization
Community-based services
Assessment and offender classification
Disposition and sentencing
Transfer to criminal court
Nature and perception of juvenile crime
Case screening procedures
Institutional treatment
Family influence and accountability

Low influence

Figure 30.1   *Continuum of likely actuarial justice influence in juvenile justice*

and oft publicly criticized system. The actuarial objective does not offer an answer to this perceived hopelessness. Instead, it takes for granted that no answer exists, and offers the placating alternative of at least managing this hopelessness in a less burdensome and more efficient fashion. In this respect, actuarial justice offers beleaguered personnel at least a chance to succeed, although only through a redefinition of goals. It is especially troubling that these changes to the criminal justice system are occurring without the benefit of adequate public discourse or scholarly investigation.

[···]

CURRENT POLICY DEVELOPMENTS IN JUVENILE JUSTICE

In this section we examine a number of key policy developments and situations within juvenile justice that help explain the evolution of actuarial justice in this purview. The extent to which they have been adopted by juvenile justice systems varies considerably across the many independent systems; however, these procedures may be aligned somewhat along a continuum indicating how apt they are to be influenced by actuarial justice objectives and techniques (see Figure 30.1). Susceptibility to adaptation of actuarial goals – which focus primarily on cost-efficiency rather than any youth-specific goal such as rehabilitation or retribution – is ranked in terms of the actuarial influence present in the means for various juvenile justice procedures. In other words, if a policy or procedure draws more heavily from the logic of actuarialism, eventually, it is more likely to be evaluated solely in terms of its cost-effectiveness and efficiency in management, in keeping with the goals of actuarial justice.

Although this schematic continuum is without fixed intervals and exact placements, it does help to order the influence of actuarial justice among many current juvenile justice reforms. At the high end, there are policy initiatives targeting juveniles that virtually exude the orientation of new penology – namely preventive detention, the growth of privately run institutions, specialization of community-based services, and risk-based classification, and dispositional assignment of youths. At the low end, there are certain features of the juvenile system with inherent barriers against the intrusion of actuarial justice aims and techniques. Recent initiatives calling for the systemic inclusion of 'at risk' parents and families, and the diverse institutional settings used in the treatment of juveniles are among those features in which the influence of actuarial justice strategies is not yet likely to be as great. At central positions along the continuum, there are juvenile policies and developments that seem susceptible to adoption of these aims and techniques. New standards for case screening, public perceptions of juvenile crime, limiting judicial discretion in certification, and determinate sentencing of juvenile offenders are likely accorded this status of vulnerability. Moving down the continuum of influence, we will now discuss the role of actuarial justice objectives and techniques in relation to each of these current juvenile justice developments.

Pre-hearing detention and public safety

In 1996, an estimated 316,368 youths were detained prior to resolution of their delinquency cases, and this number does not include youths in custody with pending cases for pending status offenses and other non-criminal juvenile law matters (NCJJ/OJJDP, 1998). Thus, preventive detention, a huge factor in the emergence of actuarial justice (Feeley and Simon, 1994; Vaughn and del Carmen, 1997), also is applicable to the juvenile process. The step from first warehousing youthful offenders for the protection of society to warehousing those offenders with the emphasis on *efficiency* is not a long one. The goal of preventive detention was affirmed as a policy by the US Supreme Court in 1984, when *Schall* v. *Martin* formalized the right to pre-trial detention of juvenile offenders perceived to be a danger to the community. This ruling allows judges to detain juveniles they perceive as 'at risk' for subsequent offending if released from detention based on subjective predictions, effectively making youths 'guilty until proven innocent' with the blessing of the Supreme Court. The *Schall* decision also legitimized the use of preventive detention for adults (Goldkamp, 1985); both the Federal Bail Reform Act and *US* v. *Salemo* were justified in part by the Court's decision in *Schall* v. *Martin*.

The objective of detention may have changed considerably, but the criteria for detaining juveniles remains unclear even in light of this new focus on prevention. Measures used to determine detention tend to be unspecified and based on the discretion of many individual decision makers, including police officers, intake court staff, and judges. The factors they consider may differ by virtue of their positions, training, backgrounds, and experience responding to youths. Research on detention practices has identified disparities resulting in disproportionate detention based on race, gender, type of offense, legal counsel, geographic location of the court, and access to a detention center (Lerman, 1997; Costello and Worthington, 1981–2; Feld, 1991, 1995b, 1999; Schwartz et al., 1991; Federele and Chesney-Lind, 1992; Frazier and Bishop, 1995; Community Research Associates, 1997). The actuarial goal of efficiently controlling the underclass is particularly apparent in the case of poor, minority youths, who may be hardest hit by disparities in detention practices (see also Feld, 1999).

There also are very few custody options, aside from a growing number of beds within secure facilities. Juveniles rarely have release on one's own recognizance, money bail, or a deposit option. Outright release means parental supervision, but other forms of third party, community-based, supervision are uncommon. This situation is likely to worsen as more opportunities for secure detention coincide with a growth in the number of private facilities, and access to new funding for construction of facilities. As Schwartz and his colleagues (1988) observed for one state, the detention situation in most juvenile justice systems does not mirror the enhanced rationality of pre-trial release decision-making in criminal justice.

After studying the *Schall* ruling, the American Bar Association concluded that continued refinement of the procedures for detention was needed (Brown *et al.*, 1985). Although still the minority, techniques that include more uniform, sometimes actuarial-based, detention guidelines instruments that identify youths as candidates for detention based on risk models, as well as classification policies that specify the type of detention, are gaining in popularity (Baird, 1984, 1985; Frazier, 1989; Weibush *et al.*, 1995).

Thus, since *Schall,* detention objectives often suggest that the perception of community safety has surpassed concern for the needs of the youth, and the unlimited discretionary procedures that still prevail make almost anything possible. Incapacitation before adjudication, particularly without any rehabilitative or retributive goal, smacks of the actuarial justice objective. The intent is simply to manage efficiently an unchangeable population (primarily poor minority males) and preserve social tranquility.

The growth of privately run institutions

Privatization of services is another area in which the juvenile system exudes both actuarial justice strategies and objectives. Federal mandates for the sight and sound separation of juveniles from adults, the removal of youths from jails, and the deinstitutionalization of status offenders in juvenile justice forced juvenile court staff to become more creative in their confinement practices. These mandates are sure to fail because of strategies of circumvention, including reclassifying status offenses as minor law violations or issuing unreasonable supervision requirements, that result in violations of court orders, which both allow for the confinement of juveniles. Another method of sidestepping the mandates involves cloaking the confinement by avoiding the use of publicly run and monitored facilities, following either a direct court order or through an informal 'negotiation' in which parents agree to 'voluntarily' commit their children to ensure an informal resolution of the case. Their creativity has resulted in an increased number of youths confined within private institutions and tremendous growth in the number of private agencies accepting youths (Schwartz, 1989; Demone and Gibelman, 1990).

One consequence of growing reliance on privatized correctional facilities is many forms of differential processing. 'Voluntary' confinement generally either requires Medicaid, a good insurance plan or money on the part of the family. Thus, the working poor are frequently excluded from private care, and comprise most of the group of youths still officially detained in juvenile institutions. The racial division that occurs largely due to socioeconomic factors also means that minority youth are less able to avoid the stigma of formal adjudication. Racial disparities also exist in involuntary confinement through formal court orders, as one study found that private treatment facilities were more often ordered for white youths, whereas public custodial facilities are more often ordered for minority youths, even when similar drug-related offending is at issue (Kempf-Leonard and Sontheimer, 1995). Breed and Krisberg (1986: 16) underscore this phenomenon: 'Tragically, juvenile justice facilities are becoming minority enclaves in which conditions of confinement are becoming ever more harsh.' Gender effects also are evident. Chesney-Lind (1995) refers to this substitute mechanism of social control as 'transinstitutionalization', and argues that middle class white girls are the principal targets of private hospitalization and treatment. The extent of girls' private institutionalization may be exacerbated by many juvenile justice professionals' preference not to work with girls, and because private facilities also accept referrals directly from families, physicians, and schools – sources known to refer girls more often (Kempf-Leonard *et al.*, 1997).

Thus, juvenile justice procedures lead to the use of different types of facilities to separate youths based on demographic profiles, in addition to consideration of their offense. Of course, crowding and resource concerns in many jurisdictions also dictate placement wherever it is available, and by whatever means it can be obtained. Under perceived ideal conditions, however, youth populations could be expected to become even more segregated and specialized given the expanded range of facilities and new recommendations for gender-specific and culturally diverse treatment.

Juvenile justice is inclined to use private incarceration as a preferred method of case disposition (Lerman, 1980, 1984; Weithorn, 1988; Coates, 1989; Schwartz, 1989). There are many different motives for confinement, including perceptions of dangerousness (more often applied to minorities), need for protection (more often applied to girls), and treatment. Regardless of the goal, incarceration is expensive and transferring the responsibility elsewhere may help alleviate limited juvenile justice funds that are already stretched to the limit by increased caseloads. Another argument for the rapid growth of privatization is that most states fail to monitor the security measures used by private facilities; therefore, private institutions may provide an option to intervene with status offenders and victims of abuse which keeps states in compliance with the federal mandate prohibiting their secure confinement. This is consistent with Gilbert's (1996: 19) contention that 'the arguments that support private prisons and jails are rooted in self-interest of correctional enterprise rather than public interest.'

In addition to the aforementioned problems with disparity and motivation, private institutions – whether operated for gain or non-profit – are a business, and thus subscribe naturally to the efficiency precepts of actuarial justice, which are based on a managerial model. Cohen (1985: 65) explained how private agencies negotiate control over youths from state-run juvenile justice systems by linking funding to promises of success akin to 'Benthamite utilitarianism.' Private for-profit institutions attempt to maximize return through the efficient custody of the juveniles in their care, just as public and non-profit institutions seek to realize cost-savings. Here, although not specifically referring to juveniles. Garland (1996: 455) commented that '[t]he most publicized aspects of [the management, business-like ethos] have been the various measures of privatization which have taken place, transferring specific criminal justice functions to commercial concerns in a new form of contract provision.'

The emphasis on organizational efficiency may overshadow that of punishment or rehabilitation – goals which are far more difficult to evaluate. Meyer and Grant (1996) suggest that the success of some private treatment may reflect selection criteria skewed toward selection of less serious cases. However, Winn (1996) calls the notion of greater efficiency 'ideology' rather than fact. In his review of 40 articles on the topic, he found that while efficiency is the primary justification given for privatization, there is little empirical support that private organizations are actually more efficient than public agencies. Mays (1996) echoes this criticism that there is a lack of program evaluation in this area. The growth of privately run institutions has eased some pressures within juvenile justice while concomitantly enabling increased numbers of youths to be confined: two outcomes which are very consistent with the ideology of actuarial justice.

Community-based services

Juvenile justice is unique in that it acts as a centralized referral agency of sorts, responding to minors in an array of situations. It differs from other social services, however, in its authority to require treatment. Previous juvenile justice reforms encouraged courts to use the least restrictive alternative in adjudicating youths (Schwartz, 1989). These initiatives, based on the traditional objective of *parens patriae*, and buttressed by the federal mandate to deinstitutionalize status offenders and victims of abuse or neglect, have spawned tremendous growth in the specialization of community-based services (Mahoney *et al.*, 1988; Lerner, 1990; Mays, 1996).

The actual nature of community-based programs and the goals they are intended to achieve vary greatly. The term is applied to programs ranging from a simple court order that the youth attend school regularly or obey a curfew to electronic monitoring as a means of in-home supervision. In their meta-analysis of evaluations of over 200 treatment programs, Lipsey and Wilson (1998) reported that the most effective community-based programs included components of individualized counseling, interpersonal skills training, other behavioral programs, and the incorporation of multiple services. Not surprisingly, programs with a longer intervention period, higher-quality services, well-trained staff, carefully designed and monitored treatment curriculums, and appropriately targeted clients also had higher levels of success. These scholars linked lower recidivism among serious juvenile offenders – particularly violent and chronic offenders – with community-based programs rather than with institutional programs. They also found that wilderness programs, vocational programs without an educational component, and shock incarceration were least effective, and sometimes associated with higher recidivism.

Besides diversity in type of service and level of supervision, there also is a wide continuum of stages across which these community-based programs are used to intervene with juveniles. In-home programs serve youths who have had no contact with traditional juvenile justice systems as a means of prevention. These community-based prevention efforts that target 'at risk' youths, families, and neighborhoods have garnered significant support (Hawkins and Catalano, 1992; Montgomery and Landon, 1994; Brewer *et al.*, 1995; Hawkins *et al.*, 1995; Howell, 1995; Greenwood *et al.*, 1996 and see Chapter 29 of this volume). However, their potential for negative labeling effects also has been criticized. For example, according to Feld:

> Because parents bear primary responsibility to raise their own children, public programs to assist other people's children stipulate that parents demonstrably must fail at the task as a prerequisite of receiving public assistance. But, stigmatizing the clients of social programs by making failure a requirement of eligibility undermines public support for those programs and ensures their inadequacy. (1999: 291)

Beyond prevention, community-based programs, often the same ones serving 'at risk' populations, are evoked at the pre-hearing stage of court processing as a diversionary strategy. These same programs also are popular with courts as a 'sentence' or formal disposition following official adjudication (see Chapter 31 of this volume). In-home supervision, once again co-mingling the type of youths and intended goals within the same programs, also has become increasingly popular as a tool in aftercare, the juvenile version of parole (Armstrong, 1991; Altschuler, 1999).

Concerning adults, Feeley and Simon (1992: 456) argue that probation and parole programs, which were long viewed as a means of reintegrating offenders into the community, are increasingly being treated as a 'cost-effective way to police and sanction a chronically troublesome population.' More generally, Gowdy (1993: 5) echoes the argument that the increasing prevalence of community-based services has occurred due to the fact that they are 'practical and affordable.' Therefore, community-based supervision for juveniles may become yet another method of control over even more juveniles; one that is chiefly motivated by the expedient use of resources.

To understand the consequences of this extended control, one must bear in mind that this form of supervision can also be viewed as an extension of the effects of labeling brought about by actuarial justice techniques. Thus, if the youth is already under the surveillance of the system – even a prevention program serving a non-offending youth from a 'high risk' neighborhood, but particularly an offender supervised intensively – he or she is far more likely to be caught offending and sanctioned sooner, and more often. Calling it a 'new diversion *into* the system,' Cohen (1985: 51) has warned how in such prevention programs, 'intervention comes earlier, it sweeps in more deviates, is extended to those not yet formally adjudicated and it becomes more intensive' (1985: 53 and see Chapter 17 of this volume). This net-widening effect is further reinforced by the revised definition of revocation as a successful indicator of systemic effectiveness, rather than the traditional definition of failure (Feeley and Simon, 1992).

Whether or not alternative forms of supervision are completed without subsequent offense, they most assuredly fit the mold cast by actuarial justice. Feeley and Simon (1992: 457) also note that 'these new forms of control are not anchored in aspirations to rehabilitate, reintegrate, train, provide employment, or the like. They are justified in more blunt terms: "variable detention depending upon risk assessment".' While the current juvenile justice aim of employing the least restrictive alternative in sentencing youths is upheld by new risk management strategies, the difference is that the goal of the process may have shifted from the best interests of the child to the best interests of a more cost-effective system.

Assessment and classification guidelines

Objective assessment instruments and classification guidelines are central to the theory of actuarial justice, and tools that are gaining ground for case processing in juvenile justice systems (Bonta, 1996). Currently, these instruments are most often used to assess youths for risk of reoffending and need for treatment, but the tools can be applied to any measurable outcome and are also used to schedule staff workloads.

Often called risk and needs classification instruments, these measures are used to assign points to various characteristics of the youth and his or her alleged offense. The points typically are derived from statistical models that identify the relative importance of each characteristic in predicting the policy outcome of interest. The range of cumulative scores is categorized according to estimates associated with their probability of the outcome, much in the manner of insurance tables which predict the likelihood of one having an automobile collision, house fire, or serious illness. The guidelines then provide a classification grid that identifies the suggested juvenile justice intervention within each category of scores.

When they exist, guidelines typically are used initially at the intake screening stage, at the point of detention, or at disposition to direct sanction and treatment (Baird, 1984, 1985; Weibush *et al.*, 1995; Bonta, 1996). Similar instruments could be adapted to other stages of traditional case processing. Risk-based classification is essential to the graduated sanctions component of the newest federal initiative in the area of juvenile justice, *The comprehensive strategy for serious, violent, and chronic juvenile offenders* (Wilson and Howell, 1993). This initiative also endorses the *Communities That Care* model of community-level assessments of risk factors related to adolescent problem behaviors in the aggregate (DRP, 1994, 1996). A promotion of this policy initiative includes the following: 'In addition to ensuring that these decisions are made in a consistent fashion, these instruments help reduce inappropriate placements, thereby reducing the costs of juvenile court sanctions' (Howell, 1995: 35).

The idea that custody and control are easier to maintain with proper classification is hardly new as a correctional technique, but in the past, classification was more often based on subjective 'clinical' diagnoses made by individual employees of the courts and correctional facilities, and seldom reviewed. According to the National Council on Crime and Delinquency, '[h]istorically, risk assessment and classification have been informal, highly discretionary procedures carried out by individuals who have varying philosophies, different levels of experience and knowledge and who use dissimilar criteria in the assessment process' (1997: 3). Somewhat more critically, James Bonta (1996: 20) has called professional judgements 'legally, ethically, and practically unacceptable.' With the incorporation of these techniques, youths can now be grouped according to information obtained from computer-generated statistical profiles of risk. Most new procedures still allow individual staff the discretion to override the guideline from the statistical model in special cases, but the exceptions require special justification and tend to be thoroughly reviewed.

In juvenile justice, this classification is increasingly based on the risk to the community because of the current emphasis on public safety objectives, rather than traditional aims directed at the needs of youths. Juveniles considered 'high risk' are more often placed in secure settings, whereas 'low risk' juveniles typically receive in-home services. Although still difficult, assessing risk of recidivism and assigning a corresponding level of supervision is an easier task than assessing specific needs and determining which mode of treatment is more likely to succeed. There are some efforts to combine risk of reoffending with needs for treatment, such as the inclusion of two types of factors associated with recidivism that are offered by Andrews and Bonta (1994). Their classification instruments include both risk factors that are inherent to the youth or a constant in the youths' life and risk factors that have the capacity to change; the latter type they label as 'criminogenic needs.'

More and more often, risk assessment increasingly is determined using criteria identified as relevant according to statistical prediction models, and by statistical experts who are new to the juvenile justice arena. As actuarial management continues to gain prominence, the success of case processing, custodial institutions, and community-based programs may be more often gauged internally, with progress measured by the efficiency of their statistical models and cost-savings initiatives, rather than enhanced safety, the production of better citizens, or other traditional goals.

Criteria for case screening

Traditionally, the majority of all juvenile cases have been handled informally. This has often translated into decisions on processing a specific case being made by police and court officers without ever consulting a juvenile court judge. Attrition from the system is less likely for adjudicated cases, which are processed formally with petitions for judicial decisions, than non-adjudicated cases, which are handled more informally. Even among formally adjudicated cases, hearings are not typically held in an adversarial setting; as such, attorneys rarely represent the legal interests of youth. Usually the whole court process is completed quickly, with few formal records, and almost never with an appellate review. Throughout the stages of case processing, juvenile justice systems have been oriented toward the youths' attitudes and behaviors, family support and structure, and general 'amenability to treatment' (Bernard, 1992). Information on these nurturing criteria is obtained primarily through lengthy interviews with youths and their parents.

The discretion associated with traditional case screening couples easily with the doctrine of *parens patriae*, including the explicit emphasis on informality and individualized treatment. However, recent introduction of formally trained attorneys and new offense-based criteria to case screening have resulted in greater amenability to both the goals and techniques of actuarial justice. In addition to the standardized assessment and classification instruments already discussed, legal sufficiency, a concept based on probable cause and once reserved for the adult legal system, has crept into the language of juvenile case processing. Many involved in the juvenile court process use criteria to establish legal sufficiency, primarily through police reports, as the means for sorting cases and guiding at least the initial processing decisions. This change has been identified as a by-product of the punitive sentiments of the day (Feld, 1993), although an alternative explanation might be the greater ease of decisions based on police reports given new court problems associated with large caseloads, crowding, youth violence, and unresponsive or inaccessible parents. These problems are particularly acute in large urban courts, where staff diversity is greater and where attorneys have recently been assigned responsibilities for intake case screening more often (American Bar Association, 1977; Aday, 1986; Shine and Price, 1992; Feld, 1993, 1995b; OJJDP, 1998).

Thus, legal sufficiency, determined fairly quickly by attorneys who are now more often involved and represent the state, coupled with increased use of standardized intake guidelines described earlier, reflect the presence of techniques, and possibly goals, consistent with the actuarial justice orientation of standardization and efficiency in processing.

Determinate sentencing in juvenile justice

Another development in adult criminal justice that has found its way into the realm of juvenile justice is determinate sentencing. Obviously, a sentencing scheme in which there is a precise price tag for each offense, offset by enhancements for repeat or particularly heinous offenses, or discounts for reduced responsibility associated with a younger offender (Feld, 1993: 288), provides a proficient mechanism consistent with achieving the actuarial justice objective. And thus, juvenile court models of determinate, or 'truth in' sentencing, typically based on the offenders' age, offense severity, and prior record, have also set the stage for the emergence of these techniques in juvenile justice. Many of the new procedures for dispositional decisions currently are linked to a 'get tough' punitive agenda. Independently, these sentencing changes also signify a new mechanism by which court staff can deflect responsibilities for case processing, including any 'failures' that garner negative publicity, to the policy instrument.

Even amidst punitive objectives, if youths are to be warehoused for specific lengths of time, without regard to their unique needs or amenability to treatments – which is precisely the point of 'blended jurisdictions' and 'youth discounts' (Feld, 1999) – then objectives of actuarial justice have made at least some inroads at the dispositional stages of juvenile justice systems. The new penology philosophy holds that incarceration has no effect upon recidivism rates (Feeley and Simon, 1992), thus delinquent youths may simply age into the adult system without attempts to divert them from this self-destructive pattern. This amounts to breeding future adult offenders void of any belief that something can, or should, be done to alter this course. If we give up on the possibility of change at such an early age, the rationale for a separate juvenile system is called into question.

Although techniques of actuarial justice are encroaching on the dispositional process of juvenile justice, evidence exists that it may not yet prevail. In 1990, the Texas Youth Commission (1991) conducted a survey of all states and discovered that only 37 per cent of these jurisdictions still employed the traditional juvenile justice model of indeterminate sentencing, compared with approximately 33 per cent of states which had a combination of determinate and indeterminate sentencing in their sentencing statutes. However, only about 17 per cent had completely abandoned the individual treatment of youths based on the *parens patriae* tradition and relied upon determinate sentencing exclusively. Of course, this study is nearly a decade old and newer data are not available so actuarial justice procedures may have advanced somewhat. Indeed, such inroads seem likely too, given that more accountability within juvenile justice processing has been a political 'hot button' issue during the decade and determinate sentencing provides a vehicle by which judges can escape blame by placing responsibility on the policy directive.

Limiting judicial discretion in certification

The movement to limit judicial discretion over transfer to criminal court is perhaps the most common reform in juvenile justice systems today. The drive for transfer, waiver, or certification of more youths is based both on a lack of confidence in juvenile justice interventions, and a more punitive political environment (Beckett, 1997). Researchers at the National Center for Juvenile Justice report that the percentage of cases waived from juvenile courts increased 68 per cent between 1988 and 1992 (Butts *et al.*, 1995). Perceptions of extreme leniency have led a skeptical public and some politicians to believe that juveniles who commit serious offenses or offend repeatedly are deserving of punishment within the 'tougher' adult system (*Criminal Justice Newsletter*, 1995; Sontheimer and Volenik, 1995).

Most new strategies involve establishing mandatory or presumptive guidelines for typical cases that should be waived, authorizing criminal court prosecutors to choose the legal venue rather than juvenile court judges, and giving adult corrections some responsibility for custody and confinement of youth (Fagan, 1995; Torbet *et al.*, 1996; Torbet and Szymanski, 1998; Tracy and Kempf-Leonard, 1998). Although less prevalent, some reforms linked to transfer policies would have all or most serious juvenile offenders processed in criminal justice and call into question the status of a separate juvenile system (Dawson, 1990; Feld, 1993). Further, wider adoption of these techniques is likely, because of new financial incentives offered by the federal government to states in which prosecutors are able to file charges directly in criminal courts against some juveniles (*House Conference Report*, 1997; OJJDP, 1998).

The criteria associated with mandates and presumptive guidelines for transfer should increase standardization and routine processing, and as such, the new policies should expedite the handling of more cases. The reformed waiver policies reflect case profiles; thus, the new penology finds yet another doorway to juvenile justice in this manner, simply by relocating youths who fit certain profiles to the adult system – where actuarial justice is already a reality (Feeley and Simon, 1992, 1994; Simon and Feeley, 1995). Cost-savings also is very likely because the new waiver policies provide a convenient vehicle by which juvenile justice can divest itself of many of the types of cases that traditionally have required the most time and resources. To illustrate this effect, Singer (1996) aptly showed how consideration of local resources affected court waiver decisions under a new law in New York. Less is known about resources allocated to confinement of youthful offenders in the so-called 'blended,' or 'dual' correctional systems.

These techniques are conducive to actuarial justice and increasing in popularity as each year more states have adopted similar reform of waiver provisions (Torbet and Szymanski, 1998). One of the impetuses for these changes has been the drive to punish juveniles, but there is evidence of significant obstacles to achieving this objective. The real difficulty is that most adult systems either are not equipped to deal with juvenile offenders or are reluctant to accept them for other reasons. In fact, many studies have revealed that certification often leads the prosecutor to drop or reduce the charges against the youth because of inadequate post-conviction alternatives (Gillespie and Norman, 1984; Sagatun *et al.*, 1985; Rudman *et al.*, 1986; Fagan *et al.*, 1987; Bishop *et al.*, 1989; Lemmon *et al.*, 1991; *Criminal Justice Newsletter*, 1995; Howell, 1996). Youthful inmates also pose unique administrative problems for adult prison staff (McShane and Williams, 1989).

Advancement of these strategies is less often fueled by public interest, as the public appears to be satisfied with the reforms for the most part, and juvenile crime is on the decline, thus providing no impetus for change based upon an actual need. The reforms will probably not be discontinued, however, simply because the goal of punishment via routine mechanisms of the adult system has proven less than a stunning success. Adult certification is likely to be adapted as routine, in large part due to the convenience it affords to juvenile justice systems. Thus, the diversion of serious, chronic juvenile offenders out of juvenile justice – regardless of whether criminal justice subsequently intervenes effectively – may be all about seeking actuarial justice.

Perception of juvenile crime

Juvenile crime is currently perceived as a major social problem. Indeed, the mere status of adolescence is equated with offending by some (for a discussion see Males, 1996).

Although recent *Uniform crime reports* indicate that the arrest rate for juvenile property crime has remained stable for more than a decade, juvenile arrest rates for violent crime, including homicide, increased dramatically until 1993, but have since fallen slightly (Federal Bureau of Investigation, 1996). According to Snyder and Sickmund (1995), the small juvenile violence rate increase in the late 1980s and early 1990s looked big because of 'the tyranny of small numbers.' In other words, a small increase in juvenile violence yields a larger percentage change because of the relatively small number of juveniles in the US population as compared to adults. Even though most crimes are committed by adults (Snyder and Sickmund, 1995), public perceptions generally hold that juvenile crime is far worse than in previous years and continuing to rise (Bernard, 1992).

It is worth noting that the media helps to shape this popular view. Consider that while the general public holds a tenacious belief that 'the [juvenile crime] problem is recent and did not exist in the "good old days"' (Bernard, 1992: 164 and see Chapter 3 of this volume), the media has profoundly reinforced this misconception in recent years, largely in response to the artful manipulation of politicians (for an excellent discussion of this phenomenon, see Beckett, 1997). The nightly news regularly reports *youthful* offenders as responsible for various crimes, a description that seems synonymous with *juvenile* offenders to the average viewer, but one that often refers to persons too old to fall within the jurisdiction of juvenile justice. Coverage more often goes to those who speculate about waves of juvenile violence (Blumstein, 1995; Fox, 1996) and 'superpredators' (DiIulio, 1996), than to those who are able to debunk such alarming reports (Zimring, 1996; Howell, 1997a). The media focus on violent and non-representative, or high profile cases (Walker, 1994) has escalated dramatically in recent years; these 'true crime' stories are reported in shocking detail, often accompanied by sweeping generalizations about the 'crime problem' (Felson, 1994). In the competition to capture the attention of an American public dulled to these routine displays of heinous violence, the added shock value of a child committing the act may seem just the ratings ticket.

Moreover, the leap from typically no media or public access to juvenile court proceedings and case dispositions to implied conclusions that juvenile courts do nothing is a reasonable scenario. Thus, it is easy to understand how the public might perceive juvenile justice as ineffective and the juvenile crime rate as skyrocketing in the absence of information on the topic. Although there has been an enormous increase in media coverage and publicity in juvenile cases in the last decade, this coverage still tends to report outlandish cases and those cases obviously bound for adult court. This situation also helps make the political climate ripe for intervention with greater numbers of youths and more accountability by the system for how cases are processed (Torbet et al., 1996). Managing large numbers of unwanted people in a way that does not attract public attention is precisely the attraction of actuarial justice.

Diverse institutional settings and treatment options

Traditional juvenile justice systems have almost unlimited sentencing options at their disposal, and many of these options resist intrusion by techniques consistent with actuarial justice through their design. For example, many of the large training schools of the past have been replaced by small, cottage-design institutions offering diverse programs to youths (Schwartz, 1989; Bernard, 1992). Wilderness camps, ranches, and restitution are other good examples of juvenile dispositions that serve specific types of youths. Other modes of specialized treatment and placement options include mental health facilities, vocational training, foster homes, intensive juvenile probation, electronic monitoring, boot camps, and a variety of residential options ranging from non-secure to secure. New federal initiatives to encourage gender-specific and culturally diverse opportunities across the spectrum of treatment suggest that an even wider variety of official responses may exist in the future. Because so many juvenile programs are geared toward helping youths with their individual problems, it seems likely that the neutral stance on rehabilitating offenders associated with actuarial justice is incompatible with the philosophy of most juvenile justice treatment options. While the availability of such options might be viewed as facilitating the efficient management of juveniles, much in the manner of classifying adult offenders to reduce friction in prisons (Brennan, 1987; Sechrest, 1987), the overriding emphasis on rehabilitation inherent in current strategies is not consistent with actuarial-based goals.

This relatively recent trend toward specialized institutions as opposed to the huge training schools of the past provides some buffer from the impact of actuarial justice. However, the trend toward early intervention and prevention, coupled with the current push for just deserts-oriented dispositions (perhaps even returning to single large custodial facilities in some locations), and a corresponding emphasis on cost-savings (Winn, 1996) all work to erode this protection.

'At risk' families and parental accountability

Finally, as politicians and policy makers scramble to appease an angry and frightened constituency (that they may have helped to create in the first place), the system has been extended to include so-called 'at risk' youths and their families. For example, a current initiative from the Federal Office of Juvenile Justice and Delinquency Prevention calls for implementing 'risk-focused' strategies aimed at 'targeted populations' (Howell, 1995). Among other causes, juvenile crime is blamed on single mothers or [those] living in certain neighborhoods, with welfare reform, urban renewal, and 'target hardening' touted as the cures.

The obvious problem with including 'at risk' parties in the scope of juvenile justice begins with case screening. As the standard for screening delinquent youths now shifts toward judgements by attorneys about probable cause and legal sufficiency, there is an obvious contradiction in intervention with families or parents who simply fit 'at risk' profiles for producing delinquent children when there is no probable cause and glaring legal insufficiency.

Although it hearkens back to the shrill laws of the early 1800s, another policy reprisal comes in the form of holding parents legally accountable through civil and criminal sanctions for the actions of their children (Mennel, 1973; Geis and Binder, 1991; Harlan and Hayes, 1992; Leo, 1995). At least 12 states enacted new parental responsibility laws during 1995 and 1996 (Nasser and Moss, 1996). Utah raised the cap for civil liability for cases in which parents are held financially responsible for property damage committed by their children to $2,000 in 1994, and Virginia to

$2,500 in 1996, on civil liability cases in which parents are held financially responsible for property damage committed by their children. Hawaii now holds parents and their children jointly liable for graffiti damages. Some states (e.g. Arizona, Idaho, Illinois, Oregon) require parents to pay court or supervision fees for cases involving their children. Other states also make parents incur costs associated with incarceration or placement of their children – as high as $10,000 in Colorado. Finally, a growing number of jurisdictions (e.g. Arizona, Arkansas, Colorado, Washington, DC, Iowa, Kansas, Utah, and Virginia) permit courts to order parents to participate in programs such as community service and parenting classes, and have ordered employers to grant parents unpaid leave to attend juvenile court hearings (Coalition for Juvenile Justice, 1996b).

This situation reveals an interesting bit of hypocrisy inherent in legal sufficiency as the method for case screening and the tendency toward greater accountability without regard to the age of the offender in general: how can juvenile justice simultaneously hold the juvenile and the parent responsible for the formers' actions? If youths are to be processed using adult criteria and held responsible for their delinquent actions as individuals capable of making rational decisions, it is an incompatible dichotomy to hold parents responsible for these capable youths as well.

The movement to include families in juvenile justice is a result of policy decisions based on public fear of unfamiliar populations and misconceptions about juvenile crime. The idea that 'it takes a village to raise a child' (Clinton, 1996) has become a popular catchall phrase for the extension of community responsibility for the actions of juveniles. It may be that this phrase speaks accurately to the societal breakdown that has reduced social controls for youths (W. Wilson, 1987). Nonetheless, its implications push juvenile justice processing ever closer to embracing actuarial justice objectives as yet another reactionary 'solution' to the problems faced by juvenile justice through further increasing the demands on an already overburdened system. This country may need to address the larger issues of community and parental responsibility, but the juvenile justice system is already responsible for addressing more issues than it can handle effectively in dealing strictly with the demands of helping the youths already assigned to its jurisdiction.

Juvenile justice systems are already beset with difficulties arising from their dual roles in social work and social control (Ferdinand, 1991; Bernard, 1992; Bazemore and Umbreit, 1995). This additional burden of adding those perceived as being 'at risk' increases the aura of ineffectiveness and hopelessness in the juvenile process, and thus may allow actuarial justice objectives to advance in the absence of an alternative cure for a system perceived as ailing.

Further, the predictive element in targeting 'at risk' families exemplifies actuarial justice strategies, as do the net-widening effects of including families in the first place. Actuarial justice models attempt to predict and circumvent crime – through incarceration and supervision – because crime is considered inevitable and criminals can, at best, only be controlled efficiently (Feeley and Simon, 1992, 1994). The inclusion of parents in case processing of juveniles obviously increases the scope of control, thereby strengthening the foothold of actuarial justice sentiments within the juvenile realm.

[…]

REFERENCES

Aday, David P., Jr (1986) 'Court structure, defense attorney use, and juvenile court decisions', *Sociological Quarterly*, 27 (1): 107–19.

Altschuler, David M. (1999) 'Issues and challenges in the community supervision of juvenile offenders', *Southern Illinois University Law Journal*, 23: 1–15.

American Bar Association (1977) *Standards relating to private counsel for private parties*. Cambridge, MA: Ballinger.

Andrews, Don and Bonta, James (1994) *The psychology of criminal conduct*. Cincinnati, OH: Anderson.

Armstrong, Troy L. (ed.) (1991) *Intensive interventions with high risk youths: promising approaches in juvenile probation and parole*. Monsey, NY: Willow Tree Press.

Baird, Christopher (1984) *Classification of juveniles in corrections: a model systems approach*. Madison, WI: National Council on Crime and Delinquency.

Baird, S. Christopher (1985) 'Classifying juveniles: making the most of an important mangement tool', *Corrections Today*, February: 32–8.

Bazemore, Gordon and Umbreit, Mark (1995) 'Rethinking the sanctioning function in juvenile court: retributive or restorative responses to youth crime', *Crime and Delinquency*, 49: 296–316.

Beckett, Katherine (1997) *Making crime pay: law and order in contemporary American politics*. New York: Oxford University Press.

Bernard, Thomas J. (1992) *The cycle of juvenile justice*. New York: Oxford University Press.

Bishop, Donna, Frazier, Charles and Henretta, John (1989) 'Prosecutorial waiver: case study of a questionable reform', *Crime and Delinquency*, 5 (2): 179–201.

Blumstein, Alfred S. (1995) 'Violence by young people', *NIJ Journal*. Washington, DC: US Department of Justice.

Bonta, James (1996) 'Risk–needs assessment and treatment', in A.T. Harland (ed.) *Choosing correctional options that work*. Thousand Oaks, CA: Sage.

Breed, Allen F. and Krisberg, Barry (1986) 'Juvenile corrections: is there a future?', *Corrections Today*, 48: 14–20.

Brennan, Tim (1987) 'Classification for control in jails and prisons', in D.M. Gottfredson and M. Tonry (eds) *Prediction and classification: criminal justice decision making*, pp. 201–48. Chicago, IL: University of Chicago Press.

Brewer, Devon D., Hawkins, J. David, Catalano, Richard F. and Neckerman, Holly J. (1995) 'Preventing serious, violent, and chronic juvenile offending: a review of evaluations of selected strategies in childhood, adolescence, and the community', in R. Howell, R. Hawkins, B. Krisberg and J. Wilson (eds) *Sourcebook on serious violent juvenile offender*, pp. 61–141. Thousand Oaks, CA: Sage.

Butts, J., Snyder, H., Finnegan, T., Aughenbaugh, A., Tierney, N., Sullivan, D., Poole, R., Sickmund, M. and Poe, E. (1995) *National Center for Juvenile Justice report*. Washington, DC: National Center for Juvenile Justice.

Chesney-Lind, Meda (1995) 'Girls, delinquency, and juvenile justice: toward a feminist theory of young women's crime', in B.R. Price and N.J. Sokoloff (eds) *The criminal justice system and women* (2nd edn), pp. 71–88. New York: McGraw-Hill.

Clinton, Hillary (1996) *It takes a village*, New York: Simon & Schuster.

Coalition for Juvenile Justice (1996b) *The transformation of juvenile justice: the state of the states*. Washington, DC: Coalition for Juvenile Justice.

Coates, Robert B. (1989) 'The future of corrections in juvenile justice', in A.R. Roberts (ed.) *Juvenile justice policies, programs, and services*. Chicago, IL: Dorsey Press.

Cohen, Stanley (1985) *Visions of social control*. Cambridge: Polity Press.

Community Research Associates (1997) *Addressing disproportionate minority confinement: a national report on state compliance with the JJDP Act*. Champaign, IL: draft report.

Costello, J. and Worthington, N. (1981–2) 'Incarcerating status offenders: attempts to circumvent the Juvenile Justice and Delinquency Prevention Act', *Harvard Civil Rights – Civil Liberties Law Review*, 16: 41–81.

Criminal Justice Newsletter (1995) 'Violent and Hard-Core Juvenile Offender Reform Act of 1995', 26 (18 (15 September)): 4–5.

Dawson, Robert P. (1990) 'The future of juvenile justice: is it time to abolish the system?', *Journal of Criminal Law and Criminology*, 81: 136–55.

Demone, Harold W. and Gibelman, Margaret (1990) '"Privatizing" the treatment of criminal offenders', *Journal of Offender Counseling, Services, and Rehabilitation*, 15: 7–25.

Developmental Research and Programs, Inc. (DRP) (1994) *Communities that care team handbook*. Seattle, WA: Developmental Research and Programs, Inc.

Developmental Research and Programs, Inc. (DRP) (1996) *Promising approaches to prevent adolescent problem behaviors*. Seattle, WA: Developmental Research and Programs, Inc.

DiIulio, John J., Jr (1996) 'They're coming: Florida's youth crime bomb', *Impact*, spring: 25–7.

Fagan, Jeffrey (1995) 'Separating the men from the boys,' in R. Howell, R. Hawkins, B. Krisberg and J. Wilson (eds) *Sourcebook on serious violent juvenile offender*, pp. 238–57. Thousand Oaks, CA: Sage.

Fagan, Jeffrey, Forst, M. and Vivona, T.S. (1987) 'Racial determinants of the judicial transfer decision: prosecuting violent youth in criminal court', *Crime and Delinquency*, 33: 259–86.

Federal Bureau of Investigation (1996) *Uniform crime reports, crime in the United States*. Washington, DC: US Department of Justice, 19 August.

Federele, Katherine and Chesney-Lind, Meda (1992) 'Special issues in juvenile justice: gender, race, and ethnicity', in I. Schwartz (ed.) *Juvenile justice and public policy: toward a national agenda*, pp. 165–95. New York: Lexington Books.

Feeley, Malcolm M. and Simon, Jonathan (1992) 'The new penology: notes on the emerging strategy of corrections and its implications', *Criminology*, 30: 449–74.

Feeley, Malcolm M. and Simon, Jonathan (1994) 'Actuarial justice: the emerging new criminal law', in D. Nelken (ed.) *The future of criminology*, pp. 172–201. Thousand Oaks, CA: Sage.

Feld, Barry C. (1991) 'Justice by geography: urban, suburban, and rural variations in juvenile justice administration', *Journal of Criminal Law and Criminology*, 82: 156–210.

Feld, Barry C. (1993) *Justice for children: the right to counsel and the juvenile courts*. Boston, MA: Northeastern University Press.

Feld, Barry C. (1995a) 'Violent youth and public policy: a case study of juvenile justice law reform', *Minnesota Law Review*, 79 (5): 965–1128.

Feld, Barry C. (1995b) 'The social context of juvenile justice administration: racial disparities in an urban juvenile court', in K. Kempf-Leonard, C. Pope and W. Feyerherm (eds) *Minorities in juvenile justice,* pp. 66–97. Thousand Oaks, CA: Sage.

Feld, Barry C. (1999) *Bad kids: race and the transformation of the juvenile court.* New York: Oxford University Press.

Felson, Marcus (1994) *Crime and everyday life.* Thousand Oaks, CA: Pine Forge.

Ferdinand, Theodore N. (1991) 'History overtakes the juvenile justice system', *Crime and Delinquency,* 37: 204–24.

Fox, James A. (1996) *Trends in juvenile violence: a report to the United States Attorney General on current and future rates of juvenile offending,* Boston, MA: Northeastern University, technical report.

Frazier, Charles (1989) 'Preadjudicatory detention', in A. Roberts (ed.) *Juvenile justice: policies, programs, and services,* pp. 143–68. Chicago, IL: Dorsey Press.

Frazier, Charles and Bishop, Donna (1995) 'Reflections on race effects in juvenile justice', in K. Kempf-Leonard, C. Pope and W. Feyerherm (eds) *Minorities in juvenile justice,* pp. 16–46. Thousand Oaks, CA: Sage.

Garland, David (1996) 'The limits of the sovereign state: strategies of crime control in contemporary society', *British Journal of Criminology* 36 (4): 445–71.

Geis, Gilbert and Binder, Arnold (1991) 'Sins of the children: parental responsibility for juvenile delinquents', *Notre Dame Journal of Law, Ethics and Public Policy,* 5 (2): 303–22.

Gilbert, Michael J. (1996) 'Making privatization decisions without "getting burned": a guide for understanding the risks', in G.L. Mays and T. Gray (eds) *Privatization and the provision of correctional services: context and consequences,* pp. 61–74. Cincinnati, OH: Anderson.

Gillespie, L.K. and Norman, M.D. (1984) 'Does certification mean prison: some preliminary findings from Utah', *Juvenile and Family Court Journal,* 35: 23–35.

Goldkamp, John (1985) 'Danger and detention: a second generation of bail reform', *Journal of Criminal Law and Criminology,* 76 (1): 1–74.

Gowdy, V.B. (1993) *Intermediate sanctions.* Washington, DC: National Institute of Justice.

Greenwood, Peter, Model, Karyn, Rydell, C. Peter and Chiesa, James (1996) *Diverting children from a life of crime.* Santa Monica, CA: Rand.

Harlan, Christi and Hayes, Arthur (1992) 'Jailing parents', *Wall Street Journal,* 18 May, B6.

Hawkins, J. David and Catalano, Richard F. Jr (1992) *Communities that care.* San Francisco, CA: Jossey-Bass.

Hawkins, J. David, Catalano, Richard F. and Brewer, Devon (1995) 'Preventing serious, violent, and chronic juvenile offending: effective strategies from conception to age 6', in R. Howell, R. Hawkins, B. Krisberg and J. Wilson (eds) *Sourcebook on serious violent juvenile offender,* pp. 47–60. Thousand Oaks, CA: Sage.

House Conference Report (1997) 'House bill, 2267: juvenile accountability incentive block grant fund'. Washington, DC: US Office of Printing.

Howell, James C. (ed.) (1995) *Guide for implementing the comprhensive strategy for serious, violent, and chronic juvenile offenders*. Washington, DC: US Department of Justice.

Howell, James C. (1996) 'Juvenile transfers to the criminal justice system: state-of-the-art', *Law and Policy* 18 (January/April): 17–60.

Howell, James C. (1997a) *Juvenile justice and youth violence*. Thousand Oaks, CA: Sage.

Kempf-Leonard, Kimberly and Sontheimer, Henry (1995) 'The role of race in juvenile justice in Pennsylvania', in K. Kempf-Leonard, C. Pope and W. Feyerherm (eds) *Minorities in juvenile justice*. Thousand Oaks, CA: Sage.

Kempf-Leonard, Kimberly, Peterson, Elicka and Sample, Lisa (1997) *Gender and juvenile justice in Missouri*. Technical report prepared for the Missouri Department of Public Safety.

Lemmon, John, Sontheimer, Henry and Saylor, K. (1991) *A study of Pennsylvania juveniles transferred to criminal court in 1986*. Commissioned by the Pennsylvania Juvenile Court Judges' Commission, Harrisburg, PA.

Leo, John (1995) 'Punished for the sins of the children', *US News and World Report* 118 (23): 18.

Lerman, Paul (1977) 'Discussion of differential selection of juveniles for detention', *Journal of Research on Crime and Delinquency*, 14: 166–72.

Lerman, Paul (1980) 'Trends and issues in the deinstitutionalization of youths in trouble', *Crime and Delinquency*, 26: 281–98.

Lerman, Paul (1984) 'Child welfare, the private sector and community-based correction', *Crime and Delinquency*, 30: 5–38.

Lerner, S. (1990) *Good news about juvenile justice: the movement away from large institutions and toward community-based services*. Bolinas, CA: Ittleson Family Foundation.

Lipsey, M.W. and Wilson, D.B. (1998) 'Effective interventions with serious juvenile offenders: a synthesis of research', in R. Loeber and D.P. Farrington (eds) *Serious and violent juvenile offenders: risk factors and successful interventions*, pp. 313–45. Thousand Oaks, CA: Sage.

McShane, Marilyn and Williams, Frank P., III (1989) 'The prison adjustment of juvenile offenders', *Crime and Delinquency*, 35 (2): 254–69.

Mahoney, Dennis, Romig, Dennis and Armstrong, Troy (1988) 'Juvenile probation: the balanced approach', *Juvenile and Family Court Journal*, 39: 1–59.

Males, Mike A. (1996) *The scapegoat generation: America's war on adolescents*. Monroe, ME: Common Courage Press.

Mays, G. Larry (1996) 'Correctional privatization: defining the issues and searching for answers', in G.L. Mays and T. Gray (eds) *Privatization and the provision of correctional services: context and consequences*, pp. 2–10. Cincinnati, OH: Anderson.

Mennel, Robert M. (1973) *Thorns and thistles: juvenile delinquents in the United States, 1825–1940*. Hanover, NH: University Press of New England.

Meyer, Jon'a F. and Grant, Diana (1996) 'The privatization of community corrections: panacea or Pandora's box?', in G.L. Mays and T. Gray (eds) *Privatization and the provision of correctional services: context and consequences*, pp. 89–102. Cincinnati, OH: Anderson.

Montgomery, Imogene and Landon, Marilyn (1994) *What works: promising interventions in juvenile justice.* Washington, DC: US Department of Justice, Office of Juvenile Justice and Delinquency Prevention.

Nasser, Haya E. and Moss, Desda (1996) 'Teen crime tosses ball in parents' court', *USA Today,* 6 August: A1.

National Council on Crime and Delinquency (NCCD) (1997) *Development of an empirically-based risk assessment instrument and placement recommendation matrix, final report.* Prepared by the National Council on Crime and Delinquency for the Maryland Department of Juvenile Justice.

NCJJ/OJJDP (1998) 'Easy access to juvenile court statistics, 1987–1996, December release'. Pittsburgh, PA: National Center for Juvenile Justice.

Office of Juvenile Justice and Delinquency Prevention (OJJDP) (1998) *Juvenile accountability incentive block grant program announcement.* Washington, DC: US Department of Justice.

Packer, Herbert (1968) *The limits of the criminal sanction.* Standford, CA: Standford University Press.

Rudman, Cary, Hartstone, Eliot, Fagan, Jeffrey and Moore, Melinda (1986) 'Violent youth in adult court: process and punishment', *Crime and Delinquency,* 32: 75–96.

Sagatun, I., McCollum, L. and Edwards, L. (1985) 'The effects of transfers from juvenile to criminal court: a loglinear analysis', *Journal of Crime and Justice,* 8: 65–92.

Schwartz, Ira M. (1989) *(In)justice for juveniles: rethinking the best interests of the child.* Massachusetts: Lexington Books.

Schwartz, Ira, Barton, W. and Orlando, Frank (1991) 'Keeping kids out of secure detention', *Public Welfare,* spring: 2–26, 46.

Schwartz, Ira, Harris, L. and Levi, L. (1988) 'The jailing of juveniles in Minnesota: case study', *Crime and Delinquency,* 34 (2): 133–49.

Sechrest, Lee (1987) 'Classification for treatment', in D.M. Gottfredson and M. Tonry (eds) *Prediction and classification: criminal justice decision making,* pp. 293–322. Chicago, IL: University of Chicago Press.

Shine, James and Price, Dwight (1992) 'Prosecutors and juvenile justice: new roles and perspectives', in I.M. Schwartz (ed.) *Juvenile delinquency: theory, practice, and law,* pp. 101–33. New York: Lexington Books.

Simon, Jonathan and Feeley, Malcolm (1995) 'True crime: the new penology and public discourse on crime', in T.G. Blomberg and S. Cohen (eds) *Punishment and social control: essays in honor of Sheldon L. Messinger,* pp. 147–80. New York: Aldine de Gruyter.

Singer, Simon (1996) *Recriminalizing delinquency.* Cambridge: Cambridge University Press.

Snyder, Howard N. and Sickmund, Melissa (1995) *Juvenile offenders and victims: a focus on violence.* Washington, DC: Office of Juvenile Justice and Delinquency Prevention.

Sontheimer, Henry and Volenik, A. (1995) 'Tough responses to serious juvenile crime includes waiver to adult court – but is that the best answer?', *Juvenile Justice Update,* 1 (February): 1–10.

Texas Youth Commission (1991) *Juvenile sentencing in the United States – a survey.* Austin, TX: Texas Youth Commission.

Torbet, P. and Szymanski, Linda (1998) *State legislative responses to violent juvenile crime: 1996–1997 update*. Washington, DC: US Department of Justice, OJJDP.

Torbet, P., Gable, R., Hurst, H., Montgomery, I., Szymanski, L. and Thomas, D. (1996) *State responses to serious and violent juvenile crime*. Washington, DC: US Department of Justice, OJJDP.

Tracy, Paul and Kempf-Leonard, Kimberly (1998) 'Sanctioning serious juvenile offenders: a review of alternative models', *Advances in Criminological Theory*, 8: 135–71.

Vaughn, Michael S. and del Carmen, Rolando V. (1997) 'The Fourth Amendment as a tool of actuarial justice', *Crime and Delinquency*, 43: 78–101.

Walker, Samuel (1994) *Sense and nonsense about crime and drugs: a policy guide* (3rd edn). Belmont, CA: Wadsworth.

Weibush, Richard, Baird, S. Christopher, Krisberg, Barry and Onek, D. (1995) 'Risk assessment and classification for serious, violent, and chronic juvenile offenders', in R. Howell, R. Hawkins, B. Krisberg and J. Wilson (eds) *Sourcebook on serious violent juvenile offender*, pp. 171–210. Thousand Oaks, CA: Sage.

Weithorn, Lois A. (1988) 'Mental hospitalization of troublesome youth: an analysis of skyrocketing admission rates', *Stanford Law Review*, 40: 773–838.

Wilson, John J. and Howell, James C. (1993) *A comprehensive strategy for serious, violent, and chronic juvenile offenders*. Washington DC: US Department of Justice.

Wilson, William J. (1987) *The truly disadvantaged*. Chicago, IL: University of Chicago Press.

Winn, Russell G. (1996) 'Ideology and the calculation of efficiency in public and private correctional enterprises', in G.L. Mays and T. Gray (eds) *Privatization and the provision of correctional services: context and consequences*, pp. 21–30. Cincinnati, OH: Anderson.

Zimring, Franklin E. (1996) 'Crying wolf over teen demons', *Los Angeles Times*, 19 August: B5.

31

The contemporary politics of youth crime prevention

Tim Newburn

Writing in autumn 1998, and reflecting on the first year or so of youth justice policy and rhetoric under New Labour, I noted that much 'of the populist punitive rhetoric of the pre-election period has now either disappeared or lessened in volume' (Newburn, 1998). Though criminologists as a whole did not appear to be especially sanguine about the prospects for enlightened youth justice under the new regime, nonetheless it appeared that some of the worst aspects of pre-election macho posturing by politicians had been toned down. The 'tough on the causes of crime' half of the New Labour mantra appeared at least to be sharing the bill with its punitive sibling. So early in the life of the new government the question was, did 'this represent the emergence of the *real* face of criminal justice policy making under New Labour or [was] it a reflection of the fact that parliamentary opposition had been almost completely absent since May 1997?' The question should be somewhat easier to answer now, despite the continued absence of effective political opposition since that time. This chapter examines the politics of recent measures introduced to reshape youth justice and youth crime prevention in England and Wales. In order to make sense of current strategies it is worth reminding ourselves of some of the recent history and politics of youth justice and crime prevention.

Unlikely as it seemed at the time, there was a significant and sustained decline in the use of custody for juveniles during the 1980s. As Rutherford (1986) commented, the paradox is that 'the decade of "law and order" was also the decade of what has been called "the successful revolution" in juvenile justice'. Underpinning this 'revolution' were the practices of multi-agency working and diversion that saw a huge expansion in the use of (informal and formal) cautioning, and an increasingly bifurcated system that distinguished the serious, the dangerous and the persistent from the rest (see Chapter 26 of this volume). How was this emergent system to be understood?

SOURCE: Commissioned for this volume. Tim Newburn is Professor of Urban Social Policy and Director of the Public Policy Research Unit at Goldsmiths College, University of London, UK.

Writing at the end of the 1980s, Pratt (1989; see also Chapter 27 of this volume) argued that the debate about justice and welfare was something of a 'sideshow' in this period, and that a new form of penological discourse and practice was emerging in juvenile justice: 'corporatism'. Efficient and effective 'management' of the offending population was now to the fore, legimated by the rediscovery that 'something works' – that 'something' being the infliction of a 'just measure of (community-based) pain' (see Chapter 28 of this volume).

The emergent managerial and actuarial discourses of the late 1980s were joined in the early 1990s by the embracing of 'populist punitiveness' by politicians of all hues (see Chapter 26 of this volume). Bottoms (1995) suggests three reasons for the attractiveness of this new 'disciplinary common sense' (Hall, 1980). First, it is popular because of the belief that increased punitiveness may be effective in reducing crime through general deterrence and/or incapacitation. Second, because it is hoped that it will help foster a sense of moral consensus around issues where dissensus or moral pluralism exists. Third, because politicians believe that it will be a vote winner. It was under these circumstances that New Labour sought to redefine itself in the law-and-order landscape. In opposition New Labour drew on the managerialism of the justice model, and added its own potent blend of communitarianism and populism (Newburn, 1998).

The consequence is, we are told, the emergence of a 'new youth justice' (Goldson, 2000), the 'broad contours' of which 'are easily described' (Pitts, 2000). It is to a more detailed exploration of the politics of contemporary youth crime prevention that we now turn.

NEW LABOUR, NEW DISCOURSE(S)?

Though the broad contours may possibly be easily discerned, in fact the precise nature of youth justice and crime prevention under New Labour is somewhat tricky to characterize. There are a number of reasons for this. One difficulty is identifying just how 'punitive' New Labour's 'populism' actually is in practice. To what extent has the Labour administration been 'tough on the causes of crime' at the same time as displaying its 'no more excuses' approach to youth crime more generally? These complications are exacerbated by the confusion sometimes engendered by the difficulty of separating rhetoric from action. As some commentators have noted, one key element of Jack Straw's style as (shadow) Home Secretary was to 'talk tough' whilst behind the scenes enabling sometimes more enlightened practices to be developed and promulgated (Savage and Nash, 2001).

One of the most significant changes, at the level of both rhetoric and practice, has been New Labour's shift away from a focus solely on 'crime' and towards 'incivilities' or, indeed, 'crime and disorder'. In terms of influence, apparently like so many areas of Labour social policy, here North America once again loomed large (Deacon, 1999; Newburn, 2002). In this particular case it was the 'broken windows' thesis associated with James Q. Wilson and George Kelling that was formative. Wilson and Kelling (1982) had argued that 'disorder and crime are usually inextricably linked in a kind of developmental sequence'. Though popular with many policy makers and criminologists (of a particular perspective), the 'broken windows' thesis became particularly influential with New Labour because of its desire to learn what it took to be the lessons of the New York 'miracle'. During the first half of the 1990s, crime, especially murder and other serious violent crimes, had declined spectacularly in Gotham (Karmen, 2000). Those policy entrepreneurs closest to the action were quick to claim that 'quality of life policing, directly influenced by Kelling's ideas, was key to the remarkable transformation of the City' (Bratton, 1998; Barrett, 2000). Some of the more strident language associated with these proselytizers of quality-of-life policing – 'zero tolerance'; cracking down on street begging, 'squeegee merchants', etc. – soon found its way into New Labour rhetoric (Fairclough, 2000; Newburn, 2002):

> The rising tide of disorder is blighting our streets, neighbourhoods, parks, town and city centres. Incivility and harassment, public drunkenness, graffiti, and vandalism all affect our ability to use open spaces and enjoy a quiet life in our own homes. Moreover, crime and disorder are linked.
>
> (Straw and Michael, 1996)

Though the term 'zero tolerance' has been bandied about by politicians, especially New Labour politicians, at a *practical* level arguably its impact has been minimal in the United Kingdom. However, the broken windows thesis with which, rightly or wrongly (Kelling, 2001), it is associated has had a much greater impact on crime control *policy* in England and Wales. This impact is most visible in both the title of the 1998 Crime and Disorder Act and its contents, particularly in the new antisocial behaviour orders, and child curfews.

ACTING ON CRIME AND DISORDER

In the area of youth justice New Labour, as it promised, 'hit the ground running' after the 1997 general election. The first six months in government were characterized by a frenzy of activity. Within the space of less than two months six consultation documents on the subject of youth crime were published (Home Office, 1997a, b, c, d, e, f). Each contained considerable discussion of various proposals that had first been outlined in Labour's pre-election document *Tackling Youth Crime, Reforming Youth Justice* (Labour Party, 1996), and the general approach was much influenced by the conclusions drawn by the Audit Commission from its own investigations of youth justice (Audit Commission, 1996).

The proposals contained in these consultation papers eventually found their way, largely unchanged, into the government's flagship legislation, the Crime and Disorder Act 1998. Several aspects of this Act deserve to be seen as the defining elements of Labour's 'new youth justice'. These are the establishment of the Youth Justice Board, the creation of youth offending teams (YOTs) and the restructuring of the non-custodial penalties available to the youth court.

This Act was without doubt the key element in New Labour's youth justice reforms in its first term. The Act made a series of far-reaching changes to both the organization and the operation of youth justice in England and Wales. For the first time the youth justice system was given an overarching aim: 'to prevent offending by children and young persons' (Section 37(1)). Moreover the legislation required those delivering youth justice to 'have regard' to those aims. The Act placed on statute several new orders of the court, including the antisocial behaviour order, the reparation order, the parenting order, the action plan order and the child safety order. Again following Audit Commission recommendations, it also radically overhauled the cautioning system. The

Act scrapped the caution (informal and formal) and replaced it with a reprimand (for less serious offences) and a final warning. As the name implied, one of the crucial characteristics of the final warning is that, except in unusual circumstances, it may be used only once. In addition to the change of nomenclature, and the more sparing manner of usage, the new system of reprimands and final warnings also set in motion a set of other activities – such as those previously associated with 'caution plus' – more frequently, and often earlier, than previously had been the case. Under the Act, all young offenders receiving a final warning are referred to a youth offending team. Offenders are then expected 'unless they consider it inappropriate to do so' to participate in a rehabilitation programme (in which reparation is expected generally to be present).

The reparation order requires the young offender to make reparation – specified in the order – either to a specified person or persons or 'to the community at large'. The underlying rationale, according to the minister of state at the time (Michael, 1998), was to avoid 'excuses' for offending: 'With the restorative approach there is no way for youngsters – or their parents – to hide from their personal responsibilities.' This rationale underpinned final warnings, reparation orders and also the new 'parenting order' and 'action plan orders'. New Labour's punitive responsibilization was imbued with the language of communitarianism.

Of all the new orders introduced by the Act, the antisocial behaviour order attracted the greatest criticism. The order was designed specifically to tackle 'antisocial behaviour [which] causes distress and misery to innocent, law-abiding people – and undermines the communities in which they live. Neighbourhood harassment by individuals or groups, often under the influence of alcohol or drugs' (Home Office, 1997a). Antisocial behaviour orders (ASBOs) are a civil court order applied for by local authorities and the police. They prohibit the defendant from doing anything described in the order for a minimum of two years. What was most controversial about the order, however, was that non-compliance is a criminal matter, triable either way and carrying a maximum sentence of five years' imprisonment. According to some of its distinguished critics (Gardner et al., 1998) it is strange 'that a government which purports to be interested in tackling social exclusion at the same time promotes a legislative measure destined to create a whole new breed of outcasts'.

Similar concerns were voiced about the provisions in the Act that allowed local authorities to introduce 'local child curfew schemes'. The introduction of curfews had been foreshadowed by proposals in the consultation paper *Tackling Youth Crime* (Home Office, 1997f) and the White Paper *No More Excuses* (Home Office, 1997d). The former described the problem thus: 'unsupervised children gathered in public places can cause real alarm and misery to local communities and can encourage one another into anti-social and criminal habits' (Home Office, 1997f, para. 114). The provisions in the Crime and Disorder Act allow local authorities, after consultation with the police and with the support of the Home Secretary, to introduce a ban on children of specified ages (though under ten) in specified places for a period of up to ninety days. Children breaking the curfew are to be taken home by the police, and a breach of the curfew constitutes sufficient grounds for the imposition of a child safety order. The new powers to introduce curfews, exclusion zones and other restrictions were described by one Home Office spokesperson as 'giving the concept of zero tolerance teeth' (quoted in Muncie, 1999).

In practice, there has been remarkable reluctance on the ground to use such powers. Despite such reluctance, and sustained criticism of curfews from some quarters, more recent legislation, the Criminal Justice and Police Act 2001, extended the powers available to impose curfews. The Act extends the maximum age at which children can be subject to a curfew from ten to 'under sixteen', and also makes provision for a local authority or the police to impose a curfew on an area and not just an individual.

The final element of the 1998 Act that drew sustained criticism (from, *inter alia*, Wilkinson, 1995; Penal Affairs Consortium, 1995) was the abolition of the presumption – rebuttable in court – that a child aged between ten and thirteen is incapable of committing a criminal offence (generally known as *doli incapax*). Whilst the United Kingdom has long been out of step with much of the rest of western Europe with its significantly lower age of criminal responsibility, the principle of *doli incapax* has protected at least a proportion of children under fourteen from the full weight of the criminal law. The Home Secretary stated his reasons for this amendment robustly: 'The presumption that children aged ten to thirteen do not know the difference between serious wrongdoing and simple naughtiness flies in the face of common sense and is long overdue for reform' (Straw, 1998).

Some of the key elements of New Labour's youth justice are visible in this raft of new measures. There are echoes of both the old 'welfare' and 'justice' models as well as signs of the influence of 'new' penological thinking (Feeley and Simon, 1992) through the drawing in of 'at risk' groups through ASBOs, parenting orders and curfews. 'Communitarian moralism' (Crawford, 1998) and a form of punitive responsibilization also run through the same measures. Perhaps the most dominant strand in New Labour youth justice, however, is managerialism or a refined form of corporatism. This is most clearly seen in the establishment of youth offending teams and the creation of the Youth Justice Board.

The core of New Labour's managerialism in this area was embodied in the creation of the Youth Justice Board. Historically, juvenile justice was a 'broad church' in which there was considerable variation in service delivery at the local level. Inspired by the excoriating criticisms of the extant system by the Audit Commission (1996), New Labour sought, as in so many areas, to impose order from the centre. Its key tool in this regard was the Youth Justice Board. The board's principal function was to monitor the operation of the youth justice system and the provision of youth justice services, together with monitoring national standards and establishing appropriate performance measures. Such arrangements exhibited all four major characteristics of 'systemic managerialism' (Bottoms, 1995) – the creation of an overall strategic plan; the construction of key performance indicators; active monitoring of aggregate information; and inter-agency co-operation in order to fulfil the overall goals of the system. This latter characteristic was also at the heart of what was, arguably, the most significant reform introduced by the Crime and Disorder Act: the establishment of youth offending teams.

Prior to the Act, youth justice teams, comprised primarily of social workers, had had primary responsibility for working with young offenders subject to non-custodial penalties, and for liaising with other criminal justice and treatment agencies in connection with that work. Stimulated by a managerialist concern with efficiency and consistency on the one hand, and by a pragmatic belief in multi-agency working on the other, New Labour's new-model youth offending teams had to include a probation officer, a local authority social worker, a police officer, a representative of the local health authority and someone nominated by the chief education officer.

As Pitts (2001) notes, the constitution of these new teams had echoes of the Multi-agency Diversion Panels of the 1980s and, indeed, the influential Audit Commission

(1996) had drawn particular attention to the Northampton diversion scheme. However, whereas the diversion schemes were the child of an earlier era – a product of the emergent 'corporatism' in juvenile justice – youth offending teams were set up not to divert but to intervene. The Home Office-funded evaluation of the YOT pilots outlined the key assumptions about offending that informed the development of the new structures:

> [The Crime and Disorder Act] has a central objective to prevent offending by children and young people and is concerned with addressing offending behaviour; with early interventions on the basis of risk assessments related to known criminogenic factors; with the systematic use of evidence-based practice; with reparation and, therefore, the needs of victims; and with the promotion of crime prevention measures.
>
> (Holdaway *et al.*, 2001)

CRIME REDUCTION AND EVIDENCE-BASED POLICY AND PRACTICE

On coming to power New Labour was determined that the 'nothing works' pessimism of previous eras would not be the hallmark of its new youth justice (or, indeed, of its penal policy and practice generally). Much of the impetus for this came from the Treasury, which not only sought to ensure value for money, but demanded an evidence base for the proposals it was being asked to fund. The Comprehensive Spending Review had resulted in a demand for the Home Office to provide a summary of 'what works' or, failing that, 'what is promising'. The result (Goldblatt and Lewis, 1998) covered everything from policing strategies to situational crime prevention. It also included a chapter on 'youth criminality prevention' (Graham, 1998). At the heart of 'criminality prevention' is the identification of 'risk factors', generally via the statistical analysis of longitudinal cohort data (Rutter *et al.*, 1998). Using such an approach to focus on 'onset' (why people start offending), 'persistence' (why they continue) and 'desistance' (why they stop) it is argued that it is possible to predict, albeit not with a high degree of accuracy, which individuals are most likely to become involved in offending (Farrington, 1997; see also Chapter 29 of this volume). The identification of those deemed to be 'at risk' – be they individuals, families or neighbourhoods – provides the basis for the targeting of interventions and, potentially, a justification for both earlier and more far-reaching interventions. Such an approach underpins the government's Youth Inclusion Programme (YIP), a £20 million initiative launched in 2001 as part of the wider Crime Reduction Programme. The Youth Inclusion Programme 'seeks to reduce offending, truancy and exclusion in disadvantaged neighbourhoods by providing assistance and support to the thirteen–sixteen year olds at most risk of offending, truancy or exclusion'. Like the bulk of the Crime Reduction Programme such projects are accompanied by evaluation. The evidence base being developed by such evaluations is centrally concerned with 'crime reduction', though also with 'cost effectiveness' (Tilley, 2001).

Such developments, it is fairly easy to see, chime with some aspects of what has been referred to as an actuarial 'new penology' (Feeley and Simon, 1992). In particular, the extension of the gaze of the youth justice system to cover 'disorder' and 'incivilities' as well as crime, the focus on those 'at risk', and their families, the continued attempts to identify and exclude the allegedly most 'persistent' offenders, and the inclusion of civil as well as criminal 'remedies', are all resonant of this alleged new paradigm. However, we would do well not to overstate the case. According to Kempf-Leonard and Peterson (see Chapter 30 of this volume) the actuarial objective requires 'that justice systems should be efficient, devoid of the traditional [aims of] treatment, deterrence, punishment, or even incapacitation'. Yet, as the discussion so far should have made clear, elements of each of those aims, and other characteristics besides, remain visible within contemporary youth justice. The contemporary reality is more complex than arguments about radical paradigm shifts might lead us to believe. Arguably, one of the key developments since the advent of New Labour to government in 1997, and one not easily subsumed under the rubric of the 'new penology', has been the attempt to incorporate aspects of restorative justice within the youth justice system.

REFERRAL ORDERS AND RESTORATIVE JUSTICE

The influence of communitarian thinking, which was very visible in the Home Office's consultation documents published immediately after the 1997 general election, found form in the central place accorded to restorative justice in New Labour's youth justice. Initially this was most visible in the place given to reparation in the Crime and Disorder Act, and to the support given to experiments such as that with restorative cautioning in Thames Valley (Young and Goold, 1999). The referral order represents the latest, and arguably most significant, attempt to draw on restorative justice principles in the youth justice arena (see Chapter 16 of this volume).

The referral order was first suggested in *No More Excuses* (Home Office, 1997d), though not called a referral order at that point. The order is mandatory for ten to seventeen-year-olds pleading guilty and convicted for the first time by the courts, unless the crime is serious enough to warrant custody or the court orders an absolute discharge. The disposal involves referring the young offender to a youth offender panel. The intention is that the panel will provide a forum away from the formality of the court. As Crawford (2002) argues, the panels draw on at least four sources: the Scottish children's hearing system (Whyte, 2000); the experience of family group conferencing (Morris and Maxwell, 2000); the history of victim–offender mediation in England and Wales (Marshall and Merry, 1990), and that of restorative cautioning (Young, 2000).

The referral order is available in the youth court and adult magistrates' courts and may be made for a minimum of three and a maximum of twelve months, depending on the seriousness of the crime (as determined by the court). The referral order constitutes the entire sentence for the offence and, as such, substitutes for action plan orders, reparation orders and supervision orders.

The Act extends the statutory responsibility of youth offending teams to include the recruitment and training of YOP volunteers, administering panel meetings and implementing referral orders. Panels consist of one YOT member and (at least) two community panel members, one of whom leads the panel. A parent or both parents of a young offender aged under sixteen are expected to attend all panel meetings in all but exceptional cases. The offender can also nominate an adult to support them. It is not intended that legal representatives acting in a professional capacity should be included in panel meetings, either directly or as an offender's supporter. To encourage the restorative nature of the process a variety of other people may be invited to attend given panel meetings. (Any participation is strictly voluntary.) Those who may attend include: the victim or a representative of the community at large; a victim supporter; a supporter of the young person and/or anyone else the panel considers to be capable of having a 'good influence' on the offender; and signers and interpreters for any of the participants in the process who require them.

Where there is no direct victim the panel may wish to invite 'someone who can bring a victim perspective' to the meeting, 'for example a local business person or an individual who has suffered a similar offence' (Home Office, 2001). The aim of the initial panel meeting is to devise a 'contract' and, where the victim chooses to attend, for the panel to meet and talk about the offence with the offender. It is intended that nego-tiations between the panel and the offender about the content of the contract should be led by the community panel members. By contrast, the YOT member's role is to advise on potential activities to be included in a contract and to ensure proportionality. Where a young offender fails to attend the youth offender panel, the YOT member should try to establish the reason and may rearrange the meeting. If no reason is forthcoming, or the reason given is unacceptable, the offender should return to court for re-sentencing. The contract should always include reparation to the victim or wider community and a programme of activity designed primarily to prevent further offending. Where possible it is recommended that reparation should have some relation to the offence itself. Once the period of the referral order is successfully completed the offender is no longer considered to have a criminal record under the Rehabilitation of Offenders Act 1974.

Though referral orders are still at the pilot stage, early reports from the evaluation indicate mixed success. On the positive side, the youth offender panels appear to have established themselves within a year of operation as deliberative and participatory forums in which a young person's offending behaviour can be addressed (Newburn *et al.*, 2001b). The informal setting of youth offender panels would appear to allow young people, their parents/carers, community panel members and YOT advisers opportunities to discuss the nature and consequences of a young person's offending, as well as how to respond to it in ways which seek to repair the harm done and to address the causes of the young person's offending behaviour. In addition, the suc-cessful integration of a large number of volunteers within the youth justice process provides an opportunity for a potentially powerful new external voice to participate and influence this arena.

The major difficulty encountered so far, as in other developments (Dignan, 2000), concerns the involvement of victims (Newburn *et al.*, 2001a, b). To date, the level of victim involvement in panels has been very low. There appear to be a number of reasons for this, though in essence they appear to concern issues of implementation rather than problems with the general principles underlying referral orders. The response of all the major participants in the process to date has been largely suppor-tive of the general principles underlying referral orders.

CONCLUSION

Though potentially problematic, the fact that there is no coherent philosophy under-pinning contemporary youth crime prevention is neither novel nor surprising. Juvenile or youth justice has an especially complicated history, with widely divergent and some-times patently contradictory tributaries flowing into the major policy and practice streams. Under New Labour, this 'melange of measures' (Muncie, 2002) that is youth justice has become even more complicated than previously. How, though, should we judge the so-called 'new youth justice'? Should we regard the policies of the Labour government on youth justice 'as simply a continuation, and in some ways a more radical extension, of the policies of its immediate Conservative predecessor' (Smith, 2000)?

As Smith (2000) recognizes, though there are clear continuities between New Labour and previous administrations, not least in some of their punitive rhetoric, there are also clear differences. Indeed, even in that regard there have been changes, for some of the populist punitiveness of the pre-1997 period has been toned down or jettisoned altogether. Similarly, the corporatist modernizing agenda, though clearly a descendant of the 1980s version, is also radically different from it. In particular, the rise to prominence of the 'what works' paradigm, and the centralizing managerialist initiatives embodied in the creation of the Youth Justice Board and youth offending teams, signal a major departure from previous arrangements. Though somewhat rarely acknowledged, there is much that is positive in such developments. Despite the often entirely pejorative way in which 'managerialism' is understood and presented, it clearly has more than one face. Though the pitfalls are well rehearsed, and the dangers are indeed real, it is rarely acknowledged that there is positive potential in such developments. In precisely this vein we should not lose sight of the fact that as a result of New Labour's 'systemic managerialism' in youth justice an organizationally more creative and coherent environment, and one that is significantly better funded, and therefore potentially better placed to deliver necessary services, has been created.

What is undeniable is that we are at an important juncture in the politics of crime prevention and community safety. In relation to crime prevention there has been 'a redrawing of what constitutes the legitimate responsibilities of individuals, collectivities, and the state' (Crawford, 1997). Central to this redrawing of boundaries and responsibilities have been the notions of 'community', 'partnerships' and 'responsibilities', all of which are clearly visible – indeed, prioritized – within the Crime and Disorder Act. New Labour youth justice, which combines the rhetoric and practice of criminality prevention and crime reduction with that of 'what works' and 'evidence-based policy', attempts to concern itself with the causes of crime and the delivery of justice whilst simultaneously focusing on probabilistic calculations of risk and harm minimization. There are clear tensions between some of the inclusionary aspirations of community safety and some of the exclusionary potential of criminality prevention. Similarly, the restorative justice-influenced reforms offer the prospect of a more participatory and deliberative form of youth justice, yet they may, inadvertently or otherwise, encourage net widening and mesh thinning. Though 'what works' can be made to sound as if it is simply an empirical question, in reality it is at least as much a question of politics. As in so much that is New Labour, the contemporary politics of youth crime prevention has a tricky balancing act at its heart.

REFERENCES

Audit Commission (1996) *Misspent Youth: Young People and Crime*, London, Audit Commission.

Barrett, W. (2000) *Rudy! An Investigative Biography of Rudy Giuliani*, New York, Basic Books.

Bottoms, A.E. (1995) 'The philosophy and politics of punishment and sentencing', in C. Clarkson and R. Morgan (eds) *The Politics of Sentencing Reform*, Oxford, Oxford University Press.

Bratton, W., with Knobler, P. (1998) *Turnaround: How America's Top Cop Reversed the Crime Epidemic*, New York, Random House.

Crawford, A. (1997) *The Local Governance of Crime*, Oxford, Clarendon Press.

Crawford, A. (1998) 'Community safety and the quest for security: holding back the dynamics of social exclusion', *Policy Studies*, vol. 19, pp. 3–4, 237–53.

Crawford, A. (2002) 'The prospects of restorative justice for young offenders in England and Wales: a tale of two Acts' in K. McEvoy and T. Newburn (eds) *Criminology and Conflict Resolution*, Basingtoke, Palgrave.

Deacon, A. (1999) 'Learning from the US? The influence of American ideas on new Labour welfare reform', *Policy and Politics*, vol. 28, no. 1, pp. 5–18.

Dignan, J. (2000) *Youth Justice Pilots Evaluation: Interim Report on Reparative Work and Youth Offending Teams*, London, Home Office.

Fairclough, N. (2000) *New Labour, New Language?* London, Routledge.

Farrington, D.P. (1997) 'Human development and criminal careers', in M. Maguire, R. Morgan and R. Reiner (eds) *The Oxford Handbook of Criminology*, Oxford, Clarendon Press.

Feeley, M. and Simon, J. (1992) 'The new penology: notes on the emerging strategy of correction and its implications', *Criminology*, vol. 30, pp. 449–74.

Gardner, J., von Hirsch, A., Smith, A.T.H., Morgan, R., Ashworth, A. and Wasik, M. (1998) 'Clause 1: the hybrid law from hell?', *Criminal Justice Matters*, vol. 31 (spring), pp. 25–7.

Goldblatt, P. and Lewis, C. (1998) *Reducing Offending: An Assessment of Research Evidence on Ways of Dealing with Offending Behaviour*, Home Office Research Study no. 187, London, HMSO.

Goldson, B. (ed.) (2000) *The New Youth Justice*, Lyme Regis, Russell House.

Graham, J. (1998) 'What works in preventing criminality', in Goldblatt and Lewis (eds) *Reducing Offending*.

Hall, S. (1980) *Drifting into a Law and Order Society*, London, Cobden Trust.

Holdaway, S., Davidson, N., Dignan, J., Hammersley, R., Hine, J. and Marsh, P. (2001) *New Strategies to Address Youth Offending: The National Evaluation of Pilot Youth Offending Teams*, RDS Occasional Paper no. 69, London, HMSO.

Home Office (1997a) *Community Safety Order: A Consultation Paper*, London, HMSO.

Home Office (1997b) *Getting to Grips with Crime*, London, HMSO.

Home Office (1997c) *New National and Local Focus on Youth Crime: A Consultation Paper*, London, HMSO.

Home Office (1997d) *No More Excuses: A New Approach to Tackling Youth Crime in England and Wales*, Cm 3809, London, HMSO.

Home Office (1997e) *Tackling Delays in the Youth Justice System: A Consultation Paper*, London, HMSO.

Home Office (1997f) *Tackling Youth Crime: A Consultation Paper*, London, HMSO.

Home Office (2001) *Implementation of Referral Orders: Guidance for Youth Offending Teams*, London, HMSO.

Karmen, A. (2000) *New York Murder Mystery: The True Story behind the Crime Crash of the 1990s*, New York, New York University Press.

Kelling, G. (2001) 'Broken windows and the culture wars: a response to selected critiques' in R. Matthews and J. Pitts (eds) *Crime, Disorder and Community Safety,* London, Routledge.

Labour Party (1996) *Tackling Youth Crime, Reforming Youth Justice*, London, Labour Party.

Marshall, T. and Merry, S. (1990) *Crime and Accountability*, London, HMSO.

Michael, A. (1998) Speech to the Crime Concern Parliamentary Discussion Group, London, 7 July.

Morris, A. and Maxwell, G. (2000) 'The practice of family group conferences in New Zealand: assessing the place, potential and pitfalls of restorative justice' in A. Crawford and J. Goodey (eds) *Integrating a Victim Perspective within Criminal Justice*, Aldershot, Ashgate.

Muncie, J. (1999) *Youth and Crime: A Critical Introduction*, London, Sage.

Muncie, J. (2002) 'A new deal for youth? Early intervention and correctionalism' in G. Hughes, E. McLaughlin and J. Muncie (eds) *Crime Prevention and Community Safety: New Directions*, London, Sage.

Newburn, T. (1998) 'Tackling youth crime and reforming youth justice: the origins and nature of "New Labour" policy', *Policy Studies*, vol. 19, pp. 3–4, 199–211.

Newburn, T. (2002) 'Atlantic crossings: policy transfer and crime control in America and Britain', *Punishment and Society*, forthcoming.

Newburn, T., Crawford, A., Earle, R., Goldie, S., Hale, C., Masters, G., Netten, A., Saunders, R., Sharpe, K. and Uglow, S. (2001a) *The Introduction of Referral Orders into the Youth Justice System*, RDS Occasional Paper no. 70, London, HMSO.

Newburn, T., Crawford, A., Earle, R., Goldie, S., Hale, C., Masters, G., Netten, A., Saunders, R., Sharpe, K., Uglow, S. and Campbell, A. (2001b) *The Introduction of Referral Orders into the Youth Justice System: Second Interim Report*, RDS Occasional Paper No. 73, London, HMSO.

Penal Affairs Consortium (1995) *The Doctrine of Doli Incapax*, London, Penal Affairs Consortium.

Pitts, J. (2000) 'The new youth justice and the politics of electoral anxiety' in Goldson (ed.) *The New Youth Justice.*

Pitts, J. (2001) 'The new correctionalism: young people, youth justice and New Labour' in R. Matthews and J. Pitts (eds) *Crime, Disorder and Community Safety,* London, Routledge.

Pratt, J. (1989) 'Corporatism: the third model of juvenile justice', *British Journal of Criminology*, vol. 29, no. 3, pp. 236–54.

Rutherford, A. (1986) *Growing out of Crime: Society and Young People in Trouble*, Harmondsworth, Penguin.

Rutter, M., Giller, H. and Hagell, A. (1998) *Antisocial Behaviour by Young People*, Cambridge, Cambridge University Press.

Savage, S. and Nash, M. (2001) 'Law and order under Blair', in S.P. Savage and R. Atkinson (eds) *Public Policy under Blair*, Basingstoke, Palgrave.

Smith, D. (2000) 'Corporatism and the new youth justice' in Goldson (ed.) *The New Youth Justice.*

Straw, J. (1998) Speech to the Magistrates' Association, Blackburn, 25 June.

Straw, J. and Michael, A. (1996) *Tackling the Causes of Crime: Labour's Proposals to Prevent Crime and Criminality*, London, Labour Party.

Tilley, N. (2001) 'Evaluation and evidence-led crime reduction policy and practice' in R. Matthews and J. Pitts (eds) *Crime, Disorder and Community Safety*, London, Routledge.

Whyte, B. (2000) 'Between two stools: youth justice in Scotland', *Probation Journal*, vol. 47, no. 2, pp. 119–25.

Wilkinson, T. (1995) '*Doli incapax* resurrected', *Solicitors' Journal*, 14 April, pp. 338–9.

Wilson, J.Q. and Kelling, G. (1982) 'Broken windows', *Atlantic Monthly. March*, pp. 29–38.

Young, R. (2000) 'Integrating a multi-victim perspective into criminal justice through restorative justice conferences' in A. Crawford and J. Goodey (eds) *Integrating a Victim Perspective within Criminal Justice*, Aldershot, Ashgate.

Young, R. and Goold, B. (1999) 'Restorative police cautioning in Aylesbury: from degrading to reintegrative shaming ceremonies?', *Criminal Law Review*, February pp. 126–38.

Index

abolition 375–8
abortion, decriminalization 265–6
accountability, legal and political 293–4
acid house/rave culture 68, 72–3, 75, 88–9
action plan orders 4, 242, 246, 320, 454, 455
actuarial justice 6, 88, 330, 401,
    431–51, 457–8
Adams, Sergeant 154
Addams, Jane 181
Adderley, C. B. 109, 110
African Americans 347
African-Caribbeans/West Indians
    alleged criminality 70
    discrimination 322
    girls 301, 308
    relations with police 55–7, 58–9, 59–60,
        61–2, 64–5
after-care 154, 167, 203, 336, 346–7
age of criminal responsibility 11, 325, 456
    1969 Act recommendations 175, 216
    England and Wales 7, 239, 240–1,
        311, 322
    Finland 280
    Ingleby recommendations 218, 219
    Scotland 7, 232, 311
    UN recommendations 318–19, 320, 322
AIDS 71, 301
Aldington Detention Centre 340
Allen, H. E. 263
Allen, Nathan 185
Allen, Stephen 181
Amending Act (1861) 167
Anderton, James 415
Andrews, Don 439
'antisocial behaviour' 9, 13, 81, 161, 314, 316,
    320, 390, 426
antisocial behaviour orders (ASBOs) 9, 10, 242,
    249, 320, 454, 455
approved schools 11, 387
Ariès, Philippe 20, 191
Ashley, Lord 28, 49, 141
Ashworth, Andrew 365, 367
Asians
    girls 308
    and illegal immigration 57–8
Astor, Mrs William 181
'at risk' groups 1, 167, 296, 434, 437,
    444–5, 456, 457
attendance centres 223, 240, 333
Auburn penitentiary 349

Audit Commission report (1996) 5, 320,
    454, 456–7
Austin, J. 261
Australia
    restorative justice 174, 244, 249
    transportation 249
authoritarianism 10–12, 293, 337, 391

Bacon, Alice 219–20
Baker, Kenneth 415
Barnett, Mary 47, 127, 128
Bauman, Zygmunt 84
Beames 105
Beccaria, Cesare 116, 130, 354
Beck, U. 85
Becker, Howard 81
Beckett, Gilbert A. 147
Beggs, Thomas 105
behaviour
    modification 408
    surveillance 408–9
Beijing rules 317, 318, 319
Bengough, G. H. 152
Bennett, H. G. 145
Bevan, James 164
Beveridge, William 210
Birmingham 48, 160
Black Acts 287
Black Power 57, 59
Black Report (1979) 276, 281
blacks
    and criminality 21, 50–67, 70
    girls 56, 297, 301, 303, 308
    male sexuality 301
Blackstone, W. 99, 143, 147
Blagg, H. 414
Blair, Tony 11, 390, 392, 396
Blake, G. F. 260
Blake, William 24
Bland, L. 300
Blantyre House 335
Bonta, James 439
boot camps 5, 11, 240, 330, 345–58
Booth, William 151
borstals 11, 205, 333, 340, 387
Bosanquet, Helen 47
Bottoms, A. E. 132, 134, 418, 453
bourgeoisie 40, 126, 128, 135, 183, 214
Bowen, Louis 181
Bowlby, John 37

Boy Scout movement 48
Brace, Charles Loring 181, 182, 184–5
Bray, Reginald 47
Brenton 129
bridewells 162, 163, 165, 169
Bristol Gaol 99, 145
Bristol riots (1980) 64
Britain *see* United Kingdom
British Association of Social Work 224
British Crime Survey (1998) 391
British National Party (BNP) 75
Brittan, Leon 339, 340
Brixton riots (1981) 45, 59
Brockway, Zebulon 189, 190, 349
Brodeur, Jean-Paul 345
'broken windows' thesis 453–4
Brougham, Lord 118–19
Brownlee, Ian 247
Buchanan, J. 105
Bulger, James 12, 19–20, 39, 240, 313, 314
Burt, Cyril 35, 53
Butler, R. A. 219, 335, 336
Butler-Sloss, Dame 314
Butterworth, James 46
Buxton, Foxwell 99
Buxton, Thomas 145

Cadogan Report (1938) 333
Cale, Michelle 168
California Juvenile Court Act (1961) 264
California Probation Subsidy 261
Calvert, Roy and Theodora 46
Cambridge Evacuation Survey 37
Cameron, Sue 68
Campbell, B. 314
Campsfield House 334–5
Canada 280, 379, 428
capital punishment (death penalty) 11,
    142, 162, 348
capitalism 25, 26, 28, 82, 89, 125, 180,
    181, 184, 186, 187, 197, 317
care orders 7, 175, 216, 223, 239, 240,
    287, 307
Carlebach, J. 128
Carnie, J. 232
Carnival riots 59, 61–2
Carpenter, Mary 29, 30, 107, 108, 109,
    110, 112, 125–6, 127–8, 129, 138,
    139, 141, 147, 148, 149, 150, 154,
    155, 164, 167, 189
case screening 440, 444
cautioning 255, 388, 389, 452, 454–5
Chadwick, Edwin 123, 149
Chapeltown riots 59
Chartism 27, 141
Chesney-Lind, Meda 436
Chesterton, G. L. 101
Child, the Family and the Young Offender,
    The (1965 White paper) 134, 221–2

child abuse 39, 168, 230, 296, 298, 299,
    303, 325
Child Guidance Clinics 36
child labour 26–8, 116, 182
child protection 229, 235, 418
child safety orders 9, 247, 320, 454
child-saving movement 116, 120,
    174, 177–92
Child Study movement 31–3
childhood 19
    'adultization' 4–5, 247, 280, 322, 392
    constructions and reconstructions 20,
        22–44
    'crisis' in 314–15, 390
    demonization 12, 315, 391–2
    and dependency 29, 104, 107, 126, 127
    determinist view 129
    distinction from adulthood 26, 28, 34, 102,
        110, 112, 138–9, 278, 279–80, 323
    fear of and for 142
    historicization 141–2
    intensive governance 2
    ontology 147–8
Children Act (1908) 98, 132, 159, 394
Children Act (1948) 37, 38
Children Act (1989) 39, 240, 320, 389
Children and Young Persons Act (1933) 7, 46,
    131, 132, 387
Children and Young Persons Act (1963) 132
Children and Young Persons Act (1969) 7, 10,
    134, 175, 216–17, 223–4, 239, 249,
    284–7, 291, 292, 307, 336, 387
Children in Trouble (1968 White Paper)
    7, 134, 223–6
children's hearings 8, 173–4, 175, 228–37,
    238, 276, 280
Children's Legal Centre 340, 341
children's rights 15, 34, 38, 257, 276, 278,
    280, 281–2, 313–14, 317–26
    girls 301
Children's Rights Movement 39
Children's (Scotland) Bill (1994) 231
Christie, N. 315, 316
Churchill, Winston 197–8, 209, 374
Chute, Charles 177
citizenship 34, 37, 197, 210–11, 212
class 315, 326, 395
    1969 Act and 223–4, 292
    law and 287, 288–9, 290, 291
    moral 146–8
    and risk-taking 86
    social classification 148–50
classical liberalism 2, 178
Clay, John 101, 105, 106, 109
Clear, T. R. 268
Cleland, A. 235
Cleveland 'crisis' 298
Code Napoleon 108
Cohen, Stanley 69, 72, 247, 317, 394–5, 436, 438

colonial expatriation 154–5, 163, 167
Colquhoun, Patrick 103
Communities that Care model 429, 439
community-based programmes 7, 316, 437–8
community correction 255, 262
Community Development Foundation 249
community service 240, 243
conferencing 174, 244–5, 249
Consedine, J. 243
Conservative Party 5, 8, 45, 68, 73, 74, 132,
      175, 219, 239–40, 286, 293, 331, 335–6,
      337–9, 388, 389, 394, 402, 403, 404, 415
Consolidating Act (1866) 110–11, 168
contagion 104, 105, 129, 145, 148, 161
Cooley, Charles 186
Cooper, Joan 223
Cordon riots 141, 142
Cornwallis 146
corporal punishment 23, 26, 31, 39, 161–2,
      190–1, 219, 333, 335–6
corporations
   and US liberal reforms 178–9, 180, 182
   use of moral panics 88
corporatism 6, 209, 320, 401–2, 404–12,
      453, 456
cost-effectiveness 5, 415, 433, 457
Covington, C. 292
Cox, Pam 169
Crawford, A. 458
Crawford, William 100, 101, 108, 111, 119
crime
   abandonment of concept 331, 384
   marketing of 89–90
   and society 141–2
Crime, Justice and Protecting the Public (1990
      White Paper) 420
Crime and Disorder Act (1998) 6, 9, 11, 95,
      241–2, 245, 246–7, 248–9, 314, 320, 323,
      324, 325, 387, 394, 454–7, 460
crime prevention *see* youth crime prevention
crime rate
   nineteenth century 103
   1989–1992: 389, 413
   see also youth crime rate
Crime Reduction Programme 457–8
'criminal classes' 126, 149, 160, 184–6
Criminal Justice Act (1855) 161
Criminal Justice Act (1948) 333, 334, 387
Criminal Justice Act (1961) 336
Criminal Justice Act (1967) 223
Criminal Justice Act (1982) 240, 339–40, 363,
      364, 366, 367, 387, 388
Criminal Justice Act (1988) 332, 387, 389
Criminal Justice Act (1991) 8, 240, 389, 417
Criminal Justice and Police Act (2001) 456
Criminal Justice and Public Order Act (1994)
      230, 240, 314, 387, 394
Criminal Justice Bill (1938) 333
Criminal Law Amendment Act (1912) 52

criminalization 10, 13, 117–18, 161, 316, 324
   challenging 311–28
   of everyday life 87–9
Crosland, Anthony 38
Crown courts 321–2
Crown Prosecution Service 368, 388–9
cultural criminology 21, 80
culture industry 72–3, 78
Cuneen, C. 15
curfew orders 9, 10, 14, 88, 242, 320, 348, 455–6
Curtis Report (1946) 37, 38

Daily Mail 64, 65, 75
Daily Mirror 62, 64
Daily Telegraph 62, 64
Daly, K. 244, 249–50
Dando, Jill 90
'dangerous' classes 30, 107, 149, 150, 155,
      163, 185, 189
Dartmoor Prison 362
Davis, Jennifer 52
Davis, Mike 84
de Haan, W. 316
death penalty *see* capital punishment
decarceration
   'progressive' mirage 387–90
   US 260–2
   welfarism and 292
decriminalization 368, 379
   of English juvenile courts 216–27
   US 264–6
Denmark 374
detention and training orders 11, 246–7, 249,
      320, 325, 387, 394
detention centres 11, 223, 240, 293, 329,
      332–44, 366, 387, 388
deterrence
   detention centres and the politics of
      329, 332–44
   individual 360
   US 266–7
deviancy amplification 69, 70, 72, 88
Dickens, Charles 115
Dickover, R. 260
Dignan, J. 246, 247
Dill, F. 261
'disorder' 9, 13, 453–4
diversion 255
   children's hearing system 234
   dangers of prosecutorial 367
   and the rise of corporatism 401, 406–7
   US 255, 259–60
   see also cautioning
Dixon, David 289
Dobash, R. 232
Docker, J. 89
doli capax/incapax 99, 108, 109, 110, 116,
      118, 142–3, 160, 240–1
   abolition 4, 242, 320, 321–2, 456

'domestic ideal' 26, 29, 38, 41
Donnison, D. 217
Donzelot, J. 198
Downes, D. 389
drug treatment orders 242
drug use 64, 72–3, 82–3
    decriminalization 264–5
due process 8, 256, 288, 293
    US 262–4, 267
Dugdale, Richard 185–6
Duster, T. 218
Duxbury, E. 260

Eardley-Wilmot, J. E. 102
Eastcourt, Thomas 101
economic policy 208, 361, 405–6
Ede, Chuter 333
'edgework' 85–7
Edgworth, Maria 25
education
    Evangelical view 25
    as preparation for labour 182, 187
    relationship with crime 106
    Rousseauian theory 24
    and social regulation 212
    stressed in US reformatories 189–90
    see also schools; social education
Education Act (1944) 38
Education Acts (1870s and 1880s)
        29, 159
eighteenth century
    classification of juveniles 163
    constructions of childhood 23–4
    use of the trial 144
Eliot, T. S. 46
Elkin, Winifred 46
Elliott, Mr 109
Ellis, John 147, 151, 152, 153
Elmira Reformatory 185, 190, 349
Emery, Fred 64
England and Wales 276, 413, 416, 418
    decriminalization of juvenile courts
        175, 216–27
    eclipse of welfare principles 239–42
    origins of youth justice 95–172
    politics of juvenile control 256, 284–95
    prison reduction 359–68, 374, 378
    restorative justice 175–6, 245–8, 249
    youth crime prevention 452–63
    youth governance 2–16
Eton 64–5
European Convention on Human Rights 10,
        312, 363
European Court of Human Rights 19–20, 231,
        314, 363
evacuation 37
Evangelicalism 25–6
Evans, Mrs Glendower 191
Evans-Gordon, William 52

Evening Standard 61
evidence-based policy and practice 6, 457–8

Fabians 132–3, 219, 223
Factory Acts 27, 28
Fagan, J. 259
families
    'at risk' 444–5
    black 57
    bourgeois 128, 214
    centrality in juvenile reform movement
        125–6, 135, 147
    domestic ideal 26, 29, 38, 41
    embodiment in juvenile courts 131–2
    Fabian, and social reconstruction 132–4
    girls as 'property' of 298–9
    Ingleby concern with 132
    investigation and inquiry 201
    'natural order' 27–8
    perceived decline 46, 47
    'problem families' 37, 133, 219, 290
    protection by Human Rights Act 10
    psychological significance 35, 36, 37
    subjection to intervention 213, 214
    targeting 9
family courts 220, 240
family group conferences 176, 244–5
'family service' 133, 219, 220, 221
Faulkner, David 390
Feeley, Malcolm 431–2, 438
Feld, Barry C. 437
Felt, Jeremy 182
feminist movement 182, 303, 306, 308
Field, John 100–1
final warnings 245, 320, 455
Financial Times 62
Finland 280
Fionda, J. 4, 323
Fletcher, Joseph 104, 106
Flew, A. 277
Fogel, R. 267
forced labour 374
Foster, Andrew 320
fostering 154
Foucault, Michel 2, 14, 200–1, 329, 341, 348
Fox, S. J. 229, 231, 232, 233
Freeden, M. 312
Freeman, M. 323–4
French Revolution 25
Fruin, D. 233
Full Metal Jacket 352–3

Gallie, W. B. 275
Gallo, E. 419–20
Gambling Act (1906) 289
Gaol Acts 163
Garland, David 3, 5, 52, 391, 432, 436
garotting panic 51–2
Gault 263, 276

Geach, H. 290
Geis, G. 265
gender 86, 315, 326, 395, 434, 436
    nineteenth century discourse 96–7, 164–7, 169
    problematizing relations 300–2
    and referral to children's hearings 231–3
Gesellschaft 404, 405
Gibbens, T. C. N. 220
Gibbons, D. C. 260
Giddens, A. 84
Gilbert, M. J. 436
Giller, H. 285, 286, 290, 292
Gillick judgement (1985) 39
Gillis, John R. 115
Gilroy, Paul 71
Gingrich, Newt 351
Girard, Stephen 181
girls and young women 12, 26, 255,
        322–3, 326
    nineteenth century delinquents 97, 164–7,
        168, 169
    private institutionalization 436
    referral to children's hearings 231–3
    'troublesome' 256–7, 296–310
Glyde, John 105–6
Gorz, André 192
Gould, E. R. L. 186
Gowdy, V. B. 438
Gramsci, Antonio 70, 125
Grant, D 436
Grunhut, M. 334–5, 336
Guardian 76

Hackney Wick Reformatory 154, 155
Hagel, A. 235
Haldeman, Harry 181
Hall, R. 153
Hall, Stanley 32
Hall, Stuart 50, 69, 70–1, 72
Hallett, C. 235
Handler, Joel 188
Harford, John 145
Harris, R. 282, 339
Hartz, Louis 178
Harvey, J. 233
Haydon, D. 15
Haymarket Riot (1866) 180
Health and Morals of Apprentices Act (1802) 27
Heathcote, C. G. 47
hegemony 70–1, 75
Hele, Henry Selby 119
Henningsen, Gustav 377
Henrotin, Ellen 181
heredity vs. environment 186–7
Hewitt, Margaret 115
Hill, Frederick 101
Hill, Matthew Davenport 98, 108, 111, 115,
        146, 148, 151, 152, 154, 189
Hill, Micaiah 28–9, 106

Hirst, F. W. 46
Hoare, Samuel 164
Hobler, Francis 162
Hofstadter, Richard 179, 183
Holdaway, S. 248
Holloway prison 362
Hollywood films 46, 70, 352, 355
Holmes, Thomas 48
Home Affairs Select Committee on Race
        Relations and Immigration
    1971–72: 55–8
    1975–76: 58–9, 59–61
homosexuality 168
    decriminalization 265
    and moral panic 71–2
Hood, R. 159
hooliganism 48, 53
House of Refuge movement 178
houses of correction 162, 163
Howard, John 99
Howard, Michael 19, 313–14, 396
Howard League for Penal Reform 341
Hudson, Barbara 307, 315–16, 317
Hulsman, Louk 368, 379, 384
Human Rights Act (1998) 10, 314
Hurd, Douglas 340
Hylton, J. H. 262

ideology 70, 71
    building socialist ideology 381
    countering ideology of prison 380–1
immigration
    early nineteenth century fears 52, 184, 185
    illegal 57–8
    Powellism 53–5
incarceration 11–12, 239, 246–7, 321, 331,
        386–400
    effects of IT Initiative 418–20
    opposition of UN Convention 319, 325
    segregative sector 206–7
    use in US 266
Industrial Conciliation Act (1896) 209
industrial model 349
industrial revolution 25, 125
industrial schools 95, 98, 109–12, 131, 155,
        167–8, 205
Industrial Schools Act (1857) 159, 386–7
industrial training 128–9, 167, 189
industrialization 26, 139, 141
Ingleby Report (1960) 132, 133, 217–20, 225
Innocent VIII 376
inter-agency working *see* multi-agency working
inter-war period
    constructions of childhood 34–6
    moral decline 45–7
intermediate treatment 223, 239, 285
    DHSS Initiative 416–20
International Crime Victimization Survey
        (1997) 391

Ipswich 105–6
Isaacs, Susan 35–6

'Jack the Ripper' 52
Jackson, Louise 168
Jameson, Fredric 140, 351
Japan
   bosozoku 86–7
   reduction of prison population 364, 367, 374
Jebb, Joshua 100, 156–7
Jenkins, Roy 222–3
Jewish settlers 52
Joad, Professor 275
Johnson, Richard 152
Johnson's Crime Commission 179, 259
Jones, Gareth Stedman 53
joyriding 87, 240
judicial discretion, limiting 441–2
'just deserts' 8, 173, 217, 315, 416, 432
   US 267–8
justice approach 1, 311–12, 416–17
   and children's rights 324
   and common sense 417–18
   compared with corporatism 404, 406–9
   effectiveness 418–20
   progressivism and 284–94
   and retributivism 256, 275–83
justice vs. welfare debate 1, 315
   and children's hearings system 229
   and emergence of corporatism 409–11, 453
   and juvenile courts 96, 131–2, 217–19
   misconceived 284, 286, 292–3, 294
   nineteenth century 154
   and provision for girls 307–8
Juvenile Court Act (1899, US) 187
juvenile courts
   and bourgeois social control 135
   decriminalization of 216–27
   erosion of rehabilitative ideals 4
   establishment 7, 131, 159
   justice vs. welfare in 96, 131–2, 217–19
   legal sufficiency 440
   and 'moral decline' 46–7
   and requirement of knowledge 201
   US 177–8, 187–8, 263, 264
   waivers 441–2
juvenile delinquency
   coining of term 138, 146
   and constructions of childhood 20, 28–30
   evolution of the concept 28, 98–114
   gender, justice and 96–7, 159–72
   and the government of a generation
      96, 138–58
   invention of 95–6, 115–22, 159, 160
   legal recognition 29, 98
   moral psychology and 35
juvenile hulks 100, 125, 129, 145, 155
Juvenile Justice and Delinquency Prevention
   Act (US, 1993) 346

Juvenile Offenders Act (1847) 159, 161
juvenile reform movement 28–30, 95, 96,
   108–12, 124–9, 129–31, 135,
   138–57

Katz, Jack 80, 81–4
Katz, Michael 189
Kay, J. P. 104
Kelling, George 453
Kelynack, T. N. 34
Kilbrandon Report (1964) 7–8, 175, 221,
   228, 233
King, M. 417, 418
King, Peter 169
King, R. 362
Kirchheimer, Otto 190
Kirkman Gray, B. 202, 204
Klein, M. 260
Kolko, Gabriel 182
Krämer, Heinrich 376
Kubrick, Stanley 352–3

labour force
   control through welfare 197–9
   education as preparation for 182, 187
   ensuring recruitment 124, 125, 152, 156
   military model invalid 351
   temporal order 354
Labour Party 7, 51, 73, 74, 132, 134, 217,
   219–20, 220–4, 225, 239, 241, 320,
   389–90, 394
   see also New Labour
LAC3 initiative 404, 407
laissez-faire 2, 26, 180, 181
Lambert, John 56
Lancaster study 287
Land, H. 341
Larceny Act (1827) 118
late modernity 5, 21, 84–7
Lathrop, Julia 181
law
   appropriation by New Right 288, 293
   first attack on classical 129
   and nation 50
   vs. norms 200–2
   progressivism and 287–90
   vs. social sciences 417–18
law and order 6, 13, 50, 61, 70, 185, 240, 314,
   337, 388, 389
lawyers 108, 183, 217, 221, 222, 225,
   255, 291
Leavis, F. R. 46
Leer-Salvesen, P. 383
Lemert, E. 261
Lerman, P. 261
lesbianism 301
Letchworth, William 189, 190–1
Lewis, P. W. 263
Liberal Party 209

liberalism
  in America 178, 179, 182
  see also classical liberalism; neo-liberalism;
    welfare liberalism
Lindsey, Ben 187
Lipsey, M. W. 437
Little, A. D. 261, 268
Littledale, Justice 116
Liverpool 105, 116, 120, 160
Lloyd Baker 150
Lloyd-George 197
local authorities 4, 6, 14, 38, 217, 242, 455
Local Authority Social Services Act (1970) 224
local child curfew schemes 14, 242, 320,
    455–6
Local Government (Scotland) Act (1994) 230
Locke, John 23
Lombroso, Cesare 185
London
  nineteenth century 48, 51–2, 104, 105,
    117–18, 160, 162, 163, 169
  street conflicts (1970s) 59, 61–2
Longford Report (1964) 133, 134, 220–1
Lyng, Stephen 85–6
Lyttleton, Lord 109

MacGregor 154
Mack, Julian 188
Magarey, Susan 161
magistrates 45, 217
  dissatisfaction with Butler's policies 335
  importance to Intermediate Treatment
    Initiative 416, 418
  nineteenth century 102, 108, 116,
    118–19, 162
  opposition to 1969 Act 225, 275, 286, 291,
    293, 336–7
  opposition to Longford Report 222
  power increased through 1982 Act 339–40
  see also summary jurisdiction
Magistrates' Association 225, 341
Mair, G. 419
Maitland, F. W. 118
Major, John 74, 389, 392
Malicious Trespass Act (1827) 117, 118, 119,
    144, 161, 162
managerialism 5–6, 12, 16, 349, 403,
    415, 436, 456, 460
Manchester 48, 76, 104, 148, 160
Mark, Robert 60–1, 62
market
  commodification of transgression 89–91
  effect of Liberal reforms 197, 208
Martin, F. M. 229, 231, 232, 233, 234
Martinson, R. 414
Marxism 70, 82, 279
Massachusetts closure programme 361, 375
Matza, David 81
May, Margaret 115, 125

May Committee 360, 362
Mayhew, Henry 105, 118, 126
Mayhew, Patrick 415
Mays, G. L. 437
McCormick, D. N. 281
McNee, David 63
media
  marketing of crime 89–90
  and moral panics 21, 68–79, 443
medical model 186, 188, 221
Medway Secure Training Centre 393
mental patients 262
Metropolitan Police 48, 52, 56, 57, 58, 59,
    60–1, 62, 117–18
Metropolitan Police Act (1829) 117,
    119, 144
Metropolitan Police Act (1839) 118
Mettray *colonie agricole* 128, 130, 167
Meyer, J. F. 436
middle class
  conception of childhood and family 23, 108,
    111, 125–6
  fear for the social order 27, 30, 109, 139
  US reformers 178–9, 180, 181, 182
Miles, W. A. 104, 148, 155
military model 348–9, 350–1, 352
Miller, D. 262
Miller, Eleanor 86
Miller, J. 387, 393
Miller, Jerome 375
Miller, P. 3
Milnes, Monckton 111
Mintz, R. 259
Miranda 263–4
modern penality, limits of 329–30, 345–58
modernity
  late 5, 21, 84–7
  military as a model for 348–9
Monday Club 340
Moore, S. 389
moral class 146–8
moral discernment 142–6
moral panics 21, 50, 80, 88, 124, 160, 162,
    315, 337
  historical perspective 20, 45–9, 69–70
  rethinking 68–79
'moral statisticians' 104
moral training 150–2, 189
More, Hannah 25–6
More, J. S. 116
Morgan, A. E. 46–7
Morgan, P. 285, 286, 287–8, 291
Morgan, R. 362
Morrell, D. H. 223
Morris, A. 277, 280, 281, 285, 286, 290
Morris, Norval 347
Morris, Terence 220
Mountbatten Inquiry 360
'mugging' 50, 55, 56, 60, 62, 63, 70

multi-agency working 3, 4, 5, 6, 407, 409,
    452, 456
Muncie, J. 316–17, 320
Mundle, C. W. K. 277
Murphy, J. G. 278–9, 281
Murray, K. 229, 231, 232, 233

NACRO 341, 393, 418
Nagel, W. G. 266
Nathan, S. 393
nation
    children and 33–4
    law and 50
National Association of Probation
    Officers 224
'national efficiency' 33, 53
National Front 63
Neal, Stephen 106
Neale, William Beaver 104, 148
neo-conservatism 9–12
neo-liberalism 2–6, 8, 12, 14, 15
Netherlands 363, 364, 365, 367, 374
'new behaviourism' 408–9, 411
New Hall detention centre 338
New Labour 4, 5, 8–9, 10, 95, 175, 241–2,
    247, 331, 390, 394–5, 403, 452–60
new penology 247, 401, 403, 431–51,
    456, 457–8
new public managerialism (NPM) 5
new punitiveness 386–400
New Right 288, 290, 291, 293, 314
New Zealand 174, 176, 244–5, 248, 249
Newburn, T. 235, 388
Newgate Prison 99, 145, 161, 166
Newman, Kenneth 63
nineteenth century
    constructions of childhood 23, 24–33
    control of working-class youth 124–31
    juvenile delinquency 95, 98–114, 115–22,
        138–58, 159–72
    moral panics 47–8, 70
    treatment of girls 194–6, 197, 297
    'un-English' criminality 51–2
    US liberal reforms 177–96
Nix, Carole Ann 353
No More Excuses (1997 White Paper) 241,
    242, 243, 246, 455, 458
normalization
    normalizing sector 203–5
    and social control 2
    of 'troublesome girls' behaviour 303–4
norms vs. law 200–2
Northampton Juvenile Liaison Bureau 407,
    408, 457
Northern Ireland 238, 276, 280
Norway 374, 379, 380, 383–4
nostalgia, willful 330, 351–5
Notting Hill riots 59, 61–2
Nottinghamshire 'linking' programme 408

offender work 382–3
offending workshops 416
O'Malley, P. 14
Orwell, George 46
Osborne, C. S. 101
Osler, Mark 348, 354–5

PACE project 408
Packman, J. 233
Palmer, Mrs Potter 181
Panitch, L. 405
parens patriae 187, 263, 437, 440, 441
parenting orders 10, 242, 249, 320, 454,
    455, 456
parenting programmes 428
parents
    and children's hearings 230, 231, 233
    crime ascribed to neglect and irresponsibility
        47, 103, 104, 106, 125–6
    duties enforced under nineteenth century
        legislation 110, 111
    new accountability laws, US 444–5
    responsibility stressed 132, 218, 240
    risk factors 426–7
    stigmatization 437
    surveillance by probation 204
    at youth offender panels 458
Parker, H. 419
Parkhurst Prison 100, 125, 154, 156,
    164, 167, 186
parole 223, 267, 349, 364, 374, 438
Parton, Nigel 39
Patten, John 417, 422
Pearson, Charles 108
Pearson, Geoff 69–70, 72, 74
Peel, Robert 117, 120, 160, 162, 163
Peirce, Bradford Kinney 190
penal welfarism 2–3, 174–5, 197–215
'perishing' classes 107, 149, 150, 155, 163
'permissiveness' 45, 49, 70, 80
persistent offenders 206, 235, 240, 242, 337,
    390, 395, 425–6
    incorrigible juveniles 96, 156–7, 206
Philanthropic Society 163, 164, 169
Pickett, Robert 178
Pinchbeck, Ivy 115
Pitts, J. 456
place of safety orders 300–1
Platt, Anthony 116, 120
police 45, 259
    and crime prevention 420
    efficiency drive 223
    and girls' 'reputations' 300–1
    intensified policing 383
    juvenile liaison programs 260
    and moral panics 69, 74, 75, 77
    opposition to 1969 Act 175, 286, 291
    'participating Miranda' technique 263–4
    relations with blacks 55–65

police *cont.*
  response to US decarceration 261–2
  social factors in 'discretion' 289
  use of corporal punishment 161–2
Police Federation 56, 57, 61
political-economic system
  increasing dysfunctionality 269
  and Romantic conception of childhood 25
  and US liberal reforms 180–1, 184
politics
  of child incarceration 386–400
  of deterrence 332–44
  of juvenile control 284–95
  and the media 77
Poor Law 33, 108, 209
'popular punitiveness' 329, 331, 390–2,
    401, 403, 452, 453, 460
positivism 129, 173
Postman, Neil 40
postmodernism 89
postmodernity 345–51
Powell, Enoch 52, 53–5
power 316–17
  adult/child relations 15, 40, 313
  family relations 298–9
Power, David 109, 151
Pratt, J. 388, 453
pre-court tribunals 406
pre-trial detention 102, 144, 161, 434–5
Presdee, Mike 87–9
pressure groups 73, 74, 78
Prevention of Crime Act (1908) 387
Preyer, Wilhelm 32
prison
  abolitionist view 331, 373–85
  association and contagion 100, 101–2, 144,
    145, 161
  costs 393
  and crime rates 100–1, 266, 393
  freeze (standstill) policy, 359–60, 373–4, 378
  increasing use 12, 267–8, 346, 396
  nineteenth century 99–102, 103, 106, 116,
    119–20, 125, 129, 130, 144, 145, 154,
    163–4, 168
  overcrowding 99, 267–8, 338, 363, 374
  population forecasting 360
  reductionist agenda 330, 359–72, 374–5
  search for alternatives 333
  segregative function 206–7
  separate juvenile provision 100, 125, 163–4
Prison Discipline Society 163–4
Prison Inspectorate 129, 130, 141, 321,
    339, 340
Prison Officers' Association 339, 341, 360
Prison Reform Trust 341
Prisons Commission 334, 335
private institutions 435–7
privatization 407–8, 435–7
probation service 154, 175, 255–6, 259, 438
  attitude to *Children in Trouble* 224

probation service *cont.*
  as cost-effective control 438
  and crime prevention 420
  deprofessionalization 402, 421–2
  IT initiative and 416, 417, 419, 420
  normalising function 203–5
  opposition to Longford Report 222
  professionalization 213
  response to US decarceration reforms 261–2
  Thatcherite hostility 415
progressivism
  the decarcerative experiment 387–90
  and the justice movement 284–94
  nineteenth century US 178–9, 182
  and the rule of law 287–90
proportionality 256, 315–16
Prosecution of Offences Act (1985) 388–9
prostitution 56, 165–6, 168, 297, 300
  legalization 265
Pryce, Ken 64
psychoanalytic theory 37, 38, 134, 216, 219,
    222, 224, 297
psychology
  associationist 101
  and conceptions of childhood 34–6, 37
  reclaiming emotionality 302
punishment 239, 240
  approach of corporatist model 408–9
  justice approach and 276–8, 291, 293, 311,
    315, 408
  liberalization of 211
  limits of modern penality 329–30, 345–58
  New Labour policies 247–8
  nineteenth century discourse 109, 129–30,
    138–9, 161–2
  separation from trial 144
  US emphasis on 5, 11, 331, 396
  vs. welfare 154, 173, 282
  see also capital punishment; corporal
    punishment; new punitiveness;
    popular punitiveness
Pursehouse, Mark 76

Quinton, D. 232

race 315, 395, 434, 435–6
  and crime 20–1, 50–67, 70, 71
  fears of degeneration 32
Race Relations Bill 368
racism 53, 55, 326
  nomenclature of 'criminal classes' 105, 185
  stereotyping 301, 308
Radzinowicz, L. 117, 120, 130, 159, 167
Rastafarian religion 64–5
Rauhe Haus 167
Rawls, J. 278
Rawson, R. W. 104
Raynor, P. 407
Redgrave, Samuel 103
Redhill Reformatory School 103, 130, 154

referral orders 4, 175, 245–6, 247, 403, 456–9
Reformation 25
reformation 162–4
  within the social 153–7
reformatories 2, 11
  correctional sector 205–6
  ethical machines 150–3
  US system 189–90
  see also industrial schools;
    reformatory schools
reformatory schools 29, 95, 98, 109–12, 128,
  139, 140, 141, 153, 154–5, 167–8, 205
Reformatory Schools Act (1857) 139, 159
Reformatory Schools (Scotland) Act (1854)
  128, 156
Reformatory Schools (Youthful Offenders) Act
  (1854) 29, 109, 110, 139, 154, 386
Refuges for the Destitute 163,
  165, 166–7
rehabilitation 256, 336, 349, 402, 403, 411, 444
  decline 413–14
Rehabilitation of Offenders Act (1974) 459
Reich, Robert 351
remand centres 387
'remoralization' 6, 9–10, 249
reparation orders 4, 246, 247, 320, 454, 455
reprimands 455
Republic of Ireland 276, 364
residential care 37, 38, 232, 299, 300, 306,
  307–8, 325
'residuum' 147, 151
resistance 14, 140
responsibilization 3–5, 331, 392
responsibility
  attack on 129–31
  serious revision 200
  see also age of criminal responsibility
restorative justice 4, 175–6, 238–53, 243–8,
  316–17, 403, 455, 458–9
retribution 256, 275–83, 314–17
rights
  conflation with policy 408
  'interest' and 'will' theories 281
  rights-based agenda 14–15, 257, 311–28
  see also children's rights
Riis, Jacob 185
risk 316
  assessment and classification 6, 438–40
  factors 5, 402, 426–7, 457
  management 85, 401, 402, 403
  see also actuarial justice; 'at risk' groups
risk-taking 85–7
Roman empire 376
Romanticism 24–5
Rose, Nikolas 2, 3
Rothman, David 354
Rousseau, Jean Jacques 24, 25
Rovner-Pieczenik, R. 259
Rowbotham, S. 305
Ruggerio, V. 419–20

Ruggles-Brise, E. 206, 211
Rusche, George 190
Rushton, Edward 105
Russell, Lord John 128, 155, 156
Russell, Whitworth 100, 101, 119
Rutherford, Andrew 242, 266, 374, 378, 379,
  388, 452
Rutter, M. 232
Ruxton, S. 386

safeguarders 229
Salazar Frias, Alonso de 377
Samuel, Herbert 98, 203
Sanborn, Frank 189
Sato, Ikuya, 86–7
Scarman Report 60
Schall v. Martin 434
Scheerer, Sebastian 376
Schlesinger, Arthur Jr. 178
Schlesinger, P. 71
schools
  and constructions of childhood 30–1
  crime prevention techniques 428
  effects of non-attendance 231–2
  inculcating state loyalty 184
  restricted curriculum and intake 107–8
  risk factors 427
  significance for Child Study
    Movement 31–2
Schrag, F. 280
Schwartz, I. 435
science and scientism 32, 33, 88, 134, 297
Scotland 341
  children's hearings 8, 173–4, 175, 228–37,
    238, 276, 280
  Kilbrandon Report 7–8, 175, 221,
    228, 233
  reformatory schools 110, 128, 156
Scott, Peter 217
Scraton, P. 15
secure training centres (STCs) 11, 235, 320,
  321, 387, 393, 394
secure training orders 240, 320, 394
Send detention centre 336, 338
sentencing
  determinate 240, 256, 267–8, 354, 440–1
  diverse options incompatible with actuarial
    justice 443–4
  emergence of age as factor 144
  inconsistency 102
  indeterminate 189, 190, 191, 255, 354
  mandatory 266
  use of least restriction sanction 365–6
Separate System 100, 101
sex offender orders 9, 242
sexual abuse 39, 168, 296, 298, 299, 303, 325
sexuality
  girls' 168, 296, 300–2, 326
  and moral panic 71–2
Shaw, Mrs 166

'short sharp shock' 240, 293, 329, 332–4, 337, 338, 340, 341, 388, 415
Sickmund, M. 443
Silent System 100
Sim, Joe 60
Simon, J. 11, 13, 14
Simon, Jonathan 431–2, 438
Singer, S. 442
single parents 6, 9, 73, 74, 75, 444
slavery 27, 53, 115
    abolition 331, 376
Slipman, Sue 73
Smith, D. 414, 460
Smith, Mrs Perry 181
Snyder, H. N. 443
social, the
    classification of 148–50
    'death' of 3, 6, 13
    emergence of concern with 146
    penal support for 199–200
    reconfiguration of 6–12
    reformation within 153–7
    reinventions of 14
'social construction' 22–3, 149
social control
    child-saving movement and 181
    emergence of hybrid forms 87–8
    and humanitarian reform 135, 139–40
    media and 77
    and 'normalization' processes 2
    and political-economic system 258, 269
    social work and 2, 285, 286, 291
social Darwinism 185–6
social and economic conditions
    1830s studies 104
    crime and 10, 133, 186, 236, 241, 249, 325, 382–3, 389–90, 427
    impact on individual subjectivity 84
    marginalized in justice approach 256, 279, 282, 315, 417, 418
    structure vs. agency 83, 392
social education
    Kilbrandon recommendations 228–9, 232
    with 'troublesome girls' 305
Social Exclusion Unit 249
social inequality, law and 288, 289–90, 291
social insurance 2, 198–9, 210
social policy
    criminalization 6–7, 13
    and needs of girls in trouble 304–9
    overlap with prison reduction 361
    regulatory effect of Liberal reforms 197–9, 208–10
social process, law as 289–90
social reconstruction 132–4
social reform, US 180–1
social regulation, welfare state strategies 208–14

social sciences 417–18
social work 2, 456
    and children's hearings system 8, 228–9, 230, 231, 233
    conflict with magistrates 225
    criticism by justice movement 255–6, 285, 286, 287, 290, 291
    emergence of generic 219
    government hostility to claims of professionalism 414
    influence on 1969 Act 217, 223–5, 225–6
    opportunities for women child-savers 183
    powers under 1969 Act 134, 284–5
    professionalization 213
    reports 14
    role in corporatism 406, 407, 408, 410
    support for Longford Report 134, 221, 222
    unification 224
    see also welfare professionals
Social Work (Scotland) Act (1968) 7, 175, 228
Socialist Workers Party (SWP) 75
society
    contesting 72–4
    crime and 141–2
    image fractured 146
    media and 76–7
'Something Works' 402, 413, 414, 421, 453
Soskice, Frank 223
Spaghetti House siege 60–1
Spanish Inquisition 377–8
specified activities order 388
Spencer, Herbert 185
Spiers, Graham 102
Spränger, Jakob 376
Star 64
state
    changes in attitude to children 110
    formation 51
    increasing interventionism 33–4
    modes of youth governance 1–16
    and parent-child relationships 30, 98, 110
    response to transgression 87–9
    right to punish 278–9
    rights obligations 312
    see also welfare state
Stern, V. 394
stigma theory 219–20, 221
Straw, Jack 320, 322, 396, 453
structure vs. agency 83, 392
Sully, James 32
summary jurisdiction 96, 118–19, 143–4, 159, 160–1, 162, 167, 169
Summary Jurisdiction Act (1847) 102
Sun 64, 65, 76
Sunday Times 64
supervision orders/requirements 216, 231, 234, 307
'sus' law 62, 289

suspended sentences 223, 366
Sweden 364, 374, 379, 380
Symons, Jelinger 109, 149
Szwed, E. 290

*Tackling Youth Crime, Reforming Youth
    Justice* (1997) 241, 454, 455
Taine, Darwin and Hippolyte 32
Taylor, I. 129
teenage parenthood 9, 299
television 40, 77, 90
Thatcher, Margaret 45, 50, 388
Thatcherism 69, 75, 388, 389, 405, 415
Thompson, E. P. 287, 354
Thompson, Robert 19–20, 313–14
Thorpe, David 286–7
Times, The 47, 64
Tobias, J. J. 115
Toxteth riots (1981) 45
'tracking' 408, 416
transportation 52, 99, 100, 154, 163
    abolition 109
trial by jury 102
Tumber, H. 79
Turner, Sydney 103, 109, 147, 150,
    151, 169

UN Committee on the Rights of the Child
    319–20, 321, 324
UN Congress on the Prevention of Crime
    (1985) 373
UN Convention on the Rights of the
    Child (UNCRC) 9, 174, 257, 312,
    313, 317–20, 323
underclass 9, 314, 434
United Kingdom/Britain 3, 4, 5,
    7, 12, 235
    child incarceration 11–12, 239, 246–7, 321,
        331, 386–400
    constructions of childhood 22–44
    corporatism 401, 404–12
    detention centres 329, 332–44
    justice model critiqued 402, 413–24
    penal strategies in a welfare state 174–5,
        197–215
    racialization of crime 20–1, 50–67
    rethinking moral panic 21, 68–79
    securing a rights-based agenda 311–28
    'troublesome girls' 296–310
    youth crime and moral decline 20, 45–9
    see also England and Wales; Republic of
        Ireland; Scotland
United States 32, 428
    actuarial justice 401, 402–3, 431–51
    'adulteration' 4–5
    boot camps 329–30, 345–58
    child-saving movement 116, 120,
        174, 177–96
    Communities that Care model 429, 439

United States *cont.*
    constitutional revisionism 276
    dialectics of criminal justice reform
        255, 258–74
    law and order discourse 13
    New York 'miracle' 453–4
    punitive values 5, 11, 331, 396
    reinventions of the social 14
    use of imprisonment 267–8, 346, 363,
        364, 396
upper classes 27, 181, 182
urban areas
    criminality and race 52–3
    'edgework' 86, 87
    nineteenth century 30, 47, 104–5,
        126–7, 146, 180
    risk factors 427
urbanization 139, 141, 160, 183
Usk Detention Centre 340–1

vagrancy 110–11, 119, 163, 167–8, 374
Vagrancy Act (1824, UK) 117, 119,
    120, 161, 162
Vagrancy Act (1900, Norway) 374
Venables, Jon 19–20, 313–14
Vernon, J. 233
victim work 381–2
victims 235
    and restorative justice 243, 244, 245, 246,
        247, 248, 249, 316, 459
Victorian
    hooligans 48
    literature 24, 99
    mindset on youthful female sexuality 168
    moral tone 297
    obsession with crime rates 98
    underworld 126
    values 47–8
video gaming 90
Vietnam War 347, 352–3
Violent Crime Control and Law Enforcement
    Act (US, 1994) 346
voluntary sector 96–7, 127, 163–4,
    165, 166–7
von Hayek 8
von Hirsch, A. 267

Waddington, P. A. J. 71
Wakefield, Edward 145
Walker, N. 277, 278
Walpole, Horace 141–2
Walton, P. 129
warnings 242
Waterhouse, L. 232
Watney, Simon 71–2
Watson, D. 277
Weber, Max 40, 87
Weeks, J. 297
Weinstein, James 182

welfare approach 1, 311
of 1969 Act 217, 286, 292, 336
centrality of social characteristics 289–90
defended 242, 292
'justice' critique 255–6, 275–7, 280–1, 285–6, 286–7
reinventions of the social 14
and restorative justice 248, 249–50
rights-based 323–4, 324–5
undercut by punitive mentality 173–4
welfare legislation
(1880–1918) 33–4
(1945–1948) 38
welfare liberalism 3
welfare paternalism 7–9
welfare professionals, work with 'troublesome girls' 296–309
welfare state 7, 37–8, 184, 210, 219, 404–5, 414
penal strategies 174–5, 197–215
welfare vs. justice debate *see* justice vs. welfare debate
Wesley, John 24
West Germany 363, 364
Wey, Hamilton 185
'what works' 5, 6, 402, 403, 457, 460
White, R. 15
Whitelaw, William 337, 338, 388, 415
Wilderspin, Samuel 126
Williams, John 101, 109
Williams, W. J. 148
Williams, William Appleman 184, 191–2
Wilson, D. B. 437
Wilson, Jackson 184
Wilson, James Q 453
Wines, Enoch 189, 190
Winn, R. G. 436–7
witch hunts 376–8
women
and the child-saving movement 182–3
work with 'troublesome girls' 306, 308
Women's Aid 303, 306
Wootton, Lady 220
Wordsworth, William 24–5
working class
bourgeois fear of 26–7
child-saving movement and 180, 182, 186, 188, 190
control of youth 123–37
delinquency as symbolic rebellion 82
girls 297, 303
Liberal reforms and 197, 209
pathological view 53
views of juvenile reform movement 29, 126, 139
'respectable' 23, 104, 152
vulnerability to law 221, 224, 289, 290, 292
World War II 45, 333, 349, 352, 355
Wormwood Scrubs 333
Worsley, Henry 146–7, 149, 150
Wright Mills, C. 269

Young, J. 129
Young, Jock 69, 74, 84
young offender institutions (YOIs) 11, 321, 325, 332, 341, 387, 389, 394
Young Offender Psychology Unit 338
Young Offenders (1980 White Paper) 388
youth
centrality in law-and-order discourse 13
desirability and threat 15–16
and the social order 96, 123–4, 142
youth courts 240, 458
youth crime 425
criminal careers 425–6
and moral decline 45–9
perception of 442–3
pleasures of 21, 80–93
research and development priorities 429
risk factors 426–7
youth crime rate
1900s: 140, 141–2, 143, 145–6, 149, 150, 159–60, 167
1939–45: 333
1955–1957: 335
post-war Scotland 228
1980s and 1990s, UK 240, 393, 420, 425
1980s and 1990s, US 443
youth crime prevention 401, 402
contemporary politics of 403, 452–63
effectiveness of justice model 420
expansion of initiatives 255
and modes of youth governance 4, 9, 13, 14
preventive detention 434–5
techniques 427–9
youth culture
and moral panic 72–3, 88–9
risk-taking 85–7
Victorian 48
youth custody centres 11, 387
youth custody orders 240, 332, 340, 388
Youth Inclusion Programme (YIP) 457
Youth Justice and Criminal Evidene Act (1999) 241, 245, 248–9
Youth Justice Boards 4, 6, 242, 394, 395, 454, 456, 460
youth offender panels 10, 175, 245–6, 247, 458–9
youth offending teams (YOTs) 4, 6, 242, 245, 248, 454, 455, 456–7, 458, 460

'zero tolerance' 13, 454